Lecture Notes in Computer Science 10489

Commenced Publication in 1973
Founding and Former Series Editors:
Gerhard Goos, Juris Hartmanis, and Jan van Leeuwen

Stefano Tonetta · Erwin Schoitsch
Friedemann Bitsch (Eds.)

Computer Safety, Reliability, and Security

SAFECOMP 2017 Workshops
ASSURE, DECSoS, SASSUR, TELERISE, and TIPS
Trento, Italy, September 12, 2017
Proceedings

 Springer

Editors
Stefano Tonetta (iD)
Fondazione Bruno Kessler
Trento
Italy

Erwin Schoitsch (iD)
Austrian Institute of Technology GmbH AIT
Vienna
Austria

Friedemann Bitsch (iD)
Thales Deutschland GmbH
Ditzingen
Germany

ISSN 0302-9743   ISSN 1611-3349 (electronic)
Lecture Notes in Computer Science
ISBN 978-3-319-66283-1   ISBN 978-3-319-66284-8 (eBook)
DOI 10.1007/978-3-319-66284-8

Library of Congress Control Number: 2017952205

LNCS Sublibrary: SL2 – Programming and Software Engineering

Printed on acid-free paper

This Springer imprint is published by Springer Nature
The registered company is Springer International Publishing AG
The registered company address is: Gewerbestrasse 11, 6330 Cham, Switzerland

Preface

For many years now, the SAFECOMP conference has had a successful add-on – the SAFECOMP workshop day, preceding the main conference. The SAFECOMP workshops have become particularly attractive since they started generating their own proceedings in the Springer LNCS series (Springer LNCS vol. 10489, the book in your hands; the main conference proceedings are LNCS 10488). This has meant adhering to Springer's standards, i.e., the respective International Program Committee of each workshop had to make sure that at least three independent reviewers reviewed the papers carefully. The selection criteria were different from the those for the main conference since authors were encouraged to submit workshop papers, i.e., on work in progress and on potentially controversial topics. In total, 39 regular papers were accepted.

All five workshops (selected from six proposals) are sequels to earlier workshops, organized by well-known chairs and respected Program Committees, which shows continuity of their relevance to the scientific and industrial community that deals with safety, reliability, and security of computer (control) systems:

- ASSURE 2017 – 5th International Workshop on Assurance Cases for Software-Intensive Systems, chaired by Ewen Denney, Ibrahim Habli, Ganesh Pai, and Kenji Taguchi (full day);
- DECSoS 2017 – 12th ERCIM/EWICS/ARTEMIS Workshop on Dependable Embedded and Cyber-physical Systems and Systems-of-Systems, chaired by Erwin Schoitsch and Amund Skavhaug (full day);
- SASSUR 2017 – 6th International Workshop on Next Generation of System Assurance Approaches for Safety-Critical Systems, chaired by Alejandra Ruiz, Jose Luis de la Vara, and Tim Kelly (full day);
- TIPS 2017 – 2nd International workshop on Timing Performance in Safety Engineering, chaired by Chokri Mraida, Laurent Rioux, Julio L. Medina, and Marc Geilen (half day);
- TELERISE 2017 – 3rd International Workshop on Technical and Legal Aspects of Data Privacy and Security, chaired by Ilaria Matteucci, Paolo Mori, and Marinella Petrocchi (full day; this workshop is new to the SAFECOMP conference series, although not the first one in its life time).

Similar to the SAFECOMP conference, the workshops provide a truly international platform for academia and industry.

It has been a pleasure to work with my general co-chair, Stefano Tonetta, my workshop co-chair Amund Skavhaug, and particularly with the publication chair Friedemann Bitsch, the workshop chairs, the workshop Program Committees, and the authors. Thank you all for your good cooperation and excellent work!

September 2017   Erwin Schoitsch

Organization

EWICS TC7 Chair

Francesca Saglietti   University of Erlangen-Nuremberg, Germany

Conference Co-chairs

Stefano Tonetta   FBK Fondazione Bruno Kessler, Italy
Erwin Schoitsch   AIT Austrian Institute of Technology, Austria

Program Co-chairs

Erwin Schoitsch   AIT Austrian Institute of Technology, Austria
Stefano Tonetta   FBK Fondazione Bruno Kessler, Italy

Workshop Chair

Erwin Schoitsch   AIT Austrian Institute of Technology, Austria

Publication Chair

Friedemann Bitsch   Thales Deutschland GmbH, Germany

Local Organizing Committee

Annalisa Armani   FBK Fondazione Bruno Kessler, Italy
Silvia Malesardi   FBK Fondazione Bruno Kessler, Italy
Stefano Tonetta   FBK Fondazione Bruno Kessler, Italy

Workshop Chairs

ASSURE 2017

Ewen Denney   SGT/NASA Ames Research Center, USA
Ibrahim Habli   University of York, UK
Ganesh Pai   SGT/NASA Ames Research Center, USA
Kenji Taguchi   AIST, Japan

DECSoS 2017

Erwin Schoitsch   AIT Austrian Institute of Technology, Austria
Amund Skavhaug   NTNU, Norway

SASSUR 2017

Alejandra Ruiz Lopez	Tecnalia, Spain
Jose Luis de La Vara	Carlos III University of Madrid, Spain
Huascar Espinoza	ESI Tecnalia, Spain

TELERISE 2017

Ilaria Matteucci	IIT-CNR, Italy
Paolo Mori	IIT-CNR, Italy
Marinella Petrocchi	IIT-CNR, Italy

TIPS 2017

Laurent Rioux	Thales R&T, France
Chokri Mraidha	CEA List, France
Marc Geilen	Eindhoven University of Technology, The Netherlands
Julio Medina	Universidad de Cantabria, Spain

Supporting Institutions

European Workshop on Industrial Computer
Systems Reliability, Safety and Security

Fondazione Bruno Kessler

Austrian Institute of Technology

Thales Deutschland GmbH

Lecture Notes in Computer Science (LNCS),
Springer Science + Business Media

European Space Agency

Austrian Association for Research in IT

Austrian Computer Society

European Research Consortium
for Informatics and Mathematics

ARTEMIS Industry Association

Electronic Components and Systems
for European Leadership - Austria

German Computer Society

European Network of Clubs for Reliability
and Safety of Software-Intensive Systems

IEEE SMC Technical Committee on
Homeland Security (TCHS)

Associazione Italiana per l'Informatica e il
Calcolo Automatico

Verband österreichischer Software Industrie –
Austrian Software Industry Association

Contents

12th International ERCIM/EWICS/ARTEMIS Workshop on Dependable Smart Embedded Cyber-Physical Systems and Systems-of-Systems (DECSoS 2017)

6th International Workshop on Next Generation of System Assurance Approaches for Safety-Critical Systems (SASSUR 2017)

3rd International Workshop on TEchnical and LEgal Aspects of Data pRIvacy and SEcurity (TELERISE 2017)

5th International Workshop on Assurance Cases for Software-Intensive Systems (ASSURE 2017)

5th International Workshop on Assurance Cases for Software-Intensive Systems (ASSURE 2017)

Ewen Denney[1], Ibrahim Habli[2], Ganesh Pai[1], and Kenji Taguchi[3]

[1] SGT/NASA Ames Research Center, Moffett Field, CA 94035, USA
{ewen.denney, ganesh.pai}@nasa.gov
[2] Department of Computer Science, University of York, York YO10 5DD, UK
ibrahim.habli@york.ac.uk
[3] National Institute of Advanced Industrial Science and Technology,
Hyogo 661-0974, Japan
kenji.taguchi@aist.go.jp

1 Introduction

This volume contains the papers presented at the 5th International Workshop on Assurance Cases for Software-intensive Systems (ASSURE 2017), collocated this year with the 36th International Conference on Computer Safety, Reliability, and Security (SAFECOMP 2017), in Trento, Italy. As with the previous four editions of ASSURE, this year's workshop aims to provide an international forum for presenting emerging research, novel contributions, tool development efforts, and position papers on the foundations and applications of assurance case principles and techniques. The workshop goals are to: (i) explore techniques to create and assess assurance cases for software-intensive systems; (ii) examine the role of assurance cases in the engineering lifecycle of critical systems; (iii) identify the dimensions of effective practice in the development/evaluation of assurance cases; (iv) investigate the relationship between dependability techniques and assurance cases; and, (v) identify critical research challenges towards defining a roadmap for future development.

2 Program

ASSURE 2017 kicked off with an invited keynote talk by Dr. Simon Burton, Chief Expert in Safety, Reliability, and Availability at the Central Research Division of Robert Bosch GmbH, Germany, on assurance of machine learning in automated driving.

Eight papers were accepted this year, covering three themes: *assurance case frameworks, assurance case tool support, and assurance cases for security.*

Papers under the theme of assurance case frameworks examined issues such as their efficacy in software life cycle improvement, and their applicability in developing security strategies and policies. The theme of assurance case tool support included papers that dealt with the integration of assurance cases with system models as applied in the context of medical device assurance, integrated model-based development of safety cases, and web-based platforms for authoring assurance arguments. Finally, the theme concerning assurance cases for security comprised papers addressing such research problems as a combined analysis of safety and security constraints, attack modeling, and the application of systems-theoretic and component-centric approaches.

Unlike the previous years' workshops which concluded with panel sessions, the workshop this year concluded with a guided discussion, where the attendees of the workshop participated in breakout sessions, discussing emerging problems and the types of challenges that should be the focus of future research within the assurance case community. The participants of ASSURE 2017 broadly represented academia, the industry, and the government.

Acknowledgments. We thank all those who submitted papers to ASSURE 2017 and congratulate the authors whose papers were selected for inclusion into the workshop program and proceedings. For reviewing the submissions and providing useful feedback to the authors, we especially thank our distinguished Program Committee members:

- Robin Bloomfield, City University and Adelard LLP, UK
- Simon Burton, Bosch Research, Germany
- Isabelle Conway, ESA/ESTEC, The Netherlands
- Martin Feather, NASA Jet Propulsion Laboratory, USA
- Jérémie Guiochet, LAAS-CNRS, France
- Richard Hawkins, University of York, UK
- Joshua Kaizer, Nuclear Regulatory Commission, USA
- Tim Kelly, University of York, UK
- Yoshiki Kinoshita, Kanagawa University, Japan
- Terrence Martin, Queensland University of Technology, Australia
- Andrew Rae, Griffith University, Australia
- Philippa Ryan, Adelard LLP, UK
- Roger Rivett, Jaguar Land Rover, UK
- Mark-Alexander Sujan, University of Warwick, UK
- Sean White, NHS Digital, UK

as well as the additional reviewers:

- Peter Bishop, Adelard LLP, UK
- Kate Netkachova, Adelard LLP, UK
- Rui Wang, LAAS-CNRS, France

Their efforts have resulted in an exciting workshop program and, in turn, a successful fifth edition of the ASSURE workshop series. Finally, we thank the organizers of SAFECOMP 2017 for their support of ASSURE 2017.

Making the Case for Safety of Machine Learning in Highly Automated Driving

Simon Burton(✉), Lydia Gauerhof, and Christian Heinzemann

Corporate Research, Robert Bosch GmbH, Renningen, Germany
{Simon.Burton,Lydia.Gauerhof,Christian.Heinzemann}@de.bosch.com

Abstract. This paper describes the challenges involved in arguing the safety of highly automated driving functions which make use of machine learning techniques. An assurance case structure is used to highlight the systems engineering and validation considerations when applying machine learning methods for highly automated driving. Particular focus is placed on addressing functional insufficiencies in the perception functions based on convolutional neural networks and possible types of evidence that can be used to mitigate against such risks.

1 Introduction

The transition from *hands-on* (Levels 1–2 of [25]) driver assistance to *hands-off* automated driving (Levels 3–5) requires a number of changes to system safety approaches. For example, a higher level of availability is required as the system cannot be simply deactivated upon detection of a component hardware fault (fail operational vs. fail safe) [20]. At a functional level, an approach to interpreting the current driving situation including environmental conditions and making judgements regarding the subsequent actions is required in order to ensure critical driving situations are avoided under all possible circumstances [26]. The use of machine learning (e.g. for perception tasks [19]) is seen as a promising answer to some of the functional challenges of highly automated driving (HAD) based on the ability to extract relevant features within an unstructured input space. However, systems based on machine learning can only be released into the public domain if they can be argued to be acceptably safe.

The conditions for being acceptably safe with respect to functional safety are set by ISO 26262 [16]. Adherence to this standard remains a necessary prerequisite for demonstrating the safety of HAD in order to ensure a reliable and fault tolerant implementation of the system with respect to random hardware and systematic failures. Nevertheless, in a number of areas the standard does not transfer well to the application of machine learning for open context systems, i.e., systems where the operational context and the environmental conditions for operation cannot be clearly defined at design time. As an example, the development and verification methods contained within part 6 of the standard do not address the problem that when applying machine learning approaches, the functionality itself is essentially embedded in highly dimensional data matrices

© Springer International Publishing AG 2017
S. Tonetta et al. (Eds.): SAFECOMP 2017 Workshops, LNCS 10489, pp. 5–16, 2017.
DOI: 10.1007/978-3-319-66284-8_1

[11] for which verification techniques such as coding guidelines and white-box code coverage [22] provide no relevant insights. In addition, the issue of the insufficiency of the system to meet the safety goals, due to inherent restrictions in sensors, actuators or the inadequacy of the target function itself is also not well addressed by ISO 26262. Extensions to the standard, such as the "Safety of the Intended Function" (SOTIF) approach currently under development aim to address some of these issues, but are mainly focused on driver assistance rather than HAD systems [3]. As a result, alternative methods must be developed and the ability of the system to meet its safety goals must be systematically argued based on "first principles" where adherence to a standard is only one part of the overall argument. An assurance case [15] provides a convincing and valid argument that a set of claims regarding the safety of a system is justified for a given function based on a set of assumptions over its operational context.

In this paper we will explore how assurance case approaches can be applied to the problem of arguing the safety of machine learning within the scope of HAD. As a basis, we analyse and discuss different uses of machine learning and their impact on arguing system safety (Sect. 2). Using a systematic analysis of claims, context and assumptions, we demonstrate that the question of safety for a machine learning function cannot be answered without a detailed understanding of the system context (Sect. 3). The argumentation path proposed in this paper will focus on mitigating the main causes of functional insufficiencies in machine learning based functions (Sect. 4). Finally, we summarise techniques that could be used to create the evidence required to support the assurance case claims (Sect. 5). We use the Goal Structuring Notation [30] to illustrate main lines of the argumentation but our example should not be seen as a comprehensive safety case. We conclude the paper with a brief examination of future work required in this area.

2   Machine Learning and Safety

The issues involved in arguing the safety of machine learning depend very heavily on the types of techniques applied and their application within the overall system context. The following perspectives are useful in evaluating the impact of machine learning on the overall safety case:

- **Scope of the Function:** Machine learning can be applied for different tasks within a HAD functional architecture. The more restricted the task, the more specific the performance criteria on the function can be defined, allowing focused validation and verification activities. Attempts have also been made at applying machine learning techniques for end-to-end learning, the scope of which covers the data fusion of various sensor inputs (e.g. camera and radar data), trajectory planning and decision making and eventual vehicle control (braking, acceleration, steering) [6]. Safety requirements for end-to-end learning approaches are by necessity more abstract due to the scope of the function (e.g. avoid collisions with other vehicles) thus making the task of formulating and validating measurable performance criteria significantly more difficult [28].

- **Learning technique:** Probabilistic inference and statistical learning techniques include methods such as Support Vector Machines [7], Gaussian Processes [23], Markov decision process [9] and Bayesian Networks [10]. These approaches build statistical models based on training data and typically exhibit a continuous behaviour with increasing accuracy of results, the more they are trained. Deep learning algorithms apply multiple processing layers, composed of multiple linear and non-linear transformations to model high-level abstractions within the input data [11]. Examples of which are Convolutional Neural Networks[1] (CNNs, [11, ch. 9]) which show significant potential for processing images [19]. These algorithms add additional challenges due to the lack of transparency and explainability [5] in the features learned at deeper layers and vulnerability to unpredictable "adversarial examples" [12].

- **Learning time:** Machine learning functions that are trained during the development phase (for example using offline supervised learning) can be validated as part of a system release strategy. Online training techniques such as reinforcement learning involve continuously adapting the function during execution (i.e. while driving). Furthermore approaches can be distinguished between centralized training (functions within different vehicles are training in the same way with the same input data) or decentralized training (in this case individual vehicles learn on their own and differ from each other in their learning progress). Techniques which continue their training online must be embedded within a context that ensures that the function remains within a safe envelope as it adapts to its environment in the field. Therefore, unless a sufficiently complete set of invariants for a safe operating envelope can be deterministically defined, decentralized, online training imposes the greatest challenges for safety validation.

- **Distance between critical events:** Events exist that must be handled correctly by the system to ensure safety goals are met (e.g., children appearing suddenly on the road or the car being close to loosing traction) but that are typically under-represented in the training data for the machine learning function. This is either because they occur rarely in reality or because the collection of sufficient training data itself represents an unacceptable risk. As a result, analysis is required to determine how such situations can be adequately covered during training and validation to ensure that they are equally well handled by the system as commonly occurring situations.

The challenges involved in providing a convincing assurance case for the system will heavily depend on the scope of the function as defined by the above dimensions. It is expected that, in practice, the initial applications of machine learning in series development of HAD systems will be for offline, centrally trained functions, implementing well specified detection tasks which can be supported by plausibility checks based on alternative channels within the system context. One such example application, which shall be referenced in the rest of this paper, is the application of CNNs to detect (i.e. classify and localize) objects based on camera images as part of a collision avoidance system for self driving vehicles.

---

[1] See https://www.youtube.com/watch?v=u6aEYuemt0M for an introduction.

3   Application Context

The *Goal G1* that forms the top-level claim of the assurance case scope addressed in this paper will focus on the contribution of the machine learning function to *functional insufficiencies* in the system and can therefore be defined as follows:

- **G1: The residual risk associated with functional insufficiencies in the object detection function is acceptable.**

Arguing the contribution to the *residual risk* due to functional insufficiencies requires a detailed understanding of the functional and performance requirements on the object detection function within the overall system context. These requirements are referenced by the following *Context element C1* of the argument:

- **C1: Definition of functional and performance requirements on the object detection function.**

An assurance case structure at the system level is required that leads to a definition of the performance requirements and risk contribution allocated to the machine learning function. An argument is also required that the contributions of systematic failures and random hardware faults are also adequately covered, for example based on an ISO 26262 related argument. The development of these arguments also lead to significant unsolved challenges in the engineering and validation of HAD systems, but are outside the scope of this paper. The derivation of performance (Safety) requirements within the system context is one of the key contributions to ensuring overall system safety and requires deep domain and system knowledge. Deriving a suitable set of requirements for open context systems is a non-trivial task in itself, systematic approaches to systems engineering are therefore indispensable.

Figure 1 illustrates how a machine learning function could be embedded within its system context. Typical requirements that might be derived at the level of the machine learning function could include for example: *Locate objects of class person from a distance of $X1$, with a lateral accuracy of $X2$, a false negative rate of $X3$ and false positive rate of $X4$.* The parameters $X1, X2, X3, X4$ can be functions that depend on the velocity of the ego vehicle or time to collision (TTC), respectively. The distance to an object $X1$ and the accuracy $X2$ might be also limited by sensor range and resolution and by estimated relevant minimum width of objects (e.g. width of infant legs), while a false negative rate of $X3$ and false positive rate of $X4$ can be tuned by training, evaluation parameters or system measures (e.g. data fusion). Such requirements provide a clear measure of performance for the machine learning environment, but also imply a number of assumptions on the system context. These assumptions might include that the braking distance and speed are sufficient to react when detecting persons for example as close as 10 m ahead on the planned trajectory of the vehicle and that other system measures are available to decrease the overall false negative and false positive rate to a sufficiently safe level, etc.

As indicated in Fig. 1, a design by contract approach is recommended whereby each functional component of the system is defined by a set of assumptions that needs to hold in order to ensure the specified behaviour. The following list contains typical assumptions that are relevant for the assurance case:

- **A1: Assumptions on the operational profile of the system's environment.** For example, the types and occurrence distribution of objects in the environment.
- **A2: Assumptions on attributes of inputs to the machine learning function.** For example, the camera resolution is sufficient to be able to detect persons from a distance of 100 m with the required accuracy.
- **A3: Assumptions on the performance potential of machine learning.** For example, the chosen CNN approach has the intrinsic potential, given the right parameterization and set of learning data to fulfil the allocated performance requirements.

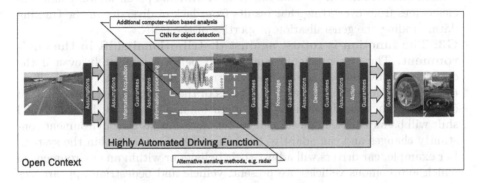

Fig. 1. Functional architecture of a HAD system

4 Causes of Functional Insufficiencies in Machine Learning

The inherent uncertainty associated with machine learning techniques coupled with the open context environment lead to different causes of hazards compared to traditional, algorithmic and control law approaches to vehicle control. In order to argue the claim that functional insufficiencies within the machine learning function (here: camera based object detection, supervised training) are minimised, it is important to understand the causes of the insufficiencies. The assurance case strategy S1 described here can thus be described as follows:

- **S1:** Argument over causes of functional insufficiencies in machine learning.

As interest in machine learning safety has grown, a number of authors [1,27,31] have investigated different causes of insufficiencies in machine learning functions. A number of causes that are applicable to the HAD use case described here are summarised below and are positively formulated as sub-goals G2-G6 within the assurance case, which is summarised in Fig. 2:

- **G2: The environmental context is well defined and reflected in training data.** One of the key differences in machine learning techniques compared to algorithmic approaches is the lack of a detailed specification of the target function. Instead, the functional specification can be seen to be encoded within the set of training data. Therefore, if the training data does not reflect the target operating context, then there is a strong likelihood that the learned function will exhibit insufficiencies. Critical or ambiguous situations, within which the system must react in a predictably safe manner, may occur rarely or may be so dangerous that they are not adequately represented in the training data. This leads to the effect that critical situations remain undertrained in the final function. Additional potential for insufficiencies comes from overfitting that results from lack of diversity in the training data, eroding the generalisation properties of the CNN.

- **G3: The function is robust against distributional shift in the environment.** The system should continue to perform accurately even if the operational environment differs from the training environment [1]. This effectively can be formulated as the robustness of the system to react in a shift of distribution between its training and operational environment. Distributional shift will be inevitable in most open context systems, as the environment constantly changes and can adapt to the behaviour of actors within the system. For example, car drivers will adjust their behaviour within an environment in which autonomous vehicles are present, vehicle and pedestrian appearances change over time, etc.

- **G4: The function exhibits a uniform behaviour over critical classes of situations.** An often cited problem associated with neural networks, is the possibility of adversarial examples [8,12,21]. An adversarial example is an input sample that is similar (at least to the human eye) to other samples but that leads to a completely different categorisation with a high confidence value. It has been shown that such examples can be automatically generated and used to "trick" the network. Although it is still unclear to what extent adversarial examples could occur naturally or whether they would be exploited for malicious purposes, from a safety validation perspective, they are useful for demonstrating that features can be learnt by the network and assigned an incorrect relevance [12]. Therefore an argument should be found to minimise the probability of such behaviour especially in critical driving situations.

- **G5: The function is robust against differences between its training and execution platforms.** Machine learning functions can be sensitive to subtle changes in the input data. When using machine learning to represent a function that is embedded as part of a wider system as described here (see Fig. 1), the input to the neural network will have typically been processed by a number of elements already, such as image filters and buffering mechanisms. These elements may vary between the training and operation environments leading to the trained function becoming dependent on hidden features of the training environment. It is therefore necessary to understand the differences between training and operational environment, including any potential weaknesses or faults in the training environment (e.g. software defects in open source training libraries) and data leakage resulting from hidden, unnoticed correlations in the environmental context of the provided training samples [17].

- **G6: The function is robust against changes in its system context.** Vehicle systems are typically developed and deployed in a wide number of system variants which may include different combinations of sensors as well as different positioning of sensors within the vehicle. In addition, over time changes are made to the system design as part of continuous improvement or cost reduction measures. However, hidden data dependencies [27] may exist by training and validating the machine learning function within a given context. Subtle differences between the original context (e.g. a particular camera lens, or installation height) for which the function was trained and the re-use context can lead to functional insufficiencies that may not appear during development and regression testing but may lead to degraded performance in the field. Furthermore, when updating the system it is also necessary to ensure a monotonic performance improvement, i.e. situations that are safely covered in a previous version of the system must also be covered in the new version, even if the overall performance is improved.

5   Sources of Evidence for the Assurance Case

Dedicated methods for validating machine learning functions, and in particular neural networks, to the level of integrity required by safety-critical systems is currently an emerging field of research. It is expected that, analogous to traditional algorithmic-based software approaches, a diverse set of complementary evidence based on constructive measures, formal analyses and test methods will be required to make a robust assurance case. In this section we discuss different categories of potential evidence and how it can support the sub-claims of the assurance case described in the previous section. Note that each sub-claim in Fig. 2 will depend on more than one source of evidence.

- **Training data coverage:** Open context systems such as HAD are defined by the fact that it is not possible to specify a priori all possible operational scenarios. Applied to the training of neural networks for image processing in HAD, this relates to the infinite dimensionality and variations in the input images. Criteria therefore need to be applied to define how much training data is required for a particular application and which data will lead to the most accurate approximation of the (unspecifiable) target function. It is expected

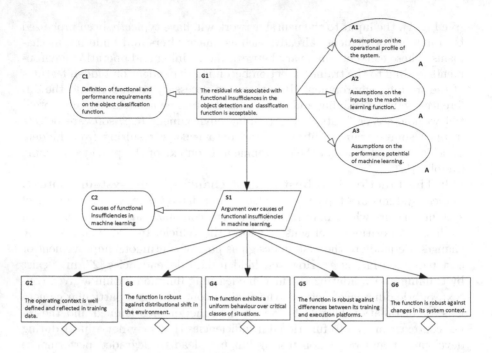

Fig. 2. Assurance Case Structure

that a combination of complementary criteria applied in parallel will be most effective and may include:

- *Training data volume*: A sufficient amount of training data is used to provide a statistically relevant spread of scenarios and to ensure a stabilization of a strong coverage of weightings in the neural network.
- *Coverage of known, critical scenarios*: Domain experience based on well understood physical properties of the system and environment as well as previous validation exercises leads to the identification of classes of scenarios that should exhibit similar behaviour in the function. Although some classes may be obvious and simple to reproduce (day and night driving, weather conditions, traffic situations), other classes may occur rarely and will require targeted data acquisition and possibly synthetic generation to ensure sufficient coverage during training.
- *Minimisation of unknown, critical scenarios*: Other critical combinations of classes will not even be known during system design [2]. A combination of systematic identification of equivalence classes in the training data and statistical coverage during training and validation will therefore be essential to adequately minimise the risk of insufficiencies due to inadequate training data.
- **Explainability of the learned function:** A key component of demonstrating the correctness of traditional safety-critical software are white-box techniques that include manual code review, static analysis, code coverage

and formal verification. These techniques allow for an argument to be formulated on the detailed algorithmic design and implementation but cannot be easily transferred to the machine learning paradigms. Other arguments must therefore be found that make use of knowledge of the internal behaviour of the neural networks. Saliency maps [4,29], based on the back propagation of results in the network to highlight those portions of an image that have greatest influence on classification results, can be used to provide a manual plausibility check of results as well as to determine potential causes of failed tests, e.g., resulting from data leakage. Another line of research tries to generate a natural language explanation referring in human understandable terms to the contents of the input image to explain which features were relevant for the classification. A recent approach in this direction has been presented by Hendricks et al. [14]. It is also conceivable that other metrics could be found for neural networks that can be used in the assurance argumentation, e.g. the extent by which weightings are affected by the training data or how well computations of the neural network have been covered by the performed tests.

- **Uncertainty calculation:** Although machine learning approaches offer a promising performance on perception tasks, false negatives (not detected objects), false positives (ghost objects), misclassification and mislocalisation may have safety critical consequences within the overall functional architecture of the system. One way to reduce the impact of these errors is considering uncertainties. Thereby, two types of uncertainties can be distinguished. Aleatoric uncertainty covers noise that is inherent in the observation (e.g. sensor or motion noise) and that cannot be reduced by increasing training data. In contrast, epistemic uncertainty captures uncertainty within the model (e.g. uncertainty of parameters) [18] and emphasises that assumptions on the model or the model itself may not represent the reality accurately enough. This has the effect that for a given input class (e.g. a particular vehicle, under similar environmental conditions), the system performs inconsistently within a particular range of error. A high classification uncertainty for a specific input class, belonging to epistemic uncertainty, could indicate inadequacies in the training data or sub-optimal parametrisation fo the neural network, etc. Uncertainty quantification can provide information that is used in plausibility and sensor fusion algorithms [18], thus improving the overall robustness and reliability of the subsequent trajectory planning tasks [26].
- **Black-box testing:** Due to the inherent restrictions of white-box approaches to verification of the trained function, a strong emphasis will need to be placed on black-box testing techniques. These techniques will include targeted testing of the software component containing the learned function including the use of systematically selected test data based on equivalence classes (see discussion of training data selection above). Based on advances in computer graphics realism as well as the possibility to generate labelled data with specific properties, the use of synthetically generated data may also play a role as demonstrated by Richter et al. [24]. This would imply the introduction of an additional assumption into the assurance case, that the synthetic data

would lead to test results that are representative of the operational environment. A combination of synthetic, real and manipulated real data, including a detailed analysis of the impact within the network due to the difference input types would be required. System-level vehicle integration tests will also need to form an essential part of the assurance case in order to validate all assumptions made during system development including whether or not sufficient understanding of critical scenarios have lead to an adequate training of the function. In reality, it will not be viable to provide assurance of the required level of system performance through driving test hours alone during the development phase. Therefore evidence will need to be provided for scenario coverage of the tests combined with statistical extrapolation techniques, field-based observations, component and integration tests (including simulation) as well as constructive safety measures.

- **Run-time measures:** An additional source of evidence for minimising the impact of functional insufficiencies will be run-time measures which make use of secondary channels, not used by the machine learning function.
    - *Run-time plausibility checks*: Plausibility checks on the outputs of the neural network could involve tracking results over time (e.g. objects detected in one frame should appear in contiguous frames, until out of view) or by comparing against alternative sensor inputs (e.g. radar or lidar reflections). Such plausibility checks may mitigate against insufficiencies that occur spontaneously for individual frames.
    - *Run-time monitoring of assumptions*: If certain assumptions regarding the operational distribution are determined to be critical, then they could also be monitored during run-time. Discrepancies between the distribution of objects detected at run-time and the assumptions could indicate either errors in the trained function or that the system is operating within a context for which it was not adequately trained. If such a situation is detected, appropriate actions for mitigating the effect of the discrepancy can be initiated. One approach in this direction are software safety cages [13].

6 Conclusions and Future Work

The main challenge for using machine learning algorithms for HAD is arguing an adequately low level of residual risk associated with functional insufficiencies resulting from imperfections of the used machine learning algorithms and the impossibility of testing all possible driving situations at design time. Such arguments are not currently supported by the relevant safety norms, most prominently ISO 26262. This paper proposed applying an assurance case approach to determine how such an argument could be formed based on "first principles" by decomposing the safety goals of the system into technical performance requirements on the machine learning function under explicit consideration of assumptions on the system (and components within the system context) environment. The assurance case would be completed by providing systematically derived and diverse evidence to support the claim that various causes of insufficiencies have been sufficiently mitigated against.

The assurance case structure presented in this paper raises several issues that require substantial future research activities. First, providing the necessary evidence for the assurance case requires the development of entirely new verification techniques including a demonstration of their effectiveness. This work will require advances in theoretical insights into machine learning as well as large scale experimental research to confirm the effectiveness of proposed measures. Further research will also include the application of dynamic safety cases for systems that apply decentralized, online reinforcement learning techniques, i.e., systems that continue to adapt their behaviour at runtime. These activities have to be integrated into a holistic system engineering approach that supports the structure of the assurance case. This technical research work needs to be complemented by activities within industry to form a consensus on risk evaluation and acceptable argumentation structures that would feed into future standards.

References

1. Amodei, D., Olah, C., Steinhardt, J., Christiano, P., Schulman, J., Mané, D.: Concrete problems in AI safety. arXiv e-prints, June 2016
2. Attenberg, J., Ipeirotis, P., Provost, F.: Beat the machine: challenging humans to find a predictive model's "unknown unknowns". ACM J. Data Inf. Qual. 1(1), 1–17 (2014)
3. Bergenhem, C., Johansson, R., Söderberg, A., Nilsson, J., Tryggvesson, J., Törngren, M., Ursing, S.: How to reach complete safety requirement refinement for autonomous vehicles. Technical report, CARS 2015 - Critical Automotive applications: Robustness & Safety, September 2015, Paris, France (2015)
4. Binder, A., Bach, S., Montavon, G., Müller, K.R., Samek, W.: Layer-wise relevance propagation for deep neural network architectures. In: Kim, K., Joukov, N. (eds.) Information Science and Applications (ICISA). LNEE, vol. 376, pp. 913–922. Springer, Singapore (2016). doi:10.1007/978-981-10-0557-2_87
5. Castelvecchi, D.: Can we open the black box of AI? Nature 538(7623), 20–23 (2016). http://www.nature.com/news/can-we-open-the-black-box-of-ai-1.20731
6. Chen, C., Seff, A., Kornhauser, A., Xiao, J.: Deepdriving: learning affordance for direct perception in autonomous driving. In: Proceedings of the 2015 IEEE International Conference on Computer Vision (ICCV), pp. 2722–2730. IEEE (2015)
7. Christmann, A., Steinwart, I.: Support Vector Machines. Springer, Heidelberg (2008)
8. Fawzi, A., Fawzi, O., Frossard, P.: Analysis of classifiers' robustness to adversarial perturbations. arXiv:1502.02590 (2015)
9. Feinberg, E.A., Shwartz, A. (eds.): International Series in Operations Research & Management Science, vol. 40. Springer, Heidelberg (2002)
10. Friedman, N., Geiger, D., Goldszmidt, M.: Bayesian network classifiers. Mach. Learn. 29(2), 131–163 (1997)
11. Goodfellow, I., Bengio, Y., Courville, A.: Deep Learning. MIT Press, Cambridge (2016)
12. Goodfellow, I.J., Shlens, J., Szegedy, C.: Explaining and harnessing adversarial examples. arXiv:1412.6572 (2015)

13. Heckemann, K., Gesell, M., Pfister, T., Berns, K., Schneider, K., Trapp, M.: Safe automotive software. In: König, A., Dengel, A., Hinkelmann, K., Kise, K., Howlett, R.J., Jain, L.C. (eds.) KES 2011. LNCS, vol. 6884, pp. 167–176. Springer, Heidelberg (2011). doi:10.1007/978-3-642-23866-6_18

14. Hendricks, L.A., Akata, Z., Rohrbach, M., Donahue, J., Schiele, B., Darrell, T.: Generating visual explanations. In: Leibe, B., Matas, J., Sebe, N., Welling, M. (eds.) ECCV 2016. LNCS, vol. 9908, pp. 3–19. Springer, Cham (2016). doi:10.1007/978-3-319-46493-0_1. http://arxiv.org/abs/1603.08507

15. IEEE: IEEE standard adoption of ISO/IEC 15026-1 - systems and software engineering - systems and software assurance (2014)

16. ISO: ISO 26262: Road vehicles - functional safety (2011)

17. Kaufman, S., Rosset, S., Perlich, C.: Leakage in data mining: Formulation, detection, and avoidance. In: Proceedings of the 17th ACM SIGKDD International Conference on Knowledge Discovery and Data Mining, pp. 556–563. ACM (2011)

18. Kendall, A., Gal, Y.: What uncertainties do we need in Bayesian deep learning for computer vision? CoRR abs/1703.04977 (2017). http://arxiv.org/abs/1703.04977

19. Krizhevsky, A., Sutskever, I., Hinton, G.E.: Imagenet classification with deep convolutional neural networks. In: Advances in Neural Information Processing Systems, pp. 1097–1105 (2012)

20. Mohan, N., Törngren, M., Izosimov, V., Kaznov, V., Roos, P., Svahn, J., Gustavsson, J., Nesic, D.: Challenges in architecting fully automated driving; with an emphasis on heavy commercial vehicles. In: 2016 Workshop on Automotive Systems/Software Architectures (2016)

21. Nguyen, A., Yosinski, J., Clune, J.: Deep neural networks are easily fooled: High confidence predictions for unrecognizable images. In: 2015 IEEE Conference on Computer Vision and Pattern Recognition, CVPR 2015, pp. 427–436 (2015)

22. Piziali, A.: Functional Verification Coverage Measurement and Analysis. Springer, Heidelberg (2008)

23. Rasmussen, C.E., Williams, C.K.I.: Gaussian Processes for Machine Learning. MIT Press, Cambridge (2006)

24. Richter, S.R., Vineet, V., Roth, S., Koltun, V.: Playing for data: ground truth from computer games. arXiv:1608.02192 (2016)

25. SAE: J3016, taxonomy and definitions for terms related to on-road motor vehicle automated driving systems (2013)

26. Tas, Ö.S., Kuhnt, F., Zöllner, J.M., Stiller, C.: Functional system architectures towards fully automated driving. In: 2016 IEEE Intelligent Vehicles Symposium. IEEE (2016)

27. Sculley, D., Holt, G., Golovin, D., Davydov, E., Phillips, T., Ebner, D., Chaudhary, V., Young, M., Crespo, J.F. Dennison, D.: Hidden technical debt in machine learning systems. Advances in Neural Information Processing Systems, 28 (NIPS 2015) (2015)

28. Shalev-Shwartz, S., Shashua, A.: On the sample complexity of end-to-end training vs. semantic abstraction training. In: arXiv:1604.06915 (2016)

29. Simonyan, K., Vedaldi, A., Zisserman, A.: Deep inside convolutional networks: visualising image classification models and saliency maps. In: arXiv:1312.6034 (2014)

30. Kelly, T., Weaver, R.: The goal structuring notation - a safety argument notation. In: Proceedings of the DSN 2004 Workshop on Assurance Cases (2004)

31. Varshney, K.: Engineering safety in machine learning. ArXiv e-prints, January 2016

A Thought Experiment on Evolution of Assurance Cases
—from a Logical Aspect

Shuji Kinoshita and Yoshiki Kinoshita[✉]

Kanagawa University, Tsuchiya 2946, Hiratsuka 259-1293, Japan
{shuji,yoshiki}@progsci.info.kanagawa-u.ac.jp

Abstract. A thought experiment on evolution of assurance argument is performed on the basis of an interview with a manufacturer that applied for a certification of conformance of their in-house software life cycle to a safety standard. The working hypothesis of the experiment is that assurance cases help find problems in arguments on software life cycle and improve the life cycle. Based on the result of the thought experiment, questions for further empirical studies are generated and the ontology of relevant information items are analysed.

Keywords: Assurance case · Assurance argument · Software assurance · Software life cycle · Evolution · Formal approach · Thought experiment

1 Introduction

Assurance arguments must change as their target item (product, system, its life cycle or service) changes. The item changes because of corrections or changes in its environment, including the system connected to the item and the relevant regulations.

The authors had an interview with a manufacturer who applied for a certification for conformance of their in-house software life cycle to a safety standard. They struggled to follow update of the standard. In some occasions, the manufacturer had a valid argument for the conformance of their initial software life cycle, but the certification body found it unacceptable and the manufacturer had to modify their life cycle in order to give an argument that the life cycle conforms to the revised standard. The manufacturer recorded their initial software life cycle but did not record their assurance argument on it in such a way that enables tracing the problem.

The authors surmised that a logical support by means of assurance cases could have reduced the struggle after the rejection. This led the authors to set up the working hypothesis that assurance cases help find logical problems in arguments on software life cycle and improve the life cycle and perform a thought experiment that explicates how assurance cases help.

© Springer International Publishing AG 2017
S. Tonetta et al. (Eds.): SAFECOMP 2017 Workshops, LNCS 10489, pp. 17–26, 2017.
DOI: 10.1007/978-3-319-66284-8_2

Logical here does not only mean "according to logical inference" but also "according to ontology" (i.e., vocabulary and basic assumptions that frames the arguments). In order to focus on logical aspects of assurance arguments and to abstract away from the irrelevant aspects, a hypothetical safety standard and hypothetical software life cycles are used in this work.

The thought experiment is performed in the following hypothetical setting. It is assumed that a software manufacturer is applying for certification that their own in-house *software life cycle*, named SLC1, conforms to a hypothetical safety standard STD (Fig. 1). Before application, the manufacturer has had an assurance argument that convinced themselves of the conformance and has developed an assurance case A1 that records the conformance argument. For that purpose, there is a need for an interpretation I1 of STD in the context of SLC1, and I1 is also documented in A1.

Unfortunately, the first application for a certification is rejected. The manufacturer has to find the reason of rejection by itself because the certification body does not provide it, as is common in certification. The assurance case A1 is examined and two possible reasons for rejection are found. To remedy these problems, the interpretation of the standard in the context of the life cycle is changed.

The manufacturer revises the interpretation and its in-house software life cycle to obtain I2 and SLC2, and the assurance case A2 is developed to record the relevant assurance argument. The scenario finishes with the success of the second application.

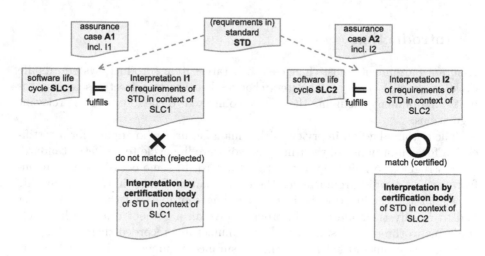

Fig. 1. Information items of the thought experiment

After the thought experiment, three questions are generated out of its result. These questions may serve as a starting point and determine a framework of further studies, which could be empirical work or other thought experiments.

The ontology of relevant information items is also analysed. Information items include standards, descriptions of items (software life cycle, in this work) to conform to the standard, and interpretations of requirements of the standard in the context of the item.

To sum up, the contribution of this work is two folds: generation of questions for further studies and analysis of ontology of relevant information items.

This paper is organized as follows. The thought experiment of assurance argument is presented in Sects. 2–7. A hypothetical safety standard STD is presented in Sect. 2. The standard, the following software life cycles and assurance cases are presented to the extent only enough for the discussion in this paper. Section 3 presents a hypothetical software life cycle SLC1 for in-house use in a manufacturer. Section 4 provides the manufacturer's interpretation I1 of requirements of STD in the context of SLC1 and assurance argument claiming that SLC1 conforms to the requirements of I1; these are compiled as the assurance case A2. Sections 6 and 7 are about the modified software life cycle and assurance case developed in response to rejection of application for a certification. This ends the presentation of the thought experiment.

Questions generated by this thought experiment and the ontology for relevant information items is discussed in Sect. 8, where relevant to this thought experiment is also analysed. Section 9 concludes with a list of related work.

2   The Hypothetical Safety Standard STD

Our hypothetical safety standard STD specifies requirements on software life cycle processes on top of the general requirements in ISO/IEC/IEEE 12207 [4]. For risk management, it contains the following requirement, among others.

(STD-1) The risk under the intended use of the target software and reasonably foreseeable misuse shall be managed. The result of risk management shall be documented.

In the sequel, we focus on conformance to this requirement.

3   The Software Life Cycle SLC1

The manufacturer has a software life cycle for its in-house use. It contains the following processes, among others. The reader is referred to Fig. 2.

(SLC1-1) Define and record stakeholder needs and requirements. The output includes the stakeholder needs and requirements, and records the intended use of the software. It also records all misuses that are identified according to the activity SLC1-0 (not shown).

(SLC1-2) Define safety requirements, which identify the requirements for safety under the intended use and misuse identified in the document. The input to safety requirements definition includes the stakeholder needs and requirements.

(SLC1-3) Manage risk. The activities include the following:

    (SLC1-3)(1) analyse risk of the system satisfying the system/software requirements,

    (SLC1-3)(2) evaluate risk analysed above, and

    (SLC1-3)(3) if the result of risk evaluation requires, provide means of controlling risk and implement it; this task includes selection of risk control measures, review of new risk introduced by the selected risk control measures, and review of risk increased by the selected risk control measures. The input to risk management includes the system/software requirements among others. All output is recorded in risk management file.

(SLC1-4) Define system/software requirements. The input includes stakeholder needs and requirements, safety requirements and risk management file, among others.

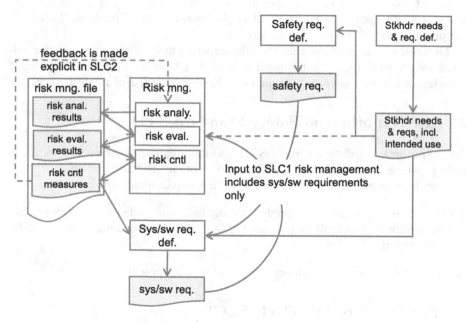

Fig. 2. Processes and their input/output

4 Assurance Case A1 that Claims Conformance of SLC1 to STD

The manufacturer interprets the requirement (STD-1) in the context of SLC1 as (I1-1)–(I1-3); this interpretation is called I1. It then developed an assurance argument that claims the conformance of SLC1 to I1 and documents the whole argument including I1 as the assurance case A1.

The target of the argument is software life cycle here, and is not to be confused with a concrete software. Therefore, for instance, we talk about whether a provision of assurance argument on the software is included in the life cycle, instead of talking about whether some concrete assurance argument on the software is valid and appropriate.

(A1-1) The following three claims are sufficient for the conformance to (STD-1).
  (I1-1) The risk of the system satisfying the system/software requirements shall be managed.
  (I1-2) Risks newly introduced by the selected risk control measures and the risks increased by the selected risk control measures shall be reviewed.
  (I1-3) The result of risk management shall be documented as the risk management file.
(A1-2) (I1-1) holds for SLC1 because the risk of the system satisfying the system/software requirements is managed (SLC1-3)(1).
(A1-3) (I1-2) holds for SLC1 because of (SLC1-3)(3).
(A1-4) (I1-3) is supported by the last statement of (SLC1-3).

5   Rejection of Certification and Improvement of SLC1

The manufacturer applies for certification of conformance of SLC1 to STD. Unfortunately, it is rejected without any reasons specified, as is often the case for certification. So the manufacturer examines A1 and concludes there can be the following two reasons for rejection.

(RR-1) (I1-1) may need to be strengthened. The requirement (STD-1) of STD requires to manage the risk under intended use and identified misuse. The requirement (I1-1) is considered appropriate as an interpretation of (STD-1) because the system/software requirements are derived from stakeholder needs and requirements including intended use and identified misuse. However, this rationale is not made explicit and may be insufficient.
(RR-2) (I1-2) may not be sufficient because then there may be no room for *iterative* realization and evaluation of the risk control measures. The new risk and increased risk found in (SLC1-3)(3) must be managed.

The interpretation I1 is updated in the following way. To resolve (RR-1), the following requirement is added in the new interpretation: to fulfill (STD-1), assurance argument for the claim shall be provided that the risk from each intended use and reasonably foreseeable misuse are managed to a sufficient level. To resolve (RR-2), the interpreted requirement (I1-2) was strengthened so that "risks newly introduced by the selected risk control measures and the risks increased by them" shall not only be reviewed but also be managed.

These changes necessitates the change of the life cycle SLC1 and argument A1. An activity that fulfills the demand for assurance argument is added to the life cycle to fulfill (I1-1). For (I1-2), the risk management process of the life cycle is made iterative so that the result of (SLC1-3)(3) is input to (SLC1-3)(1). The iteration is to be terminated when the new and increased risk is small enough so that it is acceptable as residual risk.

6   Improved Software Life Cycle SLC2

The revised software life cycle SLC2 contains the following processes. The difference from SLC1 is indicated by underline.

(SLC2-1) Define and record stakeholder needs and requirements. The output includes the stakeholder needs and requirements, and records the intended use of the software. It also records all misuses that are identified according to the activity SLC2-0 (not shown).

(SLC2-2) Define safety requirements, which identify the requirements for safety under the intended use and misuse identified in the document. The input to safety requirements definition includes the stakeholder needs and requirements.

(SLC2-3) Manage risk. The activities include the following:
  (SLC2-3)(1) analyse risk of the system satisfying the stakeholder needs and requirements,
  (SLC2-3)(2) evaluate risk analysed above, and
  (SLC2-3)(3) if the result of risk evaluation requires, provide means of controlling risk and implement it; this task includes selection of risk control measures, review of new risk introduced by the selected risk control measures, and review of risk increased by the selected risk control measures. The result of review is then input to SLC2-3)(1) to start the risk management iteratively. (This iteration is terminated when the result of risk evaluation does not require risk control measures in (SLC2-3)(3).)
The input to risk management includes the stakeholder needs and requirements and the system/software requirements among others. All output is recorded in risk management file.

(SLC2-4) Define system/software requirements. The input includes safety requirements and risk management file, among others.

(SLC2-5) For each use and misuse identified in (SLC2-1), provide an assurance argument for the claim that the risk is managed by (SLC2-3) appropriately.

7   Assurance Case A2 that Claims Conformance of SLC2 to STD

The manufacturer interprets the requirement (STD-1) in the context of SLC2 as (I2-1)–(I2-3); this interpretation is called I2. It then developed an assurance argument that claims the conformance of SLC2 to I2 and document the whole argument including I2 as the assurance case A2. The difference from A1 is indicated by underline.

(A2-1) The following three claims are sufficient for the conformance to (STD-1).
  (I2-1) The risk of the system under the intended use and identified reasonably foreseeable misuse of the target software shall be managed. Also, an assurance argument for the claim shall be provided that the risk under each intended use and reasonably foreseeable misuse are managed to the sufficient level.

(I2-2) Risks newly introduced by the selected risk control measures and the risks increased by the selected risk control measures shall be reviewed and managed.

(I2-3) The result of risk management shall be documented as the risk management file.

(A2-2) (I2-1) holds for SLC2 because the risk of the system satisfying stakeholder needs and requirements is managed (SLC2-3), the stakeholder needs and requirements include the identified intended use and reasonably foreseeable misuse (SLC2-2), and for each intended use and foreseen misuse, an assurance argument is provided for the claim that the risk is managed properly.

(A2-3) (I2-2) holds for SLC2 because of (SLC2-3)(3).

(A2-4) (I2-3) is supported by the last statement of (SLC2-3).

The second application of certification that SLC2 conforms to STD with the assurance case A2 was accepted by the certification body.

8   Discussion

8.1   Questions Generated by the Thought Experiment

Some questions arise from the result of the thought experiment.
    The first question is

How difficult or easy it would be to find the problems (RR-1) and (RR-2) if assurance case A1 were not developed?

Use of the assurance case A1 enabled finding the problem (RR-1). If assurance cases were not used, the manufacturer would have to recall the detail of their implicit argument for the reexamination after the rejection. It would have been difficult to spot the difference between the risk under intended use and identified misuse and the risk of the system satisfying system/software requirements.
    Finding (RR-2) would require similar detail. Here, the difference between only reviewing the risk and reviewing it and starting another risk management cycle is enabled by means of examination of explicit description provided by A1.
    The assurance cases clarify the ontology by distinguishing the requirements in the standard, their interpretations and the description of the life cycles. Empirical work or another thought experiments may be conducted in order to investigate whether this makes it easier to find the problems such as (RR-1) and (RR-2).
    The second question is

How could formal approach to assurance argument facilitate the manufacturer's work and the cerfitication body's work?

Formal approach to assurance arguments, as proposed in [8] would provide methods to describe ontology formally, automatic methods to check the formal ontology, and methods to experiment on the formal ontology by means of proof checkers or theorem provers. This is similar to the case in validation where the specification alone is examined but not quite the same as the case in verification where the implementation is examined with respect to the given specification.

In the presented thought experiment, it does not matter whether the assurance argument is given formally or not.

The second question may be specialised to the following third question.

How could formal approach to assurance argument facilitate to handle logical flaws in the argument?

Finding and correcting logical flaws in the argument is not included in the present thought experiment, but there are certainly those reported in authors interview with manufacturer. Formal approach obviously enables finding logical flaws, but the significance of such finding in the context of the overall assurance of total software life cycle should ultimately be examined in vivo by empirical study, by thought experiments or by other means.

These questions may serve as a starting point and may provide a framework in which further investigation may be conducted.

8.2   Information Items and Relation Between Them

In this thought experiment, the following kinds of information items appear.

(1) Top level requirements of interest (the standard STD, in this case).
(2) Item of interest (software life cycles SLC1 and SLC2).
(3) Interpretation of the top level requirements in the context of the item (I1 and I2).
(4) Assurance argument that the item of interest fulfills the interpreted requirements (A1 and A2).

Note that we do need the interpretation that instantiates the requirements in the setting (or in the vocabulary and basic assumptions) of the item of interest because the top level requirements is not usually written in the context of a specific item, i.e., in the vocabulary of the item nor under the basic assumption that should be supposed to be the case for the item.

These information items have interdependency with each other. Items are expected to *conform* to the interpreted requirements, and the interpreted requirements should be related to the top level requirement so that the conformance of any applicable item to the interpreted requirements *implies* that to the top level requirements.[1] Logical and mathematical formulation of these

---

[1] Here is a more strict but involved explanation. Items and the top level requirements are described in a different language as they are at different level of abstraction. So, fulfillment by an item of the top level requirements means fulfillment by an item of the *interpreted* top level requirements, given an interpretation of top level requirements language to items language. There are in general many such interpretations, such as the manufacturer's and certification body's in our thought experiment. Stakeholders would have their own interpretation under which they are confident that "an item fulfills the requirements" means "an item fulfills the interpreted requirements."

relations is not trivial and theories such as clones in universal algebra and Lawvere theories in category theory seems relevant. Such formulation would work as the theory behind formal approach to formulate these information items in the direction suggested in [8]. Investigation in this direction is left as future work.

In the thought experiment, typified uses of the verbal forms used in requirements and specifications of life cycle processes are of much help. For instance, requirements (top level requirements and their interpretations) are typically stated as "shall be," and life cycle processes are typically described by imperative mood, such as "Act." Some of these rules are provided in the manual for standard writing such as [3], and to follow such rules would ease mathematical formulation of the relationship between the information items.

9   Conclusion and Related Work

A thought experiment was performed, with a hypothetical setting that a manufacturer is applying for certification of conformance of their own in-house software life cycle to a hypothetical safety standard. Three questions were generated out of the result of the experiment. Approaches to the questions were suggested but the study of these questions remains as future work. Ontology of information items relevant to this experiment and to assurance arguments on software life cycles in general were also discussed.

There are works on assurance cases and conformance to standards including the following. [1] reports practical experience concerning structuring assurance case in the context of conformance to actual standards. [2] presents an explicit framework of assurance case as required by DO-178C. A similar framework is found in IEC 62853 Open systems dependability, whose Committee Draft for Vote is in the process of approval at the time of preparing this paper.

[6] discusses integration of formal arguments into system refinement in the context of system/software life cycle. It refers to the changes in connection to modularization and encapsulation of the system. [7] argues that assurance case plays an essential role in the change management for items (product including software and service). Specific example of change, however, is not given in these works. Design of system/software life cycle is not considered, either.

The thought experiment in the current work examines the change to the system/software life cycle and assurance argument on it in the context of conformance to a hypothetical standard.

[5] discusses that standards should define the properties of the target item that are expected to accrue from the use of the standard, as well as a rational that justifies the contents of the standard. This work may be regarded to proceed in the same direction as the analysis of information items in this work.

Acknowledgments. The authors acknowledge Makoto Takeyama's thoughtful comments on the draft of this paper. Koji Okuno coordinated the authors' contact with Nihon Koden Corp. that led to this work. The authors thank Kazuo Oosone, Masato Tanaka and Yuichi Kurabe for sharing their experience as software engineering experts in industry. The second author is grateful to Bengt Nordström for providing necessary facilities to prepare a draft of this paper during his stay in Göteborg.

References

1. Ankrum, T.S., Kromholz, A.H.: Structured assurance cases: three common standards. In: Ninth IEEE International Symposium on High-Assurance Systems Engineering (HASE 2005), pp. 99–108 (2005)
2. Holloway, C.M.: Explicate78: uncovering the implicit assurance case in do-178c. Technical report 20150009473, NASA Langley Research Center (2015)
3. ISO/IEC: ISO/IEC Directives, Part 2, Principles and rules for the structure and drafting of ISO and IEC documents, 7th edn. (2016)
4. ISO/IEC/IEEE: 12207 FDIS Software life cycle processes (Final Draft International Standard registered for approval)
5. Knight, J.C., Rowanhill, J.: The indispensable role of rationale in safety standards. In: Skavhaug, A., Guiochet, J., Bitsch, F. (eds.) SAFECOMP 2016. LNCS, vol. 9922, pp. 39–50. Springer, Cham (2016). doi:10.1007/978-3-319-45477-1_4
6. Moore, A.P., Klinker, J.E., Mihelcic, D.M.: How to construct formal arguments that persuade certifiers. In: Hinchey, M.G., Bowen, J.P. (eds.) Industrial-Strength Formal Methods in Practice. FACIT, pp. 285–314. Springer, London (1999). doi:10.1007/978-1-4471-0523-7_13
7. Tokoro, M. (ed.): Open Systems Dependability: Dependability Engineering for Ever-Changing Systems, 2nd edn. CRC Press, Boca Raton (2015)
8. Kinoshita, Y., Takeyama, M.: Assurance case as a proof in a theory towards formulation of rebuttals. In: Dale, C., Anderson, T. (eds.) Assuring the Safety of Systems, Proceedings of the Twenty-first Safety-Critical Systems Symposium, Bristol, UK, pp. 205–230 (2013). SCSC on Amazon ISBN 978-1-4810-18647

Using an Assurance Case Framework to Develop Security Strategy and Policies

Robin Bloomfield[1,2(✉)], Peter Bishop[1,2], Eoin Butler[2],
and Kate Netkachova[1,2]

[1] Centre for Software Reliability, City, University of London, London, UK
[2] Adelard LLP, London, UK
{reb, pgb, eb, kn}@adelard.com

Abstract. Assurance cases have been developed to reason and communicate about the trustworthiness of systems. Recently we have also been using them to support the development of policy and to assess the impact of security issues on safety regulation. In the example we present in this paper, we worked with a safety regulator (anonymised as A Regulatory Organisation (ARO) in this paper) to investigate the impact of cyber-security on safety regulation.

Keywords: Security-informed safety · Assurance cases · Regulation · Risk assessment

1 Introduction

Assurance case frameworks have been developed to reason and communicate about the trustworthiness of systems. Over the past five years or so we have been researching the impact security has on safety assurance and have been developing enhancements to the Claims, Arguments and Evidence (CAE) approach [1–3] to deal with some of the challenges posed by the need for increased rigour and complexity of systems. This supports the evaluation we have been doing of critical infrastructure security and safety e.g., [4].

Recently we have also been using the CAE framework to support the development of policy. From a broader perspective we are interested in the innovation potential of engineering methods to support decision making in large organisations and government [5, 6]. In the example we present in this paper, we worked with a safety regulator (anonymised as ARO in this paper) to "Investigate the Impact of Cyber-Security on Safety Regulation". The project developed a proposed regulatory strategy to enable this organisation to provide an adequate response to issues of cyber-security. They regulate complex systems of systems and the assessment of whether systems are safe, and the communication of that assessment to the interested stakeholders, is not complete unless security and cyber issues are taken into account.

The interest to the assurance community is perhaps twofold: one that the frameworks we are developing have a wider applicability to decision analysis and support

© Springer International Publishing AG 2017
S. Tonetta et al. (Eds.): SAFECOMP 2017 Workshops, LNCS 10489, pp. 27–38, 2017.
DOI: 10.1007/978-3-319-66284-8_3

and second that deploying approaches beyond their initial design intent can provide feedback on our approach to assurance cases.

2 Impact of Cyber Security on Safety Regulation

The project developed a proposed regulatory strategy to enable the ARO to provide an adequate response to issues of cyber-security. They regulate complex systems of systems and the assessment of whether systems are safe, and the communication of that assessment to the interested stakeholders, is not complete unless security and cyber issues are taken into account. The security aspects are increasingly important as there are:

- greater levels of threats and a changing threat in terms of nature, targets and capabilities of the attackers
- significant planned changes to systems, greater connectivity and use of supply chains and products with vulnerabilities
- changes in regulation
- requirements to communicate that effective and sufficient measures have been taken to a variety of stakeholders
- increased expectations of the public for a resilient service and associated systems

To assess the impact and to develop a programme of work we worked collaboratively with a wide range of stakeholders to establish the complex and organisational and regulatory context captured what we dubbed as an "entanglement diagram" that showed the dependencies between the stakeholders. Having established an understanding of the context we used CAE to develop the visions and objectives. We continued detailing the objectives in terms of claims until these were sufficiently detailed to establish a programme of work. There were a complex interlocking array of issues and the use of the CAE provided a vehicle for reasoning and communicating with stakeholders (government regulatory policy experts, government security agencies, domain experts, regulators and assessors).

This paper describes how we developed the vision and objectives using an assurance case approach.

2.1 Vision and Objectives

Having established the system and regulatory context, we then developed a set of structured cyber-related objectives for the ARO starting from the ARO's own strategic vision, taking into account the UK Cyber Strategy, a number of cyber frameworks and maturity models [7–9], and a focused analysis of activities in other sectors. We presented the results of this analysis in terms of a set of structured objectives or claims so that the rationale and interaction of different parts of strategy can be appraised. These are presented within a Claims Argument Evidence (CAE) framework and notation. The regulator was familiar with the notion of outcome-based regulation and the concepts of claims, arguments and evidence.

The approach to deriving the cyber programme objectives is illustrated in Fig. 1 (the nodes are discussed in detail later and are not meant to be legible in this figure).

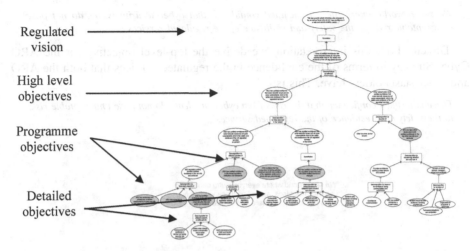

Fig. 1. Schematic of approach (Color figure online)

We started with the organisation's strategic vision and then derived high-level cyber-related objectives. We further decomposed these into more detailed objectives, identifying in orange those that form the proposed cyber programme objectives, which are numbered sequentially.

In developing the objectives in this way we can show traceability and rationale for them and also show the coverage with respect to the set of issues identified in the tree structure of Fig. 1 (some of the claims are outside the scope of the regulator but show its dependence on others).

We have also reviewed the UK Cyber Strategy objectives and from these developed specific strategic objectives that we then mapped to the proposed programme objectives to show how our proposals relate to them and provided another check for coverage of issues.

2.2   Deriving the Programme Objectives

First we derive some high level objectives from the ARO strategic vision as shown in Fig. 2 below.

High Level Objectives. The ARO's principal functions and duties are set out in primary legislation. The ARO has a strategic vision that

> *"We see a world where everyone who chooses to use these services, as well as those who do not, have confidence in a safe and secure sector that takes its responsibilities seriously, backed by a regulatory system that actively manages risk and supports consistently high performance."*

Part of this strategic vision *"We see a world where everyone [...] has confidence in a safe and secure sector [...]"* provides a starting point for the Cyber Strategy. We propose that the cyber component of this vision is interpreted as

We see a world where there is justified confidence that cyber-security issues do not pose unacceptable risks to the safety and resilience of the regulated services

Directly from this interpretation, we derive the top-level objective for the ARO Cyber Strategy in terms of the confidence in the regulated services that both the ARO and other stakeholders have. This is:

There is justified confidence that the risks from cyber incidents do not pose unacceptable risks to the safety and resilience of the regulated services

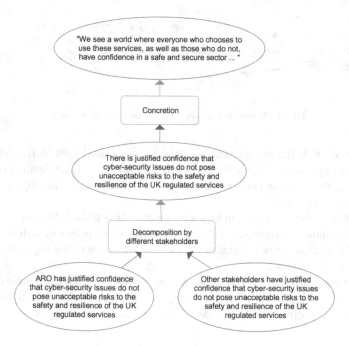

Fig. 2. Deriving the ARO objectives from the vision

ARO Confidence. Starting from the claim "There is justified confidence that the risks from cyber incidents do not pose unacceptable risks to the safety and resilience of the regulated services", we divide the top-level objective into the confidence of the ARO and that of other stakeholders. We propose that the objective for ARO is:

ARO has justified confidence that cyber-security issues do not pose unacceptable risks to the safety and resilience of the regulated services

As shown in Fig. 3 below, this is then split into two sub-objectives, one describing the present situation and another the future.

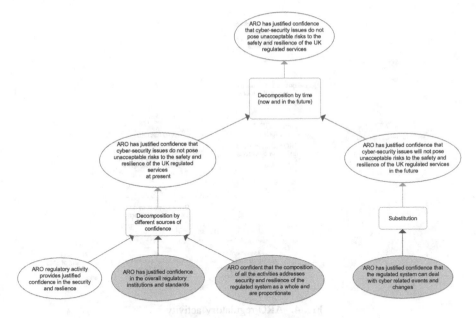

Fig. 3. Confidence now and in the future (Color figure online)

Confidence in the present situation is then further expanded in terms of the sources of that confidence, which are:

- the ARO's own regulatory assessment activities
- the overall regulatory approach, the institutions involved and the standards deployed
- a synthesis that all these activities when considered together show that risks from cyber are tolerable

The high-level objective for the future is:

ARO to have confidence that in the future the cyber risks will not undermine the safety and resilience of the regulated system

To support this, we proposed an objective that the regulated system can deal with future cyber-related events and changes. These top-level objectives are summarised in Fig. 3 in which the key programme objectives are coloured orange.

We now detail these objectives, moving left to right in Fig. 3. We first consider ARO's direct regulatory activities as shown in Fig. 4 below.

For the ARO regulatory activity to provide confidence, we identify three aspects to be addressed. The first two concern governance: the need for appropriate internal processes and procedures, and confidence that ARO has the capability to undertake its role as a regulator of cyber-security activities. These correspond to the programme objectives below:

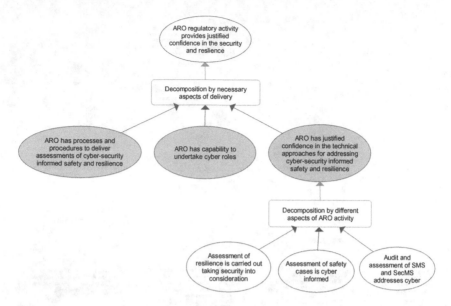

Fig. 4. ARO regulatory activity

| 1. ARO has processes and procedures to deliver assessments of cyber-security-informed safety and resilience |
| 2. ARO has capability to undertake cyber roles |

Here we note that, as well as the ARO's capability to undertake its regulatory role, the ARO needs to have the capability to ensure the cyber-security of its own processes, people and technology. Cyber-security related events within ARO, even if restricted to office systems and nothing to do with safety as such, will undermine confidence in the institution as a whole. The adversaries realise this, and as their overall goals may be to undermine confidence in the state and institutions, attacks on confidence and competency are a possibility, both directly and as part of multi-faceted attacks. There will be a need to define and adapt existing processes to deal with cyber issues, e.g. to define roles and responsibilities, multidisciplinary oversight and specialist involvement of cyber-related activities. These should address competency and the need for education, training and awareness.

The third aspect to consider is the need for technical approaches for security-informed safety and resilience. This corresponds to the next programme objective:

| 3. ARO has defined technical approaches for addressing cyber-security-informed safety and resilience |

As shown in Fig. 4, these need to support the audit and assessment of Safety Management Systems (SMS) and Security Management Systems (SeMS), the assessment of resilience, and the cyber informed review of safety case changes.

These technical approaches need to take into account that cyber-security issues impact safety assurance and associated risk analyses throughout the system and service lifecycle, with associated changes needed from requirements through development and operation to disposal. The impact varies with the nature of the systems and the extent to which they are already engineered to be trustworthy. Many safety critical components will already have had a high degree of assurance applied to them and this needs to be reviewed and augmented from a cyber perspective. Less critical systems may have minor safety significance, but due to potential connectivity, they may need substantial reengineering and analysis to address security concerns. We provided details of technical approaches to cyber-security informed assessment, vulnerabilities, standards, systemic risks and interdependencies and the need to respond to the faster tempo that security issues may demand.

Returning to the decomposition in Fig. 3, the second objective that "ARO has confidence in the overall regulatory approach, the institutions involved and the standards deployed" is detailed by considering the sources of confidence in overall regulation. This is formalised as the fourth programme objective:

4. ARO has confidence in the overall regulatory institutions and standards

This is further elaborated in Fig. 5 below.

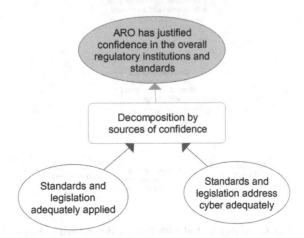

Fig. 5. Sources of confidence in regulation and standards

The confidence that the overall cyber-related risks are tolerable is based on the regulatory oversight and engagement with the regulated institutions and service providers, and the evaluations that the ARO undertakes itself, i.e.

5. ARO confident that the composition of all the activities addresses security and resilience of the regulated system as a whole and are proportionate

Confidence in the Future Safety and Resilience. Next, we elaborate the "future" branch of Fig. 3 where we define the following programme objective.

> 6. ARO has justified confidence that the regulated system can deal with cyber-related events and changes

As shown in Fig. 6 below this goal is elaborated in terms of the different types of events and changes to which the system has to respond to.

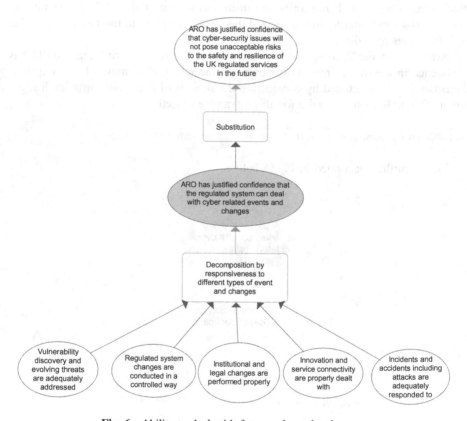

Fig. 6. Ability to deal with future cyber-related events

Some of these, such as vulnerability discovery and new threats, can be considered as changes to the environment, while others are changes to the regulated systems themselves and other innovations and changes to connectivity that redefine what "the system" actually is. There can also be institutional and legal changes that introduce different stakeholders or change the roles, and lastly there will be attacks, incidents and accidents that may have a cyber component.

Incident reporting and subsequent learning from experience is an important part of achieving safety. The tempo and changing nature of the cyber threat makes this particularly critical, and the recognition that failures may occur means that resilience and recovery in particular need to be addressed. An important component of a Cyber Strategy is therefore incident reporting and response: it is an important part of the UK Cyber Strategy and the development of the UK National Cyber Centre.

Supporting Other Stakeholders. We now return to the second part of Fig. 2 which considers confidence that other stakeholders have in the regulated system and services. We propose that ARO have responsibilities and objectives here as well as being an authoritative source of confidence for some stakeholders, e.g. the public. We propose a programme objective that

7. ARO provides other stakeholders with confidence in the regulated systems' security and resilience

We propose that the objective be achieved by communicating the ARO's confidence in the system and actively managing sources of actual and perceived risks. This is summarised in Fig. 7.

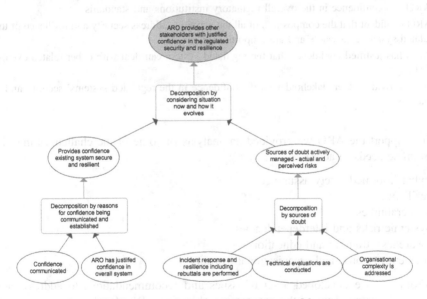

Fig. 7. Supporting other stakeholder confidence

Maintaining confidence in the ARO and for the ARO to discharge its role in supporting the confidence in the sector will need communication as an explicit part of the strategy. This communication should explain the effectiveness and the reasons why there should be confidence in the regulated systems. It should address internal communication within the industry to provide a cyber aware and knowledgeable culture and importantly it should provide expertise, either directly or in support of other spokespeople, to allow accurate reporting of cyber issues. We have already seen the need for effective communications where claims are made about cyber vulnerabilities.

3 Analysis Results and Follow-Up

The CAE-based analysis led to a structured set of objectives for the Cyber Strategy that are summarised in Table 1 below.

Table 1. Proposed objectives of ARO cyber programme

Programme objectives
1. ARO has processes and procedures to deliver assessments of cyber-security-informed safety and resilience
2. ARO has capability to undertake cyber roles
3. ARO has defined technical approaches for addressing cyber-security-informed safety and resilience
4. ARO has confidence in the overall regulatory institutions and standards
5. ARO confident that the composition of all the activities address security and resilience of the regulated system as a whole and are proportionate
6. ARO has justified confidence that the regulated system can deal with cyber-related events and changes
7. ARO provides other stakeholders with confidence in the regulated systems' security and resilience

To support the ARO we provided an analysis of some of the challenges that this programme needs to address:

- cyber-informed safety assurance
- resilience
- vulnerabilities
- systemic risks and interdependencies
- awareness, training and education
- incident response and organisational learning

From this we developed a set of issues and recommendations to address these issues, and related them to the programme objectives. We developed a preliminary regulatory maturity model to explain and structure the programme of work and to put into context the challenge: achieving these seven objectives. We combined the programme objectives with levels of our maturity model to define an indicative high-level plan. To do this we expanded on the recommendations from our analyses of the challenges to define the steps needed to go from the current "start-up" or "formative" maturity level of the regulated system with respect to cyber, to an "established" level.

4   Discussion and Conclusions

The role of the safety regulator is complex and the work highlighted the complexity and interconnectedness of the organisations involved, captured in an entanglement diagram. The issues that need to be addressed are also many and interlocking and the development and use of CAE as a presentation and reason framework helped tackle this complexity and provided a vehicle for reasoning and communicating with stakeholders (government regulatory policy experts, government security agencies, domain experts, regulators and assessors).

As shown above, we used the CAE Blocks [3] as a structuring mechanism. These were presented informally without side conditions. For decomposition blocks the names of the block is followed by the type of argument e.g. "decomposition by the sources of doubt" to indicate we were decomposing by these sources. The validity of the decomposition was assessed by stakeholder review and workshops. We also provided more succinct descriptions of some nodes to improve legibility and communication aspects: a balance has to be made between preciseness of claim and how this is described on a graphical canvas. The usage of the CAE Blocks is shown in Table 2.

Table 2. Usage of CAE Blocks

Blocks	Usage
Concretion	1 use. Stakeholder preferred "interpretation" to "concretion"
Substitution	1 use. "Not posing unacceptable risks" is substituted by "dealing with cyber events and changes"
Decomposition	A variety of uses: by types of stakeholder, sources of confidence (3), sources of doubt (1), aspects of role, aspects of delivery (2), now and future (2)
Evidence incorporation	In later part of project not reported here
Calculation	Not used

In terms of directions and future work, we hope to publish the maturity model that supports the definition of the detailed programme of work and we would like to apply the approach to different regulator in different domains. The usage of CAE Blocks provides some indications of what might be provided by more domain specific or instantiated blocks for this type of application. From a broader perspective our work can be seen as a part of a wider initiative to see how engineering methods can be used "off label" to support decision making in industry and government.

Acknowledgments. This work has been partially supported by the UK EPSRC project "Communicating and Evaluating Cyber Risk and Dependencies" (CEDRICS, EP/M002802/1), which is part of the UK Research Institute in Trustworthy Industrial Control Systems (RiTICS).

References

1. Adelard Safety Case Development Manual: © Adelard (1998). ISBN 0 9533771 0 5
2. Bishop, P.G., Bloomfield, R.E.: A methodology for safety case development. In: Redmill, F., Anderson, T. (eds.) Industrial Perspectives of Safety-Critical Systems, pp. 194–203. Springer, London (1998). doi:10.1007/978-1-4471-1534-2_14
3. Bloomfield, R.E., Netkachova, K.: Building blocks for assurance cases. In: IEEE International Symposium on Software Reliability Engineering Workshops (ISSREW) 2014, pp. 186–191 (2014). doi:10.1109/ISSREW.2014.72
4. Bloomfield, R.E., Bendele, M., Bishop, P., Stroud, R., Tonks, S.: The risk assessment of ERTMS-based railway systems from a cyber security perspective: methodology and lessons learned. In: Lecomte, T., Pinger, R., Romanovsky, A. (eds.) RSSRail 2016. LNCS, vol. 9707, pp. 3–19. Springer, Cham (2016). doi:10.1007/978-3-319-33951-1_1
5. Bloomfield, R.E., Netkachova, K., Stroud, R.: Security-informed safety: if it's not secure, it's not safe. In: Gorbenko, A., Romanovsky, A., Kharchenko, V. (eds.) SERENE 2013. LNCS, vol. 8166, pp. 17–32. Springer, Heidelberg (2013). doi:10.1007/978-3-642-40894-6_2
6. Bloomfield, R.E., Wetherilt, A.: Computer trading and systemic risk: a nuclear per-spective. Foresight study, The Future of Computer Trading in Financial Markets, Driver Review DR26. Government Office for Science (2012)
7. The UK Cyber Security Strategy: Protecting and promoting the UK in a digital world, November 2011
8. Cyber Security Capability Maturity Model (CMM) – Pilot: Global Cyber Security Capacity Centre University of Oxford (2014). http://www.oxfordmartin.ox.ac.uk
9. US Department of Energy (DOE) Cyber-security Capability Maturity Model (BuildSecu-rityIn) Department of Homeland Security (2016). https://cwe.mitre.org/top25/

Uniform Model Interface for Assurance Case Integration with System Models

Andrzej Wardziński[1,2]([✉]) and Paul Jones[3]

[1] Gdańsk University of Technology, Gdańsk, Poland
Andrzej.Wardzinski@pg.edu.pl
[2] Argevide, Gdańsk, Poland
[3] US Food and Drug Administration, Silver Spring, MD, USA
Paul.Jones@fda.hhs.gov

Abstract. Assurance cases are developed and maintained in parallel with corresponding system models and therefore need to reference each other. Managing the correctness and consistency of interrelated safety argument and system models is essential for system dependability and is a nontrivial task. The model interface presented in this paper enables a uniform process of establishing and managing assurance case references to various types of system models. References to system metamodels are specified in an argument pattern and then used for assurance case instantiation. The proposed approach permits incremental development of assurance cases that maintain consistency with corresponding system models throughout the system development life cycle.

Keywords: Assurance case · Safety case · System models · Argument pattern

1 Introduction

When developing systems, engineers necessarily rely on models to facilitate comprehension, analysis, and communication of complex development details. Such models may represent design and development processes, system component architecture, behavior, and other types of development abstractions. We refer to each of these types of models in this paper collectively as *system models*.

Assurance cases may mirror these system models to varying levels of detail and refer to their elements. It is important that these references are unambiguous, complete, and correct so that someone creating, modifying or reviewing an assurance case can be confident of being directed to the right element or property. When a few assurance cases are developed for components of the system (e.g. system of systems) it is critical to ensure that the assurance cases refer to the same concepts, system models, model interfaces, and properties.

Our goal is to develop a generic model interface between an assurance case and system models which will allow establishing and maintaining assurance case references to elements of various system models. The interface should provide system model referencing services desired by the assurance case user (developer, assessor etc.) while hiding unnecessary details that may not add to comprehension. The idea is to not have

© Springer International Publishing AG 2017
S. Tonetta et al. (Eds.): SAFECOMP 2017 Workshops, LNCS 10489, pp. 39–51, 2017.
DOI: 10.1007/978-3-319-66284-8_4

the assurance case user track model element references manually but rather to assist the user by providing required information describing the desired system model(s). The proposed model interface provides:

- A uniform way of specifying assurance case references to system model elements,
- The ability to specify restrictions in a form of relations between referenced model elements to strengthen assurance case consistency,
- A mechanism for maintenance of the argument references when the models are modified,
- The possibility to develop an assurance case incrementally when system models are evolving throughout the system life cycle (the argument instantiation does not have to be carried out all at once, some parts of the pattern may stay un-instantiated until the corresponding system models are available).

Use of a uniform model interface for establishing and maintaining assurance case relations to system models will make it simpler to manage consistency between the two. The initial cost of this approach is in the development of the model interface. It must be implemented for each system model type to which the assurance case references. The implementation will depend on the specific data format used by each type of system model. System models can be represented in XML, a database, "flat" text file or a structured document. The system model can be also managed by any application with an API offering access to the model data (for example OSLC interface – Open Services for Lifecycle Collaboration).

In the next section, we will analyze the general problem of managing relations between assurance cases and system models. The concept of a model interface is presented in the third section. Section 4 describes the process how the model interface is used in assurance case integration with system models. We summarize the approach in Sect. 5.

2   Assurance Case Integration with System Models

Assurance cases may refer to many aspects of systems like systems goals and requirements, risks and mitigations, system structure, elements properties, life cycle activities and their products. The most common approach is to use textual references and manually manage their consistency with system models and real world artefacts. For example, textual references were proposed in developing assurance cases for software model-driven development [1].

One of the initial studies on managing explicit assurance case references to external models or ontologies was described in a safety argument for hospital treatment [2]. Górski et al. used UML to represent a claim model and a related context model.

Evidence argument elements can also be used to represent elements of system models. Sljivo et al. presented an extension of assurance case metamodels enabling use of evidence element references to a system component and safety contract metamodel [3].

Currently the most advanced solution for use of models to describe the context of an assurance case is a weaving metamodel proposed by Hawkings et al. [4] and applied in the D–MILS project [5]. The weaving metamodel captures dependencies between role bindings specified in an assurance case pattern and system models. Abstract dependency information captured in the weaving metamodel is used in the argument instantiation process.

The weaving metamodel describes:

- system model classes specific for a given system perspective (e.g. AADL or FMEA model),
- relations between model classes specified as UML associations,
- role bindings in the argument patterns, that is terms used in pattern element names to denote specific system model elements (e.g. "System" in a claim "{System} safety policy is enforced"),
- relations between role bindings resulting from the pattern argument structure (they are directed relations which describe the scope of a binding role context),
- relations between role bindings and system model classes.

The approach presented in this paper is similar to the use of the weaving model, however, we use two separate elements in place of the weaving model. The first one is a model interface describing system models in a unified way and the second one is a reference table describing argument relations to system models. This approach offers new possibilities described in the next sections.

3 The Concept of the Model Interface

The concept of a model interface arose from the observation that assurance cases refer to different types of system models but assurance case developers would prefer a standard way to establish and maintain the references. The model interface has been designed to satisfy these needs and facilitate a uniform reference management process in assurance case development and maintenance. The concept has been developed as an extension of a reference mechanism described in [6].

References to system models are first specified on an abstract level when an argument pattern is developed. Argument patterns may refer to abstract concepts like subsystems, components, events or hazards. To ensure abstract references are unambiguous, they should be specified in a context of a formally defined system metamodel. UML class models can be used for such specification. References to metamodel elements will be sufficiently precise to ensure unambiguity.

The argument pattern serves as a basis for development of a "well formed" argument appropriate for a specific system model. In the assurance case instantiation process each abstract reference should be replaced with a reference to an existing system model element which satisfies the conditions imposed by the abstract reference. Use of a formally defined system metamodel in abstract references helps ensure the consistency of the instantiated argument with the referred system. The model interface should operate on both levels: abstract system metamodels and concrete system models that describe a real system.

The model interface serves as an intermediary between the assurance case and system models. As presented in Fig. 1 it provides an interface for assurance cases (on the left of the diagram) to access system models. The model interface does not keep any information on the assurance case argument references to system models. All the reference data is stored in the assurance cases in an abstract and a concrete reference table.

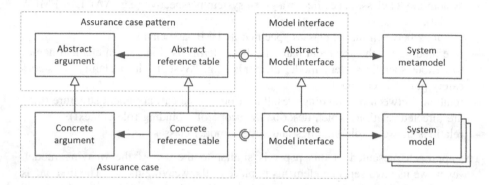

Fig. 1. Assurance case instantiation metamodel

You can notice two levels of the model interface presented on the diagram. The upper part works on an abstract level, i.e. the system metamodel used for argument pattern references. The lower part provides an interface to system models used when the concrete argument is instantiated. On the abstract level the model interface services return:

(a) a list of available model types,
(b) a list of element types for a given model type,
(c) a list of relations for a specific model element type.

Abstract functions of the model interface do not need existing system models to function because they return data on a metamodel level. To work with the concrete model interface one first needs to initiate it with a specific model (for example provide a model file name) and then the interface functions can be called to return:

(d) a list of models of a given type,
(e) a list of model elements of a given type,
(f) a list of elements which satisfy a given relation,
(g) detailed data of a given element (when its identifier is provided).

The presented set of functions is sufficient to specify abstract references in argument patterns and then instantiate them to produce concrete assurance cases. This process will be presented in the next section.

4   Process of Assurance Case Integration with System Models

The integration process consists of steps performed in two phases. The first phase is performed on the abstract level when the assurance case pattern is developed but no real system exists yet. This is what might be called a *pre-development* phase. Here, an abstract argument pattern with references to a system metamodel is established. The second phase is what might be called a *development* phase when an assurance case is instantiated with references to models of the developed system and then maintained throughout the system life cycle. In the following subsections, we will describe the steps of this process.

- Pre-development phase steps

  1. System metamodel specification
  2. Model interface development
  3. Argument pattern development

- Development phase steps

  4. System modeling
  5. Assurance case development
  6. System models and assurance case maintenance (iteration of steps 4 and 5)

The process covers the whole assurance case life cycle from the moment an argument pattern is created in the context of an abstract metamodel, to assurance case maintenance after a product has been placed on the market.

Details of the integration process are presented below with the use of a sample argument fragment that references a system risk model. The referenced system is a Patient Control Analgesia (PCA) infusion pump [7].

4.1   Step 1: System Metamodel Specification

The first step of the process is to specify a system risk metamodel and its data format to allow implementation of model interface functions.

In our example, we will use a *risk metamodel* presented in Fig. 2. as a UML class diagram (for simplicity class' attributes are not shown on the diagram). The risk model describes system hazards, their causes and control measures. The structure of the

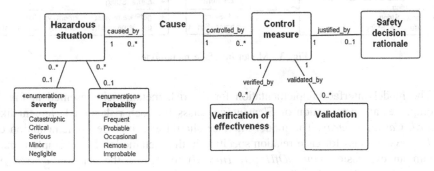

Fig. 2. The system risk metamodel

metamodel is based on the hazard table format specified in [8]. The model data format is an XML file and the XML schema is based on the presented risk metamodel.

The result of this step is a set of system metamodels along with detailed technical data on the model format necessary for implementing the model interface as described in the next step.

4.2   Step 2: Model Interface Development

A model interface is, in general, a software module that provides a uniform interface for access to any type of system models. It is assumed that the model interface is only allowed to read system models and cannot modify them. Access to system models is realized by instantiations of abstract classes *ModelType*, *ElementType* and *Expression*. An implementation of these classes is required for each system metamodel intended to be referenced from the assurance case.

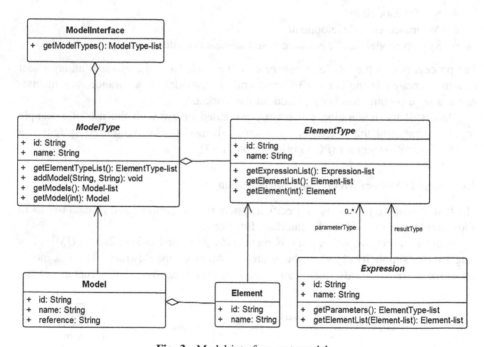

Fig. 3. Model interface metamodel

The model interface implementation for the risk metamodel presented in Fig. 2 encompasses an instantiation of *ElementType* class for each risk model element like *Hazard*, *Cause*, *Severity*. The model interface should also include implementation of the *Expression* class for each relation specified in the metamodel. For example it may contain an expression *causesOfHazard(Hazard)* to denote the relation *caused_by* between classes *HazardousSituation* and *Cause*. This interface function takes one parameter of *Hazard* type and returns a set of elements of *Cause* type. Given that the risk models are represented in XML files, we chose to use XQuery scripts to implement access to the model data.

```
for $causeId in doc($ModelRef)//relationship[@source
    =$HazardId]/@target
for $cause in doc($ModelRef)//hazardElement[@xmi:id
    =$causeId and @xsi:type="HA:Cause"]
return <result><id>{data($cause/@xmi:id)}</id>
    <name>{data($cause/@content)}</name></result>
```

The script returns the result in XML format, for example:

```
<result><id>C1</id><name>Sensor failure to detect air
bubble</name></result>
<result><id>C2</id><name>Safety subsystem failure to stop
the pump</name></result>
<result><id>C4</id><name>Pump does not stop on request
</name></result>
```

The result consists of model elements identifiers and names. This is transformed into a collection of *Element* objects and returned by the model interface. The element name will be presented for the assurance case user and the identifier will be used for traceability of the referenced model element.

The complete model interface implements all the functions specified in Sect. 3 and its scope covers all the system model classes and relations between them. The presented example refers to a risk model, but model interface implementations for other types of models (e.g. AADL, EAST-ADL) are also possible.

4.3 Step 3: Argument Pattern Development

In this step an argument pattern with references to the system metamodel is developed. The model interface should provide operations which return available system model types, their element types and relation, permitting the user to specify correct references

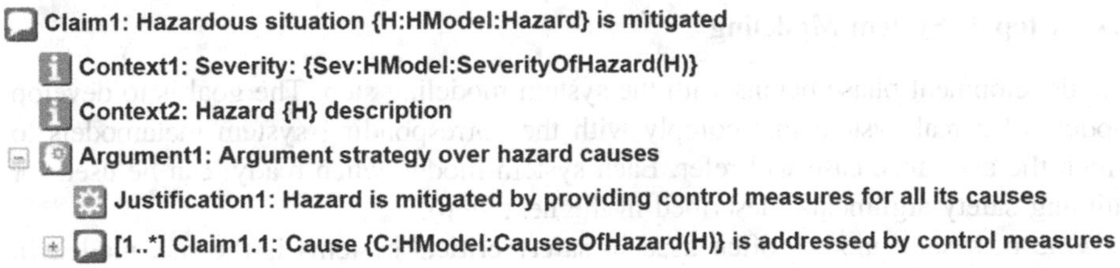

☐ **Claim1: Hazardous situation {H:HModel:Hazard} is mitigated**
　　ℹ **Context1: Severity: {Sev:HModel:SeverityOfHazard(H)}**
　　ℹ **Context2: Hazard {H} description**
　⊟ ⚙ **Argument1: Argument strategy over hazard causes**
　　　⚙ **Justification1: Hazard is mitigated by providing control measures for all its causes**
　　　⊞ ☐ **[1..*] Claim1.1: Cause {C:HModel:CausesOfHazard(H)} is addressed by control measures**

Fig. 4. Argument template

to a system metamodel. A definition of an abstract reference consists of three attributes: a reference name, a model type and an element selector. The reference name is used internally in the assurance case pattern while the model type and the element selector are used to identify the referred element of the metamodel. For example, reference "H" in *Claim1* in Fig. 4 refers to elements of the *Hazard* class in *HModel*. The presented argument fragment uses textual hierarchical notation. Labels of the argument elements indicate the type for each element.

Once a reference is specified, it can also be used for other argument elements. It can be used directly as a reference, for example *Context2* refers to the same hazard *H* as *Claim1*. A reference can also be used as a parameter for a selector. Hazard *H* is used as a parameter for references in *Context1* and *Claim1.1* (Fig. 4). This method of reference specification ensures that instantiated *Claim1.1* will refer only to causes of a hazard specified by the instantiation of its parent *Claim1*.

Model interface operation *getModelTypes()* (compare Fig. 3) helps to ensure that the argument pattern references relate to existing model types. Operations *getModelElementTypeList()*, *getExpressionList()* and *getParameterList()* assist in managing correct references to the system metamodel.

All the abstract references defined in the argument pattern are recorded in the *abstract reference table* (Table 1) which is an integral part of the assurance case pattern.

Table 1. Abstract reference table

Pattern element id	Reference name	Model type	Element selector
Claim1 Context2	H	HModel (the *risk model*)	Hazard
Context1	Sev	HModel (the *risk model*)	SeverityOfHazard(H)
Claim1.1	C	HModel (the *risk model*)	CausesOfHazard(H)

The result of the pattern development step is a complete argument pattern with references to the system metamodel represented in the abstract reference table. The pattern is not specific to any system and it can be used for developing assurance cases for a class of systems.

4.4   Step 4: System Modeling

The development phase begins with the system modeling step. The goal is to develop models of a real system that comply with the corresponding system metamodels to which the assurance case will refer. Each system model, when ready, can be used for building safety arguments (described in the next step).

One of system models often used in safety critical systems is the risk model. In Table 2 we present a fragment of the risk model in the form of a hazard table.

Table 2. Excerpt of the PCA infusion pump hazard table

Hazardous situation	Severity	Cause	Control measure
Air in line	Critical	Sensor failure to detect air bubble	Sensor failure rate 10E-6 for air bubbles with the size greater than 1 ml
		Safety subsystem failure to stop the pump	Safety subsystem failure rate 10E-6/h
		Pump does not stop on request	Pump design ensures stopping the flow in the absence of control signal

The risk model is recorded in an XML file and its file format is based on the metamodel presented in Sect. 4.1. The model interface will read these XML files to get information on referenced model elements. An XML file excerpt is presented below:

```
<hazardElement content="Air in line"
  xsi:type="HA:HazardousSituation" xmi:id="H1"/>
<hazardElement
  content="Sensor failure to detect air bubble"
  xsi:type="HA:Cause" xmi:id="C1"/>
<hazardElement
  content="Safety subsystem failure to stop the pump"
  xsi:type="HA:Cause" xmi:id="C2"/>
<relationship xsi:type="HA:CausedBy" xmi:id="S1C1"
  source="H1" target="C1"/>
<relationship xsi:type="HA:CausedBy" xmi:id="S1C2"
  source="H1" target="C2"/>
```

The result of this step of the process is a set of system models in a format readable by the model interface. One does not need to have all the system models developed before starting the argument instantiation. An assurance case can be developed incrementally and can refer to models or parts of a model that are ready at a given time.

4.5   Step 5: Assurance Case Development

The objective of this main step is to develop an assurance case based on the argument pattern (see step 3) and establish references to models of a particular system. To do this the model interface must be initialized with concrete models of a real system. The user selects an argument pattern and then specifies the file locations or links to system models to which the assurance case will refer.

The instantiation process is performed top down starting with the top pattern element. For each abstract reference and multiplication operator the user has to decide how a given pattern element should be instantiated. For each abstract reference the model interface can search existing system models for elements which satisfy the reference conditions and the user may choose a model element for instantiated (concrete) reference. When a multiplication operator is used, a separate argument section can be created for each reference value (e.g. for all causes of a hazard).

The risk model fragment presented in Table 2 consists of one hazard and three causes. The instantiation process starts with the top claim (Fig. 4). It refers to a model element *H* of class *Hazard*. The model interface function *getElementList()* returns a list of hazards defined in the hazard table and the user can select any hazard from the list. The reference can be instantiated to the hazard 'air in line' specified in the hazard table. The next argument element to be instantiated is *Context1*. It refers to a model element of Severity class in relation to hazard *H*. The model interface will return an element with value 'Critical'. For the next pattern element *Claim1.1* the multiplication operator [1..*] enables the user to choose a set of referenced elements. The model interface will return a list of causes for hazard H and all of them can be used in the claim instantiation. The result is presented in Fig. 5 (the identifiers of the instantiated argument have been reset).

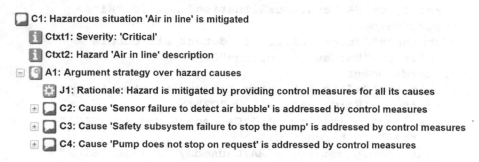

Fig. 5. Instantiated argument

The final result of this step is the instantiated argument along with the reference table describing all the relations to system models. The reference table specifies model element values and identifiers which can be used to track model changes (Table 3).

Table 3. Concrete reference table

Argument element id	Reference name	Model name	Model element id	Element name
C1 Ctxt2	H	PCAHazardTable.xml	H1	Air in line
Ctxt1	Sev	PCAHazardTable.xml	S1	Critical
C2	C	PCAHazardTable.xml	C1	Sensor failure to detect air bubble
C3	C	PCAHazardTable.xml	C2	Safety subsystem failure to stop the pump
C4	C	PCAHazardTable.xml	C4	Pump does not stop on request

4.6   Step 6: System Models and Assurance Case Maintenance

The objective of this step to accommodate the evolution of assurance cases throughout the system life cycle. An assurance case is usually not developed all at once; rather it is developed gradually during system development and is subject to many changes. System models are also developed gradually. In fact, a change in one often affects a change in the other.

Steps 4 and 5 can be repeated to gradually develop system models and the corresponding assurance case. The model interface provides features to facilitate this process in the following way:

- References to new models can be added at any time in the assurance case maintenance process. The user can change an existing reference to make it refer to a new model or add a new argument branch in the pattern where a multiplication operator is used. The new argument section can refer to new or already existing system model elements.
- Assurance case reference consistency with system models can be verified at any moment of time. For each reference the model interface functions *getElementList()* and *getElement()* (compare Fig. 3) can be used to check if the current reference value refers to a correct model element. The model interface can also return the current list of model elements which satisfy the condition specified by the abstract reference. When the system model is modified then new model elements can be reported. The user may want to add new argument elements with such new references. In some cases the model interface may report that an existing reference value is not a valid model element. Broken or inconsistent references can be reported to allow the user to correct them.
- In case the system model element name is changed, the assurance case can be automatically updated. The model element identifier stored in the reference table can be used as a parameter for the function *getElement()* to get its current data. When the system model element name is modified, it can be updated in the assurance case. In this way changes in system models can be propagated to the assurance case.

Use of a model interface allows keeping the assurance case up to date with systems models and to evolve in accordance with progress in system development throughout the system life cycle.

5   Summary

The presented concept of the model interface and the integration process facilitates assurance case consistency with system models. In particular it enables:

- A uniform process of definition and instantiation of assurance case relations to various system models independent of technical model representations (XML format, databases, files or external systems) provided that a model interface is implemented. This simplifies managing references to diverse system model types by the assurance case developer.

- Improved internal assurance case consistency by use of explicitly defined relations between system model elements. Those relations help in managing consistency between different references in the argument.
- Improved assurance case maintainability thanks to the possibility of incremental assurance case instantiation and establishing references to new system models.
- Better traceability because specified model element references can be verified for changes at any moment.
- Improved verifiability of the assurance case thanks to the possibility of analysis of consistency between the assurance case and system models.

The presented approach has been verified with a prototype tool that implements the model interface for the risk model and a subset of AADL models developed with Osate2. The prototype performs assurance case instantiation and exports the argument in XML format compliant with OMG SACM metamodel.

The model interface metamodel can be compared to the terminology classes in OMG SACM 2.0 metamodel [9]. The terminology classes in SACM consist of *Category* class which can correspond to a model type, *Term* class which can relate to model elements and *Expression* class which can be equivalent to *Expression* class in the model interface. Further research is required to determine if OMG SACM 2.0 should be extended to cover the model interface and references to models.

The presented process assumes that the argument pattern is static when the assurance case is developed for a given system. Usually system evolutionary life cycles span years requiring changes in the argument structure. Such changes would be introduced to the argument pattern as well and then propagated to the assurance case. Maintaining assurance case consistency with an evolving argument pattern may be challenging and requires further work.

The presented concept of a model interface is new to assurance case development. It offers the possibility of more robust assurance cases that map directly to system models, facilitating the development of unambiguous arguments.

References

1. Jee, E., Lee, I., Sokolsky, O.: Assurance cases in model-driven development of the pacemaker software. In: Margaria, T., Steffen, B. (eds.) ISoLA 2010. LNCS, vol. 6416, pp. 343–356. Springer, Heidelberg (2010). doi:10.1007/978-3-642-16561-0_33
2. Górski, J., Jarzębowicz, A., Leszczyna, R., Miler, J., Olszewski, M.: Trust case justifying trust in an IT solution. Reliab. Eng. Syst. Saf. **89**, 33–47 (2005)
3. Sljivo, I., Gallina, B., Carlson, B., Hansson, H., Puri, S.: A method to generate reusable safety case argument-fragments from compositional safety analysis. J. Syst. Softw. **131**, 570–590 (2017). doi:10.1016/j.jss.2016.07.034. Elsevier
4. Hawkins, R., Habli, I., Kolovos, D., Paige, R., Kelly, T.: Weaving an assurance case from design: a model-based approach. In: IEEE 16th International Symposium on High Assurance Systems Engineering (2015)
5. Compositional assurance cases and arguments for distributed MILS, D-MILS Project deliverable D4.2, University of York (2015)

6. Wardziński, A., Jarzębowicz, A.: Towards safety case integration with hazard analysis for medical devices. In: Skavhaug, A., Guiochet, J., Schoitsch, E., Bitsch, F. (eds.) SAFECOMP 2016. LNCS, vol. 9923, pp. 87–98. Springer, Cham (2016). doi:10.1007/978-3-319-45480-1_8

7. Larson B.R., Hatcliff, J.: Open Patient-Controlled Analgesia Infusion Pump System Requirements, Kansas State University, SAnToS TR 2014-6-1 (2014)

8. Jones, P.L., Taylor, A.: Medical device risk management and safety cases. Bio-Med. Instrum. Technol. **49**, 45–53 (2015)

9. Structured Assurance Case Metamodel (SACM), version 2.0 – Beta, Object Management Group (2016)

ExplicitCase: Integrated Model-Based Development of System and Safety Cases

Carmen Cârlan[✉], Simon Barner, Alexander Diewald, Alexandros Tsalidis, and Sebastian Voss

fortiss GmbH, Munich, Germany
{carlan,barner,diewald,tsalidis,voss}@fortiss.org

Abstract. Tools for creating safety cases currently on the market target safety experts, whose main concern is the management of safety cases. However, for safety assurance, safety experts should collaborate with technical experts, who have better understanding of technical and operational hazards. Thus, there should be a closer collaboration between the management of safety cases and technical expertise. Technical expertise may be retrieved, among others, from model-based system artifacts and processes. In order to close the gap between safety and technical expertise, we present ExplicitCase, an open-source tool for semi-automatic modeling, maintenance, and verification of safety cases integrated with system models. The advantage of this tool is two-fold. First, it enables its users to capture safety relevant information from model-based artifacts into safety cases. Second, it makes the safety cases rationale available to engineers in order to help them reason about design choices, while minding safety concerns. We evaluate the approach and the implemented tool based on the experiences obtained in a project use case.

Keywords: Safety cases · Goal Structuring Notation · System models

1 Introduction

In safety critical system design, certification is obtained by providing evidence that the system is acceptably safe in a defined context. Recent years have seen a marked shift in the regulatory approach to ensuring system safety away from a mere demonstration of compliance with prescriptive safety codes and standards. Now, developers and operators are asked to construct and present safety cases, i.e. well-reasoned arguments that their systems achieve acceptable levels of safety [11]. *Safety cases* constitute a technique to systematically demonstrate the safety of systems using existing information about the system, its environment and development context [6]. There are several approaches to describe safety cases, such as free text, tabular structures, claim structures, or graphical notations such as Goal Structuring Notation (GSN) [3].

Tools on the market focus on facilitating the construction of safety cases for safety engineers in a certain structural notation (e.g., GSN) and on the

© Springer International Publishing AG 2017
S. Tonetta et al. (Eds.): SAFECOMP 2017 Workshops, LNCS 10489, pp. 52–63, 2017.
DOI: 10.1007/978-3-319-66284-8_5

hyperlinking to external safety evidence artifacts [1]. Other tools focus on the automatic generation of safety case arguments from the output of formal verification tools [7]. Another approach is the automatic instantiation of safety cases patterns, i.e. templates of reusable argumentations, with information from system models [10]. Such tools target safety experts, whose main concern is the management of safety cases. However, leaving the safety assurance just in the hands of the safety experts may not be a good practice, since they may not have deep knowledge about technical and operational hazards [16]. Thus, there should be a closer collaboration between the management of safety cases and technical expertise (e.g., model-based system artifacts and processes).

In this paper, we take on the problem of *closing the gap between safety assurance and model-based system development*. First, we enable to capture safety relevant information from model-based artifacts into safety cases. Second, we make the safety cases rationale available to engineers in order to help them reason about design choices, while minding safety concerns. In order to tackle this problem, we propose a model-based approach for semi-automatic creation, maintenance, and verification of GSN-based safety cases in a tool called *ExplicitCase*.

In contrast to existing solutions, the benefit of our tool is three-fold. First, our tool does not proclaim itself as a plain GSN-based safety case editor. The most common approach for describing safety cases in the industry is free text. According to Rinehart et al., the benefit of having a structured graphical notation for safety cases is that it supports the presentation of safety cases to non-safety experts in a comprehensive manner [16]. Thus, graphical notations for safety cases seem to be used at their best when being integrating with design methods, such as model-based approaches, in order to embed in the safety case technical knowledge about the system. Therefore, our tool proclaims itself as communication means of safety concerns between safety and system engineers via integrated metamodels of safety cases and system design artifacts. Second, the proposed GSN-based safety case metamodel allows capturing the rationale behind a safety case argument structure, allowing more rigorous argument analysis. This is done by defining rules and constraints for safety case entities and relationships between these entities. Third, the tool supports the integration of our GSN-based safety case metamodel with safety system design metamodels.

In the following, we show how to capture as much safety-relevant information from system model artifacts as possible in GSN nodes via *ExplicitCase* and explain its design principles (Sect. 2). Before we conclude (Sect. 5), we report on the experience gained from using ExplicitCase in the context of a project and discuss related work (Sects. 3 and 4).

2   ExplicitCase: Design Principles and Features

ExplicitCase is an open-source application built on the Eclipse Rich Client Platform, for constructing, managing and verifying GSN-based safety cases. It is a tool integrated into the AutoFOCUS3 (AF3) open-source model-based development tool for reactive embedded systems [4]. In the following, we present its design principles and editing features.

AF3 (http://af3.fortiss.org) is a research CASE tool that allows modeling and validating concurrent, reactive, distributed, timed systems on the basis of a formal semantics [4]. It provides a graphical user interface supporting the specification of embedded systems in different layers of abstraction while supporting different views on the system model (e.g. from the model-based requirements view down to the hardware-related platform view). As an example, the *Component Architecture View* of a system is defined by means of components communicating via channels. Each component exposes defined input and output interfaces to its environment, either to other components or to the system environment. AF3 uses a message-based, discrete-time communication scheme as its model of computation that involves semantics for components sequence computation and their timing behavior. The *Technical Architecture View* describes a hardware topology that is composed of hardware units, e.g. electrical control units (ECUs), hardware ports (sensors or actuators) and buses. Furthermore, AF3 supports the specification of inter-level allocation between different models. The *Deployment view* is one example of such an allocation by mapping elements from the *component* to elements of the *technical architecture*.

Safety Case Editing. ExplicitCase is based on a metamodel derived from the GSN standard [17] and offers a graphical editor facilitating the model-based development of safety cases (see Fig. 1). Since the most common approach for describing safety cases in the industry is free text, the user can add to any modeled GSN node a reference to the document in which further explanation of the claim in the node may be found. Furthermore, the user can add a string, which depicts a reference to the paragraph from the referenced document in which the node is explained in detail.

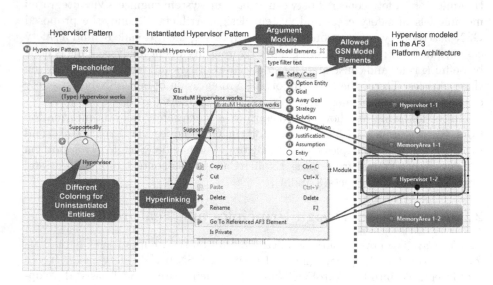

Fig. 1. An overview of the main features of ExplicitCase. (Color figure online)

Hyperlinking and Traceability. There are several types of hyperlinking offered by ExplicitCase. First, we distinguish between hyperlinking words in safety claims and linking an entire GSN node to another artifact. Second, hyperlinks can link the safety case with external documents containing safety reports, safety analysis or verification results or even system models [17] (see Fig. 2). AF3 provides the "native" internal system models that may be linked to elements of safety cases modeled in ExplicitCase. The novelty of our hyperlinking system lays in the fact that words in claims or GSN nodes are deeply integrated with the system artifacts created by the user in the AF3 model-based development tool. The user may link words in claims, or entire GSN nodes to AF3 artifacts from different phases of the safety process (e.g., *requirement* and *deployment* models), as well as implementation (e.g., *generated code*), and verification artifacts (e.g., *simulation*, *formal verification* or *testing results*). GSN-based safety arguments created in ExplicitCase may augment the traditional syntactic tracing ("depend-on") between safety process artifacts with a semantic tracing ("why?") capability. Semantic tracing provides answers to two aspects relevant for traceability: (1) how the traceability among system model elements relates to the traceability among different levels of requirements depicted in the safety case, and (2) if all the system model elements referenced in the same safety case argument are connected by a traceability link in the system models. A safety case

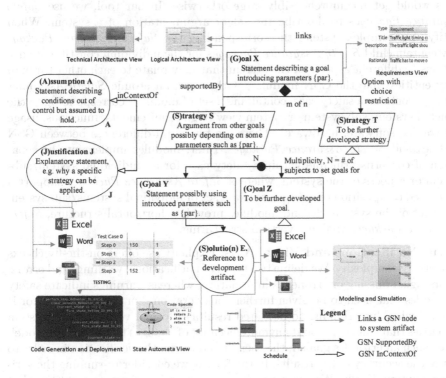

Fig. 2. Linking GSN nodes with AF3 and external artifacts (example based on [9]).

may provide an argument on how, in which context and under which assumptions the inference from one system model element to another holds. A sound safety argument should contain all the relevant information from system models. The relevant system model elements in a safety case are depicted by our safety case metamodel, via references. The metamodel has been built based on our experience from projects, on standard-mandated requirements on safety assurance artifacts and on information from related literature, such as Hawkins et al. [10]. When trying to link nodes and claims from the argument to system model elements, all related system model elements are identified. All the system model elements referenced in a safety case argument should trace to each other. After identifying all the system model elements referenced in the safety case argument, the engineer can manually check if the system model elements have a tracing link between them. If not, the software engineer should (at least) reconsider the tracing, if not even model a tracing link.

Tool-Based Support for Handling Large Arguments. In conformance with the GSN standard [3] (Annex B1), ExplicitCase supports the construction of modular safety cases [17]. Figure 3 depicts an overview of a safety case defined by a set of interrelated modules. Apart from the traditional modular structure, the tool also allows the construction of hierarchical safety argumentation structures, which is especially suitable for complex systems, where GSN structures would get incomprehensibly large otherwise. In our tool, we use *Safety Assurance Packages* to describe the safety argumentation of a system. When certifying a complex system, the corresponding top *Safety Assurance Package* may contain child *Safety Assurance Packages* for the individual constituent subsystems or different aspects of the system that may relate to each other through away entities (like the GSN modules). Otherwise, an atomic *Safety Assurance Package* contains a safety case, containing a set of modules, corresponding to the depicted system, sub-system or system view (e.g., requirements, functions, usage constraints, software, hardware). There are two main differences between GSN modules and *Safety Assurance Packages*. First, modules implement the separation of concerns principle within a safety case for an individual system/subsystem or aspects of the system, whereas *Safety Assurance Packages* support a structured composition of safety cases for a set of individual systems/sub-system or aspect of the system. Second, modules provide a horizontal structure, *Safety Assurance Packages* enable a vertical structuring.

Status Notifications and Visual Aids. ExplicitCase offers on-the-fly checks of arbitrary complexity. We define two types of notifications: warnings and errors. Errors signal missing or erroneous information, whereas warnings indicate safety case nodes that need to be given further consideration. For example, an error is signaled when hyperlinking to outdated results of formal verification of system properties that might not hold anymore because of changes to the system model. When such an error is signaled, the user should re-run the verification in order to ensure the accuracy of the results. In the future, we consider re-running the verification automatically. Warnings are, for instance, raised for option entities that cannot be left in the final version of the safety case, but must be appropriately

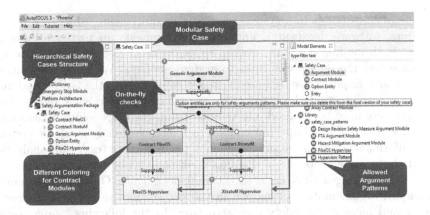

Fig. 3. An overview of ExplicitCase's modular and hierarchical safety case structure. (Color figure online)

resolved (see Fig. 3). Different coloring of GSN elements raises the safety case developer's awareness about the existence of undeveloped or uninstantiated entities. In addition, contract modules have a distinct coloring in order to distinguish them from regular argumentation modules (see Figs. 1 and 3). We do not allow users to color nodes by themselves, in order to keep a certain meaning of each coloring so that anyone can easily "read" the coloring.

Built-in Safety Case Model Constraints. Model constraints define semantic conditions that cannot be defined in the syntactic structure of a metamodel. Since different stakeholders may have different interpretations and the underlying assumptions may be overlooked, ExplicitCase requires to document goal decompositions via strategies. Therefore, a constraint on the safety case model enforces the existence of a strategy node whenever the user wants to connect two goals. ExplicitCase checks many more constraints to ensure the integrity of safety cases (e.g., to prevent the creation of invalid relationships). For example, another constraint to ensure the integrity of safety cases is that only GSN connections permitted by the GSN standard can be modeled (e.g., a context node cannot be connected to a justification node). Avoidance of circular argumentation is another built-in constraint on the semantic level.

3 Practical Experience

The DREAMS project [2] provides an architectural style for mixed-criticality systems [8], a reference platform, and a model-driven toolchain. A main goal of the project is to reduce certification costs based on modular safety cases relying on the guarantees of the DREAMS architecture (see [12,13]).

In the DREAMS project, safety engineers used the ExplicitCase tool to review and complement the system safety case for a wind power demonstrator [15]. This case study comprises five argumentation sub-packages, where each sub-package corresponds to a system view (e.g., requirements, functions, usage constraints, software, hardware), and contains from one up to ten argument modules. Each module contains between six and twenty nodes. Approximately forty percent of the nodes have links to system artifacts. We received positive feedback about ExplicitCase because (1) it is compliant with the GSN standard, and (2) one can intuitively build safety cases with it. However, some requests to extend the tool have been raised. On the one hand, the GSN solution class was extended with a *link* attribute that enables to reference already available certificates, conformance demonstration documents, test reports or test result analyses. This attribute implements one of the aforementioned types of the hyperlinking, namely hyperlinking a GSN node to external documents. On the other hand, the complex argumentation developed in the project motivated ExplicitCase's modular and hierarchical safety case structure. In the following, we consider on a product-line family [5] of the DREAMS wind turbine controller [15]. The product space is based on two variation points, namely the usage of a one or two channel safety architecture, and the usage of diagnostic units. The variation points map to *DesignChoice* strategy nodes in ExplicitCase that decompose the goal to achieve a certain Safety Integrity Level (SIL) by enforcing design constraints (e.g., constraints on the deployment model that ensure the mapping of software components to sufficiently safe hardware elements). We build a safety case argument on the fulfillment of a safety requirement (see *Goal: SIL Fulfillment*) demanding the achievement of SIL 3 for a safety function by means of the 1oo2 design pattern with diagnostic units (see Fig. 4). The *SIL Fulfillment* safety goal points to the model of the corresponding safety requirement, which provides further information on the requirement (e.g., priority, author,

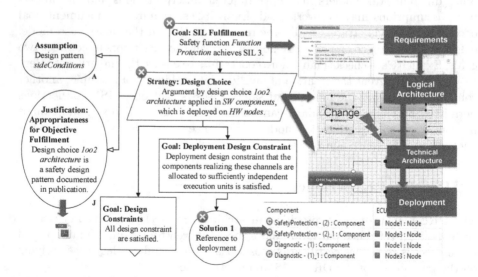

Fig. 4. Evaluation scenario: linking safety argumentation with design artifacts. (Color figure online)

status etc.). The justification node refers to a document that attests that the design choice is a known and suitable design pattern and is only valid when the associated *sideConditions* hold. Further, the strategy of implementing a design choice implies that certain *designConstraints* must be implemented in the logical and technical architecture. In Fig. 4, we only depict one such constraint. The two-channel architecture requires that the components realizing these channels be allocated to sufficiently independent execution units, satisfying the separation required by the *Deployment Design Constraint* GSN goal. The argument is deeply integrated with the system models (e.g., the safety goal refers to a safety requirement model element). The evidence that the *Goal: Deployment Design Constraint* goal is implemented by the system is given by the deployment model of the safety architecture (see *Solution 1*). AF3 offers a rich modeling language for depicting system models. Thus, hyperlinking words in safety claims with system models eliminates the need for GSN context nodes (e.g., *SW components* and *HW nodes* in *Design Choice* strategy nodes refer to elements in the logical and technical architecture of the AF3 system model). *Context* GSN nodes explain the claims of other GSN nodes. As such explanations are required for sound argumentations, the number of GSN context nodes rapidly grows, which clutters the argumentation structure. By hyperlinking safety claims to system models, certain context nodes may be eliminated. This reduces the number of GSN nodes in one argument, which is beneficial, since safety arguments tend to get very large.

The Advantages of Hyperlinking. In Fig. 4 the hyperlinks from the GSN model to system model elements are depicted, together with other traces with the system model. A change in the logical architecture affects not only the GSN node that contains the hyperlink to the logical architecture, but also other nodes. A change in the logical architecture may impact a claim about a system model element that has a trace to the logical component (e.g., *Goal: SIL Fulfillment* and *Solution 1*). The claims referencing to system model elements traced from the changed system model element should also be marked to be re-visited. For example, if a requirement is changed, the components from the logical architecture refining that requirement may also need to be changed. Thus, the claims referring to those components need to be re-visited. The tool automatically marks all the nodes which have a hyperlink to system models which have traces to or are traced from the logical architecture by different coloring (in the picture, we mark the potentially affected nodes with a red cross, signaling an error). Thus, our hyperlinking system proves to support change management in safety cases. From the safety case argument in Fig. 4 one can read that the deployment may be traced through the logical architecture, to the safety requirement implemented by the logical architecture. Hence, safety cases offer a better overview on the inherited traces throughout system models. Furthermore, the safety argument not only depicts already existing traces between system models, but also enhances them with additional information. For example, the deployment model referenced by *Solution 1* can only satisfy the requirement referenced by the *Goal: SIL Fulfillment*, if the constraints depicted by *Goal: Deployment Design Constraint* are satisfied, because only then the employed design pattern (see *Strategy: Design Choice*) may be applied. Furthermore, the side-conditions assumed for the logical and platform architecture must also hold in order for the requirement to be satisfied by the deployment. All this rationale, even though implicitly used during the modeling of the system, is now explicitly documented in the system's safety case. Making implicit rationale explicit supports the system engineers in making justified safety-aware design decisions. Also, explicitly depicting the design rationale in a safety case supports safety engineers in making the case of system safety in front of certification authorities, with the help of the rationale used by the system engineers.

4   Related Work

The most mature commercial tool to develop GSN-based safety cases is the *Adelard Safety Case Editor (ASCE)* [1]. ASCE supports, among others, the development of GSN structures in any kind of contexts. We, on the other hand, offer a solution for solely modeling based on GSN notation safety cases in the context of model-based development. One important feature of ASCE is its hypertext feature. One can have in the GSN argument structure dynamic and traceable document and web links. This enables collaboration - information from other sources being shared in the argumentation, traceability as referenced external information may be easily accessed via hyperlinks. The hypertext system also aids the change management, since changes in the linked document are highlighted in ASCE. In ExplicitCase we also have hyperlinks. The scope of our hyperlinks is to tune GSN in order to express a meaningful set of semantic constructs from the model-based development domain. This enables us also to specify semantic rules for the construction of safety arguments and also semantic analysis. In contrast to ASCE's hypertext system, we provide hyperlinking via references to elements from other metamodels. Even though our tool is open-source and much less mature than ASCE, it provides a large set of features ASCE has to offer, such as node status attributes, syntactic checks of the argumentation network, the possibility to embed in a node a link to an external artifact and modular structure. We intend to implement in the future filtering options, multiple-views which enable the rendering of the argument structure in different formats and also a narrative field for any node.

D-Case offers an Eclipse-based GSN editor focusing on the creation and manipulation of GSN arguments and patterns [14]. D-Case offers parametrized claims within nodes of GSN patterns, which allows type checking. In our tool, the user can also create parametrized claims. ExplicitCase, having as main scope supporting model-based engineers at exchanging information with safety engineers, only allows parameters to have types defined by the classes from our system metamodels. Basing the allowed types on the given metamodels helps at maintaining a domain specific language while building safety arguments. It also ensures the validity of parameter types. During instantiation, the user is only given the possibility to instantiate the parameter with model elements of such type, avoiding type errors. Thus, there is no more need of type checks.

The tool which is closest to ExplicitCase is *AdvoCATE* [7]. Both tools offer a model-based approach for creation, modular structuring and manipulation of safety cases. On the one hand, AdvoCATE focuses on creation of safety cases by automatic instantiation of safety case patterns with output from external formal verification tools. On the other hand, ExplicitCase has its main scope to support creation of safety cases based on the information from the model-based development processes. On the one hand, AdvoCATE's scope is to create and manage safety cases with an increased level of automation. It has features that perform transformations to different formats of safety case reports. On the other hand, ExplicitCase's goal is to offer an interchange of information between safety and software engineers. Thus, ExplicitCase offers transformation capabilities from safety case arguments to system design artifacts and reversely. ExplicitCase may be used for editing any safety case, however, in contrast to AdvoCATE - a standalone tool for safety case creation, its features mainly focus on building safety case arguments deeply integrated with system models and analyses available in AF3. Currently, safety cases modeled in ExplicitCase may be connected only to system models complaint to AF3 metamodels.

Hawkins et al. presented an approach for the automatic instantiation of patterns with information from system models [10]. The rationale of integrating information from system models into safety cases is in line with our research. However, while Hawkins et al. is based on an approach that is tool-independent [10] we implement our approach in a safety case editor integrated with a model-based development tool. Thus, the relation between system and safety case models is bilateral. Our approach and tool enhances the safety argument with information from system models. Furthermore, it enhances the tracing between system models with information such as why the trace is relevant for safety assurance and under which assumptions and in which context the trace is valid.

5   Conclusion and Outlook

In this paper, we present a model-based tool to develop GSN-based safety cases integrated with system design artifacts. This integration of metamodels supports the change management within a safety case. Also, we argue how a safety case may enhance the traceability between different system model elements. Rather than being a simple safety case editor, our tool's main scope is to offer an approach for (1) using system design artefacts as safety assurance evidence; and (2) reasoning via safety cases about safety design decisions. In complex projects, a safety case node may have to be linked to multiple requirements or other artifacts. Thus, as future work, we want to extend the hyperlinking features in order to support multiple linking. Based on our proposed safety case metamodel, we will explore the automatic creation of safety case artifacts, in parallel with system design artifacts. We also intend to integrate ExplicitCase with safety analysis techniques, like Failure Mode and Effects Analysis (FMEA). The critical failure modes will be then linked to safety requirements in AF3, which will then be implemented by system models and verified by model-based verification analysis in AF3. We plan to use our tool in more projects, in order to increase its usability.

Acknowledgments. The research leading to these results has received funding from the European Union's Seventh Framework Program FP7/2007–2013 under grant agreement no. 610640. We thank Fernando Eizaguirre and Carlos-F. Nicolás from IK4-IKERLAN for their valuable feedback on applying ExplicitCase in the context of the DREAMS project.

References

1. Adelard safety case editor. http://www.adelard.com/asce/
2. DREAMS FP7 project. http://dreams-project.eu
3. GSN community standard version 1, November 2011. http://www.goalstructuring notation.info/documents/GSN_Standard.pdf
4. Aravantinos, V., Voss, S., Teufl, S., Hölzl, F., Schätz, B.: AutoFOCUS 3: Tooling concepts for seamless, model-based development of embedded systems. In: Proceedings of the 8th International Workshop Model-Based Architecture Cyber-Physical Embeded System, pp. 19–26 (2015)
5. Barner, S., Diewald, A., Eizaguirre, F., Vasilevskiy, A., Chauvel, F.: Building product-lines of mixed-criticality systems. In: Proceedings of the Forum Specification and Design Languages (FDL 2016). IEEE, Bremen, September 2016
6. Bloomfield, R., Bishop, P.: Safety and assurance cases: past, present and possible future - an Adelard perspective. In: Dale, C., Anderson, T. (eds.) Making Systems Safer, pp. 51–67. Springer, London (2010). doi:10.1007/978-1-84996-086-1_4
7. Denney, E., Pai, G., Pohl, J.: AdvoCATE: an assurance case automation toolset. In: Ortmeier, F., Daniel, P. (eds.) SAFECOMP 2012. LNCS, vol. 7613, pp. 8–21. Springer, Heidelberg (2012). doi:10.1007/978-3-642-33675-1_2
8. DREAMS consortium: Architectural style of DREAMS. D1.2.1, July 2014
9. Gleirscher, M., Cârlan, C.: Arguing from hazard analysis in safety cases: a modular argument pattern. In: Proceedings of the International Symposium on High Assurance Systems Engineering, January 2017
10. Hawkins, R., Habli, I., Kolovos, D., Paige, R., Kelly, T.: Weaving an assurance case from design: a model-based approach. In: IEEE 16th International Symposium on High Assurance Systems Engineering (HASE) (2015)
11. ISO/TC 22: ISO/DIS 26262–1 - Road vehicles Functional safety Part 2 Management of Functional Safety. Technical report, Technical Committee 22, Geneva, Switzerland, July 2009
12. Larrucea, A., Perez, J., Agirre, I., Brocal, V., Obermaisser, R.: A modular safety case for an IEC 61508 compliant generic hypervisor. In: Proceedings fo the Euromicro Conference on Digital System Design (DSD), pp. 571–574. IEEE,•August 2015
13. Larrucea, A., Perez, J., Obermaisser, R.: A modular safety case for an IEC 61508 compliant generic COTS processor. In: Proceedings of the International Conference on CIT/IUCC/DASC/PICOM, pp. 1788–1795. IEEE, October 2015
14. Matsuno, Y.: D-case editor: a typed assurance case editor. University of Tokyo (2011)

15. Perez, J., Gonzalez, D., Trujillo, S., Trapman, T.: A safety concept for an IEC-61508 compliant fail-safe wind power mixed-criticality system based on multicore and partitioning. In: de la Puente, J.A., Vardanega, T. (eds.) Ada-Europe 2015. LNCS, vol. 9111, pp. 3–17. Springer, Cham (2015). doi:10.1007/978-3-319-19584-1_1
16. Rinehart, D.J., Knight, J.C., Rowanhill, J.: Understanding what it means for assurance cases to "work". Technical report, NASA/CR-2017-219582, NASA Langley Research Center, Hampton, VA, United States (2017). https://ntrs.nasa.gov/archive/nasa/casi.ntrs.nasa.gov/20170003806.pdf
17. Voss, S., Schätz, B., Khalil, M., Cârlan, C.: Towards modular certification using integrated model-based safety cases. In: Proceedings of the Workshop Verification and Assurance, July 2013

D-Case Communicator: A Web Based GSN Editor for Multiple Stakeholders

Yutaka Matsuno$^{(\boxtimes)}$

Department of Computer Engineering, College of Science and Technology,
Nihon University, Tokyo, Japan
matsuno.yutaka@nihon-u.ac.jp

Abstract. This paper presents *"D-Case Communicator"*, a web-based GSN editor which facilitates co-authoring of GSN diagrams by (possibly) remote stakeholders. D-Case Communicator is easy to use: it can be used in typical web-browsers such as Chrome, Firefox, and Safari; Editing is smooth as it is implemented using recent web technologies. This paper explains basic specification, usage, and design rationale of the tool. D-Case Communicator is available in https://mlab.ce.cst.nihon-u.ac.jp/dcase/.

1 Introduction

There are several assurance cases tools (D-Case Editor [1], AdvoCATE [2], ASCE [3], Astah GSN [4], ...). Most of the tools are stand-alone and require several steps for installation and preparation. For example, some tools require platform for the tools e.g., Eclipse, but it is not easy for ordinary users to install such platform. Recently, web-based technologies have been getting advanced and many stand-alone softwares such as Microsoft Office also have their web-based versions (Microsoft Office 365, etc.). One of the merits of web-based softwares is that they do not require any installation step and platform other than conventional web browsers.

This paper presents "D-Case Communicator", a web-based GSN (Goal Structuring Notation) [5] editor, which facilitates co-authoring of GSN diagrams by remote users. D-Case Communicator is easy to use: it can be used in typical web-browsers such as Chrome, Firefox, and Safari; Editing is smooth as it is implemented using recent web technologies (Docker, Mongo DB, Bootstrap, D3.js, etc.). Also, D-Case Communicator is secure as all data including user information and GSN diagrams are stored in Docker container, and only privileged user (knowing the architecture of the database) can access to and edit the data.

The structure of the paper is as follows. Section 2 shows basic usage of the tool. Section 3 explains design rationale of the tool. Section 4 concludes the paper.

2 Basic Usage of D-Case Comminicator

Figure 1 shows a screenshot of D-Case Communicator.

In D-Case Communicator, users can share and edit GSN diagrams remotely amongst each other via the internet. This screenshot shows

S. Tonetta et al. (Eds.): SAFECOMP 2017 Workshops, LNCS 10489, pp. 64–69, 2017.
DOI: 10.1007/978-3-319-66284-8_6

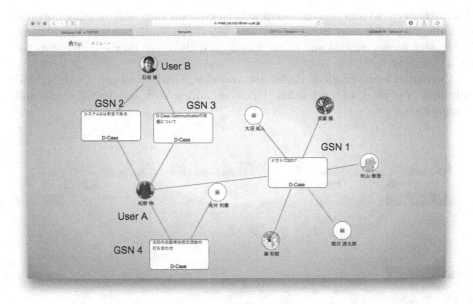

Fig. 1. Stakeholder network view of D-Case Communicator

"stakeholder network" view, which is one of the two main views of D-Case Communicator. For example, GSN 1 in Fig. 1 (robot development for mechatronics contest 2017) is a GSN diagram for a robot being developed in our laboratory, and six users (the author and his students) share the GSN diagram. In Fig. 1, there are also other GSN diagrams: GSN 2 (GSN for "System X is safe") shared by the two users (the author and one of the developers), GSN 3 (GSN for updating D-Case Communicator) shared by two users, and GSN 4 (GSN to be used in a meeting with engineers of automobile companies) shared by the author and one of the participants. The users can only look at and edit GSN diagrams directly linked to them. For example, User A (the author) can look at and edit all the four GSN diagrams, but User B can only look at and edit GSN 2 and GSN 3. Users can together edit GSN diagrams by double clicking the GSN diagrams in stakeholder network view. This stakeholder network view is for User A. In this view, all GSN diagrams which can be accessed by the user are shown.

Figure 2 shows the editing view of GSN 1 diagram. If a user creates a GSN node, moves the node, and writes a description for the node, then other users can see the editing of the GSN diagrams instantly from their own web browser. The current version does not have kinds of access control of a GSN diagram. All sharing users can freely edit the GSN diagram. If one of the users changes the description of a node, the node is instantly updated and other users can see the change after the user completes the edit; but if a user tries to move a node to right and the other user tries to move the node to left, then the node does not move. In our current testing, we observe that an access control is not necessary.

Also, other typical functions in recent web-based tools such as indicating portions of a diagram edited by other users have not been implemented. We plan to implement access control and other functions if there are user requirements for such functions.

Currently, basic kinds of nodes are available: Goal, Strategy, Context, and Solution. We plan to add other kinds of nodes such as Justification and Assumption.

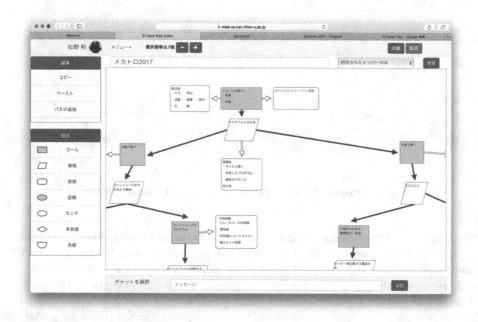

Fig. 2. Editing view of D-Case Communicator

The usage steps are as follows: User registration, searching other users, inviting other users, and co-authoring GSN diagrams. Other functions includes chatting and "agree" or "disagree" button for presenting agreement or disagreement of the GSN diagrams to other users.

D-Case Communicator was used in a GSN workshop held in Tokyo, March 2017. The lecturer and the participants can instantly share GSN diagrams via the tool, and the lecturer can easily present examples and GSN diagrams drawn by the participants using the tool and a projector. Feedbacks from the participants are positive on D-Case Communicator as it is easy to use and the function of sharing GSN diagrams in sync is useful.

D-Case Communicator is available both in Japanese and English. The website is in our laboratory's web page: https://mlab.ce.cst.nihon-u.ac.jp/dcase/login. html. Also, as it is implemented in a Docker container, D-Case Communicator can be implemented in any local server inside a company.

3   Design Rationale of D-Case Communicator

Over the past six years, we have been trying to spread assurance cases in Japan. We have been organizing assurance case meetings twice for a year, and each meeting has about 30 participants. Some participants said they like assurance cases and GSN, but the penetration of assurance cases in Japan is currently very limited. The main reasons seem to be as follows (from the voices of the participants).

- Tools are limited and not so easy to use.
- Drawing assurance cases is difficult: how to set goal, strategy, ..., are all difficult. The concept of assurance cases and GSN and other formats are easy to understand, but there is not a good guide book.

For the first reason, D-Case Communicator is designed primary for usability and been developed as a web-based tool which does not require any installation steps. For the second reason, some of basic difficulties can be listed as follows.

1. Setting the top goal.
2. Selecting a strategy for splitting the goal.
3. Setting a solution node for the goal.
4. Setting amount of description in a GSN node.
5. Setting the size of a GSN diagram.

There are several guidebooks on constructing assurance cases. However, such guidebooks are either accompanied with detailed description of risk analysis for safety-critical system [6,7] and difficult for a reader who wants to study "argumentation" first in a short time, or seem to be only show a history of safety cases, basic explanation on GSN syntax, and GSN drawing steps [8] briefly extended from the six steps shown in [9]. Unfortunately, those books have not helped us well for resolving the above difficulties.

For these basic difficulties, current our answers are as follows.

1. Setting the top goal by the concerns of the stakeholders.
2. Selecting a strategy for splitting the goal by the concerns of the stakeholders.
3. Setting a solution node for the goal by the concerns of the stakeholders.
4. Setting amount of description in a GSN node according to readability.
5. Setting the size of a GSN diagram at most twenty GSN nodes and it can be shown within one slide. If the size of a GSN (GSN A) diagram is to be more than twenty, then draw another GSN (GSN B) diagram and link it to GSN A. The stakeholders of GSN A and B might be different. For example, if GSN A is drawn by the manager of a system, then GSN B might be drawn by the developers having technical detail of the system, because lower part of a GSN diagram tends to be technical.

The format of GSN is simple and easy to understand, but too free and gives almost no restriction, thus it is difficult to draw GSN diagrams. We introduce the notion of stakeholders explicitly (Items 1, 2, and 3). Goals, strategies, solutions are chosen according to the concern of the stakeholders. Items 4 and 5 derives from our experience on using GSN: Most effective usage of GSN diagrams is to show and update GSN diagram using a PC and a projector, and discuss with less than five participants (to prevent divergence of discussion). D-Case Communicator can also be used in a meeting where the participants look at and edit the same GSN diagram on their PC in sync, and the GSN diagram is also shown in the projector. In such a use case, a GSN diagram should be with in one slide and the amount of description is limited for readability. In many cases, too big GSN diagrams (e.g., more then one hundred nodes) does not work in our experiences.

Based on the above observation, we introduce stakeholder network in D-Case Communicator. Introducing stakeholders is not a new idea as it is a common-sense in software engineering, but as far as we know, there are not assurance cases tool (currently available) which explicitly use the notion of stakeholders (In [9], stakeholder interest is briefly shown in a node other than basic GSN nodes in a figure, but the detail is not shown; it is said that in SAM (Safety Argument Manager) tool [10], stakeholder interests could be indicated, but currently the tool seems to be unavailable). Also, the interface of D-Case Communicator is designed for drawing GSN diagrams of at most twenty nodes (of course a user can draw a GSN diagram more than twenty nodes if the user wants). D-Case Communicator can link any kind of documents (including GSN diagrams drawn in the tool) on the internet to GSN nodes. Currently we are developing a dedicated linking function from a GSN diagram to another GSN diagrams (simple GSN module system [1]).

4   Concluding Remarks

This paper has presented "D-Case Communicator", a web-based GSN tool for co-authoring GSN diagrams by multiple (possibly remote) users. The tool has been designed based on our experience, and introduced stakeholder network interface. The GSN drawing function is smooth and got good feedbacks from the participants in a GSN workshop. Currently, we are writing a GSN guide-book using D-Case Communicator. Introducing the notion of stakeholder is of course not enough and we need more detailed steps according to each kind of stakeholders (designer, developer, owner, ...,). As a future work, we plan to develop automatic selecting function of goals, strategies, contexts, ..., as briefly discussed in [11]. We would like to report our progress in the near future.

Acknowledgement. This work has been supported by KAKENHI 15K15971, MEXT, Japan.

References

1. Matsuno, Y.: A design and implementation of an assurance case language. In: 44th Annual IEEE/IFIP International Conference on Dependable Systems and Networks, DSN 2014, pp. 630–641, Atlanta, GA, USA, 23–26 June 2014

2. Denney, E., Pai, G., Pohl, J.: AdvoCATE: an assurance case automation toolset. In: Ortmeier, F., Daniel, P. (eds.) SAFECOMP 2012. LNCS, vol. 7613, pp. 8–21. Springer, Heidelberg (2012). doi:10.1007/978-3-642-33675-1_2
3. Bishop, P., Bloomfield, R.: A methodology for safety case development. In: Safety-Critical Systems Symposium (SSS 1998) (1998)
4. Change Vision, Inc.: Astah GSN. http://astah.net/editions/gsn
5. Kelly, T., Weaver, R.: The goal structuring notation - a safety argument notation. In: Proceedings of the Dependable Systems and Networks 2004, Workshop on Assurance Cases (2004)
6. Adelard: Adelard safety case development manual (1998)
7. Eurocontrol: Safety case development manual (2006)
8. Spriggs, J.: GSN—The Goal Structuring Notation: A Structured Approach to Presenting Arguments. Springer, London (2012)
9. Kelly, T.: Arguing safety - a systematic approach to safety case management. Ph.D. thesis, Department of Computer Science, University of York (1998)
10. Wilson, S.P., McDermid, J.A., Kirkham, P.M., Fenelon, P.: The safety argument manager: an integrated approach to the engineering and safety assessment of computer based systems. In: IEEE Symposium and Workshop on Engineering of Computer Based Systems (ECBS 1996), pp. 198–205, Friedrichshafen, Germany, 11–15 March 1996
11. Matsuno, Y., Ishigaki, Y., Bando, K., Kido, H., Tanaka, K.: Developing SNS tool for consensus building on environmental safety using assurance cases. In: Skavhaug, A., Guiochet, J., Schoitsch, E., Bitsch, F. (eds.) SAFECOMP 2016. LNCS, vol. 9923, pp. 55–62. Springer, Cham (2016). doi:10.1007/978-3-319-45480-1_5

Towards Combined Safety and Security Constraints Analysis

Daniel Pereira[1], Celso Hirata[1(✉)], Rodrigo Pagliares[1,2],
and Simin Nadjm-Tehrani[3]

[1] Instituto Tecnológico de Aeronáutica, São José dos Campos 12228-900, Brazil
dpatricksp@gmail.com, hirata@ita.br,
pagliares@bcc.unifal-mg.edu.br
[2] Universidade Federal de Alfenas, UNIFAL-MG, Alfenas, MG, Brazil
[3] Linköping University, Linköping 581 83, Sweden
simin.nadjm-tehrani@liu.se

Abstract. A growing threat to the cyber-security of embedded safety-critical systems calls for a new look at the development methods for such systems. One alternative to address security and safety concerns jointly is to use the perspective of modeling using system theory. Systems-Theoretic Process Analysis (STPA) is a new hazard analysis technique based on an accident causality model. NIST SP 800-30 is a well-known framework that has been largely employed to aid in identifying threats event/source and vulnerabilities, determining the effectiveness security control, and evaluating the adverse impact of risks. Safety and security analyses, when performed independently, may generate conflicts of design constraints that result in an inconsistent design. This paper reports a novel integrated approach for safety analysis and security analysis of systems. In our approach, safety analysis is conducted with STPA while security analysis employs NIST SP800-30. It builds on a specification of security and safety constraints and outlines a scheme to automatically analyze and detect conflicts between and pairwise reinforcements of various constraints. Preliminary results show that the approach allows security and safety teams to perform a more efficient analysis.

Keywords: Safety analysis · Security analysis · STPA · NIST SP800-30

1 Introduction

Safety-critical systems are becoming complex with many components reused in integration of subsystems in order to reach a common goal. Cyber-security threats are becoming a growing concern while developing of safety-critical systems [1]. The use of commercial off the shelf software across the aviation, maritime, rail and power-generation infrastructures has resulted in increased number of vulnerabilities. Johnson [1] points out that existing office-based security standards cannot be easily integrated with safety-critical systems standards easily. There is an urgent need to move beyond high-level policies and address the more detailed engineering challenges. This view is supported by the ways in which cyber-security concerns undermine traditional

© Springer International Publishing AG 2017
S. Tonetta et al. (Eds.): SAFECOMP 2017 Workshops, LNCS 10489, pp. 70–80, 2017.
DOI: 10.1007/978-3-319-66284-8_7

forms of safety assessment and the ways in which safety concerns hinder the deployment of conventional mechanisms for cyber-security.

An alternative to address security and safety concerns jointly is to use the perspective of modeling using system theory. STAMP (Systems-Theoretic Accident Model and Processes) [2] is an accident causality model based on system theory. Within STAMP, safety is viewed as a control problem rather than a reliability problem. STAMP is built on top of three basic constructs: safety constraints, hierarchical safety control structures and process models. STAMP, due to its underlying basis - system theory - is a sound model that can be considered to fit not only safety concerns but also security concerns.

STPA (Systems-Theoretic Process Analysis) [3] is a safety analysis technique based on STAMP. STPA allows the identification of several factors contributing to accidents such as software flaws, decision-making errors, hazardous component interactions, and organizational, and management deficiencies. STPA has two steps. The first step identifies the unsafe control actions that can lead to system unsafe behavior. The second step identifies the potential causes of scenarios leading to unsafe control, and thereafter effectively identifying safety requirements.

There are two recent approaches, STPA-Sec [4] and STPA-SafeSec [5], which aid in the joint elicitation of functional, safety, and security requirements. However, both approaches are very recent and lack extensive experience in real case studies. We also believe that techniques and tools to support the requirement engineering of cyber-security of safety-critical systems and more investigations on integration of existing techniques are required.

NIST Special Publication 800-30 [6] is a guide for conducting security risk assessments. It provides guidance for carrying out tasks of a risk assessment process that are preparing for, conducting, communicating the results, and maintaining the assessment. The NIST SP800-30 framework uses six steps to break down its activities. The first two steps are identifying threat events/sources and vulnerabilities. Other steps consist in determining the effectiveness of security control, evaluating the adverse impact of risks as a combination of impact and likelihood. We will consider NIST SP800-30 because many organizations in the United States, particularly those in the aerospace area, align to the standard. Moreover, NIST SP800-30 is a flexible framework that provides a standard report structure. We will focus on the first two steps of NIST SP800-30.

Security concerns are relatively new in domains such as aeronautics and space. Some specific standards to address it have been developed [7]. Currently, security and safety specialists have their own processes enacted by distinct teams. We claim that security and safety teams conducting their analyses rather independently may produce inconsistent designs. The inconsistency is characterized by the existence of conflicting requirements.

Another issue is related to the satisfaction of requirements in an effective manner. *Reinforcement* is characterized by similarity of security and safety requirements, i.e. requirements that can be satisfied by similar (or same) features. We argue that safety and security requirements that have a reinforcement relationship can be addressed jointly in a more effective manner. Therefore, it is useful to have a systematic approach that aids identifying conflicts and reinforcements between security and safety requirements and addresses them in an integrated manner.

We propose a novel integrated approach for security and safety analyses of systems to analyze both concerns jointly using NIST SP800-30 and STPA. It builds on specifications to define security and safety constraints and drives a scheme to automatically analyze and detect conflicts and reinforcements between security and safety constraints. The idea is that the proposed approach aids security and safety teams to resolve conflicts early during system life cycle (concept phase), and to perform a more efficient analysis.

The remainder of this paper is organized as follows. The related work is presented in Sect. 2. Section 3 introduces our approach. Section 4 presents an example of use of the approach and Sect. 5 concludes the paper.

2 Related Work

Oates et al. present a SysML technique for security and safety using HiP-HOPS (Hierarchically Performed Hazard Origin and Propagation Studies) and SDL (Secure Development Lifecycle) [8]. They assume that there is a significant overlap between security and safety analysis activities. However, it is not clear which are those overlapping activities. They do not deal with conflicts between security and safety.

Subramanian and Zalewski [9] apply a NFR (Non-Functional Requirements) approach to evaluate security and safety properties. The NFR approach uses an ontology, which defines elements such as soft goals and contributions. Security and safety analyses occur together; in the same graph, the security and safety goals are displayed with contributions. Trade-offs between security and safety requirements are handled, but there is no distinction between which activity should be performed by the safety or security team.

Young and Leveson propose an integrated approach to security and safety called STPA-Sec [4]. The approach is based on STAMP [2] and extends STPA [3]. It helps identifying security vulnerabilities, safety hazards, requirements, and scenarios leading to violation of security and safety constraints. As a result, the analysis allows refining system concept by addressing not only technical but also organizational issues. STPA-Sec is a very recent work, with little documentation and history of usage. The approach does not describe how security and safety teams share information with each other in order to detect conflicts between security and safety constraints.

Similar to STPA-Sec, Friedberg et al. [5] present an analysis methodology for both security and safety, called STPA-SafeSec. The core contribution is the description of a generic component layer diagram to evaluate whether security constraints are assured or not. Their work provides a list with the cyber-attacks on integrity and availability at component layer to analyze the malicious effect. The methodology neither mentions the relationship between security and safety constraints nor discriminates the activities performed by security and safety teams.

Nostro et al. [10] describe a general methodology to support the assessment of safety-critical systems with respect to security aspects. The methodology defines a security threat library based on NIST SP800-53 (Security Controls). It is not clear in their methodology how the security and safety assessments are jointly performed. The authors state that there may be conflicts between security and safety concerns but they do not describe how to resolve them.

Thomas [11] presents a model-based technique to automate conflict detection between safety requirements and other functional requirements during early development of a system using the results of a hazard analysis. A conflict is defined when it is hazardous for the controller to provide and at the same time not to provide a control action. This approach neither considers security constraints nor takes into account reinforcements of constraints.

Troubitsyna [12] describes briefly a structured integrated derivation of safety and security requirements from safety goals. It relies on a widely accepted safety case technique and enables the integrated treatment of safety and security; however, conflicts are not dealt with.

Katta et al. [13] present an approach for providing traceability to an assessment method to combined harm of safety and security for information systems. Their goal is to capture the interdependencies between the safety and security requirements and to demonstrate the history and rationale behind their elicitation. Their approach does not deal with conflicts between safety and security constraints.

Netkachova et al. [14] present an approach to conduct structured safety and security analyses. Their approach creates safety cases that provide safety justification taking into consideration security issues. The approach is applied to a gateway function based on Multiple Independent Level of Security (MILS). The defined integrated policy considers safety and security domains and resolution of conflicts. However, the authors do not present how conflicts are identified and resolved. There is no information about which activity should be performed by the safety or security team respectively.

Many works investigate the relationships between NFR (Non-Functional Requirements) [15–19] using different strategies such as ontology, graph, model table, and taxonomy. There is a consensus that early identification of conflicting requirements is an important task during system development. However, most of the works [15–19] provide means to identify requirement conflicts only in the development phase of system's lifecycle. Few investigations are concerned with correlation or reinforcement of requirements. Egyed and Grunbacher [15] recognize the need to identify requirements conflict and cooperation, which is similar to our *reinforcement*. They consider requirement correlation during the analysis of conflict. Only Hu et al. [17] consider semantic modeling to identify requirement conflicts. Our proposed approach differs from the related work in the sense that detection of conflicts and reinforcements takes place during safety and security analyses at an earlier stage (concept phase). Besides, our detection is automatically performed using a specification of security and safety constraints.

3 Proposed Approach

Our approach builds on a process that allows interaction between both teams in specific stages of analysis. The interaction happens more deeply when the teams identify relationships between security and safety concerns. We claim that the joint analysis is made easier if we use constraints instead of requirements. The idea is to verify whether the satisfaction of a safety constraint affects a security constraint, and vice-versa. As indicated, the relationship between satisfaction of security and safety constraints can be a conflict or a reinforcement. When the sets of security and safety constraints do not conflict, a design that satisfies both sets is consistent (considering the current environment).

The proposed approach consists of a workflow of activities depicted in Fig. 1. We group the activities into three sets: safety, security, and integration. In Fig. 1, safety activities are depicted in the upper part while the security activities are shown in the lower part. Activities shared by security and safety teams are exhibited between the two parts.

STPA and NIST SP800-30 are safety and security techniques, which are based on systems engineering and should be deployed early in the system life cycle. Security and safety specialists usually perform their analysis independently, generating their own security and safety requirements from security and safety constraints.

With respect to the integration set, the activities require expertise of both teams: security and safety. It also requires the expertise of systems theory, to provide a theoretical foundation for the approach. The integration set includes two activities: "Define System Goals and its Context", and "Perform Integrated Analysis". The first one is related to the technical foundations and assumptions while the second activity is about performing a joint analysis of security and safety.

Before both teams begin their own analysis, a joint meeting is required. The activity "Define System Goals and its Context" establishes a context for the security and safety assessment according to stakeholder needs. This context includes identifying the purpose and scope of the assessment and identifying unacceptable losses, assumptions and constraints associated with the assessment, system boundaries, and other relevant information to perform the security and safety assessment. Once the system foundation is established, both teams can follow their own processes and discuss the security and safety constraints.

"Perform Integrated Analysis" is an activity where security and safety teams work together to identify conflicts between security and safety constraints and jointly define security measures and safety recommendations (SMSR). The inputs are the security and safety constraints and the outputs are the relationship between the security and safety constraints and the defined SMSR for each security and safety constraint, which are recorded in a document called "Security and Safety Dossier". The activity is divided into four tasks, not shown in Fig. 1: "Analyze the relationships between security and safety constraints", "Resolve conflicts", "Define security measures and safety recommendations", and "Elaborate security and safety dossier". In the example in Sect. 4, we will detail the tasks. The activities "Identify Causal Factors and Scenarios", "Determine Security Control, Adverse Impact and Risk", and "Maintaining and Monitoring Risks" are activities that security and safety teams can perform more independently. More information about these activities can be obtained elsewhere [3, 6].

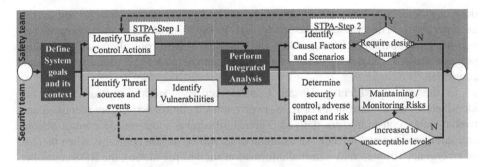

Fig. 1. The proposed integrated approach

4 Example of Use

In order to illustrate the use of our approach, we consider a simple example of a revolving door system (RDS). Figure 2 illustrates the main components of the system: (i) a revolving door that has a controller with an embedded software with a metal detection function, and a receptor device to receive commands from the remote-controller, (ii) a repository for personal belongings (including metals) and (iii) a security guard (SG) with a remote-control device. The maintenance team (not shown in the figure) can configure the metal detector's sensitivity. The SG can lock or unlock the system through a remote control or a key. The revolving door detects metal objects (e.g. gun) through the embedded software. The repository for personal belongings allows customers/employees to put their personal belongings for SG inspection. The system is used in banks and other types of office facilities. Usually there is only one door system per office facility.

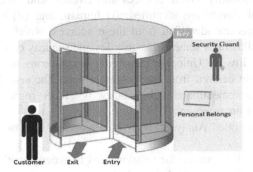

Fig. 2. Revolving door system (RDS)

For the activity "Define system goals and its context", two accidents are identified: (i) people killed or injured and (ii) damage to facility. The following hazards are identified: (i) armed and unauthorized person inside the bank branch, (ii) revolving door unlocked, (iii) disruption of power supply, and (iv) revolving door locked during an emergency. The control structure for the RDS elaborated has five components: security guard, person, RDS controller, and electrical system controllers, and controlled process. Responsibilities, process model, and mental model are identified for each controller.

In the activity "Identify Unsafe Control Actions", unsafe control actions are identified for each controller. For RDS, twelve unsafe control actions are identified and twelve safety constraints are derived. Table 1 illustrates some unsafe control actions and safety constraints of RDS. An example of identified unsafe control is when there is an emergency (triggered by external information such as fire alarm), the RDS controller has to issue unlock door command but it fails to do so (UCA-5.1). In this situation, people can be held locked in the building during a fire. The safety constraints (SaCs) are directly derived from the unsafe control actions. For instance, for the above unsafe control action, the corresponding safety constraint is "RDS must provide unlock door command when there is an emergency".

Table 1. Some unsafe control actions and safety constraints identified for RDS

Unsafe control action	Safety constraint
UCA-5.1: RDS does not provide unlock door command when there is an emergency	SaC-5.1: RDS must provide unlock door command when there is an emergency
UCA-5.2: RDS provides unlock door command when an armed person is in the entrance lane	SaC-5.2: RDS must never provide unlock door command when an armed person is in the entrance lane
UCA-6.1: RDS provides lock door command when there is an emergency	SaC-6.1: RDS must never provide lock door command when there is an emergency

In the activities "Identify Threat Sources and Events" and "Identify Vulnerabilities", two sources of threats are identified: (i) human, and (ii) environmental and physical. Seven threats are identified from these sources, which result in nine vulnerabilities. Table 2 illustrates some vulnerabilities and security constraints (SeCs). An example of vulnerability is "Unlocked revolving door during an emergency". Ten security constraints are derived from the vulnerabilities. The security constraint corresponding to the aforementioned vulnerability is "RDS must never unlock the revolving door during an emergency".

The "Perform Integrated Analysis" activity consists of four tasks as presented in Fig. 3:

The goal of the task "Analyze the relationships between security and safety constraints" is to identify the type of relationship between security constraints and safety constraints. The identification is based on the type of influence that satisfaction of one constraint has on another constraint. The influence may be positive (reinforcement) or negative (conflict).

Table 2. Some vulnerabilities and security constraints identified for RDS

Vulnerability	Security constraint
Vul-06: Incorrect parameters set up (e.g. metal detector's sensitivity)	SeC-06.1: The maintenance team must set up RDS with the correct parameters
	SeC-06.2: The maintenance team, only when authorized, must configure RDS
Vul-07: Lack of redundancy for critical activities	SeC-07: RDS must provide redundancy in critical activities
Vul-08: Lack of power supply generation	SeC-08: Electrical System must never be interrupted when the system is operating
Vul-09: Unlocked revolving door during an emergency	SeC-09: RDS must never unlock the revolving door during an emergency

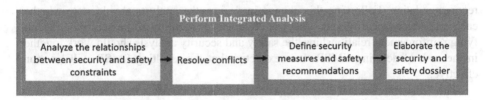

Fig. 3. Perform integrated analysis process

To identify the relationship, we employ the tokenization of safety constraint specifications proposed by Thomas [11]. The specification is expressed as four-tuple: (i) source controller that can issue control actions, (ii) type of control action (*must provide* or *must not provide*), (iii) control action, and (iv) context in which the control action must or must not be provided.

Similarly, we propose to use the tokenization for security constraint specifications with four-tuple: (i) agent that has the capability to perform an action in the asset, (ii) type of action taken by the agent (*must provide* and *must not provide*), (iii) action taken by the agent, and (iv) system and assets state when the action must or must not be provided. With the specifications, we derive an automatic scheme to detect conflicts and reinforcements.

We analyze the relationships between twelve safety constraints (SaC) and ten security constraints (SeC) using the scheme. For instance, the scheme automatically detected the conflict between the SeC "RDS must never unlock revolving door during an emergency" and SaC "SG must manually/remotely provide unlock door command during an emergency".

We suggest two alternatives to resolve conflicts. The first alternative is to redefine the components, processes, and operations of the system, so that the new constraints do not conflict. The second alternative is to refine the constraints. The idea is to take into consideration the identified conflict and refine the constraint in space and/or time to define more refined constraints that do not conflict with each other. We call the first alternative as "system redefinition" and the second, "constraint refinement". We used the second alternative for the conflict we identified earlier.

Most of the times, it is difficult to discern which emergency is going on: just security, just safety, or both. Based on that, both constraints should be redefined using the two independent lanes of the RDS to meet all types of emergency. Thus, the safety constraint should be detailed by using two independent lanes: exit and entry. During an emergency, the entry lane must be blocked and the exit lane must be controlled. Considering the decomposition, the security and safety constraints should be rewritten as follow: "SG must manually/remotely provide unlock door command for exit lane during an emergency" and "RDS must never unlock revolving door for entry lane during an emergency". The constraints do not conflict with each other any longer because there are two separate lanes.

In the task "Define security measures and safety recommendations", the security and safety teams identify and analyze the SMSR that best satisfy the security and safety constraints. In our example, in order to provide a physical implementation for the two lanes, we consider two independent doors - one for entry and other for exit – as a recommendation. Following this change in design, the analysts should state whether each constraint (security and safety) is complete or partially addressed. After identifying reinforcement relationships, the safety and security analysts should work together in the task of defining SMSR. It is expected that the resulting SMSR will be more effective.

The "Elaborate security and safety dossier" task documents the security and safety constraints and their relationships during security and safety assessments. It also documents the security measures, safety recommendations and system vulnerabilities. The security and safety dossier ensures that all identified constraints were addressed as expected by the safety and security teams through the SMSR. Verification (testing) is not covered here; however, once the SMSR are implemented, the verification activities shall be performed to check the security and safety effectiveness.

5   Concluding Remarks

We propose an integrated approach for the analysis of security and safety risks with automatic detection of conflicts and reinforcements. The joint analysis of security and safety constraints within different teams aligns with current safety and security best practice processes (STPA and NIST SP800-30 respectively). We simply augment the approaches with automatic detection of conflicts and their resolution, or identified reinforcements that may be useful in a later risk quantification and mitigation activity.

In a current work, we are applying the proposed approach in a larger and more complex system. The system is the Flight Management System (FMS). FMS is a specialized computer system that automates a wide variety of in-flight tasks, reducing the workload on the flight crew. Preliminary results [20] have shown that it is practically unfeasible to make the integrated analysis manually. We are developing a set of tools to support the analysis, including the tool for automatic detection of conflicts and reinforcements presented in this work.

Acknowledgements. The work of the last author was supported by the national projects on aeronautics (NFFP6-00917) and the research centre on Resilient Information and Control Systems (www.rics.se). The work of the second author was supported by the Conselho Nacional de Desenvolvimento Científico e Tecnológico under grant number Universal 01/2016 403921/2016-3.

References

1. Johnson C.: Why we cannot (yet) ensure the cyber-security of safety-critical systems. http://eprints.gla.ac.uk/130822/1/130822.pdf. Accessed 2017/05/14
2. Leveson, N.: Engineering a Safer World: Systems Thinking Applied to Safety. MIT Press, Cambridge (2011)
3. Leveson, N.: An STPA Primer:What is STPA? http://sunnyday.mit.edu/STPA-Primer-v0.pdf. Accessed 12 May 2017
4. Young, W., Leveson, N.: An integrated approach to safety and security based on systems theory. Commun. ACM **57**(2), 31–35 (2014)
5. Friedberg, I., McLaughlin, K., Smith, P., Laverty, D., Sezer, S.: STPA-SafeSec: safety and security analysis for cyber-physical systems. J. Inf. Secur. Appl. **34**, 183–196 (2016)
6. National Institute of Standards and Technology: NIST Special Publication 800-30 Revision 1, Guide for Conducting Risk Assessments (2012)
7. RTCA DO-326A: Airworthiness security process specification. RTCA (2014)
8. Oates, R., Foulkes, D., Herries, G., Banham, D.: Practical extensions of safety critical engineering processes for securing industrial control systems. In: 8th IET International System Safety Conference incorporating the Cyber Security Conference Proceedings, pp. 1–6. IET, Cardiff (2013)
9. Subramanian, N., Zalewski, J.: Quantitative assessment of safety and security of system architectures for cyberphysical systems using the NFR approach. IEEE Syst. J. **10**(2), 397–409 (2016)
10. Nostro, N., Bondavalli, A., Silva, N.: Adding security concerns to safety critical certification. In: IEEE International Symposium on Software Reliability Engineering Workshops Proceedings, Naples (2014)
11. Thomas, J.: Extending and automating a systems-theoretic hazard analysis for requirements generation and analysis. MIT Ph.D. dissertation, Cambridge (2013)
12. Troubitsyna, E.: An integrated approach to deriving safety and security requirements from safety cases. In: IEEE 40th Annual Computer Software and Applications Conference Proceedings, Atlanta (2016)
13. Katta, V., Raspotnig, C., Karpati, P., Stålhane, T.: Requirements management in a combined process for safety and security assessments. In: International Conference on Availability, Reliability and Security, Regensburg (2013)
14. Netkachova, K., Müller, K., Paulitsch, M., Bloomfield, R.: Security-informed safety case approach to analysing MILS systems. In: International Workshop on MILS: Architecture and Assurance for Secure Systems, Amsterdam (2015)
15. Egyed, A., Grunbacher, P.: Identifying requirements conflicts and cooperation: how quality attributes and automated traceability can help. IEEE Softw. **21**(6), 50–58 (2004)
16. Tabassum, M., Siddik, M., Shoyaib, M., Khaled, S.: Determining interdependency among non-functional requirements to reduce conflict. In: International Conference on Informatics, Electronics & Vision (ICIEV), Dhaka (2014)

17. Hu, H., Ma, Q., Zhang, T., Tan, Y., Xiang, H., Fu, C., Feng, Y.: Semantic modelling and automated reasoning of non-functional requirement conflicts in the context of softgoal interdependencies. IET Softw. **9**(6), 145–156 (2015)
18. Sadana, V., Liu, X.: Analysis of conflicts among non-functional requirements using integrated analysis of functional and non-functional requirements. In: 31st Annual International Computer Software and Applications Conference Proceedings, Beijing (2007)
19. Salado, A., Nilchiani, R.: The concept of order of conflict in requirements engineering. IEEE Syst. J. **10**(1), 25–35 (2016)
20. Pereira, D., Hirata, C., Pagliares, R., De Lemos, F.: STPA-Sec for security of flight management system. In: 2017 STAMP Workshop (2017). http://psas.scripts.mit.edu/home/2017-stamp-presentations/. Accessed 12 May 2017

Attack Modeling for System Security Analysis
(Position Paper)

Abdullah Altawairqi and Manuel Maarek$^{(\boxtimes)}$

Heriot-Watt University, Edinburgh, UK
{aha37,M.Maarek}@hw.ac.uk

Abstract. Approaches to the safety analysis of software-intensive systems are being adapted to also provide security assurance. Extensions have been proposed to reflect the specific nature of security analysis by introducing intention as a causal factor to reaching unsafe state of the system, or by introducing new layers in the system modelling to model its surface of attack.

In this paper we propose to extend these approaches by modelling the attacks perspective alongside the system. We explain how such modelling could be used to verify the coverage of the security analysis and facilitate its maintenance.

Keywords: Hazard analysis · Security analysis · Attack model

1 Introduction

The ubiquitous computing paradigm is prevalent in nowadays systems which leaves them vulnerable to faults [5]. Safety analysis is essential for safety-critical systems as it identifies the behaviour and properties that each component and the system as a whole need to satisfy. The security of computer systems is of growing concern and requires such analysis to consider external threat as well as hazard in system design, development and operation. The combination of system safety and security using advanced engineering techniques along with detailed knowledge of domains and processes has made the task extremely challenging for cyber-security professionals.

In this paper, we explore security analysis approaches inspired by safety hazard analysis methods. We then present an extension to these approaches to model the attack perspectives alongside the system and discuss how this modelling could increase the security analysis by focusing on the attacker's point of view, and could help in verifying the coverage of the security analysis and facilitate the maintenance of the analysis.

2 Safety and Security Analysis

In this section, we explore a selection of works that adapt, for security, hazard analysis methodologies developed for safety. In particular, we are looking at

© Springer International Publishing AG 2017
S. Tonetta et al. (Eds.): SAFECOMP 2017 Workshops, LNCS 10489, pp. 81–86, 2017.
DOI: 10.1007/978-3-319-66284-8_8

the base on which the analysis is built, the manner individual elements of the analysis differ, and how the coverage of the analysis is sought with the perspective of constructing a safety or security assurance case. A summary is presented in Table 1 of Sect. 2.3.

These safety analysis methodologies are Functional Hazard Analysis (FHA) and Systems-Theoretic Process Analysis (STPA) [6], part of Systems-Theoretic Accident Modeling and Processes (STAMP) [5]. For a more exhaustive survey of approaches combining safety and security analysis, see [4].

2.1 Safety Analysis

FHA. Safety analysis implies a combined systematic inspection of the system's functional specification and the conditions that could trigger hazards the system should avoid. FHA suggests a methodology to conduct such analysis by putting together a bottom-up and a to-down approaches. The bottom-up approach, Failure Mode and Effects Analysis (FMEA), exhaustively explores the ways each component of the system could fail, and the cause and safety implication of the failure. At the base of this elicitation of single point of failures are the system's components and specification. It is complemented by the top-down approach, Fault Tree Analysis (FTA), which structures the analysis of more complex scenarios that could lead to a hazard. Hazards are at the root of this tree-based analysis which explores the conditions which could trigger the hazard to occur, the conditions could be a combination of failures and events.

STPA. Due to the ever increasing complexity of systems, such systematic exploration starting from the system's architecture or from the hazards to avoid is costly to implement and maintain, and does not handle well systems with complex interactions. As part of STAMP [5] which is a more holistic approach to modelling accident causality, the hazard analysis STPA [6] was proposed as an alternative method based on a system abstraction in terms of controller and actuators. This approach allows to better model the system-wide interactions. STPA shifts the safety focus from failure to control. It regards hazard as resulting from a lack of enforcement of safety constraints rather than resulting from component failure. This focus is more relevant for software-intensive systems as software components do not fail the same way physical component fail. The goal is to control the behaviour of the components and systems as a whole to ensure that safety constraints are enforced in the operational system.

Safety constraints are enumerated by mapping hazards to the system's control actions. Accident scenarios are then derived from these constraints by looking at control factors and control flaws.

2.2 Safety Analysis Methods Adapted for Security Analysis

STAMP and STPA were presented as system-centric analysis, [1,10,11] suggests with STPA-Sec that this approach could be applied for security analysis simply by adapting its safety terminology to the security equivalent. STPA-Sec proposes a change to the traditional bottom-up approach of security analysis where threats are used to derive security requirements. A number of works [2,8] have then highlighted the limitations of this safety-oriented view and proposed ways to effectively extend STPA to match the peculiarities of security analysis. In the following we explore how safety approaches have been extended to allow for security analysis.

Threat Model Based on Intention. In [8], the authors suggest that security threats could not simply be viewed as equivalent to a list of safety hazards but that the intention, which is at the heart of a security attack, must be modelled. This follows previous work in [7] by the authors to adapt the FMEA safety method for security by including vulnerabilities, threat agent and threat mode in the failure elicitation. They named their approach Failure Mode, Vulnerabilities and Effects Analysis (FMVEA). For a security-critical analysis, four ingredients (vulnerabilities, threat agent, threat mode, threat effect) are proposed and from which an attack probability is derived.

Similarly, an approach to extend FTA with attacker's intention has been proposed in [9]. Security events are added to the fault tree with a likelihood level. Note that this probability level is to change over time depending on availability of attack capabilities.

Surface of Attack. In [2], STPA-SafeSec is proposed as another extension of STPA for combined safety and security analysis. The authors suggest that the security analysis needs to be performed on the components of the system rather than the controllers as it is done in STPA. This choices allows to base the security constraints on the system physical vulnerabilities, effectively modeling the surface of attack of the system. Methods similar to STPA are then used to derive the security constraints and attack scenarios. In STPA-SafeSec, both safety constraints and security constraints are derived.

2.3 Base, Elements and Coverage of Analysis

Table 1 summaries the analysis strategies we discussed in this paper in terms of their strategy and coverage. The coverage should be seen as central for building a security assurance case from the analysis.

3 Attack Capabilities for Security Analysis

We outline in this section our proposition to extend the approaches discussed in Sect. 2. This extension has three main features: adding dependencies to the attack surface, modelling threats from the attacker's perspective, verifying the coherence between attack models and attack dependencies. We finally enumerate the changes to the STPA-SafeSec analysis process these features imply.

Table 1. Strategy and assurance of analysis methodologies. This table gives an overview of the strategy each analysis methodology from Sect. 2 implies and the assurance it provides in terms of its coverage.

Approach	Safety	Security	Base for the analysis	Differentiation criteria for analysis elements	How coverage of the analysis could be achieved
FMEA	×		Components	Cause and effect	Enumeration of failure modes
FMVEA		×	Components	Vulnerability, threat, attack type	Enumeration of threat modes
FTA	×		Hazards	Accident scenario	Decomposition of hazard causes
STPA	×		Control actions	Accident scenario (control factors and flaws)	Enumeration of four types of unsafe control action
STPA-Sec	×	×	Control actions	Hazard scenario	Enumeration of four types of unsafe control action
STPA-SafeSec		×	Components	Hazard scenario	Enumeration of attack modes per security concern
	×		Control actions	Hazard scenario	Enumeration of unsafe control action

3.1 Extend Attack Surface with Vulnerability Dependencies

STPA-SafeSec introduces on top of STPA's control layer a component layer. Each type of component of this layer is paired with generic security constraints (or vulnerabilities) to effectively map the physical surface of attack of the system.

This surface of attack is an essential base for the security analysis, we propose to extend it with vulnerability dependencies to identify the combinations of vulnerabilities that may result in the system being compromised. A dependency between a vulnerability v_1 and a vulnerability v_2 indicates that if v_1 is exploited it makes v_2 more open to subsequent exploits. These dependencies are expressed at the component and control layer of the system to refine the physical and control interactions of the system.

3.2 Model Attack Alongside System

FMVEA and the extension of STPA-Sec suggested in [8] propose to replace safety-oriented failures with security-oriented threats to represent intentions in a security analysis.

We propose to go one step further in representing the intention by modelling attackers and attacks alongside the modelling of the system. An attack agent represents an attacker entity, and an attack mode represent an individual attack a method to exploit a vulnerability (these are respectively equivalent to

FMVEA's threat agent and threat mode). An attack gain represents the outcome of an attack from the agent's point of view, this differs from FMVEA's threat effect which is expressed in terms similar to a failure effect in safety and therefore is from the system perspective. Finally, an attack strategy is represented as an attack tree [3]. An attack strategy is attached to an agent with an attack gain objective. Individual attack scenarios within a strategy are combined with *or* nodes and comprise attack modes exploiting components which are combined with *and* nodes. Each individual attack scenario is evaluated by means of attack impact which is its hazard effect on the system.

3.3   Verification and Coverage of Analysis

The separation between the system and the attacks' point of view make it possible to perform some automated verification of coherence and coverage of the analysis. The correspondence between attack modes and vulnerabilities could help to validate the vulnerability dependencies and the attack strategies as Table 2 explains. Dependencies and strategies should strengthen the maintainability of the analysis by highlighting the impact a new vulnerability or attack mode.

Table 2. Correspondence, verification, coverage between system and attack elements

System	Mapping and analysis	Attack
Vulnerability	Mapping indicating that an attack vector could exploit a given vulnerability	Attack mode
Vulnerability dependency	Individual attack scenario make use of a combination of attack modes on components, these combinations must correspond to vulnerability dependencies, every vulnerability dependency must be illustrated in attack scenarios	Attack strategy

Table 3. Extension to STPA-SafeSec's analysis process. Note that we use the term vulnerability in place of STPA-SafeSec's security constraint

STPA-SafeSec process	Additional analysis step	
High level analysis	1.	Derive vulnerabilities
	2.	Define attack modes
	3.	Map attack modes to vulnerabilities
	4.	Define attack profiles (agents, gains)
Control loop analysis	1.	Define vulnerability dependencies
	2.	Identify attack scenarios
	3.	Verify coherence between attack scenarios and vulnerability dependencies
	4.	Evaluate individual attack scenario by means of its effect, gain and modes

3.4 Analysis Process

The extensions we suggest requires additional steps within the STPA-SafeSec [2] analysis process. These additional steps are indicated in Table 3.

4 Conclusion

We proposed in this paper to model attacks alongside the system to better capture the intention of the attacker and the attack vectors when deriving scenarios. This approach which extends previous works offers opportunities to verify the analysis and its coverage.

References

1. Abdulkhaleq, A., Wagner, S., Leveson, N.: A comprehensive safety engineering approach for software-intensive systems based on STPA. Proc. Eng. **128**, 2–11 (2015). doi:10.1016/j.proeng.2015.11.498
2. Friedberg, I., McLaughlin, K., Smith, P., Laverty, D., Sezer, S.: STPA-SafeSec: safety and security analysis for cyber-physical systems. J. Inf. Secur. Appl. Part 2 **34**, 183–196 (2016). doi:10.1016/j.jisa.2016.05.008
3. Jhawar, R., Kordy, B., Mauw, S., Radomirović, S., Trujillo-Rasua, R.: Attack trees with sequential conjunction. In: Federrath, H., Gollmann, D. (eds.) SEC 2015. IAICT, vol. 455, pp. 339–353. Springer, Cham (2015). doi:10.1007/978-3-319-18467-8_23
4. Kriaa, S., Pietre-Cambacedes, L., Bouissou, M., Halgand, Y.: A survey of approaches combining safety and security for industrial control systems. Reliab. Eng. Syst. Saf. **139**, 156–178 (2015). doi:10.1016/j.ress.2015.02.008
5. Leveson, N.: Engineering a Safer World: Systems Thinking Applied to Safety. The MIT Press, Cambridge (2011)
6. Leveson, N., Thomas, J.: An STPA Primer (2013). http://sunnyday.mit.edu/STPA-Primer-v0.pdf
7. Schmittner, C., Gruber, T., Puschner, P., Schoitsch, E.: Security application of failure mode and effect analysis (FMEA). In: Bondavalli, A., Di Giandomenico, F. (eds.) SAFECOMP 2014. LNCS, vol. 8666, pp. 310–325. Springer, Cham (2014). doi:10.1007/978-3-319-10506-2_21
8. Schmittner, C., Ma, Z., Puschner, P.: Limitation and improvement of STPA-sec for safety and security co-analysis. In: Skavhaug, A., Guiochet, J., Schoitsch, E., Bitsch, F. (eds.) SAFECOMP 2016. LNCS, vol. 9923, pp. 195–209. Springer, Cham (2016). doi:10.1007/978-3-319-45480-1_16
9. Steiner, M., Liggesmeyer, P.: Combination of safety and security analysis - finding security problems that threaten the safety of a system. In: Workshop on Dependable Embedded and Cyber-Physical Systems DECS of the 32nd International Conference on Computer Safety, Reliability and Security (2013)
10. Young, W., Leveson, N.: Systems thinking for safety and security. In: 29th Annual Computer Security Applications Conference ACSAC, pp. 1–8 (2013). doi:10.1145/2523649.2530277
11. Young, W., Leveson, N.: An integrated approach to safety and security based on systems theory. Commun. ACM **57**(2), 31–35 (2014). doi:10.1145/2556938

Reconciling Systems-Theoretic and Component-Centric Methods for Safety and Security Co-analysis

William G. Temple[1]([⊠]), Yue Wu[1], Binbin Chen[1], and Zbigniew Kalbarczyk[2]

[1] Advanced Digital Sciences Center, Illinois at Singapore, Singapore, Singapore
{william.t,wu.yue,binbin.chen}@adsc.com.sg
[2] University of Illinois at Urbana-Champaign, Champaign, IL, USA
kalbar@crhc.illinois.edu

Abstract. As safety-critical systems increasingly rely on computing, communication, and control, there have been a number of safety and security co-analysis methods put forth to identify, assess, and mitigate risks. However, there is an ideological gap between qualitative system-level methods that focus on control interactions, and more traditional methods based on component failure and/or vulnerability. The growing complexity of cyber-physical and socio-technical systems as well as their interactions with their environments seem to demand a systems-theoretic perspective. Yet, at the same time, more complex threats and failure modes imply a greater need for risk-based analysis to understand and prioritize the large volume of information. In this work we identify promising aspects from two existing safety/security co-analysis methods and outline a vision for reconciling them in a new analysis method.

1 Introduction

As information and communication technology becomes more prevalent in safety-critical systems such as automobiles, trains, and air traffic control, the safety engineering community has confronted the issue of cyber security and its relationship to hazard and risk assessment. While safety and (cyber) security were traditionally considered as separate issues to be evaluated by different subject matter experts, there has been a surge of interest in considering and assessing safety and security in a holistic manner [3,8,10]. Such assessments and the risks they identify serve an important role in system design by influencing design decisions and informing the development of assurance cases.

A number of methodologies and techniques have been proposed to integrate safety and security in risk assessment. In some cases, those methods extend familiar safety engineering approaches like failure mode and effect analysis [13] or hazard analysis and risk assessment [9], which evaluate components of a system. Those components are examined to identify hazards, failure modes, and potential vulnerabilities or threats. An alternative approach that has attracted attention in recent years eschews low level hazard and vulnerability assessment and instead focuses on system-level control loops and unsafe control actions [14,16,17].

© Springer International Publishing AG 2017
S. Tonetta et al. (Eds.): SAFECOMP 2017 Workshops, LNCS 10489, pp. 87–93, 2017.
DOI: 10.1007/978-3-319-66284-8_9

However, while there are a number methods available to analyze the safety and security of a system during the design phase, cyber security threats today are growing ever more complex: they often involve multi-stage attacks, and attackers can exploit physical phenomena in the system and the environment to indirectly cause harm. The classic example of this is the Stuxnet attack, where changes in speed set point on centrifuges caused physical damage to the assets. However the risks posed to systems by cyber-physical interaction are not limited to advanced persistent threats and highly-targeted attacks. In complex systems with hardware and software elements as well as a dynamic physical environment, complex interactions and unintended consequences can lead to hazards. For example, there have been instances of offshore oil rigs temporarily immobilized by malware [4], and a recent metro rail reliability incident in Singapore was due to complex signalling interference between trains triggering fail-safe behavior [5].

Those types of complex interactions are challenging to account for using traditional safety/security analysis methods like fault trees or failure mode and effect analysis. The Systems-Theoretic Process Analysis for Security approach (STPA-Sec) [16], with its emphasis on emergent system behavior and qualitative assessment of unsafe or insecure scenarios may offer one path to addressing these challenges. However, at the same time, more complex threats and failure modes imply a greater need for risk-based analysis to understand and prioritize safety and security issues—a practice eschewed by STPA-Sec. In this work, we seek to bridge the gap between the STPA-Sec approach and those that examine component failure and/or vulnerability in a risk-based manner to address the challenges faced by complex, cyber-physical systems.

2   Review of Safety and Security Co-analysis Methods

A number of methods have been proposed to improve the completeness of system risk assessment by covering the interactions between both unintentional/non-malicious failures, and intentional/malicious threats. Recent survey and systemization of knowledge papers [3,8,10] serve as an excellent starting point to understand the state of the art. In Table 1 we borrow a conceptual framework from recent work [3] to classify approaches as either *extending* an existing method from safety or security analysis (e.g., Fault Tree Analysis, Failure Mode and Effect Analysis), *combining* existing methods (often a safety analysis method and a security analysis method), or proposing an *alternative* method which differs substantially from existing approaches. We add a second dimension inspired by [7], which differentiates whether a method is *component-based* or *systems-based*.

The first group of methods, Security Aware Hazard Analysis and Risk Assessment (SAHARA) [9] and Failure Mode, Vulnerabilities and Effect Analysis (FMVEA) [13] extend existing safety analysis techniques from ISO 26262 [2] and IEC 60812 [1], respectively, by incorporating threat information based on the STRIDE [15] model. The second group, the Failure-Attack-CountTermeasure (FACT) Graph [12], and Extended Fault Tree (EFT) [6] are based on a combination of fault tree and attack tree methods. Combined Harm Assessment of

Table 1. Classification of related work in safety and security co-analysis

	Extend	Combine	Alternative
Component-based	SAHARA [9], FMVEA [13]	FACT Graph [12], EFT [6]	
Systems-based		CHASSIS [11]	STPA-Sec [16], STPA-SafeSec [7]

Safety and Security for Information Systems (CHASSIS) [11], which involves the combination of use/misuse cases and sequence diagrams, is classified as a systems-based approach because it places more emphasis on interactions between entities (which may include human actors) as opposed to the hardware/software structure of the system. Finally, System-theoretic Process Analysis for Security (STPA-Sec) [16] and the related STPA-SafeSec [7] approaches emphasize a top-down assessment of a system's functional control structure to identify unsafe/insecure control actions.

From Table 1, we see a clear divide between component-based methods that build on classical safety or security analysis techniques and the systems-based approaches which represent a departure from existing standards and traditional thinking. As discussed in the next section, we believe both philosophies have the ability to complement one another to better cope with emerging challenges.

3 Complexity and Unintended Consequences

Safety critical systems today operate in complex environments, with complex failure modes caused by subsystem interdependency and, in many cases, insecure communication and software-based systems. It can be challenging to thoroughly identify threats and hazards during the system design process and even meticulously engineered systems face unanticipated issues during operation. Below we use two recent real-world incidents from the maritime and rail transportation industries to motivate the need for new techniques to analyze safety and security.

Incident 1: Malware Disables Offshore Oil Platform. In a 2015 speech, an Admiral from the US Coastguard discussed an incident where a mobile offshore drilling platform had its dynamic positioning thrusters disabled by malware [4]. Dynamic positioning thrusters keep a floating drilling platform stationary on the well site by compensating for ocean currents. In this incident, crew members were plugging personal devices such as phones and laptops into the onboard computer system—the same computer system used to control the thrusters. Malware from personal devices entered the system and was able to propagate. Although this was not a targeted attack, unintended interaction facilitated by inadequate cyber security policy and protection caused an unsafe situation where the rig drifted off the well site.

Incident 2: Signalling Interference from a Nearby Train. In late 2016, the automated Circle Line train system in Singapore was afflicted with mysterious service disruptions. Trains traveling in multiple sections of the line and directions would lose the signalling network connection seemingly at random and activate the emergency brake. This persisted for weeks, leading to delays, thousands of inconvenienced passengers, and a serious public relations crisis for the operator. After a detailed investigation involving multiple government agencies and organizations, it was determined that a single train with malfunctioning signalling hardware was emitting a incorrect signals that interfered with nearby trains' connectivity [5].

Both of the above incidents raise questions about the relationship between safety, reliability, and cyber security as well as the manner in which risks to such complex systems are identified and managed. It should be noted that neither incident led to loss of life or serious injury; however system performance and reliability are critical security-related properties that are influenced by and, need to be assessed in conjunction with, system safety and fail-safe behavior.

Several safety/security co-analysis methods introduced in the previous section are intended to address how security threats impact safety. For example, SAHARA [9] and FMVEA [13] incorporate security/threat information into existing safety assessment frameworks. This is desirable from an industry adoption point of view, however are there important system-level threats and consequences that can be overlooked? This may be particularly true for human factors such as the oil rig's crew illegally downloading music, etc. on their personal devices (the reported source of the oil rig malware). Similarly, fault-tree based approaches [6,12], which are combinatorial, may be unable to adequately cope with complex interactions and interdependencies in a system of systems (e.g., the circle line metro, with multiple driverless trains, trackside power and communication infrastructure, etc.).

Conceptually, the STPA-Sec [16] approach which focuses on the functionality provided by a system, and its functional control structure, rather than on threats and attacker properties, appears well-suited to such systems. However the output of STPA-Sec analysis is qualitative in nature: a list of control actions in the system that may be unsafe or insecure, and how those control actions may lead to unacceptable losses in one or more causal scenarios. This high-level perspective has led to criticism. The authors of [14] point out that STPA-Sec may be more amenable to the early design stages of the system lifecycle since it does not fully align with current safety/security standards—a view shared by [8].

4   Toward a Hybrid Method

We believe there is an opportunity to integrate different aspects of systems-theoretic and component-centric analysis methods. Conceptually, STPA-Sec offers advantages in the identification of complex interactions in the system and environment that may create hazards. However, identifying a large number of interactions and potential sources of loss also lends itself to risk-based analysis:

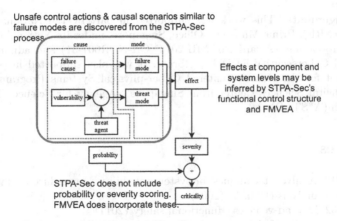

Fig. 1. Annotated FMVEA cause-effect chain highlighting areas where STPA-Sec can be incorporated.

stakeholders need a way to manage that complexity and identify which cyber attacks and/or failures are worth taking seriously. This is where STPA-Sec has limitations. We see potential for a method like FMVEA to play a complementary role in supporting the assessment of risk in a structured, semi-quantitative (i.e., numeric rating) manner that considers factors such as severity and likelihood.

We envision a new safety/security co-analysis method that begins with a systems analysis similar to STPA-Sec, which identifies the functional control structure of a system, including the relationships between human actors, the system, and the environment. This may include extensions or modifications to the original STPA-Sec to enhance its coverage of security topics, e.g., [14]. The resulting graphical model of the functional control structure will help stakeholders identify potential risks to reliability, safety, and security.

However, to prioritize and manage the resulting unsafe control actions a more detailed assessment is required. We intend to make use of the process in FMVEA, since it is based on established practices (IEC 60812). Figure 1 shows the information flow in the FMVEA cause-effect chain (see [13]) with annotation to illustrate how information from an SPTA-Sec assessment may be incorporated. Our future work will focus on refining the process for integration, including extensions of the two approaches where appropriate.

5   Conclusion

In this paper, we examine differences between systems-theoretic and component-centric safety/security co-analysis methods. Inspired by two real-world incidents we outline the vision for a hybrid method that combines elements of STPA-sec and FMVEA: two popular approaches from the systems and component side.

Acknowledgements. This work was supported in part by the National Research Foundation (NRF), Prime Minister's Office, Singapore, under its National Cybersecurity R&D Programme (Award No. NRF2014NCR-NCR001-31) and administered by the National Cybersecurity R&D Directorate. It was also supported in part by the research grant for the Human-Centered Cyber-physical Systems Programme at the Advanced Digital Sciences Center from Singapore's Agency for Science, Technology and Research (A*STAR).

References

1. IEC 60812: Analysis techniques for system reliability - procedure for failure mode and effects analysis (FMEA) (2006)
2. ISO 26262–1: Road vehicles - functional safety (2011)
3. Chockalingam, S., Hadziosmanovic, D., Pieters, W., Teixeira, A., van Gelder, P.: Integrated safety and security risk assessment methods: a survey of key characteristics and applications. In: International Conference on Critical Information Infrastructures Security, Paris, FR (2016)
4. CSIS: Coast guard commandant addresses cybersecurity vulnerabilities on offshore oil rigs. https://goo.gl/yJN4xi (2015). Accessed 12 Jun 2017
5. data.gov.sg Blog: How the circle line rogue train was caught with data. https://goo.gl/qEgy4b (2016). Accessed 12 Jun 2017
6. Fovino, I.N., Masera, M., De Cian, A.: Integrating cyber attacks within fault trees. Reliab. Eng. Syst. Saf. **94**(9), 1394–1402 (2009)
7. Friedberg, I., McLaughlin, K., Smith, P., Laverty, D., Sezer, S.: Stpa-safesec: safety and security analysis for cyber-physical systems. J. Inf. Secur. Appl. (2016)
8. Kriaa, S., Pietre-Cambacedes, L., Bouissou, M., Halgand, Y.: A survey of approaches combining safety and security for industrial control systems. Reliab. Eng. Syst. Saf. **139**, 156–178 (2015)
9. Macher, G., Höller, A., Sporer, H., Armengaud, E., Kreiner, C.: A combined safety-hazards and security-threat analysis method for automotive systems. In: Koornneef, F., Gulijk, C. (eds.) SAFECOMP 2015. LNCS, vol. 9338, pp. 237–250. Springer, Cham (2015). doi:10.1007/978-3-319-24249-1_21
10. Piètre-Cambacédès, L., Bouissou, M.: Cross-fertilization between safety and security engineering. Reliab. Eng. Syst. Saf. **110**, 110–126 (2013)
11. Raspotnig, C., Karpati, P., Katta, V.: A combined process for elicitation and analysis of safety and security requirements. In: Bider, I., Halpin, T., Krogstie, J., Nurcan, S., Proper, E., Schmidt, R., Soffer, P., Wrycza, S. (eds.) BPMDS/EMMSAD-2012. LNBIP, vol. 113, pp. 347–361. Springer, Heidelberg (2012). doi:10.1007/978-3-642-31072-0_24
12. Sabaliauskaite, G., Mathur, A.P.: Aligning cyber-physical system safety and security. In: Cardin, M.A., Krob, D., Lui, P., Tan, Y., Wood, K. (eds.) Complex Systems Design & Management Asia. Springer, Cham (2015). doi:10.1007/978-3-319-12544-2_4
13. Schmittner, C., Gruber, T., Puschner, P., Schoitsch, E.: Security application of failure mode and effect analysis (FMEA). In: Bondavalli, A., Di Giandomenico, F. (eds.) SAFECOMP 2014. LNCS, vol. 8666, pp. 310–325. Springer, Cham (2014). doi:10.1007/978-3-319-10506-2_21

14. Schmittner, C., Ma, Z., Puschner, P.: Limitation and improvement of STPA-Sec for safety and security co-analysis. In: Skavhaug, A., Guiochet, J., Schoitsch, E., Bitsch, F. (eds.) SAFECOMP 2016. LNCS, vol. 9923, pp. 195–209. Springer, Cham (2016). doi:10.1007/978-3-319-45480-1_16
15. Shostack, A., Lambert, S., Ostwald, T., Hernan, S.: Uncover security design flaws using the STRIDE approach. MSDN Mag. (2006)
16. Young, W., Leveson, N.: Systems thinking for safety and security. In: Annual Computer Security Applications Conference, New Orleans, LA, USA (2013)
17. Young, W., Leveson, N.: An integrated approach to safety and security based on systems theory. Commun. ACM **57**(2), 31–35 (2014)

12th International ERCIM/EWICS/ARTEMIS Workshop on Dependable Smart Embedded Cyber-Physical Systems and Systems-of-Systems (DECSoS 2017)

12th International ERCIM/EWICS/ARTEMIS Workshop on Dependable Smart Embedded Cyber-Physical Systems and Systems-of-Systems (DECSoS 2017)

European Research and Innovation Initiatives in the Area of Cyber-Physical Systems and Systems-of-Systems

Erwin Schoitsch[1] and Amund Skavhaug[2]

[1] Digital Safety & Security Department, AIT Austrian Institute of Technology, Vienna, Austria
Erwin.Schoitsch@ait.ac.at
[2] Department of Production and Quality Engineering, NTNU, Norwegian University of S&T, Trondheim, Norway
Amund.Skavhaug@ntnu.no

1 Introduction

The DECSoS workshop at SAFECOMP follows already its own tradition since 2006. In the past, it focussed on the conventional type of "dependable embedded systems", covering all dependability aspects as defined by Avizienis, Lapries, Kopetz, Voges and others in IFIP WG 10.4. To put more emphasis on the relationship to physics, mechatronics and the notion of interaction with an unpredictable environment, the terminology changed to "cyber-physical systems" (CPS) and "Systems-of-Systems" (SoS). The new megatrend (and hype?) IoT ("Internet of Things") as super-infrastructure for CPS as things added a new dimension with enormous challenges. Collaboration and co-operation of these systems with each other and humans, and the interplay of safety, security and reliability are leading to new challenges in verification, validation and certification/qualification. Examples are e.g. the smart power grid (power plants and power distribution and control), smart transport systems (rail, traffic management with V2V and V2I facilities, air traffic control systems), advanced manufacturing systems ("Industry 4.0"), mobile co-operating autonomous robotic systems, smart health care, smart buildings up to smart cities and the like.

Society as a whole strongly depends on CPS and SoS - thus it is important to consider dependability (safety, reliability, availability, security, maintainability, etc.), resilience, robustness and sustainability in a holistic manner. CPS and SoS are a targeted research area in Horizon 2020 and public-private partnerships such as the ECSEL JU (Joint Undertaking) (Electronic Components and Systems for European Leadership), which integrated the former ARTEMIS (Advanced Research and

Technology for Embedded Intelligence and Systems), ENIAC and EPoSS efforts. Industry and research ("private") are represented by the industrial associations ARTEMIS-IA, AENEAS (for ENIAC, semiconductor industry) and EPoSS ("Smart Systems Integration"), the public part are the EC and the national public authorities of the member states. Funding comes from the EC and the national public authorities ("tri-partite funding": EC, member states, project partners).

2 ARTEMIS/ECSEL: The European Cyber-physical Systems Initiative

This year the workshop is co-hosted by the ARTEMIS and Horizon 2020 projects

- CRYSTAL ("Critical Systems Engineering Factories", http://www.crystal-artemis. eu),
- ARROWHEAD1 ("Ahead of the Future", http://www.arrowhead.eu/),
- EMC2 ("Embedded Multi-Core systems for Mixed Criticality applications in dynamic and changeable real-time environments", http://www.artemis-emc2.eu/) and
- CP-SETIS ("Towards Cyber-Physical Systems Engineering Tools Interoperability Standards", http://cp-setis.eu/), a Horizon 2020 project, funded only by the EC, but executed by ARTEMIS-IA members.

These projects finished this year, and results are partially reported in presentations at the DECSoS-workshop.

Last year started the co-hosting ECSEL projects AMASS (Safety & Security Multi-Concern Assurance), ENABLE-S3 (Automated Vehicles), IoSENSE (IoT and Industry 4.0) and SemI40 (Semiconductor - Industry 4.0). This year are starting AQUAS (Quality, Safety, Security and Performance Multi-Concern). The projects AutoDrive (Autonomous Vehicles – Road, Rail, Aircraft) and Productive 4.0 (Smart Manufacturing, Industry 4.0), the largest ECSEL project in this field with up to now (110 partners), are so-called "Light-House projects". The first one for Mobility, the second one for Production, i.e. they should attract co-operations across project boundaries and be the core for the next generation of projects joining the "lighthouse" party. Detailed references are on the project- and EU-CORDIS web site, see also Acknowledgements at the end of the article. The DECSoS chair who is partner in most of these projects, will also provide some overview and explain some context in the workshop introduction of the workshop.

ARTEMIS was one of the European, industry-driven research initiatives and is now part of the ECSEL PPP. The last ARTEMIS projects finished this year, but work in the research fields addressed continues within the ECSEL JU. The four co-hosting ARTEMIS projects that finished their work this year are described briefly, the "new-comers" have just started last and this year, but are already referenced in some presentations.

CRYSTAL, a large ARTEMIS Innovation Pilot Project (AIPP), aimed at fostering Europe's leading edge position in embedded systems engineering by facilitating high quality and cost effectiveness of safety-critical embedded systems and architecture platforms. Its overall goal was to enable sustainable paths to speed up the maturation, integration, and cross-sector reusability of technological and methodological bricks in the areas of transportation (aerospace, automotive, and rail) and healthcare providing a critical mass of European technology providers. CRYSTAL integrated the contributions of previous ARTEMIS projects (CESAR, MBAT, iFEST, SafeCer etc.) and further developed the ARTEMIS RTP (Reference Technology Platform) and Interoperability Specification.

CP-SETIS ("Towards Cyber-Physical Systems Engineering Tools Interoperability Standards" (IOS)) was a H2020 support-action-like Innovation Action (IA). CP-SETIS created a sustainable eco-system for the IOS by finding a host and service structure (ARTEMIS-IA as hosting and funding organization, a small start-up to maintain the Database and IOS Coordination Forum (ICF) of stakeholders interested in the IOS specifications, standards and guidelines, which can be active during the next years. This is insofar a considerable achievement as very often with end of a project the activities are ceased, the follow-up not guaranteed. The ARTEMIS and ECSEL JU and their organizations differ insofar from other funding schemes as the sequence of projects builds on the preceding ones and work is continued over long-term schedules.

ARROWHEAD, a large AIPP addressing the areas production and energy system automation, intelligent-built environment and urban infrastructure, is aiming at enabling collaborative automation by networked embedded devices, from enterprise/worldwide level in the cloud down to device level at the machine in the plant. The goal is to achieve efficiency and flexibility on a global scale for five application verticals: production (manufacturing, process, energy production and distribution), smart buildings and infrastructures, electro-mobility and virtual market of energy.

EMC^2 is up to now the largest ARTEMIS AIPP bundling the power of innovation of 100 partners from embedded industry and research from 19 European countries and Israel with an effort of about 800 person years and a total budget of about 100 million Euro. The objective of the EMC^2 project is to develop an innovative and sustainable service-oriented architecture approach for mixed criticality applications in dynamic and changeable real-time environments based on multi-core architectures.

It provides the paradigm shift to a new and sustainable system architecture which is suitable to handle open dynamic systems:

- Dynamic Adaptability in Open Systems, scalability and utmost flexibility,
- Utilization of expensive system features only as Service-on-Demand in order to reduce the overall system cost,
- Handling of mixed criticality applications under real-time conditions,
- Full scale deployment and management of integrated tool chains, through the entire lifecycle.

The AIPPs ARROWHEAD and EMC^2 are addressing "Systems-of-Systems" aspects in the context of critical systems, whereas CRYSTAL and CP-SETIS are devoting their major efforts towards creating a sustainable eco-system of a CRTP (Collaborative Reference Technology Platform) and the harmonization of efforts towards an IOS (set of standards, specifications and guidelines for tool interoperability).

3 This Year's Workshop

The workshop DECSoS'17 provides some insight into an interesting set of topics to enable fruitful discussions during the meeting and afterwards. The mixture of topics is hopefully well balanced, with a certain focus on mixed-criticality and multi-core systems and concerns, cybersecurity & safety co-analysis and on collaborative and autonomous systems. Presentations are mainly based on ARTEMIS/ECSEL, EU FP7 and Horizon 2020, and nationally funded projects mentioned above and on industrial developments of partners' companies and universities.

The session starts with an introduction and overview to the ERCIM/ EWICS/ARTEMIS DECSoS Workshop setting the European Research and Innovation scene. The first session on **Critical Software Analysis and Development** comprises two presentations:

(1) "Analysis of Potential Code Vulnerabilities involving Overlapping Instructions" (Research of the University of Erlangen-Nuremberg, Germany, work funded by the German Federal Ministry for Economic Affairs and Energy, in the project SMARTEST),

(2) "Increasing dependability in Safety Critical CPSs using Reflective Statecharts", work developed and funded by the Basque government and continued now in the ECSEL-JU project Productive4.0, which was mentioned before as a "Lighthouse project" of ECSEL JU).

The second session covers **Mixed Criticality and Multi-Core Systems** by three papers:

(1) "A Survey of Hardware Technologies for Mixed-critical Integration Explored in the Project EMC²", an invited paper, providing an overview over and reflecting on hardware aspects and challenges, and on bridging solutions explored in the ARTEMIS EMC² project, therefore many co-authors are mentioned, from the different areas and industrial use cases.

(2) "Safe Implementation of Mixed-Criticality Applications in Multicore Platforms: A Model-Based Design Approach". This paper reflects also on significant results of the EMC² project, addressing the critical challenges of multi-core and hybrid architectures with respect to system's safety and safe implementation.

(3) "GSN Support of Mixed-Criticality Systems Certification". Using the Goal-Structuring Notation GSN, safety arguments are stored in an argument database to support automatic composition of safety cases for variants of products. This is an outcome of the FP7 DREAMS project, OPENCOSS and AMASS are also mentioned in this context.

The session after lunch is dedicated to **Reliability, Safety & Cybersecurity (Co-) Engineering**, a general topic nowadays for all areas of CPS and IoT in an connected (smart) world:

(1) The session starts with a presentation on reliable communication, which is a major factor in daily life and particularly for large infrastructures, autonomous driving etc. where services have to be provided and interruption may be critical:

"Concepts for Reliable Communication in a Software-defined Network Architecture" on how sharing of the internet is possible in an innovative, reliable and secure manner. The project was funded by the Austrian Federal Ministry of Transport, Innovation and Technology, projects OFSE (Open Flow Secure Grid) and OPOSSUM (SDN Open Flow-based communication system for multi-energy domains).

(2) "Combining Safety & Security Analysis for Industrial Collaborative Automation Systems" – IoT is a key enabler for collaborative automation. Safety and security assessments are gaining increasing importance, particularly when legacy equipment and devices are part of automation systems, which is regularly the case. An industrial application in Austria is demonstrated, which was developed in context of the ARTEMIS project ARROWHEAD.

(3) "Software Updates in Safety and Security Co-engineering" presents a review of safety & security standards with respect to software updates, which are on the one hand critical from the safety point of view ("safety expert: never change a certified system"), but on the other hand often necessary as countermeasure to mitigate security threats. A roadmap of relevant standards is provided as well as result of the review.

(4) "Detailed analysis of security evaluation of automotive systems based on JASO TP15002". Recent cases of hacker attacks on automotive systems revealed that "a system that is not secure cannot be save" (David Strickland, chief Administrator for the National Highway Traffic Safety Administration (NHTSA). Fortunate, they did not really endanger persons, but were done for demonstration purposes only. The paper describes security analysis according to automotive cybersecurity guidelines of the Japanese standardization organization (similar to SAE in the US and now developed in ISO/SAE JWG1 as ISO 21434 standard "Road vehicles – Cybersecurity engineering".

The last session of the day is about **Collaborative and Autonomous Systems**, a topic of increasing interest in industry, automotive, railways, drones and aircraft, and robotics:

(1) "Systematic Composition of Services from Distributed Systems for Highly Dynamic Collaboration Processes" is about collaboration processes of systems in open and dynamically changing environments, which is a challenge to shared services. Platooning of vehicles is an example – what to do if environmental conditions change in a manner influencing e.g. control (braking on wet road surface etc.), which needs adaptation to degraded conditions. "Dynamic safety contracts" are presented as a potential solution, being executed at runtime and adapting to environmental conditions, which extends the existing concept of run-time certification (which results afterwards in a stable configuration, but does not adapt system behavior continuously), which was already presented at recent workshops.

(2) "Safety Assurance for Autonomous and Collaborative Medical Cyber-Physical Systems" – this paper refers to medical CPSoS which collaborate in a flexible

manner at run-time, thus providing a higher level of functionality. Since predictability can no longer be assumed, so new models and approaches are required
to meet the new challenges, e.g. safety contracts, dynamic risk assessment etc.
Some thoughts and a coherent taxonomy will be discussed.

(3) "Safety-Aware Control of Swarms of Drones" – this paper proposes a novel
approach to ensuring safety while planning and controlling an operation of a
swarm of drones, using evolutionary algorithms for safety-aware mission planning at run-time; autonomy of each drone is not assumed, it is a more centralized
approach.

As chairpersons of the workshop, we want to thank all authors and contributors
who submitted their work, Friedemann Bitsch, the SAFECOMP Publication Chair, and
the members of the International Program Committee who enabled a fair evaluation
through reviews and considerable improvements in many cases. We want to express
our thanks to the SAFECOMP organizers, who provided us the opportunity to organize
the workshop at SAFECOMP 2017 in Trento. Particularly we want to thank the EC and
national public funding authorities who made the work in the research projects possible. We do not want to forget the continued support of our companies and organizations, of ERCIM, the European Research Consortium for Informatics and
Mathematics with its Working Group on Dependable Embedded Software-intensive
Systems, and EWICS, the creator and main sponsor of SAFECOMP, with its working
groups, who always helped us to learn from their networks.

We hope that all participants will benefit from the workshop, enjoy the conference
and accompanying programs and will join us again in the future!

Acknowledgements. Part of the work presented in the workshop received funding
from the EC (ARTEMIS/ECSEL Joint Undertaking) and the partners National Funding
Authorities through the projects ARROWHEAD (332987), EMC2 (621429), CRYS-
TAL (332830) and SafeCer (295373). Other EC funded projects are in FP7 DREAMS
(610640) and OPENCOSS (289011), and in Horizon 2020 CP-SETIS (645149). Some
projects received national funding only (see individual acknowledgements in papers).
The ECSEL JU and nationally ("tri-partite") funded projects recently started and
contributing to the work areas described here are AMASS (grant agreement 692474),
ENABLE-S3 (692455), IoSENSE (692480), SemI40 (692466), ENABLE-S3
(692455), AQUAS (737475), Productive4.0 (737459) and AutoDrive (737469).

International Program Committee

Eric Armengaud	AVL List, Graz, Austria
Jens Braband	Siemens AG, Braunschweig, Germany
Bettina Buth	HAW Hamburg, Department Informatik, Germany
Friedemann Bitsch	Thales Transportation Systems GmbH, Germany
Peter Daniel	EEWICS TC7, UK
Wolfgang Ehrenberger	University of Applied Science Fulda, Germany
Francesco Flammini (IT)	Ansaldo University "Federico II" of Naples, Italy

Janusz Gorski	Gdansk University of Technology, Poland
Hans Hansson	Mälardalen University, Sweden
Maritta Heisel	University of Duisburg-Essen, Germany
Floor Koornneef	TU Delft, The Netherlands
Willibald Krenn	AIT Austrian Institute of Technology, Austria
Erwin Kristen	AIT Austrian Institute of Technology, Austria
Dejan Nickovic	AIT Austrian Institute of Technology, Austria
Frank Ortmeier	Otto-von-Guericke-University Magdeburg, Germany
Thomas Pfeiffenberger	Salzburg Research, Austria
Francesca Saglietti	University of Erlangen-Nuremberg, Germany
Christoph Schmitz	Zühlke Engineering AG, Switzerland
Daniel Schneider	Fraunhofer IESE, Kaiserslautern, Germany
Erwin Schoitsch	AIT Austrian Institute of Technology, Austria
Rolf Schumacher	Schumacher Engineering Office, Germany
Amund Skavhaug	NTNU Trondheim, Norway
Mark-Alexander Sujan	University of Warwick, UK
Stefano Tonetta	Fondazione Bruno Kessler, Trento, Italy

Analysis of Potential Code Vulnerabilities Involving Overlapping Instructions

Loui Al Sardy, Tong Tang, Marc Spisländer,
and Francesca Saglietti(✉)

Software Engineering (Informatik 11), University of Erlangen-Nuremberg,
Martensstr. 3, 91058 Erlangen, Germany
{loui.alsardy, tong.tang, marc.spislaender,
francesca.saglietti}@fau.de

Abstract. This article proposes approaches supporting the analysis of code vulnerabilities based on overlapping machine instructions of variable length. For the purpose of focusing the search for potential malicious code it is suggested to apply first disassembling techniques allowing for a restriction of potentially exploitable memory space. Successively, testing based on heuristic optimization may be applied in order to evaluate dynamically the practicality of vulnerability exploitation.

Keywords: Security · Vulnerability · Overlapping instruction · Redirection · Testing

1 Introduction

The increasing number and scope of IT security attacks [2] demand for the design of verification techniques targeted at the early detection of security flaws before operation. The more urgent is this need in case of software-based systems automatically controlling critical technical processes, e.g. within the automotive, medical or industrial domains.

Due to the diverse nature of attacks, successful verification approaches must address different kinds of potential vulnerabilities by aiming at identifying both their presence and their practical exploitability. This question will be addressed in the following with respect to a particular attack scenario recently pointed out [6]. It involves the possibility of hiding malicious code by insider attacker(s) taking advantage of machine codes allowing for different instruction lengths.

The article is structured as follows:

Section 2 presents some initial considerations on the attack type considered by:

- introducing first the threats posed by malicious code hidden in overlapping instructions (Sect. 2.1) and
- considering successively a number of redirection techniques capable of triggering the hidden code (Sect. 2.2).

S. Tonetta et al. (Eds.): SAFECOMP 2017 Workshops, LNCS 10489, pp. 103–113, 2017.
DOI: 10.1007/978-3-319-66284-8_10

Section 3 presents a static analysis of machine code

- based on a preliminary classification of memory space reflecting the potential for hiding malicious code (Sect. 3.1) followed
- by a syntactical constraint analysis (Sect. 3.2) and
- by a disassembling analysis (Sect. 3.3)

Finally, Sect. 4 considers the application of heuristic approaches targeted at the early detection of redirection attacks, e.g. in case they were constructed to take advantage of intentional buffer overflows.

2   Attack Description: Preparation and Activation Phases

2.1   Preliminary Activities

In the following, the attack illustrated in [6] is shortly summarized (for details, the reader is kindly referred to the original article). For the attack considered to be carried out, in the following it is assumed that

- an insider attacker is involved with the development of a software-based control system in C;
- the source code manipulation remains undetected during code reviews;
- the resulting software system is run on a CISC (Complex Instruction Set Computing) processor architecture, allowing in particular for machine code instructions of variable length;
- deterministic builds guarantee that identical binary codes result from re-compilation of identical source codes.

Thanks to the variable instruction length, different start addresses (as indicated by the instruction pointer) may result in different interpretations of the same machine code, each leading to the execution of different overlapping instructions. An example is shown in Fig. 1. As illustrated in [5], this may be exploited during development by designing a backdoor which may be later executed by moving the instruction pointer to the starting address of the backdoor.

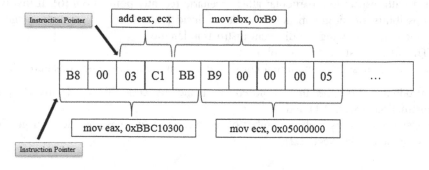

Fig. 1. Decoding overlapping instructions

The hidden code may vary in length, ranging

- from a short hidden fragment HF_1 consisting of one instruction or more sequential instructions
- up to a chain $(HF_1, \ldots, HF_n)$ of such hidden fragments linked by unconditional direct jumps (see Fig. 2).

Fig. 2. Hidden fragments linked together using unconditional direct jump instructions

Depending on the position of the fragment(s) resp. fragment chain(s), the effect of the attack may vary:

- in case of fragment(s) resp. fragment chain(s) do not reach the end of the machine code, their triggering would result in abortion, hereby supporting immediate detection, while
- the execution of fragment(s) resp. fragment chain(s) reaching the end of the machine code might remain unnoticed and provoke unsafe behaviour for a prolonged time.

2.2 Triggering the Backdoor by Redirection Techniques

In order to trigger the backdoor the attacker must redirect execution to its start address by gaining control of the instruction pointer. More precisely, the instruction pointer register containing the memory address of the next instruction to be executed by the CPU must be overwritten such as to redirect execution to the start of the (first) hidden fragment.

This can be achieved by several redirection techniques, a. o. by exploiting one of the following source code vulnerabilities [1–3, 7, 8]:

- **Buffer Overflow:**
  Writing data outside of the boundaries allocated for a buffer can be exploited to overwrite the return address of a function hereby implicitly redirecting the instruction pointer to the overwritten address.
- **Format Strings:**
  Also use of format functions such as printf can be exploited by attacker(s) in order to overwrite selected memory cells, in particular the one containing the return address. In this specific case the input format specifier %n (which provides for recording at a given location the number of characters already printed) can be misused such as to overwrite the return address with the address to which the instruction pointer is to be redirected.
- **Uninitialized Variables:**
  Let a function f overwrite memory cells $S_1, \ldots, S_n$ on its stack frame, where these cells are determined by evaluation of a local uninitialized variable V. If the attacker is

able to overwrite a memory cell SV referenced by this uninitialized variable V, the execution of function f may result in overwriting the memory cell $S_i \in \{S_1, \ldots, S_n\}$ containing its return address, hereby redirecting the instruction pointer.

A major difference between this kind of attack and meanwhile better known attack scenarios based on return-oriented programming lies in the different challenges: the former requires an a priori construction of the backdoor followed by the overwriting of one single memory cell, while the latter demands for the manipulation of a whole range of cells [13].

3   Search Space Restriction

3.1   Classification of Memory Cells

This section is devoted to static analysis techniques targeted at restricting the set of potential malicious start addresses by excluding those memory addresses which do not allow for a sound machine code interpretation.

In order to do so, let I denote the set of all syntactically valid instructions and the assembler code of program P consist of a sequence

$$(Instr_1, \ldots, Instr_n), \text{ where } Instr_i \in I \text{ for } i \in \{1, \ldots, n\}$$

of intended (i.e. benign) instructions. Then the whole set of memory addresses containing the binary code of the underlying program P can be subdivided into the following three, pair-wise disjoint sets:

- Set $\mathcal{SI}$ (Starts of Intended Instructions):
  $\mathcal{SI}$ is defined as the set consisting of all memory addresses containing the start of intended instructions (see Fig. 3). In other words:

$$\mathcal{SI} := \{SI_1, \ldots, SI_n\} \text{ where } SI_i := \text{ start } (Instr_i) \, \forall i \in \{1, \ldots, n\}$$

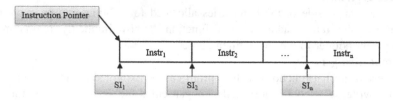

Fig. 3. Set $\{SI_1, \ldots, SI_n\}$ of start memory addresses for intended benign instructions

- Set $\mathcal{SU}$ (Starts of Unintended Instructions):
  $\mathcal{SU}$ is defined as the set consisting of all memory addresses at which a syntactically correct instruction starts which is not an intended instruction (see Fig. 4). In other words, $\mathcal{SU}$ consists of memory addresses at which hidden fragments may start. Formally:

$$\mathcal{SU} := \{SU_1, \ldots, SU_m\} \text{ where } SU_i := \text{start}\left(Instr_i^*\right)$$
$$\text{with } Instr_i^* \in I \text{ and } SU_i \notin \mathcal{SI} \, \forall i \in \{1, \ldots, m\}$$

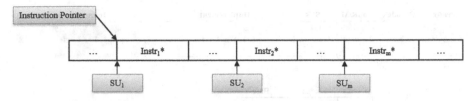

Fig. 4. Set $\{SU_1, \ldots, SU_m\}$ of start memory addresses for potentially malicious instructions

- Set $\mathcal{SV}$ (Starts of Invalid Code):
  $\mathcal{SV}$ is defined as the set consisting of all memory addresses which are neither valid instructions nor can they be completed by further addresses such as to form a valid instruction. In other words, any sequence of bytes starting at an $\mathcal{SV}$ address cannot be interpreted as a valid machine instruction (see Fig. 5).
  Formally:

$$\mathcal{SV} := \{SV_1, \ldots, SV_q\} \text{ where } SV_i \neq \text{start}(Instr) \, \forall Instr \in I \, \forall i \in \{1, \ldots, q\}$$

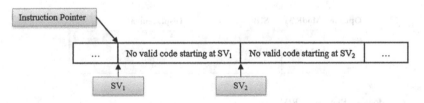

Fig. 5. Set $\{SV_1, SV_2, \ldots\}$ of start memory addresses for invalid instructions

During static analysis, the compiled binary code will be inspected in order to extract all $\mathcal{SU}$ addresses and exclude all $\mathcal{SV}$ addresses.

3.2 Search Space Restriction by Syntactical Constraint Analysis

In the following, the Intel Architecture IA-32 will be taken as the CISC architecture of reference. According to the Intel x86 Instruction Format [4], a valid instruction consists of an opcode field (1–3 bytes) possibly anticipated by a *Prefix* field and followed by further fields (see Fig. 6). *Prefix* codes are distinguishable from opcodes; therefore, when encountering a *prefix* the memory address classification can skip it and proceed to the following *opcode*. The latter determines which combinations of subsequent fields (*ModR/M, SIB, Displacement, Immediate*) are legal, while each legal combination, on its part, determines a possible instruction length.

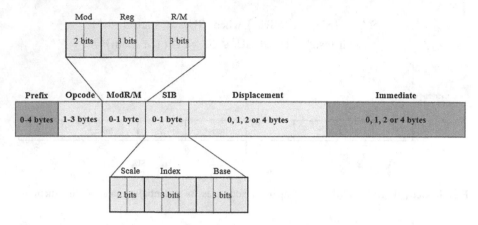

Fig. 6. Intel x86 Instruction Format (based on [4, 10])

Based on this knowledge, an evident approach to reduce the search space for potential hidden fragments relies on a preliminary evaluation of syntactical constraints posed on selected instructions (e.g. push, mov, add). The validity of such constraints can be taken as necessary evidence for $\mathcal{SU}$ memory addresses.

In the following, push instructions with *opcode **FF*** (see Fig. 7) will be considered as an example; this excludes the presence of *Immediate* fields; on the other hand, the absence of *prefixes* is assumed for the sake of simplicity (as noted above, this does not restrict generality).

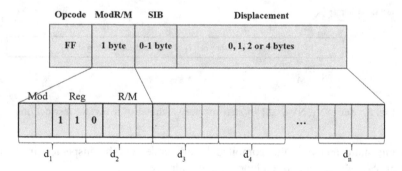

Fig. 7. Intel x86 Instruction Format for *push* operation with *opcode **FF*** (based on [4, 10])

In this case, the stream of bytes represented by the sequence $(d_1, ..., d_n)$ of hexadecimal digits following a push instruction *opcode* value ***FF*** must satisfy the following syntactical constraints:

- **Constraint 1:** the first hexadecimal digit of a Mod-Reg-R/M byte is 3, 7, B or F:

$$d_1 \in \{3, 7, \text{B, F}\}$$

- **Constraint 2:** the second hexadecimal digit of a Mod-Reg-R/M byte is a natural number between 0 and 7:

$$d_2 \in \{0, 1, \ldots, 7\}$$

- **Constraint 3:** The overall number n of digits following the *push opcode FF* can vary within the range {2, 4, 6, 10, 12}. Depending on the values of the first two digits d_1 and d_2, the value of n is given in Table 1.

Table 1. Number n of digits following the opcode *FF* of a valid push instruction

d_1 \ d_2	3	7	B	F
0	2	4	10	2
1	2	4	10	2
2	2	4	10	2
3	2	4	10	2
4	4	6	12	2
5	10	4	10	2
6	2	4	10	2
7	2	4	10	2

The example above was shown to illustrate the principle of the approach; actually, it addressed only the particular case of *push* operations utilizing the opcode *FF*. The relation between operations and *opcodes*, however, is not bijective:

- on the one hand, the same operation may allow for different *opcode* values; for example, the *push* operation can be addressed by the *opcode* values *FF, 51, 52, 53, 54, 55, 56, 57, 6A, 68;*
- on the other hand, the same *opcode* value may address different operations; the *opcode FF*, for example, can be used to address further operations like *inc, dec, call, jmp.*

In order to be exhaustive, syntactical constraints should be extracted from the machine grammar for any possible operation and for any of its instruction *opcodes*. This makes a systematic extraction of constraints rather laborious. Fortunately, for the purpose of a static analysis, this explicit extraction is not strictly necessary.

3.3 Search Space Restriction by Disassembling Analysis

In fact, the details of the non-bijective relation mentioned above are irrelevant to the final outcome of the static analysis which only concerns the presence of syntactically correct, unintended machine code fragments; for this purpose, additional information regarding the type of operations involved resp. the *opcode* used to address them is negligible.

Therefore, the effort for the identification of individual constraints can be simply avoided by making use of a classical disassembler whose function consists of interpreting - as far as possible - binary code back to assembly instructions; if a binary code cannot be interpreted, the disassembler indicates this.

In order to check whether the memory address of an arbitrary byte in a byte sequence belongs to SV, the byte sequence can be disassembled by starting with the address considered. If the result of the disassembler is negative, then this address belongs to SV; in other words, it cannot serve as the start of a backdoor fragment such that it can be excluded from further consideration.

A disassembler was used together with a bash-shell-script to analyse executable binary code given by a list $(b_1, \ldots, b_n)$ of bytes. For each byte b_i $(1 \le i \le n)$ the list $(b_i, b_{i+1} \ldots, b_n)$ is disassembled and the first disassembled instruction is outputted:

- if this instruction is invalid, then the memory address of b_i belongs to the set SV;
- if this instruction coincides (in terms of its location) with one of the regular machine code instructions, then the memory address of b_i belongs to the set SI;
- otherwise, the memory address of b_i belongs to the set SU.

As expected, when compared to the incomplete *push* constraint analysis sketched in the previous section, this approach reveals as superior in terms of considerably lower effort required and logical completeness.

Table 2 shows a few examples, among them one valid and one invalid fragment for which the *push* constraints alone are not sufficient to determine a definitive memory address classification which on the other hand is easily achievable by disassembling.

Table 2. Examples for static analysis of hidden bytes following opcode byte *FF*

Bytes following opcode byte *FF*	Instruction semantics	Outcome of push constraints analysis	Outcome of disassembling analysis
71AB	push [exc-0x55]	SU	SU
A111000000	jmp [ecx+0x11]	Invalid *push* operation, no general result	SU
E8	Invalid instruction	Invalid *push* operation, no general result	SV

The outcome of the static analysis by disassembling is

- the set SU consisting of memory addresses starting potentially executable malicious code fragments, in particular the length and position of each such fragment,
- the chains linking successive unintended code fragments by unconditional direct jump instructions, in particular their length.

Such preliminary information may help evaluate the potential effects to be expected by executing corresponding hidden fragments. What it cannot provide in general is reliable evidence for the possibility of actually executing such hidden fragments during runtime.

4   Testing for Redirection

Thorough security investigations demand for an evaluation of the practicability of the attack strategy during runtime. To be able to carry out an attack of the type considered requires

- a non-empty set $\mathcal{SU}$ and
- redirection of the instruction pointer to a memory address from $\mathcal{SU}$.

While the first aspect has been analysed so far, to address the second one may involve an analysis of undecidable program properties. For example, in general the actual occurrence of buffer overflowing during runtime cannot be proven or disproven by systematic, terminating approaches. In fact, static techniques based on integer constraint analysis [14] may help identify a basic potential for buffer overflowing without being capable, however, of determining whether and when it will actually occur.

Therefore, such approaches may be complemented by behavioural observations based on random input selection. The question how to generate test scenarios such as to optimize the chances of provoking buffer overflows poses crucial challenges.

Usually, in the absence of systematic solutions, the application of heuristic-based techniques may be considered. Evolutionary approaches based on genetic algorithms, for example, have revealed as beneficial for the automatic generation of test cases aimed at maximizing predefined testing coverage measures [9, 11]. Such algorithms are based on populations of individuals, whose adequacy to serve as a solution is preliminarily evaluated by means of a so-called *fitness function*. Based on this metric, random evolutionary operators (selection, recombination, mutation) are repeatedly applied to (part of) the individuals to yield new populations until a predefined end criterion is met. The search for test cases maximizing structural coverage criteria of a subject under test relies on the fact that evolution can be designed such as to improve (or at least to maintain) the best individuals of each generation, i.e. such that the coverage metric achieved so far is not going to decrease in future.

Unfortunately, in the context of testing for redirection, genetic algorithms may not always guarantee an evolutionary progress. For example, when testing for potential buffer overflows the buffer pointer index may arbitrarily oscillate or converge without trespassing the buffer boundary. In order to avoid this, heuristics should be trained to identify impasses, to detect their cause by data analysis and to re-initialize the search process by adapting the search algorithm to the findings. Such approaches are currently under study.

An additional challenge to this problem is posed by the fact that the search process is evidently doomed to failure whenever buffer overflowing is actually unfeasible; in such cases, testing evidence has to ensure that the scope of the unsuccessful search was broad enough to justify sufficient confidence in the testing outcome [12].

5   Conclusion

The present article considered a recently emerged type of IT attack based on overlapping instructions and proposed some considerations on static and dynamic verification techniques targeted at its detection before operation.

Disassembling processes serve to filter out machine code addresses; this filter is intended to exclude those code portions for which it can be systematically proven that they cannot possibly contain malicious fragments of the type considered.

Successively, it is suggested to test the software for redirection by adopting heuristic-based strategies as being considered within the ongoing project SMARTEST.

Acknowledgment. The authors gratefully acknowledge that a major part of the work presented was supported by the German Federal Ministry for Economic Affairs and Energy (BMWi), project SMARTEST. The project is carried out in cooperation with the partner institutions University of Magdeburg, University of Applied Sciences of Magdeburg-Stendal and AREVA GmbH.

References

1. Andriesse, D., Bos, H.: Instruction-level steganography for covert trigger-based malware. In: Dietrich, S. (ed.) DIMVA 2014. LNCS, vol. 8550, pp. 41–50. Springer, Cham (2014). doi:10.1007/978-3-319-08509-8_3
2. CAPEC (Common Attack Pattern Enumeration and Classification) Community: Overflow Buffers (CAPEC-100) (2017). http://capec.mitre.org/data/definitions/100.html
3. Cowan, C., Barringer, M., Beattie, S., Kroah-Hartman, G., Frantzen, M., Lokier, J.: FormatGuard: automatic protection from printf format string vulnerabilities. In: Proceedings of 10th USENIX Security Symposium (SSYM 2001), vol. 10. USENIX Association (2001)
4. Intel® 64 and IA-32 Architectures: Software Developer's Manual, vol. 2. Instruction Set Reference (2016)
5. Jämthagen, C., Lantz, P., Hell, M.: A new instruction overlapping technique for anti-disassembly and obfuscation of x86 binaries. In: Proceedings of Anti-malware Testing Research (WATeR 2014). IEEE Xplore (2014)
6. Jämthagen, C., Lantz, P., Hell, M.: Exploiting trust in deterministic builds. In: Skavhaug, A., Guiochet, J., Bitsch, F. (eds.) SAFECOMP 2016. LNCS, vol. 9922, pp. 238–249. Springer, Cham (2016). doi:10.1007/978-3-319-45477-1_19
7. Kilic, F., Kittel, T., Eckert, C.: Blind format string attacks. In: Tian, J., Jing, J., Srivatsa, M. (eds.) SecureComm 2014. LNICSSITE, vol. 153, pp. 301–314. Springer, Cham (2015). doi:10.1007/978-3-319-23802-9_23
8. Lhee, K., Chapin, S.: Buffer overflow and format string overflow vulnerabilities. J. Softw: Pract. Experience **33**, 423–460. Wiley (2003)
9. Oster, N., Saglietti, F.: Automatic test data generation by multi-objective optimisation. In: Górski, J. (ed.) SAFECOMP 2006. LNCS, vol. 4166, pp. 426–438. Springer, Heidelberg (2006). doi:10.1007/11875567_32
10. Paleari, R., Martignoni, L. Fresi Roglia, G., Bruschi, D.: N-version disassembly: differential testing of x86 disassemblers. In: Procdings of 19th International Symposium on Software Testing and Analysis. ACM (2010)
11. Saglietti, F., Lill, R.: A testing pattern for automatic control software addressing different degrees of process autonomy and cooperation. In: Proceedings of 19th World Congress of the International Federation of Automatic Control (IFAC), vol. 47. Elsevier (2014)
12. Saglietti, F., Meitner, M., Wardenburg, L., Richthammer, V.: Analysis of informed attacks and appropriate countermeasures for cyber-physical systems. In: Skavhaug, A., Guiochet, J., Schoitsch, E., Bitsch, F. (eds.) SAFECOMP 2016. LNCS, vol. 9923, pp. 222–233. Springer, Cham (2016). doi:10.1007/978-3-319-45480-1_18

13. Shacham, H.: The geometry of innocent flesh on the bone: return-into-libc without function calls (on the x86). In: Proceedings of 14th ACM Conference on Computer and Communications Security (CCS 2007). ACM (2007)
14. Wagner, D., Foster, J.S., Brewer, E.A., Aiken, A.: A first step towards automated detection of buffer overrun vulnerabilities. In: Proceedings of Network and Distributed System Security Symposium (NDSS 2000). The Internet Society (2000)

Increasing Dependability in Safety Critical CPSs Using Reflective Statecharts

Miren Illarramendi(✉), Leire Etxeberria, Xabier Elkorobarrutia,
and Goiuria Sagardui

Embedded Systems Research Group,
Mondragon Goi Eskola Politeknikoa (MGEP),
Mondragón, Spain
{millarramendi,letxeberria,xelkorobarrutia,gsagardui}@mondragon.edu
http://www.mondragon.edu/eps

Abstract. Dependability is crucial in Safety Critical Cyber Physical Systems (CPS). In spite of the research carried out in recent years, implementation and certification of such systems remain costly and time consuming. In this paper, a framework for Statecharts based SW component development is presented. This framework called CRESC (**C++ REflective StateCharts**), in addition to assisting in transforming a Statechart model to code, uses reflection to make the model available at Run Time. Thus, the SW components can be monitored at Run Time in terms of model elements. Our framework helps the developer separate monitoring from functionality. Any monitoring strategy needed to increase dependability can be added independently from the functional part. The framework was implemented in C++ because this programming language, together with the Statechart formalism constitute widely used choices for the Safety Critical CPS domain.

Keywords: Fault Tolerance · Monitoring · Statecharts · Safety-critical embedded systems · Cyber Physical Systems · Reflection · Introspection

1 Introduction

Cyber-Physical Systems (CPSs) integrate digital cyber computations with physical processes. These CPSs are composed of embedded computers and networks that monitor and control physical processes with sensors and actuators [1]. A Safety Critical Cyber-Physical System (SCCPS) is a system whose failure or malfunction may result in very severe consequences.

CPSs are applied in several domains including aerospace, energy, automotive, railway or health-care, which are considered safety critical domains. In comparison with CPSs, SCCPSs are more complex in terms of functionality, integration and networking interoperability, reliance on software, and the number of non-functional constraints (e.g., dependability, robustness, scalability, safety).

Functional Safety is one of the key properties of SCCPS. Safety is aimed at protecting the systems from accidental failures in order to avoid hazards. Many

S. Tonetta et al. (Eds.): SAFECOMP 2017 Workshops, LNCS 10489, pp. 114–126, 2017.
DOI: 10.1007/978-3-319-66284-8_11

safety critical CPS, are required to pass a certification process and must provide evidence that they have been developed according to the domain functional safety standards [2–6].

The scope, complexity, and pervasiveness of SCCPSs continue to increase dramatically. As the software of today assumes more of the responsibility of providing functionality and control in systems, it has became more complex and more significant to the overall system performance and dependability. Given the current state of the art, fewer development faults are committed because of the use of best practices and better tools, but not all are prevented.

Verification and validation techniques applied during development could help to reduce the errors introduced in the systems but, if we want to increase the dependability of the systems, there is still a need for Run Time Checking. There are Fault Detection and Fault Tolerance techniques that assist in this task but they are not easy to implement and require much effort as Laprie et al. stated in [7].

In a process of developing SW components, designers add the requirements to their software models in the design phase. Normally, in the next phases, most of this information is lost. Fault Detection strategies need these requirements and specification information. In the approach presented in this paper the specifications and requirements added in the design phase, when modelling the system, are kept at Run Time. The SW components generated by the CRESC framework can use the Fault Detection mechanisms to check the current internal state of the controller by means of reflection.

The contribution of this research is to introduce the CRESC framework that generates SW components based on Reflective Statecharts in C++ programming language. This CRESC framework is easy to use and the generated SW control components have the ability of introspection and adaptation.

The solution separates the functionality and safety aspects of the system. We use a combination of classic mechanisms (such as Reflection and Statecharts). However, from that combination we have created a new efficient tool to develop SW control components for SCCPSs.

In Sect. 2 of the paper the Technical Background is presented. In Sect. 3 we present the CRESC Framework. After that, in Sect. 4 a Toy Example and the Use Case for Productive 4.0 project are shown. The Conclusion of the developed Framework is presented in Sect. 5 and finally, the Future Lines section closes the paper.

2   Technical Background

In the domain of CPSs, there are different techniques to design and develop robust systems. The main aim of this research is to increase the dependability of SCCPSs.

The term dependability has been studied by different researchers and one definition by Laprie and Kanoun [8] is "trustworthiness of a computer system such that reliance can justifiably be placed on the service it delivers". Laprie classifies dependability in terms of threats, attributes and means. The means described by Laprie are based on fault prevention, tolerance, removal or forecasting.

2.1 Fault Classification and Fault Detection

Faults can be classified in many ways and different type of faults have their particular characteristics. Avizienis et al. after an extensive analysis presented a classification in [9].

In our research, we considered the following faults:

– Controller faults. These faults may be due to:
  - SW design and development faults: committed either during the system initial design, from requirements specification to implementation, or during subsequent modifications.
  - HW malfunction faults: adverse physical phenomena either internal (such as short circuits, open circuits and threshold changes) or external (such as temperature and electromagnetic perturbations).
– Environmental faults: these faults occur during the operation phase, therefore they are also called operational faults. They are caused by elements of the environment that interact with the system (such as sensors, actuators and communication systems).

Fault Detection is one of the initial and necessary steps to prevent the failure of the system. Even if other elements of a system stop a failure by using other techniques, it is important to detect and remove faults to prevent the exhaustion of the fault tolerance resources of a system.

The faults we have classified could be detected by HW Redundancy (HW and some SW faults) [10], SW Diversity (SW faults) [10] and/or Run-Time Monitoring (all the faults but specially Environmental faults) of the SW control components [11].

2.2 Run Time Verification

Although a model based checking approach in the design and development phases can give enough confidence that the implementation is correct, for SCCPSs we need to continue checking their behaviour respect to its specification also after the deployment.

Run Time verification is the study of how to design artifacts for monitoring and analyzing program executions. The information extracted from the running systems is used to asses satisfaction or violation of specified properties. Those properties are expressed formally using different notations such as finite state machines, regular expressions and linear temporal logic formulas [12].

To monitor a program, we need to log the events and the controller status while it is running. Program instrumentation consist of the addition of code for such information gathering. Different types of program instrumentation could be used to implement the error detection mechanism. These are some examples of program instrumentation: Hooks, Design by Contract approach and Assertions.

There are tools that automatically add program instrumentation by transforming source code as CIL (C) [13] or byte/object code as Valgrind (C) [14] or BCEL (Java) [15].

Some middleware or OS can also offer basic services to implement an error detection mechanism. These services use the infrastructure that is behind the application level (middleware and OS). However, it is not a platform independent solution.

2.3 Reflective Principle

Reflection makes the model used in the design phase available at Run Time. Computational reflection [16] is an approach that:

- Helps in separating the application and dependability mechanisms to reduce complexity.
- Adds the introspection capacity to increase dependability.

As an example of research in Reflection carried out in recent years, in [17,18] Lu et al. developed techniques and mechanisms to detect errors and adapt the system to change to a non error mode at Run Time. Their approach is based on multi-layered architectures using the AUTOSAR [19] standard middleware and specific OS services.

2.4 Statecharts Formalism and Development Tools

UML statechart formalism allows constructing a state-based model of the controller, describing both its internal behavior and its reaction to external events.

Ferreira and Rubira [20] created the Reflective State Pattern for finite state-machine aiming at reflecting the state structure of a component and changing its behaviour at Run Time for tolerating environmental faults. However, to the basis of our knowledge, it is Barbier [21] who first created a framework for Statechart based components that implicitly supported introspection of a component at Run Time. Based on this work, Elkorobarrutia et al. [22] defined a framework for Java that supports Run Time modification of the behaviour of a Statechart-based software component. Elkorobarrutia's solution does not consider real time constraints nor the resource limitation of the execution environments in embedded and real time systems.

There are a lot of patterns and proposals for transforming statecharts to code but as far as we know none of them is well suited for our purposes. As an example there is a framework, the Boost Statechart library [23], able to transform UML Statecharts to executable C++ code and viceversa, but they are not aimed at creating reflective code. Another drawback is that it makes an extensive use of C++ templates and it becomes impractical for large sized Statecharts.

Finally, there are many commercial tools that transform Statecharts specification to code, however this is their only aim. In addition, the transformation rules are quite tool and version specific. Therefore, they are not suitable for adding Run Time introspection.

3 Design and Development of the CRESC Framework

3.1 Selected Technology

CRESC was developed as a Framework that generates components based on Reflective Statecharts. One of the reasons for this decision was that Statecharts are accepted by the functional safety standards due to its simplicity and to the fact that they constitute a formalism widely used in SCCPSs [24–26].

Specifically we decided to use Reflective Statecharts because this way we are able to introspect SW components in term of model elements and if necessary adapt them at Run Time. Introspection and adaptability, provide the means of adding a Fault Tolerance infrastructure to SW Control Components. Additionally, the use of reflection reduces complexity as Fabre affirms in [16].

As in SCCPS domain usually they are real time and resource limited systems, we decided to implement the framework in C++. This programming language is more suitable for real time and resource limited systems than languages or execution platforms as Java. Additionally, the majority of the Functional Safety standards accept it (a subversion of C++, MISRA C++ [27]).

3.2 The Reflective Framework and Error Detection Mechanism

In the next paragraphs we are going to show the main elements of the CRESC framework. We can not explain all the details due to the space limitations.

In order to create a reflective structure for software components, first we had to define which elements of those components we want to reflect. We considered previous work developed by Elkorobarrutia [28]. This work was developed in Java and it was not thought to be used in CPSs and real time execution platforms.

First, we divided the design of the framework into two important parts: the *controller* part and the *executor* part.

In the former, we define the behaviour of the controller implemented by Statecharts. This part is the one that specifies and reflects the statechart model.

The second part is the one that executes the actions and conditions specified by the controller. In Fig. 1 we can see the relationship between the two parts.

To implement the *Controller*, the statechart model of the application is transformed to an object structure. These objects are representing concepts as states, transitions and actions of the statecharts. This object structure is the element that reflects the statechart model. Any change in this structure implies changes in the model and vice versa. Thus, our code reflects the application model.

This reflection enables us to query the status of the component at Run Time. Thus, the framework allows adding fault detection, fault tolerance and adaptability mechanisms to the SW Control components.

The framework needs some extra elements to manage the Run Time information. For that issue, the State Machine Global Repository object was developed. This object keeps Run Time information such as active states and the event currently being processed.

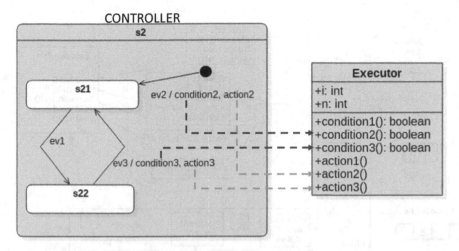

UML Statechart Notation: States, Transitions, Events, Actions, Conditions,...

Fig. 1. Controller part and its references to the Executor

The Dispatcher is the object that directs the execution of our SW components. When an event is launched, it is stored in the Buffer object. The Dispatcher gets the event from the Buffer and it checks the current status of the application. Then, the Controller orders what to do (i.e. transition to another state performing specific actions) and the Executor part executes the methods (controller's actions) that the controller orders. Figure 2 sets out the whole picture.

Based on introspection ability of the CRESC Framework, internal error detection can be added to the controllers. To this end and based on the work carried out by Lu [29], software *hooks* were used in the CRESC framework. The hooks were added in the entry and exit actions of each of the states. These hooks will log information of the current status provided by the Global Repository and this logged information will be structured using the UML statecharts notation. Thus, an Error Detection mechanism will use this information to check the correctness of the monitored system.

So we can add introspection ability in any of the objects structure and it is also possible to adapt the controller. Once an early error is detected, and before the failure is generated, the Error Recovery mechanism will be started. Depending on the safety properties of the use case and the degradation modes defined for the current application, the Error Recovery Mechanism will initiate the adaptation process to the defined degradation mode at Run Time.

As we are working in the Safety Critical CPS domain, these degradation modes have to be designed previously and the adaptation in this case must be a controlled one.

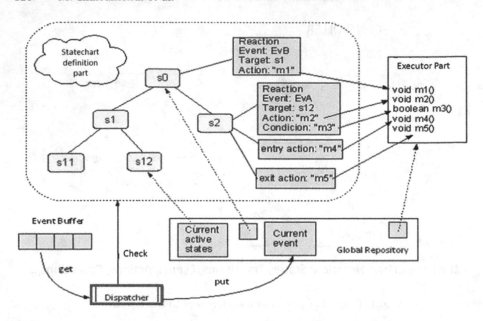

Fig. 2. Framework infrastructure

One of the benefits of the CRESC Framework is its ability to detect controller internal errors in early phases before they are transformed to erroneous output control signals.

4   Toy Example and Productive 4.0 Use Case

In this section the development of a SW Control Component that controls a distributed elevator is presented. As shown in Fig. 3 the elevator moves the load up and down by two synchronized engines. The details of this toy example were defined in [30]. Each of the synchronized subsystems is composed of an engine and different sensors: top and bottom detectors and a shaft rotation sensor that is used to infer position and speed. The elevator has two movements: up and down.

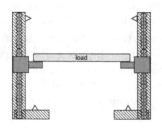

Fig. 3. Elevator toy example

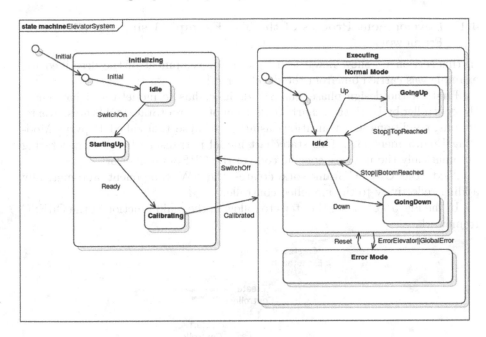

Fig. 4. Toy example statechart

As shown in the Fig. 4, the system starts in the Idle state and once the SwitchOn event is detected, it goes to the StartingUp state. Here, the controller checks all the elevators and if they are ready a new transition is performed. Next, the system goes to the Calibrating state. In this state, the controller performs the calibration action of sensors and the system is ready to work. At this moment, the initializing phase is finished and the system enters the Executing state.

The Executing state has two substates: Normal and Error Mode. The default substate is the Normal Mode. Here, there are three substates: Idle (default state), Going Up and Going Down.

The system is in the Idle state until the user sends a command (Up or Down). Once an Up or Down event is detected, a transition is performed to Going Up or Going Down state.

- If the activated state is Going Up, the system does not change until Stop, TopPositionReached or an Error event is detected.
- If the activated state is Going Down, the system does not change until Stop, BottomPositionReached or an Error event is detected.

In Normal Mode, in any of the substates, if an Error event is detected, the system performs a transition to the Error Mode. In this state, once the system is restored/reset, a Reset event is launched and the system goes to the default state, the Normal Mode (Idle).

We developed and tested the case study in a Linux machine with Ubuntu 14.04 LTS and our development environment was eClipse CDT [31].

4.1   Development Process of the Toy Example Using the CRESC Framework

In this section we show how the design and development of the described toy example was carried out from the developer role.

First, at the design phase, the SW designer has to model the behaviour of the controller by UML statecharts (definition of the rootState, subStates, events, actions, conditions and transition) using an eClipse tool called Papyrus Modeling Environment [32]. This statechart model is translated to text generating automatically the use case specific code of the CRESC framework.

Next, the CRESC framework creates the SW component automatically adding reflectivity to the modelled controller.

In the Fig. 5 we can see the steps to follow in the main function of the CRESC framework.

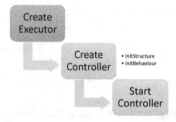

Fig. 5. CRESC: main function steps

In the first step, the developer only had to define the name of the Executor in order to identify it. The framework allows having more than one Executor (for example to use as Error Recovery Mechanisms to adapt the behaviour of the system when an error is detected). This information could be extracted from the model automatically.

In the second step, when creating the controller, the developer had to define the structure of the Controller (ToyExampleSM) using the initStructure function and the behaviour of the system by the initBehaviour function. As mentioned before, this step is carried out automatically extracting the model information.

The following extract of code was created automatically with the model to text transformation. In this case, the initStructure and initBehaviour functions were filled with the toy example specific information:

Listing 1.1. initStructure	**Listing 1.2.** initBehaviour
| ```
states="idle";
idle=new
    control::XorState(states,0);
root->addState(idle);
states="StartingUp";
startUp=new
    control::XorState(states,0);
root->addState(startingUp);
``` | ```
methName="SwitchOff";
fName[methName]=&Executor::SwitchOff;
action::Action
    *actSwitchOff=new
    action::MethodInvocation(methName);
rName="rExecuting2Idle";
control::SimpleReaction(...);
executing->addReaction(EvSOff,rExecuting2Idle);
``` |

At this point, the controller was created and the system was ready to start.

Evaluation of Results. A Toy Example was implemented in order to show how to use the CRESC framework. In the next list, some of the positive aspects found in the experiment are presented:

- runtime introspection ability is added automatically to the controller,
- easy to use framework,
- SW development process: the implementation of the solution is generated automatically from the design phase.

It is true that the listed benefits are not measurable and at this stage we are not able to specify how much the dependability and/or efficiency have been increased. In the next steps of the research we will add mechanisms that will benefit from runtime introspection ability and these benefits will be measured.

4.2 Productive 4.0 Use Case

In the project Productive 4.0 (European ECSEL project), our research group will work in the *Machinery for railway wheels* Use Case leaded by DANOBAT S.Coop (industrial partner) shown in the Fig. 6. In this Use Case, the results and future works of the presented research are going to be implemented and evaluated. For that, MGEP will develop fault tolerant and safety critical SW control components based on introspection. These components will be integrated with the manufacturing HW and devices of the Use Case.

These new SW controllers will monitor the internal signals and sensors of the machines. Different machining processes will be considered and each of them will

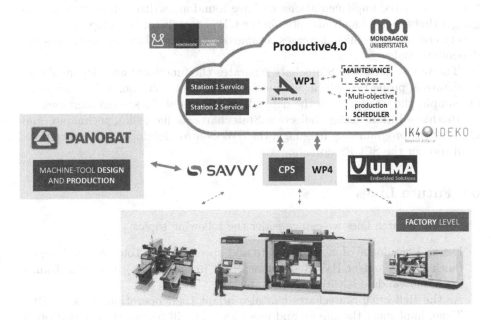

Fig. 6. Machinery for railway wheels.

have different optimization objectives and constraints. Based on those objectives and constraints, the controller will send optimized control signals such as spindle speed and/or feed rate to the machine.

The controller will be modelled by UML statecharts and automatically a CRESC SW controller component will be generated. The researchers are going to develop an evolution of the CRESC framework that will include a Run Time Monitoring and Checking infrastructure. Thus, the increased dependability of the controller will be measured and the benefits of the framework quantified.

5   Conclusion

Safety, dependability, adaptability, reliability and maintainability of CPSs are crucial issues due to the increasing complexity, development cost and the supporting Run Time environment.

In this research a framework that generates SW Control Components with introspection capacity was developed. This ability supports the addition of Fault Tolerance mechanisms.

It is true that currently there are tools that generate code automatically taking as starting point the system model. Some of them are reliable tools but the developer does not know how this transformation is carried out. They are not in control of their code and a lot of the tools are not designed for use in CPS and they are not reflective.

The presented solution is based on Reflective Statecharts and while there are other tools [22] that provide similar characteristics, they are not written in C or C++. All related implementations we have found are written in Java or in languages that are not widely accepted in the CPSs domain, or the adopted solution is very complicated which increases complexity in the solution and decreases the dependability level.

The use of Reflective Statechart separates the functional and dependability mechanisms properties which adds simplicity to the solution. When solutions are simple, the integrity and the dependability level of the system increases.

In this solution, using Reflective Statecharts as modelling technique, and C++ as the programming language, the SW Control developer has a very powerful tool for the SCCPS domain.

6   Future Lines

As future research lines we can consider the following topics:

- Define a catalogue of mechanisms to add specific Fault Tolerance techniques (such as SW and/or HW Redundancy and Recovery [33]) using this framework and validate it with experimentation.
- As the Reflective Statecharts can also adapt their operation mode at Run Time, implement the classes and modules that will permit the adaptation of operation mode at Run Time.

- Develop methodologies and tool support to help adding introspection ability and dependability mechanisms to legacy systems.
- Application and Evaluation of the results in the Productive 4.0 use case.

Acknowledgments. The project has been developed by the Embedded System Group of MGEP and supported by the Department of Education, Universities and Research of the Basque Government under the projects Ikerketa Taldeak (Grupo de Sistemas Embebidos) and LANA II ELKARTEK and by the European H2020 research and innovation programme, ECSEL Joint Undertaking, and National Funding Authorities from 19 involved countries under the project Productive 4.0 with grant agreement no. GAP-737459 - 999978918.

References

1. Derler, P., Lee, E.A., Vincentelli, A.S.: Modeling cyber-physical systems. In: Special issue on CPS, pp. 13–28. IEEE (2012)
2. IEC 61508: Functional safety of electrical/electronic/programmable electronic safety related systems (2010)
3. ISO 26262: Road vehicles- Functional Safety (2012)
4. CENELEC: EN50128 Railway applications- Communications, signalling and processing systems-Software for railway control and protection systems (2012)
5. IEC 61511: Functional safety- Safety instrumented systems for the process industry sector (2016)
6. RTCA & EUROCAE. DO-178B: Software Considerations in Airborne Systems and Equipment Certification (1992)
7. Laprie, J.-C., Arlat, J., Beounes, C., Kanoun, K.: Definition and analysis of hardware-and software-fault-tolerant architectures. Computer **23**(7), 39–51 (1990). doi:10.1109/2.56851
8. Laprie, J., Kanoun, K.: Software reliability and system reliability. In: Handbook of Software Reliability Engineering (1996)
9. Avizienis, A., Laprie, J.-C., Randell, B., Landwehr, C.: Basic concepts and taxonomy of dependable and secure computing. IEEE Trans. Dependable Secure Comput. **1**(1), 11–33 (2004)
10. Heimerdinger, W.L., Weinstock, C.B.: A conceptual framework for system fault tolerance. Technical report, Carnegie Mellon University (1992)
11. Al-Asaad, H., Murray, B., Hayes, J.: Online BIST for emebedded systems. IEEE Des. Test Comput. **15**, 17–24 (1998)
12. Havelund, K.: Reliable software: testing and monitoring. http://www.runtime-verification.org/course09
13. Necula, G.C., McPeak, S., Rahul, S.P., Weimer, W.: CIL: intermediate language and tools for analysis and transformation of C programs. In: Horspool, R.N. (ed.) CC 2002. LNCS, vol. 2304, pp. 213–228. Springer, Heidelberg (2002). doi:10.1007/3-540-45937-5_16
14. Valgrind. http://valgrind.org. Accessed 14 June 2017
15. Byte code engineering library. http://commons.apache.org/proper/commons-bcel. Accessed 14 June 2017
16. Fabre, J.-C., Killijian, M.O., Taiani, F.: Lessons learnt, robustness of automotive applications using reflective computing (2011)

17. Lu, C., Fabre, J.-C., Killijian, M.-O.: Robustness of modular multi-layered software in the automotive domain: a wrapping-based approach. In: Regular paper submitted to ETFA (2009)
18. Lu, C., Fabre, J.-C., Killijian, M.-O.: An approach for improving fault-tolerance in automotive modular embedded software. INRIA, Paris, France (2009)
19. Automotive open system architecture. https://www.autosar.org. Accessed 14 June 2017
20. Ferreira, L.L., Rubira, C.M.: Reflective design patterns to implement fault tolerance (1998)
21. Barbier, F.: MDE-based design and implementation of autonomic software components. In: International Conference on Cognitive Informatics (ICCI) (2006)
22. Elkorobarrutia, X., Muxika, M., Sagardui, G., Barbier, F., Aretxandieta, X.: A framework for statechart based component reconfiguration. In: Engineering of Autonomic and Autonomous Systems (EASE) (2008)
23. The boost statechart library (2015). http://www.boost.org
24. Banci, M., Fantechi, A.: Geographical versus functional modelling by statecharts of interlocking systems. Electron. Notes Theor. Comput. Sci. **133**, 3–19 (2005)
25. Pap, Z., Majzik, I., Pataricza, A.: Checking general safety criteria on UML statecharts. In: Voges, U. (ed.) SAFECOMP 2001. LNCS, vol. 2187, pp. 46–55. Springer, Heidelberg (2001). doi:10.1007/3-540-45416-0_5
26. Pradelly, M., Pazzi. L.: Using part-whole statecharts for the safe modeling of clinical guidelines (2010)
27. The Motor Industry Software Reliability Association. Misra C++: Guidelines for the use of the C++ language in critical systems (2008)
28. Elkorobarrutia, X.: ISCART: framework para la reconfiguracin dinamica de componentes software basados en statecharts. Master's thesis, Mondragon University (2010)
29. Lu, C.: Robustesse du logiciel embarqu multicouche par une approche reflexive: application l'automobile. Master's thesis, LUNIVERSIT DE TOULOUSE (2009)
30. Illarramendi, M., Etxeberria, L., Elkorobarrutia, X.: Educational use case final results. Reuse in safety critical systems (2015)
31. Eclipse IDE for C/C++ developers (Mars). https://eclipse.org/mars. Accessed 14 June 2017
32. Papyrus. https://eclipse.org/papyrus. Accessed 14 June 2017
33. Egwutuoha, I.P., Levy, D., Selic, B., Chen, S.: A survey of fault tolerance mechanisms and checkpoint/restart implementations for high performance computing systems. J. Supercomput. **65**, 1302–1326 (2013)

A Survey of Hardware Technologies for Mixed-Critical Integration Explored in the Project EMC^2

Haris Isakovic[1(✉)], Radu Grosu[1], Denise Ratasich[1], Jiri Kadlec[2],
Zdenek Pohl[2], Steve Kerrison[3], Kyriakos Georgiou[3], Kerstin Eder[3],
Norbert Druml[4], Lillian Tadros[5], Flemming Christensen[6], Emilie Wheatley[6],
Bastian Farkas[7], Rolf Meyer[7], and Mladen Berekovic[7]

[1] Institute of Computer Engineering, Vienna University of Technology,
Vienna, Austria
{haris.isakovic,radu.grosu,denise.ratasich}@tuwien.ac.at
[2] Institute of Information Theory and Automation, Prag, Czech Republic
{kadlec,xpohl}@utia.cas.cz
[3] Department of Computer Science, University of Bristol, Bristol, UK
{steve.kerrison,kyriakos.georgiou,kerstin.eder}@bristol.ac.uk
[4] Infineon Technologies Austria AG, Graz, Austria
norbert.druml@infineon.com
[5] Technische Universität Dortmund, Dotrmund, Germany
lillian.tadros@tu-dortmund.de
[6] Sundance Multiprocessor Technology, Chesham, UK
{flemming.c,emilie.w}@sundance.com
[7] Technische Universität Braunschweig, Braunschweig, Germany
{farkas,meyer,berekovic}@c3e.cs.tu-bs.de

Abstract. In the sandbox world of cyber-physical systems and internet-of-things a number of applications is only eclipsed by a number of products that provide solutions for specific problem or set of problems. Initiatives like the European project EMC^2 serve as cross-disciplinary incubators for novel technologies and fuse them together with state-of-the-art industrial applications. This paper reflects on challenges in scope of hardware architectures and related technologies. It also provides a short overview of several technologies explored in the project that provide bridging solutions for these problems.

1 Introduction

Cyber-physical systems (CPS) integrate computation with the physical environment [9]. A wast number of systems can be classified as CPS in various domains of implementation (e.g., consumer electronics, automotive, space, avionics) including multiple disciplines (e.g., computer science, electrical engineering, mechanical engineering, biology, chemistry). The concept of CPS was introduced to unite diverging disciplines and establish a fundamental set of rules and methodologies for the design and development of these systems. The project EMC² (Embedded

© Springer International Publishing AG 2017
S. Tonetta et al. (Eds.): SAFECOMP 2017 Workshops, LNCS 10489, pp. 127–140, 2017.
DOI: 10.1007/978-3-319-66284-8_12

Multi-Core systems for Mixed Criticality applications in dynamic and changeable real-time environments) explores different aspects of the design and development of CPS in an interdisciplinary and cross-domain approach. The goal is to unify the design process from requirements and specification phase to the validation and verification phase, such that individual processes of different disciplines are merged into a single process.

Establishing a chain of multi-disciplinary links is a highly complex task. Commonly, each discipline would provide their respective part of the system which is further integrated with the rest of the system. The goal of the CPS paradigm is to establish common guideline for multiple disciplines to co-exist and co-develop a system together. The project EMC^2 represents an incubator of different technologies which strive towards common goal of bridging gaps in design and implementation process CPSs. A common example is the mixed-criticality integration issue addressed in Sect. 2.

The paper provides a short overview of the major challenges related to hardware technologies and mixed-critical applications (see Sect. 2) and some of the techniques explored in the project EMC^2 to resolve them. Section 3 describes seven different technologies explored in the scope of the project. Section 4 provides a reflection on the effect of the technologies on the presented challenges and industrial applications. Section 5 concludes the paper.

2 Background

2.1 Mixed-Criticality Integration

Two basic conditions for the mixed-criticality integration are spatial and temporal isolation [18]. These emerging properties depend on a series of interlocked architectural properties. Respectively they represent abilities to separate applications in a system both in space and time. A spatial isolation represents distribution of system resources (e.g., memory, IO) among applications without interference between individual applications. A temporal isolation allows deterministic execution and interaction off applications without overlapping and interference. The architectural structure of the system dictates whether these properties can be achieved in hardware or in software. On conventional single-core and multi-core architectures individual applications share resources and the distribution of resources is administered by system software. However, this task is extremely simpler on a single-core processor than on the architectures with multiple processors that share multiple resources.

2.2 Performance

Main driver behind advance of general purpose computing was performance. This progression was accurately predicted by Moore's Law [14] is reaching its limits. The performance depends more and more on core and thread multiplication, rather than increase of frequency. Industrial applications require must conform to various standards and must be certified as such. A switch from single-core processors to multi-core processors for safety critical or real-time applications is an uphill battle. The COTS multi-core hardware architectures are non-deterministic and can be certified for safety-critical and real-time applications only in single-core operation mode.

2.3 Power Consumption

Optimizing for power and energy consumption has mainly been done through hardware innovation. Currently, there are no appropriate tools that can provide feedback to the software developer on how their programming choices affect the energy consumption of a system. Such feedback could help programmers, toolchains and runtime systems to utilize the available energy-saving hardware capabilities and meet strict energy budgets. Hardware energy measurements are difficult to use within the software development process and are usually insufficient for providing fine-grained energy consumption attribution to various software components. New techniques are needed that can estimate the energy consumption of software without any hardware energy measurements. These techniques must be easily integrated into existing toolchains to lift energy consumption information from the hardware, through the different software abstraction layers, and up to the programmer.

2.4 Verification

To ensure correct behaviour, systems must be verified. The complexity of EMC^2-type systems poses verification challenges, where test-based verification can easily miss bugs and formal verification can require an infeasible amount of resources. The MCENoC, discussed in Sect. 3.4, addresses this complexity by building a predictable network from simple, repeated logic components, where certain behaviours are already mathematically proven. Non-functional properties, such as total energy consumption, may also need verification. This is particularly challenging in a software context, where better tools for estimating the energy consumption of code are needed.

3 Survey of Hardware Technologies in EMC2

3.1 Asymmetric Multiprocessing with Video Processing for EMC2-DP-V2 Platform

Video processing and very fast digital I/O requires processing based on combination of standard processors and HW acceleration blocks in programmable logic. The Xilinx 28 nm Zynq devices contain two 32bit ARM Cortex A9 processors and programmable logic on a single chip. We describe accelerator designs for a standalone EMC2-DP-V2 platform developed in the EMC2 project in the Xilinx SDSoC 2015.4 environment [22].

Development Environment and the Board Support Package for the EMC2-DP-V2. UTIA developed board support package for the SDSoC compiler with support for Full HD I/Os and the asymmetric multiprocessing. The video processing algorithms have been modelled and debuged on ARM A9 processor in C. Some user-defined SW functions have been compiled by the SDSoC compiler to HW accelerator blocks together with the corresponding DMA data movers. Figure 1 presents example of video processing HW generated in the SDSoC.

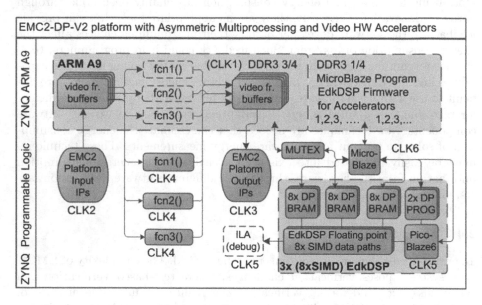

Fig. 1. AMP system with 3× (8xSIMD) EdkDSP and Full HD HDMII-HDMIO for EMC2-DP-V2

The developed board support package supports the asymmetric multiprocessing of the ARM Cortex A9 processor with the MicroBlaze processor and three runtime reprogrammable floating point accelerators. Each EdkDSP accelerator consists of a vector floating point unit and an reprogrammable sequencer. The accelerators perform sequences of vector operations in 8xSIMD floating point data paths. The run-time reconfiguration is performed by reprogramming of each sequencer.

Parameters of EMC2-DP-V2 Platform. The board can be fitted with two supported system-on-modules. Clocks $CLK1 \ldots CLK6$ are specified in Table 1 and Fig. 1. Measured performance for both supported modules is summarized in Table 2.

In case of acceleration of a motion detection algorithm, the total energy of standalone EMC2-DP-V2 board needed for processing of each Full HD frame has

Table 1. Clock frequencies

Device	CLK1	CLK2	CLK3	CLK4	CLK5	CLK6
	MHz	MHz	MHz	MHz	MHz	MHz
7z030-1I	666.7	148.5	148.5	150.0	150	125
7z030-3E	1000	148.5	148.5	200.0	200.0	142.8

Table 2. Performance

Video algorithms in Full HD	7z030-1I	7z030-3E
1× Sobel edge detection (FPS)	49.7	57.7
1× Motion detection (FPS)	42.8	51.8
Motion detection HW/SW acceleration	36×	30×
LMS adaptive filter (GFLOP/s)	0.914	1.189
FIR filter (GFLOP/s)	1.419	1.798
Peak: 3× (8xSIMD) EdkDSP (GFLOP/s)	7.2	9.6

been reduced from 6065 mJ/FRAME (ARM SW) to 177 mJ/FRAME (this is 34× for the slower module) and from 4113 mJ/FRAME to 149 mJ/FRAME (28× for the faster module). Application notes and evaluation packages describing these designs are publicly accessible from [21].

3.2 Multicore Stack Using the $EMC^2 - DP$

The EMC^2-DP, a PCIe/104 FMC carrier developed by Sundance, can be used as a stand-alone module (like in Fig. 1), but it was really intended for large-scale, stacked multiprocessing ARM/FPGA systems (see Fig. 2).

The EMC^2-DP integrates an on-board PCI Express switch allowing an infinite number of EMC^2-DP to be stacked and therefore providing large I/O solutions.

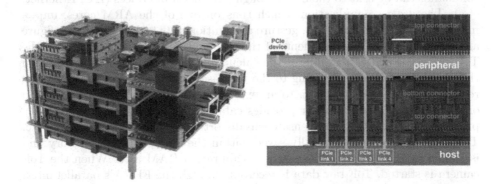

Fig. 2. EMC^2-DP stack and PCI Express switch

The PCI Express switch also provides high-speed communications between each EMC^2-DP. Moreover the EMC^2-DP can be expanded with a VITA57.1 FMC-LPC compatible Daughter Cards for I/O expansion from the FPGA fabric. The EMC^2-DP is a versatile board that can be used for various commercial, medical, industrial and military applications.

The host communicates with the FPGA modules with the PCI Express driver on Windows 7 64-bit. Each board appears as a separate device in Windows, and has its own PCI express hardware link (see Fig. 2). It is thus possible for several transfers between the host and the boards to be in progress simultaneously.

The PCIe interface software is split between the Windows device driver primarily responsible for managing communication and hardware-specific drivers implemented as embedded functions in a microblaze soft-processor in the ADC/-DAC controller FPGA. The Windows driver was written in such way that it is possible for the host application to overlap transfer operations with host-side processing hence improving the system performance. The PCI Express driver integrated DMA engine for transfers between board and host memory under control of the soft-processor controller. The board and the host share 1 GB of external DDR3 memory, as well as 128 KB of on-chip Block RAM. The DDR memory is reserved for data storage, while the Block RAM is used for coordination between the board controller and its host. The PCI Express firmware was developed with Xilinx Vivado 2015.2.

3.3   Time-of-Flight 3D Imaging on Zynq

Time-of-Flight (ToF) is a technology providing distance information by measuring the travel time of emitted infrared light with the help of photonic mixing devices (PMD), cf. [3]. However, the provided raw data of a ToF sensor requires processing in order to obtain depth data, which is typically done in software. In the following, a novel Xilinx Zynq solution is presented, which closes the gap in the field of flexible but fast hardware-accelerated ToF processing.

The Zynq SoC, depicted in Fig. 3, is designed as a supporting co-processor, thus it is controlled and operated from an external processing system. Specific commands can be sent to the SoC through peripheral interfaces (I2C, Ethernet, etc.). The use-case application, which runs on one of the ARM cores, implements the actual use-case (e.g., gesture recognition). Its task is also to configure all the other HW/SW components of the SoC and to configure and control the ToF camera. Finally, it evaluates the calculated depth data, which is saved in the *Depth Data RAM*, according to the use-case implementation and transmits results, events, commands, etc. to an external CPU. Every ToF camera based on Infineon's REAL3™ sensor provides calibration data which is used by the processing algorithms to compensate lens distortions, ToF systematic errors, etc. The calibration data is typically saved within the camera's flash memory and is loaded by the SoC into its dedicated calibration RAM area. When the ToF camera is started, ToF raw data is received through the FPGA's parallel interface. The *Video In* unit generates a video stream and forwards it to the *Video DMA* which pushes the data into the *Raw ToF Data RAM* and notifies the

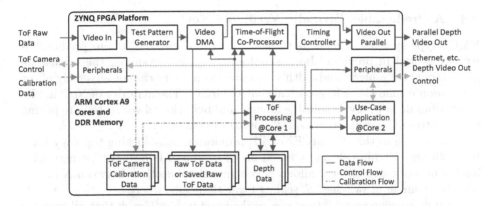

Fig. 3. PMD-based ToF processing on Zynq platform.

ToF Processing software. This software runs on a separate ARM core and utilizes the *ToF Co-Processor* for hardware-acceleration. The co-processor's control logic block interprets incoming instructions, configures the data buffers and the processing engine, and starts the hardware-accelerated operations. More than a dozen of hardware-integrated operations (such as arcus tangent or square root of two images) are supported, which are typically used by ToF algorithms. After an instruction was executed, the ToF processing software is notified through interrupts. Thanks to its efficient and fine-grained implementation, high-speed and yet flexible ToF solutions can be realized. Finally, the resulting depth data is saved in the *Depth Data RAM* and is employed by the use-case application (Table 3).

A 4-phases ToF measurement represents a typical gesture recognition use-case scenario. In this work, the implementation of the reference processing includes the following operations: depth, amplitude, 3D point cloud calculations, and the compensation of common ToF systematic errors. Compared to the high-precision reference implementation in software (using floating point operations), an average depth error (caused by the inexact hardware calculations) of only 0.08 mm is introduced. Overall, this framework sets a new benchmark for hardware-accelerated ToF processing.

Table 3. Timing results for gesture recognition use-case

Time-of-Flight algorithm	t [ms]	FPS	#HW Instr.
Reference in software	248.15	4.0	-
Reference in Zynq HW/SW	28.38	35.2	20
Optimized HW accel. processing	10.11	98.9	14

3.4   A Predictable, Formally Verifiable NoC

EMC2 type systems demand both safety and performance, where predictability is essential in providing both simultaneously. For example, there must be guarantees that a high-bandwidth video process activity cannot adversely affect the response time of a safety-critical control circuit. The majority of NoC implementations do not provide suitable latency and behavioural guarantees, requiring conservative utilisation or over-provisioning of resources.

In response to this, the MCENoC [7] provides a non-blocking topology built from simple switching elements based on Clos [2] and Beneš [1] type networks. Such a network arrangement allows N concurrent connections between N nodes, with the number of switches, S, scaling logarithmically, where $S = 2\log_2(N) - 1$.

Switches are arranged into stages as depicted in Fig. 4, such that all possible routes traverse the same number of switches. This tightly bounds the latency of all network communication to a fixed value for a given size of network.

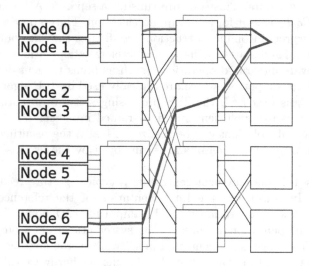

Fig. 4. Example of an eight node network using five switching stages totalling 20 switches. One possible route between node 0 and node 6 is depicted.

Formal Verification (FV) techniques are used to ensure that the design specification is robust and unambiguous, and that the implementation of switches, the total network structure, and edge interfaces, are correct with respect to the specification. System Verilog Assertion [11] language (SVA) is used in combination with the Jasper Gold FV tool to prove safety-critical properties, such as guaranteeing the routing behaviour and error responses in all possible input conditions [7]. The simple nature of the switching elements permits this, and using FV in place of test-based verification provides stronger behavioural guarantees, provided that the specification and SVA properties are adequately defined.

Implementations of the MCENoC have been targeted at the Kintex-7 FPGA, using both in-house custom hardware and the EMC2-DP. Implementation alongside 16–32 RISC-V processors is possible within a single FPGA at 100 MHz, using a configuration that provides a timing-predictable, cache-less array of processors. The MCENoC then provides a predictable network that is appropriate for use in combination with these predictable processors.

3.5   Enabling Software-Driven Energy Consumption Optimization

A novel target-agnostic mapping technique, introduced in [4], can be used to lift existing ISA resource models to higher levels of abstraction, such the Intermediate Code representation of the LLVM compiler infrastructure (LLVM IR) [10]. Mapping an ISA energy model to the compiler's IR level has significant benefits over static LLVM IR energy models. Firstly, the mapping-based approach benefits from the accuracy that ISA models can provide, because the ISA is closer to the hardware than LLVM IR. Secondly, the dynamic nature of the mapping technique can account for specific architecture and compiler behavior, such as code transformations.

The mapping technique was used together with a new target-agnostic profiling technique to retrieve energy estimations at the LLVM IR level. This profiling technique was designed to ensure that the instrumentation code required for profiling does not lead to energy overheads. The experimental evaluation on a comprehensive set of single- and multi-threaded deeply embedded programs, demonstrated that the achieved estimations had an average absolute error of only 3% compared to hardware measurements. Furthermore, the technique was able to attribute energy consumption to the various software components at the LLVM IR level, such as basic blocks and functions, and then correlate this information with the source code.

The profiling-based estimation proved to be significantly more efficient than existing instruction set simulators. The high accuracy and performance of the profiling can enable feedback-directed optimization for energy consumption. Further research is needed to improve energy-transparency techniques for energy-aware software development.

3.6   A Heterogeneous Time-Triggered Architecture on a Hybrid System-on-a-Chip Platform

As described in Sect. 2 ensuring performance for future safety critical applications and implementing mixed-critical applications on COTS hardware presents a major challenges. The proposed architecture provides an alternative approach that ensures these basic properties and adds additional functionality extremely beneficial for industrial applications.

The presented architecture [6] utilizes underlying hybrid SoC technology and time-triggered communication principles. Former allows designers to engage in design of custom hardware in an FPGA fabric, while being able to use advantages of the hard-coded processor.

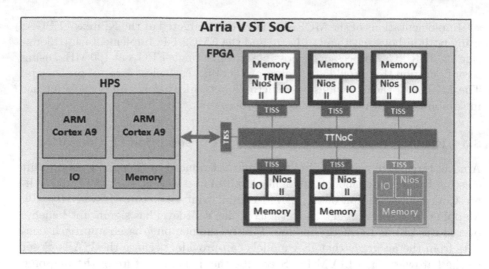

Fig. 5. Block diagram of the deterministic MPsoC architecture on hybrid SoC.

The architecture is built around a communication backbone called time-triggered network-on-a-chip (TTNoC) introduced in [18]. It is message based communication medium interfaced with a arbitrary number of computational components using a trusted interface subsystem (TISS) (see Fig. 5). The interface ensures temporal and spatial isolation of each component and provides them ability to operate in a synchronized fashion. TTNoC provides distribution of chip global time ensuring timeliness of all components.

The original architecture presented in [18] implements a homogeneous set of components implemented fully in an FPGA fabric. The architecture described in [6] and presented in this paper uses underlying hybrid SoC platform to implement a heterogeneous solution that combines hard-coded processor with FPGA based set of components, interconnected with the TTNoC.

Both architecture executions establish spatial and temporal isolation as vital properties. They enable integration of safety critical applications and non-critical applications on a single chip in a high-performance deterministic structure. The concept enables increase in performance while maintaining essential safety properties.

3.7   A Deterministic Coherent L1 Cache

Tightly-coupled multi-core systems with shared memory and central, fine-grained task scheduling can achieve the highest core utilization, provided that low-overhead inter-core communication and data sharing is guaranteed. As the number of cores grows, however, the memory bottleneck dominates and caches become indispensible for upping performance. Caches, in turn, require mechanisms for keeping shared data coherent. Conventional coherence techniques deriving from the classic MSI protocol show largely indeterministic timing behavior due to complex cache interactions, rendering them inapplicable to hard real-time systems.

A time-predictable L1-cache coherence mechanism specifically tailored to real-time systems, has been developed in [16]. The goal is to enable fast access to shared data while maintaining a tight worst-case execution time (WCET) estimate, necessary for realistic timing analysis. The key idea is to hold shared data only as long as necessary, after which it is dumped to memory and reloaded before the next access. Only one core is granted access to a shared region at a single point in time. For this strategy to provide satisfactory performance, instructions are grouped into sequences, denoted by either *shared* or *private*. The cache does not attempt to maintain coherence as long as memory accesses are marked as private. As soon as a shared block is entered, the cache switches to the afore-mentioned on-demand coherence mode. Thus, the granularity of shared/private blocks has to be carefully chosen: Smaller blocks enable finer interleaving and balancing between cores at the price of higher overhead for flushing and reloading.

The performance of the caching strategy has been analyzed in [15,17]. The algorithm has been integrated into the LEON3 caches of the SoCRocket SystemC platform [20], where we are currently testing our strategy in the context of mixed-critical applications.

3.8   Platform NoC Simulation with EMC2 SoCRocket

EMC2 SoCRocket is a virtual platform which enables early prototyping of Hardware/Software systems without the need of real hardware [19]. It eases the debugging and evaluation efforts, particularly focussing on full-system simulation. Resulting in a higher development speed for software and faster hardware exploration. The approach is tested and benchmarked with a real-world full-system example, demonstrating the overall benefits [13].

With SocRocket we assembled a platform to simulate an crosssection of the EMC2-DP hardware for special heterogeneous use cases. Said platform consists of the core components of the GRLib library with the LEON3 Processor extended by an ARM Cortex-A9 [20], MicroBlaze and for interconnection a NoC simulation executing tasks of different criticality levels [5]. The Zynq inside the EMC2-DP hardware uses an AMBA interconnect, this is replicated inside the SoCRocket simulation platform, enabling engineers to evaluate accelerator algorithms within a realistic design environment.

In the course of the project SoCRocket was extended by several features for mixed criticality development. One such feature is a standards-compliant powerful and flexible method of deriving, logging, and filtering detailed status information in different execution contexts. Another notable feature enhancement has been described in the previous section. By leveraging the coherency enhanced caches within the simulation framework we can better predict the real-time behaviour during simulation.

At the core of the simulation is a flexible scripting interface which may change all simulation parameters during run-time, thus not requiring recompilation of the to-be-simulated models [12]. The simulation with SoCRocket shows a speedup up to 160× between RTL and the approximately timed TL-Model and 1400×–2000× speedup between RTL and the loosely timed TL-Model by a simulation uncertainty of less than 10%.

4   Discussion and Future Work

The works presented in the paper provide insight in the hardware techniques for mixed-criticality integration. The heterogeneous TTNoC architecture presented in Sect. 3.6 provides can implement applications with different levels of safety and security without performance loss, while maintaining full spatial and temporal isolation. The future challenges include implementation of tools for configuration and deployment that would connect the whole development process from hardware to the application. Also, for MCENoC future work includes software and toolchain improvements, where communication needs such as bandwidth and periodicity must be known in advance. However, the fixed latency of this network simplifies resource allocation. Where dynamic network traffic is needed that cannot be known in advance, portions of network time could be dedicated TDM phases, controlled by a central unit, which has previously been demonstrated successfully on mesh networks [8]. To improve verification of energy consumption requirements, further research is needed to develop more energy-transparency techniques that can enable energy-aware software development. The EMC2 SoCRocket virtual platform can simulate real-time systems with mixed criticality tasks in a much faster way than RTL while still maintaining good enough accuracy. It can be further enhanced by speeding up the evaluation of energy requirements early in the design stage together with the software development could greatly enhance design efficiency. It provides a rapid prototyping platform for mixed-criticality applications. The asymmetric multiprocessing architecture on EMC2-DP demonstrates feasibility of the hybrid SoC platforms to carry high performance applications. The future work on this field considers full tool integration and further performance optimization. The ToF hardware/software framework enables flexible hardware-accelerated ToF processing for various types of use-case applications. It provides high-quality 3D point cloud data with nearly 100 frames per seconds while introducing an average calculation error of only 0.08 mm. The work on deterministic coherent cache memory provides ability to access data in deterministic fashion thus maintaining WCET bounds. This approach has a enormous advantage for mixed-criticality and real-time applications.

5   Conclusion

Technologies described in the paper provide hardware solution from architectural level up to the peripheral and application specific hardware. Moreover paper presents extendable multiprocessing hardware platform based on Zynq hybrid SoC, an asymmetric multiprocessing in video processing architecture, Time-of-Flight sensor and image processing architecture, predictable and verifiable Network-on-Chip (NoC), heterogeneous time-triggered NoC architecture, virtual hardware platform, software-driven energy consumption optimization techniques, and time-predictable L1 cache memory. The application of hybrid SoC platforms opposed to COTS multi-core architecture provide multiple benefits and can be seen as a viable bridging solution in the gap between single- and multi-core architectures.

Acknowledgment. This research has received funding from the ARTEMIS Joint Undertaking (JU) in European project EMC^2 under grant agreement no. 621429.

References

1. Beneš, V.E.: On rearrangeable three-stage connecting networks. Bell Syst. Tech. J. **41**(5), 1481–1492 (1962). doi:10.1002/j.1538-7305.1962.tb03990.x. http://ieeexplore.ieee.org/lpdocs/epic03/wrapper.htm?arnumber=6769814
2. Clos, C.: A study of non-blocking switching networks. Bell Syst. Tech. J. **32**, 406–424 (1952). doi:10.1002/j.1538-7305.1953.tb01433.x
3. Druml, N., Fleischmann, G., Heidenreich, C., Leitner, A., Martin, H., Herndl, T., Holweg, G.: Time-of-flight 3D imaging for mixed-critical systems. In: 13th International Conference on Industrial Informatics (INDIN), pp. 1432–1437 (2015)
4. Georgiou, K., Kerrison, S., Chamski, Z., Eder, K.: Energy transparency for deeply embedded programs. ACM Trans. Archit. Code Optim. (TACO) **14**(1), 8 (2017)
5. Horsinka, S.A., Meyer, R., Wagner, J., Buchty, R., Berekovic, M.: On RTL to TLM abstraction to benefit simulation performance and modeling productivity in noc design exploration. In: NoCArc 2014: Proceedings of the 2014 International Workshop on Network on Chip Architectures. ACM (2014). http://doi.acm.org/10.1145/2685342.2685349
6. Isakovic, H., Grosu, R.: A heterogeneous time-triggered architecture on a hybrid system-on-a-chip platform. In: 2016 IEEE 25th International Symposium on Industrial Electronics (ISIE), pp. 244–253 (2016). doi:10.1109/ISIE.2016.7744897
7. Kerrison, S., May, D., Eder, K.: A benes based NoC switching architecture for mixed criticality embedded systems. In: 2016 IEEE 10th International Symposium on Embedded Multicore/Many-core Systems-on-Chip (MCSOC), pp. 125–132 (2016). doi:10.1109/MCSoC.2016.50
8. Kostrzewa, A., Saidi, S., Ernst, R.: Slack-based resource arbitration for real-time. In: Design, Automation Test in Europe Conference Exhibition (DATE), pp. 1012–1017 (2016)
9. Lee, E., Seshia, S.: Introduction to Embedded Systems: A Cyber-Physical Systems Approach. Electrical Engineering and Computer Sciences, Lulu.com (2011). https://books.google.at/books?id=MgXvLFE7HIgC
10. LLVMorg: The LLVM Compiler Infrastructure (2014). http://www.llvm.org/
11. Mehta, A.B.: System verilog assertions. In: Mehta, A.B. (ed.) SystemVerilog Assertions and Functional Coverage. Springer, New York (2014). doi:10.1007/978-1-4614-7324-4_2

12. Meyer, R., Wagner, J., Buchty, R., Berekovic, M.: Universal scripting interface for systemc. In: DVCon Europe Conference Proceedings 2015 (2015). https://dvcon-europe.org/sites/dvcon-europe.org/files/archive/2015/proceedings/DVCon_Europe_2015_TA3_1_Paper.pdf

13. Meyer, R., Wagner, J., Farkas, B., Horsinka, S., Siegl, P., Buchty, R., Berekovic, M.: A scriptable standard-compliant reporting and logging framework for systemC. ACM Trans. Embed. Comput. Syst. **16**(1), 6 (2016). doi:10.1145/2983623

14. Moore, G.E., et al.: Cramming more components onto integrated circuits. Proc. IEEE **86**(1), 82–85 (1998)

15. Pyka, A., Rohde, M., Uhrig, S.: Performance evaluation of the time analysable on-demand coherent cache. In: 4th IEEE International Workshop on Multicore and Multithreaded Architectures and Algorithms, Melbourne, Australia (2013)

16. Pyka, A., Rohde, M., Uhrig, S.: A real-time capable coherent data cache for multi-cores. Concur. Comput.: Pract. Exp. **26**(6), 1342–1354 (2014)

17. Pyka, A., Tadros, L., Uhrig, S.: WCET analysis of parallel Benchmarks using on-demand coherent cache. In: 3rd Workshop on High-Performance and Real-time Embedded Systems (HiRES 2015) (2015)

18. Salloum, C., Elshuber, M., Höftberger, O., Isakovic, H., Wasicek, A.: The ACROSS MPSoC - a new generation of multi-core processors designed for safety-critical embedded systems. In: 2012 15th Euromicro Conference on Digital System Design (DSD), pp. 105–113 (2012). doi:10.1109/DSD.2012.126

19. Schuster, T., Meyer, R., Buchty, R., Fossati, L., Berekovic, M.: SoCRocket - a virtual platform for the european space agency's SoC development. In: 2014 9th International Symposium on Reconfigurable and Communication-Centric Systems-on-Chip (ReCoSoC), pp. 1–7 (2014). doi:10.1109/ReCoSoC.2014.6860690

20. Braunschweig, T.U.: Transaction-Level Modeling Framework for Space Applications. https://github.com/socrocket

21. UTIA: UTIA public www server dedicated to the EMC2 project (2016). http://sp.utia.cz/index.php?ids=projects/emc2

22. Xilinx Inc.: Xilinx Inc. (2016). http://www.xilinx.com

Safe Implementation of Mixed-Criticality Applications in Multicore Platforms: A Model-Based Design Approach

Pasquale Antonante[1], Juan Valverde-Alcalá[1], Stylianos Basagiannis[1(⊠)], and Marco Di Natale[2]

[1] United Technologies Research Center, Cork, Ireland
{AntonaP,ValverJ,BasagiS}@utrc.utc.com
[2] Scuola Superiore Sant'Anna, Pisa, Italy
marco.dinatale@sssup.it

Abstract. Application complexity in safety-critical systems is currently creating an immediate need to employ new model-based approaches to ensure system's safe operation in high performances. At the same time, hardware evolution through multicore and hybrid architectures, while serving performance requirements, has not been realized as a safe and technology-ready solution to be employed in critical domains. In this paper, we report our experiences on the development of a model-based design workflow for safety assurance in mixed-critical applications executed on multicore platforms. Starting from our application specification, we develop intermediate models and extract configuration parameters that help us define a task optimization problem. Tasks composing the application will be weighted according to their criticality degree, allowing us to solve an optimization problem for safe resource and time partitioning at the available multicore resources. Based on code-generation techniques, we automatically generate an optimal and safe schema to be implemented in a real-time operating system, safeguarding the multicore resources from errors while executing the tasks. Indicative results are being presented by a prototype tool developed for a case study while we reason about the applicability of the approach.

Keywords: Aerospace · Model-based design · Multicore · Safety

1 Introduction

In multiple domains such as automotive and telecommunications, embedded systems tend to be governed by multicore platforms [1]. Meanwhile, safety critical systems are composing highly complex networks of interconnected Cyber-Physical Systems (CPS) that question their performance and safety [2]. Consequently, the need for increased computational power on embedded systems' platforms raise questions on the safe usage of multicore against certification regulations. Multicore CPS are still not fully embraced by industry for safety-critical

© Springer International Publishing AG 2017
S. Tonetta et al. (Eds.): SAFECOMP 2017 Workshops, LNCS 10489, pp. 141–156, 2017.
DOI: 10.1007/978-3-319-66284-8_13

applications. For example, aerospace systems are subject to costly and time-consuming certification processes, which require a predictable behavior under certain hazardous conditions, hard to be proved in multicore platforms. The main reason is reflected on the multicore non-determinism where commercial-off-the-shelf (COTS) solutions are based on Real-time Operating Systems [3].

At the same time, model-based design processes have been acknowledged nowadays as a vital, irreplaceable process of product development in multiple industrial domains including automotive and aerospace. Despite the significant advances achieved in modeling, simulation and verification, there is still a lack of methods and integrated frameworks enabling multicore tasks safe and optimal scheduling and system-wide validation. At the component level, product development for software is driven by DO-178C [18] and for hardware by DO-254 [19]. Re-defining a multicore model-based design approach towards avionics regulations, we target on the DO-178C supplement (DO-331 [21]), where models have to generate proofs of validity during their code generation.

The challenge in this paper is to employ current model-based design techniques and tools used today in the industry and evaluate their effectiveness in determining the correctness of new prototypes. Those models will include every component relevant to the overall system behavior, such as algorithms, control logic, and device analytics. Recent studies [9] have shown that the application of model-based certification and formal verification can be a practical and cost-effective solution against regulations requirements [12]. Examples of available model-based commercial tools are Simulink® [13], SCADE Suite® [14], LabVIEW® [15] and SystemModeler® [16]. Open source academic tools may also be used, such as Scicos [17]. In this work, we employ Simulink, a de-facto model-based design standard for design, simulation, and code generation. Code generation will be based upon Embedded coder® [13], which provides a mature solution to automatically generate C code for our motor control use case. While appropriate requirements should be specified at different design phases of the product, we argue that multicore model-based development should also define a separate process to validate and verify the system validity against its requirements. Based on the later, we reason about information generated by the current work; this information includes intermediate artifacts, namely: (a) models composed by tasks forming the application based on their periodicity, (b) weight-scores for tagging the tasks depending on their criticality, (c) resource-partitioning based on the multicore platform characteristics and (d) time partitions and schedulers for safe and deterministic execution of the tasks in the allocated resources.

The rest of the paper is organized as follows: in Sect. 2 we review the related work around the area of multicore certification concerning the several domains briefly. Later on, in Sect. 3 we present the proposed model-based design methodology, depicting the tools and models used, optimization problem defined and the solution followed. As a use-case, in Sect. 4 we focus on a proof of concept multicore platform for a motor-drive, and apply its concept on a Quad-rotor, depicting the developed safe scheduling executed by the application tasks, which are partitioned to the end platform. Finally, we conclude this paper with remarks and ongoing research activities.

2   Related Work

In recent years, the industry is dominated by an increasing need for higher processing power while having a small energy footprint. It is a fact, that traditional approaches for providing more processing bandwidth such as clock frequency increment or instruction pipelining, are no longer sustainable. For this reason, embedded devices urge to transition to multicore platforms which have the potential to meet performance requirements by offering greater computational capabilities and advantages in size, weight, and power consumption (SWaP).

However, commercial domains like automotive and aerospace have special requirements to deal with, due to the high integration of systems of systems with different safety-critical levels, such as flight-critical and mission-critical functions, on a single, shared hardware device. In multicore systems, different cores share hardware resources such as caches and central memory, which were developed with a focus maximizing the overall performance; but when placed in the safety-critical context, they introduce challenges to predictability.

From an industrial point of view, safety-critical systems (e.g. aerospace) are subject to costly and time-consuming certification processes, requiring proofs of device-predictable behavior under fault-free and certain hazardous conditions. Despite these concerns, companies are moving towards a higher exploitation of COTS devices to reduce development costs [6]. For the multicore certification process, it is of paramount importance to ensure the *Execution Integrity* of its software components. This means that the application will be correctly executed in normal conditions while the system state will be predictable in non-nominal situations. Usually, not all functions have the same requirements to deal with, and this difference is expressed by their *Criticality*. A formal definition of criticality can be obtained with reference to the safety standards [4] that define the design and development processes for safety-critical embedded systems (hardware and software). The generic standard IEC-61508 requires that a *sufficient independence* is demonstrated between functions of different criticalities. A practical interpretation of this principle is the concept of *robust partitioning*. It is defined differently by several standards, without an officially agreed or common definition [5]. ARINC-653 [20] contains its interpretation of robust partitioning, quoted as: *"The objective of Robust Partitioning is to provide the same level of functional isolation as a federated implementation."* Federated architecture is the traditional design for avionic architecture where each application is implemented in self-contained units. Therefore, robust partitioning consists of the following the concepts:

- *Fault Containment.* Functions should be separated in such a way that no failure in one application can cause another function to fail. Low criticality tasks should not affect higher criticality tasks.

- *Space Partitioning.* No function may access the memory space of other functions unless explicitly configured.
- *Temporal Partitioning.* A function's access to a set of hardware resources during a period of time is guaranteed and cannot be affected by other functions.

This space partitioning concept can be implemented on multicore systems with the help of Real-Time Operating Systems or Hypervisors. Simulink provides a way to address the challenge of designing systems for concurrent execution through its *Concurrent Workflow*. It uses the process of partitioning, mapping, and profiling to define the structure of the parallel application. However, this tool is not yet mature (e.g. not ideal for mixed-criticality setting), being also complex to customize. It offers basic model-based partitioning by grouping blocks to form tasks instead of finding a way to isolate functionality towards robust partitioning.

3 Proposed Methodology

As it was already introduced in the previous sections, the main purpose of this work is to offer a design methodology that deals with the application of mixed-critical applications in multicore platforms. The proposed methodology follows a model-based design approach that covers all the development stages from the initial model and till the code generation in a multicore platform using a hypervisor. As traditional embedded system development process follows the standard V-shaped lifecycle, product development process is split into a design and an integration phase. During the design phase, the model is developed and simulated. Once the results are satisfactory, the model is tested directly on the hardware platform and then deployed. The Code Generation step is the crucial point of the process where the application is evaluated without any governing assumptions. Our contributions are positioned from the model evaluation and optimization phase till the automatic code generation. The methodology enables to run different applications with different criticality levels in multicore platforms ensuring adequate safety properties.

3.1 Hypervisor Selection, Model Development and DAG Generation

Before the actual model design and creation, several information is needed to be capture for the methodology effectiveness. The main concept for the design of a mixed-critical system is, first and foremost, the demonstration of sufficient independence among software components. System virtualization, which is the abstraction and management of system resources, facilitates the integration of mixed-criticality systems [7]. This approach results in independent virtual machines (partitions) that are fully contained in an execution environment that can not affect the remaining system. As there are plenty of commercial and open-source hypervisors, current methodology is based on PikeOS [8] from SysGO AG. It is a microkernel-based hypervisor, suitable for embedded platforms, certified for a series of common regulations (e.g. DO-178C, ARINC-653,

ISO-26262, etc.). It has been designed for functional safety and security requirements which make it also a suitable choice for our use case. Moreover, it fully supports multicore processor with some mechanism to improve performances. PikeOS execution entities are shown in Fig. 1a.

The *Resource Partitions* implement the space separation whereas the *Time Partitions* implement the temporal separation of a robust partitioned system. In this work, we consider Resource Partition as a group of one or more threads assigned to a Time Partition. This will be convenient to simplify timing analysis and improve predictability of the overall execution. The platform used for our case is a heterogeneous embedded system including a dual ARM core and an Artix-7 FPGA. For this study, the FPGA will be considered as a HW resource for the cores and its implementation is not included in the partitioning and scheduling process. In the same way, the first SW-HW partition of the application is now executed manually depending on the designer. A schematic of the simplified design process is shown in Fig. 1b.

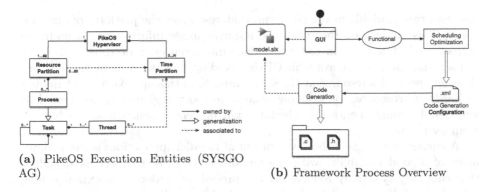

(a) PikeOS Execution Entities (SYSGO AG)

(b) Framework Process Overview

Fig. 1. Model-based design framework with Hypervisor entities

The input to the process for our example is a Simulink model. This model is completely agnostic from its final implementation, as it is crucial to allow a clear role separation among designers, such as the domain expert modeling the algorithm, till the software and verification engineer. In this way, an agnostic implementation of the end multicore platform is sought, prohibiting the platform dependent requirements to restrict designers modeling concepts. Initially, the system designer refines the division of the model in subsystems, which are considered as the unit of execution. This refinement is still a manual process since it is highly dependent on the application and the designer preferences. Once the model is divided into subsystems, a configuration step is required which includes: (a) assigning criticalities to each subsystem, (b) running an initial estimation of the execution time per subsystem and (c) load the platform model to see how the HW resources are used by each task.

The platform is a rough representation of the *uniform memory access* architecture as shown in Fig. 2. Its simpler form contains the number of CPU and

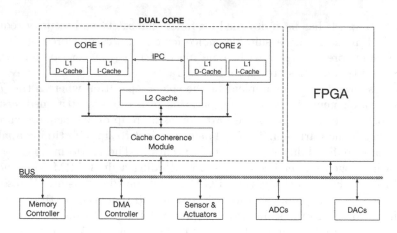

Fig. 2. Unified memory acess architecture

the resources available in the platform, that resemples the platform of our case study. This model, together with the resource usage information, is useful to correctly schedule tasks in order to reduce interferences. Indeed, the scheduler can schedule tasks on all available CPUs, avoiding that two or more tasks access the same peice of a resource at the same time. Note this approach is not limited to hardware resource, for example, shared memory regions can be treated as additional resource hence the scheduler will prevent concurrent access to that memory region.

A current challenge in the development of parallel applications is the achievement of a good scalability with the number of threads and processors. Often the scalability is heavily reduced by the precedence order of execution among threads (usually due to data dependencies). A possible approach to model the problem is through a *Directed Acyclic Graph* (DAG). The DAG is a functional representation of the model, it consists of vertices (threads) and edges (communications/precedences) among nodes. We utilize Simulink modeling API through scripting to parse the model and create a functional representation of it. While the DAG represents a *precedence graph* among threads, it should be mentioned that it also imposes a partial order of execution of the application. To automatically generate an implementation of the application entering the code generation phase, the total order of the DAG must be computed, as it will improve safety and predictability (determinism) through partitioning and scheduling. In order to perform a real-time scheduling for the tasks on multiprocessor platforms there exist two basic approaches: the partitioned approach, in which each task is statically assigned to a single processor and migration is not allowed, and the global approach, in which tasks can freely migrate and execute on any processor. Even though the global scheduling has several advantages, this paper focus on scheduled partitioning because the global scheduling would lead to preemptions and migrations, which produce more overheads and less determinism. In particular the latter might cause certification issues that primarily we would like to avoid.

3.2   Partitioning Based on Criticalities

After extracting the DAG, the framework perform its next step, executing a partitioning algorithm based on criticalities, platform model, and task periodicity. The output of this process, two hierarchical groups, are obtained represented in intermediate DAGs:

1. *P-DAG* the DAG representing all the partitions of the system and their precedence constraints.
2. *T-DAG* one for each node of the P-DAG, this DAG represent the tasks assigned to that partition along with precedence constraints.

Each partition corresponds to time and resource partitions at the hypervisor domain. The isolation of the time and resource partitions will be guaranteed by the hypervisor.

3.3   Scheduling, Resource Allocation, and Factorization

As a following step, scheduling and allocation of the tasks need to be defined. This step is divided into two phases, (a) *inter-partition scheduling*, and (b) *intra-partition scheduling*. The intra-partition scheduling takes the T-DAG of each partition and schedule, allocate and assign priorities to each task of the graph. The problem is NP-hard in the strong sense, and a solution will be obtained through a Mixed-Integer-Linear-Programming (MILP) optimization. Inter-core communications are handled by spinlocks in order to avoid overhead from operating system to re-scheduling or context switching the waiting threads. Moreover, spinlocks are proved to be efficient if threads are likely to be blocked for only short periods, which is true to some extent depending on worst-case timing (WCET) analysis reliability. The Linear-Programming (LP) optimization problem will assign priorities such that the FIFO scheduler of PikeOS correctly schedules threads under the optimal schedule solution found including additional constraints imposed by the use of spinlocks. Similarly, inter-partition scheduling part, takes the P-DAG and schedule each partition by directly assigning time-slots and execution order, for the hypervisor. PikeOS will also guaranty error containment inside partitions, in case a resource is malfunctioning (functional alteration of the resource) during the task execution.

As partitions can have different rates, it is assumed that rates are an integer multiple of a base-period. Considering the *Major Time Frame* which is the Least Common Multiplier of all rates multipliers, some partition should execute more than once. For this reason, a *factorization* phase is required. During this step, each partition in the P-DAG is repeatedly replicated in order to execute in the Major time frame. An example of factorization is shown in Fig. 3. It should be added that as the P-DAG imposes a partial order of execution among partitions, a correct time slots assignment must take into account this order. As the intra-partition scheduling is considered to be an NP-hard problem, a Branch-and-Bound optimization step is executed, taking the factorized P-DAG in order to identify optimal solution if exists. At the same time, as our focus is a

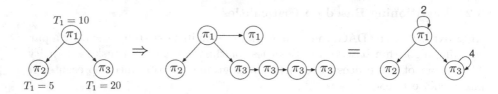

Fig. 3. P-DAG factorization example

model-based design approach towards the safe execution of the tasks led by the generated DAGs, we argue that model checking techniques (such as Simulink Design Verifier or NuSMV) could be used to exhaustively verify temporal isolation of the enumerated resources assigned to execute the tasks. Abstractions on the other hand, are necessary to describe the embedded systems platform, leading us to partial verification of the solution. Thus, from practical point of view, we utilize the certified PikeOS hypervisor solution which proves safe temporal isolation and determinism of the mixed-critical tasks execution on the available cores.

3.4 Code Generation

Once the configuration is loaded, we realize the software architecture described in the configuration file, by scripting. In particular, we have to address the communication issue between the different resources. All the threads inside a process share the same virtual memory address space, so a global variable containing an output (or input) of a thread is accessible from every thread. When the threads are scheduled inside two different partitions, this variable is no longer accessible. For solving this problem, two approaches are possible:

- Communication Primitives: use message oriented communication such as Sampling or Queuing Ports.
- Shared Memory Regions: define shared memory regions between the two partitions.

While shared memory is suitable for a large amount of data, usually a single inter-partition communication channel, which is the implementation of a Simulink Line, transfers a limited amount of bytes. After the aforementioned phases, the information obtained is:

- Time partitions schedule scheme, where each partition has one or more reserved time slots.
- For each partition, which threads it contains tagged with starting times, priorities, core mapping and specification for thread-to-thread communications.

Model Inport and Outports in Simulink that implement an inter-partition communication, need to be substituted with surrogate blocks that, respectively, implement a Read and Write on the Sampling Port. The mechanism that

Simulink provide for extending its built-in modeling functionality is the definition of Custom Blocks. Each custom block is composed of two files: an S-Function that describe the behavior of the block during simulation and a TLC file specifying the code that is going to be generated out of it. Each block has a target file that determines what code should be generated for that block. Within each target file, block functions specify the code to be output during the start function, output function and update function. After the Code generation block initialization (i.e. BlockInstanceSetup and BlockTypeSetup) different TLC function generate the resulted executable code. This partitioning configuration is stored in an XML file. It is used to drive the automatic code generation and integration with the hypervisor IDE. Initially, the model is automatically adapted to implement the software architecture described in the XML file, addressing all communication issues. The reason is the following: as all the threads inside a partition will share the same virtual memory address space, a global variable containing an output (or input) of a thread is made accessible from every thread. When the threads are scheduled inside two different partitions, this variable will no longer be available. To overcome this problem, each Simulink line that represents an inter-partition communication channel is automatically substituted with communication through *Sampling ports*. As a result, a fresh value will be present providing a validity flag on the expected refresh rate which is crucial for detecting faults occurred to one of the predecessors of the executing thread; and eventually, implement some handler for a not up-to-date value.

This operation, which is a model-to-model transformation, is fully transparent to the designer. Therefore, any Inport or Outports (which are blocks) that implement an inter-partition communication need to be substituted with other blocks that, respectively, implement a Read and Write on the Sampling Port. The mechanism that Simulink provides for extending its built-in modeling functionality, and generate the required C code, is the definition of *Custom Blocks* which has been exploited to achieve the model transformation.

Once the model has been adapted, in the second step we scan the model and generate the code for each subsystem. To drive the code generation process, a Simulink *Custom System Target File* has been developed. Using the aforementioned template, C code will be generated that will be based on code mappings populating the final source files, for every new block is encountered. The generation template also creates an additional XML file which outlines the interface of the generated code, including: (a) The list of all the source files, (b) The name of the structure containing the Inputs/Outputs for the subsystem code and every structure element (ports) with its name and dimension, (c) The name of the entry point functions.

Once the code of each subsystem is available, in the third step code generates the code for each partition. The generation is driven by all the XML file that have been generated by the Custom System Target File, enriched with the information produced by the partitioning, scheduling and allocation optimization. Each resource partition will contain a single PikeOS-Hypervisor Process which is composed by the main thread and eventually some optional child threads.

The main thread is loaded by the PikeOS kernel, and it is responsible for initializing all the children threads. Therefore, all the subsystems are glued together with the main forming partition by a custom TLC. As a result, the main generated will: 1. Create all the child threads. 2. Enter in an infinite loop where it will resume all child threads and wait for the next period activation.

Finally, through the PikeOS Integration Project we configure the generation of the PikeOS boot image, including all the partitions. The Integration Project uses an XML-based file to store all the configuration information. The generation of the whole file is complex, so, for the seek of simplicity only some XML snippets are generated. This does not lead to a loss of functionality because it is possible to develop a tool that, once an Integration Project is available, can scan it and add programmatically the snippets. With a procedure similar to the generation of the partitions, as a last step of the code generation, a TLC file will generate the XML snippets, in particular, they will cover the following sections of the configuration file: 1. *Partitions and Ports* the list of the partitions with the relative ports, 2. *Channels* the list of channels used by the ports to communicate i.e. the port connection list and 3. *Schedule Scheme* the inter-partition schedule scheme.

4 Experimental Results

After the model configuration and code generation of the optimized task allocated to the cores, we describe the experimental results driven by our platform. The hardware used for this proof-of-concept demonstrator. The selected processing unit is based on the Zynq-7000 device, a System on Chip (SoC) that includes two ARM cores and an Artix-7 FPGA fabric (Fig. 4). The motor and drive used is the FMCMOTCON2 developed by Analog Devices. The system includes a brushless DC motor (BLY171S-24V-4000) with a dynamometer, and the drive and connection boards compatible with the ZedBoard platform that contains the Zynq-7000 device.

Fig. 4. Zynq-7000 experimental platform

The implemented system consists of a speed control and Prognostics and Health Management (PHM) algorithm to perform system identification. The implementation is divided into two main parts: the SW side implemented in the multicore, includes the speed control loop, a mode control state machine and the PHM algorithm, while the HW-FPGA implementation includes the current control loop with its Clarke and Park transformations, Space Vector Modulation, and different sensor acquisition algorithms to measure current and position.

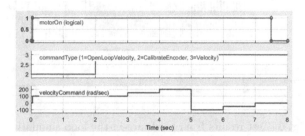

Fig. 5. Reference signal for hardware-in-the loop simulation

The system design for the FPGA is a combination of manually designed and commercial IPs and automatically generated blocks using the HDL Coder from Simulink models. To link both parts automatically, it is necessary to develop a reference design in Vivado (XILINX IDE for the Zynq-7000 device) and extract its TCL script. HDL Coder creates another TCL file with the Simulink blocks and merges them together. In order to provide to the reader a full picture of our application needs, we perform and show simulation results with and without our methodology.

Initial simulation results, show the real-time interaction between the hardware platform and the model, for a single motor control at an isolation phase. This allows a comparison with simulation results and enables the real-time interaction with the user since it is possible to change the speed set point and different operation modes during operation. Controlling one mixed-critical application on a single motor will provide us with the necessary information about the application execution coverage, periodicity, and complexity. This step is essential for the validation of the standalone control algorithms and observes differences between the FPGA and ARM implementations in the real device without changing manually VHDL or C code. This experiment is following the speed pattern shown in Figs. 5 and 6.

As the single motor control example is relatively straightforward for showing the tool capabilities on multicore, we aim to elevate the use-case to a multivariant control problem with multiple motors. Therefore, as additional example model, we consider a Quad-rotor flight control with a pan/tilt camera on it shown in Fig. 7. The models include the control of six motors, four of them for the quad-rotor itself, the last two for a pan-and-tilt camera.

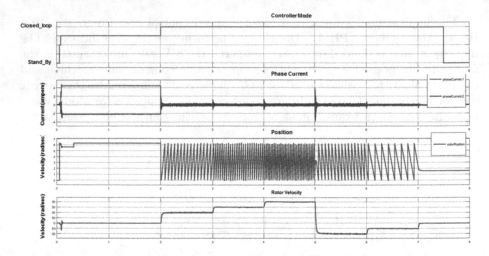

Fig. 6. Test results from hardware-in-the loop simulation

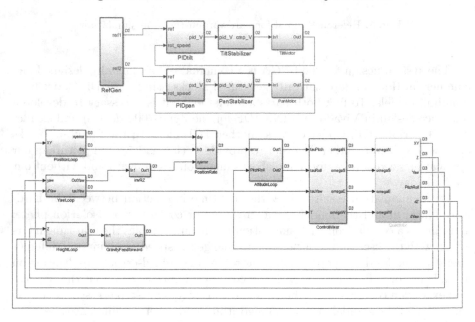

Fig. 7. Compiled Simulink model model

The adopted drone control scheme is inspired by [10] with minor changes introduced to comply with our design restrictions. The DAG in Fig. 8 is automatically extracted as the framework is started, it is then enriched with the information manually configured by the designer through the Framework Graphical User Interface (GUI) in Fig. 9. Once the configuration is complete, the designer can start the partitioning, scheduling and allocation optimization. Generated

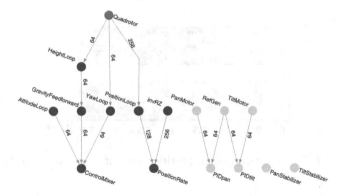

Fig. 8. Functional model task-set for quad-rotor example

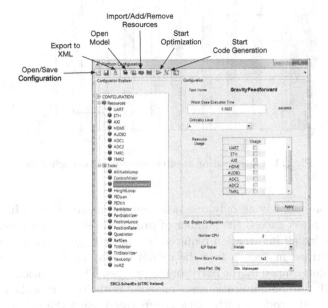

Fig. 9. Framework Graphical User Interface

scheduling and optimization diagrams are generated and given to the designer, for him to select if the design produces acceptable results. Indicative diagrams for the quad-rotor example are shown in Fig. 10 and in Fig. 11.

In order to assess our model executed on multicore platform, *speed-up* and the *efficiency* [11] techniques will be used. The Speed-up technique $(S(p))$ is defined as the ratio of the elapsed time $(E(p))$ when executing a program on a single processor to the execution time when p processors are available $(E(p) = \frac{S(p)}{p})$. Speed-up refers to each partition: in the quad-rotor example, the tasks have been scheduled on two cores obtaining a speed-up of 1.9927 for partition one and two,

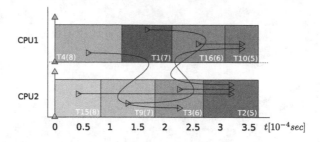

Fig. 10. Optimization results: partition one intra-partition schedule

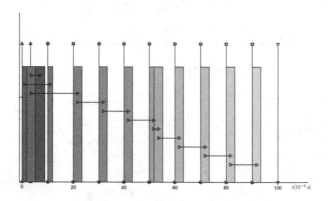

Fig. 11. Optimization results: inter-partition schedule

while partition one, having only one task, has no improvements. In theory, the speed-up can never exceed the number of processors in the best case.

At this point all information required by the code generation is made available. As described in Sect. 3, first the model is adapted to the communication architecture determined by the partitioning process. This operation is fully automatic since all the communications are encoded in the output of the partitioning problem. Then the code of each block is generated using the developed System Target and finally merged to the partitions.

The final steps only generate the code that glues together sub-systems (tasks). Indeed, inter-partition communication is generated by Simulink based on our custom blockset code generation functionality. As a result, out of the code generation and the task scheduling process, XML snippets generated will help the configuration of the PikeOS Integration Project. Due to space limitations we omit the organization information of the integration project.

5   Conclusions and Look Ahead

Automated analysis and fast verification are currently important milestones pursued by major companies for certifying their products. To this end, model-based design approaches nowadays have proven irreplaceable when designing a single aerospace device or an integrated platform. The aforementioned technique presented in this paper, provides an automated tool-assisted solution that steps into the complete development cycle for early and accurate error detection, prior to the final testing of the product. We have presented a model-based approach for the development of multicore prototypes towards safe temporal core isolation of the available resources while performance of our use case is respected. Following resource and time partitioning at a model level of the application tasks, we automatically optimize and allocate tasks to the resources, guarantying their safe execution with a COTS hypervisor solution. As a look ahead, our research activities will focus on evaluating and developing new modeling techniques, combining those with FMI-based co-simulations platforms [23] and implementing new code generation libraries and certification workflows towards the finalization of standardization efforts of manycore solutions for safety-critical domains.

Acknowledgments. This work is supported by the EMC^2 ARTEMIS project: *Embedded Multi-core Systems for Mixed Criticality applications in dynamic and changeable real-time environments'*. UTRC is supported jointly by the European Commission and the Irish Development Agency (IDA), Project Number: 621429.

References

1. Markus, L., Conte, T.: Embedded multicore processors and systems. IEEE Micro **29**, 7–9 (2009)
2. Basagiannis, S.: Software certification of airborne cyber-physical systems under DO-178C. In: 2016 IEEE International Workshop on Symbolic and Numerical Methods for Reachability Analysis (SNR), Vienna, pp. 1–6, April 2016
3. Paun, V.-A., Monsuez, B., Baufreton, P.: On the determinism of multi-core processors. In: Proceedings of 1st French Singaporean Workshop on Formal Methods and Applications (FSFMA). OpenAccess Series in Informatics, (OASIcs), vol. 31, pp. 32–46 (2013)
4. Ernst, R., Di Natale, M.: Mixed criticality systems - a history of misconceptions? IEEE Des. Test **33**(5), 65–74 (2016)
5. Jean X., Faura D., Gatti M., Pautet L., Robert, T.: Ensuring robust partitioning in multicore platforms for IMA systems. In: 2012 IEEE/AIAA 31st Digital Avionics Systems Conference (DASC), pp. 7A4-1–7A4-9, October 2012
6. Fumey, M., Jean, X., Gatti, M., Berthon, G.: The use of multicore processors in airborne systems (mulcors) (2012). https://www.easa.europa.eu/document-library/research-projects/easa20116
7. Trujillo, S., Crespo, A., Alonso, A.: MultiPARTES: multicore virtualization for mixed-criticality systems. In: 2013 Euromicro Conference on Digital System Design, pp. 260–265, September 2013
8. PikeOS Hypervisor. SYSGO AG. https://www.sysgo.com/products/pikeos-hypervisor/
9. Bhatt, D., Madl, G., Oglesby, D., Schloegel, K.: Towards scalable verification of commercial avionics software. In: AIAA Infotech@Aerospace 2010, p. 3452 (2010)

10. Corke, P.: Robotics, Vision and Control Fundamental Algorithms in MATLAB, 1st edn. Springer, Berlin (2011). doi:10.1007/978-3-642-20144-8. corr. 2. print
11. Grama, A.: Introduction to Parallel Computing. Pearson Education, London (2003)
12. Basagiannis, S., Gonzalez-Espin, F.: Towards verification of multicore motor-drive controllers in aerospace. In: Koornneef, F., Gulijk, C. (eds.) SAFE-COMP 2015. LNCS, vol. 9338, pp. 190–200. Springer, Cham (2015). doi:10.1007/978-3-319-24249-1_17
13. Simulink. http://www.mathworks.com/products/simulink/
14. SCADE Suite. http://www.esterel-technologies.com/products/scade-suite/
15. NI LabVIEW. http://www.ni.com/labview/
16. Wolfram SystemModeler. http://wolfram.com/system-modeler/
17. Scicos. http://www.scicos.org/
18. DO-178B: Software Considerations in Airborne Systems and Equipment Certification. Requirements and Technical Concepts for Aviation, Radio Technical Commission for Aeronautics (RTCA) (2012)
19. RTCA DO-254/EUROCAE ED-80: Design Assurance Guidance for Airborne Electronic Hardware. Radio Technical Commission for Aeronautics (RTCA) and EURopean Organisation for Civil Aviation Equipment (EUROCAE)
20. ARINC-653 P1 revision 3: Avionics Application Software Standard Interface. Aeronautical Radio Inc. (2010)
21. RTCA DO-331: Model-Based Development and Verification Supplement to DO-178C and DO-278A. Radio Technical Commission for Aeronautics (RTCA) (2011)
22. IEC-61508: Functional Safety of Electrical/Electronic/Programmable Electronic Safety-related Systems. International Electrotechnical Commission
23. Gorm-Larsen, P., Fitzgerald, J., Woodcock, J., Fritzson, P., Brauer, J., Kleijn, K., Lecomte, T., Pfeil, M., Green, O., Basagiannis, S., Sadovykh, A.: Integrated tool chain for model-based design of Cyber-Physical Systems: the INTO-CPS project. In: Proceedings of the 2nd International Workshop on the CPS Data Workshop, CPS-Week, pp. 1–6 (2016)
24. Nowotsch, J., Paulitsch, M.: Leveraging multicore computing architectures in avionics. In: European Dependable Computing Conference, pp. 132–143 (2012)

GSN Support of Mixed-Criticality Systems Certification

Carlos-F. Nicolas[1]([✉]), Fernando Eizaguirre[1], Asier Larrucea[1], Simon Barner[2],
Franck Chauvel[3], Goiuria Sagardui[4], and Jon Perez[1]

[1] IK4-Ikerlan, Mondragon, Spain
{cfnicolas,feizaguirre,alarrucea,jmperez}@ikerlan.es
[2] Fortiss, Munich, Germany
barner@fortiss.org
[3] SINTEF ICT, Oslo, Norway
franck.chauvel@sintef.no
[4] Mondragon Goi Eskola, Mondragon, Spain
gsagardui@mondragon.edu

Abstract. Safety-critical applications could benefit from the standard-isation, cost reduction and cross-domain suitability of current heterogeneous computing platforms. They are of particular interest for Mixed-Criticality Product Lines (MCPL) where safety- and non-safety functions can be deployed on a single embedded device using suitable isolation artefacts and development processes. The development of MCPLs can be facilitated by providing a reference architecture, a model-based design, analysis tools and Modular Safety Cases (MSC) to support the safety claims.

In this paper, we present a method based on the MSCs to ease the certification of MCPLs. This approach consists of a semi-automated composition of layered argument fragments that trace the safety requirements argumentation to the supporting evidences. The core of the method presented in this paper is an argument database that is represented using the Goal Structuring Notation language (GSN). The defined method enables the concurrent generation of the arguments and the compilation of evidences, as well as the automated composition of safety cases for the variants of products. In addition, this paper exposes an industrial-grade case study consisting of a safety wind turbine system where the presented methodology is exemplified.

Keywords: Goal Structuring Notation (GSN) · Model-based development · Safety-critical systems · Product lines · Variability

1 Introduction

Modern *Heterogeneous Computing Platform* (HCPs) enable architectural simplification and standardisation across multiple application fields (e.g., automotive, railway, avionics) to implement embedded systems with a homogeneous

© Springer International Publishing AG 2017
S. Tonetta et al. (Eds.): SAFECOMP 2017 Workshops, LNCS 10489, pp. 157–172, 2017.
DOI: 10.1007/978-3-319-66284-8_14

hardware (HW) and *software* (SW). The research on bringing determinism and fault isolation to HCP platforms enable safety-critical applications for heterogeneous processors, while also deploying non-safety-related applications. The cost reduction in multi-purpose HW components fosters a common platform development for multiple domains. However, HCPs lead to interferences in temporal and spatial domains due to their complexity, sophistication and high-performance resources. These interferences challenge the certification of modern HCPs and they are one of the main objectives of today's embedded system developers.

Certification represents the major cost driver in the project budget for developing safety-critical HCP systems. This process is a third-party attestation related to products, processes, systems or persons [14]. An attestation is the issue of a statement based on reviewer's decision that demonstrates the fulfilment of specified requirements or standards. In traditional certification, if a requirement of the systems changes, the whole system is re-assessed. This certification model increments the cost and the time-to-market. Modularity methodology enables dividing the system into independent modules which may be developed and certified with different criticality levels (e.g., Safety Integrity Level (SIL) 1 to 4 according to IEC 61508). This method enables improving the reusability and scalability of the overall system and allows the reduction of the complexity and the certification cost of mixed-criticality systems.

IEC 61508 is the safety-related standard for Electrical/Electronic/Programmable Electronic (E/E/PE) functional safety systems. This standard considers safety as an *emergent system property*, resulting from the inherent safety of its components, the system structure and the interactions between its parts, the operational context, and the development process. Safety standards rooted in IEC 61508 follow a stereotyped development work-flow (V-model development process) with interleaved analysis, refinement and review tasks. The IEC 61508 standard also recommends the use of models to assess the compliance with the established practices where the developer verifies the safety behaviour of the safety-related system.

The development process redundancy is also mandated by IEC 61508 for high integrity systems. The redundancy consists of the separation of concerns, staff roles and artefacts between the design and development and the *Verification and Validation* (V and V) activities. The process redundancy decreases the likelihood of systematic errors relying on diverse interpretations of the requirements. However, in practice, a file-based application environment does not support the concurrent and independent development, which is required to certify high-integrity *Mixed-Criticality Product Lines* (MCPLs) cost-effectively.

In the scope of the European project *Distributed REal-time Architecture for Mixed Criticality Systems* (DREAMS) [8] the safety certification of MCPLs according to the IEC 61508 standard is one of the objectives. This paper presents a shared certification artefact based on a *Database Management System* (DBMS) to overcome the limitation introduced in the previous paragraph. Furthermore, the presented solution provides support for different use-cases for collaborative safety-projects. Those collaborative projects can handle and share safety certificates, evidences and reference documents common to a MCPL.

The project can also collect the arguments and the documents concurrently and semi-automatically optimise the design and post-design of MCPLs.

The paper is organised as follows. Section 2 recalls some related works about product line development. Section 3 introduces the European DREAMS project, presents its architectural style and exposes a toolset for generating and checking safety argumentation models. Section 4 presents a Platform Based Design (PBD) work-flow to design safety product lines. Section 5 exemplifies the integration of the methodology proposed in a safety wind turbine product line system. Section 6 reflects the lessons learned. Finally Sect. 7 presents the conclusion and outlook.

2   Related Work

The key to provide modularity in safety certification are the safety cases. A safety case is a structured argument supported by a body of evidence that provides a compelling, comprehensive and valid case that a system is safe for a given application in a given operating environment. When these components are integrated into a mixed-criticality system, then, specific global safety arguments can also be assembled to show the validity of the safety claims.

The safety case approach is already accepted in safety applications domains like railway applications (according to the requirements of EN 50139 [7]) or air traffic management systems. EUROCONTROL publishes a safety case development manual [11] for aviation management applications, based on *Goal Structuring Notation* (GSN) notation [15]. Other safety standards also allow the use of safety cases, even if there is no specific guidance on the safety case structure or the overall structure for cross-reference.

GSN [15] is a safety case notation language proposed by Kelly to develop, document and maintain safety-cases. It was developed following the Toulmin approach [26]. This notation language uses the goal, strategy, solution, context, assumption and justification elements to express the safety-related requirements of a system (see Fig. 1). In addition, GSN language supports modularity [17,21],

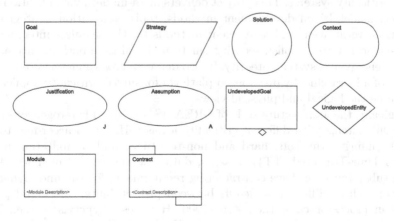

Fig. 1. GSN elements. (Source [16])

adding the module and contract elements. The module element is a package of arguments that abstract the view of the argument structure. The contract element is a package that represents the relationship between two or more modules, defining how a claim in one supports the argument in the other.

On the other hand, the OPENCOSS project [3] tackles the problem of certifying a product for multiple application domains for which different safety standards may apply. Such domain-specific safety standards differ in the definition of the safety property and its scope, as well as the compliant processes or the approval criteria from the competent certification body. OPENCOSS aimed at integration and interoperability of SW tools, including requirements management and test automation tools. To that end, it relies on DBMS repositories to build certification arguments. This project introduces:

- a common certification meta-model, the Common Certification Language (CCL) that can be transformed to the certification requirements mandated by the domain-specific safety standard
- argumentation patterns to arrange the product and process compliance arguments
- a customizable process to generate certification artefacts (e.g. documents).

The ongoing AMASS project [1] builds on OPENCOSS developments. AMASS proposes a reuse-oriented approach for architecture-driven assurance, multi-concern assurance and seamless interoperability between assurance and engineering activities. This project focuses on the loose coupling between SW design environments, retaking the Open Services for Lifecycle Collaboration (OSLC) integration.

3   European Project DREAMS

DREAMS [20] is a European project that aims at developing a cross-domain real-time (RT) architecture and design tools for complex networked multi-core mixed-criticality systems. This project delivers meta-models, virtualization technologies, model-driven development methods, tools, adaptation strategies and validation, verification and assessment methods for the seamless integration of mixed-criticality to establish security, safety and real-time performance as well as data, energy and system integrity. It also defines a cross-domain system architecture of a hierarchically distributed platform for mixed-criticality applications combining the logical and physical views.

Logically, the architecture style of DREAMS consists of heterogeneous application subsystems with different criticality levels (SIL 1 to 4 according to IEC 61508), timing (firm, soft, hard and non-real-time) and computation models such as Time-Triggered (TT) messages, data-flow and shared memory. Application subsystems can have contradicting requirements for the underlying HW platform such as different trade-offs between predictability, safety and performance in processor cores (i.e., Zynq-7000, Hercules), hypervisors (i.e., XtratuM, PikeOS), operating systems (i.e., Windows CE, Linux) and networks (i.e., on-chip network, off-chip network). They can be further split into SW components (e.g., diagnosis partitions and safety protection partitions which are responsible for executing a safety state in the case of a failure).

Figure 2 shows the architecture style defined in DREAMS project where blocks highlighted in grey represent *core platform services*, blocks with dotted boundary are the *optional platform services*, and the blocks with diagonal lines are the *application related platform services*. Partitioning establishes this system perspective, enabling the decomposition of the system into multiple application subsystems which can be independently certified to the respective level of criticality.

The HW architectural style proposed by the European project DREAMS ensures determinism and temporal independence to simplify the timing and resource analysis. Temporal predictability and low jitter also promote the quality of control of mixed-criticality systems. This architecture style is used in the following sections to define the methodology for developing mixed-criticality product lines.

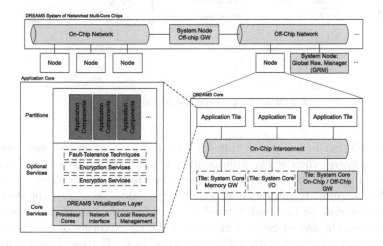

Fig. 2. The DREAMS architecture style (Source [20]).

In the scope of the DREAMS project [20] the safety certification of MCPLs according to the IEC 61508 standard is one of the objectives. The subject of this project are families of dependable mixed-criticality systems that embody variable sets of features (e.g., safety-related and non safety-related features). In DREAMS, we generate several argumentation models [18,19] which may be completed by evidences, analysis and tests results to provide a robust and verified system.

As this European project aims at providing cost-effective tools and procedures for the certification, we tackle the compilation of the whole set of safety information required by each variant of a mixed-criticality system product line.

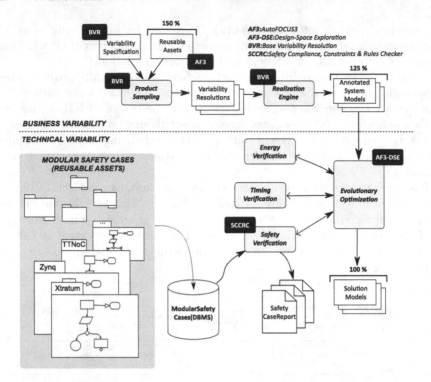

Fig. 3. Design Space Exploration (DSE).

Such compilation is costly and time-consuming, even when two variants show minor differences; their safety argumentation may share only some small fragments. To improve cost-effectiveness, we automate the construction of preliminary safety arguments, after a favourable safety evaluation of a candidate mixed-criticality system. To that end, several plug-ins for safety verification are developed based on the *Design Space Exploration* (DSE) extension of the open source model development tool *AutoFOCUS* 3 (AF3) [4,6]. Further plug-ins are also developed to give support for energy and timing verification, although they are out of the scope of this paper.

Safety related plug-ins shown in Fig. 3 may be used to capture the requirements of MCPL systems, define the variability models, sample and assess the properties of the variability models and build and refine the variant safety argumentation of those systems [9]. The plug-ins for safety developed in DREAMS projects are the following:

– *Safety Case Argumentation Generator:*
  This generator enables constructing safety case argumentations (i.e., *Modular Safety Cases* (MSCs)) by instantiating and composing a set of GSN diagram patterns. The GSN argumentation models that we generate represent the certificates as a *Solution* element, constrained by an *Obligation* (i.e. the

requirement for conformance demonstration). In the context of IEC 61508, a safety certificate usually has an accompanying mandatory report, emitted by the certification body.

The components that compose a reliable system shall be supported by reference workflows, which guide the developers to use the item safely. Therefore the project team must to justify how they manage the item, demonstrate the proper adoption of safety measures from design to integration and system validation, justify deviations from the recommended practice and execute verification activities.

In DREAMS project, these activities spread through different project phases of the development process. The proper handling of safety-compliant items is justified at the design phase.

- *Safety Case Checker:*

Once we get a safety case argumentation, the DREAMS Safety Compliance Constraints and Rules Checker (SCCARC) [9] performs sanity checks following these rules:

- *Rule 1:* Concrete argumentation shall not contain optional elements.
- *Rule 2:* The goals shall be supported by strategies.
- *Rule 3:* The strategies shall be supported by other goals or solutions.
- *Rule 4:* At the final development stage, the related goals, strategies and solutions shall be developed and instantiated.

As required in the IEC 61508 safety standard, the validation, verification and testing activities (V and V) shall be accomplished independently from the design. Therefore the V and V related information and evidences shall be provided by a separate team. The DSE tool generates a blueprint system based on custom evaluation results at its completion. After building the actual products, the properties predicted are verified, by carrying out further analysis and experiments.

- *Safety Case Documenter:*

This post-processing feature generates a detailed description of the safety arguments and exposes the results from the safety case checker in a report. The safety argumentation is generated using the safety case argument generator. The safety case documenter traverses the argumentation model for the feasible product variants, writing a LaTeX transcript with a pre-defined safety-case template. The template contains 11 chapters, including an introduction, a system description, an overall safety argumentation, an analysis of every safety argument and its evidences, assumptions, issues, limitations detected and recommendations. In addition, this template is extended with an annexe that includes a user guide of the template.

The automated generation of the preliminary safety case helps at keeping the overall documentation synchronised and eases the completion of the argumentation with new safety-relevant information collected at later development stages [15].

4   Safety Mixed-Criticality Product Line Development

Modularity methodology gives rise to the System of System (SoS) where independently useful systems are integrated into large systems with unique capabilities [23]. Concepts from SoS engineering can be helpful in Product Line Engineering (see Fig. 4). When dealing with SoS engineering, we can consider each system to be an instantiation of a product of a product line. The motivation to consider systems (in a SoS context) to be products of a product line can come from multiple causes. In many cases, a supplier of systems may have families of similar systems. Product line techniques promise considerable benefits in systematically handling such families of products. Therefore, product lines can be seen as a mechanism to develop components, sub-systems and systems in a SoS approach. From the perspective of the end user, it can be beneficial to handle groups of systems together rather than addressing them independently.

On the other hand, the DREAMS project implements modularity and provides a backup of safety argumentation models, consisting of a structured set of GSN MSCs. This set of GSN models encapsulate the MSCs in a composable mode and provide a guideline to carry out IEC 61508 compliant assessment. For instance, the MSC for an IEC 61508 compliant hypervisor and a Commercial Off-The-Shelf (COTS) multi-core device are defined in [18,19].

On the basis of the safety-related arguments defined in the MSCs and the product line hierarchy introduced at the beginning of this section, we identify the following four levels of abstraction to represent a modular mixed-criticality product line development process.

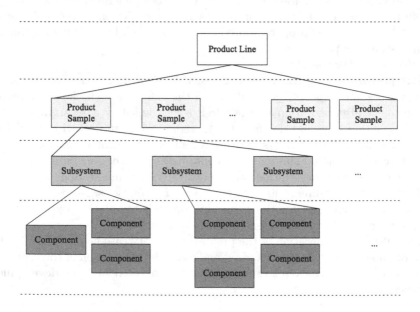

Fig. 4. Product line abstraction layers.

- the first layer represents the *safety-related arguments regarding a product line* that is based on the argument framework introduced in [13]
- the second layer defines the *safety arguments of a product sample* that may be composed of a set of components represented in the fourth layer of abstraction
- the third abstraction layer defines the *generic safety-related arguments that a safety component* shall fulfil to be considered a compliant item. This abstraction layer is the meet-in-the-middle point for developing a product line
- the last layer defines the *safety-related arguments for commercial and custom safety components* which could be used for developing a certain product sample, e.g.: a COTS multi-core device, a hypervisor, a mixed-criticality network, an operating system.

Variability is the quality, state or degree of a system to be changeable. For example, the product samples of a product line can vary depending on the safety standard (i.e., IEC 61508, ISO 26262, IEC 50126) and the level of criticality (i.e., SIL 1 to 4 according to the IEC 61508, Automotive Safety Integrity Level (ASIL) A to D according to ISO 26262).

- *Variation Points from Standards*
  DREAMS tackles the safety certification approach according to the IEC 61508 standard. IEC 61508 is the safety standard for E/E/PE functional safety systems and it is the basis for other domain-specific safety standards such as the ISO 26262 (automotive), EN 50126 (railway) or ISO 13849 (machinery). Most domain-specific safety standards require further characterization of the components, require a specific argumentation structure and provide mandatory safety-case guidelines. In general, a safety standard does not provide a fully objective evaluation guideline, and therefore, they require some subjective interpretation.
  On the other hand, there is a trend to harmonise the underlying requirements from multiple safety standards. However, no cross-domain development environment can cope completely with these differences [3].
  The work presented herein scopes the IEC 61508 safety standard, a similar approach may be used for other application domains ruled by different standards. The same may be applied to security or timing related standards.
- *Variation Points from Safety Requirements*
  Given a particular application domain (i.e., automotive, railway), safety standards set different requirements regarding the development process, the product design and the integration. In addition, the product manufacturer may target different safety levels (e.g., ASIL, SIL) for developing the product samples of a product line. In those cases, the safety requirements of those product samples may be mapped to several variation points that provide the right to choose between components with different criticality levels (e.g., SIL 1 to 4 according to the IEC 61508 safety standard). For instance, different measures and diagnostic techniques are recommended by the IEC 61508 safety standard depending on the required SIL.

The argument database may also host argument models for COTSs artefacts that may be used to implement parts of a product line safety argumentation.

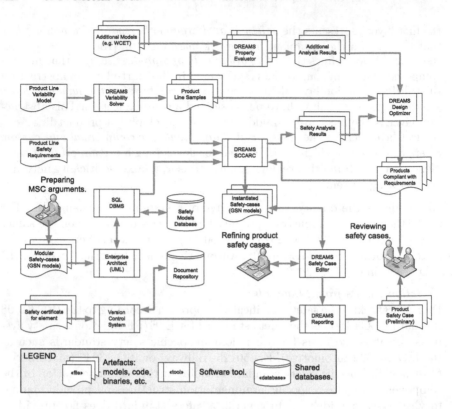

Fig. 5. DREAMS workflow to support the certification of mixed-criticality product lines.

E.g., a commercial model-based design and coding environment, a safety Programmable Logic Control (PLC). Adjoined to a certified component we usually find a certificate stating the safety score of the component, a certificate report from the certification body, detailing the context for which the certificate was granted, as well as a fault analysis, the identified risks and the prevention measures, a safety manual and a reference workflow stating how the development process accommodates specific measures required by the component. For instance, a model-to-code transformer may require the developers to subscribe or regularly check an alert service from the application manufacturer to warn about detected defects in the tool that could bring errors to the implementation.

The DREAMS modelling toolset intends to support the certification of safety-critical embedded product lines. To attain this goal, in DREAMS we define a PBD workflow that covers several possible low-level refinements [24]. PBD supports the meet-in-the-middle process [12], where successive refinements of specifications meet with abstractions of potential implementations and identification of precisely defined layers. I.e., the platforms [25]. This workflow, that is shown in Fig. 5, consists of the following steps:

- Build the argumentation meta-models for the common components.
- Set the design objectives into the design space explorer [22].
- Run the optimizer.
- When a product line configuration meets the safety requirements, a safety argumentation model is generated by the safety-validator.
- The report generator translates the argumentation model for a given design solution into a set of documents with proper references to already available information (e.g. pre-built argumentation).

The proposed workflow shares a data base (DB) store of safety cases generated using GSN notation, as well as safety certificates and related documents for commercial-of-the-shelf elements. DBs ease tool integration into a collaborative framework, collecting the pre- and post-design information contributed by actors with different roles in the safety project. AF3 extensions compose pre-built safety cases, which are generated in DREAMS according to the compliant product configurations, then document the preliminary safety cases with cross-references to either available or due documents.

5   Validation – Wind Turbine System

This section exemplifies the application of the methodology introduced in the previous section for developing industrial-grade safety product line systems. This case study consists of a wind turbine controller that bases on the DREAMS architecture style defined in Fig. 2, which is designed and deployed using the DREAMS modelling toolset shown in Fig. 5.

The HW architecture for the *Wind Turbine Controller* (WTC) is composed of the supervision, control and protection units. The WTC operates some distributed *input/output* (I/O) nodes networked over an EtherCAT field-bus (see Fig. 6). The wind turbine control system is composed of the *Galileo* and the *DREAMS harmonized platform* (DHP) platforms, which are interconnected

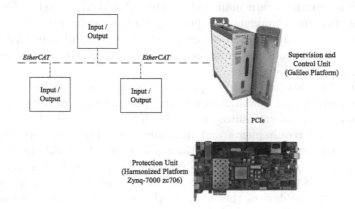

Fig. 6. Wind turbine system HW architecture.

through a Peripheral Component Interconnect (PCI) Express (PCIe) bus. The RT platform named *Galileo* that supervises and controls the wind turbine system. This platform consists of an APC 910 industrial computer [5] with the customised operating system and SW. On the other hand, the DHP intends to implement the safety-related functions of the wind turbine system. The DHP integrates a Xilinx Zynq-7000 zc706 multi-core System on a Chip (SoC), integrating into a single silicon chip a dual-core ARM Cortex A9 and a Programmable Logic (PL).

This system architecture supports the execution of functionalities with different criticality levels (such as SIL 1 to 4 according to IEC 61508). To that end, XtratuM hypervisor [2] is used, splitting the CPUs of the Processing System (PS) and the soft-core(s) of the PL into partitions where the functionalities with different criticality are executed. The protection unit of the wind turbine system communicates with external sensors (e.g., wind speed sensor) and actuators (e.g., safety relay) through a safe field bus protocol composed of a non-safe field-bus EtherCAT and a Safety Communication Layer (SCL) integrated on top of a Network-on-Chip (NoC).

The combination of the NoC and the SCL enables temporal and spatial independences, which depend if a shared memory is used or not to communicate the partitions. The NoC implemented in this case study is the STmicroelectronics' NoC (STNoC), which is complemented with the NoC SCL cross-domain pattern. The SCL guarantees a safe communication between the partitions.

Based on this HW architecture, the DREAMS toolset (safety argumentation generator, safety case checker and safety case documenter) and the variable product line development methodology presented in this paper, we present a wind turbine development process in this section.

Figure 7 presents the top abstraction layers (highlighted in grey) which are used for representing a wind turbine product line development. Those layers contain the safety argumentation of the modules that compose a product line. In addition, this figure exposes two contracts which select the optimum combination of components that should be used for composing a wind turbine (see Fig. 7). These contracts are managed by the AF3 DSE toolset, which would choose the optimum components depending on the safety arguments specified (e.g., integrity level, application environment) and the evidences that are provided by the components that compose the safety argumentation database (e.g., certification accreditation).

As defined in this paper, this representation hierarchy can be extended for include variability, thus enabling developing product lines of different application domains (e.g., railway, automotive). Each domain specific safety standard defines additional requirements and measures and diagnostic techniques that shall be met to accomplish safety certification. In addition, this representation hierarchy can be extended to develop product samples with different levels of criticality. Figure 8 presents a partial representation of the safety argumentation for COTS multi-core devices that support the variations from safety standards and safety requirements. In addition, the modular development methodology

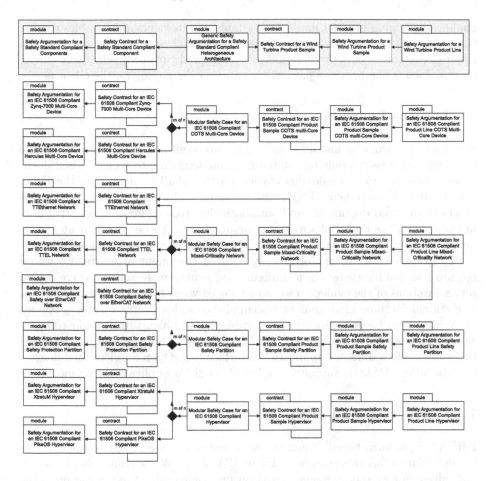

Fig. 7. Wind turbine product line representation.

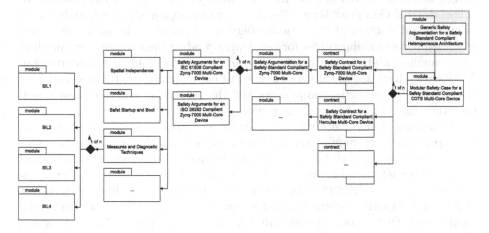

Fig. 8. Standard variable product line argumentation – Overall.

enables developing product lines with variable requirements as it enables reusing the safety argumentation blocks of the commercial and custom components. Figure 7 presents a safety requirement variable wind turbine product line where, as explained in the previous paragraph, can vary depending on the client needs.

6   Lessons Learned

The main challenge is handling an incomplete argumentation structure while splitting and cross-referencing the information according to a customised documentation structure. The documentation pattern shall be defined in the Functional Safety Management (FSM) procedure [10]. Mapping the argument fragments to the FSM documents and automatically cross-reference to existing documents -e.g. risks and faults analysis- or documents to be provided at a later development stage. E.g., a compilation of test results and their analysis.

To assemble the library of cross-referenced document artefacts, we would require a shared file system or a configuration management server, where digital representations of the evidences would be stored when available. For other tools, a relational database management system also provides a common storage point.

While these tools suffice for low-complexity products, to develop complex safety systems a better scalability would be required. This could be accomplished by switching to a different application interface (e.g. Open Services for Lifecycle Collaboration (OSLC)) supporting a loosely coupled application framework.

7   Conclusion and Outlook

DREAMS platform-based design supports re-using pre-certified components to deploy mixed-criticality systems. These HW and SW elements also enable a partially-automated design-space exploration, while easing the generation of the design rationale documentation as is required by the certification process. To this end, DREAMS provides a collection of safety arguments as a foundation to argue the satisfaction of the overall safety requirements. The safety-case approach supports modularity, yet for developing product lines where a per-product safety analysis and the justification of compliance are required to certification. Justification includes the linking analyses of the components, the freedom from interferences between the components and the prevention and tolerance of systematic errors in the development process.

A database of modular certification arguments provides a convenient information arrangement to support the modular composition of safety arguments. Our work shows how this can be even partially automated using the GSN to model the re-usable safety arguments. As an example, we developed the safety arguments for a generic IEC 61508 compliant wind-turbine product line which consist of a DREAMS wind turbine product sample composed of a set of commercial components. Furthermore, we identify several variation points that may extend the modular argumentation database. Those variation points include the variability of safety-related standards (i.e. DO 178C, ISO 26262), and the integrity level of the components (i.e., SIL 1 to 4 according to IEC 61508).

Future developments of the argumentation support would include additional attributes to represent the credibility of a given argument. Those attributes will enable capturing the subjective evaluation of the argumentation as done by a certification body. It is noteworthy that gathering this information is a challenging task. However, based on previous safety assessments and experiences with a certification body, a GSN model can represent a valuable asset to detect in advance the weakest link in the argumentation chain before actually facing the certification process.

Acknowledgement. This work was funded by the European Union's 7th Framework Programme under grant agreement No. 610640. Any opinions, findings and conclusions expressed in this article are those of the authors and do not necessarily reflect the views of funding agencies.

References

1. AMASS (Architecture-driven, Multi-concern and Seamless Assurance and Certification of Cyber-Physical Systems). http://www.amass-ecsel.eu/
2. XtratuM Hypervisor. http://www.fentiss.com/en/products/xtratum.html
3. OPENCOSS Open Platform for EvolutioNary Certification of Safety-critical Systems (2016). http://www.opencoss-project.eu/
4. Aravantinos, V., Voss, S., Teufl, S., Hölzl, F., Schätz, B.: AutoFOCUS 3: tooling concepts for seamless, model-based development of embedded systems. In: Proceedings of the 8th International Workshop Model-Based Architecting of Cyber-Physical and Embedded Systems (ACES-MB), pp. 19–26 (2015)
5. B&R Automation: Automation PC 910 (2015). http://www.br-automation.com/en/products/industrial-pcs/automation-pc-910/
6. Barner, S., Diewald, A., Eizaguirre, F., Vasilevskiy, A., Chauvel, F.: Building product-lines of mixed-criticality systems. In: Proceedings of the Forum on Specification and Design Languages (FDL 2016). IEEE, Bremen, September 2016
7. CENELEC: PD CLC/TR 50506-2: 2009 Railway applications. Communication, signalling and processing systems. Application guide for EN 50129. Part 2: Safety assurance, CENELEC (2009)
8. DREAMS: DREAMS - Distributed real-time architecture for mixed-criticality systems (2013). http://www.uni-siegen.de/dreams/home/
9. DREAMS: DREAMS 5.5.3 - Distributed real-time architecture for mixed-criticality systems - Methods for certifying mixed-criticality (2016)
10. DREAMS: DREAMS 5.6.1 - Distributed real-time architecture for mixed-criticality systems - Functional Safety Management (2017)
11. EUROCONTROL: Safety Case Development Manual version 2.2, 6 November 2006. http://www.eurocontrol.int/sites/default/files/article/content/documents/nm/link2000/safety-case-development-manual-v2.2-ri-13nov06.pdf
12. Fan Jiang, Y.Y., Kuo, J., Ma, S.P.: An embedded software modeling and process by using aspect-oritented approach. J. Softw. Eng. Appl. 4(2), 16 (2011). doi:10.4236/jsea.2011.42012

13. Hutchesson, S., McDermid, J.: Trusted product lines. Inf. Softw. Technol. **55**(3), 525–540 (2013). doi:10.1016/j.infsof.2012.06.005
14. ISO/IEC: ISO/IEC 17000 Conformity assessment - Vocabulary and general principles, June 2004
15. Kelly, T.: Arguing safety - a systematic approach to managing safety cases. Ph.D. thesis (1998). https://www-users.cs.york.ac.uk/tpk/tpkthesis.pdf
16. Kelly, T.: Concepts and principles of compositional safety case construction, May 2001
17. Kelly, T.: Modular certification: acknowledgements to the industrial avionic working group (IAWG) (2007)
18. Larrucea, A., Perez, J., Agirre, I., Brocal, V., Obermaisser, R.: A modular safety case for an IEC 61508 compliant generic hypervisor, August 2015. doi:10.1109/DSD.2015.27
19. Larrucea, A., Perez, J., Obermaisser, R.: A modular safety case for an IEC 61508-compliant COTS multi-core device. In: Proceedings of the DASC 2015 Conference, October 2015. doi:10.1109/DSD.2016.66
20. Obermaisser, R., Weber, D.: Architectures for mixed-criticality systems based on networked multi-core chips. In: Proceedings of the 2014 IEEE Emerging Technology and Factory Automation (ETFA). pp. 1–10, September 2014
21. de Oliveira, A.L., Braga, R.T.V., Masiero, P.C., Papadopoulos, Y., Habli, I.: A model-based approach to support the automatic safety analysis of multiple product line products. In: Proceedings of the SBESC 2014. IEEE (2014). doi:10.1109/SBESC.2014.20
22. Perez, J., Gonzalez, D., Trujillo, S., Trapman, T.: A safety concept for an IEC-61508 compliant fail-safe wind power mixed-criticality system based on multicore and partitioning. In: de la Puente, J.A., Vardanega, T. (eds.) Ada-Europe 2015. LNCS, vol. 9111, pp. 3–17. Springer, Cham (2015). doi:10.1007/978-3-319-19584-1_1
23. Prochnow, D., Hilton, L., Zabek, A., Willoughby, M., Harrison, C.: Systems of systems and product line best practices from the DoD modeling and simulation industry, Septemeber 2014. http://www.acq.osd.mil/se/webinars/2014_09_09-SoSECIE-Prochnow-brief.pdf
24. Sangiovanni-Vincentelli, A., Martin, G.: Platform-based design and software design methodology for embedded systems. IEEE Des. Test Comput. **18**(6), 10 (2001). doi:10.1109/54.970421
25. Sangiovanni-Vincentelli, A., Carloni, L., Bernardinis, F.D., Sgroi, M.: Benefits and challenges for platform-based design. In: Proceedings of the 41st Annual Conference on Design Automation - DAC 2004, p. 5. ACM (2004). doi:10.1145/996566.996684
26. Toulmin, S.E.: The Use of Argument, No. 241. Cambridge University Press, Cambridge (1958)

Concepts for Reliable Communication in a Software-Defined Network Architecture

Ferdinand von Tüllenburg[(✉)] and Thomas Pfeiffenberger[(✉)]

Salzburg Research ForschungsgmbH, Jakob Haringerstr. 5/3, 5020 Salzburg, Austria
{ferdinand.tuellenburg,thomas.pfeiffenberger}@salzburgresearch.at
http://www.salzburgresearch.at

Abstract. Not available services or service interruption could have different impact to our social life. Emails or messages which are not delivered in a proper time-frame could lead to omit a meeting or a discussion with colleagues. Interconnected CPS in different domains, like autonomous driving, smart grids, Industry 4.0, needs a guaranteed and safe delivery of information.

Nowadays distributed application in critical infrastructures such as transportation (e.g. air traffic management, train control, traffic management), financial services, or electricity systems, are often implemented in dedicated network infrastructures not using the public Internet. This leads to high expenditures (CAPEX and OPEX) for the companies to maintain these separated and dedicated telecommunication infrastructure.

Our approach in this work is to verify concepts to share the Internet, as a telecommunication infrastructure for critical and non-critical applications. This reduces the effort to implement and to manage different communication architectures. The present work develops and evaluates methods and procedures that enable high reliable communication between two endpoints over several shared telecommunication networks for future critical and uncritical applications. Our approach shows that it is possible to use the public Internet for future communication requirements in a converged network. Further innovations include the integration of novel network technologies, such as software-defined networks (SDN), programming protocol independent packet processors (P4), and self-adaptive and autonomous network management functions.

Keywords: Critical infrastructure · High reliable communication · Software defined networking · Network function visualisation · P4 · Self adaptive network management · NFV orchestration

1 Introduction

Recent studies predict a tremendous increase of interconnected Cyber-Physical-Systems (CPS) for the near future [11,17]. It is expected that huge numbers of sensors, actors and computer systems will be interconnected in order to

© Springer International Publishing AG 2017
S. Tonetta et al. (Eds.): SAFECOMP 2017 Workshops, LNCS 10489, pp. 173–186, 2017.
DOI: 10.1007/978-3-319-66284-8_15

provide new applications in many areas. These developments give raise to questions regarding the management of the underlying complex networks, which consists of multiple management domains, contain a large number of interconnected end systems and, operate new applications which have individual requirements for their communication quality. Main reasons for the challenges in network management are proprietary control protocols and vendor and device specific configuration interfaces for switches, routers and middle boxes such as firewall, intrusion detection system (IDS), load balancers, etc. [10]. A particular challenge when configuring the underlying communication networks is given, when end-to-end connections extend over several separate and dedicated communication networks. To maintain and manage such proprietary systems, expert knowledge is necessary for multitude of devices and applications in the network. This problem intensifies, if networks grow from local area networks (LAN) to distributed wide area networks (WAN) in central managed critical system.

In this paper, we focus especially on applications within critical infrastructures such as transportation, electricity system or financial services, which we expect (and actually noticed) to also experience the predicted developments. Applications within critical infrastructures in particular desire high-dependable communication networks. Adapting the generic definition of Avizienis et al. [4], dependability of a computer network can be defined as its capability to provide the intended data communication service (regarding functional specification) at any random time an application needs to transmit or receive data. However, this is a fairly broad definition and in order to derive a concept of dependability for communication networks used by critical infrastructures, concrete requirements need to be formulated which must be met to achieve dependable communication. In this context, Avizienis named the means to achieve dependability fault forecasting, fault prevention, fault tolerance, and fault removal.

This paper presents concepts that enable dependable communication services between two end points across multiple network domains including application-specific traffic treatment for critical and uncritical applications. In order to achieve dependable communication four reliability methods are presented, based on different redundancy-levels. For the cross-domain end-to-end connectivity a new management architecture allowing for application-specific network configuration is introduced. The provided concepts are based on novel networking technologies such as software-defined networking (SDN), programming protocol-independent packet processors (P4) [8], and self-adaptive and autonomous network management functions.

The paper is structured like follows: Sect. 2 gives a state-of-the-art overview of technologies for dependable communication. Section 3 gives a brief overview of SDN and describes the opportunities and challenges SDN has related to dependable communication. Section 4 presents the developed reliability methods and the proposed end-to-end communication architecture.

2   State of the Art for Reliable Communication

Today several technologies are available to support user requirements on a requested communication quality. Communication availability can be mapped on delay, jitter, duplicated and lost packets.

If the link is down, packets are dropped. The transport layer of the communication stack can store packets for a retransmit or send the packet over a different link.

If the quality of the communication has inappropriate values or the service level agreement (SLA) is not complied with packet drops, delay or jitter requirements for a safe performance of an application could not be guaranteed. Several methods to manage the Quality of Service (QoS) have been implemented to guarantee the SLA, such as IntServ [9] or DiffServ [5]. Also some overlay network technologies were introduced to support QoS within big network implementations like MPLS. These methods often used for Wide area networks (WAN). In Local area networks (LAN) different layer 2 and layer 3 protocols where implemented to connect switches and nodes redundant. STP/RSTP supports a mechanism to detect loops in layer 2 switching architectures. This enables to have more physical connection at the same time using only one connection at layer 2. If the active connection fails and a timer expire the system tries to find a different layer 1/2 connection to the destination. It activates the second connection and establishes a layer 2 connection. These systems are reasonable for a disconnection time in several seconds to small values of seconds. Redundancy protocols duplicate the packets and sent the packets on two or more disjunct communication paths towards the destination. Proprietary network devices receive the duplicated packets and forward only one packet to the receiving node. This duplication approach avoids packet losses through link failures up to the amount of disjunct paths.

The presented methods are often not usable on a multi domain communication infrastructure to guarantee high reliability in a shared environment.

3   Software-Defined Networks for Reliable Communication

Software-defined networking (SDN) describes an approach for programmable computer networks with the aim to support increasing dynamics in future networks together with simplified management and maintainability. Increasing dynamics in networks is a consequence of always shorter innovation cycles in networked computing environments (new technologies, new protocols, etc.) coming along with the advent of new applications (particular from the area of the Internet of Things).

The main approach of SDN is abstraction, softwarisation and centralisation of lower-level network functionality within rigorouly separated control and forwarding plane. While the forwarding plane is responsible for handling packets at network devices (forwarding, dropping, packet modification), the control plane's responsibility lies in maintaining the network's state and configuring the forwarding service of a network. Thus, the control plane logically centralizes network control functionality and is aware of all controllable devices in the forwarding plane. The control plane is implemented by a high redundant distributed SDN controller application. The general SDN concept is depticted in Fig. 1

The network state consists of topology information including detailled device information and existing links between CPS as well as traffic information including forwarding rules at network nodes, flows between network nodes and possibly bandwidth demands of flows.

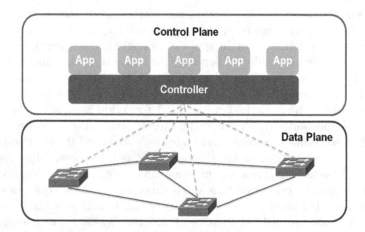

Fig. 1. SDN applications running on a central controller determine overall network behavior by deploying forwarding rules in simple network switches

Accompanied with the separation of control plane and forwarding plane, also a standardized and vendor independent configuration interface for forwarding plane devices has been introduced. The aim of this, commonly referred to as southbound interface (SBI), was to massively simplify the configuration of the forwarding behaviour within the network by making it unnecessary to configure each forwarding device using vendor specific tools and knowledge.

The separation of the control and forwarding plane also reduces the complexity of network nodes towards simple forwarding devices that are reduced to pattern matchers with the task to match incoming packets against forwarding rules and execute actions specified in these rules. The forwarding rules are created at the networks control plane making in unneccessary for forwarding devices to implement complex protocols - except of Ethernet and common wireless technologies (such as wireless LAN), which are seen as foundation of packet-switched data communication nowadays.

The following sections enlight the relationship between SDN and reliable communication in terms of opportunities and challenges.

3.1 Opportunities of SDN for Reliability

In light of the dependability concept, separation of control and forwarding plane, less complex forwarding nodes in conjunction with their abstracted configuration can be seen as a matter of fault prevention by bringing a system design in place, where several single components (network applications, standardized interface between control and data plane, forwarding devices) only need to be well developed once and can be reused several times. Of course, much effort must be put into the development of these single components in order to achieve dependable solutions.

Global view on and central programmability of the forwarding plane opens opportunities for network abstraction, which can be utilized as a means for reliable communication. SDN allows network abstraction in beyond the seven OSI layers of the Internet [12] opening opportunities to application-specific traffic treatment. This is done by introducing network slices and overlay networks for particular applications consisting only of a subset of forwarding devices, links, or even available bandwidth of a link. In doing so, each application in the network can be provided with application-specific characteristics such as network functions (Firewall, DHCP) or traffic constraints (delay, bandwidth). An example where this capability can be used for the purpose of reliable communication is, when slicing is used for the isolation of critical from non-critical traffic in the same network in order to minimize disturbing influences induced by non-critical traffic onto critical traffic.

Furthermore, the centrally maintained global network state can be utilized for verification and validation purposes under consideration of an entire network in scope of the control plane. Verification techniques run at the control plane and use a formalized model derived from the network state to examine effects of network modification onto the global network state. For instance, the side-effects (consistency of rules, safety of network configuration) a particular modification would have on the network state is computed beforehand a flow modification is actually executed on the data plane. Recent research activities tackled the concerns about flow verification in various approaches. For example, model checkers can be used in order to check if flows are correct and include no blackholes or loops, traffic isolation, or forwarding rule consistency as done by Kang et al. [13]. Another approach with a strong focus on real-time network state checking, fulfilling similar goals is presented with VeriFlow [14] and one another mainly aimed at maintaining security invariants is Flover [20].

In addition, the centralized control plane can also be actively used for validation purposes. For example, validation applications using the northbound API of the control plane can be used for active performance measurements. Such tests allow to examine the forwarding behaviour that critical traffic experiences within the network. The results of these measurements can be checked against the traffic specification and in cases of requirement violations, suitable countermeasures such as traffic rerouting can be initiated. Furthermore, fault detection and fault removal techniques employed in legacy networks frequently rely on global network information gathered by monitoring devices. In software-defined networks, these information can be more easily obtained from the central control plane.

Reliable Communication by OpenFlow. OpenFlow [18] is the most prominent implementation of a southbound interface consisting of a standardized model for functionalities of SDN-enabled forwarding plane devices. This model is an important component for network abstraction in SDN networks. Furthermore, OpenFlow also provides a communication protocol between control plane and data plane allowing controllers and controller applications to modify the forwarding behavior of SDN devices.

The main capability OpenFlow provides, is flow matching based on specifically defined header fields and defining corresponding actions to matched packets (such as forwarding to specific port or dropping a packet). With fast-failover, metering and queueing, OpenFlow provides additional capabilities particular important for achieving reliable communication.

OpenFlow's fast-failover concepts allows to define a list of ports on which a packet may be sent out in order to reach its final destination. The switch decides for each forwarding action which of these ports is used based on the liveliness of the corresponding link.

With queueing, OpenFlow (available since OpenFlow version 1.0) supports simple QoS mechanisms where flows can be mapped to queues, which in turn has been attached to ports. The queues are used to enforce a specific forwarding behavior for packets sent via that port (e.g. minimum data rate). Metering support of OpenFlow (available since OpenFlow version 1.3) can also be used to implement QoS capabilities such as rate limiting. In contrast to queues, meters are not mapped on ports but attached directly to flow entries. The meter then controls the (aggregate) rate of the flows it is attached to [18]. Using metering and queueing allows further opportunities for network slicing and traffic separation by assigning bandwidth portions to distinct applications. With this approach overallocation of bandwidth on single links can be avoided and combined with global network information available at the control plane also bandwidth control of end-to-end paths will be possible.

For certain applications static paths can be configured through the network. These paths can be established along, e.g., a chain of selected devices, or devices which provide special capabilities for traffic - such as additional middle boxes (Hardware Firewalls) which are not directly controllable by the SDN control plane. Such static paths can be configured in a way which forbids the control plane to alter them. One scenario for applying static path would be to establish flows for non-critical Internet traffic throughout the network in order to avoid influences on critical traffic.

Dependability by P4. Programming Protocol-Independent Packet Processors (P4) [8] is an upcoming technology improving packet filtering and matching at the incoming communication interface. While packet filtering and matching with OpenFlow is limited to particular specified header types up to IP layer and the used hardware, P4 allows maximum flexibility to filter and match future protocols for interconnecting CPS.

P4 defines a configuration language usable to define arbitrary header definitions which can be downloaded to the P4 enabled switch hardware. This enables P4 switches to process any arbitrary application layer protocol. This is of importance for CPS applications, as they frequently use special protocols such as MQTT [2] or SPDY/HTTP2 [6] which are more suitable for low energy devices (sensors, actuators). With P4 in place, networks can be flexibly adapted to the deployment of new CPS applications in areas such as IoT, Industry 4.0, etc. P4 definitions can be compiled against many different types of execution machines such as general-purpose CPUs, FPGAs, SoCs, network processors, and ASICs. Different vendors like Intel, Cavium, Pica8, metaswitch or small start-up companies like barefoot are developing hardware supporting P4. However, native P4 switches are currently not widely available. The P4 specification and language itself, is developed and maintained by the P4.org consortium, which ensures that future P4 developments are open to the public.

3.2   Challenges of SDN for Dependability

While decoupling the control plane from the data plane brings various opportunities for enhancing the dependability of SDN networks, the new concepts in place also raise several questions. The first concern lies in the conceptually centralized control of the network where two challenges arise. First, the logically centralized SDN controllers and their applications are prone to become single-points-of failure. Even if distributed controller architectures are used, it could happen that faults occuring in controller or application implementations affect the forwarding behaviour in an unintended and uncontrollable way. Second, the controllability of the network is highly dependend on a working connection between control plane and data plane. In common SDN architecuters, this connection is often established through a dedicated management network connecting forwarding devices to potentially multiple SDN controllers. Operating a dedicated infrastructure for management communication makes the setup of SDN networks more complex. The main problem however is, that individual switches become uncontrollable if the management network fails and neither reconfiguration nor monitoring of the forwarding behaviour is possible. Even if the multi-controller support of Open-Flow (since version 1.3) is utilized where each switch maintains connections to multiple controllers. In cases where the management network as whole becomes unreachable for a switch, none of the controllers can be reached.

Another concern lies in the limited capabilities of data plane devices regarding packet processing and monitoring. Although SDN switches are extremely fast in packet filtering and forwarding and also support simple metering and traffic engineering functionalities, they are commonly not capable of more complex operations such as high performance packet processing. While this is mainly due to the design of SDN, which centralizes network complexity at the control plane and keeps the data plane as simple as possible to achieve high performance and standardized configuration, in context of dependability, however, enhanced packet processing capabilities could have benefits.

In a common OpenFlow based SDN, fault removal and some fault tolerance functionalities can only be executed by applications running on the SDN controller or dedicated middleboxes. This requires connectivity and costs at least one RTT between switch and the corresponding application. Thus it is not suitable for fault-tolerance techniques, which require deep packet inspection or packet processing. In such cases, offloading control functions to the forwarding devices can reduce the reaction time for fault removal processes, which in turn can be vital for critical traffic flows.

Applications scenarios would be the implementation of control functions, where software components or software agents are running at forwarding devices which would allow the implementation of advanced fault-removal techniques by distributed monitoring applications such as IDS/IPS or network validation applications. Other examples are per-flow encryption or enhanced metering functionalitiy including QoS surveillance of individual flows. Until now, however, it is not clear to what extent control functionality should be off loaded to the data plane devices while preserving simplicity of the southbound interface and not to overstress the devices capabilities.

One first approach towards offloading control functionalities to forwarding devices is proposed with OpenState [7]. An approach to enhance metering functionality and dynamic network reconfiguration using software agents at forwarding devices is the sFlow network monitoring solution [1]. The sFlow solution, however, is closed source and only supported by some OpenFlow switches.

4   SDN Based Reliable End-to-end Communication

One of the outcomes of the work done in the projects OFSEGrid and OPOSSUM were four concepts for improving communication reliability, which are especially designed to be operated in software-defined networks.

4.1   Reliability Methods

The first developed concept is called "Managed Connectivity" (MC) and provides automatic switch-over capabilities in case network or link failures occur in a network. Similar to what is known from the rapid spanning tree protocol (RSTP), this concepts operates reactively: As soon as a lost link between two physical SDN nodes has been detected, all controlled traffic flows are automatically redirected over other paths as shown in [21]. The switch-over times in the area of several milliseconds originate mainly from the link failure detection. Link failure detection in this concept is based on the Link Layer Discovery Protocol (LLDP), which periodically sends link discovery packets throughout the network. In terms of fault tolerance, this concepts provide a means to overcome link failures in short time, although, connectivity interruptions are not completely ruled out.

The second concept denoted as "Fast Failover" (FF) provides a prepared alternate forwarding path for particular flows at a given SDN node. Beforehand of a flow installation, at each particular hop between the communication end-points a secondary path to forward packets is computed and installed. OpenFlow protocol specify the us of Fast Failover Groups. In contrast to the Managed Connectivity concept, link failure detection time is significantly reduced, first by using information provided by the switch firmware instead using LLDP and, second, by avoiding reactively computing new forwarding paths. The switch-over time of this approach lays within portions of milliseconds and depends on the link down dedection of the hardware. Due to this, packet loss is reduced to a minimum. The approach has some similarities to the Fast Reroute functionality of RSVP-TE.

The third concept "Mutual Interference Avoidance" (MIA) creates disjoint paths for distinct traffic flows in order to avoid mutual interference. This concept is separating the traffic from applications exposing dynamic behavoir in terms of bandwidth, sending intervals, etc., from more critical applications which would extraordinarily suffer from link congestion potentially leading to packet loss or out of time delivery. Another use case would be the separation of paths at particular applications-specific communication stages. For instance, traffic flows related to initializing a relation between client and server part of an application (e.g., TCP handshake procedure, client registering, etc.) might use another path throughout a network as data transfers during operational use of the application. Regarding to communication links, such a procedure could provide protection against flooding or denial of service attacks. Mutual Interference Avoidance is considered as proactive approach, as flow specification and pathcomputation happens before flows are actually installed.

Finally, the Controlled Duplication and Duplicate Removal (CDUP) concept uses disjoint paths throughout (parts of) a network to send network packets belonging to the same flow in parallel towards it's destination. At some prede-fined node packets are sent out on multiple interfaces at the same time (fork point). Each of the packets is following a separate path throughout the network and the paths are disjunct to each other. Another node of the network acts as conjunction point, where the separated paths ends up. At this point an application is removing duplicate packets in a way that only the first of the duplicated packets are forwarded in direction of the destination.

Duplication detection can either be based on frame analysis, where the contents of the frame are inspected and all packets with equal contents are considered as duplicates and not forwarded - this approach needs additional computing capabilities at the conjunction node and must be extended if heartbeat protocols are used. Another possibility would be to add markers in the packet payloads as duplicate identifiers. These identifiers are added at the fork point and get removed at the conjunction point, thus, computional power is required at both. This approach is a proactive approach requiring configuration of conjunction and fork points beforhand a flow is installed. A SDN-based proof-of-concept has been developed as a vendor independent replacement for Parallel Redundancy Proto-col/High availability seamless redundancy approaches. The last two concepts do not expose recovery times as they use concurrency.

In order to build a computer networking system supporting applications demanding reliable communication, multiple of these concepts can be combined within a particular network and applied even to a particular flow.

4.2   End-to-end Communication Architecture

The architecture is targeted to provide a comprehensive solution for reliable end-to-end communication in a multi-domain network environment. A main question in this aspect is how such a management solution could be designed, at least capable of:

• End-to-end path computation in correspondence to the required reliability parameters of each particular application, • measures for improving deployment and delivery times for emerging applications, and • support for potentially autonomous and self-adaptive network reconfigurations in order to deal with dynamic changes within one or multiple domains.

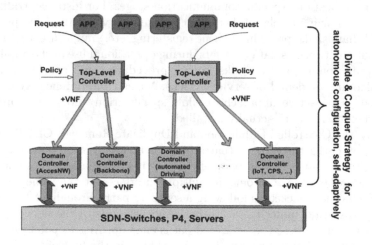

Fig. 2. Multi-domain network control architecture

Figure 2 depicts a general draft of such an architecture using a hierarchical approach to cover several domains underneath a top-level controller infrastructure. This approach allows applications to request a communication services at a top-level controller. The top-level controller has interfaces towards underlying control domains and can forward the requests according to the application requirements. The hierarchy, in general, follows a divide-and-conquer strategy for network configuration. Reliable end-to-end connectivity requires application or flow specific control capabilities finally at each particular device at the networks data plane – well integrated into a cross-domain management architecture. With SDN-enabled hardware a first step in this direction has already been taken, but with regard to reliable communication, SDN capabilities will likely not suffice to meet the requirements of future networks. For instance, the most prominent SDN configuration protocol specification OpenFlow is only capable of matching traffic flows based on packet header fields. For reliable application specific end-to-end communication, however, more fine-grained matching capabilities are required. Also more advanced computing capabilities would be beneficial to support advanced packet processing (such as deep packet inspection or packet manipulation) directly at device level. Novel network technologies, such as P4, are seen as promising candidates, but the technology itself has not been proven its operational fitness and it is currently open how practicable this P4 is and how it should be integrated in to a network control and management system.

The architecture should support self-adaption capabilities and autonomy. These are important features of future carrier networks with their ever rapidly increasing number of connected CPS and applications. Novel application have particular performance requirements regarding traffic forwarding within the network. This finally requires an application-specific configuration of the entire network. As manual configuration is infeasible raise is given to new approaches of autonomy in network control. One major goal of self-adaptively and autonomy mechanisms in network control will be providing automatisms to optimize network control corresponding to performance requirements of individual CPS and particular applications.

5 Future Work and Conclusion

The main focus of the concept is the development of a network control solution to enable reliable end-to-end connectivity across multiple network domains. The developed concept should focus to support quick deployment of critical applications in a shared communication infrastructure with strong guarantees on reliability. The main steps in future work are as follows:

Development of methodologies for reliable end-to-end communication in cross-domain environments:

The main concept of reliable communication is redundancy and the implementation of reliable end-to-end communication methods. This is based on the concepts of reactive and proactive path redundancy and packet redundancy, which has been already developed in [19]. These concepts, however, need to be adapted to the cross-domain environment.

Adoption of the Application Based Network Operations (ABNO) [15] concept providing a management solution for reliable cross-domain communication between two or more endpoints:

One main concept of ABNO is an interface allowing applications directly to interact with the network. Via this interface applications can request end-to-end connections or provide detailed information regarding their communication requirements with respect to traffic characteristics such as endpoints, bandwidth, sending interval, peak rate, burst rate, etc. The information, in turn, can be used by the ABNO system for traffic optimization processes including networks within multiple-domains. A significant contribution to this goal is also the development of a comprehensive, ABNO based, network control architecture supporting the concepts of reliable end-to-end communication needed for emerging critical applications across multiple network domains. Although ABNO hasn't been widely adopted for network management solutions so far, some results of the STRAUSS project [16] can potentially provide first inputs here.

The Integration of emerging networking technologies SDN and P4 supports global configuration capabilities and increase configuration flexibility:

The software-defined networking paradigm has been first adopted by data centres to increase the flexibility and performance of data centre networks and to reduce cost and vendor dependencies. It is currently recognizable that the concepts also get adopted in other areas of data communication such as company connection strategies with the SD-WAN paradigm and even within carrier networks, software-defined networking gets more and more prominent. The [3] project, validates a SDN integration into a carrier network. In contrast to SDN, P4 introduces three major advancements:

1. Switches are not anymore tied to a particular set of protocols;
2. The way, how switches processes packets can be reconfigured after deployment in the field;
3. Even more hardware abstraction compared to SDN-based solutions;

Thus, the introduction of P4 leads to more flexibility regarding network control and can potentially accelerate deployment of new applications and protocols within a network, which is important for increased dynamic in future networks.

Integration of network control mechanisms to enable autonomous network configuration and self-adaptive behaviour:

It is a difficult task to ensure reliable end-to-end connectivity over a potentially longer period for a particular (critical) application. During the runtime of such an application, the network is experiencing continuous change: The number of communicating applications my change over time or even the communication characteristics of present applications change. This is exactly the point addressed by mechanisms of self-adaptive or autonomous network control. A (self-)monitoring system steadily checks if policies of the network or even of particular reliable end-to-end connections are met and a re-configuration system comes into action as soon as policies are getting violated. Thus, self-adaptive/autonomous network control also requires a metering infrastructure collecting relevant data for reliable communication. Furthermore, machine-learning (ML) mechanisms will also be considered to improve self-adaptive behaviour of the network control system. ML, for instance, can provide a means for prediction of network utilization based on historical data and occurring traffic patterns. In case high utilization will be expected in some parts of the network, affected traffic flows of reliable end-to-end connections may be rerouted precautionary. Another use case of ML might be automatic traffic classification, which can also be used for prediction purposes. Furthermore, ML can provide a decision basis on which reliable communication methods will be selected for particular flows or particular network domains.

Provision of a prototypical implementation including all components necessary to show case and evaluate the developed solution:

For the evaluation of the developed overall system, a proof-of-concept implementation will be deployed in an extended testbed consisting of a lab environment and a connected optical-fiber network in production operation. The test scenarios will be focused on the implemented cross-domain network control system and especially in its performance to maintain reliable end-to-end connections in a dynamic network. The extended testbed environment with its connection to the production optical-fiber network connecting CPS and real end users (private homes and companies) provides the necessary dynamic, which allows first evaluations of the systems behavior under real-world conditions.

Acknowledgments. The work described in this paper was part of the project "Open Flow Secure Grid (OFSE-Grid)" and "SDN OpenFlow-based communication system for multi-energy domains (OPOSSUM)" which was funded by the Austrian Federal Ministry for Transport, Innovation and Technology (BMVIT).

References

1. sFlow.com. http://sflow.com/
2. Mqtt version 3.1.1, October 2014. http://docs.oasis-open.org/mqtt/mqtt/v3.1.1/os/mqtt-v3.1.1-os.pdf
3. Open flow based system for multi energy domain, June 2015. https://www.salzburgresearch.at/en/projekt/opossum-2/, Accessed 24 Jan 2017
4. Avizienis, A., Laprie, J.C., Randell, B., Landwehr, C.: Basic concepts and taxonomy of dependable and secure computing. IEEE Trans. Dependable Secure Comput. **1**(1), 11–33 (2004)
5. Baker, F., Babiarz, J., Chan, K.H.: Configuration Guidelines for DiffServ Service Classes, RFC 4594, Auguest 2006. https://rfc-editor.org/rfc/rfc4594.txt
6. Belshe, M., Peon, R., Thomson, M.: Hypertext Transfer Protocol Version 2 (HTTP/2), RFC 7540, May 2015. https://rfc-editor.org/rfc/rfc7540.txt
7. Bianchi, G., Bonola, M., Capone, A., Cascone, C., Pontarelli, S.: Towards wire-speed platform-agnostic control of OpenFlow switches. arXiv preprint arXiv:1409.0242 (2014). http://arxiv.org/abs/1409.0242
8. Bosshart, P., Daly, D., Gibb, G., Izzard, M., McKeown, N., Rexford, J., Schlesinger, C., Talayco, D., Vahdat, A., Varghese, G., Walker, D.: P4: programming protocol-independent packet processors. Comput. Commun. Rev. **44**(3), 87–95 (2014). doi:10.1145/2656877.2656890
9. Braden, R.T., Clark, D.D.D., Shenker, S.: Integrated services in the internet architecture: an overview. RFC 1633, June 1994. https://rfc-editor.org/rfc/rfc1633.txt
10. Feamster, N., Rexford, J., Zegura, E.: The road to SDN. Queue **11**(12), 20 (2013)
11. Gartner, I.: Gartner says 8.4 billion connected "things" will be in use in 2017, up 31 percent from 2016. Gartner Newsroom, February 2017. http://www.gartner.com/newsroom/id/3598917
12. ISO/IEC: Information technology - open systems interconnection - basic reference model: the basic model (1996)

13. Kang, M., Kang, E.Y., Hwang, D.Y., Kim, B.J., Nam, K.H., Shin, M.K., Choi, J.Y.: Formal modeling and verification of SDN-OpenFlow. In: IEEE Sixth International Conference on Software Testing, Verification and Validation 2013, pp. 481–482. IEEE, March 2013

14. Khurshid, A., Zou, X., Zhou, W., Caesar, M., Godfrey, P.B.: Veriflow: verifying network-wide invariants in real time. In: Presented as part of the 10th USENIX Symposium on Networked Systems Design and Implementation, NSDI 2013, pp. 15–27 (2013)

15. King, D., Farrel, A.: A PCE-based architecture for application-based network operations. RFC 7491, March 2015. https://rfc-editor.org/rfc/rfc7491.txt

16. López, V., Tsuritani, T., Yoshikane, N., Morita, I., Muñoz, R., Vilalta, R., Casellas, R., Martínez, R.: End-to-end SDN orchestration in optical multi-technology and multi-domain scenarios. In: 11th International Conference on IP + Optical Network (iPOP 2015), April 2015

17. Nordrum, A.: Popular internet of things forecast of 50 billion devices by 2020 is outdated. IEEE Spectrum, August 2016

18. Open Networking Foundation: OpenFlow Switch Specification 1.5.1, technical Specification TS-012, April 2015

19. Pfeiffenberger, T., Du, J.L., Bittencourt, P., Anzaloni, A.: Reliable and flexible communications for power systems: fault-tolerant multicast with sdn/openflow. In: 7th IFIP Soft Computing Methods for the Design, Deployment, and Reliability of Networks and Network Applications, pp. 1–6, July 2015

20. Son, S., Shin, S., Yegneswaran, V., Porras, P., Gu, G.: Model checking invariant security properties in OpenFlow. In: 2013 IEEE International Conference on Communications (ICC), pp. 1974–1979. IEEE (2013)

21. von Tüllenburg, F., Pfeiffenberger, T.: Layer-2 failure recovery methods in critical communication networks. In: von Tüllenburg, F., Pfeiffenberger, T. (eds.) 12th ICNS International Conference on Networking and Services, June 2016

Combining Safety and Security Analysis for Industrial Collaborative Automation Systems

Sándor Plósz[1]($^{(\boxtimes)}$), Christoph Schmittner[1], and Pál Varga[2]

[1] Department of Safety and Security, Austrian Institue of Technology,
1220 Vienna, Austria
{Sandor.Plosz.fl,Christoph.Schmittner}@ait.ac.at
[2] Department of Telecommunications and Media Informatics,
Budapest University of Technology and Economics, Budapest 1117, Hungary
pvarga@tmit.bme.hu

Abstract. In collaborative automation systems, providing both security and safety assessments are getting increasingly important. As IoT systems gain momentum in the industrial domain, experts stress their concerns about security and safety. Improperly or carelessly deployed and configured systems hide security threats, and even raise issues on safety, as their behavior can threaten human life. The cloud based back-ends are getting used for processing sensor data – on the other hand, legacy equipment, which may contain sensitive information, is made interoperable with broader infrastructure. Safety risks can be triggered by attacks on the backend and confidential information is at risks by attacks on legacy equipment.

In order to maintain safe and secure operations, safety and cybersecurity assessment methods have been established. There is an increased demand in modern industrial systems to perform these regularly. These methods however require a lot of time and effort to complete. A solution to this problem would be combining the assessments. This requires that proper safety and security analysis methods must be selected – those that have compatible elements.

In this paper we propose a method that combines the elements of existing methodologies, in order to make the safety and security analysis process more effective. Furthermore, we present a case study, where we verified the combined methodology.

1 Introduction

The advantages of utilizing the Internet and service-oriented information technology systems on physical systems are beyond dispute. Consequently, the physical world and the world of information technologies are converging. This results in the appearance of Cyber-Physical Systems (CPS). Industrial CPS systems (or Cyber-Physical Production Systems, CPPS) contain critical business information, which will be made accessible in the cloud. It is clear, that any weak

S. Tonetta et al. (Eds.): SAFECOMP 2017 Workshops, LNCS 10489, pp. 187–198, 2017.
DOI: 10.1007/978-3-319-66284-8_16

points in the cloud domain can cause serious reactions in the physical domain, resulting in significant impact on commercial and company values – as well as on human safety.

In order to ensure safety, security and reliability of such systems, threats and failures need to be considered on all (both physical and cyber) levels of its operation. Security is a property which expresses the ability to maintain confidentiality, integrity and availability of the system and its assets. Safety is a property which guarantees that the system cannot cause damage to life, health, property, or environment. In other words security needs to ensure the system is protected from the environment, whereas safety needs to protect the environment from the system [7].

Although well-suited and proven analysis methods exist in the IT domain, the different aspects of CPPS pose new and more strict requirements. In CPPS, security objectives such as availability and integrity are of the utmost importance – however, due to the connections with the physical world, assuring safety and reliability are just as critical. Similarly, there are established techniques to assure safety and reliability in the IT domain, but they do not consider new challenges introduced by this wide connectivity. Security threats can have impact on the safety and reliability of the system, therefore these are no longer completely independent properties. Following this finding, such a combined approach would be beneficial, which allows the analysis of the complete data path – from the industrial M2M communication to the Internet and cloud connectivity –, and considers threats and failures. The goal is that both availability and integrity be ensured on the lowest level of the machinery by closing all the weak points in the system.

For safety and reliability, the challenge is that most techniques were developed for not-connected systems, consisting of almost solely hardware parts. Electronics and software is challenging, because the calculation of risks is different than for hardware. Software does not randomly fail due to aging or environmental influences, but has built-in weaknesses that are triggered. Instead of quantitative assessments, only qualitative evaluations are possible. In addition to that, detailed analysis methods such as Fault Tree Analysis are challenged by the increasing complexity and connectivity.

To overcome these challenges we have created a combined approach, which merely requires some affordable efforts to point out the main risks in such systems, hence it is quite effective.

2   Related Work

There are a handful of existing approaches to analyze system security. A number of them is based on Threat Analysis and Risk Assessment (TARA) [4] which is a simple procedural approach. [17] presents a different approach, a framework to analyze security requirements based on fuzzy logic and calculate how security resources should be allocated.

There are several methods to perform TARA such as TVRA (Threat, Vulnerabilities, and implementation Risks Analysis), OCTAVE (Operationally Critical

Table 1. Brief summary of security analysis methods

Method	Summary
EVITA	Result of the EVITA research project; classifies different aspects of the consequences of security threats (operational, safety, privacy, and financial); classification of safety-related and non-safety-related threats differs and could thus lead to in-balances; accuracy of attack potential measures and expression as probabilities is still an open issues [10]
TVRA	Models the likelihood and impact of attacks; developed for data - and telecommunication networks; applicability for cyber physical systems is unclear [4]
OCTAVE	Developed for enterprise information security risk assessments; applicability for cyber physical systems is unclear; includes interviews and workshop with all stake holders to consider all concerns [8]
HEAVENS	Based on Microsoft's STRIDE approach; determination of threat level (TL), impact level (IL), and security level (SL) for classification of threats; does not scale easily with number of threats; requires discussion of each factor of each single threat [12]
Attack Tree Analysis (ATA)	Analogous to fault tree analysis (FTA); identifies attack paths and vectors in hierarchical manner, describes movement of an attack through the system to reach attack goal; benefits from a stable system design and known vulnerabilities; requires already identified attack goals [21]

Threat, Asset, and Vulnerability Evaluation) or Attack Trees. These methods are summarized in Table 1. The TVRA method can determine security risk based on the likelihood and impact measures of identified threats. In order to identify threats, it is best to model the system as components. The Microsoft Threat Modeling Process [20] can be used for modeling and threat identification. It describes the model elements and the meta-language for producing a threat catalog – based on the model.

The industrial sector is not aided with security standards in the same extent as the IT domain. The ISA/IEC 62443 family of standards is being developed from the ISA99 US standard family jointly by ISA (International Society of Automation) and IEC (International Electrotechnical Commission). These target Industrial Automation and Control Systems (IACS) security [6]. The concept to perform security risk assessment and management is similar to what is outlined in the ISO 27000 family [18].

In order to identify the possible safety risks in a system, safety analysis investigates potentially hazardous situations for causes and probability. Based on the severity of the hazardous situation and the probability of the cause, the risk can be calculated. The FMEA method [2] is a well known and thoroughly used method for the safety assessment.

There have been some research on performing safety and security analyses in combination. In [14] an overview of approaches and methods are given based on the SAE J3061 guidebook [5] for analyzing security in the automotive domain. Kriaa et al. developed a survey of approaches combining Safety and Security for Industrial Control Systems [13]. The challenge with most of the presented methods is that they focus only on the connected safety-critical system and not on the complete communication system, e.g. from the safety-critical system to the IT back end.

The safety domain is aware of these issues and started to tackle the new challenges of considering safety and security in an holistic way. The IEC 61508 standard [3] is applied when no domain-specific standard is available, and is used to develop domain-specific standards.

Complementing this activity, IEC workgroup TC 65/WG 20 "Industrial-process measurement, control and automation – Framework to bridge the requirements for safety and security" works on how to combine safety with security engineering and lifecycles.

3 Case Study

The Arrowhead project produced an interoperability framework for IoT automation systems. The framework has been demonstrated on different use-cases; many of them comprising CPS. We have performed safety and security assessment on an automotive use-case. The use-case scenario was to aggregate device measurement data at customer test sites into the backend of the equipment provider for statistical and diagnostic purposes in order to optimize the maintenance schedule of the measurement equipment. There have been multiple versions of the solution architecture for each of the three generations of the Arrowhead framework. We had performed risk analysis and based on the result the architecture had been refined. Beside analysis and assessment huge emphasis was also put on service level security in the Arrowhead framework [19].

The use case is a legacy system, used in automotive production for the testing of engines, which needs to communicate with the system manufacturer. The goal is to collect system status data in order to optimize maintenance, predict and increase system availability. The challenge in adopting a legacy system to meet the needs IoT and collaborative automation was to handle the increased attack surface without completely re-designing the existing system. There was no reference guides to follow for system adoption. This resulted in a sequential process of safety and security risk analysis and threat mitigation solution.

During the first assessment we identified the most critical assets. These are the configuration and test data on the test system, and the data in the backend, which must be kept confidential.

Figure 1 shows a high level data-flow model of the analyzed use-case created in the Microsoft Threat Modeling Tool. The model can be divided in two major

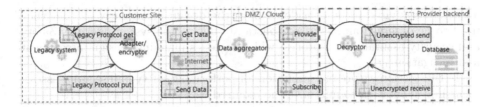

Fig. 1. Generic threat model (Color figure online)

parts, the local network and the cloud/backend network; these are outlined by red striped rectangles. These are called trust boundaries, in order to express a separation of security requirements. The other form of expressing separation of trust is a red striped line crossing data flows, in this case the Internet as the communication channel.

Most elements of the architecture are modeled as processes depicted as spheres in the figure. Processes exhibit the widest functionality but can also be affected by most of the possible threats according to the threat analysis model detailed in the next section. The model consists of three main parts:

- Customer site: includes the measurement CPS, which is the legacy system designed without extensive security measures or the need to be connected to the Internet. In the described use case it is connected through its supported legacy protocol to an adapter. This adapter provides security by encrypting the data and also implements an Internet transport protocol. Data is sent periodically to the service provider under the supervision of the customer to maintain the desired level of information privacy.
- DMZ/Cloud: the remote site in the DMZ (Demilitarized Zone), which can be in a cloud or a separated network of the service provider. The process called as data aggregator implements a publish-subscribe interface, but also acts as a firewall, authenticating the clients. The service provider can subscribe for the data of particular clients.
- Provider backend: comprised of elements on the provider network such as the decryptor which requests, receives and decrypts the data from the measurement devices, processes the data, calculates statistics and schedules maintenance of the equipment. This latter information is communicated back to the customer through another communication channel. Some of the data is put in the database unencrypted.

Even on this basic model the threat modeling tool detects 74 different security threats.

4 Safety and Security Assessment

Assuring safety and security are very crucial both in IT and industrial systems in order to avoid loss of value, damage or injury. Therefore safety and security aspects are advised to be considered from the design phase early on, but they need to be observed and assessed constantly during the system lifetime. Safety and security assurance is a process which includes planning, design, assessment and mitigation.

In this section we present a solution for performing safety and security assessment in combination to minimize the required effort.

4.1   Security Assessment

The goal of security assessment is to identify weaknesses in the system under analysis, and evaluate the risk these pose on the system. The security analysis method which we have followed is in line with security risk assessment described in ISA/IEC 62443 [6]. According to the standard, at first we identify potential vulnerabilities in the system which can pose threats; then assess the risks in terms of their consequence and likelihood; finally, the risks are communicated and understood in the form of summarizing and documenting results that can be used for evaluation and treatment. Our security analysis approach comprises several steps, which are detailed below.

Threat Modeling. The process of risk assessment generally has an initial step: modeling the system under investigation. This can be performed on many levels of detail, but usually is an iterative process by creating a simple model and iteratively refining it for the required detail. The sufficient level of detail is determined by the detail-level that the expected results should point out.

The most widely used modeling format in this domain is the Data Flow Diagram (DFD). DFDs can model system components and their interactions. Microsoft's threat modeling tool [15] allows DFD modeling of the system, as well as creating a threat catalog based on the DFD. A DFD may consist of the following elements: External Entity (EE, e.g. users), Processing Node (PN, e.g. a process), Data Store (DS) and Data Flows (DF). Assembling the threat catalog from the DFD is based on the STRIDE method [11]. The acronym stands for the six possible threat categories. Table 2 lists these categories, the security objectives that are violated by that kind of threats and the components where such threat may arise.

Table 2. STRIDE threat categories and affected security objectives

Threat	Affected security objective	Involved element
Spoofing	Authentication	EE, PN
Tampering	Integrity	DF, DS, PN
Repudiation	Non-Repudiation	EE, PN
Information disclosure	Confidentiality	DF, DS, PN
Denial of Service	Availability	DF, DS, PN
Elevation of Privilege	Authorization	PN

The idea behind building a threat catalog from a DFD is that a vulnerability is only possible due to an interaction between DFD components. The components between te endpoints of a data flow determine what kind of vulnerability may be exploited in that flow as shown in the table.

Risk Assessment. Risk assessment determines threat criticality based on the likelihood of exploitation, and the resulting impact. Several ranking schemes can be used. We have found ETSI TVRA a simple-to-apply, but sufficiently detailed method. It is a qualitative analysis method, described in standard TS 102 165-1 [4]. According to this, the likelihood measure depends on two factors, (i) the difficulty of executing a successful attack and (ii) the motivation an attacker may have behind it. This latter relates to what an attacker can gain from the attack, which can be either objective (e.g. information) but also subjective (e.g. revenge).

Table 3. Result of security risk assessment

Threat name	Type	Diffi-culty	Moti-vation	Likely-hood	Scale	Detect-ability	Impact	Risk
Improper data protection of Database	Interception	None	High	Likely	Whole NW	Low	Significant	Critical
Spoofing of Database	Masquerade	None	High	Likely	Whole NW	Low	Significant	Critical

The impact measure is determined by the scale level (extent) of the attack and detectability (and recoverability) of the attack, e.g. the difficulty to restore the system to the state prior the attack.

This standard qualifies each of the above measures in three levels. For each threat, the resulting risk can have three possible values as well, namely: minor, major or critical. In Table 3 we listed the threats which possess the most critical risk as the result of the risk assessment process.

4.2 Safety Assessment

The goal of safety assessment is to identify those risks that are related to the system, and have non-malicious and internal causes. We have found that the FMEA method can be applied to Data Flow Diagrams (DFD), the same model we use for the security assessment, and delivers results with a similar level of granularity as our security assessment approach.

Adaption of Failure Modes. FMEA was originally developed for hardware and electronic elements. For such elements, failure mode lists based on experience and probability data based on reports and testing of components exists. As an example, the Siemens Norm 29500 [16] is often used to calculate reliability and failure data for electronic components. It contains extensive lists for Failure Modes for different types of electronic components and formulas to calculate failure probability based on use and environmental conditions. In order to apply the assessment method to software and network based systems – where failure modes are more likely to be caused by software bugs than by failing resistors – some adaption is necessary. While Failure Modes for hardware components are clear failure modes, they can be much harder to define for software components. Haapanen [9] surveys different approaches for FMEA regarding software components.

Table 4. Faults and affected elements

Fault description	Element			
	Function	File/ Database	Input/ Output	Flow
Missing Data e.g. lost message, data loss due to hw failure		x		x
Incorrect Data e.g. inaccurate, spurious data		x		x
Timing of Data e.g. obsolete data, data arrives too soon for processing			x	x
Extra Data e.g. data redundancy, data over-flow		x	x	
Halt/Abnormal Termination e.g. hung or dead-locked at this point	x			
Omitted Event e.g. event does not take place, but execution continues			x	
Incorrect Logic e.g. preconditions are inaccurate; event does not implement intent	x			
Timing/Order e.g. event occurs in wrong order; event occurs too early/late	x		x	x

We have created a mapping between the list of failure modes of software components and the elements of the DFD that are prone to that failures. This mapping, shown partially in Table 4 is similar to how STRIDE defines which kind of threat affect which diagram component. This makes it possible to use a single system model for the safety and the security assessments and automate the process. This can also facilitate the exchange and cooperation between safety and security experts and to avoid differences based on different system representations.

The goal of FMEA is to consider failure modes, the effects and probability of these for all elements of a system. Starting with a system model, in our case the DFD of the use case, for each element the potential failure modes are identified based on the above table. Then potential system level effects for each failure mode are investigated and causes determined.

Table 5. Result of safety risk assessment

Element	Threat name	Type	Likely-hood	Scale	Detect-ability	Impact	Risk
Database	Error in config.	Incorr. Data	Un-likely	Whole NW	Low	Safety Critical	Critical
Adapter - test system comm.	Incorr. timing	Timing	Likely	Node	Low	Relia-bility	Major
Adapter - test system comm	Msgs. transm. twice → undef. system state	Extra data	Possible	Node	Low	Safety Critical	Critical

Risk Assessment. We utilized the basic risk assessment approach as defined in IEC 60812 [1] for the results of the FMEA analysis. While it is not possible to calculate the probability exactly like for hardware elements, we discussed each element and its *Failure Modes* with domain experts and estimated a quantitative likelihood, divided in 5 levels. In order to ease the cooperation with the security experts, we adopted a similar approach for impact assessment. The *Scale* level describes whether a *Failure Mode* only effects part of one installation or multiple installations, recoverability was adapted to include *Detectability*. This is similar as envisioned for the FMEDA, which extends the basic FMEA with a *Detectability* parameter. *Impact* ranges from no impact to safety/reliability or availability impact. Due to the connected risk, a safety-impact leads automatically to a risk-rating of critical. Table 5 shows the most critical safety threats found as the results of the safety assessment.

4.3 Combined Assessment

Performing detailed safety and security analysis on an industrial use-case is a very time-consuming task. We have found that safety and security are not completely separable properties of such systems. We have shown that security and safety analysis can be automated using a common model and risk analysis guidelines. The first step of the analysis is to create a system model. A Data Flow Diagram represents system components as interacting processes. The process is the most basic entity which can represent the encompassed state machine of both hardware and software elements. We used the STRIDE method for creating a security threat catalog, and also adapted its methodology for creating the safety threat catalog.

The combined method assembles the threat catalog based on the data flows connecting components and the constraints of those. The same way as for security we can also define safety constraints, so the algorithm for security threat generation can be extended for safety as well. This realization implies that we can use the same system model and automate the process of both security and safety assessments. There is more to deliberate on the impact and risk levels of safety threats as there can be dangers to humans involved – which obviously cannot be ranked the same level as data corruption and financial losses.

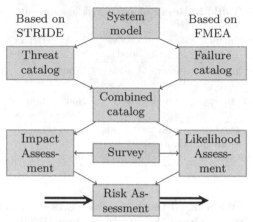

Risk on Safety and Security Objectives

Fig. 2. Combined risk assessment process

The STRIDE threat generation process puts threats into different categories according to what security objectives are affected. During risk assessment for each threat the risk level can be calculated separately for all the objectives. These objectives can however be amended with safety related ones, which solves the threat ranking issue and the fact that certain security threats can have impact on safety. This is what we have followed in our combined analysis method, which is depicted in Fig. 2.

4.4 Advantages of the Combined Assessment

The combined assessment has the following advantages.

Ruling Out Duplication of the Assessments. Safety and Security assessments have a lot of common, overlapping issues in all domains (such as hardware, information handling, etc.). As a natural advantage of the combined assessment, it saves a lot of effort by handling these commonalities at once.

Combined Safety and Security Catalog. The combined catalog is built from the Threat Catalog (of security assessment) and the Failure Catalog (of safety assessment). Its elements can be commonly addressed by the impact and likelihood assessments. This allows raising awareness on issues that has high impact or likelihood on both safety and security.

Supporting Multi-dimensional Decisions. One of the desired output of both the safety and the security assessments is to provide information on system development decisions (even if the system is deployed already). As we pointed out in the introduction, these are multi-dimensional decisions, that are supposed to find the balance between security, safety, privacy, reliability, power efficiency, and even price. The combined assessment supports this decision by handling four factors at once: beside security and safety, privacy and reliability is also assessed. Privacy issues are part of the threat catalog, reliability issues are part of the failure catalog – and these are both utilized when the combined catalog is created.

5   Conclusion

Collaborative automation systems invoke fresh motivation for safety and security assessments, since they mix issues related to physical equipment (e.g. industrial machinery), data handling (e.g. storage and networking) and virtualized IT solutions (e.g. cloud computing).

When such Cyber-Physical Systems are used in industrial applications, both safety and security issues need to be covered, otherwise the meaning of IoT would quickly inflate from Internet of Things towards Internet of Trash. CPS systems that have elements with security vulnerabilities can be a potential threat to human life. Such ideas conceived our concept of creating a combined safety and security assessment method.

Our practical experiences of utilizing various standards when assessing complex and extensive CPS systems lead to the realization of a combined safety and security assessment method, described in this paper. The method builds upon STRIDE and FMEA approaches, and it uses a combined catalog for threats and failures – in order to conduct impact and likelihood assessments as an input for assessing risk.

The advantages of this combined assessment include (i) saving effort by handling the commonalities of separate assessments at once; (ii) utilizing the combined catalog for raising awareness on issues that has high impact or likelihood on both areas, and (iii) supporting multi-dimensional decision making by decreasing the problem space through tackling security, safety, reliability and privacy issues, as well.

References

1. IEC 60812: Analysis techniques for system reliability - procedure for failure mode and effects analysis (FMEA)
2. IEC 60812: Analysis techniques for system reliability - Procedure for failure mode and effects analysis (FMEA) (2006)
3. ISO 61508: Functional safety of electrical/electronic/programmable electronic safety-related systems (2010)
4. ETSI - TS 102 165-1: Telecommunications and Internet converged Services and Protocols for Advanced Networking (TISPAN); Methods and protocols; Part 1: Method and proforma for Threat, Risk, Vulnerability Analysis (2011)
5. SAE J3061: Cybersecurity Guidebook for Cyber-Physical Vehicle Systems (2016)

6. ISA: The 62443 series of standards - industrial automation and control systems security, December 2016. http://isa99.isa.org/Public/Information/The-62443-Series-Overview.pdf

7. Bloomfield, R., Netkachova, K., Stroud, R.: Security-informed safety: if it's not secure, it's not safe. In: Gorbenko, A., Romanovsky, A., Kharchenko, V. (eds.) SERENE 2013. LNCS, vol. 8166, pp. 17–32. Springer, Heidelberg (2013). doi:10.1007/978-3-642-40894-6_2

8. Caralli, R., Stevens, J., Young, L., Wilson, W.: Introducing octave allegro: improving the information security risk assessment process. Technical report, CMU/SEI-2007-TR-012, Software Engineering Institute, Carnegie Mellon University, Pittsburgh (2007). http://resources.sei.cmu.edu/library/asset-view.cfm?AssetID=8419

9. Haapanen, P., Helminen, A.: Failure mode and effects analysis of software-based automation systems. Techncial report, Radiation and Nuclear Safety Authority, Helsinki (Finland) (2002)

10. Henniger, O., Apvrille, L., Fuchs, A., Roudier, Y., Ruddle, A., Weyl, B.: Security requirements for automotive on-board networks. In: 2009 9th International Conference on Intelligent Transport Systems Telecommunications, (ITST), pp. 641–646, October 2009

11. Howard, M., Lipner, S.: The Security Development Lifecycle. Microsoft Press, Redmond (2006)

12. Islam, M.M., Lautenbach, A., Sandberg, C., Olovsson, T.: A risk assessment framework for automotive embedded systems. In: Proceedings of the 2nd ACM International Workshop on Cyber-Physical System Security, CPSS 2016, pp. 3–14. ACM, New York (2016). http://doi.acm.org/10.1145/2899015.2899018

13. Kriaa, S., Pietre-Cambacedes, L., Bouissou, M., Halgand, Y.: A survey of approaches combining safety and security for industrial control Systems. Reliab. Eng. Syst. Saf. (2015). http://linkinghub.elsevier.com/retrieve/pii/S0951832015000538

14. Macher, G., Armengaud, E., Brenner, E., Kreiner, C.: A review of threat analysis and risk assessment methods in the automotive context. In: Skavhaug, A., Guiochet, J., Bitsch, F. (eds.) SAFECOMP 2016. LNCS, vol. 9922, pp. 130–141. Springer, Cham (2016). doi:10.1007/978-3-319-45477-1_11

15. Microsoft: Microsoft Threat Modeling Tool 2016 download page (2016). https://www.microsoft.com/en-us/download/details.aspx?id=49168

16. SN 29500: Failure rates of components 6 (1996–06)

17. Park, K.C., Shin, D.H.: Security assessment framework for IoT service. Telecommun. Syst. **64**(1), 193–209 (2017). doi:10.1007/s11235-016-0168-0 http://dx.doi.org/10.1007/s11235-016-0168-0

18. Piggin, R.S.H.: Development of industrial cyber security standards: IEC 62443 for SCADA and Industrial Control System security. In: IET Conference on Control and Automation 2013: Uniting Problems and Solutions, pp. 1–6, June 2013

19. Plósz, S., Hegedűs, C., Varga, P.: Advanced security considerations in the arrowhead framework. In: Skavhaug, A., Guiochet, J., Schoitsch, E., Bitsch, F. (eds.) SAFECOMP 2016. LNCS, vol. 9923, pp. 234–245. Springer, Cham (2016). doi:10.1007/978-3-319-45480-1_19

20. Scandariato, R., Wuyts, K., Joosen, W.: A descriptive study of Microsoft's threat modeling technique. Requirements Eng. **20**(2), 163–180 (2015). doi:10.1007/s00766-013-0195-2

21. Wiseman, D.R.: Risk, reliability and safety: innovating theory and practice. In: Attack tree analysis, pp. 1023–1027. CRC Press, September 2016. doi:10.1201/9781315374987-154

Software Updates in Safety and Security Co-engineering

Imanol Mugarza[1]([⊠]), Jorge Parra[1], and Eduardo Jacob[2]

[1] IK4-Ikerlan Technology Research Centre, Dependable Embedded Systems Area,
Po J.M. Arizmendiarrieta, 2, 20500 Arrasate-Mondragón, Spain
{imugarza,jparra}@ikerlan.es
[2] Faculty of Enginnering, University of the Basque Country UPV/EHU,
Alameda Urquijo s/n, 48013 Bilbao, Spain
Eduardo.Jacob@ehu.eus

Abstract. The application of Industry 4.0 in automation systems leads to a higher interconnectivity among machines, devices, sensors, the cloud and humans. Nevertheless, this paradigm leaves open the possibility of new cyber-security threats and attacks against industrial control systems, even for those that perform safety-critical functions. Consequently, software updates are needed in order to fix the vulnerabilities and bugs discovered on these systems. This article presents a review of safety and security standards with respect to software updates. In addition to this, a roadmap of standards for the development of safe and secure systems is provided.

Keywords: Safety · Security · Maintainability · Standards · Software updates

1 Introduction

Embedded systems are used in a wide range of applications, such as commercial, medical, industrial and military. The use of these systems has grown exponentially during the last decade. According to Embert and Jones, the worldwide market of embedded systems was around 160 billion € in 2009, with an annual growth of 9% [1]. Besides, more than 98% of all produced microprocessors were embedded microprocessors. One of the roles of these embedded systems in the industrial field such as automotive, railway or machinery sectors, is to replace or supplement physical control mechanisms. Moreover, one or more safety functions are carried out on these systems. These services prevent hazardous situations or actions which could impact on the safety of persons and/or environment.

These safety-related systems were isolated from the open communications channels. Nevertheless, within the scope of industry 4.0, the capability of sensors, machines, devices and people to be connected and communicated each other is intended. Thus, due to the high inter-connectivity among these industrial control systems, security concerns gain importance, specially for safety-critical systems. Because of the increasing number of cyber-attacks against these systems,

© Springer International Publishing AG 2017
S. Tonetta et al. (Eds.): SAFECOMP 2017 Workshops, LNCS 10489, pp. 199–210, 2017.
DOI: 10.1007/978-3-319-66284-8_17

the safety engineering community has started to address those cyber-security threats, which can alter the proper functioning of safety-related systems [2,3].

The differentiation of the safety and security terms lead to misunderstanding situations. Even some scientific and normative literature often provide different meanings for these terms. Furthermore, some languages, such as Spanish or Swedish, provide just a single word for both concepts, which are "seguridad" and "säkerhet" respectively. Thus, neither the linguistics aids to clarify these concepts. As stated by the International Atomic Energy Agency (IAEA) [4], there is not a specific distinction between the safety and security terms. Security tries to reduce malicious risks, prevent misuse and attacks in order to protect assets. On the contrary, safety attempts to prevent accidents and incidents which could impact on health.

The first significant cyber-attack compromising safety and security which targeted industrial control systems, was the Stuxnet computer virus. It was identified in 2010 and according to Ralph Langen it is possible to assume that the Natanz Uranium Enrichment plant in Iran was the only goal [5]. As stated by Kaspersky Lab [6], the number of vulnerabilities in industrial control systems keeps growing. In 2015, 189 vulnerabilities were published, where 42% of them had medium severity and 49% were critical. In order to protect safety-critical industrial control systems from cyber-attacks, such as Stuxnet, software patches and updates are needed, so cyber-security vulnerabilities, bugs, operability and reliability issues are resolved.

A patch is a piece software produced with the aim of fixing a bug or improving the usability of a computer program. These components are then used to update a given computer software. As noted by the DHS National Cyber Security Division [7], patches concerning industrial control systems have commonly addressed stability and functionality issues instead of security ones. A patch management program for asset owners is proposed, which includes the following elements: *Configuration Management Plan*, *Patch Management Plan*, *Patch Testing*, *Backup/Archive Plan*, *Incident Response Plan*, and *Disaster Recovery Plan*. Moreover, a patching analysis is provided, where first a vulnerability analysis to determine when and if a patch should be applied to the industrial control system is recommended. A patch process for industrial control systems is then suggested.

In this paper a review of standards from the point of view of software updates is provided. Concurrently, a roadmap of standards for the design, development and maintenance of safe and secure systems is also given. The aim of this work is to provide a state of the art of current industrial safety and security standards focusing on software updates.

2   Review of Standards

The IEC 61508 is the main international standard for electrical, electronic and programmable electronic safety related systems, which is contemplated as the fundamental functional safety standard [8]. The requirements for ensuring that systems are designed, implemented, operated and maintained to provide the required safety integrity level (SIL) are specified. Although the IEC 61508 standard is generic and applicable to all kinds of industry, it has been adapted to application-specific safety domains. Some of these refined standards are for example:

- Automotive: *Road vehicles – Functional safety* (ISO 26262 [9])
- Railway applications:
  - *Specification and demonstration of reliability, availability, maintainability and safety* (IEC 62278 [10])
  - *Communication, signalling and processing systems - Software for railway control and protection systems* (IEC 62279 [11])
  - *Communication, signalling and processing systems - Safety related electronic systems for signalling* (IEC 62425 [12])
- Process industry sector: *Functional safety - Safety instrumented systems for the process industry sector* (IEC 61511 [13]):

As far as security is concerned, several well-known standards are widely applied on the development, certification and management of Information Technology (IT) system and devices, such as the ISO 27000 series or Common Criteria. However, as pointed out by Paul [3], it seems that each safety standardisation institution produce their own domain-specific security regulation instead of creating generic ones for security.

The ISO 27000 series provide information security management and best practice recommendations [14]. This normative introduces the Information Security Management System (ISMS), where the purpose of it is to manage information security risks through information security controls. In addition, continuous feedback and improvements activities are incorporated to the ISMS. The aim of these adjustments is to respond to new threats and/or vulnerabilities. This framework is applicable to any kind of organization, which covers more than just cyber-security concerns. Organizations are encouraged to assess, supervise and handle their information security risks by following the guidances and recommendations defined in the standard. However, this standard does not cover the design and development of secure systems. On the contrary, the Common Criteria, also known as ISO 15408 [15], is a framework, where the functional and assurance requirements for a given product are first defined and successively evaluated by a security evaluation laboratory to determine if they actually satisfy those claims. Even it is mainly focused for IT environments, industrial control systems can also be evaluated.

In order to address security issues on industrial control systems, the International Society of Automation (ISA) created the IEC 62443 standard, which addresses the security of industrial automation and control systems. The following Fig. 1 presents the selected and analysed safety and security standards, which are depicted as undashed boxes. In addition, the diagram shows related standards which may be taken into account for the development of safe and secure systems, even if safety or security concerns are not directly addressed on them. These standards, shown as dashed elements, are not studied.

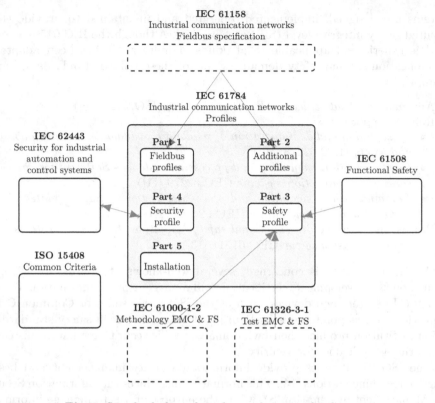

Fig. 1. Standards for safe and secure system development

In the Fig. 1 above, it can be seen that the IEC 61784 is used to associate safety and security domain standards, which is also ilustrated within the mentioned normative [16]. Even the ISO 15408 (Common Criteria) is reviewed, there is not a direct and clear association with other standards. This is the reason why this element is not connected to any other item in the diagram. The co-engineering of safety and security was also analyzed at the ITEA 3 MERgE project, where multi-concerns, particularly focused on safety and security co-engineering were tried to be efficiently handled [2,3,17].

2.1   IEC-62443

The ISA/IEC-62443 is a series of standards, technical reports, and related information that define procedures for implementing electronically secure Industrial Automation and Control Systems (IACS) [18]. This standard, created by the International Society of Automation ISA, was originally named ISA-99. Nevertheless, this normative was renumbered to ISA-62443 in 2010. The purpose of this modification was to align ISA documents with the analogous IEC standards. The IEC-62443 standards and technical reports are organized into four general categories, which are *General, Policies and Procedures, System* and *Component*:

1. **General** provides background information such as concepts, terminology and metrics
2. **Policies and procedures** addresses security and patch management policies and procedures
3. **System** provides system development requirements and guidances
4. **Component** provides product development and technical requirements, intended for product vendors

Within the scope of this normative, a special attention is given to software updates. An evidence of it is that it provides a dedicated document deferring to patch management within the **Policies and procedures** category. This technical report is the **IEC 62443-2-3: Patch management in the IACS environment**, which states that patch management is an element of a complete cyber security strategy, where cyber-security vulnerabilities, bugs, operability and reliability issues are resolved [19]. However, the standard does not differentiate among operating system, library or application-oriented patches. The aim of it is to provide a generic guidance for all type of patches. Note that, "Applying patches is a risk management decision" [19]. The software upgrade may be rejected or delayed if the cost to apply the patch is greater than the risk evaluated cost.

Two different guidances on patching are provided by the IEC 62443-2-3 technical document [19]. The first one is oriented to product suppliers, while the second one to asset owners. Once the procedure for patching is defined and documented, it can be shared with the individuals who are responsible to execute it. This task is essential, so patching activities are carried out efficiently and appropriately by the personal. This assignment is applicable for both product suppliers and asset owners. On the one hand, the product supplier guidance on patching, provides a reference procedure to develop and distribute new software updates. This guidance defines four major activities: *Discovery of vulnerabilities*, *Development of security updates*, *Distribution of security information* and *Communication and outreach*.

On the other hand, the main goal of asset owner guidance on patching is to describe patch management procedures for the asset owner. Four major activities for patch management are explained. These activities are: *Information gathering*, *Project planning and implementation*, *Procedures and policies for patch management* and *Operating a patch management system*.

In line with these patch management procedures, a patch lifecycle model is also given. This representation defines a series of states through which a patch passes from the time that is available by a third party or a product supplier until it is installed or rejected by the asset owner. Not all available patches will be approved and installed. Thus, it is important to keep the track of all available patches for an efficient patch management procedure. In addition, clear evidences will be needed to gather to ensure that the system will behave correctly functionally once the patch is applied. The following Fig. 2 depicts the patch lifecycle state model, which is divided into two main parts. The first part corresponds to the states maintained by the product supplier. In contrast, the second part conforms to the states associated with the asset owner.

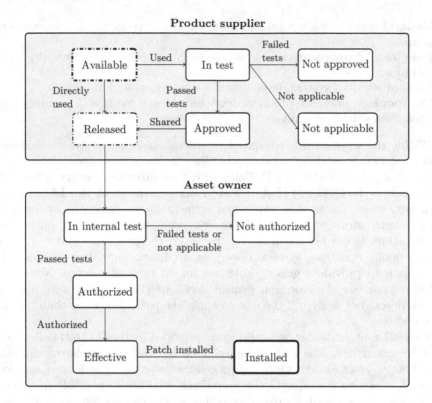

Fig. 2. Patch lifecycle model

Furthermore, as illustrated by the standard, the asset owner is also able to directly gather available patches and release, share or distribute them. This is the reason why the *Available* and *Released* states are shown as dashed elements in the Fig. 2 above. The following Table 1 gives the description of each of the states defined in the patch lifecyle model depicted in the Fig. 2 [19]:

The IEC 62443-2-3 [19] document provides adequate technical guidelines defining how software patches for industrial systems should be applied. Nevertheless, other patch management issues are not contemplated, for example how and where these software patches will be stored and tested. Procedures on how all the information and data will be handled. A security policy describing the permissions for accessing this information and performing given activities is also needed. It may be possible that an agreed authorization of several entities, such a production line supervisors or project and safety managers is necessary to approve and endorse a given software update. Tasks and responsibilities for each entity needs to be determined too.

Table 1. Patch lifecycle states

Patch state	Patch state definition	Conducted by
Available	The patch has been provided by a third party or an IACS supplier but has not been tested	Asset owner Product supplier
In test	The patch is being tested	Product supplier
Not approved	The patch has failed the testing and should not be used, unless and until the patch has been *Approved*	
Not applicable	The patch has been tested and is not considered relevant to IACS use	
Approved	The patch has passed testing	
Released	The patch is released for use or third party, or the patch may be directly applicable by the asset owner for their internally developed systems	Asset owner Product supplier
In internal test	The patch is being tested by the testing team	Asset owner
Not authorized	The patch has failed internal testing, or may not be applicable	
Authorized	The patch is released and meets company standards for updatable devices, or by inspection did not need testing	
Effective	The patch is posted for use	
Installed	The patch is installed on the system	

2.2 Common Criteria

The Common Criteria, also known as ISO 15408 or simply CC, is a framework in which users can indicate their security functional and assurance requirements (SFR and SAR respectively) through protection profiles (PP). Manufacturers can then develop their products upon the specifications described in those protection profiles and make claims about security attributes of their products. A testing laboratory would be the responsible to evaluate those products to determine if they meet the claims manifested by the vendors, where the level of confidence is also established [15,20,21]. A certification process starts with a *Security Target* (ST) document. This report identifies the security properties of the product or system which is intended to be evaluated, referred as Target Of Evaluation (TOE). It includes an overview of the product or system, possible security threats, detailed information on the implementation of all security features and any claims against a protection profile, which defines security requirements for a class of security device such as network firewalls.

Albeit the Common Criteria is mainly focused on IT environments, a protection profile for industrial systems exits, which is the *System Protection Profile for Industrial Control Systems* (SPP-ICS) provided by the National Institute of Standards and Technology (NIST) [22]. This protection profile includes security functional requirements (SFRs) and security assurance requirements (SAR). Nevertheless, as stated within the document, it has been written in such a way that it may be used as the basis for preparing a System Security Target for a specific ICS or as the basis for a more detailed SPP. Despite the fact that a new protection profile for safety-related communications in railway was proposed by [23], at the time of writing, protection profiles targeting industrial control and/or safety-critical systems are missing. Consequently, albeit this standard can be used to certify wide range of IT security products such as operative systems, databases or smart cards, protection profiles for the industrial domain are needed to be defined still.

Some of the protection profiles introduce objectives and requirements concerning software or firmware updates. An example of such profiles is the Protection Profile for *Smart Card Reader with PIN-Pad supporting eID based on Extended Access control*, created by the *Bundesamt für Sicherheit in der Informationstechnik* [24]. As defined in this document, software updates must be signed, and installed if the signature is correctly verified. On the contrary, industrial control system oriented protection profiles do not include any requirement concerning software updates. Indeed, within the Protection Profile for safety-related communication in railway automation, objectives, requirements or procedures related to software updates were not contemplated [23]. Thus, even that this frameworks provides a sound security assurance method, protection profiles, including software update requirements, are not present for industrial control systems. Indeed, these systems, such as programmable logic controllers (PLC), may also be designed to achieve, at the same time, safety certifications.

2.3   IEC-61784

The *digital data communications for measurement and control* IEC-61784 standard defines a set of protocol specific communication profiles based mainly on the IEC-61158 [16]. The purpose of the IEC-61784 is to aid to properly state the compliance to the IEC-61158 series, where fieldbuses for industrial control systems are specified. Functional safety and information security profiles are also addressed. As stated in the third part, additional security requirements are detailed in IEC 62443 series.

This standard includes several communication profile families, which specify one or more communication profiles. The specifications for the communication protocol stack are then determined for each profile, where the minimal set of required services at the *Application* layer are provided. In absence of this layer, minimal set of required services at the *Data Link* layer are indicated. Specification of options at the intermediate layers are also defined. It has to be mentioned that devices or systems complying to the same communication profile will accomplish a direct interoperability between them. The IEC-61784 standard is divided among 5 parts:

- IEC-61784-1: Profile sets for continuous and discrete manufacturing relative to fieldbus use in industrial control systems

- IEC-61784-2: Physical layer specification and service definition
- IEC-61784-3: Functional safety fieldbuses
- IEC-61784-4: Profiles for secure communications in industrial network
- IEC-61784-5: Installation

Safety communications provide a mandatory confidence in the information transportation between two or more participants in a safety-related systems and enough reliance of safe behaviour in the event of communication errors or failures. As far as profiles for secure communications in industrial network is concerned, this part of the IEC-61784 standard provides security communication profiles, where some of them permit to be used as a black channel for functional safety applications. For this purpose, the delay of the secured channel are bounded. However, it should be noted that just a draft version from 2005 of the IEC 61784-4 document has been found. The contents have been overlapped by the IEC-62443 standard.

Software updates are directly related with these communication profiles. Since, usually, when a transition from a given communication protocol to another one is required, the protocol stack needs to be modified, which is the software implementation of the networking protocols. This may be the case when a non-secure communication protocol is requested to be replaced with a secure one, or when a higher safety confidence communication protocol is wanted.

2.4   IEC-61508

The IEC-61508 normative is contemplated as the basic functional safety standard applicable to all domains. It covers the safety issues of electrical, electronic or programmable electronic systems or devices, concerns like long-term exposure to a toxic substance or an electrical shock are not within the scope of it [8,25]. It is divided among seven parts, where the first three parts contain the normative itself and the rest ones are guidelines and examples. This normative aims at reducing the risk, which is a function of frequency or probability of the hazardous event and the event consequence severity, to a tolerable level. For this purpose, safety functions are applied.

Four different safety integrity levels are established. Each level defines the risks involved in the system applications, where SIL4 is used for applications entailing high risks. For systems that operate on a low demand mode, SIL specifies an allowable probability that the system will fail to respond on demand. On the contrary, for systems that operate on continuous mode or systems that operate on high demand mode, SIL specifies an allowable frequency of dangerous failure. The standard covers the complete safety life cycle for the development of the system, consisted on sixteen main steps. They are divided among three groups: *analysis*, *realization* and *operation*. These phases specify how should be developed and maintained a safety-related system (both hardware and software).

At the hazard and risk analysis phase, the hazards, hazardous events and hazardous situations are agreed so the risks associated with those events can be determined. Due to the security threats, this evaluation needs to be extended in case of malevolent or unauthorised actions are identified. During this security threat analysis, deliberate misuse, vandalism and criminalism are taken into account [25]. However, even if safety hazards and risks probably will not change through operational period, security threats evolve continuously. This means that security issues, such as vulnerabilities and bugs need to be addressed at the *overall operation, maintenance and repair* and *overall modification and retrofit* phases. In the same manner as functional safety audits are carried out, security audits shall be performed.

In case a security issue arises, a planning for any modification or retrofit activity, and an evaluation activity to analyse the impact of those modifications on the functional safety shall be completed. On the assumption that these security issues compromise the functional safety or security properties, the standard does not specify how to deal with those security issues, and how to fix them. Thus, a security patch management system is needed, where patch management guidelines provided by the IEC 62443 standard [18,19] and the security management framework proposed by the ISO 27000 [14] may be employed or connected together with the functional safety management system.

3 Conclusions

This article provides a picture of current safety and security standards for industrial control systems. The IEC 61508 [8,25] and the IEC 62443 [18] could be considered the reference standards when it comes to the design, development and maintenance of safe and secure systems. Since the IEC 62443 addresses security issues and challenges for generic industrial control systems, it could also be applied as the security-related guide for domain specific safety standards, such as automotive, railway or process industry [9–13]. At the time of writing, the Common Criteria framework [15,20–22] provides the necessary facilities for the design, development and maintenance of secure industrial systems. However, protection profiles for industrial automation systems, which shall also define objectives and requirements with respect to software updates, are missing. In case of the ISO 27000 series [14], even that information security management and best practice recommendations are given, it does not provide any guideline, procedure and/or requirements for the design and development of secure systems.

In conclusion, concepts and methods from the Information Security Management System (ISMS) [14], and the patch management guidelines proposed by the IEC 62443-2-3 [19] technical document would be necessary to build an effective and complete patch management system for safe and secure industrial systems, where all the information and data related to the software updates shall be handled. Procedures provided by tha DHS National Cyber Security Division [7] may also be taken into account. The aim of this system is to determine which and how the available patches will be tested, approved, justified and applied to which system, and when are those activities performed, so confidentiality, integrity and availability of information and data, in addition to safety properties are ensured.

References

1. Ebert, C., Jones, C.: Embedded software: facts, figures, and future. Computer **42**(4), 0042–0052 (2009)
2. Paul, S., Rioux, L.: Over 20 years of research in cybersecurity and safety engineering: a short bibliography. In: Conference: 6th International Conference on Safety and Security Engineering (SAFE) (2015). https://www.witpress.com/elibrary/wit-transactions-on-the-built-environment/151/33367
3. Paul, S.: On the meaning of security for safety (s4s). WIT Trans. Built Environ. **151**, 379–389 (2015)
4. International Atomic Energy Agency: IAEA Safety Glossary. International Atomic Energy Agency, Vienna (2008)
5. Langner, R.: Stuxnet: dissecting a cyberwarfare weapon. IEEE Secur. Priv. **9**, 49–51 (2011)
6. Kaspersky Security Intelligence. Industrial cybersecurity threat landscape (2016). Accessed 19 Nov 2016
7. Tom, S., Christiansen, D., Berrett, D.: Recommended practice for patch management of control systems. DHS Control System Security Program (CSSP) Recommended, Practice (2008)
8. International Electrotechnical Commission and Others: Functional safety of electrical/electronic/programmable electronic safety related systems. IEC 61508 (2000)
9. ISO/DIS 26262 - Road vehicles - Functional safety. Technical report, Geneva, Switzerland, July 2009
10. International Electrotechnical Commission and Others: IEC 62278: Railway applications-specification and demonstration of reliability, availability, maintainability and safety (rams). ed. Geneva, Switzerland: IEC Central Office, pp. 21–24 (2002)
11. International Electrotechnical Commission and Others: IEC 62279, railway applications-software for railway control and protection systems. ed. Geneva, Switzerland: IEC Central Office, pp. 21–24 (2002)
12. International Electrotechnical Commission and Others: IEC 62425: Railway applications - communication, signalling and processing systems - safety related electronic systems for signalling. ed. Geneva, Switzerland: IEC Central Office, pp. 21–24 (2002)
13. IEC 61511 Functional Safety - Safety instrumented systems for the process industry sector. Technical report, International Electrotechnical Commission (2003)
14. Disterer, G.: ISO/IEC 27000, 27001 and 27002 for information security management (2013)
15. The Common Criteria Recognition Agreement Members. Common Criteria for Information Technology Security Evaluation, September 2006. http://www.commoncriteriaportal.org/
16. International Electrotechnical Commission and Others: IEC 61784: Digital data communications for measurement and control. ed. Geneva, Switzerland: IEC Central Office, pp. 21–24 (2010)
17. Paul, S., Rioux, L., Wiander, T., Vallée, F.: Recommendations for security and safety co-engineering (release n 2). ITEA2 MERgE project (2015)
18. International Electrotechnical Commission and Others: IEC 62443: Industrial communication networks - network and system security. ed. Geneva, Switzerland: IEC Central Office (2010)

19. International Electrotechnical Commission and Others: IEC 62443-2-3: Industrial communication networks - network and system security - patch management in the IACS environment. ed. Geneva, Switzerland: IEC Central Office (2010)
20. SANS Institute: Common Criteria and Protection Profiles: How to Evaluate Information (2003)
21. SANS Institute: The Common Criteria ISO/IEC 15408 - The Insight, Some Thoughts, Questions and Issues (2001)
22. Melton, R., Fletcher, T., Earley, M.: System protection profile-industrial control systems. Version 1.0, National Institute of Standards and Technology (2004)
23. Bock, H.-H., Braband, J., Milius, B., Schäbe, H.: Towards an IT security protection profile for safety-related communication in railway automation. In: Ortmeier, F., Daniel, P. (eds.) SAFECOMP 2012. LNCS, vol. 7612, pp. 137–148. Springer, Heidelberg (2012). doi:10.1007/978-3-642-33678-2_12
24. Bundesamt für Sicherheit in der Informationstechnik: Common criteria protection profile standard reader - smart card reader with pin-pad supporting eid based on extended access control," Bundesamt für Sicherheit in der Informationstechnik (2013)
25. Smith, D.J., Simpson, K.G.: Handbook, Safety Critical Systems : A Straightfoward Guide To Functional Safety, IEC 61508 2010th edn. And Related Standards, Including Process IEC 61511 And Machinery IEC 62061 And ISO 13849. Elsevier (2010)

Detailed Analysis of Security Evaluation of Automotive Systems Based on JASO TP15002

Yasuyuki Kawanishi, Hideaki Nishihara, Daisuke Souma,
and Hirotaka Yoshida(✉)

SEI-AIST Cyber Security Cooperative Research Laboratory,
National Institute of Advanced Industrial Science and Technology (AIST),
1-8-31, Midorigaoka, Ikeda, Osaka 563-8577, Japan
hirotaka.yoshida@aist.go.jp

Abstract. In response to the recent Jeep hacking and recalls based on information security vulnerability in 2015, the significance of secure system design has become increasingly important in the automotive industry. From this perspective, security guidelines such as JASO TP 15002 and SAE J3061 have been published. To realize future connected-car systems or the future autonomous driving in line with these guidelines, many automotive Original Equipment Manufacturers (OEMs) and their major suppliers are now developing key components such as central gateways (CGW), telematics, or end Electronic Control Units (ECUs), with theses security concerns in mind. In this paper, we focus on a security evaluation that consists of model definition, threat identification, and the risk analysis in JASO TP 15002. To do so we first identify gaps between an understanding of JASO TP15002 and implementation of secure system design based on it. We then present a detailed analysis which includes new methods to fill this gap using illustrative examples such as CGW. As a result, we provide a solution with an improvement in terms of work efficiency over typical methods according to the JASO TP 15002.

1 Introduction

An increasing challenge to the automotive industry has been how to deal with the external threats and therefore, how to enhance the security. Indeed, since 2010, researchers have reported attacks on real-vehicles, where the attacker can manipulate the control functions in such a way that the car can be controlled in an unintended manner [5,19]. In response to these attacks, the significance of secure system design has been recognized in the automotive industry. One particularly useful approach is to measure software attack surfaces, which indicates there susceptibility to attack. With respect to the security analysis based on the attack surface, model-based metrics have recently been developed [4], dealing with the dependability evaluations and the assurance of critical systems.

For the automotive industry, several security guidelines and methods have been proposed. SAE J 3061 [17] is a high-level guideline which includes a definition of the lifecycle process, information for existing tools, and methods. JASO

© Springer International Publishing AG 2017
S. Tonetta et al. (Eds.): SAFECOMP 2017 Workshops, LNCS 10489, pp. 211–224, 2017.
DOI: 10.1007/978-3-319-66284-8_18

TP 15002 [9,10] also deals with high-level methods, as explained in a sequel. The EVITA method [16] refines abstract attacks into concrete attacks through the construction of Attack Trees and the evaluation of the risks of abstract attacks using those Attack Trees. In the EVITA methodology, risk is evaluated by severity, which includes 4 aspects (safety, financial, privacy and operation) and attack probability based on the framework of Common Criteria (CC) in which system users can specify their security functional requirements. There is a document, the Common Evaluation Methodology for Information Technology Security Evaluation (CEM), that helps evaluators how to apply the CC when they perform formal evaluations. ISO/IEC 15408 [7] is based on the security evaluation standard developed by the CC project. The term impact in TP 15002 has the same meaning as in EVITA. Hereinafter, we will use the term impact. OCTAVE Allegro [14] is a process-driven threat assessment method. It includes methods for threat identification, risk assessment and selecting mitigation approaches.

In this paper, we analyze the JASO TP 15002 guideline. An analysis of its method is efficient enough to minimize reworking the guildeline. This saves time by using a format with organized items that allows an engineer to just write a simple description without any ambiguity.

The Need from Industry. This work is motivated by a need from industry with respect to the implementation of secure system design based on a high-level security guideline, such as JASO TP15002. This need is summarized by conducting a secure system design with appropriate efforts. With a naive implementation of JASO TP 15002, the following problems require more effort to keep the quality of the result:

- There are non-detailed matters in JASO TP 15002. Thus individual designers have to refine or instantiate these matters in their own ways.
- Typically a very large number of threats are identified, that cannot be managed by a designer.
- The quality of output, such as granularity, the amount of description, or validity depends on individual designers.

The Industrial Impact. Our work contributes to the secure development of devices such as central gateways (CGW), telematics or end ECUs that play key roles in Over-The-Air (OTA) applications. This is supported by the evidence that JASO TP 15002 is used as a risk assessment methodology in the on-going ITU-T development "Secure software update capability for intelligent transportation system communication devices" which was discussed in a WP 29 meeting in 2016 [20].

Our Contribution. In this report, we identify gaps between the descriptions in JASO TP 15002 and the actual design tasks. Furthermore we propose a systematic way for secure-design, which is consistent over phases 1, 2, and 3, in JASO TP15002. In this way, dependence on individual engineers will become lower, and more tasks can be automated. Consequently, we expect that our work will help in reducing efforts for secure system design, with sufficient quality.

Organization. In Sect. 2, we will introduce preliminary work related to this paper. In Sect. 3, we will identify the problems in previous work and then we propose our method. In Sect. 4, we conduct case studies on secure designs of publicly available automotive systems, and finally, in Sect. 5, we present our conclusion.

2 Preliminary

2.1 Common Concepts Underlying Safety and Security

In the automotive industry, it is increasing important to develop methods for evaluating multiple attributes at the same time and to provide useful information on the entire system. For instance, a methodology for modeling automotive software security, privacy, usability, and reliability has been developed by Ford [13].

The perspectives of CIA (Confidentiality, Integrity, and Availability) of security are increasingly important in safety-critical systems and that security-for-safety paradigm is necessary when hazards originate from threats. A considerable amount of published work exists in this area, for example [2,3].

Automotive systems are typically known as safety critical systems and the system development process follows the standard ISO 26262 [6], which deals with safety issues. Safety critical systems other than automotive systems have begun to consider the relationship between safety and security. In train control systems, security is considered a problem of safety violations. Thus, in train control systems, security is a part of safety analysis. In the avionic security standard DO-326A [15], security is analyzed independently. Security-related activities refer to the results of safety related activities but not vice versa.

Referring to well-established work in related disciplines [3], here we give a solid foundation for safety and security engineering by recognizing the similarities and differences in these disciplines. In [3], security and safety are defined as follows:

- Safety is the degree to which *accidental* harm is prevented, reduced, and properly reacted to.
- Security is the degree to which *malicious* harm is prevented, reduced, and properly reacted to.

As J3061 pointed out, there are some overlaps between safety and security. But the differences are not entirely clear. For instance, a malicious attack that compromises the integrity of an ECU could eventually lead to an accidental harm caused by an operation parameter change in terms of safety. A more generic quality factor that includes these two quality factors is dependability, which is defined as follows:

- Dependability [1] is the degree to which various kinds of users can depend on a work product.

Hazard is a situation that increases the likelihood of one or more related accidents [11]. In ISO 26262, a hazard is defined as a potential source of harm caused by malfunctioning behavior of the item. Note that this definition is restricted to the scope of this standard. A hazard caused by unintended failure and a threat of attacks by attackers, can cause harm to assets. More specifically, hazards and threats are defined as follows:

- Hazard is the potential source of harm to an asset due to unintended failure of the system. Note that the harm is typically restricted to humans or the environment.
- Threat is the potential source of harm to an asset due to attackers.

The information models of safety and security engineering are significantly similar. For this reason, safety and security requirements can be analyzed regarding a risk-oriented, asset-based approach that considers the accompanied hazards and threats from which these assets have to be protected.

In the above definitions, safety deals with hazards, while security deals with attacks. In order to establish a link between safety and security, the "security-for-safety" paradigm can be introduced in the sense that threats (e.g. intentional hacking attempts) cause hazards that are a potential source of harm. Thus we consider the relationship between hazards and threats, and coordinate the security development process and methods with existing safety development process and methods.

2.2   The ISO/IEC 15408 Framework in Comparison with ISO 26262

In the automotive industry, there has been an increasing need to develop a framework in which security functions are used in reference to the information system field where ISO/IEC 15408 plays a key role. The purpose of ISO/IEC 15408 is to establish security objectives and evaluation procedure for a target of evaluation (TOE), which is a statement that counters identified threats and satisfies assumptions.

In the context of the evaluation of IT products, ISO/IEC 15408 [7] provides a framework and defines security concepts. This standard uses the term TOE where there are modules employing the assets to be protected. In this paper, after defining a TOE, threat identification is conducted and security objectives regarding the major threats are considered.

Referring to [18], we explain the similarities and differences between the ISO/IEC 15408 TOE and a ISO 26262 item definition. Regarding the ISO 26262 item, most required parts of the reference, overview and description of ISO/IEC 15408 TOE, has been already described. However, ISO/IEC 15408 TOE is extended with an overview of the included security features such as the CIA (confidentiality, integrity, availability) perspectives and the functionality of the ISO 26262 item. Afterwards, hazard analysis and risk assessment are performed so that potential hazards and their operational situations are identified and an automotive safety integrity level (ASIL) is determined. Then safety goals are determined for hazardous events (the combination of a hazard and an operational situation (see, [6])).

2.3   Overview of the Security Evaluation in JASO TP 15002

Since 2012, the Society of Automotive Engineers of Japan, Inc. has developed a standard procedure for security system design specified in JASO TP 15002. The purpose of JASO TP 15002 is to describe standard procedures that define the security functions. JASO TP 15002 considers the prevention of unauthorized operations of the functions that transmit the information to control ECUs (e.g. Body domain ECUs) from servers and other devices.

In JASO TP 15002, secure system design consists of five phases, where the following three phases are related to security evaluation: TOE definition, threat analysis, and risk assessment. The tasks and deliverables for these phases are reviewed in this subsection.

Phase 1: TOE Definition. This phase clarifies a model of the TOE. This model is produced from the assets to be protected and from data flow diagrams (DFD) that specify data flows between the modules in TOE. Thus, the model shows the network structures and entry points in the TOE. In this phase, properties to protect the CIA perspectives are assigned for each asset in the module. It is important that the functions of an automotive system operate as correctly as expected, and therefore integrity or availability should be ensured for functions. Similarly, confidentiality or integrity should be ensured for the information exchanged among devices, and external central servers as well. Other information such as lifecycles and modules of the TOE are also specified in this phase. Finally, all information related to security evaluation is formalized and shared.

Phase 2: Threat Analysis. Threats together with the situations they occur in are listed exhaustively in this phase. First, assumptions are stated. Next, adverse actions that can happen at each entry point are investigated. For an adverse action, its situation is identified with $5W$ perspectives ("Who", "When", "Where", "Why", "What"), and organizational security policy is stated in this phase.

Phase 3: Risk Assessment. This phase estimates the risk levels for all the threats that have been identified in the previous phase. Two risk evaluation criteria are mentioned in JASO TP 15002, namely CRSS (CVSS v2 [8] based Risk Scoring System) and RSMA (Risk Scoring Methodology for Automotive systems). Here we review the CRSS-based one, since it is used in our case study in Sect. 4.

CRSS is a risk evaluation criterion based on CVSS v2 (Common Vulnerability Scoring System). For each threat identified in Phase 2, two metrics Exploitability and Impact are assigned, and the risk value is computed from them. Moreover, a risk for a threat is categorized into three levels according to the computed risk value: Level III (Critical), Level II(Warning), and Level I (Caution).

An example of a result at Phase 2 and 3 in JASO TP15002 is shown in Table 1.

Table 1. An example of a result at phase 2 and 3 in JASO TP15002

#	Where	Who	When	Why	What	AE	EF	Risk value
1	OBD-II	Outsider	In regular use	Maliciously	cause malfunction	3.9	9.2	6.6

3   Our Proposed Method

In this section, we propose our method by complying with JASO TP 15002. Our method includes concretizations or the improvement of activities specified in the guideline.

3.1   A Concept Model of JASO TP15002

We have reviewed the concepts in JASO TP 15002. Figure 1 shows a partial result; concepts in Phase 1, 2, and 3 are identified and related transversely. By referring to information about the entire vehicle system (*System-related information*), a model including data flows and components for security evaluation have been defined (*TOE model*). TOE is specified by the TOE model and related concepts like Lifecycle and assumptions for TOE (*TOE overview*).

As explained in Sect. 2, threats have been identified for each entry point. Next, for every threat, causes have been analyzed and risk evaluated. At last a list of threats together with causes and risk values is completed as a deliverable of Phase 3 (*Threat table*).

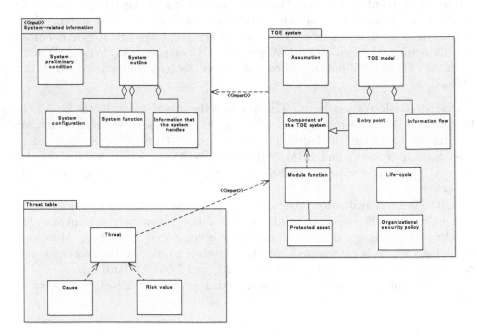

Fig. 1. Logical relations in JASO design process (Phase 1–Phase 3)

Our model makes it clear that there is in-dependency of *Lifecycle* from *TOE model*. In Phase 2, the lifecycle contributes to perspectives "who" and "when", and thus they can be dealt with independently.

3.2 A Taxonomy Problem with the JASO Design Process

Our analysis identified a problem with the JASO design process by investigating the well-known dependability taxonomy dealing with safety and security described in Sect. 2 based on [3]. The problem with the JASO design process is that the concepts of safety and hazard are not treated in an explicit manner. The JASO design process does not separate two definitions. It describes the CIA perspectives of security but it does not show the link to safety.

According to its Phase 2, each harm caused in an accidental manner is also considered a threat, rather than hazard. More specifically, each harm within the corresponding description where "why" is accidental is considered a threat.

3.3 Distinguishing Hazards from Threats

We suggest here a way to revise the JASO design process so that both of security and safety are made explicitly considered.

Although JASO TP 15002 focuses on security, its method allows us to pick up safety-related threats. Hence it is worth distinguishing safety-related threats in threat analysis, and letting safety evaluation refer to the result.

In this way, we apply the following: If the description for "why" is intentional, the corresponding harm is called a "threat". Otherwise, that is to say, if the description for "why" is accidental, the corresponding harm is called a "hazard". In this way together with the above definitions, this guideline now captures both security and safety in a explicit manner after a minor revision.

3.4 Focus on Principal Perspectives

Phase 2 of JASO TP 15002 suggests that the 5W ("Who", "When", "Where", "Why", "What") perspectives should be considered at the same time for each threat. However, we encounter a problem, namely, the difficulty in exhaustively identifying all the possible threat descriptions from the perspectives of "where" and "what".

We point out that this difficulty originates from ambiguity in the definitions of 5W characteristics. More specifically, there is a problem with the definition of "what", namely, what the attacker does. The description for "what" perspective could be *anything* such as breaking central gateway, hence, the threat identification (Phase 2) could be performed in an ad hoc manner. This could result in producing useless and unnecessary description (data) of threats for Phase 3. On the other hand, important threats could not be identified as a consequence of this ad hoc search and could end up with rework of Phase 2.

3.5   Approach for Improving Efficiency of the Total Work of Phases 2 and 3

To solve the above problems, we set a goal that is to improve efficiency of the *total* work of Phase 2 (threat identification) and phase 3 (risk evaluation).

Our approach to achieve this goal is to introduce "at" and "asset" characteristics in advance at the threat identification process. Our idea behind this approach is that the Phase-2 work identifies threats in a systematic manner and this work only outputs a list of threats whose description contain information necessary and useful for the risk-score computation in Phase 3.

The "where" perspective represents one of the entry points in TP15002, but, in our approach, the "what" perspective describes what asset of what asset container is attacked. Now we define the asset container as a module that contains the assets to be targeted as the "at" perspective (see Fig. 2).

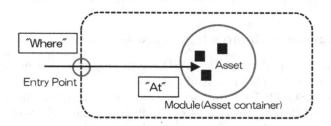

Fig. 2. Our idea of an asset container

Although these perspectives, "where", "at" and "asset", are significant parameters to cover all the possible threats at the CRSS risk evaluation, human errors during this identification are likely to occur due to the ambiguity of "what" which contains "at" and "asset" together. For example, some complex attacks which have multiple different paths through multiple modules, which may be missed when the threats are listed. Therefore, it is important to distinguish these two perspectives strictly from the beginning of Phase 2. On the other hand, only two perspectives, "where" and "what" (= "at" + "asset") are necessary to cover all threats, and the remaining three are not necessary up to Phase 3. Though a division of "what" into "at" and "asset" is added, the number of perspectives for risk analysis drops from five to three, so the workability will be increased.

In our paper, by considering the inter-dependency we described in the previous section, we propose a 2-step threat identification as follows:

- Step 1: exhaustively identify threats, each of which describes the following three perspectives: "where", "at", and "asset"
- Step 2: for the identified threats, identify associated threats each of which adds descriptions of the following three perspectives: "who", "when" and "why".

Step 1 refers to the TOE model and the module function list, both of which have been produced at the Phase 1 in JASO design process. Step 2 refers to the life-cycle list, which has been produced at the Phase 1 in the JASO design process.

After applying the above two steps, our method outputs information shown in Table 2 which includes the data produced by Phase 2 and 3 in JASO TP 15002.

Table 2. An example of data produced by our method

#	Where	Who	When	Why	What (At, Asset)	AE	EF	Risk value
1	OBD-II	Outsider	In regular use	Maliciously	cause malfunction (CGW, Control function)	3.9	9.2	6.6

Advantage of Our Method. Our method has two advantages over two advantages over a naive implementation of JASO is as follows:

– **From a working procedural perspective**, we make progress in formalizing in security evaluation work. Especially, our method can separate this work into two tasks and it enables an optimization of this work in the sense that it can re-factor in factors necessary for risk assessment.

By introducing "at (Asset container)" and "asset" to "what" perspective, the intrusion route is *clearly and systematically* identified and all assets which the destination, the attack target, contains are grasped without exception.

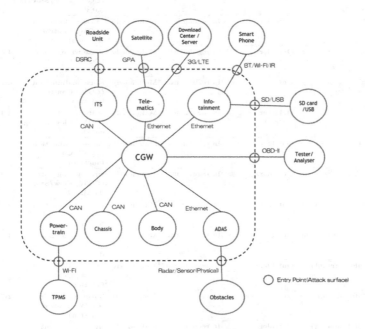

Fig. 3. Phase 1: TOE definition

– **From delivery perspective**, our method can improve the quality of the delivery (output) of security because we can remove the ambiguity from the threat descriptions.

There may be an advantage that encompassing all threats and accurate computation of risk scores for each of them can be realized.

4   Case Study

Here we present our results on a case study where the target system is a connected-car system employing CGW as a key component. We apply our method to this case study and then we show what are the prioritized threats to CGW.

Table 3. Risk analysis with respect to CGW

#	Where	Who	When	Why	What (At, Asset)	AE	EF	Risk value
64	OBD-II	Outsider	In regular use	Maliciously	cause malfunction (CGW, Control function)	3.9	9.2	6.6
65	OBD-II	Owner/User	In regular use	Maliciously	cause malfunction (CGW, Control function)	3.9	9.2	6.6
66	OBD-II	Maintenance staff	In maintenance	Accidentally	cause malfunction (CGW, Control function)	3.9	9.2	6.6
67	OBD-II	Maintenance staff	In maintenance	Accidentally	write wrong data (CGW, Flow/Storage data)	3.9	6.9	4.9
68	Wifi (TPMS)	Outsider	In regular use	Maliciously	cause malfunction (CGW, Control function)	4.4	9.2	6.8
69	Wifi (TPMS)	Outsider	In regular use	Maliciously	write wrong data (CGW, Flow/Storage data)	4.4	6.9	5.2
70	DSRC (ITS)	Outsider	In regular use	Maliciously	cause malfunction (CGW, Control function)	4.4	9.2	6.8
71	DSRC (ITS)	Outsider	In regular use	Maliciously	write wrong data (CGW, Flow/Storage data)	4.4	6.9	5.2
72	3G/LTE (Telematics)	Outsider	In regular use	Maliciously	cause malfunction (CGW, Control function)	6.8	9.2	7.9
73	3G/LTE (Telematics)	Outsider	In regular use	Maliciously	write wrong data (CGW, Flow/Storage data)	6.8	6.9	6.3
74	BT/Wifi/IR (Infotainment)	Outsider	In regular use	Maliciously	cause malfunction (CGW, Control function)	4.4	9.2	6.8
75	BT/Wifi/IR (Infotainment)	Outsider	In regular use	Maliciously	write wrong data (CGW, Flow/Storage data)	4.4	6.9	5.2
76	SD/USB (Infotainmant)	Outsider	In regular use	Maliciously	cause malfunction (CGW, Control function)	2.7	9.2	6.0
77	SD/USB (Infotainmant)	Owner/User	In regular use	Accidentally	infect with malware (CGW, Control function)	2.7	9.2	6.0
78	SD/USB (Infotainmant)	Outsider	In regular use	Maliciously	write wrong data (CGW, Flow/Storage data)	2.7	6.9	4.4

Table 4. Phase1: module function list

#	Module name	Function	Assets to be protected	C	I	A
1	Power-train	Control functions for driving vehicle related to Engine, Motor, Fuel, Battery, Transmission, etc	Control function		✓	✓
			Authentication function		✓	✓
			Authentication information	✓	✓	
			Censor information		✓	
2	Chassis	Control functions for operating vehicle related to Brake and Steering	Control function		✓	✓
3	Body	Control functions for operating vehicle body equipments related to Door lock, Air conditioner, Lights and Blinker	Control function		✓	✓
			Control input data		✓	
4	ADAS	Automatic brake, Lane-keeping contorol, Inter-vehicle distance control, etc. Functions which bring safetey and comfort working together other vehicle control functions	Control function		✓	✓
			Location information		✓	
5	CGW (Central gateway)	Functions for integration and transformation of Ethernet and CAN communication. At the same time, it acts as fault diagnosis port, OBD (On-Board Diagnostics)-II	Control function		✓	✓
			Flow/storage data		✓	
6	ITS	Functions via roadside-to-vehicle or vehicle-to-vehicle communication, ETC, ITS (Intelligent Transport System), etc	Authentication function		✓	✓
			Authentication information	✓	✓	
			Control information		✓	✓
7	Telematics	Functions for remote control services. For example, collection service of location informations, remote door-lock service, remote lighting-on service, etc	Authentication function		✓	✓
			Authentication information	✓	✓	
			Personal information	✓	✓	
			Request information to server		✓	✓
			Vehicle status information	✓	✓	
8	Infotainment	Functions for information and entertainment. For example, car navigation system, audio equipments, key-less entry system, etc	Authentication function		✓	✓
			Authentication information	✓	✓	

4.1 Phase 1: TOE Definition and Threat Identification

Based on the vehicle architecture shown in [12] we define a TOE as shown in Fig. 3.

4.2 Results of Phase 2 and 3

We present the results on our security evaluation where CGW is the asset container by applying our method. Before performing this evaluation, we assume that no *security functions* are employed in CGW because our position is that the security functions to be employed will be made clear after the implementation of the final phase of JASO TP 15002. Our study makes clear how we can prioritize the CGW-related threats and hazards, by considering all of them related to the entire vehicle structure, which we take as the ToE model.

Our study identified 145 threats and hazards in total, partly shown in Table 5. 9 threats and hazards are classified as the highest-risk (Level III). 93 threats and hazards are classified as the second-highest-risk (Level II). 43 threats and hazards are classified as the relatively-low-risk (Level I). Note that our method outputs information which includes the data produced by Phase 2 and 3 in JASO TP 15002.

Table 5. Threat and hazard overview list

#	Where	At	Asset	Who	When	Why	What
1	OBD-II	Power-train	Control function	Maintenance staff	In maintenance	Accidentally	cause malfunction
6	Wifi (TPMS)	Power-train	Control function	Outsider	In regular use	Maliciously	cause malfunction
10	DSRC (ITS)	Power-train	Control function	Outsider	In regular use	Maliciously	cause malfunction
31	3G/LTE (Telematics)	Chassis	Control function	Outsider	In regular use	Maliciously	cause malfunction
32	BT/Wifi/IR (Infotainment)	Chassis	Control function	Outsider	In regular use	Maliciously	cause malfunction
34	SD/USB (Infotainment)	Chassis	Control function	Owner/User	In regular use	Accidentally	infect with malware
52	Wifi (TPMS)	ADAS	Control function	Outsider	In regular use	Maliciously	cause malfunction
55	DSRC (ITS)	ADAS	Location information	Outsider	In regular use	Maliciously	write wrong data
56	3G/LTE (Telematics)	ADAS	Control function	Outsider	In regular use	Maliciously	cause malfunction
64	OBD-II	CGW	Control function	Outsider	In regular use	Maliciously	cause malfunction
69	Wifi (TPMS)	CGW	Flow/Storage data	Outsider	In regular use	Maliciously	write wrong data
70	DSRC (ITS)	CGW	Control function	Outsider	In regular use	Maliciously	cause malfunction
72	3G/LTE (Telematics)	CGW	Control function	Outsider	In regular use	Maliciously	cause malfunction
75	BT/Wifi/IR (Infotainment)	CGW	Flow/Storage data	Outsider	In regular use	Maliciously	write wrong data
77	SD/USB (Infotainment)	CGW	Control function	Owner/User	In regular use	Accidentally	infect with malware

With respect to CGW, Our study makes the followings clear:

- Regarding the attack path, the entry point via the telematics leads to a Level III threat. This was not expected before our study. Intuitively, the OBD interface might lead to this kind of threat. However, this is not the case. Some connected cars have already had updated software (and firmware) over the air (OTA) by using telematics, and the number of cars updated over the air will certainly increase in the future. Attackers will be use the OTA update mechanism to reprogram ECUs to take control of the vehicle. To prevent this attack, authenticity and integrity need to be updated and implemented in CGW. Threats from telematics and attacks to CGW control functions impact safety mechanisms.
- From our risk analysis result with respect to CGW, there is no significant bias among the 15 related threats and hazards with respect to the interface. This implies that uniform security countermeasures are necessary, in contrast to focusing on protecting attacks via one or a few interfaces (Table 3).

4.3 Information on Our Case Study

Here we present the information lists which we define in our case study (Table 4).

5 Conclusion

We have investigated the promising security JASO TP15002 guideline. In light of existing work, we have identified a problem with this guideline and have suggested a way to revise its design process in which both of security and safety are made explicitly considered. As a part of our on-going work, we have identified the difficulty in carrying out the actual design tasks based on JASO TP15002 and we have proposed a systematic way of secure-designing which should solve the problems of design-cost reduction in secure-system design in such a way that the degree of human dependability is made smaller and the degree of automation is made larger. We have provided a case study to examine the efficiency and usefulness of our method. As a result, we found some hazards, which seem unintentional in JASO TP15002.

As a work-in-progress, our next step is to conduct a more in-depth analysis of JASO TP15002 at the concept level regarding safety-security co-engineering, as well as at the practical level, by means of further study that coves the final phase of security requirement selection.

Acknowledgements. The authors would like to thank the anonymous reviewers for their helpful comments.

References

1. Algirdas, A., et al.: Basic concepts and taxonomy of dependable and secure computing. IEEE Trans. Dependable Secure Comput. **1**(1), 11–33 (2004)

2. Dobbing, B., Lautieri, S.: SafSec Methodology: Standard (Issue 3.1), S.P1199.50.2, Praxis High Integrity Systems (2006)
3. Firesmith, D.G.: Common Concepts Underlying Safety, Security, and Survivability Engineering, CMU/SEI-2003-TN-033, Software Engineering Institute (2003)
4. Hatzivasilis, G., Papaefstathiou, I., Manifavas, C.: Software security, privacy, and dependability: metrics and measurement. IEEE Softw. **33**(4), 46–54 (2016)
5. Koscher, K., et al.: Experimental security analysis of a modern automobile. In: IEEE Symposium on Security and Privacy (2010)
6. ISO 26262: Road vehicles - Functional safety (2011)
7. ISO/IEC 15408: Information technology - Security techniques - Evaluation criteria for IT security (2009)
8. ITU-T X.1524: Cybersecurity information exchange - Vulnerability/state exchange, Common weakness enumeration (2012)
9. JASO TP15002: Guideline for Automotive Information Security Analysis (2015)
10. JASO TP15002: Guideline concerning automotive information security (2015). (in Japanese)
11. Leveson, N.: Safeware: System Safety and Computers. Addison-Wesley, Reading (1995)
12. Miyashita, Y., et al.: On-vehicle compact and lightweight multi-channel central gateway unit. SEI Techn. Rev. **83**, 5–9 (2016)
13. Prasad, K.V., Giuli, T.J., Watson, D.: The case for modeling security, privacy, usability and reliability (SPUR) in automotive software. In: Broy, M., Krüger, I.H., Meisinger, M. (eds.) ASWSD 2006. LNCS, vol. 4922, pp. 1–14. Springer, Heidelberg (2008). doi:10.1007/978-3-540-70930-5_1
14. Richard, C., et al.: Introducing OCTAVE allegro: improving the information security risk assessment process. CMU/SEI-2007-TR-012 (2007)
15. RTCA: DO-326A Airworthiness Security Process Specification (2014)
16. Ruddle, A., et al.: Security requirements for automotive on-board networks based on dark-side scenarios. E-safety vehicle intrusion protected applications (EVITA) Deliverable D2.3 (2009)
17. SAE J3061: Cybersecurity Guidebook for Cyber-Physical Vehicle Systems (2016)
18. Schmittner, C., Ma, Z.: Towards a framework for alignment between automotive safety and security standards. In: Koornneef, F., Gulijk, C. (eds.) SAFE-COMP 2015. LNCS, vol. 9338, pp. 133–143. Springer, Cham (2015). doi:10.1007/978-3-319-24249-1_12
19. Valasek, C., Miller, C.: Adventures in Automotive Networks and Control Units. DEFCON 21 (2013). http://illmatics.com/car_hacking.pdf
20. World Forum for Harmonization of Vehicle Regulations (WP.29): UN Task Force on Cyber security and OTA issues (CS/OTA): Draft Recommendation on "Secure software update capability for intelligent transportation system communication devices" (2016). CS/OTA 1st session https://www2.unece.org/wiki/pages/viewpage.action?pageId=40829523

Systematic Composition of Services from Distributed Systems for Highly Dynamic Collaboration Processes

Sebastian Müller(⊠) and Peter Liggesmeyer

Lehrstuhl für Software Engineering: Dependability,
Technische Universität Kaiserslautern, 67653 Kaiserslautern, Germany
{sebastian.mueller,liggesmeyer}@cs.uni-kl.de

Abstract. Establishing collaboration processes of systems in an open and dynamically changing environment like the automotive domain will inescapably lead to a varying availability of shared services. A vivid example is driving in a platoon, where smaller distances between vehicles are made possible due to additional safety related runtime guarantees provided by surrounding vehicles. In such collaboration scenarios environmental conditions can change, driving behavior from surrounding vehicles may not be adequate or hardware/software failure of involved systems may occur. For safety critical use cases like platooning, such degraded or even missing collaboration capabilities can rapidly lead to hazardous situations due to the highly dynamic context. When such events occur, only an immediate and situation adapted reaction behavior can prevent physical or material damage. For the certification of such described dynamic collaboration processes, it is therefore essential to develop a conclusive safety concept for each individual system, which also considers the return to a safe mode. The presented "Dynamic Safety Contracts" approach enables a systematic composition of available services at runtime to extend or reduce allowed degrees of freedom for a system involved in a dynamic collaboration scenario.

Keywords: Collaborative systems · Emergent behavior · Dynamic safety contracts · Safety · Certification · Distributed embedded systems · Dynamic environment · Runtime adaptation · Condition monitoring · Open and adaptive systems

1 Introduction

The increasing use of embedded systems in combination with technically matured inter-system communication will alleviate classical boundaries of system applications. Previously separated systems will be able to establish ad-hoc connections during operation and to initialize emergent collaboration processes according to their needs. By integrating shared services based on emergent collaboration networks, capabilities of single system devices could be exceeded, while flexibility for involved system to adapt to changing situational requirements could be maintained. Under the notion of Cyber-Physical Systems and Systems of Systems an increasingly important research

© Springer International Publishing AG 2017
S. Tonetta et al. (Eds.): SAFECOMP 2017 Workshops, LNCS 10489, pp. 225–236, 2017.
DOI: 10.1007/978-3-319-66284-8_19

area evolved. The overall objective is to boost a better connectivity of previously segregated system functionalities. At the same time, we witness in the automotive domain a strong shift to automated driving functionalities, mainly possible due to the integration of a complete software backbone with high-performance sensors and computing devices. This development trend opens the possibility to introduce comprehensive collaboration concepts between separated vehicle platforms (V2V) and infrastructural devices (V2I). Promising scenarios become possible like platooning on highways, coordinated crossing of intersections or establishing vehicle fleets with so-called master-slave arrangements, for instance in the agricultural domain. However, establishing higher-level functionalities in a dynamic environment requires additional degrees of freedom for involved systems to change their effective and deterministic behavior accordingly. In many application domains, runtime adaptation of system behavior is safety critical and an appropriate safety assurance technique is still missing. Unsafe actions, which are triggered during collaboration of systems, could lead to physical or material damage.

The core solution concept are dynamic safety contracts (DSCs), which specify the correct merging of internal and shared (external) safety related runtime data for a dedicated system in a certain collaborative mode. DSCs contain a prioritized sequence of demand-guarantee relationships, which can be composed and dynamically evaluated at runtime. An evaluated output of a safety contract module represents a valid runtime safety guarantee considering collaborative knowledge, which is part of the decision whether the current operational situation is safe or not. Typically, several DSC modules are rigidly interconnected, in a predefined way at development time, to continuously evaluate top-level system safety properties for a collaboration process at runtime. The top-level safety properties are monitored in the DSC module "Safe Collaboration Manager" (Fig. 4). Based on this module, the additional allowed degrees of freedom for a system involved in a collaboration process can be specified like a virtual safety cage based on internal and external safety related runtime data. The current operational situation has strictly to comply with these evaluated situational degrees of freedom while collaborating. If this is not the case, the current state is detected to be unsafe. In consequence, an adjusted safe reaction behavior is initialized as part of the collaboration process description. It should bring the system as optimally as possible back to a safe operation mode. Additionally, a regular mode specifies coupling and decoupling processes of systems in the dynamic context, provided that no safety-critical event occurs. This mode should be the normal case, but, as it was already described in the problem statement, it cannot be guaranteed due to the open and dynamically changing context.

Recently, we published a framework that enables safety assurance and certification for collaboration processes of open adaptive systems in a highly dynamic context [1]. For the key aspects of specification and implementation of DSCs a comprehensive insight and tool support was provided in [2]. In this paper we want to delve deeper into this approach, provide an enhanced application example and show our validation activities. Sound mechanisms and tool support like a dedicated GUI have been developed to establish DSCs with required features and transform them to computable representations. In addition, a comprehensive 3D simulation environment with V-REP (Virtual Robot Experimentation Platform) was established, which provides a profound insight to the DSC evaluation and the resulting overall system behavior for the pla-tooning scenario. Today's applied safety engineering methods were considered to support a sound safety engineering backbone. In [2] it was already shown how the ConSerts approach could be applied for the DSC modeling with a joint development process. By this means openness for previously unknown collaboration partner could be enabled. In this paper the utilized simulation framework is shown, which was developed to validate the feasibility of DSC/ConSerts integration according the required mechanisms. Please note that a detailed description for the CACC (Cooperative Adaptive Cruise Control) platooning scenario related to the published DSC modules can be looked up in [1].

2 State of the Art

In the last few years runtime trust assurance [3] and runtime safety certification [4] in open and adaptive systems (OAS) are upcoming research topics since there is a rising demand for more flexible technical products, which can be adapted to user needs, to dynamic changes in service/device availability or resource situations. The demand for shifting parts of the safety evaluation from development time to runtime results from technical systems, which are not fully known at design time. For system concepts like Industry 4.0 a flexible modular architecture is a key factor for a high performance of the assembly line. In such technical systems safety certified modules with predefined functions should be combined in a most flexible way at runtime to adapt the system to rapidly changing customer demands and to accelerate repair times. Ideally, diverse previously unknown modules could be added in an easy way like plug and play and the overall integrated system functionality should be evolved at runtime.

To enable safety assurance for such OAS scenarios, Schneider introduced the Conditional Safety Certificates (ConSerts) [3]. It becomes possible to evaluate at runtime an integrated safety certified higher level functionality. The evaluation is based on available static safety guarantees of submodules and Runtime Evidences (RtEs) as a proof for the correct operation of the evolved entire system. For the DSC approach ConSerts are utilized to address openness. Based on the ConSerts approach an optimal collaborative mode for previously unknown collaboration partner can be found. Merging safety related runtime data of distributed systems to assure safety for highly dynamic collaboration processes was not in the scope of his work.

Recently the specific challenges of hazard analysis and risk assessment for operational situations in the automotive domain were outlined in [5]. The latest version of the ISO 26262 [6] standard for automotive safety does not consider safe collaboration processes of distributed systems. Oestberg dealt with the question how to integrate shared safety related runtime data of vehicles into standards like AUTOSAR [7]. As a result he suggested to introduce an individual data base to each vehicle, where safety related vehicle sensor data is stored. In the next step, the data bases are synchronized between the collaborating vehicles to optimize their safety assessment. Based on that he concluded a safety contract concept for dynamic safety assessment is needed, but he provided no concrete one. Also Priesterjahn introduced a runtime safety analysis for collaborating vehicles based on failure propagation models [8]. But in this approach only development time knowledge about failure rates was considered. This could be seen as a more conservative approach compared to the presented one. However, as it was outlined in the previous section, we propose a collaboration where involved collaboration partner are able to adapt themselves to shared runtime services to optimize their system functionalities. As a conclusion for this section it can be stated that there is at the moment no appropriate approach for powerful collaborations available, which tackles the specific demands of collaborative functionalities in a highly dynamic context regarding safety assurance and performance.

3   Dynamic Safety Contracts

3.1   The Principle of System Collaboration Using DSCs

In this section the process of establishing a collaboration of systems using DSCs is explained in an illustrative way. The system platform on the left side in Fig. 1 represents a system, which tries to collaborate with an arbitrary number of surrounding systems. In a platooning scenario like the presented CACC scenario the system platform would be the follower vehicle, while the surrounding systems would be the front vehicle and the communicating infrastructure. The objective of this collaboration scenario is to make shared safety related sensor data available for the system behavior generation of the following vehicle. This can be interpreted as a horizontal collaboration of systems on a very basic level. The considered system platform only collects data from surrounding systems, it does not execute tightly integrated functionalities, in the sense of mutual influences on driving behavior. No system actively influences other systems like a remote controller or has the role of a system integrator. We believe, in such a case the legal enforceability would be much more difficult, especially if we consider liability issues regarding responsibility for physical or material damage.

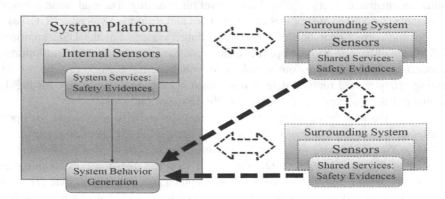

Fig. 1. Considering external services to optimize individual behavior

The first step to a collaboration based on shared data, however, is to find out the optimal collaborative mode to integrate data from currently available collaboration partner. Naturally, this has to be done in accordance with safety specifications in a safety critical domain. In Fig. 2 a set of potential collaborative modes is displayed as "Certified Collaborative Modes". We decided to facilitate a two-step approach, where the first step determines a suitable collaborative mode before operation (Fig. 2), and the second step performs a safety assurance during operation in a collaborative mode (Fig. 3). For the safe determination of an optimal collaboration mode (Fig. 2) a negotiation process (see also Fig. 8) based on ConSerts is applied. For this purpose the static hardware guarantees of systems like SIL classifications of sensors are introduced to the negotiation process based on the ConSert specification.

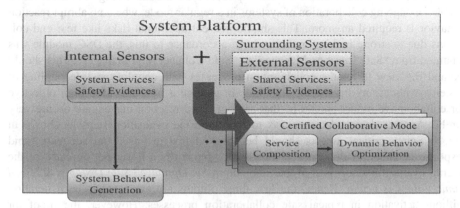

Fig. 2. Safe determination of a collaborative mode

If a certified collaboration mode is identified, the second step of ongoing collaboration is initialized (Fig. 3). This is the active integration of external sensor data, which is continuously forwarded from surrounding systems according to the demands of the collaboration mode. Internal and external services are continuously composed based on DSC evaluation and the individual system behavior is optimized accordingly.

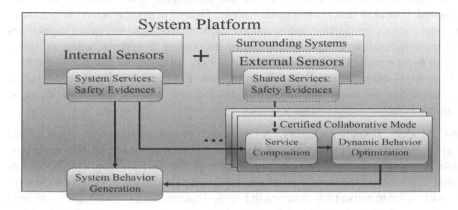

Fig. 3. Safe composition of services to optimize individual behavior

3.2 Dynamic Safety Contract Modules

The evaluation procedure of DSC modules as well as their distinction between qualitative and quantitative module types (metric) was already clarified in [1, 2]. This section focuses on enhancements of DSC modeling. In the following we discuss modifications done for the top-level DSC module "Safe Collaboration Manager", the "Detection Quality" module as well as the overall composition of DSC modules in accordance to the CACC platooning scenario.

Safe Collaboration Manager. Considering the presented top-level DSC module in [2] we implemented some refinements. The top-level DSC module in Fig. 4 is modified to enable an ongoing collaboration of systems in a regular mode, where no abrupt reaction behavior is required anymore. This should prevent additional risks like rear-end collisions due to strong braking manoeuvre. In accordance to this, the DSC module was renamed from "Safe Reaction Manager" to "Safe Collaboration Manager". This should expand the view to regular collaboration processes with coupling and decoupling of systems without any hazardous situations. In general a fundamental design objective for collaborative modes should be that safety related reaction manoeuvre occure very rarely. Another design decision was to rearrange the evaluation steps as shown in Fig. 4. Safety critical aspects should be checked first to ensure an adequate rapid response behavior. A drawback of this rearrangement is a lower performance of the overall evaluation since most of the time output *Set Optimized Safe Distance & Speed Limit Values* is active. Hence, the first three outputs are evaluated in each iteration without activation in typical safe collaboration processes. However, the proof for non-existence of hazards in combination with guarantees for an allowed activation of a collaborative behavior is still favorable. To highlight the operating principle of this module the first three outputs from left to right are summarized as "Rapid Response Mode" while the remaining two outputs are summarized as "Regular Mode".

As already mentioned, the fourth output is typically active. It specifies the allowed safe distance to a front vehicle as well as max. speed in a dynamic way. One input demand is the *CACC Collaboration Approved*, which checks if all involved collaboration partner still want to be part of this collaboration group. If this is not the case, the mentioned input demand is not fulfilled and the related collaborative mode is not activated. Instead of that, the last mode with the *Default* demand is active. In this mode the target values for distance and speed are reduced and set to individual capabilities without collaboration. It represents a regular decoupling of systems, where no safety critical event occurs. The follower vehicle is slowly enlarging the distance to the front vehicle to dissolve the integrated vehicle platoon. If a hazardous event occurs before the decoupling process is finalized, e.g. individual safe distance is reached, the rapid response behavior could still be activated.

DSC Module: Detection Quality. A key benefit of collaboration with safety related quality attributes is that an active fault detection between collaborating systems is possible. Safety related sensor data can be compared at runtime and inconsistencies can be found. To show this, the already introduced logic of the DSC module "Detection Quality" [2] is extended to active fault detection in Fig. 5. Three evaluation results are considered based on a safe mutual detection in combination with a distance measurement based on

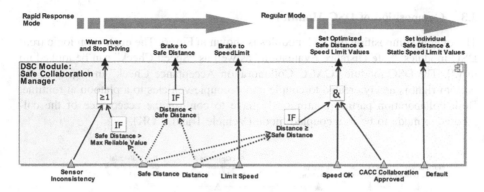

Fig. 4. DSC module: safe collaboration manager

the located position. The evaluation result *Sensor Inconsistency* is active, if both vehicles are confident that they have safely detected each other, but located each other in a wrong place. The result *Safe redundant Detection of V1 & V2* means that both vehicle can confirm the relative position to each other in a correct way. The *Default* mode describes the grey zone, where doubts are existent because the measurement inaccuracy hinders a definitive statement.

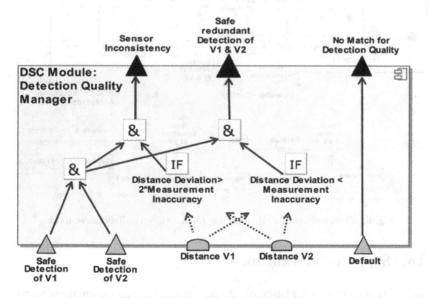

Fig. 5. DSC module: detection quality

3.3 Composition of DSC Modules

The overall composition of DSC modules is shown in Fig. 6. The evaluation logic from DSC modules "Safe Distance Evaluation" as well as "Speed Check" can be looked up in [2]. The DSC module "CACC Collaboration Acceptance Check" in Fig. 6 on the bottom right is newly created to couple and decouple vehicles to a platoon at runtime. Both collaboration partner continuously have to confirm the acceptance of the collaborative mode to be in a coupled mode (Vehicle 1 and 2 OK).

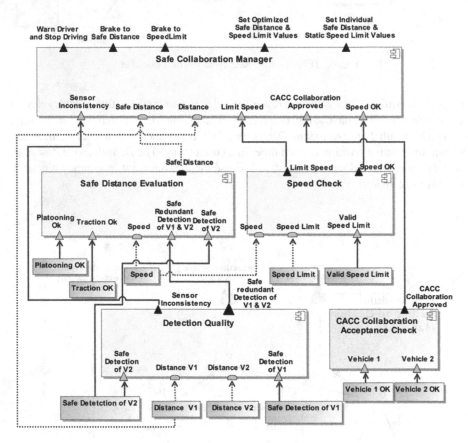

Fig. 6. Composition of DSC modules for a certified collaborative mode

4 Tool Support and Validation

Recently we developed a GUI based on Magic Draw to support the engineering process of DSC modules. It was utilized to create the figures of DSC modules presented in this paper. It is now possible, to automatically generate executable code from the graphical representation.

The executable DSC modules are validated in a virtual test environment in cooperation with RRLab at TU Kaiserslautern. Their department developed the realtime robot control framework Finroc [9], which is linked to the V-REP simulation environment based on a distributed control architecture. A holistic environmental model can be utilized to check the environment detection and reaction capabilities of a certain system. Sensor data from the V-REP simulation is forwarded to the robot control framework Finroc. There the actuator activation is computed and forwarded to the V-REP simulation again. Additionally the propagation of safety related quality attributes between DSC modules can be observed with a graphical visualization in the Finroc framework. We implemented the platooning scenario with a master-slave arrangement of two vehicles. The simulation of collaboration scenarios enables to prove the intended collaborative behavior and additionally enables the identification of hazardous situations. For this purpose the master vehicle is controlled with a virtual control panel, which enables any desired driving behavior. The slave vehicle is following in an autonomous way by interpreting its environment based on sensor fusion with an integrated behavior-based control (iB2C) [10]. Comparable to the described platooning use case, safety related services from the master vehicle are made available for the follower vehicle. To consider a varying service availability for collaboration processes, real-world environmental influences were implemented to the V-REP simulation. Examples are hilly landscapes and static objects like gras, bushes and trees. All these environmental aspects could have a negative impact on the mutual detection capability. In the test framework is also a manual degradation of shared services with a dedicated control panel implemented. In this way, we can simulate for instance communication problems between collaborating vehicles or effects like a slippery surface. Such events should force an adequate reaction behavior. This in turn enables the validation and optimization of specified DSC modules in an iterative process based on achieved experience during testing.

Lately also a JADE-based simulation framework (Fig. 7) was developed by Daniel Hillen at our SEDA department. The main objective was to validate openness for collaborative modes with DSCs considering previously unknown collaboration partner. To facilitate this, the ConSerts approach from Schneider was utilized. The integration of DSCs and ConSerts with a graphical illustration can be looked up in [2]. The main features and functionalities of the simulation framework are summarized in the following. Basically the platooning simulation framework in Fig. 7 can be subdivided into 6 main segments. These are "Vehicle Runtime Data" (1/2/3), "Collaborating Systems" (4/5), "Test Environment" (6), "ConSerts" (7), "DSCs" (8) and "Change Log" (9). In the initial state, there is already one vehicle placed in segment (6). Later on it should represent the following vehicle in a platoon. Segments (7) and (8) are still empty.

In the first step, systems, which should collaborate with the vehicle already placed in (6), are chosen from (4/5) and added to (6) via drag and drop. This can be one front vehicle (V2V) and one collaborating infrastructural element (V2I) like a flexible speed limitation or a controlled intersection crossing. The following vehicle has a database with ConSerts and requests the other systems within the communication range (simulated as placed in 6) to provide their SIL certification for possible collaborative services. These incoming guarantee certificates are introduced to a negotiation process based on ConSerts to find the most suitable collaboration mode. (This step is necessary

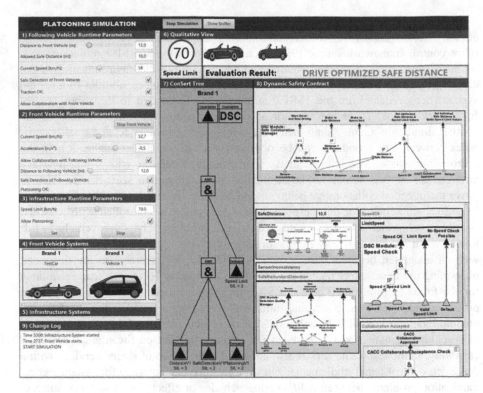

Fig. 7. Platooning simulation framework

for a safe determination of a collaborative mode. ConSerts were especially designed for such a safety certification at runtime.) If a suitable ConSert for this hardware configuration of safety related components is found, in terms of fulfillment of all demands, the associated DSC next to the ConSert guarantee is evaluated. The active ConSert and DSC configuration is displayed in (7) and (8). From this moment on, the collaboration mode is activated. The safety assurance during operation of this collaborative mode is done with DSCs. Shared services during collaboration can be modified in (1/2/3). In (8) the propagated safety related quality attributes between DSC modules are visualized. The resulting driving behavior (Parameter: speed, distance) can be observed in a qualitative way in (6) referring to enlarging or minimizing the distance between both vehicles. The detailed quantitative parameters and timestamps can be checked in the change log. Furthermore the detailed time series charts for performed V2X communication (Fig. 8) can be checked separately. This is particularly relevant for analyzing the worst case execution time for the rapid response behavior in hazardous situations.

Overall, the validation activities show that the DSC approach is a promising solution to enable safe collaboration scenarios for distributed systems in highly dynamic collaboration processes.

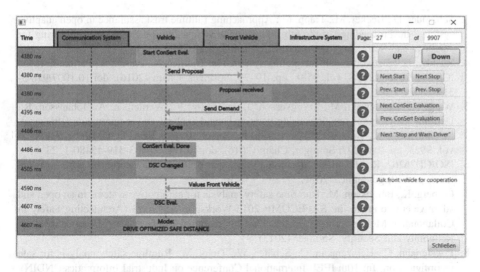

Fig. 8. Time series chart for V2X communication

5 Conclusion and Future Work

In this paper we argue that future collaboration processes of systems in a highly dynamic context like platooning with V2V and V2I communication is a new challenge for safety assurance. When provided runtime services from collaboration partners are suddenly degraded, hazardous situations could arise if collaborating system are in a coupled collaboration mode. We propose a method that can help to tackle such events with a pre-engineered individual reaction behavior based on safety considerations for a certain collaborative mode. With DSCs safety related quality attributes from internal and external system services can be systematically composed. This enables a continuous runtime calculation of allowed degrees of freedom. If the current state of ongoing collaboration doesn't comply to this safety restrictions, a safe reaction behavior associated to this collaboration mode is initialized. In our future work, we want to provide comprehensible guidelines and techniques for a traceable decision-making to support the engineering process of DSC-modules.

References

1. Müller, S., Liggesmeyer, P.: Dynamic safety contracts for functional cooperation of automotive systems. In: Skavhaug, A., Guiochet, J., Schoitsch, E., Bitsch, F. (eds.) SAFECOMP 2016. LNCS, vol. 9923, pp. 171–182. Springer, Cham (2016). doi:10.1007/978-3-319-45480-1_14
2. Müller, S., Liggesmeyer, P.: Safety assurance for emergent collaboration of open distributed systems. In: Software Reliability Engineering Workshops (ISSREW), pp. 249–256. IEEE (2016)

3. Schneider, D., Becker, M., Trapp, M.: Approaching runtime trust assurance in open adaptive systems. In: Proceedings of the 6th International Symposium on Software Engineering for Adaptive and Self-managing Systems, pp. 196–201. ACM (2011)
4. Rushby, J.: Trustworthy self-integrating systems. In: Bjørner, N., Prasad, S., Parida, L. (eds.) ICDCIT 2016. LNCS, vol. 9581, pp. 19–29. Springer, Cham (2016). doi:10.1007/978-3-319-28034-9_3
5. Warg, F., Gassilewski, M., Tryggvesson, J., Izosimov, V., Werneman, A., Johansson, R.: Defining autonomous functions using iterative hazard analysis and requirements refinement. In: Skavhaug, A., Guiochet, J., Schoitsch, E., Bitsch, F. (eds.) SAFECOMP 2016. LNCS, vol. 9923, pp. 286–297. Springer, Cham (2016). doi:10.1007/978-3-319-45480-1_23
6. ISO/CD26262. Road vehicles, functional safety part 6: Product development at the software level, part 10, guidelines (2011)
7. Östberg, K., Bengtsson, M.: Run time safety analysis for automotive systems in an open and adaptive environment. In: SAFECOMP 2013-Workshop ASCoMS (Architecting Safety in Collaborative Mobile Systems) of the 32nd International Conference on Computer Safety, Reliability and Security. Springer (2013)
8. Priesterjahn, C., Heinzemann, C., Schäfer, W., Tichy, M.: Runtime safety analysis for safe reconfiguration. In: 10th IEEE International Conference on Industrial Informatics (INDIN), pp. 1092–1097. IEEE (2012)
9. Reichardt, M., Föhst, T., Berns, K.: Introducing finroc: a convenient real-time framework for robotics based on a systematic design approach. Robotics Research Lab, Department of Computer Science, University of Kaiserslautern, Kaiserslautern, Germany, Technical report (2012)
10. Proetzsch, M., Luksch, T., Berns, K.: Development of complex robotic systems using the behavior-based control architecture iB2C. Robot. Auton. Syst. 58(1), 46–67 (2010)

Safety Assurance for Autonomous and Collaborative Medical Cyber-Physical Systems

Fabio L. Leite Jr.[2,3]([⊠]) [iD], Rasmus Adler[1], and Patrik Feth[1]

[1] Fraunhofer IESE, Kaiserslautern, Germany
{rasmus.adler,patrik.feth}@iese.fraunhofer.de
[2] Department Software Engineering: Dependability,
University of Kaiserslautern, Kaiserslautern, Germany
[3] Center for Strategic Health Technologies – NUTES,
Paraíba State University (UEPB), Campina Grande, PB, Brazil
fabioleite@cct.uepb.edu.br

Abstract. Medical Cyber Physical Systems of Systems (MCPSoS) refer to a set of systems that flexibly collaborate at runtime in order to render higher level functionality. Most systems in a MCPSoS offer a generic piece of functionality so that they can contribute to many totally different collaboration scenarios. Consequently, it is unknown at design time which systems will how collaborate at runtime. This unpredictability leads to new challenges for the assurance of safety, because established approaches always build on the assumption that systems and their environments are completely known. We believe that the safety research community has to pull together in order to tackle the challenge of unpredictability and that this requires an appropriate taxonomy in order to establish a common understanding of the challenge and related solutions. To this end, we propose enhancements based on a widely accepted taxonomy for dependable computing with respect to the system-of-systems aspect. Further, we will use the taxonomy to reflect on the new challenge of unpredictability and related solutions from the state-of-the-art, namely, safety contracts and dynamic risk assessment. Finally, we motivate an integration of the safety contracts and dynamic risk assessment and present some ideas on this integration. Throughout the paper, we use a real-world example to exemplify our proposed taxonomy and our thoughts.

Keywords: Medical Cyber-Physical Systems · System of systems · Safety assurance · Modular safety certification · Dynamic risk analysis

1 Introduction

Most existing medical devices can be roughly classified into two categories. The first category provides information about the patient in order to support the diagnosis and the selection of a therapy. Examples are devices for measuring the temperature, the heart rate, oxygen concentration or other concentrations in the blood, and so on. The medical devices from the second category do not only deliver information about the

S. Tonetta et al. (Eds.): SAFECOMP 2017 Workshops, LNCS 10489, pp. 237–248, 2017.
DOI: 10.1007/978-3-319-66284-8_20

status of the patient but also influence the status of the patient, for example by infusing some medication [19].

Following the trend towards cyber-physical systems of systems [3, 10, 19], the next generation of medical systems will use such measuring devices to make autonomous decisions about the control of the devices that affect the health and wellbeing of the patient. The market prospects for these so-called Medical Cyber-Physical Systems of System (MCPSoS) are very promising, but the issue of safety assurance currently limits their high potential.

The traditional way to assure safety for functions is hardly applicable if we transition from simple medical devices to MCPSoS. This is true for the traditional way of performing a hazard and risk assessment of a function as well as for the traditional way of dealing with critical function failures identified in the hazard and risk assessment.

To support discussions on the new challenges and related solutions, we present a taxonomy that is based on a very popular taxonomy for dependable computing. This shall facilitate discussions on safety challenges and solutions for systems of systems and thus contribute to enabling the safety research community to revise traditional safety engineering with respect to the new challenges. As a concrete contribution for such a revision, we use the taxonomy to highlight a fundamental new challenge, reflect on related solutions from the current state of the art, and motivate the integration of these solutions.

This paper is structured as follows. First, we will introduce a running example in Sect. 2. In Sect. 3, we will present a taxonomy for dependable computing with respect to the system-of-systems aspect. In Sect. 4, we will use the taxonomy to discuss safety challenges and solutions for MCPSoS. Finally, we will summarize our main thoughts and give an outlook on our future work in Sect. 5.

2 Running Example

Much effort has been spent by academia, industry, and standard bodies on developing numerous MCPSoS to cope with common problems that a single device is not capable of solving, such as airway-laser surgery [9], alarm coordination [20], closed-loop infusion pumps [1, 16], and so on.

In this work, we consider smart infusion for different scenarios, such as intensive care units, medical surgery, pediatrics, neonatal care, etc. [22]. Infusion pumps works in two ways: it provides (basal) time-programmed doses and (bolus) additional required doses. For bolus doses, the infusion pump provides a handheld device for the patient so that he/she can administer extra doses of opioids according to the current pain level. This technique is used for patient-controlled analgesia (PCA).

Although infusion pumps have improved the quality of care for the patients, several types of accidents in very different situations have been attributed to their use [4]. Thus, different organizations have developed projects to provide new techniques, tools, and documentations in order to improve the safety of infusion pumps, for example the FDA Infusion Pump improvement initiative [24].

The main goal is to safely manage the flow of intravenous (IV) medication delivered by an infusion pump for patients undergoing such therapies. Hence, an integrated clinical environment (ICE) monitors the patient's vital signs data in order to detect any respiratory distress signal, which is a side-effect caused by the continuous usage of IV opioids (e.g., heparin, dopamine, fentanyl) (Fig. 1). If the ICE identifies any respiratory distress signal, it autonomously sends a stop command to the infusion pump and sounds an alarm for the caregivers. System configurations vary according to the patient status assessment strategy and the respective monitoring systems, which may include:

- **pulse oximeter** – In [1, 16], the authors consider only the pulse oximeter sensor for monitoring SpO2 (blood saturation oxygen) and heart rate (Fig. 1 Area 1);
- **respiration sensors** – In [13], the authors used capnography sensors to collect respiration rate and end tidal CO2 data (EtCO2) (see Fig. 1 Area 2);
- **or both combined** – In the standard ASTM International STAM F2761-2009 [6], it is proposed that both data from respiration sensors and from a pulse oximeter should be combined in order to detect signals of respiratory failure (see Fig. 1 Area 2).

Each of these systems might implement different techniques to collect their respective data or infuse medication. For example, there are transmissive-based and reflectance-based pulse oximeters. There are also numerous approaches to respiration monitoring (classified as either contact-based or non-contact-based approaches), which include acoustic sensors, airflow methods, chest and abdominal movement, etc. Likewise, there are different infusion techniques such as syringe pumps, pumps with peristaltic feed, with volume chamber, and so on. Thus, different kinds of devices perform their service with different types of guarantees (e.g., accuracy or frequency), which has an implication on the challenges regarding safety assurance for MCPSoS.

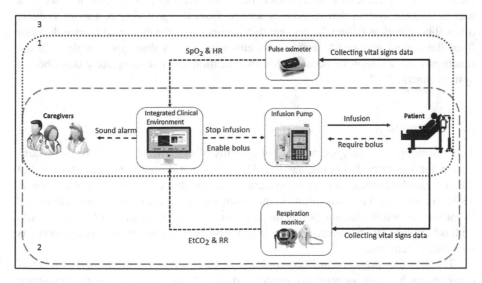

Fig. 1. Potential system configurations for joint functions of smart PCA infusion

3 Taxonomy

The smart infusion system can hardly be seen as system as it is described in the very popular taxonomy for dependable computing in [2]. We often refer to this taxonomy in order to explain problems and solutions regarding dependability and safety. However, to discuss the problems and solutions of smart infusion, we need some extensions of the taxonomy with respect to the system of systems aspect. For this reason, we will first present some relevant parts of the existing taxonomy before introducing some extensions that we will use throughout the course of this paper.

3.1 Taxonomy of Laprie

"A **system** in our taxonomy is an entity that interacts with other entities, i.e., other systems, including hardware, software, humans, and the physical world with its natural phenomena. These other systems are the environment of the given system. The system boundary is the common frontier between the system and its **environment**. From a structural viewpoint, a system is composed of a set of components bound together in order to interact, where each component is another system, which may again be composed of other systems, etc. The recursion stops when a component is considered to be atomic. The **function** of such a system is what the system is intended to do and is described by the **functional specification** in terms of functionality and performance. The **behavior** of a system is what the system does to implement its function and is described by a sequence of states" [2]. Please note that correctness is inherent to a function if we consider these definitions. A functional specification, however, may be incomplete or incorrect and may lead to an unintended behavior. "The **service** delivered by a system (in its role as a provider) is its behavior as perceived by its **user**(s); a user is another system that receives a service from the provider. A **service failure**, often abbreviated as failure, is an event that occurs when the delivered service deviates from the correct service. A service fails either because it does not comply with the functional specification or because this specification did not adequately describe the system function" [2].

3.2 Extension

This taxonomy defines systems, but not systems of systems. As there are many definitions for a system of systems, e.g. [14, 15], we do not propose another definition but rather relate the existing ones to the system definition above. As a system of systems is a system, we should find something in the definition that also fits to a system of system. What we see as this common part is that a system of systems is an "entity that interacts with other elements" because a system of systems also has a usage context and interacts with other elements.

The part that does not fit in our opinion is that a system is composed of a set of components, because we want to consider systems of systems where the single systems are so loosely coupled that they can enter and leave the collaboration field. Naturally, at some point in time, a system of systems will always be composed of a set of systems, but it might always be unclear which systems will enter or leave in the future. Accordingly, we can hardly define a system of systems via its systems. If it is not the composing systems that uniquely define a system of systems, the question arises what, then, uniquely defines a system of systems. Considering our focus on safety of the overall functionality achieved by collaboration, we see this overall functionality as the major aspect. We use the term "**joint function**" in order to refer to this desired outcome of a collaboration or to what a dynamic collaboration shall do or achieve. Furthermore, we use the term **individual function** for what a system should do as an individual and not as part of a dynamically changing composition implementing a joint function. In order to refer to what a system should do not as an individual but as a social entity in order to contribute to (possibly unknown) joint functions, we use the term **social function**. The contribution can either be that the system implements a task completely (e.g., a sensor measuring some information) or that it implements it only partially and breaks it down into other tasks (deriving some required information from some other information). We call the former a **basic social function** and the latter a **conducting social function**. We see the realization of a joint function as a tree-like composition of social functions. The leaves of the tree are basic social functions and the rest are conducting social functions. At design time, it is not clear, however, which tree structures will appear in order to realize a joint function.

In our running example, we have a safety-critical joint function "smart stop infusion", which shall stop the infusion before the risks due to respiratory distress become inacceptable. Such a joint function is not implemented by one single system but realized by a collaboration of several systems. These systems are the ICE, various currently available monitoring devices, and an infusion pump. Each monitoring system has an individual function gathering vital signs from the patient and showing them on the human-machine interface. For example, the pulse oximeter presents in its screen the SpO2 and heart rate data. Furthermore, each monitoring system has a social function, as it has an open interface to other systems so that they can access the data. This social function is a basic social function as the measuring devices require no other systems to provide the data to other systems. The infusion pump also has an individual function and a basic social function. The individual function is used when the infusion is controlled manually by a human and the social function is used by other systems in order to implement a joint function (smart infusion). The ICE has no individual function, as it cannot be used as a stand-alone system. It has a conducting social function, which is based on the basic social functions of the measuring devices and the basic social function of the infusion pump, and which generates the joint function "smart opioid infusion".

So far, we have introduced new attributes for the term function. As the other terms in the taxonomy are based on the term function, we will enhance them accordingly: **Joint behavior** is what a dynamic collaboration actually does to implement a joint function. **Individual behavior** is what a system does to implement its individual function. **Social behavior** is what a system does to implement its social function. The **joint service** delivered by some collaborating systems (in their role as a provider) is their joint behavior as perceived by their **user**(s). The **individual service** delivered by a system (in its role as a provider) is its individual behavior as perceived by its **user**(s).

The **social service** delivered by a system (in its role as a provider) is its social behavior as perceived by its **user**(s). A (joint, individual, basic social, or conductive social) **service failure**, often abbreviated as failure, is an event that occurs when the delivered service deviates from the correct (joint, individual, basic social, or conductive social) service.

In our example, the joint behavior is defined by one of the three classes of collaborations that realizes the joint function "smart stop infusion". The ICE interacts with each single monitoring device (pulse oximeter, respiration sensor, or both) to gather a patient's data and assess his or her physiological status. The data that is delivered at runtime by a monitoring device as a service. From the perspective of the ICE, it is a required service and from the perspective of a device, it is a provided service. A service failure occurs if the delivered data deviates from the intended data.

Based on the delivered data, the ICE shall decide whether further infusion is acceptable. If it is not acceptable, then it shall command the infusion pump to stop immediately. If the generated command at runtime is not as intended even though the received data was as intended, then we have a conductive social service failure.

The infusion pump shall actuate the command of the ICE. If the pump actuates something else, then we have a basic social service failure of the infusion pump.

If the runtime collaboration does not stop infusion before some risks due to respiratory distress become unacceptable, we have a joint service failure. A cause of this joint service failure is one of the aforementioned service failures.

4 Problem, Solutions, and Ideas on Integrating Solutions

After having defined a terminology, we will in the following present the challenges for safety assurance for MCPSoS, give solution ideas from the state of the art, discuss the need to integrate the solutions, and present some ideas for this integration.

4.1 Problem: Unknown Realization of the Joint Function

The fundamental problem is that we do not know how the joint function will be realized at runtime. We do not know which systems will be involved. Furthermore, we do not know how the joint behavior will emerge from the social behavior of the involved systems.

This is problematic for safety assurance as we cannot analyze at design time which failures in the realization of the joint function may cause critical failures of the joint function. Thus, we can hardly come up with a safety concept that appropriately addresses these failures with fault avoidance, fault tolerance, and fault removal.

In the running example, we considered three alternative ways of realizing the joint function "smart stop infusion". According to the three variants, we were able to specify the joint function as follows [13]:

```
If ( (heart rate <50 beats/min or >120 beats/min
OR SpO2 <90 percent)
OR (RR <10 breaths per minute OR EtCO2 >60 mmHg
OR apnea >30 seconds) )
then alert caregivers and stop infusion.
```

This could be the basis for implementing the social function of the ICE so that the ICE would require heart rate, oxygen level, and other patient parameters as input. In a system of systems scenario, it is, however, unknown which devices collaborate how in order to provide the ICE with the required information. This shows that we face a lot of unpredictability even if we come up with a specification of the joint function that already limits the realization to three concrete variants.

4.2 Solution: Safety Contracts

A promising solution approach for this problem is given by contract-based design in general and by safety contracts in particular [8, 17, 18]. The general idea here is to modularize the safety concept according to the way the joint function is modularized by the social functions.

The concept of contract-based design is used to specify for the conductive social function what is guaranteed depending on some modular demands. For the basic social functions, it is only specified what is guaranteed.

This specification technique can then be used to constrain the collaboration at integration time, that is, the point in time when systems meet at runtime. In the beginning, the systems with basic social behavior offer their guarantees. Afterwards, all systems with conductive social functions check what they can do with these guarantees. They evaluate which demands of their guarantee-demand interfaces are satisfied and which guarantees they can thus offer to other social functions. In this way, the aforementioned tree structure is built in a bottom-up manner. The first layer is given by the basic social functions. The second layer is formed by the conductive social functions whose safety demands are fulfilled by the safety guarantees of the basic social functions. The third layer is formed by the conductive social functions whose safety demands are fulfilled by the safety guarantees of the conductive social functions from the second layer, and so on.

The engineering approach for specifying these safety guarantees and demands includes a hazard and risk assessment for the provided services. The problem here is the unknown usage context of the services. The usage context is of crucial importance for determining the criticality of a failure and deriving appropriate guarantees for these failures. In particular for the basic social services, it is not known how they will be used at runtime to generate a joint service. The cause-effect relation between failures of the basic social services and failures of some joint services is thus unknown.

This situation is similar to a scenario where the component of an automotive supplier is built into different vehicles of different OEMs. In this scenario, the supplier estimates which failures of his component might cause critical failures of the vehicle. From the estimated criticality, he derives some safety requirements for his "safety element out of context (SEooC)" as it would be called in terms of the automotive safety standard ISO 26262. Once the SEooC is integrated into its concrete context, it is checked carefully whether the estimated and implemented safety requirements are sufficient for the concrete context. This check is what the ConSerts approach shifted to integration time by formalizing the guarantee-demand interface. Accordingly, the principle for deriving the necessary guarantees for a social service with unknown usage context is similar to the principle of deriving safety requirements for an SEooC. There are obviously some differences, but a detailed discussion of these differences is beyond the scope of this paper.

A fundamentally different hazard and risk assessment is implemented for systems that are not integrated into others but which are directly used by humans, like a vehicle. Due to this difference, ConSerts introduces the term "application services". By means of our taxonomy, we can investigate this aspect. First, any individual service is an application service. Considering the social services, a single service never has an application for a human. The application emerges from the composition. Thus, we have to consider joint services. Here we can distinguish between application joint services and "generic" joint services. An **application joint service** refers to a (complete) tree where the root provides some services that have an application to a human. A generic joint service refers to any subtree. As we believe that application joint services can, in principle, be used by other systems to generate other joint functions, we considered introducing "application joint service" in our taxonomy but not "generic joint service".

4.3 Solution: Dynamic Risk Management

Another related solution approach is given by dynamic (runtime) risk management [11]. The approach is used if the behavior is hardly predictable or not predictable at all. A prominent example of this is given by an implementation based on artificial intelligence (AI). If AI is used for implementation, then it is generally not predictable how the system will behave at runtime, and typically there is no clear functional specification regarding what the system is intended to do.

In the automotive domain, dynamic risk management is enabled by the use of risk metrics as time to collision. If the value of such a metric falls below a previously defined threshold, the situation can be considered as unsafe. For safety supervision, this can be used by checking if an intended action of an autonomous system would lead to such a critical value of a risk metric. In that case, a Safety Supervisor (SSV), as a technical system, would not allow the intended action and thus ensure a safe state of the system.

We see potential to adapt such a Safety Supervisor approach to handle the problems regarding autonomy of medical CPS. A great barrier along that path is the definition of meaningful risk metrics for a dynamic risk assessment in the medical domain. In the automotive domain, the issue is limited to finding one appropriate metric for determining the risk due to "collisions" as this is the major hazard of concern. In the medical domain, we have to consider a huge variety of therapy-specific ways how a patient or even personnel (in case of radiation therapy) can be harmed. Even if we limit our focus to the field of infusion, we have a huge variety of critical effects on the patient depending on that what is infused. In order to come to a meaningful set of hazardous situations for the patient, the applications have to be studied carefully by domain experts. The existing knowledge, the do's and don'ts, need then to be formalized to allow a dynamic risk assessment of intended actions of the autonomously acting system.

Going back to our example of automated infusion of opium for pain relief, we have found the above-mentioned conditions on the status of the patient that have to be fulfilled in order to allow further infusions. As these conditions involve parameters such as the level of oxygen in the blood or the heart rate, we see an analogy to the risk metrics defined in the automotive domain. In both cases, the parameter constraints enable partitioning of the situation space with respect to the risk of performing some behavior, such as infusion or acceleration. The situation partition where all risks are acceptable gives the safe space in which a Safety Supervisor would allow the behavior. The rest of the situation space can be partitioned into different levels of unacceptable risk. The higher the level, the more confidence is needed in the early detection of risky situations and in the mechanism for avoiding their occurrence. Figure 2 illustrates the partitioning of the space of situations. The unpredictable behavior shall not cause a transition from the safe space to any unsafe space. The stability of the borders with regard to avoiding such transitions refers to the different levels of confidence that are required for the different levels of unacceptable risk.

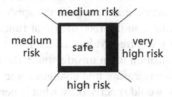

Fig. 2. Space of situations classification according to the criticality

The approach is strongly related to the "Safety Bag" presented in IEC 61508 [23] or the safety cage presented in [7]. The term safety cage refers to the picture of putting a cage around the unpredictable behavior in order to show that it will stay within "behavioral boundaries", which assure safety.

The authors of [12] present a methodology for deriving a functional specification for such a safety cage or SSV. The dynamic risk management of an SSV is also presented in [11].

4.4   Need for Integrating the Solutions

We see the need to combine contract-based design with dynamic risk management in order to deal with the unpredictability of the joint behavior. The reason why contract-based design approaches are in many cases not sufficient is the complexity of specifying safety guarantees that constrain the unpredictable joint behavior only to what is safe but provide maximized freedom for realizing the joint function.

Particularly if the joint function includes complex decision making, such as making the decision about whether to allow the patient to have some medication, the conflict between maximizing freedom for realization and minimizing freedom for safety assurance is problematic. It might be possible to come up with a simple rule that refers to some observable information about the patient, like the current oxygen concentration in his blood. However, it has to be considered that this simple rule might not be the only way to find out if further medication is acceptable. If some alternatives are imaginable, then the simple rule would lead to demands that constrain the flexibility of collaboration more than necessary.

The problem that we are facing here is exactly the same as the one we address with dynamic risk management. The reason why dynamic risk management is not a sufficient solution on its own is simply that it has to be implemented as a joint function.

4.5   Ideas for Integrating the Solutions

So far, we have no concrete approach for the integration of safety contracts and dynamic risk assessment. However, we have two concrete ideas for approaching our vision.

First, the safety guarantee for the application joint function could refer to a high-level hazard such as respiratory depression and claim that the risks due to this hazard are always acceptable.

Second, the top-level social function could break this guarantee down into some demands by means of a risk metric that partitions the space of possible situations into different risk partitions. To calculate the risk metric at runtime, it would demand that other social functions deliver the current values of the risk metric. If the current values are such that we might get transition to an unsafe space, then it would call other social functions to implement a countermeasure that changes some risk parameters so that the risk is reduced. In doing so, it would specify only what is needed and give the maximal freedom to deliver the required information and to implement the required countermeasures.

5   Summary and Conclusion

Medical Cyber-Physical Systems of System (MCPSoS) refer to collaboration of systems that is unknown at design time. This unpredictability is a big challenge for the assuring safety of such systems. To formulate these challenges more precisely, we have presented an extension of the taxonomy of Laprie [2]. We enhanced the meaning of the terms Function, Functional Specification, Behavior, and Service with respect to collaboration. Based on this enhancement, we reflected on the challenge of unpredictability and presented safety contracts and dynamic risk management as solution concepts. Safety contracts define a guarantee/demand interface for the systems in a system of systems, which allows constraining the flexibility of runtime collaboration to what is safe. It is, however, only a language, and it is challenging to specify the design space of safe collaboration behavior with this language. We thus reflected on dynamic risk management and the general idea of limiting unpredictable behavior by assessing the risk of a particular behavior in the current situation online. We believe that this general idea is also applicable for limiting unpredictable collaboration.

There are several related issues which were not the focus of this work. A fundamental challenge for safety assurance is who is responsible to assure the safety of MCPSoS. In [21] the authors claim that despite of relevant analyzed regulation efforts (such as IEC, ISO, NHS) focused on manufacturers, the safety of resulting integrated systems (e.g. MCPSoS) can only be assured if health-care providers are appropriately involved. Moreover, the evidence provided by both manufacturer and health-care providers must be accessible and integrated. The lack of adequate communication between stakeholders and unavailability of integrated safety assurance evidence however poses several challenges for the safety certification of integrated systems like MCPSoS.

Even the health-care providers often have integration problems due to the lack of appropriate standards and guidance to build integrated health IT products within their environment. However, the solutions provided by the combination of contract-based design with dynamic risk management will provide a valuable technological foundation to face the indicated issue. For example, semi-automated generation of safety case argument-fragments from safety contracts could be enhanced by the risk management strategies.

While writing this paper and creating the proposed taxonomy, this belief was strengthened and some concrete new ideas came up. We conclude thus that it is worth to investigate further how safety contracts and dynamic risk assessment relate to each other and to reason how they can be harmonized and integrated in order to tackle the challenge of unpredictable collaboration behavior of medical cyber physical system.

Acknowledgements. The ongoing research that led to this paper is funded by the Brazilian National Research Council (CNPq) under grant CSF 201715/2014-7.

References

1. Arney, D., et al.: Toward patient safety in closed-loop medical device systems. In: Proceedings of the 1st ACM/IEEE International Conference on Cyber-Physical Systems - ICCPS 2010, p. 139. ACM Press, New York (2010)
2. Avizienis, A., et al.: Basic concepts and taxonomy of dependable and secure computing. IEEE Trans. Dependable Secur. Comput. 1(1), 11–33 (2004)
3. Bondavalli, A., et al.: Cyber-Physical Systems of Systems: Foundations – A Conceptual Model and Some Derivations: the AMADEOS Legacy. Springer, Heidelberg (2016)
4. Brief, E.: Top 10 Health Technology Hazards for Top 10 Health Technology Hazards for 2017 (2016)
5. Goldman, J.M.: Getting connected to save lives. Biomed. Instrum. Technol. 39(3), 174 (2005)
6. Goldman, J.M.: Medical devices and medical systems - essential safety requirements for equipment comprising the patient-centric integrated clinical environment (ICE) - Part 1: general requirements and conceptual model (2009)

7. Heckemann, K., Gesell, M., Pfister, T., Berns, K., Schneider, K., Trapp, M.: Safe automotive software. In: König, A., Dengel, A., Hinkelmann, K., Kise, K., Howlett, R.J., Jain, L.C. (eds.) KES 2011. LNCS, vol. 6884, pp. 167–176. Springer, Heidelberg (2011). doi:10.1007/978-3-642-23866-6_18

8. Kaiser, B., et al.: Contract-based design of embedded systems integrating nominal behavior and safety. Complex Syst. Inform. Model. Q. 4, 66–91 (2015)

9. Kim, C., et al.: A framework for the safe interoperability of medical devices in the presence of network failures. In: Proceedings of the 1st ACM/IEEE International Conference on Cyber-Physical Systems - ICCPS 2010, p. 149. ACM Press, New York (2010)

10. King, A.L., et al.: Towards assurance for plug & play medical systems. In: Koornneef, F., van Gulijk, C. (eds.) SAFECOMP 2014. LNCS, vol. 9337, pp. 228–242. Springer, Cham (2015). doi:10.1007/978-3-319-24255-2_17

11. Kurd, Z., Kelly, T., McDermid, J., Calinescu, R., Kwiatkowska, M.: Establishing a framework for dynamic risk management in 'intelligent' aero-engine control. In: Buth, B., Rabe, G., Seyfarth, T. (eds.) SAFECOMP 2009. LNCS, vol. 5775, pp. 326–341. Springer, Heidelberg (2009). doi:10.1007/978-3-642-04468-7_26

12. Machin, M., et al.: SMOF: a safety monitoring framework for autonomous systems. IEEE Trans. Syst. Man Cybern. Syst. 99, 1–14 (2016)

13. Maddox, R.R., et al.: Continuous Respiratory Monitoring and a "Smart" Infusion System Improve Safety of Patient-Controlled Analgesia in the 'Postoperative Period. Agency for Healthcare Research and Quality (US), Rockville (2008)

14. Maier, M.W.: Architecting principles for systems-of-systems. Syst. Eng. 1(4), 267–284 (1998)

15. Nielsen, C.B., et al.: Systems of systems engineering: basic concepts, model-based techniques, and research directions. ACM Comput. Surv. 48(2), 1–41 (2015)

16. Pajic, M., et al.: Model-driven safety analysis of closed-loop medical systems. IEEE Trans. Ind. Inform. 10(1), 3–16 (2012)

17. Schneider, D.: Conditional safety certification for open adaptive systems. (Ph.D. theses in Experimental Software Engineering). Fraunhofer Verlag (26 March 2014), Kaiserslautern (2014)

18. Schneider, D., Trapp, M.: Conditional safety certification of open adaptive systems. ACM Trans. Auton. Adapt. Syst. 8(2), 1–20 (2013)

19. Sokolsky, O., et al.: Challenges and research directions in medical cyber-physical systems. Proc. IEEE 100(1), 75–90 (2012)

20. Stevens, N., et al.: Smart alarms: multivariate medical alarm integration for post CABG surgery patients. In: Proceedings of the 2nd ACM SIGHIT Symposium on International Health Informatics - IHI 2012, p. 533. ACM Press, New York (2012)

21. Sujan, M.A., et al.: Safety cases for medical devices and health information technology: involving health-care organisations in the assurance of safety. Health Inform. J. 19(3), 165–182 (2013)

22. Williams, C.K., et al.: Application of the IV medication harm index to assess the nature of harm averted by "Smart" infusion safety systems. J. Patient Saf. 2(3), 132–139 (2006)

23. BS EN 61508-1: 2010 BSI Standards Publication Functional safety of electrical/electronic/programmable electronic safety-related systems Part 1 : General requirements (2010)

24. Infusion Pump Improvement Initiative. https://www.fda.gov/MedicalDevices/ProductsandMedicalProcedures/GeneralHospitalDevicesandSupplies/InfusionPumps/ucm202501.htm

Safety-Aware Control of Swarms of Drones

Amin Majd[1], Elena Troubitsyna[1(✉)], and Masoud Daneshtalab[2]

[1] Åbo Akademi University, Turku, Finland
{amin.majd, elena.troubitsyna}@abo.fi
[2] KTH Royal Institute of Technology, Stockholm, Sweden
masoudd@kth.se

Abstract. In this paper, we propose a novel approach to ensuring safety while planning and controlling an operation of swarms of drones. We derive the safety constraints that should be verified both during the mission planning and at the run-time and propose an approach to safety-aware mission planning using evolutionary algorithms. High performance of the proposed algorithm allows us to use it also at run-time to predict and resolve in a safe and optimal way dynamically emerging hazards. The benchmarking of the proposed approach validate its efficiency and safety.

Keywords: Safety · Autonomous systems · Evolutionary algorithms · Route planning · Dynamic safety assurance

1 Introduction

Swarms of drones are increasingly used in a variety of applications such as surveillance, inspections, good delivery, rescue operations etc. Strong business incentives drive fast development and deployment of the drone technology. However, the problem of ensuring *motion safety, i.e., the ability of a system to avoid collisions* still remains unresolved.

In this paper, we propose a novel approach to ensuring motion safety of swarms of drones. Our approach combines safety-explicit route planning with the run-time safety monitoring and route recalculation aiming at increasing safety and minimizing travelling distance. We start by explicitly defining the conditions that should be verified to ensure motion safety of a swarm: swarms do not collide with the static objects and each other. We consider the route planning as an optimization problem that aims at maximizing safety while minimizing the length of the path of each drone.

To solve such a complex multi-criteria optimization problem, we rely on evolutionary computing paradigm [1]. As a basis of our solution, we take the Imperialist Competitive Algorithm (ICA) [2]. The algorithm iteratively generates the solutions that progressively maximize the value of the defined fitness function. In our definition of the fitness function, we explicitly introduce safety as an argument, i.e., ensure that our route planning finds the safest shortest route for each drone.

Safety-aware route planning is augmented with the run-time monitoring and control. They deal with the dynamically emerging hazards caused by the deviations while executing the planned mission, e.g., caused by drone transient failures. Our solution

© Springer International Publishing AG 2017
S. Tonetta et al. (Eds.): SAFECOMP 2017 Workshops, LNCS 10489, pp. 249–260, 2017.
DOI: 10.1007/978-3-319-66284-8_21

allows the system to proactively recalculate the routes of the drones to ensure that the swarm continues its mission execution in a safe and efficient manner.

The proposed approach is implemented as a parallel algorithm, which ensures high performance and scalability required for controlling highly dynamic systems. The algorithm is benchmarked in a number of simulation experiments representing different safety-related challenges. We believe that our approach proposes a novel solution enhancing the motion safety of the swarms of drones.

The paper is organized as follows. In Sect. 2, we discuss the problem of motion safety and define the conditions that should be verified to ensure collision avoidance. In Sect. 3, we overview the principles of the evolutionary algorithms and, in particular, ICA. In Sect. 4, we present the proposed approach and give small examples illustrating the main steps. We also present the results of benchmarking and validation of our implementation. In Sect. 5, we discuss the related work and conclude.

2 Safety Constraints in Route Planning and Mission Execution

The swarms of drones are increasingly used for surveillance, inspections, shipping, rescue etc. A *swarm* is a group of autonomously functioning drones that, in a coordinated manner, provide the required services. Ensuring motion safety should become a key parameter in route planning and control of the drones. We can formulate the following two types of safety requirements to be imposed of the swarms:

Req 1. The drones do not collide with the static objects (obstacles).
Req 2. The drones do not collide with each other.

The swarms should execute certain missions. For simplicity, we assume that a mission defines the destinations to be reached by the drones of the swarm. During the mission planning all obstacles (mountains, tall constructions etc.) are defined on the drone fly map and the initial swarm routing is calculated. While the drones are en route, the adherence to the defined mission plan is continuously monitored. Whenever a deviation is detected, the routing is recalculated to maintain safety while mimimising the travelling distance of drones.

A route planning of a swarm is typically considered to be an optimization problem, which is often solved using evolutionary algorithms (EAs) [1]. They take the initial (or current) positions of the drones and the required destinations as the input and produce the routes that meet a number of optimization criteria and constraints, e.g., minimization of distance and energy consumption, avoiding or visiting certain locations etc.

Let us consider *Req 1* – a collision avoidance with the static objects. Since the terrain of the flying zone is known for each mission, we should guarantee that the obstacles occurring on the flying altitude of the drones are faithfully introduced as the constraints of the planning algorithm and no unsafe routes are planned.

Let $SWARM = \{d_1, ..., d_N\}$ be a set of drones in the swarm. Furthermore, let the mission fly zone be represented by a finite set of locations $AREA = \{l_1,.., l_M\}$. Assume that there are M obstacles located in the fly zone. An obstacle Obs_i can be represented by a subset of locations that it occupies, i.e., $Obs_i \subseteq AREA$. Correspondingly, the locations occupied by all the obstacles are $\bigcup_{i_1..M} Obs_i$. A route of a drone is defined as a sequence of locations, i.e., for a drone d_i

$$route_i = <l_{in}, ..l_{fin}> , \tag{1}$$

such that $ran(route_i) \subseteq AREA$, where ran denoted the function range.

The requirement **Req 1** can be verified by checking that

$$\forall i,j.i \in 1..N \wedge j \in 1..M \Rightarrow ran(route_i) \bigcap \left(\bigcup_{J=1}^{M} Obs_j \right) = \emptyset \tag{2}$$

Note, that in case of **Req 1**, we have a complete a priory knowledge of the constraints (the potential collision points) and hence, if each drone (location-wise) follows the planned route, the main strategy of ensuring safety is to verify (2).

Overall, to ensure that the requirement **Req 1** is satisfied, we should guarantee that

(1) Obstacles are correctly represented as the input constraints of the route planning algorithm.
(2) Each planned route avoids obstacles, i.e., the formula (2) is satisfied.
(3) While en route, the accuracy of the position estimate is monitored and in case of a deviation, the faulty drone is stopped and navigated in a controlled rather than autonomous way.

Now let us discuss **Req 2** – drones do not collide with each other. While planning a swarm routing, we should guarantee that at any instance of time, each location is occupied by at most one drone. Let *CurLoc* be a function that returns the current position of a drone at a particular instance of time, i.e.,

$$CurLoc : SWARM \times [0..maxtime] \rightarrow AREA \tag{3}$$

where $[0..maxtime]$ is the interval covering the entire duration of a mission. (The duration of a mission is the maximal time *maxtime* required for all drones in the swarm to reach the required destinations.) Then we should guarantee that

$$\forall d_i, d_j, t.d_i, d_j, \in SWARM \wedge t \in [0..maxtime] \Rightarrow CurLoc(d_i,t) \\ \neq CurLoc(d_j,t) \tag{4}$$

Since, as a result of route planning, the paths of all drones are known in advance, we also have a complete a priory knowledge of the safety constraints, yet with a certain degree of uncertainty. The cause of uncertainty is the potential deviations of the drones from the planned routes, e.g., due to the transient faults.

Let us consider the following scenario: as a result of the route planning, it is established that the drones *d1* and *d2* cross at the location *l*. Since the speed of each drone and distance from the initial point till *l* are known, we calculate that *d1* will reach point *l* at time *t1* and *d2* at time *t2* and *t1−t2 > Δ*, were *Δ* is a constant defining time gap derived from the safe proximity distance. However, while the mission is in progress, due to some internal failure, $d1$ moves slower than expected and can reach point l at time $t1'$, such that $t1-t2 < \Delta$, i.e., the likelihood of collision increases.

To handle dynamically emerging safety hazards, we can undertake two types of actions. Firstly, we introduce safety consideration into the route planning. Secondly, we have to complement the safety aware route planning with the run-time mechanisms of safety monitoring. Such mechanisms should monitor compliance with the predefined routes, recalculate them and activate controlled coordinated cross-point passing in case the risk of a collision is detected. Overall, to guarantee that *Req 2* is satisfied, we should ensure that

(1) Safety maximisation is taken as one of the objectives of route planning optimization. It is achieved by minimizing the number of the cross-points and giving a preference to the cross-points with the longer time gaps between drones passing.
(2) Safety monitoring detects dynamically emerging hazards – the potential collisions at a cross point and activates controlled cross-point passing for the drones of concern.
(3) The controlled cross-point passing mechanism is verified to preserve condition (4).

3   Evolutionary Algorithms

Evolutionary computing comprises a set of optimization algorithms, which are inspired by a biological or societal evolution [1]. An example of the former is Imperialist Competitive Algorithm (ICA) [2]. The algorithm simulates a human social evolution. Its parallel implementation [3] shows a remarkable performance in comparison with the other EA and offers a promising solution supporting computationally intensive tasks of controlling swarm systems.

ICA starts by a random generation of a set of countries – the chromosomes (an encoding of the possible solutions) – in the search space of the optimization problem. The fitness function determines the power of each country. The countries with the best values of the fitness function become *Imperialists,* the other countries become *Colonies.* The Colonies are divided between the Imperialists and hence the overall search space is divided into empires. An association of a Colony with an Imperialist means that only the chromosomes of the Imperialist and its associated colonies will be used to crossover.

The mutation and crossover are implemented by Assimilation and Revolution operators. Mutation is a unary operator applied to a chromosome to produce a (slightly) modified mutant – a child (offspring). Mutation is stochastic, i.e., the child depends of the outcomes of random choices. For instance, a mutation of a chromosome represented by a bit-string can be achieved by a random flip of a bit. Recombination (or crossover) merges the information from two parent genotypes into offspring genotype. Similarly to mutation, the recombination is also stochastic – the choice of parents' chromosome parts and the way of combining is random. Intuitively, a recombination is mating two individuals with the different but desirable features to produce an offspring that combines both of those features.

Assimilation moves colonies closer to an imperialist in its socio-political characteristics. It can be implemented by a replacement of a bit of a Colony chromosome by the corresponding bit (or a certain function over such a bit) of the Imperialist.

Revolution is implemented by a random replacement of a certain bit in the Colony chromosome. As a result of assimilation and revolution, a colony might reach a better position and has a chance to take the control over the entire empire, i.e., to replace the current imperialist. This can happen only if the evaluation of the fitness function of such a colony gives a higher value (if we are solving a maximization problem) than the value of the fitness function of the current imperialist.

The next step of the algorithm is to compute the power of each empire and implement the Imperialistic Competition, which corresponds to the selection of the survivals process. The power of an empire is computed as a sum of the value of the fitness function of imperialist and a weighted value of the sum of the fitness functions of the colonies.

The imperialists try to take a possession of colonies of other empires, i.e., the weakest empire loses its weakest colony. Indeed, the weakest empire does not offer a promising solution in the search space and further assimilation of colonies to the current imperialist would not bring any significant improvement. Therefore, it is practical to reallocate the weakest colony to a more promising empire.

In each step of the algorithm, based on their power, all the empires have a chance to take control of one or more of the colonies of the weakest empire. The steps of the algorithm are repeated until a termination condition is reached. As a result, the imperialist of the strongest empire will give us the most optimal solution.

The benchmarking experiments demonstrate that the parallel implementation of the proposed algorithm significantly outperforms the similar parallel algorithms. Therefore, it guarantees that at each control cycle the algorithm will generate a desired optimal swarm routing as discuss next.

4 Safety-Aware Routing Planning and Run-Time Safety Monitoring

Our approach to ensuring collision avoidance in the swarm combines parallel ICA-based route calculation with the run-time monitoring. As we discussed in Sect. 2, the fly area including the positions of the drones can be represented by the set of locations *AREA*. We assume that the entire fly zone is represented by a grid, i.e., the distances between a pair of neighboring locations are the same, as shown in Fig. 1(a). The initial and the destination positions are known for all drones. The drones move from a location to location. Our goal is to find an optimal *routing*, where routing is defined as a union of each individual drone route, i.e., routing represents a plan of a mission for all drones.

We give an ID to each routing and define the set of phenotypes as a set of routing IDs. To explain the principle of defining a chromosome, let us consider an example shown in Fig. 1(b). For the drone *d1* the shortest path from the initial location to the destination is a sequence <20, 19, 18, 17, 16, 11, 6> , corresponding the shortest paths for the drone *d2* is <21, 22, 17, 12, 7, 2, 3> and for *d3* <11, 12, 13, 14, 9, 10, 15> .

We note that the path of each drone can be succinctly represented by a "turning" point – we call it a middle point, which would be 16 for *d1*, 12 ford *d2*, and 9 for *d3*. Hence, a chromosome representing such a routing can be represented as a triple ≪16, 12, 9≫. In general, for n drones a chromosome is an n-tuple consisting of the middle points of the corresponding drones. The turning points are generated randomly.

To ensure collision avoidance with the static objects, we should explicitly define the locations, which are occupied by the obstacles.

Our route planning starts by generating all shortest paths between each pair of locations in our grid and storing them in a database. The database of the shortest paths is then used to compose the routes of the individual drones as a concatenation of the route from current to the middle point and from the middle point to the final destination.

The shortest routes are computed using the algorithm proposed by Dijkstra [4]. For each given source node in the graph, the algorithm finds the shortest path between that node and all other nodes. As an input to our implementation of Dijkstra's algorithm, we define the adjacency matrix of the fly zone *AREA* with the explicit representation of the obstacles.

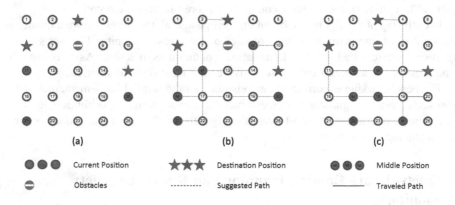

Fig. 1. Example of routing planning

Now we should define the fitness function to evaluate the fitness of each country (chromosome). As we discussed in Sect. 2, our goal is to devise an algorithms that optimizes the safety/efficiency ratio. To achieve this, while evaluating fitness of each routing, we should not only evaluate the corresponding path lengths, but also the number of cross points between all drone as well as the time gap associated with them.

The first argument of our fitness function is the distance metric:

$$Distance\,Metric = \sum_{i=1}^{nd}(Distance_{Current_i \to Middle_i} + Distance_{Middle_i \to Destination_i}) \quad (5)$$

It defines the total length of the drone routes according to the given routing. For instance, for our example in Fig. 1(b) the distance metric of the routing defined by the chromosome <<16, 12, 9 >> is the sum of the lengths of the drone paths: 6 + 6 + 6 = 18.

The second argument defines the number of cross points associated with the given routing. For our example the number of cross points is 3: in the location 17 between the routes 1 and 2, in the location 12 between the routes 2 and 3, and in the location11 between the routes 1 and 3 correspondingly.

The third argument of the fitness function is the safety level of the time gap at the cross point. We introduce three safety levels: 0 if there is no cross points, 1 if the time gap at the cross point is above the safety threshold and 2 if the time gap is below the threshold. For instance, for our example at Fig. 1(b) the time gap at cross point 17 is 1, because the drones arrive at that point at times 3 and 1, the time gap for the cross point 12 is 2, because the drones arrive there at times 3 and 1, and for the cross point 11 it is 5. As a matter of illustration, we can assume that the time gaps below threshold 2 are classified as level 2, while the time gaps at and above threshold 2 as level 1. Hence, the cross point 17 obtains level 2, while the cross points 11 and 12 the level 1.

We define our route optimization task as a minimization problem with the following fitness function:

$$Fitness\ Function = Distance\ Metric + \alpha \times Number\ of\ Cross\ Point + \beta \times Level \quad (6)$$

here α and β are the weight coefficients defined as follows:

$$1 \le \alpha \le nd/2 \qquad 1 \le \beta \le \sqrt{np} \times nd \qquad (7)$$

where nd is the number of drones and np is the total number of points. These values allow us to adapt the fitness function evaluation based on the level of complexity of the flying zone and the number of drones.

For our example in Fig. 1(b) the value of the fitness function is computed as follows: $18 + 1, 5 \times 3 + 5 \times 3 = 37, 5$. The evaluation of the fitness function for the initial population is shown in Fig. 2.

In our large scale experiments, after evaluating the fitness values of the initial population, we have chosen the imperialists – the countries with the fitness function values smaller than a certain threshold – and the colonies – the other countries. Due to a very small size of the population in our example, we skip this step and explicitly pairwise compare the fitness values. The chromosomes with the lowest fitness values are chosen for cross over and mutation, as shown in *Tournament Number* and *Mating Pool* columns in Fig. 2.

The next column defines the probabilities of cross over *rc* and the results of applying cross over operator are shown in the *Offspring after Crossover* column. In the similar way, we define the probabilities of mutation. The *Offspring after Mutation* column shows the results of mutation operator applied to the offspings.

Now we calculate the fitness function for the mutated offsprings. To produce the new generation, from the initial population and the pool of mutated offsprings, we chose the chromosomes with the lowest values of the fitness function. After that we start the next iteration of the algorithm with the new generation as the current population. After several iterations of the algorithm, we find the routing that achieves our

Current Position	Initial Population	Total Distance	# Cross Point	Critical Level	Fitness	Tournament Number	Mating Pool	r_c	Offspring after Crossover	r_m	Offspring after Mutation
20 21 11	17|24| 13	18	4	1	39	1, 3	17|24|1 3	0.6	16|22|16	0.2	17|24|13
	09|17| 18	20	4	2	56	2, 4	16|12|1 9		17|14|18	0.6	17|14|18
	13|09|23	22	5	1	44.5	1, 4	16|12|1 9	0.9	16|12|19	0.1	13|09|23
	16|12|90	18	3	1	37.5	2, 3	13|09|2 3		13|09|23	0.4	16|12|09

Total Distance	# Hot Point	Critical Level	Fitness	Next Generation	Best	Current Position	Total Distance	# Cross Point	Critical Level	Fitness	Tournament Number
18	6	2	57	17|24|13	16|12|0 9	18	14	1	1	30.5	2, 4
20	3	1	39.5	17|14|18		22	17	2	2	50	1, 3
22	4	2	58	13|09|23		12	18	4	1	39	1, 4
18	2	1	44.5	16|12|09			14	2	2	47	3, 2

Mating Pool	r_c	Offspring after Crossover	r_m	Offspring after Mutation	Total Distance	# Cross Point	Critical Level	Fitness	Next Generation	Best
16|12|09	0.5	17|09|09	0.1	17|09|11	16	4	2	52	17|24|13	17|24|13
17|24|13		16|21|14	0.3	16|21|14	14	1	1	30.5	16|21|14	
17|24|13	0.7	18|09|23	0.4	18|09|23	18	3	1	37.5	18|09|23	
13|09|23		12|24|13	0.8	12|24|13	14	2	1	32	12|24|09	

Fig. 2. An example of the two iterations of algorithm

goal – minimizes the distance of travelling and associated danger, i.e., maximizes safety. The pseudocode of the entire approach is shown in Fig. 3.

Let us now illustrate the deviation scenarios. In Fig. 1(c), we present a snap-shot of drone positions after one unit of time has elapsed. Drone 2 and Drone 3 have moved according to the planned routes with the planned speed. However, due to some internal problems, Drone 1 moved twice as fast as it was supposed to. If Drone 1 regains the planned speed and the initial routing is not changed then the Drone 1 and Drone 2 will collide in location 17. Hence, we should recalculate the routes.

This goal is achieved using our proposed algorithm. As shown in Fig. 1(c), the new routing avoids crosspoint 17 by rerouting Drone 2 to the route <22, 23, 24, 29, 24, 9, 4, 3> and finding shorter path for drone 3 <12, 13, 14, 15> .

If a collision is predicted between the drones then the priority to move to the next position is given to the drone that is closer to the cross point. Then after the safe time gap, the next drone moves to the next position and the situation is reassessed. If the collision danger is removed then the routing is recomputed and the autonomous flying mode is resumed.

Due to the lack of space, we present only the results of two extreme benchmarks. The first benchmarks focuses on resolving the problem of the high number of potential cross points, as shown in Fig. 4 (left). The drones should fly in the opposite directions and hence, there is a high risk of collision between each other. Our algorithm has success-fully and efficiently managed to solve the collision avoidance problem: no collisions occurred and the travel distance has increased only by 5.5% as shown in Table 1.

The second case aims at validating the algorithms under the challenging flying zone topology: the static objects (e.g., mountains) are densely located and leave only narrow curved corridors for flying as shown in Fig. 4 (right). The algorithm has succeeded in finding a safe and efficient routing – the resulting increase in the travel distance is 7.3%.

1. **BEGIN**
//**Offline Part*
2.   **Call** *Dijkstra' Algorithm to Compute the Shortest Path between all nodes*
3.   **Read** *Current Position of all Drones.*   **Call** *Generate Countries*
4.   **Call** *Evaluation Operation*
5.   **Select** *the Best Routes*
//**Online part*
6.   **While** (*all Drones has not arrived to their Destinations*) **Do**
7.   **Begin**
8.   **IF** (*# Cross point (Best Routes)* == 0)   //**No cross point and only monitoring
9.   **Begin**
10.   **While** (*the Best routes and current positions match*) **Do** *only monitoring*
11.   **Call** *Evaluation Operation*
12.   **End**
13.   **Else IF** (*the Dangerous level==2*)   //**Risk of collision*
14.   **Begin**
15.   **Run** *Critical Navigation Instructions*
16.   **Go to 8.**
17.   **End**
18.   **Else**
19.   **Begin**   //**Finding better routes*
20.   **Call** *Assimilation and Revolution Operations*
21.   **Call** *Evaluation Operation*
22.   **Run** *Competition Operation*
23.   **Go to 8.**
24.   **End**
25.   **End**
26. **END.**

Fig. 3. The pseudocode of the overall algorithm

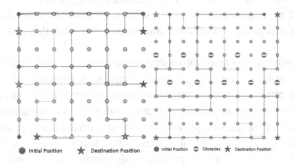

Fig. 4. Illustration of the benchmarking cases

Table 1. Benchmarking statistics

	Number of obstacles	Number of drones	Number of points	Shortest distance without safety	Shortest distance with safety	Difference distance
Benchmark 1	0	6	64	72	76	5.5%
Benchmark 2	8	4	100	68	73	7.3%

5   Related Work and Conclusions

Currently, the problem of motion safety of autonomous robotic systems attracts significant research attention. A comprehensive overview of the problems associated with mobile robots is given in [5]. The analysis carried out in [6], shows that the most prominent routing schemes do not guarantee motion safety. Our approach resolves this issue and ensures not only safety but also efficiency of routing.

Macek et al. [7] have proposed a layered architectural solution for robot navigation. They focus on a problem of safe navigation of a vehicle in an urban environment. Similarly to our approach, they distinguish between a global route planning and a collision avoidance control. However, in their work, they focus on the safety issues associated with the navigation of a single vehicle and do not consider the problem of route optimization that is especially acute in the context of swarms of robots.

A formal approach that employs formal verification to ensure motion safety has been proposed by Aniculaesei et al. [8]. They employ UPPAAL to verify that a moving robot engages brakes and safely stops upon detection of an obstacle. Since in our work we have focused on finding an algorithm that optimizes safety/efficiency ratio, our solution is more performant and flexible – it allows the system to dynamically recalculate the route to prevent a collision and avoids unnecessary stopping of drones.

Petti and Fraichard [9] have proposed an approach that relies on a partial motion planning to ensure safety. They state that a calculation of an entire route is such a complex and computationally-intensive problem that the only viable solution is a computation of the next safe states and navigation within them. The solution is proposed for the navigation of a single vehicle. In our work, to overcome the problem of heavy computational costs and hence insufficiently quick response, we have on the one hand, discretized the search space, and on the other hand, developed a highly performant algorithm that guarantees the desired responsiveness. As a result, we could not only calculate the entire safe and efficient routes, but also solve this task for a swarm of drones.

Our solution relies on the assumption that the algorithm is sufficiently fast to control the swarm of drones in real time, i.e., the worst case execution time is shorter than the control cycle. We can verify this assumption using the approach proposed in [10].

To verify safety, we can represent a swarm of drones as a multi-agent system and rely on the rigorous techniques employing formal specification and proofs as proposed in [11–16]. An integration of formal specification would allow us to increase the confidence in the correctness of the proposed algorithm and guarantee that safety is ensured despite possible deviations, e.g., caused by drone failures.

Since safety is often assessed probabilistically, an integration of stochastic reasoning using the techniques defined in [17–20] constitutes one of the important research directions. This would allow us to evaluate the probability of drone failures and correspondingly their impact of safety. In its turn, such an assessment would enable further fine-tuning of the proposed algorithm.

While defining the overall architecture of the control system, we implicitly structured the behavior of the system using the notion of modes. Indeed, the drones fly in the autonomous mode until a danger of collision is detected. Then the controlled collision avoidance mode is activated. Verification of mode logic using the approach proposed in [21, 22] would allow us to ensure correctness and safety of the proposed system architecture.

In this paper, we have proposed a novel approach to ensuring motion safety of swarms of drones. Our approach relies on the use of evolutionary computing that allows us to formulate safe routing as an optimization problem. We have made several technical contributions. Firstly, we have defined the main principles of safety-aware route planning for swarms using evolutionary algorithms. Secondly, we have proposed and verified a parallel algorithm that guarantees high performance in solving routing problem for a swarm of drones. Thirdly, we have defined and validated an architecture that combines the route planning with the run-time safety monitoring consisting of proactive collision avoidance and coordinated navigation. A distinctive feature of the approach is its ability to foresee a risk of a collision and proactively recalculate the routing of the entire swarm to maximize safety and efficiency. To the best of our knowledge, this issue has not been addressed before.

We believe that our work has offered a promising solution to the problem of ensuring motion safety of swarms of drones. The benchmarking results have demonstrated that out algorithm is able to handle challenging routing conditions, guarantees safety while introducing only a small overhead to achieve it.

As a future work, we are planning to test our algorithm in real-life scenario – a video surveillance of a rescue operation.

References

1. Eiben, A.E., Smith, J.E.: Introduction to Evolutionary Computing. Springer, Heidelberg (2003)
2. Atashpaz-Gargari, E., Lucas, C.: Imperialist competitive algorithm: an algorithm for optimization inspired by imperialistic competition. IEEE Congress Evol. Comput. **7**, 4661–4666 (2007)
3. Majd, A., Lofti, S., Sahebi, G., Daneshtalab, M., Plosila, J.: PICA: multi-population implementation of parallel imperialist competitive algorithms. In: 24th Euromicro International Conference of Parallel, Distributed and Network-Based Processing, pp. 248–255. IEEE (2016)
4. Dijkstra, E.W.: A note on two problems in connexion with graphs. Numer. Math. **1**, 269–271 (1959)
5. Siegwart, R., Nourbakhsh, I.R.: Introduction to Autonomous Mobile Robots. MIT Press, Cambridge (2004)
6. Fraichard, T.: A short paper about motion safety. In: The IEEE International Conference on Robotics and Automation (2007)
7. Macek, K., Vasquez, D., Fraichard, T., Siegwart, R.: Safe vehicle navigation in dynamic urban scenarios. In: 11th International IEEE Conference on Intelligent Transportation Systems, pp. 482–489, Beijing, China (2008)
8. Aniculaesei, A., Arnsberger, D., Howar, F., Rausch, A.: Towards the verification of safety-critical autonomous systems in dynamic environments. In: 1st International Workshop on Verification and Validation of Cyber Physical Systems – V2CPS, EPTCS 232, pp. 79–90 (2016)

9. Petti, S., Fraichard, T.: Partial motion planning framework for reactive planning within dynamic environments. In: The IFAC/AAAI International Conference on Informatics in Control, Automation and Robotics (2005)

10. Iliasov, A., Romanovsky, A., Laibinis, L., Troubitsyna, E., Latvala, T.: Augmenting Event-B Modelling with real-time verification. In: FormSERA@ICSE, pp. 51–57. IEEE Computer (2012)

11. Troubitsyna, E.: Stepwise development of dependable systems. PhD Thesis. Turku Centre for Computer Science TUCS (2000)

12. Iliasov, A., Romanovsky, A., Arief, B., Laibinis, L., Troubitsyna, E.: On rigorous design and implementation of fault tolerant ambient systems. In: 10th IEEE International Symposium on Object and Component-Oriented Real-Time Distributed Computing – ISORC 2007, pp. 141–145 IEEE (2007)

13. Sere, K., Troubitsyna, E.: Hazard analysis in formal specification. In: Felici, M., Kanoun, K. (eds.) SAFECOMP 1999. LNCS, vol. 1698, pp. 350–360. Springer, Heidelberg (1999). doi:10.1007/3-540-48249-0_30

14. Pereverzeva, I., Troubitsyna, E., Laibinis, L.: Formal development of critical multi-agent systems: a refinement approach. In: 9th European Dependable Computing Conference – EDCC 2012, pp. 156–161. IEEE (2012)

15. Laibinis, L., Troubitsyna, E., Iliasov, A., Romanovsky, A.: Rigorous development of fault-tolerant agent systems. In: Butler, M., Jones, Cliff B., Romanovsky, A., Troubitsyna, E. (eds.) Rigorous Development of Complex Fault-Tolerant Systems. LNCS, vol. 4157, pp. 241–260. Springer, Heidelberg (2006). doi:10.1007/11916246_13

16. Troubitsyna E.: Integrating Safety Analysis into Formal Specification of Dependable Systems. In: International Symposium on Parallel and Distributed Processing, IEEE, (2003)

17. Sere, K., Troubitsyna, E.: Probabilities in action systems. In: 8th Nordic Workshop on Programming Theory, pp. 373–387 (1996)

18. Troubitsyna, E.A.: Reliability assessment through probabilistic refinement. Nordic J. Comput. 6(3), 320–342 (1999)

19. Tarasyuk, A., Troubitsyna, E., Laibinis, L.: Towards Probabilistic Modelling in Event-B. In: Méry, D., Merz, S. (eds.) IFM 2010. LNCS, vol. 6396, pp. 275–289. Springer, Heidelberg (2010). doi:10.1007/978-3-642-16265-7_20

20. Tarasyuk, A., Troubitsyna, E., Laibinis, L.: Integrating Stochastic Reasoning into Event-B Development. Formal Aspects Comput. 27(1), 53–77 (2015)

21. Iliasov, A., Troubitsyna, E., Laibinis, L., Romanovsky, A., Varpaaniemi, K., Ilic, D., Latvala, T.: Developing Mode-Rich Satellite Software by Refinement in Event-B. Sci. Comput. Program. 78(7), 884–905 (2013)

22. Iliasov, A., Troubitsyna, E., Laibinis, L., Romanovsky, A., Varpaaniemi, K., Ilic, D., Latvala, T.: Developing Mode-Rich Satellite Software by Refinement in Event B. In: Kowalewski, S., Roveri, M. (eds.) FMICS 2010. LNCS, vol. 6371, pp. 50–66. Springer, Heidelberg (2010). doi:10.1007/978-3-642-15898-8_4

6th International Workshop on Next Generation of System Assurance Approaches for Safety-Critical Systems (SASSUR 2017)

6th International Workshop on Next Generation of System Assurance Approaches for Safety-Critical Systems (SASSUR 2017)

Alejandra Ruiz[1], Jose Luis de la Vara[2], and Tim Kelly[3]

[1] TECNALIA, Madrid, Spain
alejandra.ruiz@tecnalia.com
[2] Universidad Carlos III de Madrid, Madrid, Spain
jvara@inf.uc3m.es
[3] University of York, York, UK
tim.kelly@york.ac.uk

SASSUR 2017 is the 6th edition of the International Workshop on Next Generation of System Assurance Approaches for Safety-Critical Systems. SASSUR 2017 continues consolidating and keeping the main objectives of the workshop while also updating and extending its scope with new challenges and trends in system assurance. This is in line with our intention to explore new ideas on compositional, evolutionary, multi-concern, and efficient assurance and certification of safety-critical systems.

New systems characteristics such as connectivity, autonomy, and collaboration, and recent situations such as crashes of autonomous vehicles, delays in aircraft delivery due to insufficient confidence in system safety, and unclear regulatory needs and requirements for system assurance of systems with advanced features, all motivate the need for novel and cost-effective assurance approaches. The topics of interest of the workshop include, among others, industrial challenges for safety assurance and certification, challenges for assuring safety and security in autonomous systems, cross-domain product certification, integration of process-centric and product-centric assurance, management of compliance with standards and regulations, multi-concern system assurance, evolutionary approaches for safety and security assurance, tool support for safety and security assurance, evolution of standards and trends on regulations, human factors in safety and security assurance, mixed-criticality system assurance, and safety assurance for adaptive systems.

The program of SASSUR 2017 consists of six high-quality papers. We have divided the papers into two categories based on their focus and the topics that they cover:

- Safety standards

  1. Process Assessment in Supplier Selection for Safety-Critical Systems in NuclearDomain by Timo Varkoi and Risto Nevalainen
  2. Representation of Safety Standards with Semantic Technologies Used in IndustrialEnvironments by Jose Luis de La Vara, Álvaro Gómez, Elena Gallego, Gonzalo Génova and Anabel Fraga

- Safety and cybersecurity engineering

  1. Automotive SPICE, Safety and Cybersecurity Integration by Georg Macher, Alexander Much, Andreas Riel, Richard Messnarz and Christian Kreiner
  2. Safety and Security Co-Engineering and Argumentation Framework by Helmut Martin, Robert Bramberger, Christoph Schmittner, Zhendong Ma, Thomas Gruber,Alejandra Ruiz and Georg Macher

- Runtime Assessment

  1. A Runtime Risk Assessment Concept for Safe Reconfiguration in Open Adaptive Systems by Nikita Bhardwaj and Peter Liggesmeyer
  2. Assuring Degradation Cascades of Car Platoons via Contracts by Irfan Sljivo, Barbara Gallina and Bernhard Kaiser

Acknowledgements. We are grateful to the SAFECOMP organization committee and collaborators for their support in arranging SASSUR. We also thank all the authors of the submitted papers for their interest in the workshop, and the steering and programme committees for their work and advice. Finally, the AMASS project supports the workshop (H2020-ECSEL grant agreement no. 692474; Spain's MINECO reference PCIN-2015-262)

Workshop Committees

Organization Committee

Alejandra Ruiz	TECNALIA, Spain
Jose Luis de la Vara	Universidad Carlos III de Madrid, Spain
Tim Kelly	University of York, UK

Steering Committee

John Favaro,	Intecs, Italy
Huascar Espinoza	TECNALIA, Spain
Fabien Belmonte	ALSTOM, France

Programme Committee and Reviewers

Morayo Adedjouma	CEA-List, France
Jose María Álvarez	Universidad Carlos III de Madrid, Spain
Paulo Barbosa	Universidade Estadual da Paraiba, Brazil
Markus Borg	RISE SICS, Sweden
Marc Born	ANSYS medini Technologies, Germany
Barbara Gallina	Mälardalen University, Sweden

Ibrahim Habli	University of York, UK
Garazi Juez	TECNALIA, Spain
Zhendong Ma	AIT Austrian Institute of Technology, Austria
Jürgen Niehaus	SafeTRANS, Germany
Paolo Panaroni	Intecs, Italy
Mehrdad Sabetzadeh	University of Luxembourg, Luxembourg
Christoph Schmittner	AIT Austrian Institute of Technology, Austria
Erwin Schoitsch	AIT Austrian Institute of Technology, Austria
Irfan Sljivo	Mälardalen University, Sweden
Kenji Taguchi	AIST, Japan
Stefano Tonetta	Fondazione Bruno Kessler, Italy
Fredrik Warg	RISE SPS, Sweden
Gereon Weiss	Fraunhofer ESK, Germany
Marc Zeller	Siemens, Germany

Representation of Safety Standards with Semantic Technologies Used in Industrial Environments

Jose Luis de la Vara[1(✉)], Álvaro Gómez[1], Elena Gallego[2],
Gonzalo Génova[1], and Anabel Fraga[1]

[1] Departamento de Informática, Universidad Carlos III de Madrid,
Leganes, Spain
{jvara,ggenova,afraga}@inf.uc3m.es,
alvarogomez.menendez@gmail.com
[2] The REUSE Company, Leganes, Spain
elena.gallego@reusecompany.com

Abstract. Understanding and following safety standards with their text can be difficult. Ambiguity and inconsistency, among other issues, can easily arise. As a solution, several authors argue for the explicit representation of the standards with models, which can be created with semantic technologies such as ontologies. However, this possibility has received little attention. The few authors that have addressed it have also only dealt with a subset of safety standard aspects and have used technologies not usually applied for critical systems engineering. As a first step towards addressing these issues, this position paper presents our initial work on the representation of safety standards with Knowledge Manager, a tool used in industrial environments that exploits semantic technologies to manage domain information. The proposal also builds on prior work on the specification of safety compliance needs with a holistic generic metamodel. We describe how to use Knowledge Manager to specify the concepts and relationships of the metamodel for a given safety standard, and discuss the application and benefits of the corresponding representation.

Keywords: Safety-critical system · Safety standard · Representation of safety standards · Ontology · Model · Knowledge Manager

1 Introduction

Most safety-critical systems must comply with safety standards as a way of assuring that they do not pose undue risks. Examples of these standards [7] include IEC 61508 for a wide range of industries, DO-178C in avionics, EN 50128 in railway, and ISO 26262 in automotive.

Safety standards are typically large textual documents that consist of hundreds of pages and define thousands of criteria for compliance. The resulting complexity can hinder the comprehension of a standard. Ambiguity and inconsistencies are also usual in their text [6], and practitioners have indeed acknowledged issues in understanding and applying the standards [1, 7]. This can lead to certification risks, as a system

© Springer International Publishing AG 2017
S. Tonetta et al. (Eds.): SAFECOMP 2017 Workshops, LNCS 10489, pp. 265–272, 2017.
DOI: 10.1007/978-3-319-66284-8_22

supplier might miss or misinterpret some criteria and thus not develop a compliant system. As a solution, several authors (e.g. [5]) argue that the use of structured representations of safety standards can help practitioners understand and follow them.

These representations have most often been UML or UML-based models such as a class diagram or a UML profile [2]. Nonetheless, the representations can also be developed with semantic technologies, e.g. as an ontology that includes the main concepts of a safety standard and the relationships between the concepts. Some authors have used this representation format in order to exploit semantic technology capabilities for safety assurance and certification.

Gallina and Szatmári [3] propose the creation of ontology-based models to ease the comparison of safety standards. They represent ISO 26262 and EN 50128 with OWL 2.0 and Protegé to later generate safety-oriented product lines in SPEM. The ontology focuses on the standards' activities. Jost et al. [4] propose the formalisation of ISO 26262 with an ontology to enable semi-automated selection of the standard's requirements. This way, ISO 26262 can be tailored to a given project. Jost et al. combine OWL and SPEM, and manage the ontology with Protegé and Pellet, focusing on the standard's terminology. Luo et al. [5] propose a model-based approach for compliance with safety standards and to facilitate assurance reuse. They use Protegé and OWLGrEd to specify and visualise, respectively, conceptual models of safety standards, and combine them with UML and SPEM. The approach is applied to ISO 26262, and the ontology focuses on the standard's terminology.

We find three main weaknesses in the state of the art. First, little attention has been paid to the use of semantic technologies to represent safety standards, thus its benefits (e.g. automatic reasoning) have been barely studied. Second, the proposed technologies have focused on specific aspects of the standards, namely their activities and terminology. Compliance however requires the consideration of more aspects [2], e.g. artefacts to manage and relationships between them. Therefore, no proposal has been made yet that provides an integrated ontological representation. Third, the semantic technologies adopted in the literature are seldom or not used in industry for critical systems engineering, which results in a gap between research and practice. We are not aware of any company using OWL or Protegé in real projects, and related studies on the state of the practice [1, 7] do not provide evidence of their use.

We are working towards addressing these issues by investigating how Knowledge Manager [8] (KM) can be used to represent safety standards and later exploit the resulting representation. KM is a tool used in industrial environments for critical systems engineering to represent domain knowledge with ontologies. These ontologies cover several aspects, from system terminology to system specification patterns, and can be used for different purposes, e.g. system specification, system artefact quality analysis, and system information reuse. KM usage in practice focuses on system-specific characteristics, e.g. system structure, but we argue that such usage can be extended to support compliance with safety standards.

This position paper presents our initial work on the representation of safety standards with KM. We use as a basis an existing holistic generic metamodel to specify safety compliance needs [2]. We describe how the compliance information in a safety standard can be specified with KM according to the metamodel. This requires both a specific configuration of KM and the subsequent specification of the compliance information in KM. We further discuss how the resulting representation could be exploited to facilitate compliance with safety standards and related activities.

The rest of the paper is organised as follows. Section 2 presents our proposal and Sect. 3 discusses it. Section 4 summarises our main conclusions.

2 Proposal to Represent Safety Standards with KM

Our proposal to represent safety standards with semantic technologies is based on two main elements: KM, as supporting approach and tool for semantic specification of a standard's information, and a holistic generic metamodel for the specification of safety compliance needs. The metamodel indicates the element types that must be considered when having to demonstrate compliance with safety standards, as well as the relationships between them. The overall purpose of our proposal is to provide guidance about how a standard's terminology, data items of the element types, and relationships between the items can be represented with KM.

An excerpt of the metamodel is shown in Fig. 1. The metamodel supports the specification of the different types of safety compliance needs: information about safety assurance requirements, artefacts, and activities, and about their applicability. This also includes additional information about roles, techniques, artefact attributes, artefact relationships, and relationships between the element types. All the classes in the metamodel specialise Reference Element, and Reference Activity, Reference Artefact, Reference Role, and Reference Technique specialise Constrained Reference Assurable Element. Further information about the metamodel can be found in [2].

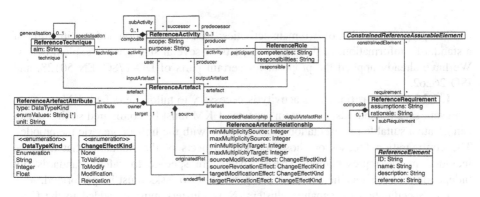

Fig. 1. Excerpt of the metamodel for the specification of safety compliance needs [2]

Figure 2 shows the structure of an ontology in KM. An ontology consists of several layers, each depending on and extending the semantic information of the inner layer. The most inner layer (Terminology) corresponds to the terms of a domain together with their syntactic information. Relationships between the terms can be specified in the Conceptual model layer, as well as their semantics with clusters; e.g. the semantics of the terms 'car' and 'truck' can be 'system', and they specialise 'vehicle'. Patterns can then be developed to provide templates (aka boilerplates) for system information specification; the patterns refer to aspects of the two underlying layers. The Formalization layer includes information about how system information that matches a pattern will be semantically formalised and stored. Finally, at the Inference rules layer the data in all the other layers can be exploited for the specification of rules to derive new information, e.g. about the correctness of a system specification. At its current state, the proposal only deals with the Terminology and the Conceptual model layers. More information about these layers is provided in the next paragraphs when describing the proposal, and more information about KM is available in [8].

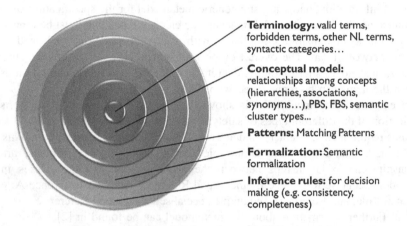

Terminology: valid terms, forbidden terms, other NL terms, syntactic categories...

Conceptual model: relationships among concepts (hierarchies, associations, synonyms...), PBS, FBS, semantic cluster types...

Patterns: Matching Patterns

Formalization: Semantic formalization

Inference rules: for decision making (e.g. consistency, completeness)

Fig. 2. Ontology layers in KM

The proposal consists of two main activities: KM configuration and specification of a standard's information. Each activity consists of several steps, as we explain below. We have already applied the proposal for certain parts of DO-178C, EN 50128, and ISO 26262.

1. KM Configuration. This activity is necessary to tailor the default KM usage to represent safety standards, i.e. certain aspects of KM must be configured so that a user can create a suitable representation in accordance with the holistic generic metamodel. The configuration focuses on those semantic aspects of the standards that must be included in the representation. These aspects are specific to safety standards but independent of the specific standard to represent. Two tasks must be performed.

1.1. <u>Specification of semantic clusters</u>. New clusters must be added to the Conceptual model layer to be able to indicate the type of information that a term represents. First, a cluster with the name of the safety standard to be represented is necessary to later specify that a term falls within the scope of the standard. Second, semantic clusters must be added for Reference Artefact, Reference Artefact Attribute, Reference Activity, Reference Role, and Reference Technique, a cluster for each. These clusters are part of another new cluster called Reference Assurance Framework. The semantic clusters will be used to further categorise certain terms.

1.2. Specification of relationship types. KM also supports the specification of relationship types between terms. To represent a safety standard, a relationship type has to be created for each association in the metamodel between the metaclasses for which the new clusters have been added, e.g. for 'user-inputArtefact' between Reference Activity and Reference Artefact. This does not apply to the compositions, e.g. between Reference Artefact and Reference Artefact Attribute. KM has a predefined relationship type for composition, as well as for specialisation (to specify e.g. taxonomies) and for equivalence (to specify e.g. synonyms), among others. Another relationship type called 'Reference Artefact Relationship' must be added to be able to relate different Reference Artefacts in KM. The specification of the relationship types also includes the specification of the roles of the relationship ends.

2. Specification of a Standard's Information. This activity results in the specific representation of a given safety standard. Two tasks can be distinguished. The tasks will usually be executed iteratively to incrementally represent a safety standard.

2.1. Specification of a standard's terminology. This task has two main aspects to address. First, most standards have some glossary or vocabulary section. The corresponding terms and definitions, abbreviations, and acronyms must be added to the Terminology. Each time a term is added, it is necessary to (1) specify its syntactic category (e.g. noun or acronym) and (2) associate it with the semantic cluster that corresponds to the name of the standard; e.g. the term 'algorithm' would be added as a DO-178C noun. Next, the text of the standard must be analysed to identify terms that correspond to Reference Artefact, Reference Artefact Attribute, Reference Activity, Reference Role, or Reference Technique. Each time a term is identified, it is added to the Terminology and, in addition to the clusters for the glossary terms, the semantic cluster of the element type is associated; e.g. 'Software Requirements Data' is a DO-178C noun that also corresponds to a Reference Artefact.

2.2. Specification of the conceptual model of a safety standard. Once all the relevant terms have been introduced and classified, relationships between them can be specified in the Conceptual model. These relationships will be classified according to the available relationship types in KM, both the default ones and those created during KM configuration. A user must conform to the holistic generic metamodel when specifying relationships, i.e. only terms that correspond to the ends of a given association in the metamodel must be related. For example, 'Software Requirements Data' is an 'output' of 'Software Requirements Process' in DO-178C.

The user also needs to decide whether the relationships between Reference Artefacts should be specified as specialisations, as compositions, or with the Reference Artefact Relationship type. It is also possible to define specialisations of this relationship type if a user decides so, e.g. because it is a recurrent Reference Artefact Relationship. For instance, it is common that artefacts have to 'conform to' some plan or standard. Finally, it can also be necessary to specify specialisation and equivalence relationships between terms; e.g. 'MC/DC' and 'Modified Condition/Decision Coverage' are equivalent for DO-178C.

Figure 3 shows part of the resulting representation for DO-178C.

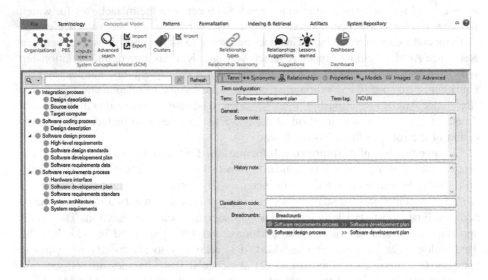

Fig. 3. Example of specification of a standard's information with KM

3 Discussion

Once the proposal has been described, this section discusses how the representation of a safety standard with KM can be exploited for specific safety assurance and certification purposes. Within the overall purpose of demonstrating alignment or compliance with a safety standard, we currently envision six main possibilities to take advantage of the representations.

(a) **Quality analysis of the text of a safety standard.** KM is part of a tool suite [8] that supports, among other features, system artefact quality analysis, including textual artefacts. More concretely, the suite can analyse artefact correctness, completeness, and consistency. Considering the text of a safety standard as an example of artefact, its text quality could be determined. This would be valuable because text quality is one of the most often weaknesses that practitioners find in safety standards. Parts that could be better specified or should be clarified could be identified.

(b) **System specification alignment.** When specifying information for a specific system or analysing the information, the degree to which the specification is aligned with a given standard could be assessed. First, the system could be specified, e.g. its system requirement, according to patterns that refer to the semantic clusters added or to standard-specific terms. Second, an ontology of the system could be linked to the ontology of the standard, e.g. to specify that a given part of the system corresponds to the DO-178C component concept.

(c) **Compliance assessment.** An ontology of a safety standard created with KM could be used to assess process and product compliance. The tool suite capabilities could be used to compare process or product information with the ontology, in order to determine compliance gaps. The information could correspond to artefacts of different nature: textual specifications, documents, diagrams, spreadsheets...

(d) Comparison of standards. The text or ontology of a safety standard could be compared with the ontology of another, in order to identify commonalities and differences. This usage can be regarded as an extension of (a) and is similar to [3].

(e) Reuse of compliant system information. If a system's information (e.g. a system model) is linked with the ontology of a safety standard to declare compliance with the standard, it would be possible to search for compliant system information and, when found, to reuse it. It could even be possible to analyse system information reuse between safety standards if the ontologies of the different standards are linked. The linking of a system's information with the ontology could be based on (b).

(f) Specification of standard-specific metrics. Specific metrics could be designed within the Inference rules layer based on the semantic information of a safety standard represented in KM. The metrics could assess (1) general compliance with the standard (e.g. the amount of Reference Artefacts that have been provided) and (2) artefact-specific characteristics that a standard defines (e.g. architecture specification consistency). Although the metrics would often not be directly declared in the safety standard (e.g. for the latter example), the standards' information would drive their definition by indicating the areas for which metrics could be designed and possible aspects to consider.

We do not provide further details about the exploitation possibilities due to page limitations. How these possibilities can be finally enacted is part of our ongoing and future work, which might include the exploitation of further benefits.

4 Conclusion

The use of explicit structured representations of safety standards has been proposed to facilitate compliance with the standards, and semantic technologies can be used to create such representations. However, further work on the topic is necessary, and it must be linked with and based on industrial practices.

This position paper has presented our initial work towards representing safety standards with semantic technologies already used in industrial environments. We have described how to create ontologies of safety standards with the Knowledge Manager (KM) tool, and according to a holistic generic metamodel to specify safety compliance needs. The proposal consists of two main activities: KM configuration and specification of a standard's information. We currently envision six main usage scenarios: quality analysis of the text of a safety standard, system specification alignment, compliance assessment, comparison of standards, reuse of compliant system information, and specification of standard-specific metrics.

The proposal represents a novel usage of KM and an attempt towards bridging the gap, for safety assurance purposes, between the benefits that semantic technologies can enable and how they are used in critical systems engineering practice.

The proposal is at an initial stage and further work is necessary to fully develop it. We plan to enact the usages presented in Sect. 3, which might allow us to identify improvement opportunities. The new capabilities that KM will have in the future (e.g. libraries of ontologies) can also enable further usages. Finally, the work is being performed within the scope of AMASS (http://amass-ecsel.eu/), which is a large H2020-ECSEL industry-academia project on assurance and certification of cyber-physical systems. We will thus be able to apply the proposal in industrial case studies.

Acknowledgments. The research leading to this paper has received funding from the AMASS project (H2020-ECSEL no. 692474; Spain's MINECO ref. PCIN-2015-262).

References

1. de la Vara, J.L., et al.: An industrial survey on safety evidence change impact analysis practice. IEEE Trans. Softw. Eng. **42**(12), 1095–1117 (2016)
2. de la Vara, J.L., et al.: Model-based specification of safety compliance needs for critical systems: a holistic generic metamodel. Inf. Softw. Technol. **72**, 16–30 (2016)
3. Gallina, B., Szatmári, Z.: Ontology-based identification of commonalities and variabilities among safety processes. In: Abrahamsson, P., Corral, L., Oivo, M., Russo, B. (eds.) PROFES 2015. LNCS, vol. 9459, pp. 182–189. Springer, Cham (2015). doi:10.1007/978-3-319-26844-6_13
4. Jost, H., et al.: Towards a safer development of driver assistance systems by applying requirements-based methods. In: ITCS 2011, pp. 1144–1149 (2011)
5. Luo, Y., Brand, M., Engelen, L., Favaro, J., Klabbers, M., Sartori, G.: Extracting models from ISO 26262 for reusable safety assurance. In: Favaro, J., Morisio, M. (eds.) ICSR 2013. LNCS, vol. 7925, pp. 192–207. Springer, Heidelberg (2013). doi:10.1007/978-3-642-38977-1_13
6. Nair, S., et al.: An extended systematic literature review on provision of evidence for safety certification. Inf. Softw. Technol. **56**(7), 689–717 (2014)
7. Nair, S., et al.: Evidence management for compliance of critical systems with safety standards: a survey on the state of practice. Inf. Softw. Technol. **60**, 1–15 (2015)
8. The REUSE Company. https://www.reusecompany.com/

Automotive SPICE, Safety and Cybersecurity Integration

Georg Macher[1]($\boxtimes$), Alexander Much[2], Andreas Riel[3], Richard Messnarz[4], and Christian Kreiner[5]

[1] AVL List GmbH, Graz, Austria
georg.macher@avl.com
[2] Elektrobit Germany, Erlangen, Germany
alexander.much@elektrobit.com
[3] EMIRAcle, Grenoble, France
andreas.riel@grenoble-inp.fr
[4] ISCN GesmbH/LTD, Dublin, Ireland
rmess@iscn.com
[5] Graz University of Technology, Graz, Austria
christian.kreiner@tugraz.at

Abstract. Currently developed automotive systems exhibit an increased level of automation as well as an ever-tighter integration with other vehicles, traffic infrastructure and cloud services. Thus, just as safety became a critical part of the development in the late 20th century, the automotive domain must now consider cyber-security as an integral part of the development of modern vehicles. Novel features, such as advanced driver assistance systems or automated driving functions drive the need for built-in security solutions and cyber-security aware system design. Unfortunately, there is still a lack of experience with security concerns in the context of safety engineering in general and in the automotive safety departments in particular. A European partnership developed a skill set, training materials and best practices for ISO 26262 in the context of the EU project SafEUr. This working party (SoQrates working group) shares knowledge and experiences and integrated the Automotive SPICE assessment model with functional safety requirements, which was further used in integrated Automotive SPICE and safety assessments. The members of the SoQrates working group are, to a large extent, certified Automotive SPICE assessors dealing with security-related project in practice. From 2016 onwards, the SoQrates working party started to analyse the SAE J3061 cyber-security guidebook and integrated the additional requirements of SAE J3061 into this assessment model. This paper will summarise the previous results and extensions of the assessment model and the working group's vision, how an Automotive SPICE assessor can support also the auditing of projects with close security relation.

Keywords: Automotive SPICE · ISO 26262 · SAE J3061 · Automotive · Security analysis

© Springer International Publishing AG 2017
S. Tonetta et al. (Eds.): SAFECOMP 2017 Workshops, LNCS 10489, pp. 273–285, 2017.
DOI: 10.1007/978-3-319-66284-8_23

1   Introduction

In recent years, cyber-security is no longer just part of the computer's domain, but plays a more and more important role in the development of connected cars. Some vehicles became famous in the last few years by mischance for being hacked remotely [2]. In many cases major safety critical elements, such as the brakes, become vulnerable and did not work as intended. Therefore, society is evolving and is getting more and more concerned about the automotive security as well. One of the major lessons learned with these incidences was that vulnerabilities are part of the design of the system.

As a result of the mentioned hacks, the society and the automotive industry became more aware of these new challenges. The idea of safety and security co-design has become a major trend of current publications and it is expected to appear also in the second edition of the ISO 26262 standard [7]. However, one of the main challenges of this merging of safety and security disciplines is their different level of maturity of standards and the available knowledge in the domain. Therefore, appropriate systematic approaches to support the development of these properties are thus required.

At the working party SoQrates [1] a large group of Tier 1 and automotive engineering companies share knowledge and experiences and focus on the integration of the Automotive SPICE assessment model [23] with functional safety requirements coming from ISO 26262 [7] and cyber-security requirements from SAE J3061 [24]. From 2016 onwards the working party started to analyse the SAE J3061 cyber-security guide-book and integrated the additional requirements of SAE J3061 into their integrated Automotive SPICE and safety assessments model. This integrated assessment model was used in 2011 in trial assessments at Tier 1 supplier.

In the course of this paper, we present the SoQrates assessing model and the working group's vision, how an Automotive SPICE assessor can support also the auditing of projects with close security relation. The aim of this work is to provide an exemplary electronic steering system which shall be assessed according to Automotive SPICE 3.0 standard integrated with additional questions to cover functional safety (based on ISO 26262) and cyber-security (based on SAE J3061).

This paper is organized as follows: Sect. 2 reviews recommendations and guidelines related to automotive cyber-security engineering. In Sect. 3 the exemplary electronic steering system is described and Sect. 4 describes how the electronic steering system architectural design will be analysed and related development processes will be assessed to cover both, functional safety and cyber-security at the same time. Finally, Sect. 5 concludes the work.

2   Automotive Cyber-Security Approaches

Safety and security engineering both focus on system-wide features and need to be integrated adequately into the existing process landscape. Safety engineering is already an integral part of automotive engineering and safety standards, such as the road vehicles functional safety norm ISO 26262 [7] and its basic norm IEC 61508 [3], are well established in the automotive industry. Safety assessment techniques, such as failure mode and effects analysis (FMEA) [4] and fault tree analysis (FTA) [5], are also specified, standardized, and integrated in the automotive development process landscape.

IEC 61508 Ed 2.0 provides a first approach of integrating safety and security; security threats are to be considered during hazard analysis in the form of a security threat analysis. However, this threat analysis is not specified in more detail in the standard and Ed 3.0 is about to be more elaborated on security-aware safety topics. In addition, ISO 26262 Ed 2.0, which is still in progress, is likely to include recommendations for fitting security standards and appropriate security measurement implementations.

Other standards, such as IEC 62443 [6], are not directly applicable in practice for the automotive domain in their current state. An analysis done by SoQrates Security AK [1] indicates that the available standards are frequently fragmented or incomplete, and typically assume that their open issues are covered by other guidelines or standards. For this reason also, several researchers and research projects have recently made efforts to combine security and safety engineering approaches; and also the International Organization for Standardization (ISO) is focusing on cyber-security standards for the automotive domain (such as *ISO/TC 22 N 3586* and *ISO/TC 22 N 3556*).

The recently published SAE J3061 [24] guideline establishes a set of high-level guiding principles for cyber-security by: (a) defining a lifecycle process framework, (b) supporting some basic guiding principles on cyber-security, and (c) summarizing further standard development activities in this context. SAE J3061 states that cyber-security engineering requires an appropriate lifecycle process, which is defined analogous to the process framework described in ISO 26262. Except for this, no further restrictions or recommendations are given on whether to maintain separate processes for safety and security engineering with appropriate levels of interaction or to attempt direct integration of the two processes.

Additionally, the concern of the International Electrotechnical Commission (IEC) TC65 on the impact of cyber-security, reliability and related system properties on functional safety, has led to the creation of three IEC TC65 Ad-Hoc Groups (AHG):

- IEC TC65 AHG1: Framework towards coordinating safety, security (in industrial automation),
- IEC TC65 AHG2: Reliability of Automation Devices and Systems,
- IEC TC65 AHG3: Smart Manufacturing Information Models.

Besides this several OEM standards (such as BMW group standard GS 95014 or VWs standard) state requirements for cyber-security and functional safety engineering. The SS 7740 [8] provides an assessment model for functional safety processes within the automotive industry, supporting ISO-26262. The main purpose of the SS 7740 assessment model is to standardize assessments of functional safety processes including well-defined capability levels, i.e. an ISO 26262 functional safety audit with standardized capability levels known from Automotive SPICE. This approach has also been focused by the SoQrates assessment model presented in [21] and further been extended for the assessment of cybersecurity related system development. Additional related work of the working group regarding the integration of safety and security in the automotive context can be found in [9–19,22]

3   Exemplary Automotive Use-Case

This section of the document an electronic steering system is used as an example to explain the steps to analyse the safety-critical item according to the ISO 26262. The exemplary electronic steering system is depicted in Fig. 1. The driver actuates the steering wheel and the interaction of the driver is measured by a steering angle sensor (integrated into the steering column) and a steering torque sensor. The ECU controls an e-motor to provide the requested torque and measures the achieved angle position by a rotor position sensor (with a rotor angle, motor torque, and a calculated index position which determines the position of the steering rack). In the hazard and risk analysis (HARA) of the item (a high level design with control unit, software, electronic elements and their interfaces), ASIL (Automotive Safety Integrity Level) levels are assigned to hazardous events and safety goals are formulated. The Table 1 shows the example rating one of the most hazardous events (2.1 with ASIL-D). The shown ratings require a safety goal 'SG1: unwanted steering must be prohibited' with an ASIL D (2.1) (and ASIL B in resulting from 2.2) classification.

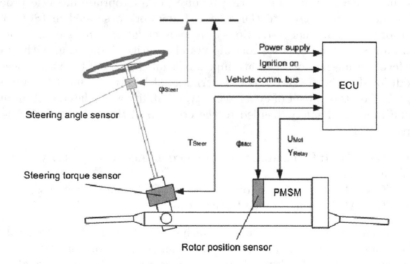

Fig. 1. Item definition of the electronic steering system example

Table 1. Excerpt of hazard analysis and risk assessment of the electronic steering system

Hazard Identification		Classification of Hazardous Situation					
ID	Hazardous situation	S	Argument	E	Argument	C	Argument
2.1	Unwanted actuation of steering system, fully occupied vehicle, high speed	3	Can cause unstable vehicle, life threatening injuries	4	Regular driving situation	3	Unstable driving mode cannot be controlled
2.2	Unwanted actuation of steering system, city, many vehicles on road, low speed	3	Other drivers and pedestrians could be affected, life threatening injuries	4	Regular driving situation	2	Due low speed driver can stop within adequate time

During the development of the system, this safety goal needs to be broken down to system safety requirements. The safety experts and system analyst usually look at the potential faults that can lead to this failure (e.g. using the FMEA as a source) and define requirements to diagnose and avoid these faults. The following paragraphs describe some illustrative examples of the electronic steering system concept on different levels.

Functional Safety Concept Level. The steering angle must be measured with ASIL-D quality.

Technical Safety Concept Level. The internal steering angle calculated from the rotor angle and index position is to be provided with ASIL-D quality.

Technical Safety Design Level. The internal steering angle calculation is done with two rotor position sensors, which are checked against each other for plausibility. Each must fulfil the ASIL-B quality goals and the comparison is done with an ASIL-D rated ASIC. The ASIC shall deliver sin and cos angle information and index counter. Remark: Here a decomposition took place where an ASIL D rated part (steering angle) was decomposed into two redundant and diverse ASIL-B rated elements. Diversity must be proved by hardware (not having same fault behaviour) and algorithms (sin and cos function). The diversity aspect is only used for ASIL-D.

Technical Software Requirement. Measuring every 1 ms the sin and cos and index counter and calculate a steering angle. Both steering angles must be same within an e.g. 5° range (plausibility-check). This comparison must be independently running and monitored.

In general, the safe electric steering systems are limiting the torque so that not more torque than requested by the driver can be put onto the motor by the ECU. Therefore it is clear that the torque sensor is required to be ASIL-D conform as well. Such an electric steering systems serves as a basis for future application with advanced driver assistant systems (ADAS) and automated driving functions (ADF). When considering ADAS and connected car functions which can also affect steering manoeuvres and overrule driver inputs, this approach will not work any more for a full ADAS mode, when the steering angle demand can come from the vehicle infrastructure and will be considered as the main input. Considering fully automated driving cars, (expected the latest in 2030) it is not possible to give the control back to the driver any more. This will have massive impacts: (a) the controllability factor of the ASIL classification will have no further impact on the safety classification, (b) safety goals will need to be changed (possible differentiation between networked and internal requests), and (c) safe states will be required to continue service (fail-operational and possible other limp home approaches).

4   Automotive SPICE, Safety and Cybersecurity Integration

This section describes the SoQrates approach of an integrated Automotive SPICE assessment model with functional safety and cyber-security addons. This assessment model implies the working group's vision, how an Automotive SPICE assessor can support also the auditing of safety-critical projects with close security relation.

Automotive SPICE [23] is widely used in an integrated approach with functional safety in the engineering life cycle of most European automotive companies. The ISO 26262 safety requirements are traced using the same concepts of traceability as for normal functional requirements. Fig. 2 outlines the traceability relation between customer and system requirement level for the safety relevant electric steering system example. The dotted parts highlight the additional specifications, which are required for the ISO 26262 standard fulfilment. The HARA assigns the required ASIL and formulates the related safety goals, which are further refined in the FMEA/FMEDA and result in measures to be taken in the system design to cope with the standards requirements. The resulting safety requirements for the electric steering system will then be treated like other system requirements.

For cyber-security related projects the STRIDE [20] analysis of potential attacks scenarios must additionally be applied. Here, the SAHARA method [9,12], a combined HARA and STRIDE analysis method specially developed for automotive needs, may be used. The findings of this analysis are linked with safety goals and traceable links according to Automotive SPICE are established (Fig. 3) [14].

For the SoQrates assessment approach the existing Automotive SPICE 3.0 standard has been integrated with additional questions to cover functional safety (based on ISO 26262 [7]) and cyber-security (based on SAE J3061 [24]). Thus, an assessment of the electric steering system would follow an Automotive SPICE conforming assessment of the process capability on the development of

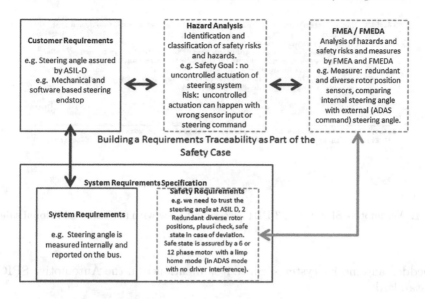

Fig. 2. Traceability of ISO26262 related artifacts and Automotive SPICE assessment model

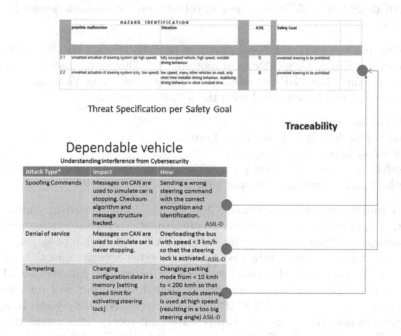

Fig. 3. Depiction of traceable links between safety goals and cyber-security attack schema

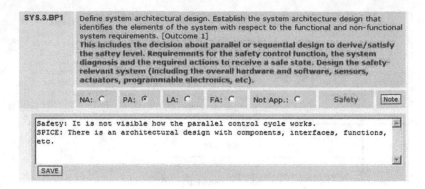

Fig. 4. Automotive SPICE SYS3.PB1 assessment view with activated additional safety view

embedded automotive systems. Since it is mentioned in the Automotive SPICE 3.0 standard:

> If processes beyond the scope of Automotive SPICE are needed, appropriate processes from other process reference models such as ISO/IEC 12207 or ISO/IEC 15288 may be added based on the business needs of the organization.

For this paper we describe the base practices (BP) BP1 for process SYS.3 System Architectural Design (see Table 3) in more details. During an assessment of the process and the related BPs an additional 'Functional Safety View' and 'Cyber-Security View' can be activated with the following effects:

- BP will have additional criteria
- generic practices include additional criteria
- new safety practices will appear
- a safety methods table per process can be opened to consider the use of methods when assessing the practices.

Table 3 summarizes the requirements for SYS.3.BP1 as stated in Automotive SPICE [23], as well as cyber-security recommendations for the system architectural design and their related sections of the SAE J3061 guide book [24].

In the different views dedicated safety or cyber-security practices, which relate to the previously described strategy of extending Automotive SPICE to cover also safety and cyber-security related development will be assessed. For instance, Fig. 4 shows SYS.3.BP1 and the activated safety view. It is also important to note that each view can be rated differently. This means that e.g. SYS.3.BP1 could be rated 'Fully' in Automotive SPICE but have only a 'Partially' rating in the extended safety view (which can be seen in Table 2).

In Table 2 the process SYS.3 BP1 of the exemplary use-case is assessed using the SoQrates approach for Automotive SPICE process assessments.

Table 2. Automotive SPICE 3.0 SYS.3.BP1 assessment findings

SYS.3 System Architectural Design
SYS.3.BP1: Define system architectural design
Automotive SPICE assessment measure: **FULLY**
System architecture design identifies the elements of the system with respect to the functional and non-functional system requirements
System decomposition is at adequate level
Functional safety measure: **LARGELY**
Technical safety concept includes not only requirements but a technical safety architecture
Design of hardware based on safety requirements and required fit rates and redundancies. The safety-relevant hard- and software parts and safety functions are identified and marked
Design of exception handling and diagnose system on different levels adequate. Diagnose levels and the three-layer monitoring concept used
Amount of self- diagnose covered by the ASIC processor architecture not provided; the amount of additional control measures needed to protect against processor failures (ECU) sufficient
Subsystem requirements are derived from the technical safety requirements/ concept and the system design and bi-directionally linked
Cyber-security measure: **LARGELY**
Traceable links of the Functional and Technical cyber-security Requirements to Elements of the Systems Architecture
System-level Vulnerability Analysis executed with SAHARA approach
Most significant risks to a potential cyber-security event covered
Defence-in-depth strategy developed according to automotive defence layer concept
Technical decisions of the system design made traceable
ECU identification via trusted platform module (TPM)
Security Mechanisms implemented and largely aligned with FSC
Trust boundaries identified in HW-SW interface (HSI) definition

Representative excerpts of the review notes of the assessment are provided to support the individual metrics. As the table indicates, the system architectural design is fully in line with SYS.3.BP1; nevertheless, functional safety as well as cyber-security measures indicate only a 'largely' implementation, and mention some findings and also some improvement recommendations.

Table 3. Automotive SPICE 3.0 SYS.3.BP1 assessment view excerpt

---

SYS.3 System Architectural Design

SYS.3.BP1: Define system architectural design

Establish the system architecture design that identifies the elements of the system with respect to the functional and non-functional system requirements. [Outcome 1]

NOTE 1: The system might be decomposed into several subsystems on different system levels, if necessary

NOTE 2: For changes to the stakeholders requirements SUP.10 applies

---

Functional Safety View Extension (skipped for lack of space)

Related to ISO 26262 clauses ISO 26262-4 7.4.1 - 7.4.7

Cyber-Security View Extension

Related to SAE J3061:2016, clauses 8.3.7

Is a Technical cyber-security Concept/Design developed?

Are there links of the Functional and Technical cyber-security Requirements to Elements of the Systems Architecture

---

Related to SAE J3061:2016, clauses 8.4.3

How is the System-level Vulnerability Analysis executed?

What are the identified System Functions that are at most risk relative to a potential cyber-security event?

Isolation of specific functions?

Use of countermeasures (e.g., encryption, decryption)?

Defence-in-depth strategy, etc.

Is the Technical Cyber-security Concept linked with the Functional Cyber-security Concept?

Traceability of the technical decisions into the system design evident?

Related to SAE J3061:2016, Appendix F

Which vehicle network each ECU (and sensors with hardware I/O) will be located on?

How each ECU will be identified?

Which ECUs should be authenticated in order to perform their functions? If so how will this be done?

Which messages will be created by which ECUs

Required hardware features for specific ECUs

Security Mechanisms implemented?

Related to SAE J3061:2016, clause 8.4.4

Is there a catalogue of specific functions (e.g., activation of airbags, braking, steering, etc.) which will be performed by the system?

Is the System Context created to define the interfaces and functions within the system? These include: (a) Hardware and software interfaces, (b) Data flows, (c) Data storage, (d) Data processing, (e) functions that support Cyber-security functionality

Is there a dynamic communication model considering the cyber-security technical requirements?

Does the design cyber-security related signal/communication flows consider the cyber-security technical requirements?

5   Conclusion

To conclude, the convergence of engineering methods towards a combined safety and cyber-security engineering for the entire development lifecycle is a challenging task. Currently available security standards, such as IEC 62443 [6], or security guidelines, such as SAE J3061 [24], are still incomplete or often fragmented and have different maturity level than the functional safety standard ISO 26262 [7]. Nevertheless, for a usable solution, best practices of cyber-security and functional safety engineering must be integrated appropriately in the existing process landscape, which is mainly Automotive SPICE related in the European area.

Hence, the SoQrates working party [1] focused on the integration of the Automotive SPICE assessment model [23] with functional safety requirements coming from ISO 26262 [7] and cyber-security requirements from SAE J3061 [24]. In this publication this combined assessing model and the working group's vision, of how an Automotive SPICE assessor can support also the auditing of projects with close security relation has been presented. To that aim, an exemplary electronic steering system has been provided and has been exemplary assessed according to Automotive SPICE 3.0 standard integrated with additional questions to cover functional safety (based on ISO 26262) and cyber-security (based on SAE J3061).

Acknowledgments. This work is supported by the EMC^2 project. The research leading to these results has received funding from the ARTEMIS Joint Undertaking under grant agreement nr 621429 (project EMC^2).

Furthermore, we would like to express our thanks to our supporting partners, the experts of the SoQrates working group.

References

1. SOQRATES Task Forces Developing Integration of Automotive SPICE, ISO 26262 and SAE J3061. http://soqrates.eurospi.net/
2. Greenberg, A.: Hackers Remotely Kill a Jeep on the Highway-With Me in It, July 2015. wired.com
3. ISO: International Organization for Standardization: IEC 61508 Functional safety of electrical/electronic/programmable electronic safety-related systems (2010)
4. ISO: International Organization for Standardization: IEC 60812 Analysis techniques for system reliability - Procedure for failure mode and effects analysis (FMEA) (2006)
5. ISO: International Organization for Standardization: IEC 61025 Fault tree analysis (FTA), December 2006
6. ISO: International Organization for Standardization: IEC 62443 - Industrial Communication Networks Network and System Security (2009)
7. ISO: International Organization for Standardization: ISO 26262 Road vehicles Functional Safety Part 1–10 (2011)
8. ISO: International Organization for Standardization: SS 7740 Road Vehicles Functional Safety Process Assessment Model (2012)

9. Macher, G., Sporer, H., Berlach, R., Armengaud, E., Kreiner, C.: SAHARA: a security-aware hazard and risk analysis method. In: Design, Automation Test in Europe Conference Exhibition (DATE), 2015, pp. 621–624, March 2015

10. Macher, G., Armengaud, E., Brenner, E., Kreiner, C.: A review of threat analysis and risk assessment methods in the automotive context. In: Skavhaug, A., Guiochet, J., Bitsch, F. (eds.) SAFECOMP 2016. LNCS, vol. 9922, pp. 130–141. Springer, Cham (2016). doi:10.1007/978-3-319-45477-1_11

11. Macher, G., Armengaud, E., Kreiner, C., Brenner, E., Schmittner, C., Ma, Z., Martin, H., Krammer, M.: Integration of security in the development lifecycle of dependable automotive CPS. In: Druml, N., Genser, A., Armin, K., Menghin, M., Hoeller, A. (eds.) Handbook of Research on Solutions for Cyber-Physical Systems Ubiquity. IGI Global, Hershey (2017)

12. Macher, G., Höller, A., Sporer, H., Armengaud, E., Kreiner, C.: A combined safety-hazards and security-threat analysis method for automotive systems. In: Koornneef, F., Gulijk, C. (eds.) SAFECOMP 2015. LNCS, vol. 9338, pp. 237–250. Springer, Cham (2015). doi:10.1007/978-3-319-24249-1_21

13. Macher, G., Höller, A., Sporer, H., Armengaud, E., Kreiner, C.: A comprehensive safety, security, and serviceability assessment method. In: Koornneef, F., Gulijk, C. (eds.) SAFECOMP 2015. LNCS, vol. 9337, pp. 410–424. Springer, Cham (2015). doi:10.1007/978-3-319-24255-2_30

14. Macher, G., Messnarz, R., Armengaud, E., Riel, A., Brenner, E., Kreiner, C.: Integrated safety and security development in the automotive domain. In: SAE Technical Paper. SAE International (2017). http://papers.sae.org/2017-01-1661/

15. Macher, G., Riel, A., Kreiner, C.: Integrating HARA and TARA - How Does this Fit with Assumptions of the SAE J3061. Software Quality Professional (2016)

16. Macher, G., Sporer, H., Brenner, E., Kreiner, C.: Supporting Cyber-Security Based on Hardware-Software Interface Definition. In: Kreiner, C., O'Connor, R.V., Poth, A., Messnarz, R. (eds.) EuroSPI 2016. CCIS, vol. 633, pp. 148–159. Springer, Cham (2016). doi:10.1007/978-3-319-44817-6_12

17. Messnarz, R., König, F., Bachmann, V.O.: Experiences with trial assessments combining automotive spice and functional safety standards. In: Winkler, D., O'Connor, R.V., Messnarz, R. (eds.) EuroSPI 2012. CCIS, vol. 301, pp. 266–275. Springer, Heidelberg (2012). doi:10.1007/978-3-642-31199-4_23

18. Messnarz, R., Kreiner, C., Bachmann, O., Riel, A., Dussa-Zieger, K., Nevalainen, R., Tichkiewitch, S.: Implementing functional safety standards – experiences from the trials about required knowledge and competencies (SafEUr). In: McCaffery, F., O'Connor, R.V., Messnarz, R. (eds.) EuroSPI 2013. CCIS, vol. 364, pp. 323–332. Springer, Heidelberg (2013). doi:10.1007/978-3-642-39179-8_29

19. Messnarz, R., Kreiner, C., Macher, G., Walker, A.: Extending automotive SPICE 3.0 for the use in ADAS service architectures. J. Softw.: Evolution Process 29, 17–27 (2017)

20. Microsoft Corporation: The STRIDE Threat Model (2005). http://msdn.microsoft.com/en-us/library/ee823878%28v=cs.20%29.aspx

21. Messnarz, R., Kreiner, C., Bachmann, O., Riel, A., Dussa-Zieger, K., Nevalainen, R., Tichkiewitch, S.: Implementing functional safety standards – experiences from the trials about required knowledge and competencies (SafEUr). In: McCaffery, F., O'Connor, R.V., Messnarz, R. (eds.) EuroSPI 2013. CCIS, vol. 364, pp. 323–332. Springer, Heidelberg (2013). doi:10.1007/978-3-642-39179-8_29

22. Riel, A., Bachmann, V.O., Dussa-Zieger, K., Kreiner, C., Messnarz, R., Nevalainen, R., Sechser, B., Tichkiewitch, S.: EU project SafEUr – competence requirements for functional safety managers. In: Winkler, D., O'Connor, R.V., Messnarz, R. (eds.) EuroSPI 2012. CCIS, vol. 301, pp. 253–265. Springer, Heidelberg (2012). doi:10.1007/978-3-642-31199-4_22
23. The SPICE User Group: Automotive SPICE Process Assessment/Reference Model V3.0, July 2015. http://www.automotivespice.com/fileadmin/software-download/Automotive_SPICE_PAM_30.pdf
24. Vehicle Electrical System Security Committee: SAE J3061 Cybersecurity Guidebook for Cyber-Physical Automotive Systems, http://standards.sae.org/wip/j3061/

Safety and Security Co-engineering and Argumentation Framework

Helmut Martin[1]([⊠]), Robert Bramberger[1], Christoph Schmittner[2],
Zhendong Ma[2], Thomas Gruber[2], Alejandra Ruiz[3],
and Georg Macher[4]

[1] VIRTUAL VEHICLE Research Center, Graz, Austria
{helmut.martin, robert.bramberger}@v2c2.at
[2] Austrian Institute of Technology, Vienna, Austria
{christoph.schmittner, zhendong.ma,
thomas.gruber}@ait.ac.at
[3] TECNALIA/ICT Division, Derio, Spain
alejandra.ruiz@tecnalia.com
[4] AVL List GmbH, Graz, Austria
georg.macher@avl.com

Abstract. Automotive systems become increasingly complex due to their functional range and data exchange with the outside world. Until now, functional safety of such safety-critical electrical/electronic systems has been covered successfully. However, the data exchange requires interconnection across trusted boundaries of the vehicle. This leads to security issues like hacking and malicious attacks against interfaces, which could bring up new types of safety issues. Before mass-production of automotive systems, arguments supported by evidences are required regarding safety and security. Product engineering must be compliant to specific standards and must support arguments that the system is free of unreasonable risks.

This paper shows a safety and security co-engineering framework, which covers standard compliant process derivation and management, and supports product specific safety and security co-analysis. Furthermore, we investigate process- and product-related argumentation and apply the approach to an automotive use case regarding safety and security.

Keywords: Safety and security co-engineering · Process- and product-based argumentation · Process and argumentation patterns · Automotive domain · ISO 26262 · SAE J3061

1 Introduction

The market and the society are requesting safe vehicles. Upcoming vehicle functions require external sensor data and communication across vehicle boundaries. Furthermore, software updates with new vehicle features can increase road safety, but these topics introduce the additional challenge on cybersecurity. Security issues are starting to be in the front line in the automotive business because more and more problems at the market occurred and have been published by various media. In 2015 the

© Springer International Publishing AG 2017
S. Tonetta et al. (Eds.): SAFECOMP 2017 Workshops, LNCS 10489, pp. 286–297, 2017.
DOI: 10.1007/978-3-319-66284-8_24

Jeep Cherokee become unfortunately famous for being hacked remotely [1]. Lately vulnerabilities in Tesla [2] have also become real. In both cases core safety-critical elements such as the brakes became vulnerable. The main lessons learned with these experiments are that vulnerabilities are hidden in the inner design of the system. Security has to be considered at early stages of the concept design [3].

The industry and standardization committees are moving forward a collaborative approach between safety and security disciplines. Currently, automotive safety and security disciplines are not similarly mature - security is less mature than safety [4]: While the SAE guidebook regarding automotive cybersecurity is available in the first edition, for the established automotive functional safety standard ISO 26262 [5] the preparation of edition 2 is ongoing. Both documents note interaction points of functional safety and cybersecurity[1], but only in an informative way. The standards focus on guidance to solve the challenges in the specific safety and security lifecycle. One of the challenges identified in the ISO 26262 standard is the need of a safety case, which provides argumentation in a clear and comprehensive way that a system achieves a reasonable level of functional safety to operate in a given context. While functional safety refers to safety against failures in electrical/electronic (E/E) components, in the future there has to be argumentation where not only safety but also security and probably other dependability aspects are covered.

The paper at hand deals with a concept that covers standard compliant process- and product-based argumentation in context of safety and security. Just by following the standards procedures, automotive systems are not guaranteed to be free of risks. Standards are considered a compilation of best practices, which describe industry-wide accepted concepts, methods and processes. The paper is structured as follows: Sect. 2 describes the state of the art and previous approaches for this problem. Section 3 presents the safety and security co-engineering framework proposed by the authors. Section 4 demonstrates how the approach is put into practice by using specific tools. Section 5 provides conclusions and an outlook on further work.

2 Background and Related Work

ISO 26262 is the automotive functional safety standard, describing a safety lifecycle for the development of safety-related automotive systems (targeting passenger cars and minivans). The first edition was published in 2011 and is currently in a revision phase. A new informative annex will define potential interaction and communication channels between functional safety and cybersecurity. The same concept of safety and cybersecurity interaction points is presented in SAE J3061 [6]. The security lifecycle specified in SAE J3061 proposes communication paths between safety and security engineering. Figure 1 provides an exemplary overview of the interaction between safety and security engineering during the concept phase. The lifecycles itself are clearly described in the standards, but the interaction and cooperation is currently based

---

[1] The term "safety" refers functional safety according to ISO 26262, and "security" refers to cybersecurity according to SAE J3061.

on informative annexes, which suggest approaches and potential cooperation topics. There is a need to define activities to force interaction between the standards. Based on SAE J3061 a joint working group between ISO and SAE was started with the goal of developing an SAE/ISO "Standard for Automotive Cybersecurity". For safety and security co-analysis in different lifecycle phases multiple methods have been developed, e.g. STAMP (Systems-Theoretic Accident Model and Processes) [7] a theoretic model for safety, SAHARA (Security-Aware HARA) [8], an extension of the HARA method (Hazard And Risk Analysis) or FMVEA (Failure Modes, Vulnerabilities and Effects Analysis) [9], a combination of threat modeling and failure modes and effects analysis. But methods like these need to be embedded in a larger lifecycle framework.

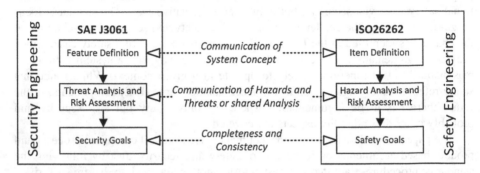

Fig. 1. Comparison of safety- and security engineering

For safety and security it is required to provide evidence and argumentation to show that system development was done compliant to relevant standards and that the system satisfies safety and cybersecurity goals. The final documentation has to be provided by the assurance case including safety and cybersecurity.

ISO 26262 mentions the possibility to use a graphical notation **Goal Structuring Notation (GSN)** to create the safety case. GSN's initial intention was to support safety case management [10]. Ray and Cleaveland proposed to apply GSN for constructing security assurance cases of medical cyber-physical systems [11]. The graphic structure of the security assurance case starts with a top-level security claim node accompanied by context information node and then breaks into layers of sub claim nodes that argue over different stages and aspects of the development lifecycle. Each sub claim is supported by a set of evidence nodes that explain the validity of the claim. Basically, GSN for assurance case is a graphic way to organize narrative information of claim, context, strategy, argument and evidence according to the GSN convention.

Patterns assist in reusing best practices systematically [17]. They are a suitable way to support argumentation that safety and security related requirements are fulfilled. Menon et al. [12] demonstrate how patterns are used to provide argumentation structures for software safety arguments. The authors define the structure consisting of GSN elements and its applicability. Patterns are usable on all development levels. Preschern et al. [13] examine the relationship between security and functional safety. The authors present an approach to categorize threats related to the impact to safety-critical functions. Taguchi et al. [14] define and compare different types of patterns concerning safety and security.

3   Safety and Security Co-engineering Framework

Figure 3 shows the main steps of the proposed methodology, which considers all process steps necessary in an automotive safety and security related development project:

Regulations and Standards (I) and Process Definition (II). In a first step we identify all relevant regulations and standards. In our automotive use case we deal with ISO 26262 regarding road vehicles functional safety and SAE J3061. It is challenging to match these two topics because they are influencing each other. Process definition has to consider that elaborated process steps are not only in parallel but also highly interactive, especially when we have to handle functional safety and cybersecurity. In addition, processes have to incorporate special analysis methods, which handle safety and security aspects in one common analysis methodology. Integrated processes which are basis for co-engineering unite safety with security activities. They lead to integrated requirements, work products and argumentation.

Process Management (III). The core of the framework is the distinction between functional safety and security related process and product requirements and the identification of interactions. Process requirements describe activities and steps, which are demanded by standards, while product requirements are requirement derived from the system under development. In order to manage the processes and support the processes execution, appropriate tools are useful, which assist developers with requirement and work product management. Work products are process outcomes representing different types of evidence. Evidence shows capability and maturity of the development process, compliance to the underlying standards and safety as well as security of the developed products. In addition, evidence is used to support arguments, which are related to requirements.

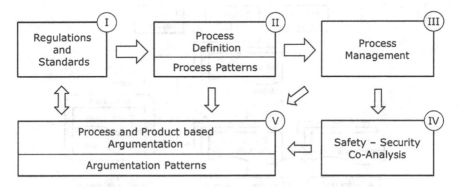

Fig. 2. Safety and security co-engineering framework

Safety and Security Co-analysis (IV). The intention of the proposed framework is to integrate functional safety and security. For that reason we have to deal with special analysis methods (see Sect. 3.2), which handle safety and security aspects in one common analysis (co-analysis) methodology.

Process- and Product-Based Argumentation (V). Consequently the argumentation demonstrates that the item under consideration contains no unreasonable risk and consolidates functional safety and security. To visualize these relationships between requirements and work products we use GSN. A more detailed description of the argumentation approach can be found in [17, 18].

To recapitulate we consider a loop (depicted in Fig. 2) in which every activity is supported by a tool: We create processes, which are modelled, instantiated and executed. The process output is evidence to argue that activities for the development of a specific product have been performed and are compliant to specific regulations. Once the process has integrated various disciplines, like safety and security, project managers have support to coordinate their cooperative actions.

3.1 Process Management

The requirements-driven workflow during process management starts with capturing requirements derived from the system artefacts, from standards, and possibly other, e.g. domain specific sources. The goal is a valid combined safety and security case, which requires evidences for the arguments it is composed of. The next step in the process is the definition of the necessary assurance activities, for which appropriate tools and methods are assigned. Finally, the assurance activities are processed - as far as possible automatically by a workflow engine. Successful assurance activities yield the necessary evidences. In case of negative results the faulty system element needs to be amended and then the assurance activity needs to be re-processed. When all assurance activities have been processed successfully the combined safety and security case is complete and valid.

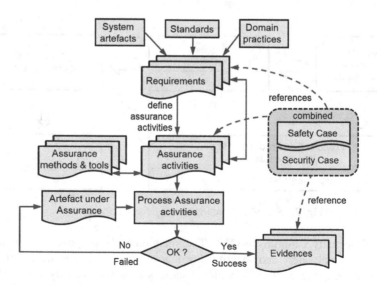

Fig. 3. Workflow model supporting compositional safety and security case

3.2   Safety and Security Co-analysis

Integrated development processes have to deal with requirements concerning functional safety and security. They affect not only safety related methods (e.g. HARA), they also demand methods for joint safety and security analysis (e.g. STAMP, STPA-Sec, FMVEA).

STAMP approach is used in this framework for co-analysis to model systems as hierarchical structures. Higher level controllers in the hierarchy control the processes at lower levels via actors, while the lower levels send feedback to the higher levels via sensors. It provides support to identify root causes for accidents in modern complex systems. Therefore, safety accidents should be viewed as a result of a lack of control, instead of a chain or sequence of events (i.e. Swiss cheese model). System-theoretic Process Analysis (STPA) is a novel analysis approach derived from STAMP.

STPA uses a control theory based system consideration. STPA for Security (STPA-Sec) [19] extends the safety-focused method to cover security. In STPA-Sec, each control action is analyzed under different possible conditions and guidewords are used to identify loss scenarios. A loss is a situation of insufficient or missing controls or safety constraints. STPA-Sec consists of following steps:

- Step 1. System description (scope, control model, accidents and hazards).
- Step 2. Identification of unsafe control actions (using control actions from Step 1 and guidewords to identify unsafe control actions in all system states and environmental conditions). Control action not given, given incorrectly, wrong timing or order, stopped too soon or applied too long.
- Step 3. Identification of scenarios which can cause unsafe control actions: identify scenarios how unsafe control action can be caused, based on control loop.
- Step 4. Design controls and countermeasures based on scenarios.

3.3   Patterns for Process and Argumentation

Patterns are a concept which spreads out in various development areas. We are using patterns to provide process and argumentation frameworks, which represents most of the recurring steps. The intention is to spend time once and reuse the elaborated patterns many times. Especially the integration of activities related to functional safety and security is a challenging work. We created patterns that provide process- and argumentation-templates. Process patterns simplify creating development processes because they already bring together functional safety and security activities. Argumentation patterns are corresponding to the process and exhibit the line of argumentation using the created work products. They include argumentation concerning functional safety and security and the interaction between them. Both types of patterns have to be instantiated for the specific development project. Instantiation for example means to select project specific methods like STPA-Sec for co-analysis. In parallel, the corresponding line of argumentation has to be selected. The purpose of creating patterns within the framework is to simplify the process definition, where the elaboration of evidence and adequate fitting arguments supports claims related to requirements.

4 Application to the Use Case

The automotive hybrid powertrain use-case provides the basis for the analysis of safety and security aspects based on state-of-the-art material[2]. An integral part of the hybrid powertrain system is the high voltage (HV) battery system, which consists of the battery management system (BMS), the battery satellite modules (grouping battery cells in modules and communicating via dedicated bus), and a fan control for cooling of the battery cells. The BMS is the main E/E system inside of an HV battery to power electric or hybrid electric vehicles. The BMS consists of several input sensors (see Fig. 5) for cell voltages, cell temperatures, output current, output voltage, and actuators like HV contactors for disconnection. This system is connected to various powertrain control units, the charging interface (enabling the communication with battery charging stations), the on-board diagnostic interface, and via a dedicated gateway to the vehicle infotainment systems (including the human machine interface and a wireless infotainment internet connection).

For the demonstration of the applicability of the presented co-engineering framework we had to use existing tools, which have been extended for specific needs of the presented approach:

EPF-C[3] (Eclipse Process Framework – Composer) is used for tool-support regarding the safety and security process modelling (II).

WEFACT (Workflow Engine for Analysis, Certification and Test) [16], web-based distributed platform for requirements-based testing with continuous impact assessment in order to support the safety case with evidences. Test workflow was extended to a workflow for safety certification and in the EMC[2] project the attribute of security was integrated (III).

XSTAMPP (eXtensible STAMP Platform) [20] is an Eclipse RCP (Rich Client Platform) based tool, which guides users through the Safety and Security Co-analysis by STPA-Sec process and supports the modelling of control loops and the definition of constraints (VI).

OpenCert is an open source tool for product and process assurance/certification management to support the compliance assessment and certification of safety-critical systems in sectors such as aerospace, railway and automotive [15]. OpenCert supports creation of GSN structures and mapping of evidence to requirements demanded by underlying standards (V).

In the following, the main parts the framework in scope of the EMC[2] project will be described in more detail.

4.1 Process Definition and Process Execution

Efficient safety certification implies a process model, which guides the user through the certification process and allows efficient compositional re-certification in the event of

---

[2] Technology-specific details have been abstracted for commercial sensitivity and presented analysis results are not intended to be exhaustive.

[3] Eclipse Process Framework, www.eclipse.org/epf/.

changes in the system. EPF-C provides elements to model phases and individual activities of the safety and security process. It allows modelling specific standards in a formal way, which enables automating the certification workflow.

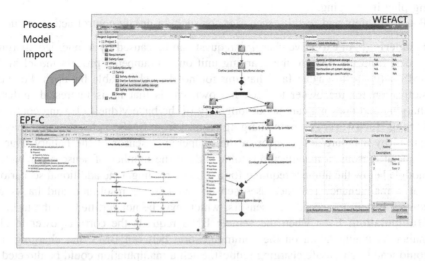

Fig. 4. Screenshots showing process modelling and execution (Tools: EPF-C, WEFACT)

WEFACT imports the process model including the activities modeled in EPF-C. Figure 4 shows safety- and security-related parts of the assurance process. The modeled assurance activities (small squares in the model diagram) are imported as so-called V-Plans and displayed as hierarchical list in the project explorer (left part of the GUI window). The upper right section of the window shows the assurance ("V&V") activities contained in the selected V-Plan. The V-Plan can be associated with the respective assurance tools (lower right corner). Finally, the assurance activities are processed by the workflow engine and deliver evidences for the requirements. During workflow execution, the status of the assurance activities changes whenever an activity is completed; the altered status is indicated by different highlighted colors in the list of activities.

4.2 Safety and Security Co-analysis Using STPA-Sec

The main accidents related to the BMS are fire/explosion of the battery systems and collision with an object:

- Fire/explosion of the battery system could be caused on the one side by charging conditions which are due to manipulation or failures outside of the safe range, but also by a modification or error in the operating parameters (e.g. spoofing on CAN bus, malicious firmware updates).
- Modified or erroneous operating parameter of the battery system or the control module, which provides power to the engines, could lead to undesired acceleration or deceleration. This could cause a collision.

Figure 5 shows the representation of the system architecture in the XSTAMPP tool used for co-analysis. We focused on the control action "Charging Request" and identified the following unsafe control action, based on the guide phrase "Control Action given incorrectly": Excessive charging request is transmitted to charging unit during plug-in charging.

Potential safety and security scenarios for such an unsafe control action include:

- **Tampering:** An excessive charging request can be caused by a modified charging request from the BMS to the charging unit due to tampered process model in the BMS software to enable fast charging for not fast chargeable batteries. Potential motivation for the owner to hack his own car is that he is interested in faster charging and does not care about longevity of the battery due to leasing contracts.
- **Wrong Hardware:** A wrong charging request from BMS to charging unit may be caused by a failure/design error in the temperature sensor of the battery. Due to financial reasons, a manufacturer could reduce the number of sensors per battery module below the number required for a reliable reading. One additional scenario is that a maintenance provider uses sensors with lower resolution and hacks the control system to accept such sensors, which may be not certified for the task.
- **Manipulation:** Even when the vehicle BMS requests the correct power level a malicious manipulation on the communication between BMS and charging unit could lead to an unsafe charging request. Such a manipulation could be directed at the charging unit or at the BMS.

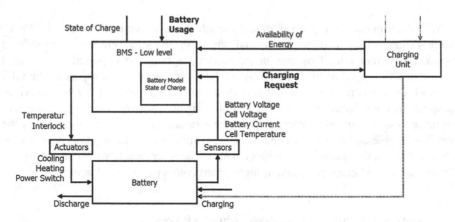

Fig. 5. Part of control loop of the battery management system (Tool: XSTAMPP) [21]

Supported by the tool XSTAMPP, we identify potential safety-related accidents based on potential causes regarding safety and security, e.g. failures and malicious manipulations by an attacker. In an independent analysis the focus of security would be on the classical CIA properties (confidentiality, integrity and availability). The feedback of safety relevance of these certain properties is missing. Safety specific analysis focuses only on safety issues caused by faults of E/E systems. Scenarios in which a user modifies the vehicle and causes a potential safety hazard would be missed. Co-analysis connects the domains and supports the identification of safety goals and safety-related security goals.

4.3   Process- and Product- Based Argumentation

Application of the methodology during the development of a BMS starts with selection of underlying standards. In this use case we consider ISO 26262 and SAE J3061, which are modeled in EPF-Composer as standard compliant integrated process model. The intention is to consider interacting functional safety and security activities. Based on the process model we examine the concept phase, which includes the Hazard Analysis and Risk Assessment (HARA). Results of the HARA are "Automotive Safety Integrity Levels" (ASIL), safety goals to mitigate potential safety-critical hazards and high level safety requirements. The necessary process steps based on SAE J3061 have to be added to the existing process model. In other words, the process model based on ISO 26262 has to be extended with steps demanded by SAE J3061 to define a co-engineering process. Executing this process means to perform co-analysis using STPA-Sec method. One result of the co-analysis is the hazard "overcharging battery during plug-in charging" for which developers have to implement an adequate countermeasure. Overcharging will be possible if an attacker modifies the BMU parameters. To document the relationship between requirements (represented as goals) and measures (declared in evidence documents) we use the OpenCert GSN editor. On the one hand the argumentation covers the safety and security process and on the other hand it deals with the product specific decision how to prevent "battery overcharging". From the security process point of view the top level claim is "define functional cybersecurity requirements to prevent unauthorized changes to BMU parameters". These requirements are listed in the corresponding project specific document "HV_Batt_SecReq" stored in the project repository. From the product point of view the BMU needs capabilities to detect and prevent unauthorized change of parameters. The documentation of these capabilities is evidence and usable as product-based argumentation.

4.4   Results of Investigation

The presented co-engineering framework was demonstrated by application to a hybrid electric vehicle powertrain use case. The application of the methodology showed a possible way how functional safety and security should correspond. Interaction between safety and security was forced by additional activities. The co-analysis method STPA-Sec was used and supported by the tool XSTAMPP. Product specific safety and security measures were coordinated to prevent unwanted interaction.

The usage of patterns speeded up the process definition activities and supported creation of argumentation fragments by GSN, which connect processes and evidence with argumentation. The graphical depiction of links between these elements improves the stakeholder's understanding and shows how the dependencies between safety and security are organized. The tool OpenCert provides the possibility to manage patterns and to create GSN structures. The execution of the assurance activities by the workflow engine WEFACT allowed widely automated generation of evidences for the combined safety and security case.

5 Conclusion

Today's interconnected world needs special care to consider safety and security aspects. Although there are approaches treating the interaction between safety and security adequately they are still immature. This paper presented a safety and security co-engineering framework. A comprehensive combined safety and security argumentation methodology for the automotive domain has been developed. Its application in the automotive domain within the standards constraints provides useful information and can be considered as the next step for a wide application in development lifecycles. The following important benefits of the presented methodology for argumentation apply to the automotive domain: Usage of patterns improves process definition; the GSN structures connect process- and product-related evidence with argumentation; the graphical depiction of links between these elements improves the stakeholder's understanding of relevant safety and security aspects. In the HEV powertrain use case we showed the benefit of combined analysis of safety and security issues and the preparation of an assurance case for safety and security. The question, what is a compelling argument regarding the coordination of functional safety and security measures has not been answered in a satisfactory manner and needs further investigation.

The idea of safety and security co-engineering is becoming an accepted approach and it is required to appear in a specific standard regarding safety and security co-engineering activities and shall be treated in a normative manner. Experience gained in EU projects like EMC^2 and AMASS will try to reach standardization committees and influence developments of future editions of standards with the goal of supporting assurance case establishment.

Acknowledgment. This work is supported by the projects EMC^2 and AMASS. Research leading to these results has received funding from the EU ARTEMIS Joint Undertaking under grant agreement no. 621429 (project EMC^2), project AMASS (H2020-ECSEL no 692474; Spain's MINECO ref. PCIN-2015-262) and from the COMET K2 - Competence Centres for Excellent Technologies Programme of the Austrian Federal Ministry for Transport, Innovation and Technology (bmvit), the Austrian Federal Ministry of Science, Research and Economy (bmwfw), the Austrian Research Promotion Agency (FFG), the Province of Styria and the Styrian Business Promotion Agency (SFG).

References

1. Greenberg, A.: Hackers remotely kill a jeep on the highway—with me in it. Wired, **7**, 21 (2015). https://www.wired.com/2015/07/hackers-remotely-kill-jeep-highway/
2. Yan, C., Wenyuan, X., Liu, J.: Can you trust autonomous vehicles: contactless attacks against sensors of self-driving vehicle. DEF CON (2016)
3. Borchert, J., Slusser, S.: Automotive (R)evolution: defining a security paradigm in the age of the connected car. Infineon Report Web, November 2014
4. Glas, B., Gebauer, C., Hänger, J., Heyl, A., Klarmann, J., Kriso, S., Wörz, P.: Automotive safety and security integration challenges. In: Automotive-Safety & Security (2014)

5. International Organization for Standardization. ISO 26262 - Road vehicles – Functional safety, Part 1–10. ISO/TC 22/SC 32 - Electrical and electronic components and general system aspects, 15 November 2011

6. SAE: J3061 Cybersecurity Guidebook for Cyber-Physical Vehicle Systems (2016)

7. Leveson, N.: A new accident model for engineering safer systems. Saf. Sci. **42**(4), 237–270 (2004)

8. Macher, G., Sporer, H., Berlach, R., Armengaud, E., Kreiner, C.: SAHARA: a security-aware hazard and risk analysis method. In: Design, Automation & Test in Europe Conference & Exhibition (DATE), pp. 621–624. IEEE, March 2015

9. Schmittner, C., Gruber, T., Puschner, P., Schoitsch, E.: Security application of failure mode and effect analysis (FMEA). In: Bondavalli, A., Di Giandomenico, F. (eds.) SAFECOMP 2014. LNCS, vol. 8666, pp. 310–325. Springer, Cham (2014). doi:10.1007/978-3-319-10506-2_21

10. Goal Structuring Notation Working Group, GSN Community Standard Version 1, 16 November 2011. www.goalstructuringnotation.info

11. Ray, A., Cleaveland, R.: Security assurance cases for medical cyber-physical systems. IEEE Des. Test **32**(5), 56–65 (2015)

12. Menon, C., Hawkins, R., McDermid, J.: Interim standard of best practice on SW in the context of DS 00-56 Issue 4. SSEI, University of York, Standard of Best Practice (1) (2009)

13. Preschern, C., Kajtazovic, N., Kreiner, C.: Security analysis of safety patterns. In: Proceedings of the 20th Conference on Pattern Languages of Programs, p. 12. The Hillside Group, October 2013

14. Taguchi, K., Souma, D., Nishihara, H.: Safe & sec case patterns. In: Koornneef, F., van Gulijk, C. (eds.) SAFECOMP 2014. LNCS, vol. 9338, pp. 27–37. Springer, Cham (2015). doi:10.1007/978-3-319-24249-1_3

15. Ruiz, A., Larrucea, X., Espinoza, H.: A tool suite for assurance cases and evidences: avionics experiences. In: O'Connor, R., Umay Akkaya, M., Kemaneci, K., Yilmaz, M., Poth, A., Messnarz, R. (eds.) Systems, Software and Services Process Improvement. CCIS, vol. 543, pp. 63–71. Springer, Cham (2015). doi:10.1007/978-3-319-24647-5_6

16. Kristen, E., Althammer, E.: FlexRay robustness testing contributing to automated safety certification. In: Koornneef, F., Gulijk, C. (eds.) SAFECOMP 2015. LNCS, vol. 9338, pp. 201–211. Springer, Cham (2015). doi:10.1007/978-3-319-24249-1_18

17. Macher, G., Armengaud, E., Kreiner, C., Brenner, E., Schmittner, C., Ma, Z., Krammer, M.: Integration of security in the development lifecycle of dependable automotive CPS. In: Druml, N., Genser, A., Krieg, A., Menghin, M., Hoeller, A. (eds.) Handbook of Research on Solutions for Cyber-Physical Systems Ubiquity. IGI Global, in press

18. Martin, H., Krammer, M., Bramberger, R., Armengaud, E.: Process-and product-based lines of argument for automotive safety cases. In: ACM/IEEE 7th International Conference on Cyber-Physical Systems (2016)

19. Young, W., Leveson, N.: Systems thinking for safety and security. In: Proceedings of the 29th Annual Computer Security Applications Conference, pp. 1–8. ACM (2013)

20. Abdulkhaleq, A., Wagner, S.: XSTAMPP: an eXtensible STAMP platform as tool support for safety engineering (2015)

21. Schmittner, C., Ma, Z., Puschner, P.: Limitation and improvement of STPA-sec for safety and security co-analysis. In: Skavhaug, A., Guiochet, J., Schoitsch, E., Bitsch, F. (eds.) SAFECOMP 2016. LNCS, vol. 9923, pp. 195–209. Springer, Cham (2016). doi:10.1007/978-3-319-45480-1_16

Process Assessment in Supplier Selection for Safety-Critical Systems in Nuclear Domain

Timo Varkoi[(⊠)] and Risto Nevalainen

Finnish Software Measurement Association – FiSMA ry,
Tekniikantie 14, 02150 Espoo, Finland
{timo.varkoi, risto.nevalainen}@fisma.fi

Abstract. Nuclear power plants set strict requirements for their suppliers. Need for digital systems containing software increases as analog technology is maintained and replaced. We have used process assessments to evaluate safety-related systems development and developed a tailored assessment method for that. Selection of a capable supplier is a key to successful system delivery and qualification. Process assessments are found to be a cost-efficient way to analyze systems development. This paper provides a practical example in applying a process assessment method in supplier evaluation. A similar approach could be exploited in other domains, where domain specific requirements are essential. Benefits of the approach are discussed based on the experiences so far.

Keywords: Safety · Systems engineering · Process assessment · Nuclear SPICE

1 Introduction

The nuclear domain is very demanding for system developers and suppliers. Requirements are set in international domain specific standards and regulatory guides. In addition, strict functional and safety requirements are set by nuclear power plants. Candidate suppliers struggle with the abundance of requirements and nuclear power plants have difficulties in finding capable suppliers. Introduction of digital instrumentation and control systems that include software, increases the concerns. Qualification of the systems is expensive and time-consuming; hence new cost-efficient methods are needed.

In general, process assessment is a well-established method to analyze quality of the development processes. The aim is to increase trust between suppliers and acquirers, and reduce risks in system deployment. Process assessment in a safety-critical domain requires an appropriate assessment model and a robust assessment process.

Nuclear SPICE is a recently developed process assessment method. It is based on ISO/IEC process assessment standards, domain specific safety standards and regulatory requirements. The method has already been used in several assessments of safety-critical systems development projects. The latest version of Nuclear SPICE

© Springer International Publishing AG 2017
S. Tonetta et al. (Eds.): SAFECOMP 2017 Workshops, LNCS 10489, pp. 298–308, 2017.
DOI: 10.1007/978-3-319-66284-8_25

contains systems engineering processes. The method has been developed within a large safety research project in Finland.

This paper presents a practical application of the Nuclear SPICE method for supplier selection. A number of sources for requirements is studied, and an appropriate set of processes is defined to enable efficient supplier evaluation. The benefits of the approach are also discussed based on the preliminary experiences of the assessors and other stakeholders.

Next, in Sect. 2, we present the safety-related process assessment models and the developed Nuclear SPICE method for process assessment. Section 3 describes the use of the assessment method in supplier selection, including a recommended set of processes. Section 4 categorizes the anticipated benefits of the method.

2 Process Assessment in Safety-Critical Domains

2.1 Model-Based Process Assessment

Systems and software engineering is becoming increasingly complex. Software systems and platforms are overloaded with features, and interfaces between the systems and system layers multiply. Development teams may be distributed and in-depth expertise is scattered. Criticality of the systems adds requirements for development skills and competences. One way to approach these issues is process assessment, which may help to ensure adequate quality of the systems development and safety assurance.

Empirically we have found that process assessment is a cost-efficient method to address quality aspects of engineering processes. Process assessment is a well-structured approach both in evidence collection and in presentation of results. In general, process assessment models are well documented; training and guidance are available for assessors, both for generic and domain specific models. The standards define also assessor competency requirements including education, training and experience. Use of standards based assessment models ensures that assessment results are comparable.

Generally, process assessment may serve two purposes: first, to determine the quality of the processes against a selected set of requirements (e.g. capability); and second, to provide input for process improvement within an organization. Assessors can be external to the organization or internal. Typically, capability determination is carried out by an external assessor, especially if the result is used for supplier selection or organization's recognition. Process improvement assessments are often internal.

Process assessments are used in a number of safety-critical domains. Space and automotive industries are the first developers of domain specific assessment models. Recently, medical devices and nuclear power domains have got their own assessment models.

The Nuclear SPICE method is developed within the Finnish Research Program on Nuclear Power Plant Safety, SAFIR2018 [1]. Nuclear SPICE assessment method [2] was first published in 2014 with a focus on software engineering processes. Development of the method now continues within SAFIR2018, where research cooperation involves a broad network of stakeholders that can benefit of the standards based, yet domain specific process assessment method.

Automotive SPICE® [3] is one of the first domain specific assessment models based on ISO/IEC 15504. Automotive SPICE has its own Process Reference Model (PRM) and Process Assessment Model (PAM). Especially within the German car industry, the model is considered mandatory, providing objective process evaluation and findings for process improvement both on project and organizational level. Automotive SPICE does not specifically consider safety-related issues – functional safety is considered in other domain specific standards.

MDevSPICE® is a framework for medical device software process assessment [4]. It integrates generic software development best practices with medical device standards' requirements enabling consistent assessment of medical device processes. MDevSPICE® can be used by software companies evaluating their readiness for regulatory audits as well as by large medical device manufacturers for selecting suitable software suppliers.

2.2   Nuclear SPICE for Systems Engineering

International standards provide a solid basis to develop process models for systems engineering. Process assessment, too, can be based on standards. International standards are well-known and widely accepted presentations of state-of-the-practice in their respective domains. Especially, in safety-critical environments many aspects of system quality need to be considered to mitigate risks and to gain required trust in the systems [5].

The Nuclear SPICE method is based on the latest ISO/IEC standards and is applicable to systems and software engineering process. Earlier Nuclear SPICE versions emphasized the software engineering viewpoint. Practice has shown that most often the assessments address embedded systems development where the system platform dictates a great deal of the technical development.

Nowadays Nuclear SPICE covers also systems engineering processes. The recent revision of ISO/IEC 15288 standard [6] provides the process reference model including activities, tasks and information products as assessment indicators. ISO/IEC 15288 provides a common process framework for describing the life cycle of systems created by humans, adopting a Systems Engineering approach. It focuses on defining stakeholder needs and required functionality early in the development cycle, documenting requirements, then proceeding with design synthesis and system validation while considering the complete problem. The purpose of the standard is to provide a defined set of processes to facilitate communication among acquirers, suppliers and other stakeholders in the life cycle of a system. The related information product characteristics are described in detail in ISO/IEC 15289 [7].

A small but significant addition in the Nuclear SPICE assessment process defines a new activity: compliance evaluation. The activity is an important part of the assessment, since compliance to the requirements of the domain standards is a key issue in qualification.

Process Reference Model. Systems and safety engineering process reference model (PRM) in Fig. 1 is based on the systems engineering processes of ISO/IEC 15288, but additional process groups may be used to complete the framework as needed. One added module from the earlier Nuclear SPICE 2014 model is the set of safety processes which originate from ISO/IEC 15504-10 [8]. When software engineering is the main discipline to assess, more detailed software development processes are available in the 2014 model. This modularity enables flexible planning of assessments and also easy development of company specific assessment models.

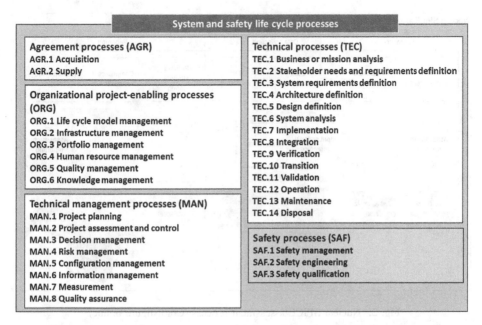

Fig. 1. Nuclear SPICE systems and safety engineering process reference model

Process Assessment Model. Nuclear SPICE Process Assessment Model (PAM) is a two-dimensional model of process quality. In one dimension, the process performance dimension, the processes are defined and classified into process categories. Each process is described with its identification, full name, purpose and a set of outcomes. Additionally, the assessment model defines more detailed assessment indicators (base practices and information products) that are evaluated and rated to derive the assessment result.

In the other dimension, the process capability dimension, process attributes are grouped into capability levels from 0 to 5. The process attributes provide the generic and measurable characteristics of process capability as defined in the standard ISO/IEC 33020 [9]. Each process capability attribute is described with a list of desirable achievements. The assessment results are expressed as achieved capability levels for each assessed process.

Assessment Process. The generic SPICE assessment process has three main phases: Planning, Data collection and Reporting. Each phase is further divided into activities. The Nuclear SPICE assessment process is mainly based on the ISO/IEC 33030 standard [10]. Each activity of the assessment process consists of tasks and related output work products. The Nuclear SPICE assessment process is presented in Fig. 2 [5]. Each activity of the assessment process consists of tasks and related output work products. The activities are supported by advanced document templates, which are presentation slides (yellow), spreadsheets (green), or text documents (blue).

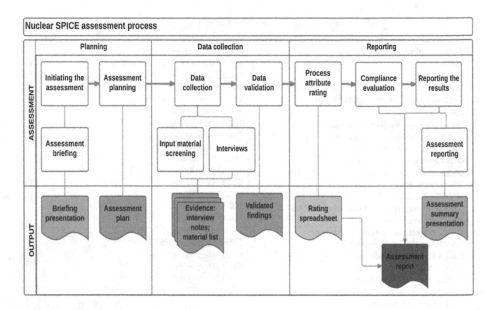

Fig. 2. Nuclear SPICE assessment process (Color figure online)

The main difference to the standard assessment process in Nuclear SPICE is the Compliance evaluation activity. It is needed to evaluate the domain specific requirements that originate from the domain safety standards or regulatory requirements. Assessment evidence is reviewed to find impacts on safety requirements, either strengths or weaknesses. Compliance evaluation is not intended to be used to determine compliance to a standard, however it may provide evidence on achievement of individual requirements [5].

Possible issues with the assessed processes are identified and reported based on the lead assessor's expert judgment of the analyzed processes. Compliance evaluation does not imply any compliance of the actual software product. This activity is optional depending on the assessment goal.

3 Use of Process Assessment for Supplier Selection

3.1 Requirements for Supplier Selection in Nuclear Domain

In this paper, we focus on requirements that are relevant to acquisition of digital instrumentation and control (I&C) systems, including software. Typically, software is a relatively small part of the systems used in nuclear power plants, and software oriented practices are few in the I&C systems engineering.

Problems in supplier selection are well recognized in all domains. Often, supplier evaluation and selection is based on an in-house approach. A typical method is a standardized checklist, which is filled by focused interviews and document reviews. Supplier selection is also a basic concept and requirement in well-known standards, for example ISO9001:2015. Focus is on necessary controls to keep promises and agreements between acquirer and supplier. In the nuclear power domain, additional requirements for suppliers are set in compliance with standards and in high rigor of safety and overall quality. Suppliers are an important source of evidences for system qualification. For these reasons, supplier selection is even more important in nuclear domain than in most other industries.

In our case, the most important nuclear specific sets of requirements for supplier selection and management are the Finnish national regulatory guide YVL A.3 [11], and the nuclear safety standards IEC 61513 [12], IEC 60880 [13] and IEC 62138 [14]. Common Position 2014 guidance [15] is also relevant, because it is detailed in the software related requirements. Other relevant sources for supplier selection requirements are e.g. IAEA Safety Standards [16] and ISO/IEC 15026 standards for assurance [17].

Requirements for supplier selection in guides and standards can be management, process and/or product requirements. If the supplier candidate manages the whole system engineering lifecycle and does not use subcontractors, then a large number of requirements for nuclear utility and system qualification are relevant to them. If the supplier candidate delivers only subsystems or components, then the set is more limited. External software components are often called COTS, PWS or PDS[1].

YVL A.3 has a direct requirement for supplier selection, requirement #626: "*The requirements for the selection of suppliers and the selection procedures shall be defined. These shall include the requirements pertaining to the supplier's management system and its quality management*". YVL A.3 has about ten other requirements for suppliers, many of them address quality planning and adequate system documentation. Nuclear SPICE is proficient to verify these requirements.

Nuclear standards IEC 60880 and 62138 are software requirements in safety classes 1–3. Supplier selection is not a clear topic, but COTS/PDS is. IEC 62138 says about PDS in clause 5.2.1.1: "*Pre-developed software shall have documentation giving the information necessary for using the software in the I&C system*." Numerous other PDS related requirements are included. Operational experience is required to measure

---

[1] COTS = Commercial off the Shell, PWS = Pre-existing Software (in Common Position 2014), PDS = Pre-developed Software (in IEC 60880). These can be considered as synonyms.

software quality and reliability. Nuclear SPICE is suitable in verifying compliance with quality assurance and system documentation.

Common Position 2014 has only a few requirements for suppliers, and they are mostly focused on PSW. There is a warning of external components in clause 1.4.2.2: *"It is doubtful that evidence will be available to demonstrate that the PSW has been developed and produced in accordance with a defined safety life cycle such as outlined in IEC 60880".*

3.2 Supplier Selection Process Set

We have defined a process set for supplier selection to simplify assessment planning. In Table 1, the processes are described with process purposes from ISO/IEC 15288 [6] to give an idea of the assessment scope. Of course, the Nuclear SPICE assessment model describes the processes in greater detail.

The selected set is based on our analysis of normative regulatory requirements and domain safety standards. Quality management (ORG.5) can be considered as an optional process to this list. Typically, Quality management is reviewed separately in a supplier audit, but can be assessed as a process, too. The presented set is a recommendation and may, naturally, be modified according to assessment needs.

The assessment may be a part of the acquisition preparation or a request for proposal. Main purposes of the supplier selection process set are to provide comparable

Table 1. Supplier selection process set

ID	Process name	Process purpose (as defined in ISO/IEC 15288)
MAN.1	Project planning	To produce and coordinate effective and workable plans
MAN.2	Project assessment and control	To assess if the plans are aligned and feasible; determine the status of the project, technical and process performance; and direct execution to help ensure that the performance is according to plans and schedules, within projected budgets, to satisfy technical objectives
MAN.4	Risk management	To identify, analyze, treat and monitor the risks continually
MAN.5	Configuration management	To manage and control system elements and configurations over the life cycle. CM also manages consistency between a product and its associated configuration definition
MAN.6	Information management	To generate, obtain, confirm, transform, retain, retrieve, disseminate and dispose of information, to designated stakeholders
MAN.7	Measurement	To collect, analyze, and report objective data and information to support effective management and demonstrate the quality of the products, services, and processes
MAN.8	Quality assurance	To help ensure the effective application of the organization's Quality management process to the project
SAF.1	Safety management	To ensure that products, services and life cycle processes meet safety objectives

information for supplier selection and to minimize risks in project implementation. This set is most suitable for fast collection of comparable information about the supplier candidates. When a supplier has already been selected, this set can be used to prepare the supplier for the project and thereby control the risks of the project. This is sometimes called pre-qualification.

The supplier selection set is most useful when used prior to a possible contract. It helps to set realistic expectations on both supplier and acquirer sides. It also prepares suppliers to address the nuclear domain requirements. The following set of processes is selected to provide a meaningful view to supplier candidates' quality and project management capabilities.

We have defined another process set for Project evaluation. It addresses mainly the need to collect system qualification material and is typically used during a delivery project. This set consists mainly of the technical processes (TEC group in Fig. 1).

Both predefined process sets support assessment planning, especially when performing assessments is a new thing. These process sets are appropriate to satisfy common process assessment goals related to the I&C system lifecycle in the nuclear domain. The process sets support repeatability of the assessments that is a key factor for both results comparability and assessment efficiency.

3.3   Performing an Assessment for Supplier Selection

So far, the use of the Nuclear SPICE method has concentrated on supplier selection or preparation of the supplier to meet the project requirements, including qualification needs. Based on this experience, we can reliably estimate resources and timetable needed to perform an assessment. Here we describe a typical implementation of an assessment for supplier selection.

Every nuclear power plant is responsible for qualification of all systems they use. Therefore, the presented supplier selection assessment usually starts with an agreement with the acquirer. Next, an assessment planning session is arranged with a candidate supplier. An appropriate assessment instance is agreed upon and the timetable is fixed. One competent lead assessor can carry out the assessment, but often an expert from the acquirer participates. When the acquirer is involved, the use of the assessment result is more efficient, too.

A supplier selection assessment with one process instance can be performed in four weeks from planning to reporting. It requires two to three days' visit on-site, where the supplier's experts are interviewed (approximately two hours per process). Usually there is no need to collect evidence for compliance evaluation, which reduces the time needed for the assessment. Data validation and assessment result preparation take about a week, including a detailed assessment report. Reporting and feedback sessions are kept for both the supplier and acquirer.

In total, the required lead assessor effort is five to seven working days, including the reporting. The acquirer is involved in planning, interview and reporting. Supplier's personnel participate in planning, material collection, interviews and reporting. Often also supplier's quality organization is interested in observing the assessment.

4 Benefits of Process Assessment Approach

These findings are based on assessors' extensive experience, interviews of both assessed organizations and assessment owners, and discussions with other stakeholders. Due to the confidentiality of the assessment results and the limited number of Nuclear SPICE assessments so far, we can only present experimental findings.

Process assessment is an effective method to check and verify in advance if a supplier has necessary capability to deliver what is required for. This way a major risk in the delivery project can be eliminated. Of course, some gaps, non-compliances and potential risks may remain and their mitigation should be included in the final contract. The power of process assessment depends also on the safety class of the system. In lower safety classes, process assessment may be the main method to collect evidence for qualification, both during supplier selection and in delivery project phases. Higher rigor safety class requires system/product centric methods, for example safety assessment, type tests and formal proofs. Even then, process assessment is an effective method to collect evidences and can be an evidence itself, since evaluation of supplier's design processes is a requirement. Based on our experiences, benefits from using Nuclear SPICE as a supplier evaluation method can be categorized in three groups:

- *Immediate benefits.* These are, for example, cost savings in comparison with other verification methods. Evidence collection in process assessment is systematic, focused and professional, because the method has been trialed and developed further based on the experiences.
- *Prevention of potential problems and risks.* If a systematic supplier selection is not done, major problems can occur in delivery, acceptance, qualification and licensing phases. As a consequence, heavy iteration cycles may be needed, or in worst case, cancellation of the whole delivery in a late phase. Assessment conclusions can be included in the final purchasing order or project plan to add visibility and control of known problems and risks.
- *Reuse of assessment results.* Early assessments help in the next phases of system development and delivery. When a delivery contract is signed and the technical work begins, it is very advisable to start the system qualification as a parallel activity. Evidences from the supplier evaluation can be reused directly in qualification.

According to a customer feedback from a nuclear power utility, the first benefit has been in finding a supplier whose engineering and implementation processes are capable enough, so that the nuclear specific standards and YVL requirements for processes can be achieved. After a Nuclear SPICE assessment, the risks associated with the choice of different suppliers as well as the potential impact on the overall cost and qualification possibilities are evaluated. The assessment results have reduced the risk of selecting a wrong supplier and potential delivery failure. Nuclear SPICE assessment also increases supplier's understanding of the documentation needs in the qualification process. Gaps in the processes have been recorded in the contract for required improvement. This has improved the confidence that the supplier will, and is able to, deliver a product that can be qualified and used in the nuclear power plant. In addition, the use of Nuclear SPICE has improved customer's own processes and understanding of the need of evidence collection to show that the nuclear specific requirements can be met in qualification.

Main benefit for the suppliers seems to be the support for their internal process improvement and systematic and objective presentation of strengths and weaknesses by an external assessor. Obviously, access to a demanding market offers commercial rewards, too.

5 Summary

Process assessment is a cost-efficient way to address also a wider range of systems engineering processes, and to enable systematic collection of evidence. Process assessment is especially useful in supplier selection, when objective evidence for comparison of suppliers' capabilities can be collected with a reliable and effective method.

We presented a special application of process assessment for supplier selection in the nuclear power domain. The approach provides comparable and repeatable information that can be used to reduce risks in system delivery. A similar approach can be applied in other domains, too. Consideration of domain specific requirements should to be planned in advance and the assessment process should be tailored to address compliance needs. Depending on the level of detail in the domain specific requirements, the assessment models might require amendments.

Expected benefits can be categorized in three groups: immediate benefits; prevention of potential problems and risks; reuse of assessment results. The benefits of the approach include cost savings, promptness of the results, risk reduction, and improved management and control of the projects. As one customer says: *"All our projects where Nuclear SPICE has been used have been successful and qualified to use in the nuclear power plant"*.

Acknowledgements. This work has been jointly funded by the Finnish national nuclear safety program SAFIR2018 (http://safir2018.vtt.fi/) and Finnish Software Measurement Association, FiSMA (www.fisma.fi).

References

1. Finnish Research Program on Nuclear Power Plant Safety. SAFIR2018. http://safir2018.vtt.fi
2. Varkoi, T., Nevalainen, R., Mäkinen, T.: Toward nuclear SPICE – integrating IEC 61508, IEC 60880 and SPICE. J. Softw.: Evol. Process **26**, 357–365 (2013). Wiley
3. Automotive SPICE®. http://www.automotivespice.com/. Accessed 11 May 2017
4. Lepmets, M., McCaffery, F., Clarke, P.: Development and benefits of MDevSPICE, the medical device software process assessment framework. J. Softw.: Evol. Process **28**(9), 800–816 (2016). Wiley
5. Varkoi, T., Nevalainen, R., Mäkinen, T.: Process assessment in a safety domain - assessment method and results as evidence in an assurance case. In: Proceedings of QUATIC 2016, Lisbon, Portugal, 6–9 September 2016, pp. 52–58. IEEE Computer Society (2016)

6. ISO/IEC/IEEE 15288:2015 Systems and software engineering—System life cycle processes
7. ISO/IEC 15289:2015 Systems and software engineering—Content of life cycle information products (documentation)
8. ISO/IEC TS 15504-10:2011 Information technology – Process assessment – Part 10: Safety extension
9. ISO/IEC 33020:2015 Information technology – Process assessment – Process measurement framework for assessment of process capability
10. ISO/IEC TS 33030:2017 Information technology – Process assessment – An exemplar documented assessment process
11. STUK: Radiation and Nuclear Safety Authority, Management system for a nuclear facility, YVL A.3 (2014)
12. IEC 61513:2011 Nuclear power plants - Instrumentation and control for systems important to safety - General requirements for systems
13. IEC 60880:2006 Nuclear power plants – Instrumentation and control systems important to safety – Software aspects for computer-based systems performing category A functions
14. IEC 62138:2004 Nuclear power plants – I&C Systems Important to Safety – Software aspects for computer-based systems performing category B or C functions
15. Common Position 2014. Licensing of safety critical software for nuclear reactors. Common position of international nuclear regulators and authorised technical support organisations. Western European Nuclear Regulators' Association (2014)
16. Leadership and Management for Safety, General Safety Requirements. IAEA Safety Standards No. GSR Part 2. IAEA 2016
17. ISO/IEC 15026-4:2012 Systems and software engineering – Systems and software assurance – Part 4: Assurance in the life cycle

A Runtime Risk Assessment Concept for Safe Reconfiguration in Open Adaptive Systems

Nikita Bhardwaj$^{(\boxtimes)}$ and Peter Liggesmeyer

Chair of Software Engineering: Dependability, University of Kaiserslautern,
Kaiserslautern, Germany
{bhardwaj,liggesmeyer}@cs.uni-kl.de

Abstract. Adaptivity is a consequential requirement for software systems that allow integration of components or devices at runtime. Dynamic integration of components and a subsequent reconfiguration during operation causes change in both functional and non-functional properties of the system. Since these systems often operate in Safety-Critical environment, safety becomes a crucial characteristic to be taken under consideration during reconfiguration. In this paper, we introduce a dynamic metrics based runtime risk assessment approach for safe reconfiguration in open adaptive systems. We combine design time safety analysis and runtime monitoring to evaluate risk factors of potential configurations of an adaptive component at runtime. Based on the evaluated risk factors the configurations are assigned a dynamic rank in an increasing order of their risk. During reconfiguration the adaptive component conforms to the ranking, thereby activating the configuration with lowest associated risk.

Keywords: Open adaptive systems · Safety assurance · Runtime risk assessment · Safe reconfiguration · Dynamic metrics

1 Introduction

Openness apropos of dynamic integration of components has become a fundamental characteristic of software systems used in application domains and technologies like Cyber Physical Systems [6], Ubiquitous Computing [10] and Service-Oriented Architectures [9]. Open systems are capable to integrate assorted components, devices, or other systems at runtime to provide an emergent and collaborative functionality as a whole. As a consequence, it becomes crucial that these systems have the capability to adapt to the dynamic changes in the system or its environment and operate accordingly.

Openness can, therefore, be defined as the ability of the system to allow integration of new (sub-)systems at runtime whereas, *Adaptivity* is the ability of the system to adjust its behaviour with respect to the changes occurring in itself or its context during operation [1,4]. Systems that are capable of *Openness* and *Adaptivity* are thus known as Open Adaptive Systems (OAS).

© Springer International Publishing AG 2017
S. Tonetta et al. (Eds.): SAFECOMP 2017 Workshops, LNCS 10489, pp. 309–316, 2017.
DOI: 10.1007/978-3-319-66284-8_26

Adaptivity is a consequential requirement for open systems. Dynamic integration of new components or devices at runtime causes change in both functional and Non-functional properties. Since OAS often operate in Safety-Critical domains like: Car2Car, Autonomous-Agriculture, avionics and medical care, one crucial characteristic that comes conjointly is safety. Owing to the dynamic changes in system structure and its characteristics at runtime, safety assurance has become a challenging task for OAS.

Traditional safety analysis and certification techniques demand entire system to be available at design time. However, in case of OAS it is not possible because system components are modified and composed at runtime [4,8]. Therefore, traditional techniques for safety analysis like Fault Tree Analysis (FTA), Hazard and Operability Analysis (HAZOP) and Failure Mode Effect (Criticality) Analysis (FMECA) are though necessary, but not sufficient. A recent work on Runtime certification [8] and Dynamic Safety Cases [5] try overcome these limitations by explicitly constructing assurance cases for system properties (e.g. Safety) that must be monitored and fulfilled at runtime, thereby providing safety assurance and certification throughout system lifecycle.

At runtime hazardous situations might occur due to random errors like wear&tear of physical components e.g. an old speed sensor generates speed with a certain time delay. Under such circumstances, changes in system structure due to integration of new components and subsequent reconfiguration modifies not only the influence of such hardware faults on the system but also the severity of their consequences. This in turn changes the risk associated with the entire system. Thus, one potential way to ensure safe operation of OAS is to perform risk management at runtime so that the system is able to reconfigure with respect to changes in the risk caused by unplanned or erroneous behaviour of system components.

The work of Priesterjahn and Tichy [2] addresses the issue of safe reconfiguration in self-* systems. They refine the structural adaptation behaviour of the system by performing checks that determine whether reconfiguration is allowed with respect to the associated damage after the reconfiguration and the maximum risk defined by the system. However, unlike our approach, they do not use the notion of dynamic metrics and have not considered dynamic complexities of individual configurations for their risk evaluation.

The use of dynamic metrics for risk assessment was introduced by Yacoub and Ammar [11] to determine the overall risk factor of system architecture based on the risk factors of its constituting components. In contrast to our approach, they do not address adaptive components of an OAS that have different potential configurations and can reconfigure at runtime.

In this paper, we introduce an approach that uses dynamic metrics to measure the risk associated with different potential configurations of an adaptive component based on the services associated with them. Configurations of an adaptive component can differ from one another in terms of services they render and the components they collaborate with in order to render those services. Any unplanned and erroneous behaviour of the collaborating component(s) influence the behaviour of the configuration, thereby influencing its risk. Since risk of an adaptive component depends upon the configuration it activates, deviations in the services associated with its potential configurations play a significant role in safe reconfiguration.

To this end, we exploit these risk dependencies between the configuration and deviations in the services of its collaborating components. We compute the risk factors of all potential configurations of an adaptive component as a product of its dynamic complexity and severity associated with the services. The dynamic complexities and the severity values, are determined at design time and are stored in a *Knowledge Base* to be used during system operation. At runtime, when an adaptive component has to reconfigure, *Service Monitor* monitors the operational status of the services associated with the potential configurations of the adaptive component. Subsequently, their corresponding severities are extracted from the knowledge base and together with the dynamic complexities risk factors are computed at runtime.

In Sect. 2, we present our approach followed by an illustration using a simple example of Tractor-Implement-Automation (TIA) from agricultural domain. In Sect. 3, we conclude our work with discussions regarding the planned future work.

2   Runtime Risk Assessment for Safe Reconfiguration

2.1   Evaluating Dynamic Complexity

In terms of software metrics dynamic complexity is a measure of complexity of a set of a code that is being executed when a system is performing a specific functionality [7]. Similarly, we define dynamic complexity of a configuration as a measure of complexity of the activated configuration that is executing in order to render the services[1] requested by the adaptive component.

In 1981, Henry and Kafura introduced the notion of information flow complexity (IFC). It is used to measure the complexity of a program and defined is as:

$$IFC = Length \times (FanIn \times FanOut)^2 \qquad (1)$$

where, *Length* is the cyclomatic complexity of the program, *FanIn* is the number of components that called this component and *FanOut* is the number of components called by this component during program execution. With reference to configuration of an adaptive component, we define *FanIn* as the number of components that depend upon this configuration for their required services and *FanOut* is the number of components the configuration depend upon to render its services.

Cyclomatic complexity introduced by McCabe in 1976 is calculated from control flow graphs and is defined as $CC = e - n + 2$, where e = number of edges

---

[1] A *service* is a behaviour that can be provided by any component for the use by any other component [4].

and n = number of nodes in the graph. To determine CC of a configuration we use state chart diagrams to represent the dynamic behaviour of a configuration. Depending upon the collaboration scenario, a configuration traverses a set of states and transitions. If e_k and n_k are the set of nodes and transitions traversed by configuration k (C_{F_k}) in collaboration scenario i (CS_i) then CC of the configuration is defined as:

$$CC_{C_{F_k}}^{CS_i} = e_k^{CS_i} - n_k^{CS_i} + 2 \tag{2}$$

We have used sequence diagrams to represent the interactions between a configuration and its collaborating components. *FanIn* and *FanOut* for a configuration of an adaptive component is the sum of all incoming interactions (messages) received by the configuration and the sum of all outgoing interactions sent to other components. The dynamic complexity (DC) of C_{F_k} is thus defined as:

$$DC_{C_{F_k}}^{CS_i} = CC_{C_{F_k}}^{CS_i} \times \left(II_k^{CS_i} \times OI_k^{CS_i} \right)^2 \tag{3}$$

A configuration interacts with different set of components in different collaborating scenarios. Due to this dynamic behaviour it has different dynamic complexities. Thus, if n is the total number of different collaboration scenarios of C_{F_k} then the normalized dynamic complexity (NDC) is evaluated as:

$$NDC_{C_{F_k}}^{CS_i} = \frac{DC_{C_{F_k}}^{CS_i}}{\sum\limits_{i=1}^{n} DC_{C_{F_k}}^{CS_i}} \tag{4}$$

2.2 Hazard and Severity Analysis

Sometimes a component with low complexity values can result in hazardous situations with highly severe consequences. As a result of which, evaluation of complexity of a configuration (or component) is not sufficient to determine risk associated with its failure [11]. Therefore, in our approach, we also consider severity associated with the configuration for risk assessment purposes. We define severity of a configuration as the severity of the consequences of the hazardous situations caused due the deviations in the services of its collaborating components.

A service, both rendered and required by a component, can have several different deviations from its planned behaviour. Each deviation has a set of potential causes, their corresponding consequences and the severities associated with them. To determine the cause-consequence relationships and the severities of a deviation, we employ the Hazard and Operability (HAZOP)-type analysis (Table 1).

A configuration consists of a set of required and provided services i.e. it is mostly associated with more than one service. In order to choose the severity of the configuration w.r.t. its associated services we take into consideration the *worst-case* consequence of all the services. Based on hazard analysis [3], we categorize the severities into following classes along with the following values: Negligible (0.10), Minor (0.25), Marginal (0.50), Critical (0.75) and Catastrophic (0.95).

Table 1. HAZOP-type analysis for *VSpeed* service of configuration *AutoSwathScCf1*

Service	Failure Mode	Direct Consequences	Direct Severity	Propagated Consequences	Propagated Consequence Severity
VSpeed *Context: The tractor performs baling operation in the autonomous mode. The tractor must decrease the speed because the bale is too heavy and this is the last section of the swath left.*	The speed of the tractor is not generated when requested.	The volume flow rate of the swath cannot be generated thereby *SwathVolFlow* can't be rendered.	Marginal	The target speed and acceleration of the tractor cannot be determined. Thereby the tractor either: - doesn't stop or - doesn't start moving or - doesn't decrease the speed when requested. ...	Critical
	The speed of the tractor is generated but x seconds after the request.	Delay in determining the volume and flow rate of the swath thereby the rendering of *SwathVolFlow*.	Marginal	The target speed & the acceleration of the tractor is set with a delay. Thus the tractor either: - stops late or - starts moving late or ...	Critical
	The speed of the tractor is determined when not requested.	N/A	-	-	-
SwathVolFlow	The volume flow rate of swath is not generated.	The target speed & acceleration of the tractor cannot be evaluated..	Critical	The tractor: - doesn't stop or - doesn't decrease the speed when requested. ...	Critical
	...	...	...		...

2.3   Runtime System Monitoring and Risk Factor Evaluation

Once the dynamic complexities and the severities of a configuration are known, the information is stored in a *Knowledge Base*. The knowledge base acts like a repository that contains system information about services, their potential deviations, cause-consequence relationships and their severities. We assume that the system is employed with a *Service Monitor* that is capable to monitor the operational status of all its services at runtime i.e. each time a service deviates from its planned behaviour the service monitor is able to detect it.

At runtime, when an adaptive component has to reconfigure, service monitor monitors the operational status of the services associated with its potential configurations. Subsequently, their corresponding severities and dynamic complexities are extracted from the Knowledge Base and sent to *Configuration Evaluation Module* to evaluate the *Risk Factors* at runtime. Risk Factor (RF) of a configuration C_{F_k} is evaluated as:

$$RF_{C_{F_k}}^{CS_i} = NDC_{C_{F_k}}^{CS_i} \times SVT_{WCSv \in CF_k}^{CS_i} \tag{5}$$

where, $SVT_{WCSv \in CFk}$ is the worst case severity of all the associated services of C_{F_k} in collaboration scenario CS_i. Based on them configurations are assigned ranking from best to worst in an increasing order of risk.

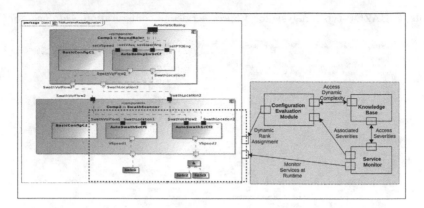

Fig. 1. Safe reconfiguration of an adaptive component using runtime risk assessment

2.4 Case Study

To illustrate our approach, we have considered a simple case study from TIA domain. The system considered in our case study belongs to the category of *pre-engineered variability* [4] of open systems[2].

The system consists of three components: Tractor, round baler and a swath scanner. Round baler is an implement that can be attached to the TIA capable tractor at runtime to automate the process of baling. In order to do so, baler requires swath scanner that provides information about swath location and volume. In the rest of the paper, round baler will be referred to as Comp1 and swath scanner as Comp2 (Fig. 1).

Comp1 uses its configuration *AutoBalingSwScCf* to render the application service *AutomaticBaling*. To do so, it requires *SwathVolFlow* and *SwathLocation* services rendered by Comp2. Comp2 further requires *VSpeed* i.e. the information about the speed of the vehicle which is provided by the speed sensors *SpSr* attached to the vehicle. Comp2 consists of two configurations labelled as *AutoSwathScCf1* and *AutoSwathScCf2*. Both configurations of Comp2 are potentially capable to provide services required by Comp1. The only difference between the two is the type and number of speed sensors used to measure the vehicle speed.

We evaluate the dynamic complexities of *AutoSwathScCf1* and *AutoSwath-ScCf2* using their state chart and sequence diagram representations at design time. The normalized dynamic complexities of the two configurations are NDC_{F_1} = 0.072 and NDC_{F_2} = 0.2. The severities of potential deviations occurring in the services are also determined at design time using HAZOP-type analysis as shown in Table 1.

For the use case, we assume a scenario where due to wear&tear *SpSr1* of *AutoSwathScCf1* generates speed information *200* ms late. As the required

---

[2] An open system with pre-engineered variability explicitly knows how its overall goals, both functional and Non-functional, can be achieved at runtime.

service *VSpeed1* gets delayed, the evaluation and rendering of the provided services *SwathVolFlow* and *SwathLocation* will suffer the delay too. On the basis of hazard and severity analysis performed at design time (Table 1) the severity value of *marginal*, associated with the delay, is extracted from knowledge base. Since speed sensors *SpSr2* and *SpSr3* of *AutoSwathScCf2* function fine without any deviations, the severity associated with the configuration is *negligible*.

At runtime, when Comp1 broadcasts a request for *SwathVolFlow* and *SwathLocation* services Comp2 being a potential provider begins the evaluation of its two configurations. To this end, service monitor detects the delay in *SpSr1* and requests for the corresponding severity from knowledge base. It then sends the severity to the configuration evaluation module. Subsequently, the module requests for the corresponding dynamic complexities of the two configurations and computes the risk factors accordingly. The risk factors of the two configurations are: $RF_{C_{F_1}} = NDC_{F_1} \times SVT_{VSpeed \in CF1}$ i.e. $0.072 \times 0.50 = 0.036$ and $RF_{C_{F_1}} = 0.2 \times 0.10 = 0.02$. Based on the calculated risk factors, *AutoSwathScCf1* is ranked lower due the deviation in *SpSr1* and *AutoSwathScCf2* is ranked 1. As a result, Comp2 selects *AutoSwathScCf2* for activation and terminates the configuration evaluation procedure.

3 Conclusion and Future Work

Open adaptive systems modify their behaviour in order to adapt to the dynamic changes caused either by integration of new components or changes in the environment at runtime. Consequently, they need an adaptation mechanism that determines a new configuration to handle these changes and aid in reconfiguration of system structure. Since these systems mostly operate in safety critical environment, safety becomes a crucial characteristic to be taken under consideration during reconfiguration.

To this end, we introduce an approach to determine risk of different potential configurations of an adaptive component using their dynamic complexity and severity associated with the hazardous situations at runtime. The idea behind is to integrate design time safety analysis and runtime system monitoring to ensure safe reconfiguration at runtime. The approach allows an adaptive component of pre-engineered variability to evaluate and compare its configurations based on the current operational condition of their collaborating components, thereby selecting the configuration with lowest associated risk.

We currently work on evaluating our model using assorted case studies and different failure scenarios. Additionally, the presented approach only estimates the risk factors of a configuration of an adaptive component. In our future work, we plan on extending the approach to estimate risk factors of all adaptive components involved in a scenario, and thus determine the risk associated with the entire collaboration scenario rendering an application service.

References

1. Cheng, B.H.C., et al.: Software engineering for self-adaptive systems: a research roadmap. In: Cheng, B.H.C., Lemos, R., Giese, H., Inverardi, P., Magee, J. (eds.) Software Engineering for Self-Adaptive Systems. LNCS, vol. 5525, pp. 1–26. Springer, Heidelberg (2009). doi:10.1007/978-3-642-02161-9_1
2. Pristerjahn, C., Tichy, M.: Modeling safe reconfiguration with the FUJABA real-time tool suite. In: Proceedings of the 7th International Fujaba Days, pp. 14–20 (2010)
3. Sundararajan, C.: Guide to Reliability Engineering, Data Analysis, Application, Implementation and Management. Van Nostrand Reinhold, New York (1991)
4. Schneider, D.: Conditional safety certification for open adaptive systems. Ph.D. thesis (2015)
5. Denney, E., Pai, G., Habli, I.: Dynamic safety cases for through-life safety assurance. In: Proceedings of the 37th IEEE/ACM International Conference on Software Engineering ICSE, pp. 587–590 (2015)
6. Lee, E.: Cyber physical systems: design challenges. Berkeley Technical report no. UCB/EECS-2008-8
7. Munson, J.C., Khoshgoftaar, T.M.: Software metrics for reliability assessment. In: Handbook of Software Reliability Engineering, pp. 493–529. McGraw-Hill, Inc., Hightstown (1996)
8. Rushby, J.: Runtime certification. In: Leucker, M. (ed.) RV 2008. LNCS, vol. 5289, pp. 21–35. Springer, Heidelberg (2008). doi:10.1007/978-3-540-89247-2_2
9. Bell, M.: Introduction to Service-Oriented Modeling. Service-Oriented Modeling: Service Analysis, Design, and Architecture. Wiley, Hoboken (2008)
10. Weiser, M.: Some computer science issues in ubiquitous computing. Commun. ACM **36**(7), 75–84 (1993). doi:10.1145/159544.159617
11. Yacoub, S.M., Ammar, H.H.: A methodology for architecture-level reliability risk analysis. IEEE Trans. Softw. Eng. **28**(6), 529–547 (2002). doi:10.1109/TSE.2002.1010058

Assuring Degradation Cascades of Car Platoons via Contracts

Irfan Sljivo[1(✉)], Barbara Gallina[1], and Bernhard Kaiser[2]

[1] Mälardalen University, Västerås, Sweden
{irfan.sljivo,barbara.gallina}@mdh.se
[2] Berner & Mattner Systemtechnik GmbH, Munich, Germany
bernhard.kaiser@berner-mattner.com

Abstract. Automated cooperation is arriving in practice, for instance in vehicular automation like platoon driving. The development and safety assurance of those systems poses new challenges, as the participating nodes are not known at design time; they engage in communication at runtime and the system behaviour can be distorted at any time by failures in some participant or in the communication itself. When running on a highway, simply switching off the function is not an option, as this would also result in hazardous situations. Graceful degradation offer a systematic approach to define a partial-order of less and less acceptable operation modes, of which the best achievable is selected in presence of failures. In this work we propose an approach for assurance of the degradation cascades based on mode-specific assertions, captured by assumption/guarantee contracts. More specifically, we share our experiences and methodology for specifying the contracts for both the nominal safe behaviour as well as the less safe but acceptable behaviour in presence of failures. Furthermore, we present an argument pattern for adequacy of the degradation cascades for meeting the global safety goals based on the contracts. We illustrate our approach by a car platooning case study.

1 Introduction

Cooperative systems represent the cornerstone of the fourth industrial revolution [1]. A typical example are vehicle platoons, where an automated fleet of vehicles join via Car2Car connection to achieve a cooperative function such as Cooperative Automated Cruise Control (CACC). Many of such systems are safety-critical. Accordingly, a technical safety concept is mandatory for discussing technical design solutions for all potential failure modes and their tolerance through detection and reaction mechanisms. When releasing the individual vehicle for road usage, an argument (called safety case) must be provided that the system is actually safe to the safety integrity level that has been claimed. The number of operation modes and of failure possibilities of the cooperative system as a whole explodes due to the combinatorics of operation and failure modes of all individual participants, plus failure modes of the communication link that can occur at any time. A safety argument must be designed at design

© Springer International Publishing AG 2017
S. Tonetta et al. (Eds.): SAFECOMP 2017 Workshops, LNCS 10489, pp. 317–329, 2017.
DOI: 10.1007/978-3-319-66284-8_27

time for each possible configuration at runtime, and onboard-mechanisms must execute corresponding failure mode detection and reaction in every configuration. As the number of combinations would make this unmanageable, usage of abstraction techniques is necessary, focusing only on the relevant assertions on black-box-level.

Moreover, these systems are often safe-operational systems (e.g. a car platoon on a highway, driving automatically without the drivers being ready to react at short notice), which means that the reaction on failures cannot be as primitive as just switching off the function in one of the participating cars, but its partial functioning should be ensured instead. Dynamic system adaptation [2] is an approach to reconfigure the system to the best achievable operation mode in case of failures, thereby trading off between safety, availability and functionality provided. Which operation mode is the best can be determined by ordering the operation modes in a degradation cascade [3,4]. An ordered set of rules determines when a certain operation mode or system configuration should be activated, triggered by failure detection, typically issued by model-based health monitors for sensors and other critical system parts.

Contract-based approaches have been frequently used for compositional verification and also offer means to specify and verify the reconfiguration rules in terms of contracts. They allow both checking of valid system configurations and checking refinement between the different hierarchical levels. A contract is a pair of assertions in form of assumptions and guarantees, where a component guarantees its own behaviour provided that the environment fulfils the assumptions. As reconfigurable components are characterised with different behaviours, we distinguish between strong and weak contracts [5]. A strong contract must hold in every environment, while a weak one is not required to hold in every environment. Only when, besides the strong assumptions, the weak assumptions are also met, the component offers the behaviour in the weak guarantees.

In our previous work we presented FLAR2SAF (Failure Logic Analysis Results to Safety Argument-Fragments) [6] – a partially tool-supported method that uses CHESS-FLA [7] to derive contracts and generate safety case argument-fragments. The basis for the argument generation is the connection of a contract with the corresponding safety requirement. Specifying requirements by stating *"X shall always happen"* is inadequate for degradation cascades where the requirements should describe a cascade stating what shall happen if for example X is not always possible [8]. We see weak contracts as a way to capture behaviour described in these complex safety requirements for degradation cascades.

In this work we propose systematic design and pattern-based safety assurance of degradation cascades using contracts. To derive contracts, we examine potential failures of initial system architecture using standard approaches, define failure detection mechanisms and the resulting operation mode changes through degradation cascade requirements. Based on the specified degradation cascade requirements and domain knowledge we derive degradation cascade contracts, which can be used to build an argument for assuring adequacy of degradation cascade to address the corresponding hazard. Finally, we illustrate the usage of the approach in a CACC case study.

The rest of the paper is organised as follows: In Sect. 2 we present background information. We present the assurance of degradation cascades using contracts in Sect. 3. In Sect. 4 we present the CACC case study. We present the related work in Sect. 5, and conclusions and future work in Sect. 6.

2   Background

In this section, we briefly recall the basic notions regarding component contracts and degradation cascades.

2.1   Assumption Guarantee Component Contracts

A traditional component contract $C = \langle A, G \rangle$ is composed of assumptions (A) on the environment of the component and guarantees (G) that are offered by the component if the assumptions are met. Strong $\langle A, G \rangle$ and weak $\langle B, H \rangle$ contracts [5] provide support for capturing variable behaviour of reusable components. The strong contract assumptions (A) are required to be satisfied in all contexts in which the component is used, hence the corresponding strong guarantees (G) are offered in all contexts in which the component can be used. The weak contract guarantees (H) are offered only when in addition to the strong assumptions, the corresponding weak assumptions (B) are satisfied as well.

Contracts can be used to (semi)-automatically instantiate existing safety case argument-patterns based on the SEooCMM metamodel [6] that captures the relations between the contracts, the supporting evidence and the safety requirements allocated on the component. Every contract is supported by one or more evidence items and every allocated safety requirement is addressed by at least one contract such that satisfaction and confidence in the associated contracts supports satisfaction of the corresponding requirement. We use Goal Structuring Notation (GSN) [9] – a graphical argumentation notation – to represent the argument-fragments. The GSN elements used in this paper are shown in Fig. 1.

2.2   Degradation Cascades

Graceful degradation is seen as a way to improve dependability of a system by degrading its performance proportionally to the failures of its components [4]. Degradation cascades represent a partial order over a labelled set of operation modes where system degrades its performance based on the presence of certain failures, while always choosing the most convenient available mode at any time. As an ordering scheme, existing classifications like the SIL or ASIL (Automotive Safety Integrity Level) according to safety standards such as ISO 26262 or the Severity factor (S) known from Failure Mode and Effects Analysis (FMEA) may be used for labelling the operation modes in terms of safety criticality. The labelling can be denoted graphically by different colours ranging, for instance, from green (fully functional and safe) over yellow (degraded function, but still safe) and orange (emergency function, hazard of low severity) to red (hazardous).

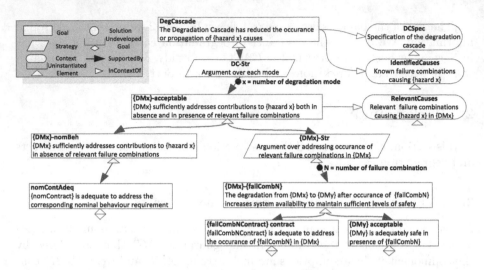

Fig. 1. Degradation cascades (DC) argument pattern in GSN

Representing degradation cascades in terms of safety requirements is not as straightforward as stating *"The system shall do X"*. Rather, if X is not available, system should do something else by going to a degraded state. Furthermore, if that degraded state cannot be maintained, the system should further degrade its performance, until the final state is the uncontrollable failure that should be sufficiently unlikely to occur. Hence complex requirement structuring mechanisms are proposed for capturing degradation cascades where each degradation mode is represented by an if-else style "sub-requirement" [3]. Each of these "sub-requirements" addresses a single degradation mode by listing under which conditions should the particular degradation mode become active. For example, for a simple Lane Keeping Assist (LKA) system [3], the nominal requirement would be that *RQ1: "When active and no input failures the LKA system shall guide the vehicle in the middle of the lane with allowed tolerance of 0.5 m"*. And its alternative requirement *RQ2: "If the system cannot achieve that (e.g., because it cannot detect the lane borders), then the vehicle shall keep in the middle of the neighbouring vehicles and issue an urgent take over"*.

3   Car Platooning Degradation Assurance via Contracts

In this section we first sketch a contract-based approach for design of degradation cascades for car platooning. Then we present the argumentation pattern for degradation modes based on the captured degradation mode contracts.

3.1   Contract-Based Design of Degradation Cascades

Unlike for traditional cars, the term failure comprises for cooperative systems:

1. Technical Failures in the local car (e.g. sensor failures, actuator failures, controller failures);

2. Technical Failures in another participating car (remote failures), impairing the integrity of any information provided by this car;
3. Failures in the communication between any cars (e.g. message loss, message delay, message corruption).

The safety case will have to show that for any combination (!) of platoon configurations, environmental situations (listed and classified before) and failure modes (neglecting multiple failures, at first) the safety goal is not violated.

Combining our previous works on contract-based design [10], structured design of degradation cascades [8] and contract-based safety case argument generation [6], we propose a combined design and safety assurance of degradation cascades using component contracts. Just as in our previous works [6,10], we follow the same generic safety assurance process using component contracts. We model the fault-free architecture, perform safety analysis to identify the needed extensions in terms of safety measures, and then derive contracts from results of such analyses. Finally we use the contracts to instantiate the corresponding argumentation pattern. We detail the process for the case of deriving the contracts for car platooning degradation cascades:

1. Model the local controller chain and the local operation state machine of each car for the failure-free case, using SysML and, if applicable, contracts (strong contracts for now), in a similar way as described in Sect. 3.3 of [10]. Validate the platoon use cases (e.g., join platoon) by simulation (building the product state-space would be unmanageable for humans, but could in the future offer the possibility for model checking);
2. Examine potential failures (local/remote/communication) and their consequences using standard approaches such as Failure Mode and Effects Analysis (FMEA) and define detection mechanisms (e.g. range checks for sensors, timeout and CRC checks for communication link). Failure classes can be used to structure this, and failures can be interpreted as violations of the initial contracts, as shown in Sect. 4 of [10]. Note: technically, this is implemented by observers or monitors as separate Simulink blocks, and captured by separate sub-state machines that report a Boolean failure state. Define safety mechanisms that change the operation mode (and therefore, the controller structure and/or the controller parameters, e.g. distance-to-predecessor setpoint) in case of detected failures. When doing so, try to fall back to the best performing, but yet safe operation mode, leading to a degradation cascade (denoted as a partial order of colours ranging from green to red, with which the operation modes are labelled, as shown for a local system in [8];
3. Collect degradation mode contracts for each local operation mode and adjust the parameters and controller configurations for each mode (and, thereby, the resulting guarantees) so that for each valid operation mode, the overall safety goal is implied.

3.2 Degradation Cascades Safety Argument Pattern

We use the degradation mode contracts to assure that the safety of the degradation cascade is adequate. We define the degradation cascades argument pattern

(Fig. 1) that can be instantiated from such contracts using the technique from our previous work [6]. The argument assures that the degradation cascade has adequately addressed the causes leading to the corresponding hazards (*Deg-Cascade* goal in Fig. 1). This means that the unreasonable risk of the hazard should be absent in each operation mode, both during nominal behaviour (*{DMx}-nomBeh*) and in presence of failures (*{DMx}-Str*). Hence, we develop the argument for each operation mode specified in the degradation cascade by looking into the identified failure combinations relevant for that particular mode. First, we assure that the mode is adequately safe under nominal conditions (when the identified relevant causes are absent). Then, we assure that increasing the system availability by switching to a degraded mode keeps the system acceptably safe when a relevant failure combination occurs (*{DMx}-{failCombN}*). In particular, we need to argue not only that the condition triggering the degradation (as described in the corresponding contract) is adequate (*{failCombNContract}Adeq*), but also that the target operation mode is adequate in presence of the particular failure combination (*{DMy}Acceptable*). We develop the lower-level parts of the argument (*nomContAdeq* and *{failCombNContract}Contract*) related to the confidence in such contracts based on the contract satisfaction pattern [11].

4   CACC and Platooning Case Study

In this case study we use degradation cascade contracts on a CACC system. We first describe the system, and then apply the process described in Sect. 3.1.

4.1   CACC and Car Platooning

A typical example of a cooperative safety-critical system is CACC – smart cruise control guided by a predecessor vehicle via a Car2Car link, as well as vehicle platooning as an extension of CACC, where additional Car2Car connection is established to the leader vehicle (the first vehicle of the platoon) that coordinates the whole platoon. Figure 2 explains the different operation modes. As a case study in the AMASS research project [12], we have built up a fleet of autonomous model cars in the scale 1:8 that can run autonomously and sense the road and any other cars or obstacles by means of camera and ultrasonic sensors. Additionally, the cars can establish a WIFI connection to one another at runtime to exchange Car2Car messages. When doing so, several cars can transit to CACC mode, and in a next step form a platoon where other cars can join in, thereby forming a system-of-systems (SoS). Several use cases have been modelled and implemented, such as "create platoon", "join platoon", "leave platoon" etc. Apart from manual driving (for model cars, this means: operated by a radio remote controller), there are the operation modes CC (cruise control, i.e. running alone with fixed speed), ACC (adaptive CC, i.e. perceiving the predecessor car with local distance sensors and adjusting speed accordingly), CACC (cooperative ACC, i.e. with radio connection established to the predecessor car, which informs about its

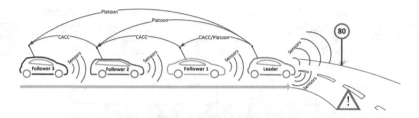

Fig. 2. Explanation of CACC and platoon driving

position, speed and manoeuvre intentions), and platoon (same as CACC, but all participants being informed via radio by the platoon leader vehicle, not just the immediate predecessor).

4.2 Safety Aspects of CACC and Platoon Driving

The SoS such as CACC and car platooning come with different hazards. We choose the rear collision as our running example. Note that, in contrast to today's road vehicles, safety standards such as ISO 26262 cannot be applied directly to vehicle platoons, because this standard allocates the overall safety responsibility to the system manufacturer, but a platoon has no manufacturer, as the participating cars come from different carmakers. However, global safety goals can be stated in a similar way as in traditional safety engineering, such as *"Any two cars shall always maintain a front-rear-distance of at least 2 m to each other"* (of course, the scaling has to be adapted from real world to model cars). It has to be proven that the safety condition holds for each mode of operation, and for each expectable environmental situation (e.g. sudden strong braking of the leading vehicle, which can be constrained by an assumption about physically reasonable deceleration values), even in presence of failures.

To explain the process of failure analysis and degradation chain creation, we show in Fig. 3 a simplified excerpt of the application state machine of one particular vehicle (reduced to the case that this vehicle is not the platoon leader, but any of the follower cars). The abstraction (in comparison to the technically implemented state machine) leaves out technically necessary states (such as waiting for WLAN connection) and directs the attention to the overall operation modes, which form a degradation cascade (marked by the different colours). This abstraction is adequate for safety considerations, and also the reduction to the state machine of one single vehicle is appropriate for the hazard of rear collision.

In this state machine we can see some external events (operator commands, presence of another vehicles) as trigger events for operation mode transitions, but also some failure events (cf. Section 4 of [8]). For instance, the transition from manual drive to ACC is triggered by a user intervention (activation button pressed), the transition from ACC to CACC by Car2X engaged, i.e. a connection has been established and both vehicles have agreed upon who is preceding and

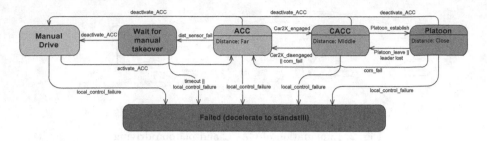

Fig. 3. Simplified application state machine including degradation (Color figure online)

who is following vehicle. The transitions back are the complementary events (e.g. deactivation button pressed), but also some failure events: When, for instance, the communication by radio gets lost in CACC or platoon mode, the fall-back is ACC (just using the front distance sensor to adjust oneself with respect to the vehicle in front). As we will see, this includes in this case not so much a change of the speed and distance controller *structure*, but rather of some *parameter* (the distance setpoint), because the simultaneous information that the vehicle in front is about to brake is no longer available. The front distance sensor (ultrasonic based in case of the model car) also allows recognising the effect of a braking manoeuvre, but with a great deal of a delay, leading to a rear collision without sufficient safety distance. If the communication does not break down, but the predecessor or platoon leading vehicle reports an error via Car2X, a similar transition happens. When, as another example, the front sensor fails in ACC mode, the only remaining degradation level (above failed) is a manual takeover, so the vehicle goes into a transition state (orange coloured, because hazardous if pertaining too long) and prompts for takeover. If the takeover (user intervention) occurs in time, the car is back in manual mode (yellow, because safe, but not really a state of preference), but if a timeout occurs, the car changes to failed (red), which means that the car carefully decelerates to standstill. Of course, there are many other faults (all of them local faults) that lead to an immediate transition to the failed state, e.g. sensor problems with the wheel encoders or motor sensors, or any other kind of controller or actuator failures. In this case, no reasonable degradation is possible any more. Note that, for the purpose of safety analysis by simulation as described in [8], it may be useful to model more discrete states as shown in the figure (reflecting the technical implementation): when a mode change due to a failure occurs, there is a short time interval where the distance setpoint has already been increased, but the controller takes some time to increase the actual distance between the cars. Technically, this is not an extra state, just the setting time that every controller exhibits. For safety analysis, this is a state that must be considered (and coloured in orange, i.e. hazardous to some degree), because a braking manoeuvre of the predecessor car in this situation could lead to a rear crash. Therefore, an estimate for the frequency and duration of these states must be derived and compared to the acceptable hazard rates. Of course, the shown simplification to a single car does not consider effects like the chain-stability of the whole platoon (e.g., one car avoids the accident, but only by strong braking, which causes subsequent cars to crash). A part of these questions has been investigated by simulation in [13].

4.3 Specifying Degradation Cascade Contracts

Before specifying the degradation cascade contracts, we first state the overall degradation cascade safety goal in terms of a strong contract presented in Table 1. The overall safety goal contract guarantee should be implied by each mode. While the stated strong assumptions are the basis for calculations done when establishing the thresholds for each of the degradation modes. The safety goal here is a simplification, as the original Safety Goal deals with the distance between any two cars, may they be part of a platoon or not.

Table 1. The strong contract representing the overall safety goal

A_1:	No car can decelerate with more than $8\,m/s^2$ AND A nominally performing car can decelerate with at least $5\,m/s^2$
G_1:	Maximum deceleration is within $[5\,m/s^2, 8\,m/s^2]$ AND (Platooning, CACC or ACC mode active) $\rightarrow$ The distance between the considered car and its predecessor car is always greater than $2\,m$

Table 2. A subset of the degradation cascade contracts for platoon and CACC modes

B_{P1}:	Platoon active AND no local control failure AND no distance sensor failure AND no car2x failure AND Braking of the predecessor vehicle is recognised within $30\,ms$
H_{P1}:	The distance to the predecessor vehicle is always greater than $20\,m$ AND A sudden braking manoeuvre of the preceding vehicle does never lead to a resulting distance of less than $2\,m$
B_{P2}:	Platoon active AND no local control failure AND no distance sensor failure AND no car2prec failure AND car2leader failure
H_{P2}:	Transition to CACC mode within $10\,ms$
B_{P3}:	Platoon active AND no local control failure AND no distance sensor failure AND car2x failure
H_{P3}:	Transition to ACC mode within $10\,ms$;
B_{CACC1}:	CACC active AND no local control failure AND no distance sensor failure AND no car2pred failure AND Braking of the predecessor vehicle is recognised within $60\,ms$
H_{CACC1}:	The distance to the predecessor vehicle is always greater than $30\,m$ AND A sudden braking manoeuvre of the preceding vehicle does never lead to a resulting distance of less than $2\,m$
B_{CACC2}:	CACC active AND no local control failure AND distance sensor failure
H_{CACC2}:	Transition to ACC mode within $10\,ms$

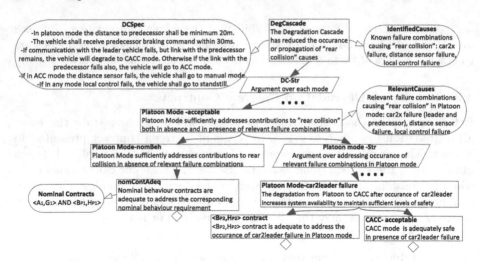

Fig. 4. Car platooning degradation cascades argument-fragment

For the individual degradation modes, we have then collected sets of weak assumptions and guarantees. We have not formally proven the guarantees, but validated them by simulation. The parameters depend on the performance (accuracy and dead time, in particular) of the local sensors or the information transfer via Car2X, respectively, and could only be estimated conservatively. We present some simplified examples of the degradation mode contracts based on our domain knowledge regarding the controller structure in Table 2. A part of the instantiated argument based on the presented pattern is shown in Fig. 4. The example covers only a portion of the platoon mode argument.

5   Related Work

Shelton et al. [4] present a framework for graceful degradation of distributed embedded systems based on the idea of configuration space that forms a product family architecture. Instead of specifying and designing degradation for every possible combination of failures individually, they propose a framework for focusing only on valid component configurations to reduce the number of failure combinations to examine. Similarly, in our work we use contracts to focus and specify only the valid configurations of the cooperative SoS and not all possible states. Schneider and Trapp [14] introduce Conditional Safety Certificates (Con-Serts) specified by directed acyclic graphs that besides demands and guarantees also contain runtime evidence, gates and directed edges. To move part of assurance at runtime with ConSerts, it is important to formulate different ConSert variants at development-time such that the ConSert conditions can be resolved at runtime and the corresponding safety requirements in terms of guarantees established. Strong and weak contracts associated with requirements and the supporting evidence work in a similar way. In our work, we focus on the degradation cascades and propose how such conditional assurance can be achieved using contracts. Assumption/guarantee contracts that support specification of variable behaviour [5,15] have been used to promote reuse of assurance artefacts. In this work, we utilise the possibility of specifying not design-time, but runtime variable behaviour such as behaviour exhibited by different degradation modes. Iliasov et al. [16] formally define notions of modes and their refinement in Event-B state-based formalism. These notions allow for describing system operation modes using assumptions to capture system conditions and guarantees to express the behaviour expressed under those conditions. We define the contracts for degradation cascade in a similar fashion and use them as the basis for degradation cascade assurance.

6   Conclusion and Future Work

In this paper we have sketched a design and safety assurance approach for cooperative SoS exhibiting degradation cascades. More than traditional non-distributed systems, cooperative systems need to cope with not just the local failures, but also ones in other peers that are announced by the communication link, and in the communication link itself. Many of such systems can cause hazards and therefore need safety properties to be ensured, which involves the introduction of safety mechanisms. A total shutdown in case of any failure is often not acceptable, so a structured way of defining degradation cascades is mandatory, but hard to verify. To address these challenges, we have combined and extended some recent research contributions: the argument-fragment generation technique FLAR2SAF, a structured design approach for degradation cascades, and an approach of contract-based design. The particular thing about using contracts in our approach is that we use weak contract - originally proposed for facilitating the reuse of components in new environments - at runtime to define contract for different levels of degradation. Thereby, the process of selecting the best strategy to fulfil a given guarantee under varying assumptions is shifted from design time to runtime. Yet we can prepare the safety argument at design time by iteration over all possible degradation levels and arguing by assumption/guarantee matching that the guaranteed behaviour is acceptably safe. We have applied our approach to a fleet of autonomous model cars that perform CACC and platoon driving and successfully validated it by experiments. It should be noted that the approach is not only applicable to vehicle systems, but to any kind of cooperating cyber-physical systems, e.g., sensor networks or distributed automation systems. As a next step plan to formalise the contracts in OCRA language to prove the safety properties and the correct decomposition and allocation of contracts. To address verification of the atomic components (i.e. the implementation) and properties in the environment (e.g. that a certain distance between cars is sufficient to prevent collisions under all conditions), we plan to integrate other verification approaches such as model checking or simulation. To make our approach applicable to industries, we will need to build a tool chain that helps evaluating the possible configurations and their global guarantees at design time and to create software code for safety arbiters that evaluate the contracts at runtime on board the vehicle and select the appropriate degradation mode.

Acknowledgements. This work is supported by EU and VINNOVA via the ECSEL Joint Undertaking project AMASS (No. 692474).

References

1. Kagermann, H., Helbig, J., Hellinger, A., Wahlster, W.: Recommendations for implementing the strategic initiative INDUSTRIE 4.0: securing the future of German manufacturing industry. Forschungsunion (2013)
2. Adler, R., Schaefer, I., Trapp, M., Poetzsch-Heffter, A.: Component-based modeling and verification of dynamic adaptation in safety-critical embedded systems. ACM Trans. Embed. Comput. Syst. **10**(2), 1–39 (2011)
3. Kaiser, B.: From "safe state" to "degradation cascades" - structured and quantified requirements for automated driving systems. Presentation at VDA Automotive SYS, Berlin, Germany (2016)
4. Shelton, C.P., Koopman, P., Nace, W.: A framework for scalable analysis and design of system-wide graceful degradation in distributed embedded systems. In: 8th International Workshop on Object-Oriented Real-Time Dependable Systems, pp. 156–163. IEEE (2003)
5. Sljivo, I., Gallina, B., Carlson, J., Hansson, H.: Strong and weak contract formalism for third-party component reuse. In: 3rd International Workshop on Software Certification, pp. 359–364. IEEE, November 2013
6. Sljivo, I., Gallina, B., Carlson, J., Hansson, H., Puri, S.: A method to generate reusable safety case argument-fragments from compositional safety analysis. J. Syst. Softw.: Spec. Issue Softw. Reuse **131**, 570–590 (2016)
7. Gallina, B., Javed, M., Muram, F., Punnekkat, S.: Model-driven dependability analysis method for component-based architectures. In: 38th Euromicro Conference on Software Engineering and Advanced Applications, pp. 233–240. IEEE, September 2012
8. Kaiser, B., Nejad, B.M., Kusche, D., Schulte, H.: Systematic design and validation of degradation cascades for safety-relevant systems. In: To Appear in The Annual European Safety and Reliability Conference ESREL, June 2017
9. Goal Structuring Notation Working Group: GSN Community Standard Version 1. Origin Consulting (York) Limited (2011)
10. Kaiser, B., Weber, R., Oertel, M., Böde, E., Nejad, B.M., Zander, J.: Contract-based design of embedded systems integrating nominal behavior and safety. Complex Syst. Inform. Model. Q. **4**, 66–91 (2015)
11. Sljivo, I., Gallina, B., Carlson, J., Hansson, H.: Generation of safety case argument-fragments from safety contracts. In: Bondavalli, A., Di Giandomenico, F. (eds.) SAFECOMP 2014. LNCS, vol. 8666, pp. 170–185. Springer, Cham (2014). doi:10. 1007/978-3-319-10506-2_12
12. ECSEL-JU-692474: AMASS - Architecture-Driven, Multi-concern and Seamless Assurance and Certification of Cyber-Physical Systems. http://www.amass-ecsel. eu/
13. Ghodratbaki, A.: Modellierung lose gekoppelter System-of-Systems am Beispiel eines Cooperative Adaptive Cruise Control (CACC) Fahrerassistenzsystems. Master's thesis (2017)

14. Schneider, D., Trapp, M.: Conditional safety certification of open adaptive systems. TAAS **8**(2), 8:1–8:20 (2013)
15. Oertel, M., Schulze, M., Peikenkamp, T.: Reusing a functional safety concept in variable system architectures. In: 7th International Workshop on Model-Based Architecting and Construction of Embedded Systems, pp. 16–25, September 2014
16. Iliasov, A., Romanovsky, A., Dotti, F.L.: Structuring specifications with modes. In: LADC, pp. 81–88. IEEE Computer Society (2009)

3rd International Workshop on TEchnical and LEgal Aspects of Data pRIvacy and SEcurity (TELERISE 2017)

3rd International Workshop on TEchnical and LEgal Aspects of Data pRIvacy and SEcurity (TELERISE 2017)

Ilaria Matteucci, Paolo Mori, and Marinella Petrocchi

This book contains the proceedings of the 3rd International Workshop on TEchnical and LEgal aspects of data pRIvacy and SEcurity (TELERISE), held in Trento, Italy, on September 12th, 2017, in conjunction with the International Conference on Computer Safety, Reliability and Security (SAFECOMP).

The TELERISE workshop provides a forum for researchers and engineers, both from academia and industry, to foster an exchange of research results, experiences, and products in the area of privacy-preserving and secure data management, from a technical and legal perspective. The ultimate goal is to conceive new trends and ideas on designing, implementing, and evaluating solutions for privacy-preserving information sharing, with an eye to the cross-relations between ICT and regulatory aspects of data management.

Information sharing is essential for today's business and societal transactions. Nevertheless, such a sharing should not violate the security and privacy requirements either dictated by Law to protect data subjects or by internal regulations provided both at organisation and individual level. An effectual, rapid, and unfailing electronic data sharing among different parties, while protecting legitimate rights on these data, is a key issue with several shades. Thus, the main goal of the TELERISE workshop is to carry forward innovative solutions, such as the design and implementation of new software architectures, software components, and software interfaces, able to fill the gap between technical and legal aspects of data privacy and data security management.

The workshop received a total of 14 submissions, from 46 authors of 8 countries. Each paper was reviewed by at least 3 Program Committee members and evaluated according to criteria of relevance, originality, soundness, maturity and quality of presentation. Decisions were based on the review results: 10 submissions were accepted, 6 as regular papers and 4 as short papers. Papers were grouped into three sessions according to the three aspects of data sharing the workshop aims to cover: Security, Legal, and Privacy aspects.

We would like to thank the SAFECOMP 2017 Workshops Organization Committee, for their precious help in handling the organizational issues related to the workshop. Our next thanks go to all the authors of the submitted papers, who manifested their interest in the workshop. With their participation, TELERISE 2017 becomes a real success and an inspiration for future workshops on this area of research. Special thanks are finally due to the Program Committee members, for their high quality and objective reviews.

Workshop Organizers

Ilaria Matteucci   IIT-CNR, Italy
Paolo Mori   IIT-CNR, Italy
Marinella Petrocchi   IIT-CNR, Italy

Program Committee

Benjamin Aziz   University of Portsmouth, UK
Gianpiero Costantino   IIT-CNR, Italy
Vittoria Cozza   University of Padova, Italy
Francesco Di Cerbo   SAP, France
Ioanna Dionysiou   University of Nicosia, Cyprus
Carmen Fernandez Gago   University of Malaga,Spain
Sorren Hanvey   Lero - The Irish Software Research Centre, Limerick,
                           Ireland
Kuan Hon   Queen Mary University, UK
Jens Jensen   STFC, UK
Erisa Karafili   Imperial College London, UK
Mirko Manea   HP Italia, Italy
Aaron Massey   Georgia Institute of Technology, USA
Kevin McGillivray   Dept. of Private Law, University of Oslo, Norway
Andrea Saracino   IIT-CNR, Italy
Daniele Sgandurra   Royal Holloway - University of London, UK
Jatinder Singh   Computer Laboratory, University of Cambridge, UK
Debora Stella   Bird & Bird, Italy
Slim Trabelsi   SAP, France

Public Disclosure of Cyber Threat Information: Risks and Benefits (Abstract of an Invited Paper)

Francesco Di Cerbo

Security Research, SAP Labs France, 805, Av. du Docteur Maurice
Donat 06250 Mougins, France
francesco.di.cerbo@sap.com

Abstract. A growing number of actors perpetrate cyber attacks to various targets, be them public entities, ISPs, enterprises or citizens. Supported by governments or aiming at criminal activities, attackers dispose of channels for sharing and obtaining undisclosed vulnerabilities, attack toolkits and information. On the other hand, attack targets need to react quickly and effectively but they risk to be alone if they do not join forces with others. However timely reactions depend on the quality and timeliness of interactions among peers (e.g. CERTs, public security bodies, ISPs, service providers). There is a need for automated cyber information preparation, sharing and consumption, being fulfilled by initiatives like CybOX [4], STIX [2], Taxii [5] and MISP [1]. However, concerns exist, related to confidential details withing cyber threat information reports, their usage as well as potential data protection laws violations. These constraints render the actual collaboration quite limited in terms of scope. A number of initiatives are focussing on CTI sharing, tackling the most significant obstacles and aiming at bringing benefits to all stakeholders involved in the process.

In the talk, risks and benefits will be presented, together with an overview of existing initiatives active in the field.

Keywords. Cyber security · Cyber threat information · Information sharing · Privacy

Cyber attacks targets (also potential) are maturing awareness that collaboration is necessary to counter menaces effectively. Be them direct attacks like DDOS or more subtle like Active Persistent Threats, interactions are sought among enterprises, national CERTS, public security and ISPs. Too often, however, these interactions happen in restricted circles of trust, due to the risk presented by the information disclosure. Cyber threat information (CTI) may be extremely sensitive: for example, they may disclose internal details of a target's network or they may be used to understand which vulnerability was used for a successful attack, before the application of countermeasures. In other cases, personal information of citizens may be part of the CTI (for example, a list of the IP addresses of a botnet may be used to identify the identities associated to those addresses in conjunction with datasets coming from ISPs) and their processing by arbitrary third parties may be forbidden, leading to potential liability issues. The mentioned risks normally lead to restricting CTI sharing operations only among trusted peers, sometimes through unstructured channels or manually created artefacts.

There is therefore a need for high quality, machine-processable, low-sensitivity CTI exchanges. Such exchange should not be limited to CERTs, ISPs and public law enforcement bodies. Security software providers and security researchers may enormously benefit from CTIs prepared in this manner. This would lead to the development of new security solutions or to the improvement of existing one; as example, one can consider the improvements brought to rule-based engines, pattern recognition and machine learning solutions. During the talk, a number of initiatives for CTI sharing will be presented (for example, CSSA [6] and the EU-funded H2020 project C3ISP [3]), starting from the analysis of risks and benefits for the main stakeholders involved in the process. A Design Thinking [7] exercise will also take place, in order to elaborate together the best strategies for achieving effective multi-party CTI sharing in communities where limited or no trust exists.

Acknowledgements. This work was partly supported by the C3ISP project, funded under the EUHorizon 2020 Programme (H2020) [grant n. 700294].

References

1. Andre, D., Dereszowski, A., Dulaunoy, A., Iklody, A., Vandeplas, C., Vinot, R.: MISP - open source threat intelligence platform and open standards for threat information sharing. http://www.misp-project.org/. Accessed 04 June 2017
2. Barnum, S.: Standardizing cyber threat intelligence information with the structured threat information expression (stix). MITRE Corporation 11 (2012)
3. C3ISP Consortium. Collaborative and con_dential information sharing and analysis for cyber protection (C3ISP) - eu horizon 2020 programme (h2020) grant agreement n 700294 (2016). http://c3isp.eu/. Accessed 04 June 2017
4. Casey, E., Back, G., Barnum, S.: Leveraging cybox to standardize representation and exchange of digital forensic information. Digit. Invest. 12, S102–S110 (2015)
5. Connolly, J., Davidson, M., Schmidt, C.: The trusted automated exchange of indicator information (taxii). The MITRE Corporation (2014)
6. CSSA Community. Cyber security sharing and analytics (cssa) (2016). https://www.cssa.de/en/index.html. Accessed 04 June 2017
7. Plattner, H., Meinel, C., Weinberg, U.: Design-Thinking. Springer, Heidelberg (2009)

Transparent Personal Data Processing:
The Road Ahead

Piero Bonatti[1], Sabrina Kirrane[2]([⊠]), Axel Polleres[2,3], and Rigo Wenning[4]

[1] Universita' di Napoli Federico II, Naples, Italy
[2] Vienna University of Economics and Business, Vienna, Austria
sabrina.kirrane@wu.ac.at
[3] Complexity Science Hub Vienna, Vienna, Austria
[4] W3C, Sophia-Antipolis, France

Abstract. The European General Data Protection Regulation defines a set of obligations for personal data controllers and processors. Primary obligations include: obtaining explicit consent from the data subject for the processing of personal data, providing full transparency with respect to the processing, and enabling data rectification and erasure (albeit only in certain circumstances). At the core of any transparency architecture is the logging of events in relation to the processing and sharing of personal data. The logs should enable verification that data processors abide by the access and usage control policies that have been associated with the data based on the data subject's consent and the applicable regulations. In this position paper, we: (i) identify the requirements that need to be satisfied by such a transparency architecture, (ii) examine the suitability of existing logging mechanisms in light of said requirements, and (iii) present a number of open challenges and opportunities.

1   Introduction

The European General Data Protection Regulation (GDPR), and *Articles 12–15* in particular, calls for technical means to support the obtaining of explicit consent from data subjects and the provision of transparency with respect to personal data processing and sharing. In order to provide said transparency, companies need to record details of personal data processing activities and personal data transactions (i.e. who shared what data with whom, for what purpose and under what usage conditions). From a technical perspective there is a need for a transparency architecture that records metadata (i.e. policies, event data, context), that can be used to verify that data is processed according to the wishes of the data subject and the applicable regulations.

From a high level perspective such a transparency architecture needs to enable: (i) data subjects to verify that data processors are complying with usage policies; and (ii) data processors to demonstrate that their business processes comply both with the policies accepted by the data subject and the obligations set forth in the GDPR. As a first step towards realising this goal, in this position

© Springer International Publishing AG 2017
S. Tonetta et al. (Eds.): SAFECOMP 2017 Workshops, LNCS 10489, pp. 337–349, 2017.
DOI: 10.1007/978-3-319-66284-8_28

paper, we examine the suitability of existing logging and transparency mechanisms as the basis for developing such a system. There exists a variety of logging mechanisms that either represent events in local logs [2,7,10,14,15], in global logs entrusted to one or more third parties [1,6,11,12], or distribute event logging across a number of peers [16,19,21]. Ideally it should be possible to use some of these logging mechanisms together with access/usage policies in order to automatically verify compliance of existing business processes with the GDPR. The contributions of the paper can be summarised as follows: we (i) identify a list of requirements relevant for transparent processing and sharing of personal data; (ii) examine the degree of support, with respect to said requirements, offered by the different logging architectures (i.e. ledgers); and (iii) discuss the open research challenges and opportunities.

The remainder of the paper is structured as follows: Sect. 2 discusses the requirements that are relevant for data usage transparency frameworks. Section 3 identifies a number of candidate approaches and examines their suitability in terms of support for the identified requirements. Section 4 points to several Resource Description Framework (RDF) vocabularies that can be used to represent data processing and sharing events and highlights a number of open research questions. Finally, we present our conclusions and some interesting directions for future work in Sect. 5.

2   Data Processing Transparency Requirements

Before discussing the different logging architectures (i.e. ledgers) we first provide a concrete motivating scenario and identify several data processing and sharing transparency and robustness requirements.

2.1   A Motivating Scenario

Sue buys a wearable appliance for fitness tracking from BeFit. She is presented with an informed consent request, comprised of a data usage policy that describes which data shall be collected, and how they will be processed and transmitted in order to give her fitness-related information. The policy says that the device records biomedical parameters such as heart rate; these data are stored in BeFit's cloud; and processed for two purposes: (i) giving Sue feedback on her activity, such as calories consumption; (ii) (optional) creating an activity profile that will be shared with other companies for targeted ads related to fitness. Sue opts in for (ii) in order to get a discount. The usage policy, signed by both Sue and BeFit, is stored in a *transparency ledger*. After one year, the device stops working. After two years, Sue starts receiving annoying SMS messages from a local gym that advertise its activities. Fortunately, all the data collection, processing, and transmission operations have been recorded in the transparency ledger. By querying the ledger, Sue discovers the following facts: (i) the gym has an activity profile referring to Sue, that due to the appliance's malfunctioning reports that she is not doing any physical exercise; (ii) the gym received the profile from BeFit, associated with a policy that allows the gym to send targeted ads to Sue based on the profile; (iii) BeFit built the profile by mining the data collected by the appliance; and (iv) all these operations are permitted by the consent agreement previously signed by Sue and BeFit. Using the information contained in the ledger, BeFit and the gym can prove that they used Sue's data according to the agreed purposes. However, Sue can now ask both BeFit and the gym to delete all of her data. The information contained in the ledger indicates precisely which pieces of information she is referring to, so they can be automatically deleted in real time.

2.2 Ledger Functionality and Robustness

In order to enable scenarios such as that described above and to provide the technical basis for companies to demonstrate that their business processes comply with the consent, transparency, rectification and erasure obligations specified in the GDPR, a fundamental first step is to create a ledger of all data transactions (i.e. who shared what data with whom, for what purpose and under what usage conditions) and to record what happened to the data (e.g. processing, anonymisation, aggregation). In order to provide transparency with respect to data processing to the data subject, while at the same time allowing companies to demonstrate that they are complying with the regulation the following core functions are required.

Ledger Functionality

Completeness: All data processing and sharing events should be recorded in the ledger.

Confidentiality: Both data subjects and companies should only be able to see the transactions that involve their own data.

Correctness: The records stored in the ledger should accurately reflect the processing event.

Immutability: The log should be immutable such that it is not possible to go back and reinvent history.

Integrity: The log should be protected from accidental and/or malicious modification.

Interoperability: The infrastructure should be able to transcend company boundaries, in the sense that the data subject should be able to easily combine logs that they get from multiple companies.

Non-repudiation: When it comes to both data processing and sharing events it should not be possible to later deny that the event took place.

Rectification and Erasure: It should be possible to rectify errors in the stored personal data and/or delete data at the request of the data subject.

Traceability: In the case of processing it should be possible to know about any previous processing of the data. As such it should be possible to link events in a manner that supports traceability of processing.

Ledger Robustness

Availability: Availability is the process of ensuring the optimal accessibility and usability of the ledger irrespective of whether the log is stored locally or globally. Here there is also a link to security as it is imperative that a breach of security does not hinder ledger operations.

Performance: When it comes to the processing of the event data, various optimisations such as parallel processing and/or indexing should be used to improve processing efficiency.

Scalability: Given the volume of events and policies that will need to be handled, the scalability of event data processing is a major consideration.

Storage: In order to reduce the amount of information stored in the log, the data itself should be stored elsewhere and only a hash of the data and a pointer to the actual data itself should be stored in the ledger.

3   Candidate Transparency Ledgers

The overarching goal of this section is to examine the potential solutions proposed in the literature in order to understand the strengths and limitations of existing proposals and to identify challenges that still need to be addressed. A summary of the degree of support offered by the candidate transparency architectures is provided in Tables 1 and 2.

Table 1. Candidate architectures and ledger functionality gap analysis

	Local log	Global log + TTP	Global log + P2P
Completeness	-	-	-
Confidentiality	MAC [2,7,14,15], FssAgg [10], PKI [7,10]	MAC [1,6,11,12], PKI [20], unlinkability [6,11,12]	MAC [15], PKI [16], compound identities [15,21]
Correctness	-	-	-
Immutability	Cipher chains [2], hash chains [7,15]	Hash chains [7,15]	Network of peers [16,19] blockchain [21]
Integrity	Forward integrity [2,7,10,14,15] MAC security proof [2]	Forward integrity [1,6,11,12]	Forward integrity [15]
Interoperability	-	-	-
Non-repudiation	-	-	-
Rectification and Erasure	-	-	-
Traceability	-	Event trails [20]	-

Table 2. Candidate architectures and ledger robustness gap analysis

	Local log	Global log + TTP	Global log + P2P
Availability	-	-	-
Performance	Logging and verification [2,7], signature generation and verification [10]	Logging [11,12], throughput [11,12]	-
Scalability	Encrypting records [7,10]	-	-
Storage	Key and signature [10]	Resource restricted devices [1]	-

3.1 The Status Quo

When it comes to the persistence of provenance records there are three high level options, that are not necessarily mutually exclusive: each company maintains a local ledger, which may be backed up remotely; a global ledger could be maintained by one or more trusted third parties; or a global ledger could be distributed across a number of peers.

Local Ledger: Each peer could store its provenance records locally, including information pertaining to data sharing (both incoming and outgoing). While, remote logging to a trusted third party (TTP) could be used to guarantee recoverability of data if the machine where the log is stored is compromised. Bellare and Yee [2] and Schneier and Kelsey [15] demonstrated how a secret key signing scheme based on Message Authentication Codes (MACs) together with a hashing algorithm can be used to generate chains of log records that are in turn used to ensure log confidentiality and integrity. MACs are themselves symmetric keys that are generated and verified using collision-resistant secure cryptographic hash functions. Bellare and Yee [2] discuss how a MAC secret key signing scheme together with evolving MAC keys (whereby each record is encrypted with a different key that is derived from the old key) can be used to ensure: (i) the confidentiality of the log; (ii) that previous log entries cannot be changed; and that (iii) the deletion of a log entry can be detected. In such a scenario the base MAC key, which is needed to verify the integrity of the log is entrusted to a TTP. Schneier and Kelsey [15] also use MACs however the log is composed of hash chains as oppose to cipher block chains. Whereas, Holt [7] propose an alternative that combines public key cryptography with hash chains. These approaches are further enhanced by Ma and Tsudik [10] who demonstrate how individual log entry signatures can be combined into a single aggregate signature that can be used to verify the component signatures and to protect against log truncation. While the previously mentioned works focused on logging in general, Sackmann et al. [14] apply it specifically to data protection by demonstrating how a secure logging system can be used for privacy-aware logging. Additionally, they introduce the "privacy evidence" concept and discuss how such a log could be used to compare data processing to the users privacy policy.

When it comes to the robustness requirements, both Bellare and Yee [2] and Holt [7] evaluate the performance and scalability of the proposed logging and verification algorithms, while Ma and Tsudik [10] compare alternative signature generation and verification algorithms.

Global Ledger and Trusted Third Party: Alternatively, the ledger may contain provenance records that are maintained by one or more TTPs. Accorsi [1] demonstrate how MAC-based secure logging mechanisms can be tailored so that they can be used by resource restricted devices that may need to log data remotely. Wouters et al. [20] highlight the fact that data often flows between different processes, and as such events cannot be considered in isolation, thus giving rise to the need to store a trail of events. The authors demonstrate how public key cryptography can be used to log events in a manner whereby the data subject can verify the process status. Hedbom et al. [6], Peeters et al. [11], Pulls et al. [12] also provide logging mechanisms that provides transparency to data subjects. The protocol, which is based on MAC secure logging techniques, ensures confidentiality and unlinkability of events and is designed so that it can be distributed across several servers. In the case of [11,12], each log is composed of a user block, a processor block and the encrypted data. A trusted third party is responsible for generating the MAC, encrypting it with the users public key, signing it with their own private key and sending it to the data subject via the data processor. The data processor block is generated in a similar manner. Both the log and the personal data are encrypted in a manner that only the data subject and the processor can access them. In the case of data sharing a new blinded public key is created (in a manner such that the data subjects private key can decrypt any data encrypted with the blinded public key). The blinded key, which will be used by the second data processor, also serves to ensure the unlinkability of the logs.

Peeters et al. [11], Pulls et al. [12] both evaluate the performance of the proposed algorithms and examine the logging throughput from a local and a remote perspective. The authors conclude that encryption and signing are expensive operations and as such the log entry generation time does not scale linearly with the size of the logged data. They also highlight that the decryption and verification processed are also expensive.

Global Ledger and Peer-to-Peer Network: Alternatively, the ledger may be distributed across several physical ledgers (i.e. a virtual global ledger), whereby provenance records are replicated by each peer. Schneier and Kelsey [15] highlight the vulnerability associated with using a single TTP and discuss how n untrusted machines could be used to replace the TTP, with m untrusted machines required to reproduce the base MAC secret key. Weitzner et al. [19] also discuss how transparency and accountability can be achieved via distributed accountability peers that communicate using existing web protocols. These accountability peers would be responsible for mediating access to data, maintaining audit logs and facilitating accountability reasoning. Unfortunately the authors only touch upon the required features and no concrete architecture is proposed. Seneviratne and Kagal [16] build on this idea by describing how a distributed network of peers can be used to store a permanent log of encrypted transactions. The replication of log entries at each peer optimises both redundancy and availability. Although the authors describe how a distributed network of peers can be used to store a permanent log of transactions, they focus primarily on helping users to conform to policies by highlighting not only usage restrictions but also the implications of their actions, as opposed to investigating the functional and technical challenges of the proposed transparency architecture itself. An alternative distributed architecture based on blockchain technology, which can be used to manage access to personal data is proposed by Zyskind et al. [21]. The authors discuss how the blockchain data model and Application Programming Interfaces (APIs) can be extended to keep track of both data and access transactions. Data that is encrypted using a shared encryption key, is sent to the blockchain, which subsequently stores the data in an off-blockchain key value store and a pointer to the data in the form of a hash in the public ledger. Compound identities are used to ensure that only the user and service providers that have been granted access to the data can decrypt the data. One of the primary drawbacks is the fact that the authors focus on how to repurpose the blockchain as an access-control moderator as opposed to exploring the suitability of the proposed architecture for data transparency and governance.

In comparison to local or global approaches that employ a third party the robustness of the proposed approaches has not been explored to date, therefore it is difficult to assess the effectiveness of P2P ledgers or blockchains from a non-functional perspective.

3.2 Gap Analysis

Although the main goal of the analysis was to investigate the opportunities and the limitations of each of the candidate architectures, in the end we were able to observe that the primary technical challenges are common across all candidate architectures (cf. Tables 1 and 2).

Correctness, Completeness and Non-repudiation: Although both *correctness* and *completeness* are very desirable features, irrespective of the choice of architecture, when it comes to data processing events neither can be guaranteed as there is no way to prevent companies from logging incorrect information or not entering the information into the log. Although fair exchange protocols could potentially be used to ensure *non-repudiation* of data transactions (i.e. neither party can deny the transaction took place), to date they have not been used in connection with existing logging mechanisms.

Confidentiality and Integrity: The combination of MAC together with cipher or hash chains appears to be the prevailing mechanism used to ensure the confidentiality and forward integrity of logs. Although Schneier and Kelsey

[15] highlight that it could be feasible to replace the TTP with n untrusted machines whereby any m are required to reproduce the base MAC secret key, no concrete details are provided. Additionally, in the context of our use case the secure logging verification schemes would need to be extended to cater for *rectification and erasure* without affecting the overall integrity of the log.

Immutability, Rectification and Erasure: Although it should not be possible for a company to go back and reinvent history, the GDPR stipulates that data subjects have the right to *rectification and erasure* (often referred to as the right to be forgotten). This could potentially be seen as a hard delete whereby the data needs to be erased from both the system and the logs. This would mean that we need to be able to update and delete records from the log without affecting the overall integrity of the log. One potential solution would be to employ a cryptographic delete and to provide support for updates via versioning.

Interoperability and Traceability: Another consideration is the interoperability of the log with other logs. Considering that existing logging research has primarily focused recording operating system and application events it is not surprising that interoperability has received very little attention to date. Although there has been some research on *traceability*, the focus has primarily been on linking processing events in a single log.

Performance and Scalability: Considering the potential volume of events that will need to be handled by the transparency ledger, the scalability of existing logging mechanisms will be crucial to their adoption. When it comes to the processing of event data, various optimisations such as parallel processing and/or indexing may improve processing efficiency. Data transfer speed could be improved via exchanging a compressed version of the data payload. Inherently querying and updating logs over distributed databases is a computational challenge.

Storage: In practice it may not be feasible for a single log server or each peer in a distributed network to store all provenance records. One possibility is to split the provenance records into multiple ledgers, distributed among TTPs or peers. However, such an architecture would need to be fault tolerant in the case of peers disconnecting from the network. Relevance criteria and careful forgetting may help too, insofar as storage requirements may be reduced by storing only the information that is needed for compliance checking in the specific domain of interest, and deleting other information.

Availability: Clearly from an availability perspective it is important that the best practices are employed in order to protect the security of the log host. Additionally the log should be backed up to a secure location on a regular basis. It is worth noting that when it comes to log recovery, rather than relying on a TTP a hash of the log could be submitted to a publicly available blockchain (such as Bitcoin). However, unlike trusted third parties public blockchains do not come with Service Level Agreements (SLAs).

4   Challenges and Opportunities

Although in this paper we primarily focus on transparency, our long term goal is to use the ledger together with access/usage policies in order to automatically verify compliance of existing business processes with the GDPR, to this end it is necessary to model both policies and events in a machine readable manner.

4.1   The Ledger

The Resource Description Framework (RDF), which underpins the Linked Data Web (LDW), is used to represent and link information, in a manner which can be interpreted by both humans and machines. Particularly, the power of RDF is revealed in combination with agreed and extensible meta-data vocabularies to describe provenance and events related to data records in a log as metadata, in semantically unambiguous terms. By employing RDF techniques to represent the provenance events stored in the ledger we shall be able to support not only interoperabiliy between ledgers, but also traceabiliy between events in a manner that facilitates automatic compliance checking. To this end, there are a number of existing vocabularies that can be adapted/extended. For example the *PROV*[1] and *OWL-Time*[2] ontologies can be used to represent *provenance* and *temporal* information respectively. The former may require extensions of PROV to model particular aspects related to processing of personal data. The latter is particularly relevant if ledger-information is distributed. For example, when tracking audit trails potentially distributed over different systems, synchronisation of timestamps and ensuring sequentiality are major issues. Apart from the actual representation of time, reasoning and querying about time and temporal aspects is still an issue that needs more research in the Semantic Web arena. Different proposals for temporal extensions of RDF and querying archived, temporal information in RDF exist, cf. for instance [5] and references therein. Additionally there exists a number of general event vocabularies such as the *Event*[3] ontology and the *LODE*[4] ontology [13] that could potentially be adapted/extended in order to model our data processing *events*.

An additional benefit of Linked Data is that it provides a simple, direct way of associating policies with data. However, such integration needs to be done in a way that ensures scalability. Several techniques can be exploited for this purpose. As an example, we mention knowledge compilation approaches that "compile" semantic metadata into a compact but self-contained policy that can be more efficiently enforced, without any further access to the knowledge repository (cf. the approaches based on partial evaluation in [3]). The usage of RDF and URIs shall enable the deployment of a linked network of distributed ledgers instead of a single, monolithic (central or P2P ledger). Here it would be interesting to look

---

[1] PROV, https://www.w3.org/TR/prov-overview/.

[2] OWL-Time, https://www.w3.org/TR/owl-time/.

[3] Events, http://motools.sourceforge.net/event/event.html.

[4] LODE, http://linkedevents.org/ontology/.

into efforts for modularising and linking between distributed ledgers such as the recent interledger protocol [8] proposal.

4.2 Ledger Integrity and Reliability

Ensuring the ledger's integrity and reliability is of course essential for compliance checking and for enhancing the subjects' trust in the transparency architecture. Reliability is partly the result of *voluntary compliance*. In the countries with strong data protection regulations, due to the sanctions and the loss of reputation and customers that may result from data abuse, data processors are willing to comply with the regulations, and feel the need for technical means to ensure compliance. In such scenarios, a correct and complete ledger is an extremely useful tool for the data processors, that can exploit it both for verifying their internal procedures, and for demonstrating compliance to data subjects and data protection authorities. This incentivises the creation and maintenance of a correct and complete ledger. As a further incentive to correctness, the event records should be signed by the parties involved in the recorded operation. In this way, the ledger's records become formal declarations that constitute evidence with legal strength (in the countries where digital signatures have legal value), that may be exploited in case of disputes. As a special case, some of the ledger's records may represent data usage consent declaration, in the form of a usage policy signed by the data subject and the data processor. Such records are very close to a contract that none of the two parties can repudiate, due to the properties of digital signatures.

Creating a reliable record for joint operations, and creating records with multiple "simultaneous" signatures, require the adoption of *fair exchange protocols* to guarantee that the operation is completed (e.g. data are transferred) if and only if all the involved parties sign the record and the record is included in the ledger. An extensive survey of fair exchange protocols can be found in [9]. Ideally, the protocol should not involve centralised nodes such as TTP, but the existing approaches of this kind, based on multiparty computations, currently do not scale to the volume of data expected in the scenarios of interest. There are, however, protocols with *offline TTP*, that involve the trusted third party only in case of malfunctioning (like lost or corrupted messages) or protocol violations. As of today, we regard such protocols as the most promising.

4.3 Immutability, Rectification and Erasure

When it comes to transparent personal data processing *immutability* is a very desirable feature as it can be used by companies to prove that they have not gone back and reinvented history. However, said immutability seems to be in direct contention with the right to *rectification and erasure* according to the GDPR. Considering the focus of this paper, we restrict our discussion to the rectification and erasure of the log entries and do not give any special consideration to the Line of Business (LOB) application. By only storing a hash of the data and a pointer to the actual data itself in the ledger it is possible to decouple the data from the log and indeed delete data. Another motivation for doing so is the *storage* requirements can be reduced considerably. In the case of rectification it may suffice to update data in the LOB application(s) and enter a new record in the log indicating that the data was updated at the request of the data subject, including a reference to the old – deleted – records hash that confirms that said record was updated in mutual agreement. Likewise, in terms of erasure, we assume that there are scenarios like rectification where it will suffice to delete data from the LOB application(s) and enter a new record in the log indicating that the data was deleted at the request of the data subject. Although this would result in a dangling pointer from the initial log entry by following the audit trail it would be possible to find out that the dangling pointer is the result of an authorised delete. However, there may also be scenarios where delete means a hard delete that needs to be propagated to the log (e.g., where it is possible to identify the individual from the log entry). One option would be to investigate the application of cryptographic deletes (where the old data should not be available anymore) to the ledger. However, it would need to be possible to distinguish between authorised deletes (at the request of the data subject) and log tampering. As such, any delete or update request needs to be strongly coupled with a request from the data subject. So far, cryptographic deletion has been considered only in cloud computing environments, where files are replicated across virtual and physical nodes, and whatever remains of the files after their standard deletion (which is logical) could be later recovered by an attacker, cf. [4,17,18]. We propose a novel use of cryptographic deletion as a means to harmonise mandatory preservation requirements and the right to deletion, so as to avoid extreme solutions where one requirement overrides the other.

5   Conclusion and Future Work

Transparency with respect to the collection, processing and sharing of personal data is a key enabler for data controllers and processors to achieve GDPR compliance. In this paper, we identified several requirements that are important for enabling transparent processing of personal data at scale. Following on from this, we analysed a number of candidate logging mechanisms and discussed their suitability in light of said requirements. Based on the gaps highlighted by this analysis, we discussed some of the open challenges and opportunities for future research. In particular we identified at least three interesting questions that call for more work: how to ensure ledger interoperability and usage traceability across organisation borders; how to obtain ledger integrity and reliability; and how to reconcile the conflict between the log immutability requirement and the data subjects' right to rectification and erasure. In future work, we will develop a system that enables data subjects to associate sticky usage policies with their personal data and companies to demonstrate compliance both with the usage policies specified by the data subject and obligations set forth in the GDPR.

Acknowledgments. Supported by the European Union's Horizon 2020 research and innovation programme under grant 731601.

References

1. Accorsi, R.: On the relationship of privacy and secure remote logging in dynamic systems. In: Fischer-Hübner, S., Rannenberg, K., Yngström, L., Lindskog, S. (eds.) SEC 2006. IIFIP, vol. 201, pp. 329–339. Springer, Boston, MA (2006). doi:10.1007/0-387-33406-8_28
2. Bellare, M., Yee, B.: Forward integrity for secure audit logs. Technical report, Computer Science and Engineering Department, University of California at San Diego (1997)
3. Bonatti, P., De Capitani di Vimercati, S., Samarati, P.: An algebra for composing access control policies. ACM Trans. Inf. Syst. Secur. (TISSEC), **5**(1) (2002)
4. Cachin, C., Haralambiev, K., Hsiao, H., Sorniotti, A.: Policy-based secure deletion. In: 2013 ACM SIGSAC Conference on Computer and Communications Security, CCS 2013 (2013)
5. Fernández Garcia, J.D., Umbrich, J., Knuth, M., Polleres, A.: Evaluating query and storage strategies for RDF archives. In: 12th International Conference on Semantic Systems (SEMANTICS), ACM International Conference Proceedings Series (2016)
6. Hedbom, H., Pulls, T., Hjärtquist, P., Lavén, A.: Adding secure transparency logging to the PRIME Core. In: Bezzi, M., Duquenoy, P., Fischer-Hübner, S., Hansen, M., Zhang, G. (eds.) Privacy and Identity 2009. IAICT, vol. 320, pp. 299–314. Springer, Heidelberg (2010). doi:10.1007/978-3-642-14282-6_25
7. Holt, J.E.: Logcrypt: forward security and public verification for secure audit logs. In: Proceedings of the 2006 Australasian Workshops on Grid Computing and e-Research, vol. 54 (2006)
8. Hope-Bailie, A., Thomas, S.: Interledger: creating a standard for payments. In: Proceedings of the 25th International Conference Companion on World Wide Web (2016)
9. Kremer, S., Markowitch, O., Zhou, J.: An intensive survey of fair non-repudiation protocols. Comput. Commun. **25**(17) (2002)
10. Ma, D., Tsudik, G.: A new approach to secure logging. ACM Trans. Storage (TOS) **5**(1) (2009)
11. Peeters, R., Pulls, T., Wouters, K.: Enhancing transparency with distributed privacy-preserving logging. In: Reimer, H., Pohlmann, N., Schneider, W. (eds.) ISSE 2013 Securing Electronic Business Processes, pp. 61–71. Springer, Wiesbaden (2013). doi:10.1007/978-3-658-03371-2_6
12. Pulls, T., Peeters, R., Wouters, K.: Distributed privacy-preserving transparency logging. In: Proceedings of the 12th ACM Workshop on Privacy in the Electronic Society (2013)
13. Rinne, M., Blomqvist, E., Keskisärkkä, R., Nuutila, E.: Event processing in RDF. In: Proceedings of the 4th International Conference on Ontology and Semantic Web Patterns, vol. 1188 (2013)
14. Sackmann, S., Strüker, J., Accorsi, R.: Personalization in privacy-aware highly dynamic systems. Commun. ACM, **49**(9) (2006)
15. Schneier, B., Kelsey, J.: Cryptographic support for secure logs on untrusted machines. In: USENIX Security (1998)
16. Seneviratne, O., Kagal, L.: Enabling privacy through transparency. In: 2014 Twelfth Annual International Conference on Privacy, Security and Trust (PST) (2014)
17. Waizenegger, T.: Secure cryptographic deletion in the swift object store. In Datenbanksysteme für Business, Technologie und Web (BTW) (2017)

18. Waizenegger, T., Wagner, F., Mega, C.: SDOS: using trusted platform modules for secure cryptographic deletion in the swift object store. In: Proceedings of the 20th International Conference on Extending Database Technology, EDBT (2017)
19. Weitzner, D.J., Abelson, H., Berners-Lee, T., Feigenbaum, J., Hendler, J., Sussman, G.J.: Information accountability. Commun. ACM **51**(6) (2008)
20. Wouters, K., Simoens, K., Lathouwers, D., Preneel, B.: Secure and privacy-friendly logging for egovernment services. In: Third International Conference on Availability, Reliability and Security, 2008, ARES 2008 (2008)
21. Zyskind, G., Nathan, O., et al.: Decentralizing privacy: using blockchain to protect personal data. In: Security and Privacy Workshops (SPW), 2015. IEEE (2015)

The Use of Data Protection Regulatory Actions as a Data Source for Privacy Economics

Aaron Ceross$^{(\boxtimes)}$ and Andrew Simpson

Department of Computer Science, University of Oxford, Oxford, UK
{aaron.ceross,andrew.simpson}@cs.ox.ac.uk

Abstract. It is well understood that security informatics is constrained by the availability of reliable data sources, which limits the development of robust methods for measuring the impact of data breaches. To date, empirical data breach analysis has largely relied upon the use of economic and financial data associated with an organisation as a measure of impact. To provide an alternative, complementary approach, we explore monetary fines resulting from data protection regulatory actions to understand how the data can inform the evaluation of data breaches. The results indicate where context matters and also provide information on the wider challenges faced by organisations managing personal data.

1 Introduction

By most accounts, instances of data breaches have continued to rise in the past decade, yet the scope and range of data concerning these events has remained difficult to obtain [6]. While it is understood that the causes for these data breaches are rooted in a culmination of failures in an organisation's security and privacy measures, ranging from technical implementation [11] to organisational approaches to risk [12], defining generalisable metrics has proved challenging [15]. To this end, the impacts of data breaches have been measured in economic terms, considering the expenditure and loss of earnings [10]. In order to establish costs for a data breach, past studies such as [2,14] have extrapolated the financial burdens that a data breach event entails, supplemented by press releases, public financial data and surveys. Such studies inevitably have limitations in the kinds of conclusions that may be drawn, as the sample sizes tend to be small, with few variables to consider.

We consider monetary penalties from a data protection authority as a potential, complementary data source through examining data breach costs related to the regulatory fine. The data protection authority in question (the United Kingdom's Information Commissioner's Office (ICO)) examines a wide range of cases, giving rise to a richer data set than might be available through, for example, a voluntary survey. This may offer several benefits. First, it provides an accessible alternative source of data to investigate consequences. Second, it has the potential to provide a wider perspective with regards to characteristics of data breaches. By using information related to monetary penalties for data

S. Tonetta et al. (Eds.): SAFECOMP 2017 Workshops, LNCS 10489, pp. 350–360, 2017.
DOI: 10.1007/978-3-319-66284-8_29

breaches from the ICO, we seek to address three questions: what are the features of the cases in which the data protection authorities has levied fines?; which of these features are correlated with the quantum of the fine?; and what are the trends, if any, of regulatory action? The results of this work contribute to the literature relating to the empirical analysis of data breaches. More importantly, while this work is inevitably limited in scope, as it is restricted to one national data protection authority, we perceive the work as illustrating the potential of a novel data set — regulatory fines — in examining data breaches.

2 Background

2.1 Regulatory Action in Data Protection is a Recognised Cost

Regulatory action regarding failures to adequately protect personal data have been increasing. Such actions are features across a number of jurisdictions, and it is becoming increasingly difficult to ignore them. To enact such penalties, the relevant authorities are empowered to investigate the nature and causes of the data breach. The imposition of a penalty, as well as the quantum of such a penalty, may be viewed as a metric when attempting to analyse the impact of a failure of data security. Such penalties and the consequent analysis of such does, of course, perform another role: to act as a driver toward the adoption of better organisational and technical practices for data security.

The European Union has adopted the General Data Protection Regulation (GDPR), which will replace Member State implementation of the Data Protection Directive.[1] The GDPR has stringent penalties, including a maximum fine of €20 million or 4% of global turnover of the preceding financial year, whichever is greater. In the US, past fines have been substantial, with, for example, $800,000 being levied for improper data collection,[2] as well as a $1.6 million fine for the loss of 36 million user details in a data breach.[3]

2.2 The Information Commissioner's Office

The ICO is the data protection authority for the UK, tasked with ensuring that data controllers collect, process and store personal information in a secure manner that protects the informational privacy rights set out in the Data Protection Act of 1998 (DPA, or 'the Act'), the UK's implementation of the EU's Data Protection Directive.[4] Within the legislation, a *data controller* is any recognised entity that determines the purposes and manner in which *personal data*

---

[1] The Data Protection Directive (Directive 95/46/EC) required EU Member States to harmonise national legislation on data protection.

[2] https://www.ftc.gov/news-events/press-releases/2013/02/path-social-networking-app-settles-ftc-charges-it-deceived.

[3] https://www.ftc.gov/news-events/press-releases/2016/12/operators-ashleymadisoncom-settle-ftc-state-charges-resulting.

[4] The legislation may be found at http://www.legislation.gov.uk/ukpga/1998/29/contents.

are processed. Within the DPA, the personal data of an individual includes any information that allows for identification of the individual. The Act also describes a special category of personal data called *sensitive personal data*, which relates to specific attributes including health information, sexual orientation, religious and political beliefs.

There is no general obligation for data controllers to report data breaches to the ICO. A consequence of this is that the ICO primarily gathers intelligence on contraventions to the DPA through an online self-reporting system. In most cases, the reporter is the data controller itself, who has the responsibility to ensure the security of the records. The DPA empowers the ICO to issue monetary penalties of up to £500,000 for violations of the duties and obligations described in the Act. In determining a quantum for a monetary penalty, the size, sector and resources of the data controller are taken into account [7]. The ICO does not give a penalty for every reported instance of data breach. To be liable for a fine, the data controller must have failed in observing the data security principle of the DPA, which pertains to the maintenance of security of personal data. If it has been determined that a cases exists, the investigators will further consider: (i) the type of data lost; (ii) the cause of the breach; and (iii) the number of individuals affected.

2.3   Related Work

A survey of the existing literature on empirical analysis of data breaches highlights two consistent themes: a scarcity of data sources and the types of data contained in such sources; and that the lack of robust data sources limits the types of analysis that may be conducted, restricting the scope of available measures of impacts of data breaches.

Data tends to come from three main sources: news media, surveys, and open data sets derived from a combination of the previous two. The lack of relevant, robust data affects the types of analysis and the resultant conclusions, particularly when attempting to derive validated, generalisable metrics [6, 15]. Empirical analysis of data breaches has therefore been limited by data sources in the sort of analysis that may be undertaken. Various studies make use of news media to identify the number and specifics of cases (see, for example, [1,3]). A limitation of this approach is that the scope of the data set is curtailed by the interest of the media, which may only report on larger entities or larger number of records lost, as these may be more 'newsworthy'. These may not represent all types of data processing entities, nor all types of losses. Often this type of study achieves a data set of tens of firms. In a similar fashion, the UK Government publishes an annual *Cyber Security Breaches Survey* report. In 2016's study,[5] the methodology included a random probability survey of 1,008 businesses within the country, followed up with qualitative interviews with 30 respondents. A limitation of this approach is that the information derived is fixed to the data controller's perspective, ignoring the fact that there may be other factors that businesses do

---

[5] https://www.gov.uk/government/publications/cyber-security-breaches-survey-2016.

not consider. Further, the qualitative analysis reflects only those firms who wish to disclose practices and experiences, which may result in a biased view of widespread practice.

Much of the work on data breach impact has focused on event studies, which measure how the market reacts to announcement of a security event. The intuition is that a larger firm with a larger breach will result in a more significant financial impact. Cavusoglu et al. [3] concluded that the size and type of firm experiencing a data breach has an effect on the market's valuation of the firm. However, it has been shown that it is not necessarily possible to use this to predict trends within data breaches. Edwards et al. [5] acknowledged that, while there exist a number of data breach reports purporting to track the trends in data breaches, the variance in the data used produces faulty results when aggregated. Furthermore, the magnitude of the effect has also been shown to be variable. Acquisti et al. [1] provided an early empirical study on data breaches, assessing whether it was feasible to ascribe a cost to a violations of privacy derived from data breaches. The results showed that, while a firm experiences a statistically significant negative impact from a data breach, the effect is moderate in respect to expectation. Campbell et al. [2] found that sensitivity of the information subject to a data breach was significant in assessing the economic impact on a firm. Relatedly, in this paper we do not evaluate stock prices or extrapolate wider costs, but instead attempt to identify the attributes of reported data breaches and use the fine received as a measure of impact.

3   Methods and Data Description

Our study makes use of two data sets provided by the ICO. The first data set is the civil penalties data set, which includes all issued fines for data breaches. This is regularly updated with the ICO's regulatory actions and is available on the ICO's website.[6] The data set includes all civil penalties issued by the ICO from November 2010 to 4th March 2017. This includes a total of 118 entries within the data set. In addition to the civil penalties data set, there is also a data set on reported breaches to the ICO between April 2015 and March 2016. The data set is the result of a freedom of information request [8]. The data contains reported data breaches, the sector in which the data controller operates, and the type cause of the breach. The provided information covers data breaches in 21 sectors and 12 causes. It contains neither information regarding the type of personal data affected nor the number of records.

For the purposes of this study, we use a more data protection-focused definition of the term *data breach* — which we consider to be any access or use of data that is not intended by the data subjects or the data controller. This requires a loss of security or control over the data by an entity other than the data controller. Other misuses of data, for example unauthorised processing, are

---

[6] https://ico.org.uk/media/action-weve-taken/csvs/1042752/civil-monetary-penaltie s.csv.

included within this definition, as it allows for the inclusion of improper disclosures, wherein a data controller inadvertently sends personal information to other entities. We use exploratory data analysis to examine the civil penalties and data incident reporting data sets, with a view to examining the relationships between the categorical variables relating to sector, cause and category of personal data, as well as between the number of records lost and the fines received. The data analysis gives summary statistics with regards to the quantum of fines levied, as well as to the records that were affected by the breaches. We are also interested in the density of the fines. There are also frequency tables for the sectors in which the data controllers operate, the ascribed causes of the data breach, and the category of breached data.

4   Results

4.1   Monetary Penalties

As of March 2017, the ICO has levied £6.8 million in fines for data breaches, from a total of 60 instances. As described in Sect. 2.2, the value of each fine reflects the severity of the breach, taking into account the resources of the data controller, and serves as a deterrent against poor data management practices. The fines range from £5,000 to £400,000, with a mean fine of £113,717. The ICO has not yet used its maximum possible fine of £500,000. Examining the count of causes in Table 1b shows that, out of issued fines, disclosure error accounts for more than half of the data breach causes (55%), having more instances than all other categories combined. The next top three causes concern management of hardware and physical media (loss, theft, and improper disposal) — constituting 38% of fines. Security failures account for 5% of cases, having been the cause of only three instances.

Table 1. Description of sectors (a), causes (b), fines (c), and records (d).

Sector	Count
Local government	24
Healthcare	13
Finance	5
Justice	5
Non-retail	4
Central government	3
Retail	2
Telecom	2
Marketing	1
Regulators	1
Total	60

(a) Civil penalties given by sector.

Cause	Count
Disclosure error	33
Loss	9
Theft	9
Disposal	5
Security failure	3
Sale	1
Total	60

(b) Causes of data breaches.

Cause	Total fine
Disclosure error	£3,058,000
Loss	£1,050,000
Disposal	£950,000
Theft	£835,000
Security failure	£800,000
Sale	£130,000
Total	£6,823,000

(c) Total fine by cause

Cause	Total records
Security failure	4,320,996
Disclosure error	2,435,307
Loss	2,029,443
Disposal	175,100
Theft	106,732
Sale	21,500
Total	9,095,078

(d) Total records by cause

The civil penalties data set captures information pertaining to data breach incidents from nine different sectors (Table 1b). Almost two-thirds of the data breach incidents (61%) come from two sectors: local government and healthcare. The local government authorities account for the largest share (40%), followed by healthcare (22%). This highlights a strong disparity between public and private entities: when grouped together, public entities (local government, central government, healthcare, justice, and regulators) account for 46 out of the 60 entities (77%).

Of the 60 cases, only 54 have information regarding the number of records affected by the breach. The total number of records breached in ICO civil penalty cases between 2010 to 2017 is over nine million. Table 1a shows that security failure accounts for nearly half of all total records (48%). Disclosure error, which is the most frequent cause of data breach within the data set, is the second largest contributor providing 27% of the breached records.

The total fines awarded match the count of causes in Table 1b. For example, disclosure error fines represent 45% of all fines given, followed by loss and disposal. The most frequent cause, disclosure error, has the lowest average fine: £92,666. The average disclosure error fine (£92,667) is less than half that of the security failure (£266,667). Telecommunications and technology services have the highest mean of fines (£325,000).

As observed in Fig. 1a, the majority of fines remain under £100,000, with few fines exceeding £200,000. When considering sectors in which the fines are levied, it becomes evident that the most fined sector — local government — largely receives fines of just £100,000. When considering total fine amounts by sector, the fines levied against central government eclipses those in other sectors. The density of fines do not surpass £200,000.

Telecommunications and technology companies have received a high quantum of penalties when compared to other sectors, although these are only account for four of the fines. The largest fine (of £400,000) was given to TalkTalk, a telecommunications provider, for failing to take precautions against a simple SQL injection attack [9]. Healthcare has the largest range of fines, with a minimum of £25,000 and a maximum of £325,000 in Fig. 1a. This sector is also associated with the most causes — which is unique as most of the sectors are associated

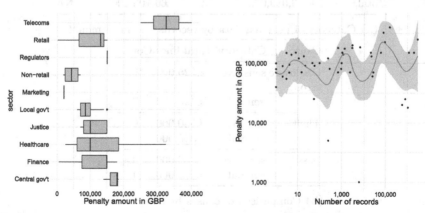

(a) Boxplot of civil penalties issued by sector.

(b) Relationship between total number of records and fines for data breaches $n = 54$.

Fig. 1. Analysis of ICO civil penalties.

with a single cause. The fines received by technology and telecommunications data controllers is confined to the upper limits of the range of fines.

In some popular surveys on data breaches, there is a claim that the number of records has a determination on the financial impact on the organisation.[7] We examine this claim in relation to regulatory action using local polynomial regression [4]. Figure 1b shows number of records has a very marginal effect on the total quantum of the fine.

In Sect. 2.2, we distinguished between *sensitive personal data* and a broader *general* class. Within the civil penalties data set, there are 54 cases with available information on the number of records and types of case. Table 2a shows that more than two-thirds of fines (68%) are associated with sensitive data and comprise more than half of the total fines (57%). The mean fine and mean records illustrate a strong indication that context is more influential than the number of records breached in determining the final penalty amount. Sensitive records account for 2.3% of the total amount of records breached, but comprise 64% of the total fines.

When considering only those causes that are present in both sensitive and general breaches, this includes only disclosure error, theft and loss. Table 2b shows that disclosure error penalties have been issued three times more than for disclosure errors of general data. Disclosure errors of sensitive data constitute 65% of penalties levied for sensitive data and 37% of all penalties levied.

Table 2. Tables comparing data breaches, controlling for type of personal data (a) and comparison of shared causes (b). Fine amounts are in GBP.

Category	Count	Records	Mean records	Total fines	Mean fine
sensitive	36	208,242	5,790	£3,905,000	£108,472
general	18	8,880,836	493,380	£1,548,000	£122,111
Total	54	9,089,078	NA	£6,103,000	NA

(a) Category of personal data by records and fine amount.

Cause	Category	Total fines	Count
Disclosure error	sensitive	£2,125,000	22
	general	£493,000	7
Theft	sensitive	£530,000	6
	general	£305,000	3
Loss	sensitive	£300,000	3
	general	£470,000	4

(b) Comparison of causes by category.

---

[7] Ponemon Institute: Cost of Data Breach Study: United Kingdom. http://www-03.ibm.com/security/data-breach/.

To further explore the number of records and fines, general and sensitive personal data were separated and their corresponding relationship between number of records and fines are analysed in Fig. 2. When controlling for category of data breached, the upward trajectory is more pronounced for sensitive data (see Fig. 2b). While the amount of records has somewhat of an effect on quantum of penalty, this relationship seems stronger within sensitive data breaches.

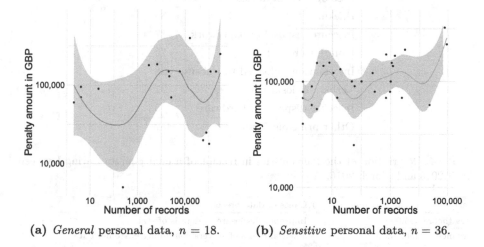

(a) *General* personal data, $n = 18$.   (b) *Sensitive* personal data, $n = 36$.

Fig. 2. Relationship between amount of records breached and fines, controlling for category of data.

4.2 Data Breach Reporting

Using the second data set, we examine the types of cases that have been reported to the ICO in regards to data breach. Over the course of a year, the ICO received 1,895 reports of data breaches within the UK. Table 3 shows that the largest category (24% of all reports) are listed as some other type of data security failure. The vast majority of reports have to do with data mismanagement, with causes ranging from loss of media or paperwork to inadvertent disclosure via email, posting or conversation. Failures of security, including the consequences of hacking, account for 8% of the reported breaches. Within this data set, there is no indication of the number of records that have been affected.

Although forming a small portion of data breach reports, security failures has been a primary concern in the literature (see, for example, [13]). Within security failures, general business is a source of a quarter of all reports, with telecommunications forming 11% of reports, and retail accounting for 10%. The low representation of security breaches may be due to the lack of obligation on the part of data controllers to report these instances to the ICO. When correlated with the civil penalties data, there are four entities that were fined for data breaches, totalling £470,000. Table 4 describes the penalties for data breaches which arose during the reporting period. Each of the cases has improper disclosure as a cause.

Table 3. Causes of data breach April 2015 to March 2016, $n = 1,895$.

Cause of data breach	Count
Loss or theft of paperwork	355
Post to incorrect recipient	347
Email to incorrect recipient	248
Loss or theft of device	108
Hacking	158
Insecure disposal of paperwork	77
Failure to redact	75
Information uploaded to website	38
Verbal disclosure	27
Insecure disposal of hardware	5
Other principle 7 failure	457

Table 4. Description of the four entities in receipt of a civil penalty during between April 2015 and March 2016.

Sector	Penalty amount (GBP)	Cause of data breach
Healthcare	185,000	Improper disclosure of details of staff
Finance	180,000	Theft and loss of servers containing customer data
Healthcare	25,000	Personal details of patients were erroneously emailed
Police	80,000	A victim's personal details were passed to the suspect in error

5   Discussion and Conclusions

This work provides an exploratory analysis of a novel data set, in order to evaluate how that data may facilitate analysis of data breaches. Within the monetary penalty data set, there is a noted difference between public and private entities — with the public sector being fined more often. There may be a number of reasons for this, including intelligence-gathering practices by the ICO or effective reporting mechanisms within the public sector. Other entities, such as telecommunications services, must report, but have only been fined in two instances. Security failure is the cause of the biggest loss of records within the civil penalties data set, but that may eclipse other conclusions relevant to data security practice. Negligence can be harmful as it results in small, constant losses rather than one large event. Poor organisational practice leads to a greater frequency of data breach incidents than external attacks. This is not meant to diminish the risk and threat of malicious, external actors, but, instead, to draw attention to a clear challenge that data controllers are experiencing in developing the appropriate operational controls to prevent negligent, internal action. In the past year, there were 158 external 'hacking' attacks reported to the ICO. This is in contrast to 595 incidents reported of posting personal data to incorrect recipients or five devices not disposed of in a correct manner or 108 reports of lost, unencrypted devices containing personal data.

Our results demonstrate that context is an important feature in a data breach. With an upper limit of £500,000, the overall average of fines is around £110,000. This figure is not meaningful in and of itself, as it covers a range from £1,000 to £400,000 (both given for security failures). The overall average fine for general data breaches was not much higher than for data breaches concerning sensitive data, despite many more records being lost in the former. Controlling for sector and cause, the sensitivity of the data appeared to increase the quantum of the monetary penalty. This may be due to the over-representation of sensitive disclosure error types of cases, especially as public sector institutions in the UK include hospitals.

It is necessary to point out the limitations of this study. First, the civil penalty data set is focused on a specific subset of data breaches. The fines are levied where the ICO has deemed that the data controller's actions did not reach an adequate level of diligence. Therefore, only a small portion of reported breaches are fined, as demonstrated in the two analysed data sets. It should be noted that, while negligence is a factor, data breaches may occur even when such diligence is observed. Second, the wide scope of the term *data breach* may include factors and considerations that are not present in other studies.

The results show that privacy is more affected by gaps and failures of operational practice than from attackers. While security failures have resulted in more records being lost, the frequency of non-security causes of data breaches is much higher. This highlights that data security is not in and of itself sufficient to address the challenges within data privacy.

Acknowledgement. AC would like to thank the EPSRC and the Oxford Radcliffe Scholarship for financial support. The authors would like to thank the anonymous reviewers for their helpful and constructive feedback.

References

1. Acquisti, A., Friedman, A., Telang, R.: Is there a cost to privacy breaches? An event study. In: ICIS 2006 Proceedings, p. 94 (2006)
2. Campbell, K., Gordon, L.A., Loeb, M.P., Zhou, L.: The economic cost of publicly announced information security breaches: empirical evidence from the stock market. J. Comput. Secur. **11**(3), 431–448 (2003)
3. Cavusoglu, H., Mishra, B., Raghunathan, S.: The effect of internet security breach announcements on market value: capital market reactions for breached firms and internet security developers. Int. J. Electron. Commer. **9**(1), 70–104 (2004)
4. Cleveland, W., Grosse, E., Shyu, W.: Local regression models. In: Statistical Models in S, pp. 309–376. Chapman & Hall, London (1991)
5. Edwards, B., Hofmeyr, S., Forrest, S.: Hype and heavy tails: a closer look at data breaches. J. Cybersecur. **2**(1), 3–14 (2016)
6. Heitzenrater, C.D., Simpson, A.C.: Policy, statistics and questions: reflections on UK cyber security disclosures. J. Cybersecur. **2**(1), 43 (2016). doi:10.1093/cybsec/tyw008

7. Information Commissioner's Office: Information Commissioners guidance about the issue of monetary penalties prepared and issued under section 55C (1) of the Data Protection Act 1998 (2015). https://ico.org.uk/media/1043720/ico-guidance-on-monetary-penalties.pdf
8. Information Commissioner's Office: ICO Disclosure Log - Response IRQ0630777. https://ico.org.uk/about-the-ico/our-information/disclosure-log/irq0630777/
9. Information Commissioner's Office: TalkTalk Telecom Group PLC Monetary Penalty Notice, October 2016. https://ico.org.uk/media/action-weve-taken/mpns/1624087/talktalk-mpn-20160324.pdf, https://ico.org.uk/media/action-weve-taken/mpns/1625131/mpn-talk-talk-group-plc.pdf
10. Ishiguro, M., Tanaka, H., Matsuura, K., Murase, I.: The effect of information security incidents on corporate values in the Japanese stock market. In: International Workshop on the Economics of Securing the Information Infrastructure (WESII) (2006)
11. Johnson, M.E., Willey, N.: Usability failures and healthcare data hemorrhages. IEEE Secur. Priv. 9(2), 35–42 (2011)
12. Liginlal, D., Sim, I., Khansa, L.: How significant is human error as a cause of privacy breaches? An empirical study and a framework for error management. Comput. Secur. 28(3), 215–228 (2009)
13. Phua, C.: Protecting organisations from personal data breaches. Comput. Fraud Secur. 2009(1), 13–18 (2009)
14. Schatz, D., Bashroush, R.: The impact of repeated data breach events on organisations market value. Inf. Comput. Secur. 24(1), 73–92 (2016)
15. Verendel, V.: Quantified security is a weak hypothesis: a critical survey of results and assumptions. In: Proceedings of the 2009 Workshop on New Security Paradigms Workshop, pp. 37–50. ACM (2009)

Automated Legal Compliance Checking by Security Policy Analysis

Silvio Ranise and Hari Siswantoro[✉]

Fondazione Bruno Kessler, Trento, Italy
{ranise,siswantoro}@fbk.eu

Abstract. Legal compliance-by-design is the process of developing a software system that processes personal data in such a way that its ability to meet specific legal provisions is ascertained. In this paper, we describe techniques to automatically check the compliance of the security policies of a system against formal rules derived from legal provisions by reusing available tools for security policy verification. We also show the practical viability of our approach by reporting the experimental results of a prototype for checking compliance of realistic and synthetic policies against the European Data Protection Directive (EU DPD).

1 Introduction

Security-by-design is an approach to security that allows for injecting security into every part of the IT management process, starting already in the design phase. Several automated techniques have been proposed for the verification of security policies—in particular those expressing access control requirements—ranging from scenario finding to change impact analysis (see, e.g., [13] when access control policies are specified in XACML). Tools implementing such techniques are capable of assisting humans in the difficult and error prone tasks of designing and maintaining access control policies that evolve over time. These are crucial—not only for ensuring basic properties such as confidentiality and integrity—but also for compliance with respect to legal provisions concerning data protection and privacy; such as the EU DPD to name but one. The hardest challenge in maintaining the compliance of security policies against legal provisions is not deploying technical security mechanisms, but rather maintaining alignment of evolving security policies with legal provisions over time. This problem is particularly pressing in current software systems (in particular those deployed in the cloud) where code updates are performed weekly and infrastructure is scalable. The only hope to ensure continuous compliance is to adopt a compliance-by-design approach supported by automated techniques and tools to ascertain compliance of evolving security policies against formal rules derived from legal provisions. Unfortunately, automated techniques for legal compliance checking have received much less attention than those for policy analysis. As a result, security and legal requirements evolve independently and give rise to situations in which an organization has a strong secure posture with little or no attention to compliance (it is thus exposed to fines) or, vice versa, it is compliant but its security posture is weak (it is thus exposed to security breaches).

To alleviate these problems, we present an approach to extend available tools for automated policy analysis with the capability of performing legal compliance checks by a reduction to policy refinement. For concreteness, we use the EU DPD and report our experiments with a prototype tool showing the utility and scalability of our approach. To derive the formal rules (from the EU DPD) against which compliance must be checked, we reuse the methodology in [8] to which the interested reader is pointed for details. Because of the trend in building tools for policy analysis by using efficient automated reasoning tools, called Satisfiability Modulo Theories (SMT) solvers, as back-end solvers [2,13], we show how to reduce legal compliance checking to policy refinement that, in turn, is reduced to SMT solving. However, we notice that the approach can be adapted to exploit algorithms for policy refinement that use any symbolic representation of security policies.

Related Work. Since policy analysis problems have been thoroughly studied in the literature about security analysis (see, e.g., [2,13]), here we focus on closely related works about legal compliance. Our approach differs from [6], because we focus on design time rather than runtime, use simpler specification languages, and use static analysis techniques to ensure compliance by construction. Compared to [7] that examine business process compliance against specific and detailed regulation, our method works on a more generic regulation (EU DPD).

Structure of the Paper. Section 2 recalls the basic notions underlying security policy analysis, in particular policy refinement. Section 3 summarizes the methodology to derive formal rules from legal provisions (in particular the EU DPD) and how these can be instantiated to security policies for a particular software system design. Section 4 describes our technique to reduce legal compliance checking to policy refinement and describes how to implement it in a way to return detailed reports about violations (if the case). Section 5 reports our experience with a prototype implementation on realistic and synthetic legal compliance checking problems. Section 6 presents conclusions and future work.

2   An Overview of Security Policy Analysis

We take Attribute Based Access Control (ABAC) [9] as the model underlying our policies. The reason for this choice is the flexibility of ABAC that allows us to specify a wide range of access control policy idioms together with their combinations [11].

In ABAC, access rights are permitted or denied depending on the security-relevant characteristics—called attributes—of the entities involved in access control: a *subject* (e.g., a user or an application) asking to perform an *action* (e.g., read, write, update) on a *resource* (e.g., a file, a document, or a database record) in an *environment*, i.e. a collection of contextual information (e.g., location, time of day). The tension between the specification of access rights (i.e. actions that subjects can perform on resources) and safety (i.e. no subject can get permissions that compromise some security goals) requires to identify the authorization queries known to be permitted, denied, and unregulated (i.e. neither permitted nor prohibited) [10]. Formally, let S, A, R, and E be sets of subjects, actions, resources, and environments, respectively. Following [2], we regard these entities as records whose fields are their attributes. An entity is uniquely identified by the values associated to its attributes, thus S, A, R, and E are the Cartesian products of the set of possible values of each attribute (this is uniquely determined according to an arbitrary order over the attributes). An *access control policy* is a tuple (S, A, R, E, P, D) where S, A, R, E are as defined above while P and D are sub-sets of $AQ = S \times A \times R \times E$, whose elements are called *authorization queries*. P is the set of *permitted* authorization queries—i.e. s is allowed to perform a on r in e when (s, a, r, e) is in P—and D is the set of *denied* ones—i.e. s is not allowed to perform a on r in e when (s, a, r, e) is in D. For any policy (P, D), we assume that P and D are non-empty and disjoint. It may be the case that the union of P and D do not contain all possible authorization queries, i.e. $(P \cup D) \subset AQ$ (this is known as the open-world assumption [5]). An authorization query in the set $U = AQ \setminus (P \cup D)$ is *unregulated*. When complementing a set X w.r.t. AQ, we write X^c; e.g., $U = (P \cup D)^c$.

It is well-known how to encode security analysis problems—such as policy refinement and subsumption, change impact, and scenario finding (see, e.g., [13]) as set-theoretic expressions by using the sets P and D in an ABAC policy (P, D). For instance, consider the notion of *policy refinement* introduced in [3], namely *"one policy refines another if using the first policy automatically also fulfills the second policy,"* which is in turn equivalent to requiring that a policy $\pi_1 = (P_1, D_1)$ refines another policy $\pi_2 = (P_2, D_2)$ if whenever π_2 returns Permit (or Deny), π_1 returns the same decision. So, policy refinement can be encoded as the set-theoretic expression

$$P_1 \subseteq P_2 \text{ and } D_1 \subseteq D_2. \tag{1}$$

Notice that there are no requirements on the unregulated queries of the policies π_1 and π_2, i.e. $(P_1 \cup D_1)^c$ and $(P_2 \cup D_2)^c$, respectively.

We observe the availability of automated tools capable of solving the security analysis problems considered above for variants of the ABAC model such as those described in [13] for XACML or the one in [2] for a high-level declarative language. In the rest of this paper, we show how to use the capability of these tools to perform policy refinement checks for mechanizing legal compliance analysis.

3   Reducing Legal Compliance to Policy Refinement

In [8], we have described a methodology to derive a formalization of legal provisions expressed in natural language by using the methodology depicted in Fig. 1. The (dashed) L-shaped box at the top-left corner of the picture shows legal and IT security experts that collaborate to identify the parts of the regulation (in our case the EU DPD) that are amenable to formalization, make it explicit any simplifying assumptions restricting the scope of applicability of the rules, use

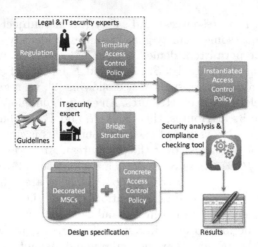

Fig. 1. Our approach to legal compliance checking

the declarative framework to derive a mathematical model, and compile a set of guidelines (in natural language) that should help IT system designers to bridge the gap between technical and legal levels. The remaining of the figure shows what an IT security experts (possibly complementing the designs of IT system architects) should do in order to come up with a privacy-friendly IT system design. First of all, she produces a (decorated) version of the MSCs describing the main processes in the system and associates each one of them with a purpose. Second, she designs the (concrete) access control policies that the various entities in the MSC should respect in order to send or receive messages. Third, by using the guidelines made available by the group of experts that produced the formal model of the regulation, she specifies a so-called bridge structure that allows her to instantiate the (formal) model of the legal provisions to a policy applicable to the system under design. At this point, she can use an available tool for automated policy analysis to answer several questions about the security of the system design (such as "is this authorization query permitted or denied?") and, most importantly, checking compliance, i.e. answering the question': "is the (concrete) access control policy compliant with the (formalization of the) regulation?" We will show how—under reasonable assumptions on the capabilities of the policy analysis tool—it is possible not only to return a yes/no answer to the question but also scenarios explaining why the legal provisions are violated (if the case).

3.1   The Formal Model for Legal Provisions

We briefly summarize the main features of the formal model obtained by applying the approach in Fig. 1 to a dramatically simplified version of the EU DPD as shown in Table 1(a). (Readers interested in the details of the methodology used to derive the formalization of the EU DPD are pointed to [8].) Column Eff(ect) reports when p(ermitting) and d(enying) to *Process* some Personal Data (*PD*) by some entity under the control of the Data Subject (*DS*), Data Controller (*DC*), or the Data Processor (*DP*) for a certain *Pur*pose (when needed) according to what is described in the column Condition. *PD* are information relating to an identified or identifiable natural person (e.g., the profile information of an employee). *DC* is a natural or legal person which alone or jointly with others determines the purposes and means of the processing of PD (e.g., ITOrg is the DC in the system considered above). *DS* is an individual that is the subject of the PD held by a DC (e.g., an employee is the DS). *DP* is any individual or organization that processes PD on behalf of DC (e.g., both ITOrg Fin Dept and ACME are DPs). The first three lines of Table 1(a) contains the conditions permitting an action to be performed while the last three lines shows the conditions denying the action the right to be executed. More precisely, the condition in the first line of the table specifies that a *DS* can *Proc*ess the *PD* provided that a *DC* has *Emp*owered her with the possibility to do so. While the EU DPD stipulates that—regardless of the purpose—a DS can perform any action on her PD, an information system is usually designed to provide only a sub-set of all possible actions that a DS is entitled to do. For this reason, we introduced *Emp* to express which actions the DS can perform when interacting with the system. The condition in the second line of the table specifies that a *DC* can *Proc*ess *PD* for a given *Pur*pose provided that the *DS* has given her *Cons*ent. The condition in the third line of the table specifies that a *DP* can *Proc*ess *PD* for a given *Pur*pose provided that a *DC* has *Man*dated it to do so. This formalizes one of the principles stated in the EU DPD that a *DC* can delegate (part of) the operations to one or more *DPs* in order to carry out the processing required to achieve a given purpose. The conditions in the last three lines of the table correspond to (some of) the negative versions (i.e. rules denying access) of those in the first three. How such negative rules are derived from the text of the EU DPD (that considers only conditions permitting access) is explained in [8]. In the case of a *DS* trying to *Proc*ess her *PD* if a *DC* has not empowered her to do so, this is sufficient to deny access (fourth line). Similarly, a *DC* cannot *Proc*ess *PD* if the *DS* has not given her consent (fifth line) and a *DP* cannot *Proc*ess *PD* if a *DC* has not mandated it to do so (last line).

In summary, the EU DPD is formalized as a pair $(\mathbb{P}, \mathbb{D})$ of Boolean formulae over a set $\mathbb{V}$ of variables corresponding to the main notions introduced in the

Table 1. (a) Formalization of the EU DPD and (b) policy to produce salary slips

(a)

Eff	Condition
p	$DS \wedge Proc \wedge PD \wedge Emp$
p	$DC \wedge Proc \wedge PD \wedge Pur \wedge Cons$
p	$DP \wedge Proc \wedge PD \wedge Pur \wedge Man$
d	$DS \wedge Proc \wedge PD \wedge \neg\, Emp$
d	$DC \wedge Proc \wedge PD \wedge \neg\, Pur \wedge Cons$
d	$DP \wedge Proc \wedge PD \wedge Pur \wedge \neg\, Man$

(b)

	pro	fin_pro	s_fin_pro	sal	sal_slip
Empl.	r,w,u				r
ITOrg	r	w			
FDept		r	w	r	w
ACME			r	r,w,u	

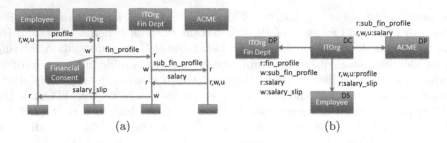

Fig. 2. (a) MSC for the salary slips computation and (b) related bridge structure

text. The idea to obtain an instance of $(\mathbb{P}, \mathbb{D})$ corresponding the instantiation of the EU DPD to a particular system, the only thing to do is to map each variable in $\mathbb{V}$ to the concrete entities in the system under scrutiny.

3.2   Instantiation of the Formal Model

We are now left with the problem of instantiating the formal rules $(\mathbb{P}, \mathbb{D})$ in Table 1(a) to the system whose compliance should be checked. We illustrate this on a simple scenario that involves the processing of personal data to produce the salary slips of employees in an Italian organization, named ITOrg. The process is described by the Message Sequence Chart (MSC) of Fig. 2 that specifies how ITOrg acquires basic personal information about each one of its Employee (e.g., name, surname, number of kids), processes the data in its Financial Department which outsources the actual computation of the salary slip to an external company, called ACME. The exact description of the various steps in the process is not very important. The interesting part are three. First, the sequence of send and receive messages defines a plan for achieving the purpose of computing salary slips (below, abbreviated with 'salary_comp'). This requires us to adopt a purpose-aware access control model [1] where the meaning of a purpose is the sequence of actions needed to achieve certain goals [12]. Second, one of the most important legal provisions of the EU DPD amounts to requiring the consent for processing personal data from a given subject; cf. the call out marked 'Financial consent' in the MSC of Fig. 2(a). So, the MSCs we consider are decorated with call outs formalizing the condition that subjects should have given their consent to process their personal data for the given purpose (i.e. that such data are processed as specified in the MSC). To formalize these two aspects, we assume that the environments in an ABAC policy have (at least) the following two attributes: *purpose* ranging over the (finite) set of possible purpose identifiers and *consent* ranging over Boolean functions telling whether the subject has given its consent to process a given message (resource). The third aspect to observe in the MSC is that the various entities in it are required to have certain rights—namely, the annotations r(ead), w(rite), and u(pdate) near the sources and targets of the arrows in Fig. 2(a)—to be entitled to send or receive a certain message. Indeed, the conditions under which the entities are permitted or denied such rights are specified in a (purpose-aware) access control policy. Table 1(b) can be seen as a specification of an access control policy for the MSC in Fig. 2(a) characterizing the rights of each subject (row) with respect to every resource (column) in the context of the process whose purpose is 'salary_slip,' which is left implicit for the sake of brevity (in the same spirit, profile has been shortened to pro, salary to sal, and ITOrg has been dropped from ITOrg Fin Dept).

We now explain how to instantiate the formal rules $(\mathbb{P}, \mathbb{D})$ of Table 1(a) to the system described by the MSC in Fig. 2(a) and the (purpose-aware) access control policy (P, D) derived from Table 1(b). The crux is a labeled directed graph, shown in Fig. 2(b) and called bridge structure, mapping the legal roles— such as Data Subject (DS), Data Controller (DC), and Data Processor (DP)— to the entities in the system (e.g., Employee and ITOrg) and describing the *Emp*ower and *Man*date relationships between DC and DS or DP, respectively. So, in Fig. 2(b), an Employee, ITOrg, ITOrg FDept (short of ITOrg Financial Department), and ACME play the legal roles DS, DC, DP, and DP, respectively. The *Emp*ower relation is identified by the arrow from ITOrg to Employee which is labeled by the pairs 'r,w,u:profile' and 'r:salary_slip' saying that an Employee is entitled to r(ead), w(rite) and u(pdate) the profile and to r(ead) the salary_slip. The *Man*date relation is identified by the two arrows from ITOrg to ITOrg Fin Dept and ACME which are labeled by 'r:fin_profile,' 'w:s_fin_profile', 'r:salary' and 'w:salary_slip' for the former and 'r:s_fin_profile' with 'r,w,u:salary' for the latter saying that ITOrg Fin Dept is delegated the permissions to r(ead) the fin_profile and the salary as well as to w(rite) the s_fin_profile and salary_slip, that ACME is delegated to r(ead) sub_fin_profile and to r(ead), w(rite) and u(pdate) the salary.

It is not difficult to see that the bridge structure induces a mapping ι from the set $\mathbb{V}$ of Boolean variables in the formalization of the EU DPD $(\mathbb{P}, \mathbb{D})$ to sub-sets or relations over the sets of subjects S, resources R, actions A, and environments E of the policy specified in Table 1(b). For instance, $\iota(DS)$ is the sub-set of subjects that are Employee and $\iota(DC)$ is the sub-set of subjects that act on behalf of the organization ITOrg. Similarly, $\iota(Emp)$ is the relation containing the tuples (ITOrg, Employee, w, profile) and (ITOrg, Employee, u, profile) saying that the Data Subject (Employee) is entitled to write or update its profile by the Data Controller (ITOrg) and $\iota(Man)$ the tuple (ITOrg, ACME, r, s_fin_profile) saying that the Data Processor (ACME) is delegated by the Data Controller (ITOrg) to read (part of) the financial profile of an employee date. It is then possible to lift the definition of ι over the Boolean expressions in $\mathbb{P}$ and $\mathbb{D}$ by interpreting disjunction as set-theoretic union, conjunction as set-theoretic intersection, and negation as set-theoretic complement to derive the ABAC policy $(\iota(\mathbb{P}), \iota(\mathbb{D}))$ that is precisely the instantiation of the formalization of the EU DPD to the system under consideration that we were looking for.

4   Automating Legal Compliance Checking

The crux of our approach is to reduce the problem of checking whether a certain (purpose-aware) ABAC policy (P, D) is compliant with the (formalization of the)

EU DPD $(\mathbb{P}, \mathbb{D})$, given a certain bridge structure inducing a mapping ι, to that of policy refinement between (P, D) and $(\iota(\mathbb{P}), \iota(\mathbb{D}))$. According to (1) in Sect. 2, this is equivalent to check if

$$P \subseteq \iota(\mathbb{P}) \text{ and } D \subseteq \iota(\mathbb{D}). \tag{2}$$

In order to mechanize the check in (2), a pre-requisite is to have symbolic representations for the sets P, D, $\iota(\mathbb{P})$ and $\iota(\mathbb{D})$ of authorization queries. Because of the trend in building tools for policy analysis by using efficient automated reasoning tools, called SMT solvers, as back-end solvers, we assume that each set of authorization queries is represented as a set-comprehension of the form $\{(s, a, r, e) | \varphi(s, a, r, e)\}$ for φ a formula of First-Order Logic (FOL) whose variables are the attributes of the entities s, a, r, and e. However, we notice that our approach can be adapted to (virtually) any symbolic representation of the ABAC policy. For instance, assuming that $P = \{(s, a, r, e) | \varphi_P(s, a, r, e)\}$ and $D = \{(s, a, r, e) | \varphi_D(s, a, r, e)\}$, checking that $P \cap D = \emptyset$ (i.e. that the ABAC policy (P, D) is conflict-free) is equivalent to checking if $\varphi_P \wedge \varphi_D$ is unsatisfiable in FOL. Similarly, the problem of checking if (2) holds is equivalent to check the validity in FOL of the following two formulae: $\varphi_P \Rightarrow \iota(\varphi_\mathbb{P})$ and $\varphi_D \Rightarrow \iota(\varphi_\mathbb{D})$ where P and D are as before and $\mathbb{P} = \{(s, a, r, e) | \varphi_\mathbb{P}(s, a, r, e)\}$ $\mathbb{D} = \{(s, a, r, e) | \varphi_\mathbb{D}(s, a, r, e)\}$. Since SMT solvers are able to check unsatisfiabilty of FOL formulae, we need to reduce validity to satisfiability by refutation, i.e. we consider the equivalent problem of verifying that

$$\varphi_P \wedge \neg\varphi_\mathbb{P} \text{ and } \varphi_D \wedge \neg\varphi_\mathbb{D} \text{ are both unsatisfiable in FOL.} \tag{3}$$

In [8], we have shown that the compliance checking problem (and other security analysis problems such as those listed in Sect. 2) is decidable and NP-complete under reasonable assumptions that allow to encode a wide range of authorization conditions (the interested reader is pointed to [8] for details). Here, we emphasize that NP-completeness is not a hindrance to the practical applicability of our approach as shown by the experimental results discussed in Sect. 5.

4.1   Implementation

We have implemented a tool capable of automating compliance checking by refining the approach described above. It is implemented in Python and use the PySMT library[1] API to invoke the SMT solver MathSAT[2] to tackle refinements of the satisfiability problems (3) as well as others corresponding to the security analysis problems listed in Sect. 2. The tool takes ABAC policies and bridge structures in a JSON format similar to the one adopted to specify the access control policies in Amazon.[3]

We explain how we have refined the satisfiability problems (3) to enable the tool to return more interesting results when checking for compliance. By using

---

[1] https://github.com/pysmt/pysmt
[2] http://mathsat.fbk.eu.
[3] http://docs.aws.amazon.com/IAM/latest/UserGuide/access_policies.html.

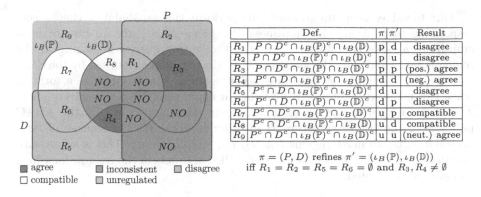

$$\pi = (P, D) \text{ refines } \pi' = (\iota_B(\mathbb{P}), \iota_B(\mathbb{D}))$$
$$\text{iff } R_1 = R_2 = R_5 = R_6 = \emptyset \text{ and } R_3, R_4 \neq \emptyset$$

Fig. 3. Venn diagram for compliance checking

the Venn diagram in Fig. 3, we consider all possible relations between the four sets P, D, $\iota_B(\mathbb{P})$, and $\iota_B(\mathbb{D})$ so that we can establish when $P \subseteq \iota_B(\mathbb{P})$ and $D \subseteq \iota_B(\mathbb{D})$. There is a total of $2^4 = 16$ Venn regions of which 7 (marked with 'NO') can be disregarded because we assume that the ABAC policies (P, D) and $(\iota(\mathbb{P}), \iota(\mathbb{D}))$ are conflict-free (notice that ensuring this requires to solve two satisfiability problems as discussed above; such checks are indeed supported by the tool as a pre-processing step when parsing ABAC policies).

The remaining 9 cases are listed in the table at the right of the Venn diagram in Fig. 3: the first column shows the region identifier, the second reports the set-theoretic definition of the regions in terms of the four sets of authorization queries involved, the third and fourth contain the result of evaluating an authorization query belonging to a region—namely p(ermit), d(eny), or u(nregulated)—and the last column shows the impact on the refinement relation of the fact that the region is non-empty. The fact that (i) R_1 or R_6 are non-empty means that refinement fails as there exists an authorization query on which π and π' disagree because it is permitted by a policy and denied by the other; (ii) R_2 or R_5 are non-empty means that refinement fails as there exists some authorization query that is unregulated by π' and permitted or denied, respectively, by π; (iii) R_3, R_4, and R_9 are non-empty means that refinement may succeed as there exist authorization queries on which π and π' positively, negatively, and neutrally (respectively) agree (i.e. such queries are permitted, denied, or unregulated, respectively, by both π and π'); and (iv) R_7 and R_8 are non-empty means that refinement may succeed as there exist authorization queries that are unregulated by π' and permitted or denied, respectively, by π. Notice the difference between the case corresponding to regions R_2 and R_5 with that of regions R_7 and R_8: the former is problematic for refinement whereas the latter is not because π should be at least as restrictive as π'; this implies that there should not be queries that are unregulated by π that are regulated by π' while the vice versa may happen. To summarize, π is compliant with $(\mathbb{P}, \mathbb{D})$ under the bridge structure B when π refines $\pi' = (\iota_B(\mathbb{P}), \iota_B(\mathbb{D}))$ iff regions R_1, R_2, R_5, and R_6 are empty and regions R_3 and R_4 are not so.

Our tool has been programmed to perform the satisfiability checks corresponding to verifying the emptiness of regions $R_1, \ldots, R_9$. In case of nonemptiness, a table containing a list of authorization queries belonging to the region is generated from the assignments to the attributes returned by the SMT solver. (The capability of returning assignments to the variables in a formula when this is found satisfiable is available in many available SMT solvers.) The authorization queries can be used by system designers to modify the ABAC policy π or the bridge structure B in order to eliminate the sources of noncompliance, i.e. to make regions R_1, R_2, R_5, and R_6 empty. This is a first substantial step to build tools that return detailed accounts of the reasons for which compliance is violated.

5   Experimental Evaluation

We have tested our tool with respect to two dimensions: evaluating its utility in realistic scenarios and experimenting its scalability on synthetic benchmarks.

Realistic Benchmarks. Besides the system in Sect. 3.2, we have considered three other situations: one involves the sharing of customer information acquired by a (cloud) service provider with third-party applications and two other concern eHealth services. For lack of space, we sketch the intended use of our tool in only one of the three scenarios, namely the one about telemedicine data processing of diabetic patients. The description is deliberately over-simplified by considering just one purpose to fit into the page limit; more details can be found at https://goo.gl/GQi8xr.

A patient enters a set of information regarding her health status (*patient_diabetes_data*) into a Personal Health Record (PHR) system using a mobile app. Within the PHR, run by the Local Health Care Provider (LHCP), the patient shares this information with her diabetic Specialist (Spec). The Spec can—using a dedicated dashboard of the PHR—access the data entered by the Pt and provide her with medical and therapeutic information (*medical_indication_data*).

To illustrate, we show just one rule of the ABAC policy:

$$s.role = Spec \wedge (a = r \vee a = w \vee a = u) \wedge$$
$$r.type = med\_indic\_data \wedge e.purpose = telemedicine \tag{4}$$

We ask our tool to check compliance for the scenario described above. It returns that regions R_1, R_3 and R_4 of the Venn diagram in Fig. 3 are non-empty. While the non-emptiness of R_3 and R_4 implies that the policy of the system agrees with the EU DPD, the fact that R_1 is also non-empty is a source of non-compliance since the queries in this region are permitted by the policy but are denied by the directive. Besides saying that R_1 is non-empty, the tool is able to show the list of queries that are in the region. By inspection of the list, the policy designer can see that the Spec can read, write or update *med_indic_data* regardless of the fact that the patient has given her consent. This means that the conjunct $e.consent = true$ must be added to (4). At this point, we re-run the tool with the updated policy and follow the same approach to resolve any non-compliance

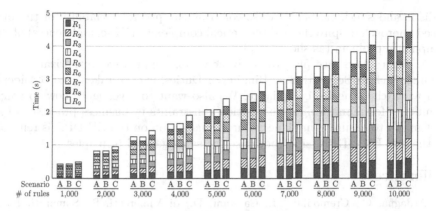

Fig. 4. Results on synthetic compliance problems

issue if the case. This iterative process allows us resolve non-compliance issues by focusing on one problem at a time.

Synthetic Benchmarks. As said above, compliance problems are NP-complete. Available SMT solvers have proved quite efficient on a variety of verification problems including those derived from policy analysis [2,13]. To confirm this is the case also for compliance checking, we have designed a set of three synthetic benchmarks that allow us to increase the number disjuncts (also called rules) in the formulae describing an ABAC policy (P, D) by increasing the values of a set of parameters. This corresponds to common practice in the field of policy analysis; see, e.g., [2] for a discussion on this. Figure 4 shows the results of our experiments on the synthetic benchmarks: the x-axis report the number of disjuncts (called rules) in the formulae for three set of scenarios (A, B and C), while the y-axis show the timings to check the emptiness of the 9 regions $R_1, ..., R_9$. The results were obtained on a PC with Intel i5-3340M 2.7 GHz processor and 4 GB of RAM, running Debian Linux with kernel version 4.7; the Python and PySMT version are 2.7.12 and 0.6.0, respectively, and the version of MathSAT is 5.3.13. These results clearly show the scalability of our approach since (a) the plot suggests a linear behaviour for the solving time in the number of rules and (b) less than 5 s are needed to perform a detailed evaluation of the compliance of a policy with 10, 000 rules.

6   Conclusions and Future Work

In [8], we have introduced an approach to support the specification of information system designs, purpose-aware access control policies, and legal requirements. The compliance checking problems in the framework can be automated by using existing tools for security policy analysis. In this paper, we have described the techniques that make this possible and an implementation that uses tools for policy analysis based on efficient SMT solvers. An experimental evaluation on realistic and synthetic benchmarks confirms the practical viability of the proposed approach despite the bad theoretical complexity (NP-completeness) of the compliance problem (as shown in [8]).

As future work, we plan to study how more expressive authorization constraints, such as Separation or Binding of Duties, can be taken into consideration when checking for compliance. We also want to investigate how to adapt techniques for monitoring authorization constraints in business processes (e.g., that in [4]) to ensure compliance. Our formalization on the EU DPD is reusable on the new EU GDPR, since both use the same general principles.

References

1. Ardagna, C., Cremonini, M., Capitani, D., di Vimercati, S., Samarati, P.: A privacy-aware access control system. JCS 16(4), 369–392 (2008)
2. Armando, A., Ranise, S., Traverso, R., Wrona, K.: SMT-based enforcement and analysis of NATO content-based protection and release policies. In: ABAC@CODASPY, pp. 35–46. ACM (2016)
3. Backes, M., Karjoth, G., Bagga, W., Schunter, M.: Efficient comparison of enterprise privacy policies. In: Proceedings of the 2004 ACM Symposium on Applied Computing, pp. 375–382. ACM (2004)
4. Bertolissi, C., dos Santos, D., Ranise, S.: Automated synthesis of run-time monitors to enforce authorization policies in business processes. In: Proceedings of the ASIACCS. ACM (2015)
5. Capitani, D., di Vimercati, S., Foresti, S., Jajodia, S., Samarati, P.: Access control policies and languages. IJCSE 3(2), 94–102 (2007)
6. Fatema, K., Debruyne, C., Lewis, D., OSullivan, D., Morrison, J.P., Mazed, A.: A semi-automated methodology for extracting access control rules from the European data protection directive. In: SPW 2016, pp. 25–32. IEEE (2016)
7. Governatori, G., Hoffmann, J., Sadiq, S., Weber, I.: Detecting regulatory compliance for business process models through semantic annotations. In: Ardagna, D., Mecella, M., Yang, J. (eds.) BPM 2008. LNBIP, vol. 17, pp. 5–17. Springer, Heidelberg (2009). doi:10.1007/978-3-642-00328-8_2
8. Guarda, P., Ranise, S., Siswantoro, H.: Security analysis and legal compliance checking for the design of privacy-friendly information systems. In: Proceedings of the 22nd ACM on SACMAT, pp. 247–254. ACM (2017)
9. Hu, V.C., Ferraiolo, D., Kuhn, R., Friedman, A.R., Lang, A.J., Cogdell, M.M., Schnitzer, A., Sandlin, K., Miller, R., Scarfone, K.: Guide to ABAC Definition and Considerations (Draft). No. 800-162 in NIST (2013)
10. Jaeger, T., Tidswell, J.E.: Practical safety in flexible access control models. ACM Trans. Inf. Syst. Secur. 4(2), 158–190 (2001)
11. Jin, X., Krishnan, R., Sandhu, R.: A unified attribute-based access control model covering DAC, MAC and RBAC. In: Cuppens-Boulahia, N., Cuppens, F., Garcia-Alfaro, J. (eds.) DBSec 2012. LNCS, vol. 7371, pp. 41–55. Springer, Heidelberg (2012). doi:10.1007/978-3-642-31540-4_4
12. Tschantz, M.C., Datta, A., Wing, J.M.: Formalizing and enforcing purpose restrictions in privacy policies. In: IEEE Symposium on Security and Privacy, pp. 176–190 (2012)
13. Turkmen, F., den Hartog, J., Ranise, S., Zannone, N.: Analysis of XACML policies with SMT. In: Focardi, R., Myers, A. (eds.) POST 2015. LNCS, vol. 9036, pp. 115–134. Springer, Heidelberg (2015). doi:10.1007/978-3-662-46666-7_7

Access Control Policy Coverage Assessment Through Monitoring

Antonello Calabrò, Francesca Lonetti(✉), and Eda Marchetti

ISTI-CNR, 56124 Pisa, Italy
{antonello.calabro,francesca.lonetti,eda.marchetti}@isti.cnr.it

Abstract. Testing access control policies relies on their execution on a security engine and the evaluation of the correct responses. Coverage measures can be adopted to know which parts of the policy are most exercised. This paper proposes an access control infrastructure for enabling the coverage criterion selection, the monitoring of the policy execution and the analysis of the policy coverage assessment. The framework is independent from the policy specification language and does not require the instrumentation of the evaluation engine. We show an instantiation of the proposed infrastructure for assessing the XACML policy testing.

1 Introduction

Nowadays, the criticality and the importance of ruling the access and the usage of the different distributed resources is becoming a stringent need. Episodes in which the cloud private profiles have been violated and personal data distributed[1], are unfortunately a more frequent part of our daily-news. Security problems motivate the research and industry to find solutions for data protection that involve the improvement of the security mechanisms and the policy specification. Security testing and assessment has also gained a lot of attention in order to avoid security flaws and violations inside the systems or applications. Indeed, as detailed more in the rest of this paper, policy-based testing is the process to ensure the correctness of policy specifications and implementations. By observing the execution of a policy implementation with a test input (i.e., an access request), the testers may identify faults in policy specifications or implementations, and validate whether the corresponding output (i.e., an access decision) is as intended. However, most of the test cases generation approaches available in literature for access control policies are based on combinatorial methodologies [3,11,16], thus the generated number of test cases can rapidly grow to cope with the policy complexity. Considering the strict constraints on testing budget, it is extremely important to focus the testing activity in the generation or selection of the test cases that cover the most important features and/or policy constructs. The purpose is to reduce as much as possible the number of tests to be executed

---

[1] http://edition.cnn.com/2014/10/02/showbiz/celebrity-news-gossip/nude-celeb-photos-google-hack/.

© Springer International Publishing AG 2017
S. Tonetta et al. (Eds.): SAFECOMP 2017 Workshops, LNCS 10489, pp. 373–383, 2017.
DOI: 10.1007/978-3-319-66284-8_31

trying, from one side, to maximize the fault detection effectiveness, and from the other, to cover the most important elements/aspects defined into the policy itself. In this paper, we focus on the testing of the access control policies and in particular on the coverage assessment of the derived test suites. In literature, the available coverage facilities are divided into two groups: those that are embedded in the execution engine such as [8,14] and those that can be integrated into the execution framework as an additional component such for instance [1,7]. Both the solutions have specific advantages. For sure, an embedded solution reduces the performance delay of the execution framework. The main disadvantage of these last approaches is the lack of flexibility both in the data collection, coverage measures definition and language adopted. Moreover, any change requires to redesign or improve the execution engine itself, preventing in such manner the possibility of dynamic modification.

In this paper, we would like to overcome the above mentioned issues by proposing a solution through which the implementation of the access policy can be made more transparent for coverage purposes, while maintaining the flexibility and access control language independency. The proposed access control policy infrastructure is based on an external monitoring facility and enables language independent coverage measurements. The basic behavior of the proposed infrastructure consists into the derivation of the relevant coverage information from the policy specification, the collection of events during the policy execution by means of a monitoring facility, and the analysis of them so to assess the coverage level reached by a test strategy. Additionally, some corrective actions could be triggered in case of violations or problems without modifying the structure of the policy execution engine, enabling to dynamically update or modify the policy when necessary. The type of data to be collected during the execution is independently specified by the execution engine and is not linked to the specific notation used for the policy specification.

The contribution of this paper can be summarized into: (i) the integration for the first time of a monitoring framework into an access control system architecture; (ii) the definition of the architecture of the Policy Assessment Infrastructure enabling the coverage criterion selection, the policy analysis, the monitoring of the policy execution, and the policy coverage assessment; (iii) an instantiation of the proposed architecture on the XACML access control language.

The remainder of this paper is structured as follows: Sect. 2 introduces the basic concepts of access control systems and coverage testing; Sect. 3 presents the architecture of the Policy Assessment Infrastructure; Sect. 4 presents an instantiation of the proposed infrastructure on the XACML context; finally, Sect. 5 concludes the paper also hinting at future work.

2   Basic Concepts

Access control is one of the most adopted security mechanisms for the protection of resources and data against unauthorized, malicious or improper usage or modification. It is based on the implementation of access control policies expressed by a specific standard such for instance the wildly adopted eXtensible Access Control Markup Language (XACML) [15]. The recent approaches for testing access control systems can be classified into [9]: (i) Policy testing which includes fault models and mutation based proposals [4], testing criteria based on structural coverage [2,6] and proposals exploiting the access control policies structure [3,11]; (ii) testing the policy enforcement to discover its possible security vulnerability [9,14]; (iii) testing the evaluation engine by means of model-based approach [5,7] or combination of access control policies values [3].

In this paper, we focus on the testing of the access control policies and in particular on the coverage assessment of the derived test suite. Here below some basic concepts about the XACML-based access control system and the coverage testing used for the specific instantiation of the proposed Policy Assessment Infrastructure presented in Sect. 4.

XACML [15] is a platform-independent XML-based language for the specification of access control policies. Briefly, an XACML policy has a tree structure whose main elements are: PolicySet, Policy, Rule, Target and Condition. The PolicySet includes one or more policies. A Policy contains a Target and one or more rules. The Target specifies a set of constraints on attributes of a given request. The Rule specifies a Target and a Condition containing one or more boolean functions. If the Condition evaluates to true, then the Rule's Effect (a value of Permit or Deny) is returned, otherwise a NotApplicable decision is formulated (Indeterminate is returned in case of errors). The PolicyCombiningAlgorithm and the RuleCombiningAlgorithm define how to combine the results from multiple policies and rules respectively in order to derive a single access result.

The main components of an XACML based access control system are shown in Fig. 1: the Policy Administration Point (PAP) is the system entity in charge of managing the policies; the Policy Enforcement Point (PEP), usually embedded into an application system, receives the access request in its native format, constructs an XACML request and sends it to the Policy Decision Point (PDP); the Policy Information Point (PIP) provides the PDP with the values of subject, resource, action and environment attributes; the PDP evaluates the policy against the request and returns the response, including the authorization decision to the PEP.

Measurement of test quality is one of the key issues in software testing and coverage measures represent an effective mean for evaluating the different testing approaches. Adequacy criteria evaluate the testing strategy through the percentage of exercised set of elements in the program or in the specification. Usually, test coverage can be used for different purposes: (i) improve the test suite so to exercise elements that have not been tested; (ii) test suite augmentation and test suite minimization in case of regression testing; (iii) test cases selection, prioritization and test suite effectiveness evaluation. A systematic review of coverage based testing is presented in [17]. Many proposals for test coverage measurement and analysis, embedded directly in the evaluation engine, have been proposed depending on the adopted policy specification language. Considering

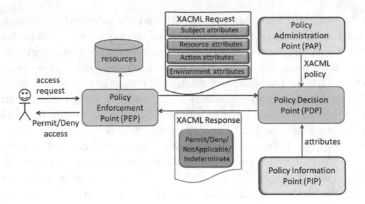

Fig. 1. Access control system architecture

in particular the XACML context, in [6,12] the authors propose PDP embedded solutions for coverage analysis and selection, while [10] focuses on regression test selection techniques.

3   Coverage Testing Framework

In this section, we propose a possible architecture of Policy Assessment Infrastructure based on an on-line monitor. The proposal has been conceived to be independent from the language adopted for the policy specification and flexible enough to be adapted to the different testing purposes. In particular, Fig. 2 (part A) shows the main components of the proposed Policy Assessment Infrastructure (top left component), referring to a generic structure of an access control system (top right component):

- *Test case generator* is in charge of test cases generation starting from the policy specification. In literature, depending on the access policy language there are several proposals such for instance XCREATE [3] and Targen [11] focused on XACML-based combinatorial approaches;
- *Test case executor* takes in input the test suite derived by the *Test case generator*, and sends one by one the test cases to the *Policy executor engine*. Moreover, it extracts the required information by each test case and transforms them into events readable by the *Monitor infrastructure*.
- *Trace generator* is in charge of implementing the different policy coverage criteria. It takes in input the policy from the *Policy Administration Point* and, according to the selected coverage criterion, derives all the possible policy traces. Usually, the traces extraction is realized by an optimized unfolding algorithm that exploits the policy language structure. Intuitively, the main goal is to derive an acyclic graph, defining a partial order on policy elements. Several proposals are available such as [6,12] for XACML policy specification. Once extracted, the traces are provided to the *Monitor infrastructure*.

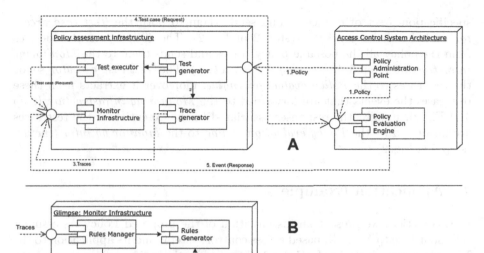

Fig. 2. Policy Assessment Infrastructure

- *Policy evaluation engine* is in charge of the execution of the policy and the derivation of the associated response. It communicates with the *Monitoring infrastructure* though a dedicated interface such as a REST one.
- *Monitoring infrastructure* is in charge of collecting data of interest during the run-time policy execution. There can be different solutions for monitoring activity. In this paper, we rely on Glimpse [1] infrastructure which has the peculiarity of decoupling the events specification from their collection and processing. As detailed in Fig. 2 (part B), the main components of Glimpse are: (i) *Complex Events Processor (CEP)* which analyzes the events and correlates them to infer more complex events; (ii) *Response Dispatcher* keeps track of the monitoring requests and sends back the final coverage evaluation; (iii)*Rules Generator* generates the rules using the templates stored into the *Rules Template Repository* starting from the derived policy traces to be monitored. A generic rule consists of two main parts: the events to be matched and the constraints to be verified, and the events/actions to be notified after the rule evaluation; (iv) *Rules Template Repository* stores predetermined rules templates that will be instantiated by the *Rules Generator* when needed; (v) *Rules Manager* instructes the CEP by loading and unloading the set of rules. We refer to [1] for a more detailed description of the Glimpse architecture.

In a typical workflow of the proposed framework, the *Policy Administration Point* sends the policy both to the *Test case generator* and the *Policy evaluation engine* (step 1 of Fig. 2). The *Test case generator* derives from the policy specification a set of test cases and sends them to both the *Test case execu-tor* and the *Trace generator* (step 2 of Fig. 2). The *Trace generator* derives from the policy all the possible policy traces and sends them to the *Monitoring infrastructure* (step 3 *Monitoring infrastructure*). The *Test case executor* sends the test cases to the *Policy evaluation engine*, moreover it extracts from these test cases the events that are forwarded to the *Monitoring infrastructure* (step 4 of Fig. 2). Finally, the responses associated to the execution of the test cases are forwarded by the *Policy evaluation engine* to the *Monitoring infrastructure* (step 5 of Fig. 2).

4   Application Example

In this section, we present an instantiation of the proposed Policy Assessment Infrastructure to XACML based access control systems and its application to the XACML policy showed in Listing 1.1. Specifically, the policy defines the accesses to a library. It includes a policy set target (line 3) that is empty; a policy target (lines 5–12) allowing the access only to the *books* resource; a first rule (*ruleA*) (lines 13–30) with a target (lines 14–29) specifying that this rule applies only to the access requests of a *read* action of *books* resource with any environment; a second rule (*ruleB*)(lines 31–46), which effect is *Deny* when the subject is "Julius", the action is "write", the resource and environment are any resource and any environment respectively; a third rule (*ruleC*) (lines 47–69) that allows subject "Julius" the action "write", if he is also "professor" or "administrator"; finally, the default rule (line 70) denies the access in the other cases.

The *Test cases generator* has been implemented by X-CREATE tool [3] using the available *Simple-Combinatorial* test generation strategy. Specifically, it derives an XACML request for each of the possible combinations of the sub-ject, resource, action and environment values taken from the policy and some additional requests containing random values. Listing 1.2 shows an example of a request generated by *Simple-Combinatorial* strategy: the subject *Julius* wants to *write* the *books* resource. Each generated XACML request is then transformed into an event by the *Test case executor* and sent to the *Monitor infrastructure*. The *Trace generator* has been implemented using the *XACML smart coverage* approach presented in [6] which focuses on the policy rules coverage. Briefly, the criterion computes the *Rule Target Set*, i.e., the union of the target of the rule, and all enclosing policy and policy sets targets. The main idea is that in order to match the rule target, the requests must first match the enclosing pol-icy and policy sets targets. For instance, the *Rule Target Sets* of Listing 1.1 are presented in Table 1. We refer to [6] for the definition of the *XACML smart coverage* criterion. Each *Rule Target Set* is sent to the *Monitoring Infrastructure* as a event. The *Policy evaluation engine* is instantiated with the XACML Sun' Policy Decision Point (PDP) [13] which executes the XACML requests against the XACML policy and sends the corresponding XACML responses to the *Mon-itor infrastructure*. The *Monitor infrastructure* observes the on-line execution of the XACML policy on the PDP, and, according to the values of the requests, the responses and the set of traces generated from the XACML policy, assesses the coverage of the XACML requests on the traces.

Table 1. *Rule Target Sets* of Listing 1.1

$T_1 = \{(\emptyset, \emptyset, \emptyset, \emptyset), (\emptyset, \{books\}, \emptyset, \emptyset),(\emptyset, \{books\}, \{read\}, \emptyset), Permit\}$
$T_2 = \{(\emptyset, \emptyset, \emptyset, \emptyset), (\emptyset, \{books\}, \emptyset, \emptyset),(\{Julius\}, \{books\}, \{write\}, \emptyset), Deny\}$
$T_3 = \{(\emptyset, \emptyset, \emptyset, \emptyset), (\emptyset, \{books\}, \emptyset, \emptyset),(\{Julius, professor\}, \{books\}, \{write\}, \emptyset), Permit\}$
$T_4 = \{(\emptyset, \emptyset, \emptyset, \emptyset), (\emptyset, \{books\}, \emptyset, \emptyset),(\{Julius, administrator\}, \{books\}, \{write\}, \emptyset), Permit\}$
$T_5 = \{(\emptyset, \emptyset, \emptyset, \emptyset), (\emptyset, \{books\}, \emptyset, \emptyset),(\emptyset, \emptyset, \emptyset, \emptyset), Deny\}$

As an example, in Listings 1.3 there is a rule definition for trace T_3 of Table 1. The monitor infrastructure extracts from the payload of the event *Glimpse-BaseEventRequest* the field data that contains the values for the (*Subjects, Resources, Actions, Environments*) and checks if they are included in the sets of *policySet, policy* and *rules* target values of the trace T_3 (lines [21–37]). If this is verified the monitoring infrastructure extracts from the same trace the *Response* value and checks whether it is equal to the corresponding PDP response (line 43). If this is true the trace is considered covered (line 49).

In this application example, we executed the XACML policy of Listing 1.1 with all the requests generated by the *Simple-Combinatorial* strategy and we reached a coverage of 60% (only T_1, T_2, T_5 were covered). Specifically, the request of Listing 1.2 is able to cover T_2 trace. Similarly, other requests having *read* as action, *books* as resource and any value for subject are able to cover T_1 trace; whereas requests having any subject, action, resource, and environment are able to cover T_5 trace. From the analysis of the coverage assessment results, it was evident that, by construction, the test suite derived from *Simple-Combinatorial* strategy can only cover traces including only one subject, resource, action and environment value. The coverage of traces T_3 and T_4 requires XACML requests having more than one subject, resource, action and environment values because the effect of the corresponding XACML policy rule (*Rule C*) is simultaneously dependent on more than one constraint.

This simple experiment evidences that the *Simple-Combinatorial* strategy is not effective enough to reach 100% coverage of the traces and should be enriched. By the identification of not covered traces, the Policy Assessment infrastructure provides important hints to testers and can guide them in the generation of ad hoc test cases or selection of more effective test strategies.

```
1    <PolicySet PolicySetId=''policySetExample''
2    PolicyCombiningAlgId=''first-applicable''>
3      <Target/>
4      <Policy PolicyId=''policyExample'' RuleCombiningAlgId=''first-applicable''>
5        <Target>
6          <Resource>
7            <ResourceMatch MatchId=''anyURI-equal''>
8              <AttributeValue DataType=''anyURI''>books</AttributeValue>
9              <ResourceAttributeDesignator AttributeId=''resource-id'' DataType=''anyURI''/>
10           </ResourceMatch>
11         </Resource>
```

```
12    </Target>
13    <Rule RuleId=''ruleA'' Effect=''Permit''>
14     <Target>
15      <Resources>
16       <Resource>
17        <ResourceMatch MatchId=''anyURI-equal''>
18         <AttributeValue DataType=''anyURI''>books</AttributeValue>
19         <ResourceAttributeDesignator AttributeId=''resource-id'' DataType=''anyURI''/>
20        </ResourceMatch>
21       </Resource>
22      </Resources>
23      <Actions><Action>
24       <ActionMatch MatchId=''string-equal''>
25        <AttributeValue DataType=''string''>read</AttributeValue>
26        <ActionAttributeDesignator AttributeId=''action-id'' DataType=''string''/>
27       </ActionMatch>
28      </Action></Actions>
29     </Target>
30    </Rule>
31    <Rule RuleId=''ruleB'' Effect=''Deny''>
32     <Target>
33      <Subjects><Subject>
34       <SubjectMatch MatchId=''string-equal''>
35        <AttributeValue DataType=''string''>Julius</AttributeValue>
36        <SubjectAttributeDesignator AttributeId=''subject-id'' DataType=''string''/>
37       </SubjectMatch>
38      </Subject></Subjects>
39      <Actions><Action>
40       <ActionMatch MatchId=''string-equal''>
41        <AttributeValue DataType=''string''>write</AttributeValue>
42        <ActionAttributeDesignator AttributeId=''action-id'' DataType=''string''/>
43       </ActionMatch>
44      </Action></Actions>
45     </Target>
46    </Rule>
47    <Rule RuleId=''ruleC'' Effect=''Permit''>
48     <Target>
49      <Subjects><Subject>
50       <SubjectMatch MatchId=''string-equal''>
51        <AttributeValue DataType=''string''>Julius</AttributeValue>
52        <SubjectAttributeDesignator AttributeId=''subject-id'' DataType=''string''/>
53       </SubjectMatch>
54      </Subject></Subjects>
55      <Actions><Action>
56       <ActionMatch MatchId=''string-equal''>
57        <AttributeValue DataType=''string''>write</AttributeValue>
58        <ActionAttributeDesignator AttributeId=''action-id'' DataType=''string''/>
59       </ActionMatch>
60      </Action></Actions>
61     </Target>
62     <Condition FunctionId=''string-at-least-one-member-of''>
63      <SubjectAttributeDesignator SubjectCategory=''access-subject'' AttributeId=''Role
                '' DataType=''string''/>
64      <Apply FunctionId=''string-bag''>
65       <AttributeValue DataType=''string''>professor</AttributeValue>
66       <AttributeValue DataType=''string''>administrator</AttributeValue>
67      </Apply>
68     </Condition>
69    </Rule>
70    <Rule RuleId=''ruleD'' Effect=''Deny''/>
71   </Policy>
72  </PolicySet>
```

Listing 1.1. An XACML policy

```
1   <Request xmlns=''urn:oasis:names:tc:xacml:2.0:context:schema:os''>
2    <Subject>
3     <Attribute AttributeId=''subject-id1'' DataType=''string''>
4      <AttributeValue>Julius</AttributeValue>
5     </Attribute>
6    </Subject>
7    <Resource>
8     <Attribute AttributeId=''resource-id'' DataType=''string''>
9      <AttributeValue>books</AttributeValue>
10    </Attribute>
11   </Resource>
12   <Action>
13    <Attribute AttributeId=''action-id'' DataType=''string''>
14     <AttributeValue>write</AttributeValue>
15    </Attribute>
16   </Action>
17   <Environment/>
18  </Request>
```

Listing 1.2. An XACML request

```
1   import it.cnr.isti.labsedc.glimpse.event.GlimpseBaseEventAbstract;
2   import it.cnr.isti.labsedc.glimpse.event.GlimpseBaseEventRequest;
3   import it.cnr.isti.labsedc.glimpse.event.GlimpseBaseEventPdpResponse;
4   import it.cnr.isti.labsedc.glimpse.engine.xacml.TraceEngine;
5   import it.cnr.isti.labsedc.glimpse.utils.Notifier;
6
7   declare GlimpseBaseEventAbstract
8       @role( event )
9       @timestamp( timeStamp )
10  end
11
12  rule ''policySetExampleRule''
13      no-loop true
14      salience 20
15      dialect ''java''
16  when
17      $aEvent : GlimpseBaseEventRequest(
18          this.isConsumed == false,
19          this.isException == false,
20
21      //policySetCheck
22          this.data.getSubjectsSection().areValidForPolicySetOfTrace(''T3''),
23          this.data.getResourcesSection().areValidForPolicySetOfTrace(''T3''),
24          this.data.getActionSection().areValidForPolicySetOfTrace(''T3''),
25          this.data.getEnvironmentSection().areValidForPolicySetOfTrace(''T3''),
26
27      //policyCheck
28          this.data.getSubjectsSection().areValidForPolicyOfTrace(''T3''),
29          this.data.getResourcesSection().areValidForPolicyOfTrace(''T3''),
30          this.data.getActionSection().areValidForPolicyOfTrace(''T3''),
31          this.data.getEnvironmentSection().areValidForPolicyOfTrace(''T3''),
32
33      //rulesCheck
34          this.data.getSubjectsSection().areValidForRulesOfTrace(''T3''),
35          this.data.getResourcesSection().areValidForRulesOfTrace(''T3''),
36          this.data.getActionSection().areValidForRulesOfTrace(''T3'')),
37          this.data.getEnvironmentSection().areValidForRulesOfTrace(''T3''));
38
39      $bEvent : GlimpseBaseEventPdpResponse(
40          this.isConsumed == false,
41          this.isException == false,
42          this.data.getId().compareTo($aEvent.getId().toString())) == 0,
43          this.data.getResponse.compareTo(TraceEngine.getTraceResponse(''T3'')) == 0,
44          this after $aEvent);
45
46  then
```

```
47        $aEvent.setConsumed(true);
48        $bEvent.setConsumed(true);
49        Notifier.setPolicyMatch($aEvent.data.getId(), ''T3'');
50        update($aEvent);
51        retract($aEvent);
52        update($bEvent);
53        retract($bEvent);
54   end
```

Listing 1.3. Monitoring rule

5   Discussion and Conclusions

In this paper, we presented an access control infrastructure for enabling the coverage criterion selection, the monitoring of the policy execution and the analysis of the policy coverage assessment. We provided an instantiation inside the XACML-based access control systems. The preliminary obtained results showed the effectiveness of the proposed infrastructure in evaluating the coverage of an XACML policy. Moreover, traces analysis highlighted weaknesses in the test suite and provided hints for the generation of ad-hoc test cases.

The application of the proposed access control infrastructure is not limited to the coverage policy assessment as shown in this paper, but can be used to detect on-line criticalities of the policy execution. Indeed, the monitoring infrastructure is able to detect some inconsistencies between the responses belonging to the not covered traces and the corresponding PDP 'responses. These inconsistencies could evidence potential flaws either in the policy specification or in its implementation. Moreover, the proposed access control infrastructure could be used in real word environments for profiling the resource usage and the user behaviors. This could be a very important starting point for identifying the most critical policy traces and improving their security enforcement.

Concerning threats to validity of the presented experiment, three aspects can be considered: the test case generation, the traces generation and the policy evaluation. Indeed, the tools adopted and the algorithms implemented may have influenced the reported results. It could be that different choices might have provided different effectiveness results.

We are currently working to include in the access control infrastructure more coverage criteria. We plan also to enhance the monitor infrastructure with facilities for proactively detecting, by the off-line trace analysis, possible security inconsistencies of the tested access control policy. Other future work deals with the instantiation of the proposed infrastructure by considering different access and usage control policy specification languages.

Acknowledgements. This work has been partially supported by the GAUSS national research project (MIUR, PRIN 2015, Contract 2015KWREMX).

References

1. Bertolino, A., Calabrò, A., Lonetti, F., Di Marco, A., Sabetta, A.: Towards a model-driven infrastructure for runtime monitoring. In: Troubitsyna, E.A. (ed.) SERENE 2011. LNCS, vol. 6968, pp. 130–144. Springer, Heidelberg (2011). doi:10.1007/978-3-642-24124-6_13
2. Bertolino, A., Daoudagh, S., El Kateb, D., Henard, C., Le Traon, Y., Lonetti, F., Marchetti, E., Mouelhi, T., Papadakis, M.: Similarity testing for access control. Inf. Softw. Technol. **58**, 355–372 (2015)
3. Bertolino, A., Daoudagh, S., Lonetti, F., Marchetti, E.: Automatic XACML requests generation for policy testing. In: Proceedings of ICST, pp. 842–849. IEEE (2012)
4. Bertolino, A., Daoudagh, S., Lonetti, F., Marchetti, E.: Xacmut: Xacml 2.0 mutants generator. In: Proceedings of ICST Workshops, pp. 28–33 (2013)
5. Bertolino, A., Daoudagh, S., Lonetti, F., Marchetti, E., Martinelli, F., Mori, P.: Testing of polpa-based usage control systems. Software Qual. J. **22**(2), 241–271 (2014)
6. Bertolino, A., Le Traon, Y., Lonetti, F., Marchetti, E., Mouelhi, T.: Coverage-based test cases selection for xacml policies. In: Proceedings of ICST Workshops, pp. 12–21 (2014)
7. Carvallo, P., Cavalli, A.R., Mallouli, W., Rios, E.: Multi-cloud applications security monitoring. In: Au, M.H.A., Castiglione, A., Choo, K.-K.R., Palmieri, F., Li, K.-C. (eds.) GPC 2017. LNCS, vol. 10232, pp. 748–758. Springer, Cham (2017). doi:10.1007/978-3-319-57186-7_54
8. Daoudagh, S., Lonetti, F., Marchetti, E.: Assessment of access control systems using mutation testing. In: Proceedings of TELERISE, pp. 8–13 (2015)
9. Felderer, M., Büchler, M., Johns, M., Brucker, A.D., Breu, R., Pretschner, A.: Chapter one-security testing: a survey. Adv. Comput. **101**, 1–51 (2016)
10. Hwang, J., Xie, T., El Kateb, D., Mouelhi, T., Le Traon, Y.: Selection of regression system tests for security policy evolution. In: Proceedings of ASE, pp. 266–269 (2012)
11. Martin, E.: Automated test generation for access control policies. In: Proceedings of OOPSLA, pp. 752–753 (2006)
12. Martin, E., Xie, T., Yu, T.: Defining and measuring policy coverage in testing access control policies. In: Ning, P., Qing, S., Li, N. (eds.) ICICS 2006. LNCS, vol. 4307, pp. 139–158. Springer, Heidelberg (2006). doi:10.1007/11935308_11
13. Microsystems, S.: Sun's XACML implementation (2006)
14. Mouelhi, T., El Kateb, D., Le Traon, Y.: Chapter five-inroads in testing access control. Adv. Comput. **99**, 195–222 (2015)
15. OASIS: extensible access control markup language (XACML) version 2.0 (2005)
16. Pretschner, A., Mouelhi, T., Le Traon, Y.: Model-based tests for access control policies. In: Proceedings of ICST, pp. 338–347 (2008)
17. Shahid, M., Ibrahim, S., Mahrin, M.N.: A study on test coverage in software testing. Advanced Informatics School (2011)

Try Walking in My Shoes, if You Can: Accurate Gait Recognition Through Deep Learning

Giacomo Giorgi, Fabio Martinelli, Andrea Saracino$^{(\boxtimes)}$,
and Mina Sheikhalishahi

Istituto di Informatica e Telematica, Consiglio Nazionale Delle Ricerche, Pisa, Italy
{Giacomo.Giorgi,Fabio.Martinelli,Andrea.Saracino,
Mina.Sheikhalishahi}@iit.cnr.it

Abstract. Human gait seamless continuous authentication, based on wearable accelerometers, is a novel biometric instrument which can be exploited to identify the user of mobile and wearable devices. In this paper, we present a study on recognition of user identity, by analysis of gait data, collected through body inertial sensors from 175 different users. The mechanism used for identity recognition is based on deep learning machinery, specifically on a convolutional network, trained with readings from different sensors, and on filtering and buffering mechanism to increase the accuracy. Results show a very high accuracy in both recognizing known and unknown identities.

1 Introduction

Wearable technology is advancing at a fast pace, with a large interest in industrial and research world. More and more additional computing capacity and sensors are incorporated into smartphones, tablets, (smart) watches, but also shoes, clothes, and other wearable items. These enhanced objects act as enablers of pervasive computing [1], collecting data used to provide additional smart services to their users.

Several of these smart devices come equipped with built-in accelerometers and gyroscopes, which can be exploited to register the body motion of users, which inspired the research interest in using the motion characters of human body for various tasks, spanning from clinical condition monitoring [2], action or gesture categorization [3], to user authentication and identity recognition.

In particular, accelerometer-based identity recognition with the use of body motion seems a promising technique in preventing the misuse of smart devices and the systems linked with them, by ensuring that the device functionalities are not available to other persons different from the owner. However, the majority of current solutions for sensor based authentication, are mainly based on active behavioral mechanisms, which require direct user interaction [4], having thus limited advantages compared to classical authentication mechanisms, such as PIN, passwords, or finger pattern recognition.

S. Tonetta et al. (Eds.): SAFECOMP 2017 Workshops, LNCS 10489, pp. 384–395, 2017.
DOI: 10.1007/978-3-319-66284-8_32

Considering that each individual person has a unique manner of walking, *gait* can be interpreted as a biometric trait and consequently, the aforementioned inertial sensors have great potential to play an important role in the field of biometry [5]. If correctly exploited, the gait can be used as a method for seamless continuous authentication, able to authenticate users of wearable devices continuously during time, without requiring any active interaction.

In this paper, we present a study on gait analysis for identity recognition based on inertial sensors and deep learning classification. The presented methodology exploits a public dataset [6] collected on a set of 175 users through five body sensors, presenting the design and implementation of a convolutional neural network for deep learning-based classification. Moreover, it will be detailed the techniques used to filter and augment data for improving the dataset quality, together with the sampling techniques used to improve classification accuracy. Through experimental evaluation, we show the effectiveness of the methodology in recognizing single user on which the convolutional network has been trained on and also the ability of the presented system to understand if the monitored gait belongs to an unknown person. The results show an accuracy close to 1, demonstrating the feasibility of the presented approach as a methodology for seamless continuous authentication, which can be exploited by mobile and wearable smart devices.

The rest of the paper is organized as follows: Sect. 2 reports background notions on the gait analysis and on deep learning. Section 3 describes the presented framework, the used dataset and the design of the convolutional neural network. Section 4 reports the classification results and describes the sampling methodology in operative phase for improved accuracy. Section 5 lists some related work. Finally Sect. 6 briefly concludes proposing some future directions.

2 Background Knowledge

In this section we present some background notions exploited in the present work.

2.1 Gait Analysis

Gait is the motion of human walking, whose movements can be faithfully reflected by the acceleration of the body sections [6]. Human gait recognition has been recognized as a biometric technique to label, describe, and determine the identity of individuals based on their distinctive manners of walking [7]. Basically, due to the fact that walking is a daily activity, human gait can be measured, as a user identity recognition technique, in daily life without explicitly asking the users to walk. This fact distinguishes gait from other accelerometer measurable actions, like gestures, as well as other commonly used biometrics, such as fingerprints, signatures, and face photos, whose data collection usually interrupts the users from normal activities for explicit participation [6]. Moreover, since portable or wearable accelerometers are able to monitor gait continuously during arbitrary time period, accelerometer-based gait recognition would be especially great tool in continuous identity verification [8].

2.2 Deep Learning

A neural network is a class of machine learning algorithms, in which a collection of *neurons* are connected with a set of *synapses*. The collection is designed in three main parts: the input layer, the hidden layer, and the output layer. In the case that neural network has multiple hidden layers, it is called *deep* learning. Hidden layers are generally helpful when neural network is designed to detect complicated patterns, from contextual, to non obvious, like image or signal recognition. Synapses take the input and multiply it by a weight, where it represents the strength of the input in determining the output [9]. The output data will be a number in a range like 0 and 1.

In forward propagation, a set of weights is applied to the input data and then an output is calculated. In back propagation, the margin of error of the output is measured and then the weights accordingly are adjusted to decrease the error. Neural networks repeat both forward and back propagation until the weights are calibrated to accurately predict an output [9].

3   Framework

In what follows, we present in detail the process of user identification through wearable accelerometer devices, with the use of deep convolutional neural network.

3.1   Dataset Description

In this study, we utilize the publicly available dataset provided in [10]. This dataset contains the gait acceleration series of records collected from 175 subjects. Out of these 175 series, we use the records of 153 subjects, which are reported in two sessions, such that the first session represents the first time that data has been collected, while the second session shows the second time that the data has been recorded. The time intervals between first and second data acquisition varies from one week to six months, for different subjects. For each subject, six records are presented in each session, where every record contains 5 gait acceleration series simultaneously measured at the right wrist, left upper arm, right side of pelvis, left thigh, and right ankle, respectively as we can see in Fig. 1.

Fig. 1. Sensors considered on the body

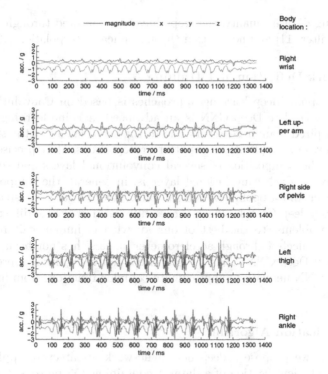

Fig. 2. Acceleration series of a gait record

The acceleration readings have been measured at 100 Hz in straightly walks, through a level floor of 20 m length. The raw data for each recording are composed by the x, y and z acceleration series during time. Figure 2 reports the single readings in the time domain done on each axis for each accelerometer sensor, as specified on the right hand side of the picture.

3.2 Data Processing

The data processing part can be summarized in three main steps, namely *cycles extraction*, *filtering*, and *normalization*, respectively.

Cycles Extraction. The *gait cycle* is used to simplify the representation of complex pattern of human walking. It starts with initial contact of the right hell and it continues until the right hell contacts the ground again. When the hell touches the ground, the association between the ground reaction force and inertial force, together make the $z - axis$ signal strongly to change, which forms peaks with the high magnitude. Those peak points are utilized to identify the gait cycles. The ZJU dataset provides the manual annotations of the step cycles of each gait record. Each gait cycle differs in terms of duration, due to the different speed which varies during walking, but not in shape. In ZJU dataset, the majority of cycles have lengths between 90 and 118. For reducing noise and improving dataset quality, the steps have been filtered through a low pass *butterworth* filter [11] and normalized through linear interpolation [12].

3.3   Network Definition and Training

One of the popular deep learning approaches is based on Convolution Neural Networks (CNN). The Deep CNN is an advanced machine learning technique which has inspired many researchers due to the achievement in the state of the art results in several applications of pattern recognitions. More precisely, a CNN is defined as the composition of several convolutional layers and several fully connected layers. Each convolutional layer is, in general, the composition of a non-linear layer and a pooling or sub-sampling layer to get some spatial invariance. Although deep CNN has been successfully used in several difficult pattern recognition problems, to the best of our knowledge, human gait recognition, when data is collected through accelerometer signals, has not been recognized with the use of Deep CNN. Thus, we propose a gait recognition approach based on a specific CNN network to approximate complex functions from high dimensional signals.

3.4   Identification Algorithm

In this paper, we propose a deep neural network architecture applied to the problem of gait identification of a dataset containing 153 persons. Given a gait cycle, the task is to determine to which person the cycle belongs. Our network architecture has been shown in Fig. 4. The network consists of the following layers: two layers of convolution, followed by a single max pooling and two fully connected layer followed by a softmax layer used to estimate the belonging class.

For the input layer, the different signals filtered and normalized belonging to each sensor are stacked in order to a matrix of dimension 15×118, in which each group of three rows correspond respectively to the x, y and z axes of a single sensor. 118 is the length of the normalized cycles.

The first two layers of our network are convolution layers, which we use to compute higher-order features. As shown in Fig. 4, in the first convolution layer we pass the 2D input data of 15×118 through 128 learned filters of size (1×3) performing a 2D convolution on each single component of each sensor. This convolution is useful to extract the low level feature maintaining separated each component of each sensor. The resulting shape obtained after convolution is three-dimensional feature maps of size $12 \times 15 \times 61$.

In the second convolution the result obtained is passed to 512 convolutional filters of size (3×3) which perform a 2D convolution used to extract the mid level features combining the components within each sensor. $512 \times 5 \times 33$ is the resulting shape obtained. Each one of convolution layer are passed through a rectified linear unit (ReLu).

The second convolutional feature maps are passed through a max-pooling kernel that halves the width and height of features with filters of size (1×3). The functionality is to reduce the spatial size of the representation reducing the amount of parameters of the network (Fig. 3).

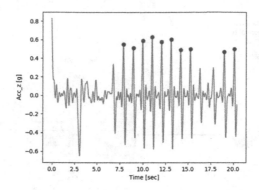

Fig. 3. Gait cycles of a walking record

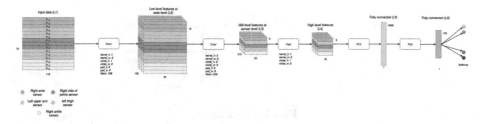

Fig. 4. Deep convolutional gait recognition network

Finally, we apply two fully connected layers: the first one uses 4096 nodes providing a feature vector of size 4096, these outputs are then passed to another fully connected layer containing 153 softmax units which represent the probability of similarity for each indentity to recognizes.

Training the Network. Our re-identification problem is posed as a classification problem. Training data are groups of accelerometer data labeled with the owner identity. The optimization objective is average loss over all the identities in the data set. As the data set can be quite large, in practice we use a stochastic approximation of this objective. Training data are randomly divided into mini-batches. The model performs forward propagation on the current mini-batch and computes the output and loss. Backpropagation is then used to compute the gradients on this batch, and network weights are updated. We perform stochastic gradient descent to perform weight updates. We start with a base learning rate of $\eta^{(0)} = 0.001$ and gradually decrease it as the training progresses using an inverse policy: $\eta^{(i)} = \eta^{(0)}(1 + \gamma \cdot i)^{-p}$. Where $\gamma = 10^{-4}$, $p = 0.75$, and i is the current mini-batch iteration. We use a momentum of $\mu = 0.9$ and weight decay $\lambda = 5 \cdot 10^{-4}$. With more passes over the training data, the model improves until it converges. We use a validation set to evaluate intermediate models and select the one that has maximum performance (Fig. 5).

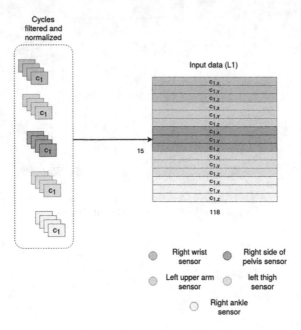

Fig. 5. Input layer

Data Augmentation. In order to improve the performance of the deep learning network and to prevent overfitting, we have artificially increase the number of training examples by data augmentation. Data augmentation is the application of one or more deformations applied to the labeled data without change the semantic meaning of the labels. In our case, the augmentation is produced varying each signal sample with translation drawn from a uniform distribution in the range $[-0.2, 0.2]$. As shown in Fig. 6 this process produces a copy of the original gait cycle different in values but with an equal semantic of the walking cycle.

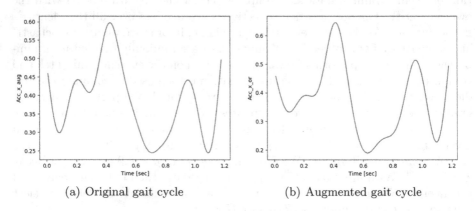

(a) Original gait cycle   (b) Augmented gait cycle

Fig. 6. Augmentation of a gait cycle

Starting from, approximately 95 gait cycles per identity, with augmentation we reach until 190 gait cycle per identity, passing from 14573 training data to 29146.

Network training converges in roughly 30 min without augmentation and 1 hour with augmentation on NVIDIA GTX1050 GPU.

4 Experiments

The classification framework has been implemented through the *Caffe* [13] deep learning framework. The experiments are conducted considering one single session of the walking records. The session has six different walking records for each one of the 153 identities belonging to the dataset. We used the first five records of each identity for training and the last record for testing. This setting is better suited for deep learning because it uses 84% of the data for training, 7295 training samples (about 47 gait cycle per identities), and roughly 16% for testing, 1465 testing samples. After the augmentation the number of training samples becomes 21885 (about 142 gait cycle per identities). We use a mini-batch size of 120 samples and train the network for 4000 iterations.

The Fig. 7 plots the re-identification accuracy of our model measured as the mean number of gaits recognized correctly for each identity in the first, second and third similarity results returned from the network. Our network reach 0.94% of accuracy in the most similar results returned without augmentation and the 0.95% with data augmentation.

In particular the graph shows the accuracy in correctly identifying the identity among the best (1NN), the two best matches (2NN) and the 3 best matches (3NN) extracted by the CNN. In the following only the 1NN case will be considered. It is worth noting the beneficial effect of augmentation for what concerns the accuracy.

Another important statistics to consider are the mean value and standard deviation of the probabilities of similarity related to the first result returned

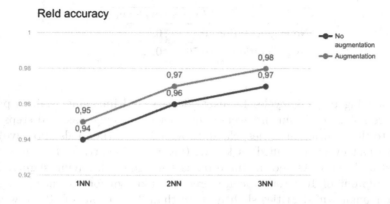

Fig. 7. Accuracy of reidentification.

by the network. We computed these values for the true positives (gait cycles identified correctly) $\overline{P_{T1NN}}$, and false positives (gait cycles identified incorrectly) $\overline{P_{F1NN}}$, in a test set composed by 153 known identities with 10 steps each one. The results are reported in Table 1.

Table 1. Similarity classification for known identities

	P_{T1NN}	$StDev_{T1NN}$	P_{F1NN}	$StDev_{F1NN}$
No augmentation	0.92	0.12	0.13	0.08
Augmentation	0.93	0.11	0.13	0.08

Hence, to correctly classify known identities, setting a probability threshold of 0.82, i.e. average similarity value with augmentation, minus the standard deviation, and filtering out all values lower than the threshold, grants an accuracy of 1 for the classification.

However, the CNN is only able to classify identities on which it has been trained on. Hence, if presented with a set of steps coming from an unknown identity, the CNN will try to match the new gait with a known one. However, we argue that is still possible exploiting the CNN to understand if a set of steps is belonging to an unknown identity rather than to a known one. It is worth noting that such a feature would be useful in the design of anti-theft applications for mobile and wearable devices. As shown in Table 2, the mean value of similarity for unknown identities is lower than the value for known ones, antecedently shown in Table 1. It is worth noting that in this case the overall accuracy is lower when augmentation is considered. This is because, the altered steps added through the augmentation procedure, increase the likelihood of generating steps which might be similar to the ones of the unknown identities.

Table 2. Similarity for unknown identities

	P_{F1NN}	$StDev_{F1NN}$
No augmentation	0.82	0.18
Augmentation	0.76	0.22

Considering ten gait cycles for each identity and imposing again a probability threshold, we obtain the average number of wrongly classified steps with respect to the known gait cycles, classified as unknown (i.e., False Positive) and unknown gait cycles classified as known (i.e. False Negative). The results are reported in Table 3. As shown, the error is quite limited, having slightly more than 1 step out of 10 wrongly considered as unknown for an known identity, whilst for unknown identities slightly more than 3 steps out of 10 are wrongly classified as known. Hence, having a sampling window of 10 steps and exploiting

Table 3. False Positives and False Negatives on ten gait cycles per identity

Threshold	FP	FN
0.93	1.02	3.27
0.95	1.11	2.93

a majority-based approach, is possible to filter away the classification error. It is also possible moving the error toward False Positive or False Negatives by changing the threshold value, in accordance to the application requirement.

5 Related Work

In [14], people are identified in video based on the way they walk (i.e. gait). To this end, convolutional neural networks (CNN) is applied for learning high-level descriptors from low-level motion features (i.e. optical flow components). The average accuracy of the result equals to 88.9%. Muramatsu et al. [15] authenticate a person through cross-view gait recognition which exploits a pair of gait image sequences with different observation views. In [16] a two-phase view-invariant multiscale gait recognition method (VI-MGR) is proposed which is robust to variation in clothing and presence of a carried item. In phase 1, VI-MGR uses the entropy of the limb region of a gait energy image (GEI) to determine the matching gallery view of the probe using 2-dimensional principal component analysis and Euclidean distance classifier. In phase 2, the probe subject is compared with the matching view of the gallery subjects using multiscale shape analysis. In [17], the three types of sensors, i.e. color sensors, such as a CCD camera, depth sensors, such as a Microsoft Kinect, or inertial sensors, such as an accelerometer, are combined for gait data collection and gait recognition, which can be used for important identification applications, such as identity recognition to access a restricted building or area. Being based on deep learning, the accuracy of our framework is increased if the training is performed with a larger and diverse dataset. However, real data collection could be an issue which also brings privacy concerns. In [18] a framework for privacy preserving collaborative data analysis is presented, which could be exploited by our framework to increase the accuracy, without violating users' privacy.

In [19] a new method for recognizing humans by their gait using back-propagation neural network. Here, the gait motion is described as rhythmic and periodic motion, and a 2D stick figure is extracted from gait silhouette by motion information with topological analysis guided by anatomical knowledge. A sequential set of 2D stick figures is used to represent the gait signature that is primitive data for the feature extraction based on motion parameters. Then, a back-propagation neural network algorithm is used to recognize humans by their gait patterns.

In [10], an accelerometer-based gait recognition, named *iGait*, is proposed. The core function of iGAIT is exploited to extract 31 features from acceleration data, including 6 spatio-temporal features, 7 regularity and symmetry features, and 18 spectral features. The proposed framework has been used to analyze the gait pattern of 15 control subjects, where a (HTC) phone was attached to the back of participants by belts. In each trial, participants walked 25 m along a hallway at their preferred walking speed. The first advantage of our approach comparing to what is proposed by Yang et al [10] is that deep-learning-based approaches learn features gradually. Hence, our methodology finds the most discriminating features through self training process. The second advantage is related to time needed to reach to 100% accuracy. In our approach 10 steps is enough to identify a person while in [10] 25 min walk is required. At the end, the proposed approach in [10] is evaluated through 15 subjects, whilst our technique is evaluated through 175 persons.

The accelerometer-based gait recognition approach proposed in [6] is evaluated on the same dataset we exploited in our experiments. In this work, Zhang et al. first addresses the problem of step-cycle detection which suffer from failures and intercycle phase misalignment. To this end, an algorithm is proposed which makes use of a type of salient points, named signature points (SPs). Experimental results on the equivalent dataset of our experiment shows rank-1 accuracy of 95.8% for identification and the error rate of 2.2 % for user verification. However, this accuracy is obtained on 14 steps, while in our proposed approach 100% is achieved in 10 steps.

6   Conclusion and Future Work

We have presented in this paper a preliminary study performed by means of deep learning classification, to identify people exploiting the gait collected through inertial sensors. The presented results show that this approach is promising in finding a tool for seamless continuous authentication of users for mobile and wearable devices. As future work, we plan to apply the proposed methodology on data collected through smartphones and smartwatches, also measuring the similarity with the data acquired from 2 out of the 5 sensors considered in this work.

Acknowledgements. This work has been partially funded by EU Funded projects H2020 C3ISP, GA #700294, H2020 NeCS, GA #675320 and EIT Digital HII on Trusted Cloud Management.

References

1. Wu, Z., Pan, G.: SmartShadow: Models and Methods for Pervasive Computing. Springer Publishing Company, Incorporated, Heidelberg (2013)
2. Ren, Y., Chen, Y., Chuah, M.C., Yang, J.: User verification leveraging gait recognition for smartphone enabled mobile healthcare systems. IEEE Trans. Mob. Comput. **14**(9), 1961–1974 (2015)

3. Bao, L., Intille, S.S.: Activity recognition from user-annotated acceleration data. In: Ferscha, A., Mattern, F. (eds.) Pervasive 2004. LNCS, vol. 3001, pp. 1–17. Springer, Heidelberg (2004). doi:10.1007/978-3-540-24646-6_1
4. Buriro, A., Crispo, B., Delfrari, F., Wrona, K.: Hold and sign: a novel behavioral biometrics for smartphone user authentication. In: 2016 IEEE Security and Privacy Workshops (SPW), pp. 276–285, May 2016
5. Sprager, S., Juric, M.B.: Inertial sensor-based gait recognition: a review. Sensors 15(9), 22089–22127 (2015)
6. Zhang, Y., Pan, G., Jia, K., Lu, M., Wang, Y., Wu, Z.: Accelerometer-based gait recognition by sparse representation of signature points with clusters. IEEE Trans. Cybern. 45(9), 1864–1875 (2015)
7. Alotaibi, M., Mahmood, A.: Improved gait recognition based on specialized deep convolutional neural networks. In: 2015 IEEE Applied Imagery Pattern Recognition Workshop (AIPR), pp. 1–7 (2015)
8. Gafurov, D., Bours, P., Snekkenes, E.: User authentication based on foot motion. SIViP 5(4), 457 (2011)
9. LeCun, Y., Bengio, Y., Hinton, G.: Deep learning. Nature 521(7553), 436–444 (2015)
10. Yang, M., Zheng, H., Wang, H., Mcclean, S., Newell, D.: iGAIT: an interactive accelerometer based gait analysis system. Comput. Methods Prog. Biomed. 108(2), 715–723 (2012)
11. van Vollenhoven, E., Reuver, H., Somer, J.: Transient response of butterworth filters. IEEE Trans. Circuit Theory 12(4), 624–626 (1965)
12. Coursey, C.K., Stuller, J.A.: Linear interpolation lattice. IEEE Trans. Sig. Process. 39(4), 965–967 (1991)
13. Jia, Y., Shelhamer, E., Donahue, J., Karayev, S., Long, J., Girshick, R.B., Guadarrama, S., Darrell, T.: Caffe: convolutional architecture for fast feature embedding. CoRR abs/1408.5093 (2014)
14. Castro, F.M., Marín-Jiménez, M.J., Guil, N., de la Blanca, N.P.: Automatic learning of gait signatures for people identification. CoRR abs/1603.01006 (2016)
15. Muramatsu, D., Makihara, Y., Yagi, Y.: View transformation model incorporating quality measures for cross-view gait recognition. IEEE Trans. Cybern. 46(7), 1602–1615 (2016)
16. Choudhury, S.D., Tjahjadi, T.: Robust view-invariant multiscale gait recognition. Pattern Recogn. 48(3), 798–811 (2015)
17. Zou, Q., Ni, L., Wang, Q., Li, Q., Wang, S.: Robust gait recognition by integrating inertial and RGBD sensors. CoRR abs/1610.09816 (2016)
18. Martinelli, F., Saracino, A., Sheikhalishahi, M.: Modeling privacy aware information sharing systems: a formal and general approach. In: 2016 IEEE Trustcom/BigDataSE/ISPA, Tianjin, China, pp. 767–774, 23–26 August 2016
19. Yoo, J.H., Hwang, D., Moon, K.Y., Nixon, M.S.: Automated human recognition by gait using neural network. In: Image Processing Theory, Tools and Applications, IPTA 2008, pp. 1–6 (2008)

Security Flows in OAuth 2.0 Framework: A Case Study

Marios Argyriou[1], Nicola Dragoni[1,2], and Angelo Spognardi[1,3(✉)]

[1] DTU Compute, Technical University of Denmark, Lyngby, Denmark
angsp@dtu.dk
[2] Centre for Applied Autonomous Sensor Systems, Örebro University,
Örebro, Sweden
[3] Dipartimento Informatica, Sapienza Università di Roma, Rome, Italy

Abstract. The burst in smartphone use, handy design in laptops and tablets as well as other smart products, like cars with the ability to drive you around, manifests the exponential growth of network usage and the demand of accessing remote data on a large variety of services. However, users notoriously struggle to maintain distinct accounts for every single service that they use. The solution to this problem is the use of a Single Sign On (SSO) framework, with a unified single account to authenticate user's identity throughout the different services. In April 2007, AOL introduced OpenAuth framework. After several revisions and despite its wide adoption, OpenAuth 2.0 has still several flaws that need to be fixed in several implementations. In this paper, we present a thorough review about both benefits of this single token authentication mechanism and its open flaws.

1 Introduction

The wide adoption of smart portable devices in our daily routine climbs to a new high pick every month. As a result of this growth, the demand of accessing remote data on several different services. However, users find it hard to maintain different accounts on every single service they use. The solution to this problem is the OpenAuth 2.0 framework, that makes use of a single account to identify users throughout the different services, without sharing or transferring passwords. In this way, users can access multiple web sites and services by maintaining a single account, a thing that boosts simplicity and efficiency. Users should only memorize the credential for a limited number of profile accounts, while their assets are secured by another entity.

The goal of this paper is to stress the security risks related to OAuth and explore potential fixes. The motivation of this paper is to raise security awareness for the use of OAuth 2.0 framework. We urge the attention of both developers and users towards a safer implementation that would build up the desired levels of security.

© Springer International Publishing AG 2017
S. Tonetta et al. (Eds.): SAFECOMP 2017 Workshops, LNCS 10489, pp. 396–406, 2017.
DOI: 10.1007/978-3-319-66284-8_33

The rest of the paper is structured as follows: next Sect. 2 presents a brief history and an overview of the framework. Section 3 introduces an analysis of known vulnerabilities and attacks of the framework. Section 4 presents an evaluation and Sect. 5 concludes this work.

2 Background

OAuth has been firstly described in December 2006 [2], to promote the re-use the user accounts for several, distinct, services, without the need of password exchanges. In April 2007, AOL introduced *OpenAuth* framework, followed by *Google's OpenAuth group*, and by the second version of the framweork to assess the emerged security flaws, released in October 2012 [3]. It considers a client-server authentication model, where the client requests access to restricted resources on the server by authenticating herself on the server using her credentials. OAuth framework employs an authorization server for issuing security tokens to different users who request access to protected resources.

As a single sign on (SSO) framework, in which the user needs to authorize web sites to act on her behalf [4], OAuth 2.0 is also used to provide authentication, where users log themselves in a web service using their identity managed by a third-party service. The authentication process is also widely used by mobile applications to access the application server back-end [15].

The main authentication schema has four entities [3]: (1) *the client*, namely the application used by the user when requiring access to the protected data/service; (2) the *the resource owner* (also referred as the *relying party*), namely the end user or a host acting on her behalf with the ability to request access to protected resources; (3) *the authorization server*, that is the issuer of access tokens and the one that assures the authenticity of the owner; and (4) *the resource server*, that is the host of the restricted data and consumer of the *access tokens*. Resource server and authorization server are generally the same host and are also called identity provider (**IdP**) server, while the Resource Owner (*RO*) is the main actor that is grant access to the IdP resources from the client. Before any client application can interact with one of the identity providers, the client requires registration at the providers side, with the generation of the credentials (a public client ID and a client secret) during the authentication process [5]. A high level sketch of the authentication schema is depicted in Fig. 1 and can be summarized as:

1. The client requests access for data belonging to the resource owner.
2. The resource owner replies by sending the **authentication grant**. The reply contains, among others, the chosen grant type, the preferable authentication server to be used and which is server holds the resources.
3. The client forwards the authentication grant to the authentication server, asking for the access token.
4. The authentication server validates the received grant and then sends back an **access token**, which represents the resource owner and states that the authorization has been approved.

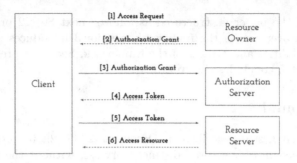

Fig. 1. Abstract authentication schema for desktop applications [3]

5. The client asks the permission to access the protected resources from the server that contains the data by providing the access token.
6. The resource server receives the token and validates it, returining the requested data.

The OAuth framework heavily relies on the concept of bearer tokens, that are cryptographic tokens, used to present proof-of-possession. Clients are using these tokens to request access to protected resources. They are generated once users successfully authenticate their identity. In OAuth, there are two types of bearer tokens [3]: the *Access Token*, that represents the credentials required to access protected resources and that defines scope and duration of the access in the authorization grant (described later); and the *Refresh Token*, that are used to obtain new access tokens when the old ones expire or become invalid.

In the OAuth terminology, endpoints are the URIs used to send the request packets [11]: the *Authorization* Endpoint is used by the client to obtain resource authorization from the owner of the resource, *Token* Endpoint is used by the client to retrieve access or refresh token and the *Redirection* Endpoint is used by authorization server to redirect the client the after authorization process.

Finally, there is the concept of grant that specifies the type of operational mode required by the client, namely the type of authentication and authorization mechanism. OAuth has four types of grants [3]. The *Authorization Code* mode is used when the client wants to authorize the Resource Owner to access their data on the IdP and requires the Resource Owner to be redirected to the IdP and to perform several message exchanges. The *Implicit* is a simplified version of the above mode, where the client mediates the exchange between the Resource Owner and the IdP. In the *Resource Owner Password Credential* mode, the client does not communicates with the IdP, but it sends its credential directly to the Resource Owner in order to prove her identity with the IdP. The prerequisite for this mode is the strong trust between the two entities [11]. Then, in the *Client Credential* mode, the client and the resource owner are the same entity or there was a prior arrangement between the owner and the authentication server on which way to act when asking for protected resources [11].

Fig. 2. OAuth in use

3   Framework Analysis

Many websites rely on the OAuth framework to provide access to external protected resources, like *Google, Facebook, Renren, Amazon* and *Paypal* [1]. These websites support as many as 10 different IdPs. Using some basics for the probabilistic theory, the probability of one IdP providing unbreakable source code and assuring secure communication will never be 1. Having 10 IdPs for the same objective rises dramatically the prospect of having user accounts compromised. When we take into account potential cross site misconfigurations, this probability grows even more.

Figure 2 shows how the login page of web sites using OAuth looks like. The left one is from www.dailymail.co.uk and the right from www.theguardian.com. As we can see, the two web sites act as RO. *Facebook, Twitter* and *Google* have the role of IdP. In the context of those two specific ROs, OAuth is used only for authentication but not for accessing protected resources. It is adopted to increase usability without the need of native account creation.

To give mobile applications the authorization to access their data, service providers offer OAuth framework implemented in software development kits (SDK) that developers can use to integrate in their apps [14]. In this way, apps supporting OAuth do not need to share users' credentials with third-party apps.

3.1   Vulnerabilities

HTTP Protocol. Despite trials to formally verify the correctness of the OAuth's framework [12], the main cause of OAuth's vulnerabilities come straight from the underlying HTTP protocol, as it does not impose strict policies to be followed. With the variety of methods accomplishing the same action (HTTP authorization header, HTTP POST body, URL query parameter), the developer has the freedom to choose which way the packet exchange procedure will follow and which status codes will be used. There are various implementations of the services that this framework supports, a thing which increases the obscurity. Moreover, OAuth framework tries to avoid the need of using HTTPS requests and rely mainly on open channel.

Inadequacy of Formalization. Another source of vulnerabilities, caused by developers as well, is the lack of compliance to the rules that compose the framework itself [4]. To be fair, both the framework and developers could be pledged guilty. From one side, the framework does not have a set of strict rules to follow when it comes to input validation. From the other one, developers fail to offer safe solutions as a legit random string generator or thorough monitoring of the exchanged values.

Credential Storage. Credentials are stored in a safe location in order to prevent misuse. When the client is a web application, responsible for the secure storage is the server. When the client is a desktop application, credentials are stored at client side [9]. At this case responsible for securing them is the desktop environment, thus the user. This makes them susceptible to many kinds of attack; an adversary could break in the system and steal this credential or get access to the executable carrying the load of securing them and reverse engineer it. Apart from gaining access to user's protected resources, the attacker could issue re-generation of credential which would lead to further damage.

Invocation of Supported Services. OAuth offers a great variety of services and solutions for different type of use. There is the basic service to generating an access token for authorizing a user and there is the complex scenario of exchanging protected resources [9]. Web and app developers, guided by the lack of thorough insight, tend to support all of them even if they just need to use the simplest ones. Publishing code that nobody can assure of its capabilities and functionality creates unquestionably security holes.

Unsupported Packages. Although the developers of OAuth suggest some standard libraries to be used along the framework (`AppAuth`), there are plenty alternatives that supply the same functionality. For example, the official Android SDK uses the `AccountManager` packet while Java encourages the use of `GoogleCredential` and `GoogleAuthorizationCodeFlow` [15]. Every misconfiguration of those libraries and packets gives the aspiring adversaries opportunities to break in. Furthermore, packages might get deprecated and unsupported at any time without prior notice.

3.2   Attacks

OAuth 2.0 is considered to be the most reliable choice among other frameworks offering the same functionality, yet security issues rise on the different implementations. Resource providers have to arrange a prior agreement with the identity providers on the exchange data. Every identity provider offers a different way to authenticate the user and authorize access. Moreover, there is no global approved standard specifying the communication primitives. Developers are allowed to provide solutions according to what they believe the best approach is.

The following attacks are based on the misconfiguration of the authentication framework between the entities of RO and IdP. The authorization code and implicit grant types are susceptible to this attacks.

HTTP 307 Redirect Attack. The goal of this attack is to learn the credential of a legitimate user. The attacker runs a malicious RO and relies on the wrong HTTP redirection status code used by the IdP. This is the first and only attack found that demonstrates itself due to 307 status code.

Attack. The user tries to connect to an RO that is owned by the attacker. Subsequently, the user is redirected to an IdP in order authenticate herself by issuing a POST request to send her credentials [5]. The IdP checks whether the credential are legit and replies by sending an HTTP 307 redirect status, informing the user which is the redirection point of the RO to follow. Since code 307 is used for redirect, user's browser will issue a POST request to the redirection URI with the same body as the one he sent earlier to the IdP which still contains her credential.

Fix. Change the implementation of the IdP server to eliminate the 307 status code. Instead, the use of 303 status code is encouraged, because it is the only one that drops the body of an HTTP POST request.

Cross Site Request Forgery. In this type of attack, the adversary takes advantage of the established session between user's browser and the RO. After the successful, legitimate authentication of the user to an IdP, the RO creates a pair locally that contains information about the user account and the IdP managed account [10]. This is done by using the unique, random generated value (*state*) produced by the IdP. Both user's browser and RO are targeted by the attacker. It begins when the attacker forces user's browser to initiate a request to the RO and the desired outcome is to make the RO execute actions without involving the user.

Attack. The attack can begin when the user's browser is logged in to an RO. Both entities are targeted by the attacker, who needs to find a way to trigger some unintended actions to the browser. This can happen by luring the victim to visit a malicious site or by following a link on the target RO's site. Then, the browser of the victim sends a request to the RO containing a new binding value, valid for correlating the attackers binding with her IdP. If this request manage to pass the validation, the attacker is able to log in to the victim's RO.

Fix. This attack is made plausible due to defective validation of the *state* value, produced by the IdP. The error can be found both in ROs and in IdPs. Many developed solutions for ROs do not consider at all this value; they rely only on its presence to assure validity of the action [10]. From the other hand, IdP's use an easy-to-guess string of a constant length to represent this value. Instead, hash functions producing random length values should be used in order to make the *state* value not guessable. ROs must always check the correctness of this value.

Mixing IdP Redirect End-Point. This attack applies to the authorization and implicit modes. The adversary aims to confuse the RO on which IdP was chosen to be followed by the user. As explained earlier, RO will follow the redirect end-point of any IdP, even when it lacks prior knowledge for this IdP. This action is allowed due to framework's applicable standards. Its goal is to obtain the authorization token and thus impersonate the legit user [5].

Attack. In this scenario, the attacker acts both as an RO and an IdP (ARO and AIdP respectively). The user initiates a session by issuing a POST request to select the honest IdP she wants to use. This request is intercepted by the ARO, where the attacker substitutes the IdP redirect point with his own. After this manipulation, the request is forwarded to the RO. The response of the RO is intercepted again and modified again by the attacker in order to reflect user's legit choice before been transmitted back to her. The authentication among user and honest IdP procedure is left intact. After successful authentication, the user sends a POST request to the RO containing values that will be used to create the authentication token. Upon the reception of the *code* and *state* values, the RO initiates the access token generation session by omitting to the AIdP. The attacker now can proceed by sending the received values to the honest IdP and ultimately gain access to user's protected resources.

Fix. This attack is possible due to lack of transmitted identification values. The RO does not recognize the validity of the provided redirect end-point. Additionally, when the user transmits the *code* and *state* values, she does not specify her identity. Thus, the RO believes that it is the same user that started the session. Solving this problem requires these values to be added to the body of the exchanged packages.

Session Wrapping Attack. The attacker manipulates the RO to use protected resources that belong to him rather than the ones belonging to the authenticated user. In this way, the attacker can confuse the RO and guide it to succeed his own purposes, mainly hurt the public image of the victim. This method is supplementary to the CSRF attack; when all the checks are done in place, the attacker can still find out the values of the *state* value [8].

Attack. After the IdP has performed all necessary checks to determine the authenticity of the user, it sends back a 3xx redirect request to the user. This tells to the user browser to perform a POST request with the *state* and *code* values to the RO in order for the RO and IdP to agree on a freshly generated access token. The final response of the IdP contains the URI of the protected resource that was asked in the first place. The attacker manipulates this URI to one that points to a malicious web-site run by him. Upon the reception of this request to his website, he inspects the request. In there, he finds the *Referrer* header which contains the values of *status* and *code*.

Fix. A possible fix to address this attack is to restrict the referrer policy. In particular, *"origin-when-cross-origin"* policy, specifies which values are sent when making same-origin requests [9]. When a request is received from an unauthorized entity (the attacker) the values of interest will not be visible. Another solution is to always exchange a unique identifier alongside legitimate requests. A third solution is to use single use *state* values. This would force the IdP to generate fresh values every time the RO asks for access to a protected resource. Another way to tackle the problem, is to set an expiration time to the exchanged *status* values. Researchers suggest that 60 to 80 min is an acceptable time limit [8].

Brute Force Attack Against the IdP. In this attack, the adversary is part of the network and able to eavesdrop on the traffic. It aims on reducing the availability of the IdP server [9]. In order to do so, the framework uses the HTTP and not the HTTPS protocol.

Attack. Inspecting the exchanged traffic, the attacker finds out specific request parameters and attributes exchanged between the two entities. Even in the absence of the authorization tokens (they may be transmitted encrypted), the attacker can launch a brute force attack against the IdP server.

Fix. A certain mindset comes to the rescue for brute force attacks: try to make it as hard as possible for the adversary to understand the captured packets. Substituting HTTP to HTTPS is a valid solution. Creating long, random and brute-force resistant tokens is another.

3.3 Identified Cases

Facebook. A flow exploitation that leads to complete take over of any account on this social network was discovered by researcher Goldshlager [6]. By exploiting this flaw, the researcher could steal unique access tokens that provide full control over any Facebook account. This flow is based on the principle that OAuth is used by Facebook to communicate between applications and its users, where a user must accept the application's request to access her account during the initialization phase of the communication. To make this exploit work, the victim is lured to visit a web-page, specially crafted to look like FB's genuine site. To do so, Goldshlager modified the URL string of Facebook's OAuth service. The URL forced the browser to redirect in his own website, exchange a pre-issued access token and eliminate the authentication pop-up. After, he was able to grant himself access to the account. Nir Goldshlager published his findings. In turn, Facebook patched its servers to eliminate this threat.

Twitter. In 2015, security researcher Pranav Hivarekar managed to fool twitter's OAuth service to steal contacts from other accounts. Twitter uses third party OAuth integrations to allow users to import contacts to their personal profiles. When the user clicks on the button to import contacts, OAuth replies with a URL containing a `redirect_uri` parameter [13]. Hivarekar manipulated this parameter to point at any internal twitter url, in the form of `*.twitter.com`. Next, he observed the `response_type=code`, which yields at server-side OAuth flow implementation. After receiving the code, twitter makes a request to the server and collects `access_token`. Using this `access_token` twitter imports contacts. Hivarekar stole the code value by attacking to the referrer header of the HTTP packet. After some trials, he realized that twitter drops the referrer header in the final step, as a security mechanism against this kind of attack. In order to bypass this, he created his own application which employed twitter as an IdP.

He initiated a session and right before the completion of the import, he canceled it. By doing so, he had an active `oauth_token`. He used this token to manually craft a URI and then send it to twitter users. When the user clicked on it, Hivarekar obtained the code via the referrer headed and used it to import contacts from other users. Twitter denied the recognition of this vulnerability at first but after some time they accepted it and rewarded the researcher. In 2016 they issued a press release which was announcing alteration to their internals servers to patch OAuth flaws.

Insecure Mobile Implementations. The failure of imposing strict rules and techniques for mobile implementations of OAuth leads to degradation of the offered SDK implementations [14]. Application developers, unknowingly, provide untrusted services and applications. Common cases of poor implementations appear to be:

- identity providers respond by sending user's identity information aside the legitimate OAuth `access_token`. Back-end servers login the users based on these information.
- identity provider's signature, used to sign users' profiles, stands unverified. Instead, user's personal information is extracted from the payload of the request.
- applications which rely on their build in identification system in order to identify the user. Instead, they ought to contact the identity provider employed in an external server.

During Black Hat EU, 2016 researchers from the Chinese University of Hong Kong demonstrated an attack, in which the attacker could take control of an account without any involvement or awareness of the victim [15]. The attack was performed on mobile devices and could ran on both Android and Apple devices. In order to expose the vulnerability, they developed an exploit to examine the implementations of 600 top-ranked US and Chinese Android Apps which make use of the OAuth2.0-based authentication service. They found out that almost 45% of them (undisclosed for security reasons) were susceptible to this attack. The attack is based on the observation that the id of the user is the only value used to identify early adopters of a 3rd party mobile application.

4   Evaluation

In this section, we rely on three important values of any security scheme, *authorization*, *authentication* and *session integrity*. Authorization refers on the access of the protected resources, authentication on the identity of the user and session integrity on the mutual agreement to access protected resources and on following the correct redirect endpoint [5].

So far, there is no official or independent authority responsible for testing authorization and authentication services based on OAuth 2.0. Analysis and practical testing is based on the framework, not on services implementing the framework and it is done either for educational purposes (researchers) or by individual users. Pen-testing on each different service implementation is done mainly by developers themselves [7].

Although OAuth is not the only available solution for providing secure access to protected resources, it is the one employed the most [15]. Its rivals, like Flickr Auth, Yahoo BBAuth and Facebook's Auth offer protected access only on the context of specific web-sites. OAuth managed to establish an inter-operable framework which enables a third-party application to obtain access. It is not dependent on the actual implementation or platform as it provides modules for diverse scripting and programming languages.

One of the main focuses of the team that designed the framework was to make it appealing to other developers. As so, OAuth fails to set hard rules, leaving space for misinterpretations [9]. This design decision has drawn criticism from the security community, however it is difficult to maintain the right balance between security and usability, while the demand of user-friendly solutions increases.

5   Conclusion

In this paper we have presented an overview of the OAuth 2.0 framework and investigated the relevant literature. We described the known vulnerabilities and how they exploit and jeopardize the authentication, authorization and session integrity properties. Since the OAuth 2.0 framework is widely adopted, this paper confirms and supports the urgent adoption of the proposed mitigation techniques to tackle each known issue.

References

1. Boshmaf, Y., Muslukhov, I., Beznosov, K., Ripeanu, M.: Key Challenges in defending against malicious socialbots. In: Proceedings of the 5th USENIX Conference on Large-Scale Exploits and Emergent Threats, LEET 2012. USENIX Association, Berkeley (2012)
2. Campbell, B., Mortimore, C., Jones, M., Goland, Y.: Assertion framework for OAuth 2.0 Client Authentication and Authorization Grants. RFC 7521 (Proposed Standard), May 2015
3. Hardt, D. (Ed).: RFC 6749: The OAuth 2.0 Authorization Framework. Annalen der Physik (2012). Accessed 12 Dec 2016
4. Ferry, E., O Raw, J., Curran, K.: Security evaluation of the OAuth framework. Inf. Comput. Secur. **23**(1), 73–101 (2015)
5. Fett, D., Küsters, R., Schmitz, G.: A comprehensive formal security analysis of OAuth 2.0. In: Proceedings of the 2016 ACM SIGSAC Conference on Computer and Communications Security, CCS 2016, New York. ACM (2016)
6. Goldshlager, N.: How i hacked Facebook OAuth to get full permission on any account. http://www.nirgoldshlager.com/2013/02/how-i-hacked-facebook-oauth-to-get-full.html. Accessed 15 Dec 2016
7. HTH: Common OAuth2 vulnerabilities and mitigation techniques. https://least privilege.com/2013/03/15/common-oauth2-vulnerabilities-and-mitigation-techniq ues/. Accessed 15 Dec 2016

8. Jones, M., Bradley, J., Sakimura, N.: OAuth 2.0 mix-up mitigation. https://tools. ietf.org/html/draft-ietf-oauth-mix-up-mitigation-01. Accessed 05 2017

9. Kiani, K.: Four Attacks on OAuth - How to secure your OAuth implementation. SANS - Working Papers in Application Security (2016)

10. Li, W., Mitchell, C.J.: Security issues in OAuth 2.0 SSO implementations

11. Lodderstedt, T., McGloin, M., Hunt, P.: OAuth 2.0 threat model and security considerations. RFC 6819 (Informational), January 2013

12. Pai, S., Sharma, Y., Kumar, S., Pai, R.M., Singh, S.: Formal verification of OAuth 2.0 using alloy framework. In: Proceedings of the 2011 International Conference on Communication Systems and Network Technologies, CSNT 2011. IEEE Computer Society, Washington (2011)

13. Pranav, H.: Twitter's bug - importing contacts (oauth flaw). https://prana vhivarekar.in/2015/01/29/twitters-bug-importing-contacts-oauth-flaw/. Accessed 15 Dec 2016

14. Shehab, M., Mohsen, F.: Securing OAuth implementations in smart phones. In: Proceedings of the 4th ACM Conference on Data and Application Security and Privacy, CODASPY 2014. ACM, New York (2014)

15. Wing, R.Y., Lau, C., Liu, T.: Signing into One Billion Mobile App. Accounts Effortlessly with OAuth2.0. The Chinese University of Hong Kong (2015)

PolEnA: Enforcing Fine-grained Permission Policies in Android

Gabriele Costa[1], Federico Sinigaglia[1,2]([✉]), and Roberto Carbone[2]

[1] DIBRIS, University of Genova, Genova, Italy
gabriele.costa@unige.it
[2] Security & Trust Unit, FBK-ICT, Trento, Italy
{sinigaglia,carbone}@fbk.eu

Abstract. In this paper we present PolEnA, an extension of the Android Security Framework (ASF). PolEnA enables a number of features that are not currently provided by the ASF. Among them, PolEnA allows for the definition of fine-grained security policies and their dynamic verification. The runtime enforcement of the policies is supported by a state-of-the-art SAT solver. One of the main features of our approach is the low invasiveness as it does not require modifications to the operating system.

Keywords: Android Security · Runtime Enforcement · Dynamic Verification

1 Introduction

In the last years, the Android security framework received many criticisms. In particular, several authors pointed out the poor expressiveness of the permission framework. Permissions are labels that developers attach to their software when they want it to access some platform resources. Then, the user revises them and authorizes the application at installation time. Installed applications are granted with access privileges corresponding to their permissions.

This approach has several drawbacks. The most evident are the following.

- Permissions are coarse-grained. As a matter of fact, a single label, e.g., INTERNET, denotes a variety of operations and behaviors.
- User authorization is all-or-nothing. When downloading an app, the user can either grant all the permissions or interrupt the installation. Only some permissions can be revoked dynamically.
- Developers are not provided with a policy framework. The only available mechanisms, i.e., the intent filters, is way too weak to express meaningful policies. Thus, the developers have to code their own protection systems.

As a consequence, the Android permission system often became the source of security misunderstandings and vulnerabilities.

In [1] we presented an extension of the Android security framework that allows developers to apply their own security policies over applications executions

© Springer International Publishing AG 2017
S. Tonetta et al. (Eds.): SAFECOMP 2017 Workshops, LNCS 10489, pp. 407–414, 2017.
DOI: 10.1007/978-3-319-66284-8_34

and interactions. Summarizing, the main features of the proposed approach are listed below.

Default Permission System. We do not redefine the existing permissions and their syntax. Developers and users deal with data items they are already familiar with.

Fine-grained Policies. Security policies are defined through a formal language that significantly extends the basic security framework. Also, policies are attached to each component, thereby allowing developers to define local security requirements.

Multiple Policy Scopes. Application components can carry *local* as well as *global* policies. Moreover, policies can be *sticky* (i.e. affecting other components after an invocation).

No Runtime Errors. Illegal interactions among components are dynamically verified before invocation and cannot generate security violations.

No OS Customization. Although feasible, our solution does not require modifications to the Android OS. PolEnA can run on any existing Android device and can be applied to any app.

Users Cannot Make Mistakes. Users can only select application components from a list of safe ones, i.e., those that, according to the current policies, cannot lead to violations.

In this paper, we describe PolEnA, the implementation of the approach presented in [1]. The aim of the approach is to provide an improvement of Policy Enforcement and Management in Android systems. Our solution includes an application rewriting framework allowing to rewrite existing applications in such a way to be compatible with our tool.

This Paper is Structured as Follows. In Sect. 2 we recall the core components defined in [1] for the policy enforcement. Section 3 describes our application rewriting framework. Section 4 presents the overall architecture of PolEnA. Finally, Sect. 5 presents the related work, while Sect. 6 concludes the paper.

2   SCP Components

In this section we briefly recall the policy enforcement framework presented in [1] and its core features. An implementation of the framework, called *safe component provider* (SCP), is available online.[1]

Computational Model. Android applications consist of a collection of *components* that are responsible for handling a specific task or part of the application logic. They belong to the following four categories: (*i*) **Activities**, user interface components which may include controls that the user can interact

---

[1] https://github.com/SCPTeam/Safe-Component-Provider.

with, (*ii*) **Services**, that carry out background computation, e.g., the interaction with a remote server, (*iii*) **Content Providers**, that offer access to the data of the application, e.g., by interacting with a local database and (*iv*) **Broadcast Receivers**, which are notified with inter-process communications (IPCs), a.k.a. intents, and handle them.

Android uses an activity stack to allow the user to browse among the GUI of the running applications. SCP extends this notion to that of *component stack*, i.e. a data structure representing the running components and the order they launched each other. At runtime, SCP keeps in memory the system configuration amounting to a finite collection of component stacks, i.e. a multi-stack. Each stack provides the execution context of a single application that has been launched, e.g., by the user. Each layer of a stack contains the details of the corresponding component and, in particular, its permissions and policies. When a component invokes another one, e.g., by sending an intent, a new layer is added to its stack (push). Instead, when a component terminates its life cycle, the corresponding layer is removed (pop).

Policy Framework. The policy framework extends the basic Android permission system in three ways.

1. It introduces a fine-grained policy language that permits to express both local and global policies. Moreover, it supports sticky policies that affect a component even after its carrier has been terminated.
2. It implements a policy enforcement mechanism that relieves the user from any security-critical decision and effectively prevents policy violations.
3. It redefines the Android manifest structure by allowing for component-level permission requests and policy specifications.

The policy enforcement framework works by encoding the configuration validity problem into a corresponding boolean satisfiability problem (SAT). As showed in [1], SAT problems generated in this way can be efficiently solved by means of state-of-the-art SAT solvers (as [6]).

Architecture. SCP is implemented by means of three interacting elements that we recall below.

SCPcore is the central element of the architecture. It stores the system configuration, i.e., the component multi-stack, and keeps it updated. Moreover, it hosts a database of all the known components which is updated every time an application is installed or uninstalled. It is notified with every component invocation request and binds them to the actual component to be invoked. To do that, it carries out the SAT encoding and solving.

SCPlib is the library allowing an application to interact with SCPcore. The library wraps the relevant Android classes, e.g., Intent and Activity, with classes mimicking their functionalities. The wrapping classes bypass the Android IPC mechanism and dispatch the requests to SCPcore.

SCPclient allows the user to inspect the SCPcore configuration. Intuitively, it works similarly to a task manager and application installer. In particular, it displays the multi-stack configuration, allows the user to kill a stack (or part of it) and to inspect the installed components.

In order to properly check and enforce policies, SCP relies on a SAT solver implementation for Java. In particular, the Sat4J[2] library has been employed. This library, indeed, includes a Java implementation of Minisat and manages the translation to Java native language (via the Java Native Interface).

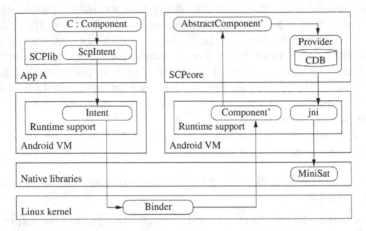

Fig. 1. A component request in SCP.

Figure 1 depicts the flow for a component request in SCP. Initially, a component C of application A sends a ScpIntent (instead of a standard Intent). The ScpIntent is sent to SCPcore in unicast mode. Then, SCPcore collects the list of components that might answer the request from its local Component Database (CDB). The policies and permissions of each of them are combined with the current configuration, passed through JNI and submitted to the Minisat SAT solver. Depending on the solver output, SCPcore prompts the user with a list of components that can legally serve the request.

3 App Rewriting

As stated in the previous section, the policy enforcement framework requires the application to include and properly use SCPlib. Clearly, all the existing applications would be incompatible with it. To overcome this limitation, we adopt an application rewriting technique. Generally, one could argue that rewriting an application might bring some security concerns related to the trustworthiness of the process executor. In our case, though, no additional trust on an external agent is required: the process is indeed performed by an extension of SCP, which is implicitly assumed trusted. In this section we hence describe the key concepts of the proposed rewriting technique.

Bytecode Instrumentation. The bytecode, usually obtained from the compilation of Java sources, is the language interpreted by the Java VM. Bytecode

---
[2] Sat4j, the boolean satisfaction and optimization library in Java: www.sat4j.org.

Table 1. A fragment of Java code before (left) and after (right) instrumentation.

```
Intent i = new Intent();      ScpIntent i = new ScpIntent();
i.setAction(/* ... */);       i.setAction(/* ... */);
                              i.putExtra("scp.caller", this);
Context c = getContext();     ScpContext c = new ScpContext(getContext());
c.sendBroadcast(i);           c.sendBroadcast(i);
```

instrumentation is a common approach often used to adapt a piece of code to the requirements of its execution environment. For instance, in [3] the authors presented a bytecode instrumentation procedure for injecting security checks in standard Java applications. Similarly, in [4] bytecode manipulation is used to enable JavaME application monitoring on smartphones.

Our approach follows the same line. To highlight the behavior of the instrumentation process, consider the snippets of code of Table 1. The code on the left hand side (which we assume is part of a class extending **android.view.View**) creates an Intent and sends it in broadcast mode[3]. The code on right hand side performs the same operation using the SCPlib classes. Notice that SCPlib only introduces two differences: (*i*) replacing Intent and Context with the corresponding wrappers ScpIntent and ScpContext (resp.) and (*ii*) setting few extra fields in the ScpIntent (e.g., to identify the intent caller).

The instrumentation process crawls the application code, finds the invocations to be modified and rewrites them. This process is not carried out at Java source code level, but directly on the application bytecode. At bytecode level, fragment on the left of Table 1 looks similar to the following.[4]

```
$r0 := @this: View; $r1 = new Intent; specialinvoke $r1.<Intent:
void <init>()>(); virtualinvoke $r1.
    <Intent: Intent setAction(String)>(/* ... */);
$r2 = virtualinvoke $r0.<View: Context getContext()>();
virtualinvoke $r2.<Context: void sendBroadcast(Intent)>($r1);
```

The $r0, $r1 and $r2 symbols denote local registers. The creation of a new Intent is carried out in two steps, i.e., the creation of a new Intent object (`$r1 = new Intent;`) and its initialization through the constructor **<init>**. Then, method **setAction** is invoked on the register $r1 and a Context object is obtained through method **getContext** and stored in $r2. Finally, **sendBroadcast** is invoked on $r2 (Context) with parameter $r1 (Intent). On this code, the instrumentation procedure follows these steps:

1. replace the type Intent with ScpIntent;
2. inject the code for the additional intent contents (**putExtra**);
3. create and initialize the ScpContext;
4. replace the usages of Context with ScpContext.

During this process, some new temporary registers might be necessary. We indicate them with $t0, $t1, ... The instrumented version of the bytecode given above is the following.

---

[3] Notice that we use **sendBroadcast** to send an explicit intent to the SCPcore. To do that we rely on a special permission having protection level "signature" (see https://developer.android.com/guide/topics/manifest/permission-element.html).

[4] For the bytecode we use the Jimple notation [9].

```
$r0 := @this: View; $r1 = new ScpIntent; specialinvoke
$r1.<ScpIntent: void <init>()>(); virtualinvoke $r1.
  <ScpIntent: Intent setAction(String)>(/* ... */);
$t0 = virtualinvoke $r0.<String: Object toString()>(); virtualinvoke
$r1.
  <ScpIntent: Intent putExtra(String, String)>(''scp.caller'', $t0);
$r2 = virtualinvoke $r0.<View: Context getContext()>(); $t1 = new
ScpContext; specialinvoke $t1.<ScpContext: void
<init>(Context)>($r2); virtualinvoke $t1.
  <ScpContext: void sendBroadcast(ScpIntent)>($r1);
```

Manifest Rewriting. The approach presented in [1] includes a Manifest extension for expressing fine-grained policies. The adoption of these additional specifications, though, can be expected on apps that originally include the SCPlib. The rest of the app, instead, will not be compatible with SCP. For overcoming this compatibility limitation, our rewriting procedure is also applied to the application manifest. In particular, the following steps are necessary: (*i*) assign permissions requests to each component of the manifest and (*ii*) replace broadcast receiver permission filters with policies. Notice that the first step can be implemented with different strategies. Here we assign to each component the full list of permissions required by the application.

To clarify the rewriting operation, consider the simplified instance of a manifest file of Table 2 (left). Notice that the broadcast receiver "my.app.receiver" requires the caller to have the CAMERA permission. This requirement is translated into the policy on the right hand side. The policy translation operation is detailed in [1].

Table 2. A manifest file before (left) and after (right) the rewriting procedure.

```
<manifest package="my.app">   <manifest package="my.app">
 <uses-permission
   name="INTERNET"/>
 <uses-permission
   name="MICROPHONE"/>
 <application>                  <application>
  <activity                      <activity
    name="my.app.activity">        name="my.app.activity">
                                    <uses-permission name="INTERNET"/>
                                    <uses-permission name="MICROPHONE"/>
  </activity>                     </activity>
  <receiver                      <receiver
    name="my.app.receiver"         name="my.app.receiver">
    permission="CAMERA">           <uses-permission name="INTERNET"/>
                                    <uses-permission name="MICROPHONE"/>
                                    <policy scope="direct">
                                    CAMERA
                                    </policy>
  </receiver>                    </receiver>
 </application>                 </application>
</manifest>                    </manifest>
```

4 Overall Architecture

The architecture depicted in Fig. 2 implements the components described in the previous sections. Following the same approach presented in [2], we employ a meta-market (SCP Market) for distributing the rewritten apps. In this way, the standard flow for installing an app on the user's device does not change, as shown in [2]. The SCP Market takes as input the apps from the Play Store and generates the corresponding signed rewritten apps. To this aim, the original apk is fetched from the Play Store and given as input to Soot [7]. This tool is designed for Java app instrumentation, providing notations for the bytecode (like Jimple) and a framework for manipulating it. Firstly, Soot processes the apk through the *Decompiler*. Then, the apk is rewritten by the *Inliner instrumenter*, that receives the instrumentation instructions and the SCPlib JAR (for including the SCP classes in the apk). Finally, the apk is repackaged via the *Packager*.

Once the APK file is modified and repackaged, it is necessary to update its signature. For executing this task, we created a script that leverages the *apksigner* tool (provided by the Android SDK) for successfully signing the apk.

The apps (obtained with the aforementioned procedure) can then be installed on the user's device, where they can interact with the previously installed SCP-client and SCPcore components (described in Sect. 2).

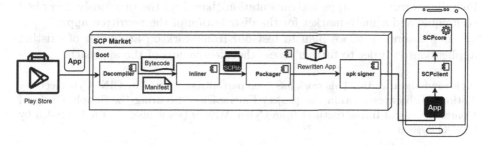

Fig. 2. The proposed Architecture integrating SCP.

5   Related Work

In the last few years, many authors have proposed several tools for empowering the security mechanisms offered by Android.

The APEX tool [8], for instance, allows a user to selectively grant permissions to applications (during their installation process) and impose constraints on the usage of resources. As PolEnA, APEX proposes an extension of the Android Security Framework. In the case of Apex, though, the Application Context class and the Package Manager service have to be modified. Moreover, if compared to our tool, the policies specified with Apex are less expressive.

The Aurasium tool [10], instead, repackages Android application attaching code for policy enforcement. Differently from PolEnA, the app has to be given by the user (in a form of apk file). As reported by other authors, one big limitation of this tool is that the instrumented run-time monitor is executed in the same process as the app. For this reason, it could be possibly circumvented.

COMBdroid [5] is another tool for enforcing fine-grained, user-defined policies. As PolEnA, COMBdroid rewrites an application, chosen by the user, for monitoring the compliance to the policy. With this tool it is possible to specify whitelists, blacklists and policies for limiting the usage of specific resources.

The tools mentioned so far, especially COMBdroid and Aurasium, are mainly focused on enforcing policies for preventing malicious operations and behaviors. Differently from PolEnA, moreover, these tools do not consider the interaction between applications (and components) with different permissions, nor the configuration of the whole system.

6   Conclusions

In this paper we presented an implementation of the Android Security Framework extension presented in [1]. This new extension, called PolEnA, supports the specification and enforcement of fine-grained security policies. Our implementation aims to integrate this approach in an environment allowing normal apps to interact with the policy checker. To do this, we proposed a rewriting technique (based on bytecode instrumentation) for making any app able to interact with the aforementioned components. Finally, we presented an overall architecture, including a server for apps instrumentation (based on the previously described technique) and a meta-market for the distribution of the rewritten apps.

As a future work, we plan to test our framework on a number of existing applications in order to further assess the effectiveness of the approach.

Acknowledgements. This work has been partially supported by CINI Cybersecurity National Laboratory within the project FilieraSicura: Securing the Supply Chain of Domestic Critical Infrastructures from Cyber Attacks (www.filierasicura.it) funded by CISCO Systems Inc.

References

1. Armando, A., Carbone, R., Costa, G., Merlo, A.: Android permissions unleashed. In: IEEE 28th Computer Security Foundations Symposium, pp. 320–333 (2015)
2. Armando, A., Costa, G., Merlo, A., Verderame, L.: Enabling BYOD through secure meta-market. In: Proceedings of WiSec 2014, pp. 219–230 (2014)
3. Bartoletti, M., Costa, G., Zunino, R.: Jalapa: securing Java with local policies. Electron. Notes Theor. Comput. Sci. **253**(5), 145–151 (2009)
4. Costa, G., Martinelli, F., Mori, P., Schaefer, C., Walter, T.: Runtime monitoring for next generation Java ME platform. Comput. Secur. **29**(1), 74–87 (2010)
5. Cotterell, K., Welch, I., Chen, A.: An android security policy enforcement tool. Int. J. Electron. Telecommun. **61**, 311–320 (2015)
6. Eén, N., Sörensson, N.: An extensible SAT-solver. In: Giunchiglia, E., Tacchella, A. (eds.) SAT 2003. LNCS, vol. 2919, pp. 502–518. Springer, Heidelberg (2004). doi:10.1007/978-3-540-24605-3_37
7. Lam, P., Bodden, E., Lhoták, O., Hendren, L.: The soot framework for Java program analysis: a retrospective. In: Cetus Users and Compiler Infrastructure Workshop (2011)
8. Nauman, M., Khan, S., Zhang, X.: Apex: extending android permission model and enforcement with user-defined runtime constraints, ASIACCS (2010)
9. Vallee-Rai, R., Hendren, L.J.: Jimple: Simplifying Java bytecode for analyses and transformations. McGill University, Sable Research Group (1998)
10. Xu, R., Saïdi, H., Anderson, R.: Aurasium: practical policy enforcement for android applications. In: 21st USENIX Security Symposium, pp. 539–552 (2012)

Fast Estimation of Privacy Risk in Human Mobility Data

Roberto Pellungrini[1](✉), Luca Pappalardo[1,2], Francesca Pratesi[1,2],
and Anna Monreale[1]

[1] Department of Computer Science, University of Pisa, Pisa, Italy
roberto.pellungrini@gmail.com, lucapappalardo1984@gmail.com,
anna.monreale@unipi.it
[2] ISTI-CNR, Pisa, Italy
francesca.pratesi@isti.cnr.it

Abstract. Mobility data are an important proxy to understand the patterns of human movements, develop analytical services and design models for simulation and prediction of human dynamics. Unfortunately mobility data are also very sensitive, since they may contain personal information about the individuals involved. Existing frameworks for privacy risk assessment enable the data providers to quantify and mitigate privacy risks, but they suffer two main limitations: (i) they have a high computational complexity; (ii) the privacy risk must be re-computed for each new set of individuals, geographic areas or time windows. In this paper we explore a fast and flexible solution to estimate privacy risk in human mobility data, using predictive models to capture the relation between an individual's mobility patterns and her privacy risk. We show the effectiveness of our approach by experimentation on a real-world GPS dataset and provide a comparison with traditional methods.

1 Introduction

In the last years human mobility analysis has attracted a growing interest due to its importance in several applications such as urban planning, transportation engineering and public health [10]. The availability of these data has offered the opportunity to observe human movements at large scales and in great detail, leading to the discovery of quantitative patterns [8], the mathematical modeling of human mobility [9,14] etc. Unfortunately mobility data are sensitive because they may reveal personal information or allow the re-identification of individuals, creating serious privacy risks if they are analyzed with malicious intent [12]. Driven by these sensitive issues, researchers have developed methodologies and frameworks to mitigate the individual privacy risks associated to the study of GPS trajectories and Big Data in general [1]. These tools aim at preserving both the right to individual's privacy and the effectiveness of the analytical results, trying to find a reasonable trade-off between privacy protection and data quality. They allow the definition of infrastructures for supporting privacy and of technical requirements for data protection, enforcing cross-relations between

© Springer International Publishing AG 2017
S. Tonetta et al. (Eds.): SAFECOMP 2017 Workshops, LNCS 10489, pp. 415–426, 2017.
DOI: 10.1007/978-3-319-66284-8_35

privacy-preserving solutions and legal regulations, since assessing privacy risk is required by the new EU General Data Protection Regulation. To this aim, Pratesi et al. [11] propose a framework for the privacy risk assessment of individuals in mobility datasets. Although frameworks like the one presented in [11] are effective in many scenarios, they suffer a drawback: the privacy risk assessment has a high computational complexity (non-polynomial in time) because it computes the maximum privacy risk given an external knowledge that a malicious adversary may have, i.e., it considers all the possible ways the adversary can try to re-identify an individual. Moreover, the privacy risks must be recomputed every time new data become available and for every selection of individuals, geographic areas and periods of time.

In this paper we propose a data mining approach for privacy risk assessment that overcomes the computational limitations of existing frameworks. We first introduce some possible re-identification attacks on mobility data, and then we use linear regression to predict the privacy risk of an individual based on her mobility patterns, and we compute the individual privacy risk level according to the re-identification attacks. We then train a regressor on such data to estimate in polynomial time the privacy risk level of *previously unseen* vehicles based just on their individual mobility patterns. In a scenario where a Data Analyst asks a Data Provider for mobility data to deploy an analytical service, the Data Provider (e.g., a mobile phone carrier) can use the regressor to immediately identify individuals with a high privacy risk. Then, the Data Provider can select the most suitable privacy-preserving technique (e.g., k-anonymity, differential privacy) to mitigate their privacy risk and release only safe data to the Data Analyst. Our experiments on GPS data shows that our approach is fairly accurate in predicting the privacy risk of unseen individuals in an urban area.

The rest of the paper is organized as follows. In Sect. 2 we define the data structures to describe human mobility data according to different data aggregations. In Sect. 3 we introduce the framework used for the privacy risk assessment, while Sect. 4 describes the data mining approach we propose. In Sect. 5 we show the results of our experiments and we discuss them. Section 6 presents the main works related to our paper and finally Sect. 7 concludes the paper proposing some lines of new research.

2   Data Definitions

The approach we present in this paper is tailored for human mobility data, i.e., data describing the movements of a set of individuals. This type of data is generally collected in an automatic way through electronic devices (e.g., mobile phones, GPS devices) in form of raw trajectory data. Every record has the following fields: the identifier of the individual, a geographic location expressed in coordinates (generally latitude and longitude), a timestamp indicating when the individual stopped in or went through that location. Depending on the specific application, a trajectory can be aggregated into different data structures:

Definition 1 (Trajectory). *The trajectory T_u of an individual u is a temporally ordered sequence of tuples $T_u = \langle (l_1, t_1), (l_2, t_2), \ldots, (l_n, t_n) \rangle$, where $l_i = (x_i, y_i)$ is a location, x_i and y_i are the coordinates of the geographic location, and t_i is the corresponding timestamp, $t_i < t_j$ if $i < j$.*

Definition 2 (Frequency Vector). *The frequency vector W_u of an individual u is a sequence of tuples $W_u = \langle (l_1, w_1), (l_2, w_2), \ldots, (l_n, w_n) \rangle$ where $l_i = (x_i, y_i)$ is a location, w_i is the frequency of the location, i.e., how many times location l_i appears in the individual's trajectory T_u, and $w_i > w_j$ if $i < j$. A frequency vector W_u is hence an aggregation of a trajectory T_u.*

We denote with D a mobility dataset, which we assume is a set of a one of the above data types (trajectory or frequency vector).

3   Privacy Risk Assessment Framework

In this paper we consider the work proposed in [11], which allows for the privacy risk assessment of human mobility data. This framework considers a scenario where a Data Analyst asks a Data Provider for data to develop an analytical service. The Data Provider must guarantee the right to privacy of the individuals whose data are recorded. First, the Data Analyst transmits to the Data Provider the data requirements for the service. With these specifications, the Data Provider queries its dataset $\mathcal{D}$, producing a set of datasets $\{D_1, \ldots, D_z\}$, each with different data structures and data aggregations. The Data Provider then reiterates a procedure until it considers the data delivery safe:

(1) *Identification of Attacks*: identify a set of possible attacks that an adversary might conduct in order to re-identify individuals in the datasets $\{D_1, \ldots, D_z\}$;
(2) **Privacy Risk Computation**: simulate the attacks and compute the set of privacy risk values for every individual in the mobility datasets $\{D_1, \ldots, D_z\}$;
(3) *Dataset Selection*: select a mobility dataset $D \in \{D_1, \ldots, D_z\}$ with the best trade-off between the privacy risks of individuals and the data quality, given a certain level of tolerated privacy risk and the Data Analyst's requirements;
(4) *Risk Mitigation and Data delivery*: apply a privacy-preserving transformation (e.g., generalization, randomization, etc.) on the chosen mobility dataset D to eliminate the residual privacy risk, producing a filtered mobility dataset D_{filt}. Deliver D_{filt} to the Data Analyst when the D_{filt} is adequately safe.

In this paper we focus on improving step (2), i.e., Privacy Risk Computation, which is the most critical one from a computational point of view. Computing the privacy risk of an individual means simulating several possible attacks a malicious adversary can perform and computing the privacy risks associated to each attack. The privacy risk of an individual is related to her probability of re-identification in a dataset w.r.t. to a set of re-identification attacks. A re-identification attack assumes that an adversary gains access to a dataset. On the basis of some background knowledge about an individual, i.e., the knowledge of a subset of her mobility data, the adversary tries to re-identify all the records in the dataset regarding the individual under attack. In this paper we use the definition of privacy risk (or re-identification risk) introduced in [13].

A background knowledge represents both the kind and quantity of information known by an adversary. Two examples of kinds of background knowledge are a subset of the locations visited by an individual (spatial dimension) and the specific times an individual visited those locations (spatial and temporal dimensions). We denote with k the number of the elements known by the adversary. So for example a specific background knowledge is the knowledge of three specific locations visited by the individual under attack. We denote a set of background knowledge of size k with B_k and a specific background knowledge with b.

Let $\mathcal{D}$ be a database, D a mobility dataset extracted from $\mathcal{D}$ as an aggregation of the data on specific dimensions (e.g., an aggregated data structure and/or a filtering on time and/or space), and D_u the set of records representing individual u in D, we define the probability of re-identification as follows:

Definition 3 (Probability of Re-identification). *Given an attack, a function* matching(d, b) *indicating whether or not a record $d \in D$ matches the background knowledge b, and a function $M(D,b) = \{d \in D | matching(d,b) = True\}$, we define the* probability of re-identification *of an individual u in dataset D as: $PR_D(d = u|b) = \frac{1}{|M(D,b)|}$ that is the probability to associate record $d \in D$ to individual u, given background knowledge b.*

Note that $PR_D(d = u|b) = 0$ if the individual u is not represented in D. Since each background knowledge b has its own probability of re-identification, we define the risk of re-identification of an individual as the maximum probability of re-identification over the set of possible background knowledge:

Definition 4 (Risk of re-identification or Privacy risk). *The risk of re-identification (or privacy risk) of an individual u given a set of background knowledge B_k is her maximum probability of re-identification $Risk(u, D) = \max PR_D(d = u|b)$ for $b \in B_k$. The risk of re-identification has the lower bound $\frac{|D_u|}{|D|}$ (a random choice in D), and $Risk(u, D) = 0$ if $u \notin D$.*

An individual is hence associated to several privacy risks, each for every background knowledge of an attack. Every privacy risk of an individual can be computed using the following procedure: *(i)* define an attack based on a specific background knowledge, *(ii)* given an individual and fixing k, compute all the possible $b \in B_k$ and the corresponding probability of re-identification, and *(iii)* select the privacy risk of the individual for a set B_k as the maximum probability of re-identification across all $b \in B_k$.

3.1 Computational Complexity of Privacy Risk Computation

The procedure of privacy risk computation has a high computational complexity. We assume that the adversary uses all the information available to her when conducting a re-identification attack on an individual. The maximum possible value of k is len, the length of the data structure of an individual. Since it is unlikely that an adversary knows the complete movement of an individual (i.e., all the points), we have to reason about different and reasonable values of k. To compute all $b \in B_k$ we have to compute a k-combination of elements from the original data structure. We need all b to correctly compute the risk of re-identification, since we have to know all the possible probabilities of re-identification. This leads to a high overall computational complexity $\mathcal{O}(\binom{len}{k} \times N)$, since the framework generates $\binom{len}{k}$ background knowledge b and, for each b, it executes N matching operations by applying function $matching$. While some optimizations can be made depending on the kind of attack simulated, the overall complexity of the procedure is dominated by the $\binom{len}{k}$ term.

4 Fast Privacy Risk Assessment with Data Mining

Given its computational complexity, the privacy risk computation becomes unfeasible as the size of the dataset increases. This drawback is even more serious if we consider that the privacy risks must be necessarily re-computed every time the mobility dataset is updated and for every selection of individuals, geographic areas and periods of time. In order to overcome these problems, we propose a fast and flexible data mining approach. The idea is to train a regression model to predict the privacy risk of an individual based solely on her individual mobility patterns. The training of the predictive model is made by using a dataset where every record refers to an individual and consists of *(i)* a vector of the individual's mobility features and *(ii)* the privacy risk value of the individual. We make our approach parametric with respect to the predictive algorithm: in our experiments we use a Random Forest regressor, but every algorithm available in literature can be used for the predictive tasks. Note that our approach is constrained to the fixed well-defined set of attacks introduced in Sect. 4.2, which is a representative set of nine sufficiently diverse attacks tailored for the data structures required to compute standard individual human mobility measures. Our approach can be easily extended to any type of attack defined on human mobility data by using the privacy framework proposed by [11].

4.1 Individual Mobility Features

The mobility dynamics of an individual can be described by a set of measures widely used in literature. The number of visits V of an individual is the length of her trajectory, i.e., the sum of all the visits she did in any location during the period of observation [8]. By dividing this quantity by the number of days in the period of observation we obtain the average number of daily visits $\overline{V}$, which is a measure of the erratic behavior of an individual during the day [9]. The length $Locs$ of the frequency vector indicates the number of distinct places visited by an individual during the period of observation [14]. Dividing $Locs$ by the number of available locations on the considered territory we obtain $Locs_{ratio}$, which indicates the fraction of territory exploited by an individual in her mobility behavior. The maximum distance D_{max} traveled is defined as the length of the longest trip of an individual [19], while D_{max}^{trip} is defined as the ratio between D_{max} and the maximum possible distance between the locations in the area. The sum of all the trip lengths is defined as D_{sum} [19]. It can be also averaged over the days in the period of observation obtaining $\overline{D}_{sum}$. The radius of gyration r_g is the characteristic distance traveled by an individual during the period of observation [8]. The mobility entropy E is a measure of the predictability of an individual's trajectory [6]. Also, for each individual we keep track of the characteristics of three different locations: the most, the second most and the least visited location. The frequency w_i of a location i is the number of times an individual visited i during the period of observation, while the average frequency $\overline{w}_i$ is the daily average frequency of i. We also define w_i^{pop} as the frequency of location i divided by the popularity of i in the whole dataset. The quantity U_i^{ratio} is the number of distinct individuals that visited location i divided by the total number $|U_{set}|$ of individuals in the dataset, while U_i is the number of distinct individuals that visited i during the period of observation. Finally, the location entropy E_i is the predictability of i, defined as a variation of the Shannon entropy.

Every individual u in the dataset is described by a mobility vector $\overline{m}_u$ of the 16 mobility features described above. It is worth noting that all the measures can be computed in linear time on the size of the corresponding data structure.

4.2   Privacy Attacks on Mobility Data

In this section we describe the attacks we use in this paper:

Location Attack. In a Location attack the adversary knows a certain number of locations visited by the individual but she does not know the temporal order of the visits. Since an individual might visit the same location multiple times in a trajectory, the adversary's knowledge is a multiset.

Location Sequence Attack. Here, the adversary knows a subset of the locations visited by the individual and the temporal ordering of the visits.

Visit Attack. In a Visit attack the adversary knows a subset of the locations visited by the individual and the time the individual visited these locations.

Frequent Location and Sequence Attack. We introduce two attacks based on location knowledge applied to frequency vectors. In the Frequent Location attack the adversary knows a number of *frequent* locations visited by an individual, while in the Frequent Location Sequence attack the adversary knows a subset of the locations visited by an individual and the relative ordering with respect to the frequencies (from most frequent to least frequent). The Frequent Location attack is similar to the Location attack but in frequency vectors a location can appear only once. The Frequent Location Sequence attack is similar to the Location Sequence attack, but a location can appear only once in the vector and locations are ordered by descending frequency and not by time.

Frequency Attack. We introduce an attack where the adversary knows the locations visited by the individual, their reciprocal ordering of frequency, and the minimum number of visits of the individual. This means that, when searching for specific subsequences, the adversary must consider also subsequences containing the known locations with a greater frequency.

Home and Work Attack. In the Home and Work attack the adversary knows the two most frequent locations of an individual and their frequencies. It assumes the same background knowledge of Frequency attack but related only to two locations. This is the only attack where the set of background knowledge is fixed and composed of just a single 2-combination for each individual.

4.3   Construction of Training Dataset

Given an attack i based on a specific set of background knowledge B_j^i, the regression training dataset TR_j^i can be constructed by the following procedure: first, given a mobility dataset D, for every individual u we compute the set of features described in Sect. 4.1 based on her mobility data. Every individual u is hence described by a mobility feature vector $\overline{m}_u$. All the individuals' feature vectors compose mobility matrix $F = (\overline{m}_1, \ldots, \overline{m}_n)$, where n is the number of individuals in D. Second, for every individual we simulate the attack with B_j^i on D, in order to compute a privacy risk value for every individual. We obtain a privacy risk vector $R_j^i = (r_1, \ldots, r_n)$. The regression training set is hence $TR_j^i = (F, R_j^i)$;

Every regression dataset TR_j^i is used to train a predictive model M_j^i. If $0 \le i \le I$ where I is the number of different kinds of attack and $0 \le j \le J$ where J is the number of different sets of possible background knowledge, we have a total of $J \times I$ models. For example, if we consider sets of background knowledge ranging in size from $j = 1$ to $j = 5$ for 7 different attacks, we would have $I = 7$ and $J = 5$. The predictive model will be used by the Data Provider to immediately estimate the privacy risk value of *previously unseen* individuals, whose data were not used in the learning process, with respect to attack i, set of background knowledge B_j^i and dataset D.

Example 1 (Construction of Regression Training Set). Let us consider a mobility dataset of trajectories $D=\{T_{u_1}, T_{u_2}, T_{u_3}, T_{u_4}, T_{u_5}\}$ corresponding to five individuals u_1, u_2, u_3, u_4 and u_5. Given an attack i, a set of background knowledge B_j^i and dataset D, we construct the regression training set TC_j^i as follows: first, for every individual u_i we compute the 21 individual mobility measures based on her trajectory T_{u_i}. Every individual u_i is hence described by a mobility feature vector of length 21 $\overline{m}_{u_i} = (m_1^{(u_i)}, \ldots, m_{21}^{(u_i)})$. All the mobility feature vectors compose mobility matrix $F=(\overline{m}_{u_1}, \overline{m}_{u_2}, \overline{m}_{u_3}, \overline{m}_{u_4}, \overline{m}_{u_5})$; second, we simulate the attack with B_j^i on dataset D and obtain a vector of five privacy risk values $R_j^i = (r_{u_1}, r_{u_2}, r_{u_3}, r_{u_4}, r_{u_5})$, each for every individual.

4.4   Usage of the Regression Approach

The Data Provider can use a regression model M_j^i to determine the value of privacy risk with respect to an attack i and a set of background knowledge B_j^i for: *(i) previously unseen* individuals, whose data were *not* used in the learning process; *(ii)* a selection of individuals in the database already used in the learning process. It is worth noting that with existing methods the privacy risk of individuals in scenario *(ii)* must be recomputed by simulating attack i from scratch. In contrast, the usage of regression model M_j^i allows for obtaining the privacy risk of the selected individuals immediately. The computation of the mobility measures and the regression of privacy risk can be done in polynomial time as a one-off procedure. To clarify this point, let us consider the following scenario. A Data Analyst requests the Data Provider for updated mobility data about a new set of individuals with the purpose of studying their characteristic traveled distance (radius of gyration r_g) and the predictability of their movements (mobility entropy E). Since both measures can be computed by using a frequency vector, the Data Provider can release just the frequency vectors of the individuals requested. Before that, however, the Data Provider wants to determine the level of privacy risk of the individuals with respect to the Frequency attack (F) and several sets of background knowledge B_j^F. The Data Provider uses the regression model M_j^F previously trained to obtain the privacy risk of the individuals. So the Data Provider computes the mobility features for the individuals in the dataset and gives them in input to the regression model, obtaining an estimation of privacy risk. On the basis of privacy risks obtained from M_j^F, the Data Provider can identify risky individuals, i.e., individuals with a high privacy risk. She then can decide to either filter out the risky individuals or to select suitable privacy-preserving techniques (e.g., k-anonymity or differential privacy) and transform their mobility data in such a way that their privacy is preserved.

5   Experiments

For all the attacks defined except the Home and Work attack we consider four sets of background knowledge B_k with $k = 2, 3, 4, 5$, where each B_k corresponds to an attack where the adversary knows k locations visited by the individual. For the Home and Work attack we have just one possible set of background knowledge, where the adversary knows the two most frequent locations of an individual. We use a dataset provided by Octo Telematics[1] storing the GPS tracks of 9,715 private vehicles traveling in Florence, a very populous area of central Italy, from 1st May to 31st May 2011, corresponding to 179,318 trajectories. We assign each origin and destination point of the original raw trajectories to the corresponding census cell according to the information provided by the Italian National Statistics Bureau [8]. We first performed a simulation of the attacks computing the privacy risk values for all individuals in the dataset and

---

[1] https://www.octotelematics.com/.

for all B_k.[2] We then performed regression experiments using a Random Forest regressor.[3] Table 1 shows the average Mean Squared Error (mse) and the average coefficient of determination R^2 resulting from the regression experiments for all the attacks. The results are averaged over $k = 2, 3, 4, 5$, since the empirical distributions of privacy risk are fairly similar across different values of k. Also, mse and R^2 are almost identical for each kind of attack. The best results are obtained for the Frequent Location Sequence attack, with values of mse $= 0.01$ and $R^2 = 0.92$, while the weakest results are obtained for the Home and Work attack, with values of mse $= 0.07$ and $R^2 = 0.50$. Overall, the results show good predictive performance across all attacks, suggesting that regression could indeed be an accurate alternative to the direct computation of privacy risk.

Table 1. Results of regression experiments.

Predicted variable	mse	r2
Frequent location sequence	0.01	0.92
Visit	0.01	0.89
Frequency	0.02	0.88
Location	0.02	0.90
Location sequence	0.02	0.84
Frequent location	0.03	0.73
Home and work	0.07	0.50

Execution Times. We show the computational improvement of our approach in terms of execution time by comparing in Table 2 the execution times of the attack simulations and the execution times of the regression tasks.[4] The execution time of a single regression task is the sum of three subtasks: *(i)* the execution time of training the regressor on the training set; *(ii)* the execution time of using the trained regressor to predict the risk on the test set; *(iii)* the execution time of evaluating the performance of regression. Table 2 shows that the execution time of attack simulations is low for most of the attacks except for Location Sequence and Location, for which execution times are huge: more than 1 week each. In contrast the regression tasks have constant execution times of around 22 s. In summary, our approach can compute the risk levels for all the 33 attacks in 179 s (less than 3 min), while the attack simulations require more than two weeks of computation.

---

[2] The Python code for attacks simulation is available here: https://github.com/pellungrobe/privacy-mobility-lib.

[3] We use the Python package `scikit-learn` to perform the regression experiments.

[4] For a given type of attack we report the sum of the execution times of the attacks for configurations $k = 2, 3, 4, 5$. We perform the experiments on Ubuntu 16.04.1 LTS 64 bit, 32 GB RAM, 3.30 GHz Intel Core i7.

Table 2. Execution times of attack simulations and regression tasks.

Variable ($\sum_2^5 k$)	Simulation	Regression
Home and work	149 s (2.5 m)	7 s
Frequency	645 s (10 m)	22 s
Frequent location sequence	846 s (14 m)	22 s
Frequent location	997 s (10 m)	22 s
Visit	2,274 s (38 m)	16 s
LocationSequence	> 168 h (1 week)	22 s
Location	> 168 h (1 week)	22 s
Total	**> 2 weeks**	**172 s**

Discussion. The preliminary work presented above shows some promising results. The coefficient of determination and the execution times suggest that the regression can be a valid and fast alternative to existing privacy risk assessment tools. Instead of re-computing privacy risks when new data records become available, which would result in high computational costs, a Data Provider can effectively use the regressors to obtain immediate and reliable estimates for every individual. The mobility measures can be computed in linear time of the size of the dataset. Every time new mobility data of an individual become available, the Data Provider can recompute her mobility features. To take into account long-term changes in mobility patterns the recomputation of mobility measures can be done at regular time intervals (e.g., every month) by considering a time window with the most recent data (e.g., the last six months of data).

6   Related Works

Human mobility data contains personal sensitive information and can reveal many facets of the private life of individuals, leading to potential privacy violation. To overcome the possibility of privacy leaks, many techniques have been proposed in literature. A widely used privacy-preserving model is k-anonymity [13], which requires that an individual should not be identifiable from a group of size smaller than k based on their quasi-identifiers (QIDs), i.e., a set of attributes that can be used to uniquely identify individuals. Assuming that adversaries own disjoint parts of a trajectory, [17] reduces privacy risk by relying on the suppression of the dangerous observations from each individual's trajectory. In [20], authors propose the attack-graphs method to defend against attacks, based on k-anonymity. Other works are based on the differential privacy model [5]. [7] considers a privacy-preserving distributed aggregation framework for movement data. [3] proposes to publish a contingency table of trajectory data, where each cell contains the number of individuals commuting from a source to a destination. [21] defines several similarity metrics which can be combined in a unified framework to provide de-anonymization of mobility data and social network data. One of the most important work about privacy risk assessment is the LINDDUN methodology [4], a privacy-aware framework, useful for modeling privacy threats in software-based systems. In the last years, different techniques for risk management have been proposed, such as NIST's Special Publication 800-30 [16]. Unfortunately, many of these works do not consider privacy risk assessment and simply include privacy considerations when assessing the impact of threats. In [18], authors elaborate an entropy-based method to evaluate the disclosure risk of personal data, trying to manage quantitatively privacy risks. The *unicity* measure proposed in [15] evaluates the privacy risk as the number of records/trajectories which are uniquely identified. [2] proposes a risk-aware framework for information disclosure which supports runtime risk assessment, using adaptive anonymization as risk-mitigation method. Unfortunately, this framework only works on relational datasets since it needs to discriminate between quasi-identifiers and sensitive attributes. In this paper we use the privacy risk assessment framework introduced by [11] to calculate the privacy risks of each individual in a mobility dataset.

7   Conclusion

Human mobility data are a precious proxy to improve our understanding of human dynamics, as well as to improve urban planning, transportation engineering and epidemic modeling. Nevertheless human mobility data contain sensitive information which can lead to a serious violation of the privacy of the individuals involved. In this paper we explored a fast and flexible solution for estimating the privacy risk in human mobility data, which overcomes the computational issues of existing privacy risk assessment frameworks. We showed through experimentations that our approach can achieve good estimations of privacy risks. As future work, it would be necessary to test our approach more extensively on different datasets and to evaluate the importance of mobility features with respect to the prediction of risk. Another possible extension of our method would be to apply more refined data mining techniques to assess the privacy risk of individuals. Moreover, our approach provides a fast tool to immediately obtain the privacy risks of individuals, leaving to the Data Provider the choice of the most suitable privacy preserving techniques to manage and mitigate the privacy risks of individuals. It would be interesting to perform an extensive experimentation to select the best techniques to reduce the privacy risk of individuals in mobility datasets and at same time ensuring high data quality for analytical services.

Acknowledgments. Funded by the European project SoBigData (Grant Agreement 654024).

References

1. Abul, O., Bonchi, F., Nanni, M.: Never Walk Alone: Uncertainty for anonymity in moving objects databases. In: ICDE, pp. 376–385 (2008)
2. Armando, A., Bezzi, M., Metoui, N., Sabetta, A.: Risk-based privacy-aware information disclosure. Int. J. Secur. Softw. Eng. **6**(2), 70–89 (2015)

3. Cormode, G., Procopiuc, C.M., Srivastava, D., Tran, T.T.L.: Differentially private summaries for sparse data. In: ICDT 2012, pp. 299–311 (2012)
4. Deng, M., Wuyts, K., Scandariato, R., Preneel, B., Joosen, W.: A privacy threat analysis framework: supporting the elicitation and fulfillment of privacy requirements. Requir. Eng. **16**(1), 3–32 (2011)
5. Dwork, C., McSherry, F., Nissim, K., Smith, A.: Calibrating noise to sensitivity in private data analysis. In: Halevi, S., Rabin, T. (eds.) TCC 2006. LNCS, vol. 3876, pp. 265–284. Springer, Heidelberg (2006). doi:10.1007/11681878_14
6. Eagle, N., Pentland, A.S.: Eigenbehaviors: identifying structure in routine. Behav. Ecol. Sociobiol. **63**(7), 1057–1066 (2009)
7. Monreale, A., Wang, W.H., Pratesi, F., Rinzivillo, S., Pedreschi, D., Andrienko, G., Andrienko, N.: Privacy-preserving distributed movement data aggregation. In: Vandenbroucke, D., Bucher, B., Crompvoets, J. (eds.) Geographic Information Science at the Heart of Europe. LNGC, pp. 225–245. Springer, Cham (2013). doi:10.1007/978-3-319-00615-4_13
8. Pappalardo, L., Simini, F., Rinzivillo, S., Pedreschi, D., Giannotti, F., Barabasi, A.-L.: Returners and explorers dichotomy in human mobility. Nat. Commun. **6**, 1–8 (2015)
9. Pappalardo, L., Simini, F.: Modelling spatio-temporal routines in human mobility. CoRR abs/1607.05952 (2016)
10. Pappalardo, L., Vanhoof, M., Gabrielli, L., Smoreda, Z., Pedreschi, D., Giannotti, F.: An analytical framework to nowcast well-being using mobile phone data. Int. J. Data Sci. Anal. **2**(1), 75–92 (2016)
11. Pratesi, F., Monreale, A., Trasarti, R., Giannotti, F., Pedreschi, D., Yanagihara, T.: PRISQUIT: a system for assessing privacy risk versus quality in data sharing. Technical report 2016-TR-043. ISTI - CNR, Pisa, Italy. FriNov20162291 (2016)
12. Rubinstein, I.S.: Big Data: The end of privacy or a new beginning? International Data Privacy Law (2013)
13. Samarati, P., Sweeney, L.: Generalizing data to provide anonymity when disclosing information (Abstract). In: PODS, p. 188 (1998)
14. Song, C., Koren, T., Wang, P., Barabasi, A.-L.: Modelling the scaling properties of human mobility. Nat. Phys. **6**(10), 818–823 (2010)
15. Song, Y., Dahlmeier, D., Bressan, S.: Not so unique in the crowd: a simple and effective algorithm for anonymizing location data. In: PIR@SIGIR, pp. 19–24 (2014)
16. Stoneburner, G., Goguen, A., Feringa, A.: Risk Management Guide for Information Technology Systems: Recommendations of the National Institute of Standards and Technology. NIST special publication, vol. 800 (2002)
17. Terrovitis, M., Mamoulis, N.: Privacy preservation in the publication of trajectories. In: MDM, pp. 65–72 (2008)
18. Trabelsi, S., Salzgeber, V., Bezzi, M., Montagnon, G.: Data disclosure risk evaluation. In: CRiSIS 2009, pp. 35–72 (2009)
19. Williams, N.E., Thomas, T.A., Dunbar, M., Eagle, N., Dobra, A.: Measures of human mobility using mobile phone records enhanced with GIS data. PLoS ONE **10**(7), 1–16 (2015)
20. Yarovoy, R., Bonchi, F., Lakshmanan, L.V.S., Wang, W.H.: Anonymizing moving objects: how to hide a MOB in a crowd? In: Proceeding of the EDBT Conference, pp. 72–83 (2009)
21. Ji, S., Li, W., Srivatsa, M., He, J.S., Beyah, R.: Structure based data deanonymization of social networks and mobility traces, pp. 237–254 (2014)

Security and Privacy in the Automotive Domain: A Technical and Social Analysis

Zhendong Ma[1](✉), Walter Seböck[2] (ID), Bettina Pospisil[2] (ID),
Christoph Schmittner[1], and Thomas Gruber[1]

[1] AIT Austrian Institute of Technology,
Donau-City-Strasse 1, 1220 Vienna, Austria
zhendong.ma@ait.ac.at
[2] Danube University Krems, Dr. Karl-Dorrek-Straße 30, 3500 Krems, Austria

Abstract. The automotive domain is undergoing a tremendous transformation in the speed and depth of technological development in recent years. Most of the innovations are based on electronics and ICT. As it is the case for most ICT-based systems, there are increasing concerns about security and privacy in the automotive domain. In this paper, we present a technical and social analysis of this issue using a methodological scenario building approach. We believe that current and future solutions must take both technical and social aspect into consideration. Our analysis provides stakeholders with such a view.

Keywords: Autonomous drive · Cooperative Intelligent Transport System (C-ITS) · Security · Privacy · Social impact

1 Introduction

Due to rapid technology development and new business opportunities, automotive systems are undergoing a tremendous transformation turning into "computers on wheels". The inherent problems of Information security and privacy become realistic in the automotive domain. The main factors for security and privacy concerns come from recent innovations in autonomous drive and cooperative Intelligent Transport Systems (C-ITS). Autonomous drive takes partial or full control of a car from a human driver. At the same time, the computer-based automotive systems consume and generate a large amount of data. C-ITS enables data exchange among the cars and between the vehicle on the road and any host in the transportation systems or any device connected to the Internet. The implication of the transformation from isolated mechanical systems to "Internet of Things" is enormous on technical front as well as on the social aspect. Automotive systems collect data about driving behavior and locations and communicate with central systems in order to optimize the overall traffic flow. While it would be beneficial for privacy to sanitize the data of all personally identifiable information (PII) there is a need to retain a minimal set of information about the sender in order to ensure authenticity and trustworthiness of the data. In addition global optimization works best if near real-time information is always available. For privacy we would like to minimize the number of times position data is transmitted in order to hinder the

S. Tonetta et al. (Eds.): SAFECOMP 2017 Workshops, LNCS 10489, pp. 427–434, 2017.
DOI: 10.1007/978-3-319-66284-8_36

generation of movement profiles. Driving data is also interesting for insurance provider in order to offer contracts based on driving behavior.

To ensure security and privacy in the era of autonomous driving vehicle with C-ITS environment, the society is facing multiple technical challenges [1], which also influence the trust and acceptance of the general public. Many works have been done focusing on various topics such as communications [2] and on-board system design [3]. However, from a macro point of view, many questions remain unanswered. Automobile is a part of transport systems for people and freights. As a part of the critical infrastructures, failures of transport systems will have devastating effect on critical sectors and people's life at national and international level. In a general sense, future transport will be underlain by an ICT infrastructure from the back-end to individual cars. Security and privacy is thus to consider potential threats from cyberattacks and misuse of personal data. Due to the increase in complexity, functionality and connectivity, modern and future transport systems have increased vulnerabilities and weakness with respect to Information security and privacy. The complex infrastructure is highly distributed and difficult to protect. Any new technologies or use case will introduce potentially new threats and risks, and inter-dependency. Security and privacy in automotive domain require considerations in multiple dimensions, from technical to social, from IT infrastructure to software in embedded systems in the car. In this paper, we present our work on the analysis of automotive security and privacy across the technical and social aspects. Our focus is on the identification of current and near-future scenarios based on the technical development and social concerns to date. The research results are envisioned to provide a ground for stakeholders and decision makers to plan and design measures accordingly. With an in-depth analysis of security and privacy challenges facing automotive domain, we aim at using existing development and facts in order to identify specific challenges and their impact on Austrian society.

Previous studies already showed that the human factor should not be left unattended when talking about autonomous vehicles and privacy. If society does not trust in and accept autonomous vehicles it is not going to use them and an implementation will failure [4–6]. As a first systematic approach to all of these concerns in Austria, the KIRAS funded "CybSiVerkehr" study conducted an in-depth analysis of cybersecurity challenges in the context of the global industrial and technological development. Within the study the research team illustrated existing developments of C-ITS and autonomous cars in order to identify specific challenges and their impact on Austrian society with respect to cybersecurity. Moreover besides the theoretical considerations in form of a meta-analysis, the findings should also be revised and extended by the opinions of experts and stakeholders on the identified issues and concerns covering both technical and societal aspects. These opinions are going to be collected in the context of qualitative focus groups. The aim of the study is to draft comprehensive recommendations to the stakeholders on how to prepare and react to cybersecurity challenges of future transport systems. The study will provide guidance on relevant topics including risk management, prevention, cyber situation awareness, legal and social readiness, and user privacy.

2 Security and Privacy Analysis from a Technical and Social Perspective

Automotive domain is under dramatic transformation and development. It is a challenge to identify and analyze various facts and prognoses in a dynamic setting. For this purpose, we apply the principles and techniques of scenario building. Scenario building is a useful tool to identify and predict possible progression of events and their outcomes in the future in the planning phase. Our scenarios building is based on the following steps: first, we identify the basic components of a scenario. The sequence of the components that consist of a security and privacy scenario in automotive domain include threat actor, motivation, attack vector, value at risk, business impact, and social impact; second, we populate each of the components with elements based on the State of the Art. The definition of the elements is based on literature survey; third, we select one or more elements from each of the scenario components and chain them to form a basic sketch of a scenario. Multiple scenario sketches are created in brain storming sessions; and finally, we select the most representative scenario sketches and enrich them with more facts. The purpose of the enriched scenarios is to describe it in a structured and narrative way such that non-technical people can also understand. Furthermore, more details are brainstormed and added to the scenarios. The final results follow the same structure according to the scenario component, similar to a textual use case description. These scenarios provide a basis to raise awareness and communicate to various stakeholders to elicit feedback.

2.1 Technical Scenario Description

This section gives a subset of the identified security and privacy scenarios that is or will likely to be happening based on the methodological identification of the building blocks. The subset includes scenarios that we deem as representative or important to be considered. Due to the space limitation, we present the scenarios in compact paragraphs, which follow the structure of title, threat actor, motivation, target, attack scenario, and business impact, as well as our rationale.

Political Assassination Covered as a Car Accident. Nation state. Cover a politically motivated assassination in a car accident to avoid jurisdiction or international law. Targeted individuals such as politicians, journalists, or political activists. Implant malware in ECUs that control safety-critical functions of a targeted car (e.g. speed, steering wheel, brake) through direct physical access via OBD port when the car is at a garage; or exploit vulnerabilities in the OTA update process to push malware downstream in a normal update. Afterwards, the malware is triggered by some predefined conditions such as the time after leaving the garage or the speed of the car. The activated malware cause one or more ECUs or the in-car network to malfunction, causing the car to travel at high speed or lose control and a crash. It can also cause the malfunctioning of the autonomous drive function. After the accident, the malware removes itself from the ECU so there is no trace left for forensics. Loss of human life and collateral damages of other road user or infrastructure. The recent Wikileaks disclosure shows that nation state is likely to have the capability for such an attack[1].

Automotive Ransomware, Organized Crime, Hacker Group. Extort money from car manufacturers or car owners. ECUs and infotainment systems, whose loss of function will lead to the loss of mobility or function. Exploit vulnerabilities in OTA update process which leads to a car to down-load ransomware. Or distribute fake Update for a specific brand to trigger a car owner to download and install it on his or her car. Afterwards, the rasomware activates itself after some time. It can lock users out of their cars, or lock users in their cars; freeze the ignition; encrypt critical software in the in-car system; block the update function; or brick some ECUs to make them totally unusable. The ransomware maker extorts money from car manufacturers or car owners to pay in order to unlock the car entrance, unlock the ECUs; decrypt the software. Financial loss maybe small for each car, but it becomes big when a large amount of cars is affected. It also damages reputation and market share for manufacturers. There is already speculation of vehicle-targeted ransomware[2]. The recent rampage of WannaCry can only confirm this view[3].

Car Theft by Defeating Anti-theft Mechanisms. Organized crime or car thief. Steal a car. Car with keyless entry or radio immobilizer. Exploit the weakness in the keyless entry system to drive the car away. Or exploit the weakness in the keyless entry system to steal the valuable belongings from the car. Financial loss of car owner or insurance company. The proof of concept of such attack is already published by different security researchers[4,5].

Cause Road Accidents to Disrupt Traffic. Hacker group, prankster/script kiddie, terrorist. Causing embarrassment of government and road operator, activism campaign, brag right, cause harm to civilians and disrupt the traffic to the targeted region or government. ITS infrastructure such as traffic light, road-side warning systems, the RF channel. Manipulate RSU traffic signals/signs/information (traffic light, speed limit, traffic flow). Or send out fake traffic warning signals such as road construction, speed limit, traffic jam; or fake messages through traffic broadcast systems to cause chaos and driver panic. Or jam the RF channel so no Car2X communication is possible, causing chaos on the road. Or attack the IT system at the traffic management center, make it no longer possible to manage traffic from the traffic management center. Financial loss due to disruption of transportation. Detailed analysis has been given in the EVITA project[6].

---

[1] http://www.nzherald.co.nz/world/news/article.cfm?c_id=2&objectid=11814476.

[2] http://blog.caranddriver.com/ransomware-the-next-big-automotive-cybersecurity-threat/.

[3] https://arstechnica.com/security/2017/05/an-nsa-derived-ransomware-worm-is-shutting-down-computers-worldwide/.

[4] https://www.adac.de/_mmm/pdf/Keyless_Liste-gepr%C3%BCfte-Fahrzeuge%2020170317_257944.pdf.

[5] https://conference.hitb.org/hitbsecconf2017ams/sessions/chasing-cars-keyless-entry-system-attacks/.

[6] https://rieke.link/EVITAD2.3v1.1.pdf.

Mass Surveillance by Collecting Vehicle Users' Personal Data Related to Mobility. Operator, marketing and adverting company. Collect personal data from vehicle user in order to make targeted business offerings, or infer business opportunities. Personal data such as mobility trance, location visited, driving behavior transmitted in Car2X communication. Deploy wireless receivers that receive Car2X communication messages at strategic intersections along the road. Or capture Car2X communications from passing by cars. Or data analysis, correlate the location data to identify spatial and temporal patterns, combine with other data source (social media, census data) to identify the driver, the passengers in the car, and to profile the individuals and their social behavior and interactions. Loss of privacy. Privacy in Car2X communication has been studied in the past [7].

Cause Accidents of a Particular Brand to Cause Massive Financial and Market Loss of Its Car Manufacturer. Hacker group or security researchers. Gain business advantage on market share, product sale over competitor. Safety-critical ECUs systems in car. Support research that leads to the discovery of serious security flaws in a competitor's product line. Or leak inside information to hacker groups about a competitor's system. Consequently the security flaws are exploited by various groups, cause serious road accidents. Mass recall and liability law suit against the manufacturer of the car. Car manufacturer has massive financial loss. Chrysler Jeep's 1.4 million vehicles recall.

Falsify Data in Order to Evade Liability in an Accident or Traffic Regulation. Car owner, maintenance person. Avoid traffic regulation. In-car blackbox or data recorder. Tamper event-recorder for recording speed or other parameters in normal driving and accident through direct physical access. Modify related data. Present falsified data in a dispute of violation of traffic laws or responsibilities in an accident. Existing traffic regulations are bypassed due to lack of evidence. How to determine responsibility and liability when human and computer are both involved will be a challenge to existing legal framework.

Copy and Reverse Engineering Vehicle Software Data. Hacker group, organized crime, OEMs, third-party application developer. Business advantage. Obtain software in a car by purchasing it from open market. Or obtain software by copying it from head unit or ECUs. Reverse engineering the software and understand its inner working. Replicate the function of the software, either use it for the car or sell it to the competitors. Market and financial loss of the original software manufacturer. In-car software is a target of attack for various reasons[7].

2.2 Social Scenario Description

While on the one hand threats on the technical side are short- and medium-term and have therefore a similar short- and medium term solution period, social scenarios on the other hand are completely decoupled from the technical security risks and represent a long term, substantial change concerning the societal security. Among other scenarios, we identified two societal scenarios.

---

[7] https://motherboard.vice.com/en_us/article/why-american-farmers-are-hacking-their-tractors-with-ukrainian-firmware.

The 1st scenario in this context refers to the higher physical driving density of autonomous vehicles ("platooning"). This will allow using the roads more intensively by radically reducing the distances between the vehicles. Therefore, the traffic will need less space and this will enable to rebuild the lanes in order to use them for pedestrians, cyclists or for social and urban needs [8].

The 2nd scenario focuses on the individuality of today's automobile versus a future pragmatic use of cars. In the case of the scenario of fully autonomous vehicles, the importance of ownership will decline because vehicles would have similar high availability as todays "services on demand". In this case, the respective use of the vehicle would be in the foreground and no longer, as now, the prestige oriented property. This would merge the prestige oriented vehicle purchase and the pragmatic use of the vehicle. In the future, the use of autonomous, collectively used common vehicles, such as public transport buses or trains with autonomous individual traffic (such as those used for holidays or family weekends or business trips) will alternate.

Economic Impact. The economic impact of these two scenarios are diametrical and therefore the extremes of the continuum (if the possibility of the prohibition of individual traffic is not considered, because a prohibition seems unrealistic from the current perspective).

In scenario 1, private transport will continue to grow as in the past decades, ownership of the vehicle continues to exist and the productivity of the vehicle manufacturers is increasing. A decline in the number of employees in the automotive sector is only possible in the case of manufacturing process efficiency improvements or in the area of the sales chain. However, the number of jobs concerned is low. Only in the field of sales, the discontinuation of the traditional dealer distribution structure can eliminate jobs which would be compensated by the development of a new structure (Rental or similar structures).

In scenario 2, the market for individual vehicle ownership would disappear in the long term, since only public transport and individual rental variants or similar structures exist. Since, in this case, municipalities or fleet managers are the owners of the vehicles, this oligopolistic market position increases the negotiating potential versus the automobile industry with regard to durability and guarantee possibilities.

Following the laws of market power, the vehicles would become more durable on the one hand, and secondly more reliable, on the other. This reduces the number of units sold and guarantees a higher TCO for the owners. The increased availability and the permanent use of the vehicles increase the effectiveness of individual traffic. Vehicles currently standing 20–23 h per day will be permanently used which will reduce the necessary parking and traffic areas and make them available in favor of the social community.

The negative effect of scenario 2 would be the elimination of individual vehicle ownership. This can lead to a breakdown of relevant vehicle sales [9]. According to this study, vehicle sales in the US could drop by 60% over the next 25 years. This would reduce the total number of vehicles in the US to 100 million vehicles. Currently 250 million vehicles are on the road in the USA. A similar result was found by researchers at the University of Michigan[8].

---

[8] http://www.umich.edu/~umtriswt/PDF/UMTRI-2015-3_Abstract_English.pdf.

Taking over a subsuming economic view, what all scenarios do have in common is that technical failures or successful attacks directly harm the prestige of the producer, will therefore cause a loss of profits and lead to a loss of market share. Moreover people get harmed in the scenarios. This ranges from a loss of human life and injuries to limitations of human mobility when a car is stolen or a road is impassable. The result is a loss of economic-power for the nation. Another major impact would be the repair costs after such an accident including the costs of a retrieval and such to rebuild the damaged infrastructure. By talking about a lack of privacy, the result is that companies provide themselves an economic advantage over their customers.

Social Impact. The social outcome in scenario 2 is dramatic. If 60% of sales are eliminated [9], this would lead to the dismantling of approximately 50–75% of the jobs and the remaining jobs will be shifted to low-cost countries. This entails the outflow of purchasing power, thereby initiating a lethal economic downward spiral.

By taking a subsuming social view, the similarity of all cases is that if such scenarios happen, people get harmed. Because the probability of an attack now appears taller to the people, this leads in most cases to a rejection of the new technology, even if the technology was not the weak point in this case [10]. The result is the rejection of implementing autonomous vehicles. Moreover the scenarios lead to a new threat situation, because vulnerability raises and often the cause of accident is unclear. This kind of attacks could be used to resolve (inter)national conflicts hidden. Therefore new ways of investigations and countermeasures are necessary. Because of the non-traceable accidents, on the one hand the question what or who is going to be blamed responsible, if an accident happens, raises. On the other hand this leads to the societal wish for a legal regulation and international security standards [11]. Another social impact of the scenarios is the differentiation of two kinds of people. While one part of society got the knowledge to understand the technique of the autonomous vehicles, the other ones do not have these skills. Thus the one group has to believe what experts and maybe insurance companies tell them, the other group has the ability to intervene in the technique of the autonomous vehicles for the reason of personal advantage and also for destructive reasons. In other words the individual responsibility for every person rises enormous. This developments leads to the establishment of a new career-model called "The Hacker". Because everybody wants to get out the best, the crime-character of "Hackers" actions gets trivialized. In case of a privacy lack, the personal privacy and the data protection are violated and one result could be surveillance. The data can be used against the interests of customers and for commercial reasons.

3   Conclusion and Possible Solutions

This paper presents a technical and social analysis of security and privacy in automotive domain within the Austrian CybSiVerkehr project. Solutions for improving cybersecurity are currently under development and will be further elaborated. An essential aspect is to obtain and continuously maintain assurance that all planned and reasonably practicable cybersecurity measures are in place. Assurance has to target the processes and the system equally, because both are potential sources of increased cybersecurity and privacy risks.

Solutions for cybersecurity have to tackle the problem at several levels, which include the occurrence of vulnerabilities, the frequency of exploits, the certainty that found vulnerabilities are fixed, the timely detection of intrusions and their neutralization, the restriction of attack effects on a limited region, the neutralization and removal of malware, and system availability in the event of successful attacks. For these aspects, measures on system-technical as well as on social level are recommendable, which will be partially addressed in our next step.

Acknowledgments. This research is supported by the project "CybSiVerkehr" funded by the Austrian security research fund KIRAS of the Federal Ministry for Transport, Innovation and Technology (BMVIT).

References

1. Schoitsch, E., Schmittner, C., Ma, Z., Gruber, T.: The need for safety and cyber-security co-engineering and standardization for highly automated automotive vehicles. In: Schulze, T., Müller, B., Meyer, G. (eds.) Advanced Microsystems for Automotive Applications 2015. LNM, pp. 251–261. Springer, Cham (2016). doi:10.1007/978-3-319-20855-8_20
2. Papadimitratos, P., Buttyan, L., Holczer, T., Schoch, E., Freudiger, J., Raya, M., Hubaux, J. P.: Secure vehicular communication systems: design and architecture. IEEE Commun. Mag. **46**(11), 100–109 (2008)
3. Schmittner, C., Ma, Z., Reyes, C., Dillinger, O., Puschner, P.: Using SAE J3061 for automotive security requirement engineering. In: Skavhaug, A., Guiochet, J., Schoitsch, E., Bitsch, F. (eds.) SAFECOMP 2016. LNCS, vol. 9923, pp. 157–170. Springer, Cham (2016). doi:10.1007/978-3-319-45480-1_13
4. Verberne, F.M., Ham, J., Midden, C.J.: Trust in smart systems sharing driving goals and giving information to increase trustworthiness and acceptability of smart systems in cars. Hum. Factors: J. Hum. Factors Ergon. Soc. **54**(5), 799–810 (2012)
5. Cunningham, M., Regan, M.A.: Autonomous vehicles: human factors issues and future research. In: Proceedings of the 2015 Australasian Road Safety Conference (2015)
6. Dinev, T., Hu, Q.: The centrality of awareness in the formation of user behavioral intention toward protective information technologies. J. Assoc. Inf. Syst. **8**(7), 386 (2007)
7. Wiedersheim, B., Ma, Z., Kargl, F., Papadimitratos, P.: Privacy in inter-vehicular networks: why simple pseudonym change is not enough. In: 2010 Seventh International Conference on Wireless On-demand Network Systems and Services (WONS), pp. 176–183. IEEE (2010)
8. Silberg, G., Wallace, R., Matuszak, G., Plessers, J., Brower, C., Subramanian, D.: Self-driving cars: the next revolution. White Paper KPMG LLP Cent. Automot. Res. (2012)
9. Johnson, B.: Barclays Research Insights on Disruptive Mobility – A scenario for 2040. Barclays Research Department (2015)
10. Slaby, M. Urban, D.: Differentielle Technikakzeptanz, oder: Nicht immer führt die Ablehnung einer Technik auch zur Ablehnung ihrer Anwendungen: eine nutzentheoretische und modell-statistische Analyse. University Stuttgart (Ed.), Stuttgart (2001)
11. Maurer, M., Gerdes, J.C., Lenz, B., Winner, H. (eds.): Autonomous Driving: Technical, Legal and Social Aspects. Springer, Heidelberg (2016). doi:10.1007/978-3-662-48847-8

One Click Privacy for Online Social Networks

Philipp Hehnle[1], Pascal Keilbach[1], Hyun-Jin Lee[1], Sabrina Lejn[1],
Daniel Steidinger[1], Marina Weinbrenner[1], and Hanno Langweg[1,2(✉)]

[1] Department of Computer Science, HTWG Konstanz University of Applied
Sciences, Konstanz, Germany
{philipp.hehnle,pascal.keilbach,hyun-jin.lee,sabrina.lejn,
daniel.steidinger,marina.weinbrenner,hanno.langweg}@htwg-konstanz.de
[2] Department of Information Security and Communication Technology,
Faculty of Information Technology and Electrical Engineering,
NTNU, Norwegian University of Science and Technology, Gjøvik, Norway

Abstract. We present an approach to reduce the complexity of adjusting privacy preferences for multiple online social networks. To achieve
this, we quantify the effect on privacy for choices that users make, and
simplify configuration by introducing privacy configuration as a service.
We present an algorithm that effectively measures privacy and adjusts
privacy settings across social networks. The aim is to configure privacy
with one click.

Keywords: Privacy · Social networks · Metrics for privacy · Configuration

1 Introduction

Nowadays, social networks are an integral part of everyday life. Recently, the
number of users has dramatically increased and the trend continues [1]. Social
networking sites allow an easy distribution of information but it is not always
easy to delimit the recipients of the information and what kind of information
they receive. Moreover, many users are not aware of the consequences that the
revelation of personal data could have. The disclosure of private information
can be critical and to some extent could be a threat, since "Likes" and other
sympathy notices, pictures and location statements reveal a lot more information
about a person than it seems at the first sight. In addition, social networks often
provide confusing terms of use or make it difficult for users to keep track of their
privacy settings.

For this reason, users of social networks should be aware of the consequences
that come with privacy disclosure. The aim of our approach is to simplify the
configuration of social networks. The main task is to quantify privacy of social
networks and provide a tool to support the user to protect his privacy adequately.

© Springer International Publishing AG 2017
S. Tonetta et al. (Eds.): SAFECOMP 2017 Workshops, LNCS 10489, pp. 435–442, 2017.
DOI: 10.1007/978-3-319-66284-8_37

2   Related Work

The basic requirement for such a tool to work is to be able to somehow measure privacy. If a privacy level can be measured, values can be compared and conclusions about improvement or worsening of the privacy level can be drawn, even across multiple social networks. The challenging aspect is, that so far, no general method for measuring privacy has been established or approved by an institution.

2.1   Configuration as a Service

People tend to use managed IT services instead of managing everything by themselves. The concept is called "everything as a service" and the most popular example is "software as a service". Cloud storage services or music streaming services are common services which people use every day. Since privacy is a complex topic and managing privacy settings can be challenging, the idea is to provide users a privacy configuration as a service. We analysed some tools that follow a similar approach.

MyPermissions (https://mypermissions.com/de/) is an app that allows users to monitor their applications that have access to their social networking sites. As the name says, it is only about permissions and does not change any privacy settings.

Reclaim Privacy scans the user's privacy settings on Facebook and indicates with colours if privacy settings are considered good or bad. Furthermore, the user could adjust the relevant settings. A similar approach is followed by Facebook Privacy Watcher (http://www.daniel-puscher.de/fpw/) by TU Darmstadt. While using Facebook, the tool indicates with a colour scheme the privacy level for each published item, such as posts, pictures, comments, etc. When users want to change the visibility e.g. of a post, a colour wheel opens and instead of adjusting the setting, the user picks a colour according to the desired privacy level. Unfortunately, these tools have been discontinued due to different reasons. Most projects were leisure projects. Since maintaining the tools took too much time, developers were compelled to stop their projects.

The most advanced approach is done by Trend Micro. They provide two possibilties for a fee for checking the privacy settings: a anti-virus software and an app. For the paper, the app "Trend Micro Mobile Security - Web Protection" was examined. With the app, it is possible to change settings in Facebook and Twitter. The user has to authenticate through the Trend Micro app with its credentials. However, the user cannot choose a desired privacy level. Instead, he has to follow privacy recommendations by Trend Micro.

None of the tools provides a way to effectively measure and change privacy settings across social networks. Reasons for failure of these tools may be explained through the complexity of privacy, social networks continuously changing their settings and a lack of measure privacy efficiently.

2.2   Privacy Measurement Index

To measure privacy, Wang and Nepali introduce a privacy index (PIDX) in [4]. The basic concept of the model uses actors, that represent a social entity (e.g. people or organisations) in a social network, and attributes to describe an actor. Each attribute has an impact on the user's privacy level, which is called the sensitivity of an attribute. Depending on the settings of the user, each attribute is to some extend visible. Therefore, the value of visibility is used. Within the simplified scope of the paper, we define the following values according to [4]:

- **Sensitivity** describes the impact of an attribute on a user's privacy level. Sensitivity is described by $S = \{s_1, s_2, s_3, \ldots, s_n\}$ and has a value between 0 and 1, where 1 indicates that the attribute describes highly sensitive information.
- **Visibility** describes the disclosure of an attribute. It is described by $V = \{v_1, v_2, v_3, \ldots, v_n\}$ and has a value between 0 and 1, where 1 indicates a publicly known attribute.

S and V represent the sensitivities and visibilities of all attributes of an actor in a social network. Wang and Nepali propose three different Privacy Indexes: $wPIDX$, $mPIDX$ and $cPIDX$.

To get the weighted privacy measurement index $wPIDX$, the first step is to multiply the sensitivity and visibility of each known attribute. Then, those values are accumulated. Finally, the $wPIDX$ is calculated by putting the accumulated result in relation to all available attribute's sensitivities and multiplying by 100. Thus, $wPDIX$ results in a value between 0 and 100, with 100 being the highest possible privacy disclosure level [4]. This leads to Eq. (1).

$$wPIDX == \frac{\sum_{j=1}^{m} v'_j s'_j}{\sum_{j=1}^{n} s_j} * 100 \tag{1}$$

Wang and Nepali also introduce the Maximum Privacy Index $mPIDX$ and the Composite Privacy Index $cPIDX$. $mPIDX$ returns the attribute that has the maximum privacy impact. $cPIDX$ combines both $wPIDX$ and $mPIDX$, giving $mPIDX$ most impact but also considers all other disclosed attributes.

For the current prototype implementation, it was decided to use $wPIDX$, because the handling with easy-structured $wPIDX$ reduces testing effort, but still considers all attributes and thus leads to insightful results. However, the question remains which one of the PIDXes leads to optimum results for our purposes.

Furthermore, if certain attributes are combined, it is possible that they further disclose privacy. For example, knowing any single component of an address (street name, house number and city) does not disclose a lot of personal data. However, knowing all of them has a higher impact on the privacy level. For this reason, Wang and Nepali introduce the concept of virtual attributes [4]. It has to be evaluated if this is applicable for our purposes.

Since the described model uses entities and instances that are valid across multiple social networks, the approach of Wang and Nepali [4] seems very promising for the project and was used to measure the privacy level.

3 One Click Privacy Concept

The concept shall provide a method that enables the user to choose a privacy level. Once the user sets a privacy level, the algorithm must guarantee the adherence to the desired privacy level. If the algorithm optimises the settings in the way that there is a better privacy level than required, this will be accepted. Nevertheless, the optimised privacy level shall be as close as possible to the desired privacy level. If, for instance, the desired privacy level was 40 and the algorithm's result was a privacy level of zero, the requirements would be fulfilled. However, the algorithm's goal to get close to the desired privacy level would not be achieved. Note that our project does not aim to achieve maximum privacy, but to enable the user to retain control of who can see his shared data. This implies the user's free choice on the degree of his privacy.

A further requirement is that personal information with high sensitivity shall not exceed the privacy level and be offset by personal information with low sensitivity that is below the privacy level limit. It is acceptable that personal information with low sensitivity exceeds the privacy level limit. This is even mandatory when complying with the previous requirements. Since it is not possible to set each preference in a way that the actual privacy level equals the desired privacy level, the desired privacy level for personal data with high sensitivity must be below the desired privacy level. If each information was below the limit, the entire privacy level would vary widely from the desired limit. For this reason, personal information with low sensitivity may exceed the limit under certain conditions which are explained in the following.

The algorithm's first step is to define the desired privacy level P_d. Afterwards, the algorithm needs to compute the limit for each personal piece of information. When using $wPIDX$, the limit for each information can be calculated like this:

$$z = \frac{P_d * \sum_{i=0}^{N} s_i}{N * 100} \qquad (2)$$

Consequently, z is the limit for each personal data item, whereas N is the amount of settings and s_i is the sensitivity for the setting i. A simple approach is to check for each setting if the visibility multiplied with the given sensitivity is equal to or below z. If this is not the case, the setting must be adapted. The consequences would be that the actual privacy level would deviate substantially from the desired privacy level. Therefore, each time there is a remainder $R = z - v * s > 0$ for an item with high sensitivity, an item with low sensitivity can exceed the limit by the remainder. This leads to the algorithm displayed in Fig. 1.

First, the desired privacy level P_d for the entire profile is defined. Then, the limit z is calculated. Now, there are two loops. Before the first loop starts, the

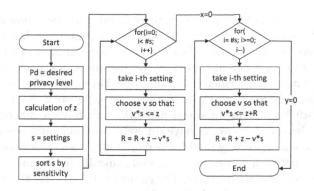

Fig. 1. Settings optimisation algorithm

settings are sorted by their sensitivities descending. The first loop runs until each setting in the set has been considered, beginning with the setting that has the highest sensitivity. In each loop run, the setting's visibility is adapted. The visibility is chosen in such a way that $v * s <= z$. Afterwards, the remainder R is calculated with $R = R + z - v * s$. In the next run, the algorithm chooses the next setting and the procedure repeats. This guarantees that those settings with the highest sensitivities are below z. The second loop starts with the last element of the set. This means that the setting with the lowest sensitivity is chosen. The algorithm checks whether the setting can be changed, since the former limit z can be shifted by the remainder. So, there is a new limit for the settings now. As a consequence, the algorithm can adapt the setting so that $v * s <= z + R$. This means, it is checked whether it is possible to worsen this setting concerning privacy. Actually, $v * s$ with the visibility that was chosen in the first loop for this setting should be added to $z + R$, too. For the sake of clarity, this has been omitted in the figure. Since the second loop starts with those settings that have the lowest sensitivities, there is no serious privacy impact if those personal data items exceed the privacy limit. After having adapted the setting, the algorithm calculates the new remainder $R = R + z - v * s$. The next setting is chosen from the set and the procedure repeats. When the remainder R is not greater than zero, z is the limit again.

4 Prerequisites for the Implementation

This section describes the necessary steps that need to be done to prepare the implementation. Since we want to provide a tool that manages privacy across multiple social networks, it has to be decided which networks will be considered. Social networks are chosen by number of users and region [2,3]. For global networks, our focus is on Facebook, Twitter, Google+ and LinkedIn. For national networks, XING for Germany, QZone for China and vKontakte for Russia were chosen.

Since the tool should be able to change settings in the relevant social networks, it is necessary to analyse the relevant settings and which attributes they will affect. Therefore, the settings of each network were summarised in a single file and clustered into ten different topics: my profile, messages, posts, detectability, location, account, announcement, blocking and hiding, security as well as specific topics that only apply to the respective social network. Nearly all settings are described differently in all social networks and have a different meaning. Furthermore, the social networks have different functions and possibilities. For example, Facebook is primary used for personal life, it serves for connecting and communicating between private persons, and LinkedIn for business. Thus, every social network has its own features. For example, QZone has the possibility to specify a security question. With the right answer a user can see certain information of the other user. QZone has a restriction, because it is the only social network which is not available in English, only in Chinese.

After clustering and managing all the settings, the sensitivity of the affected attributes was added. Here the problem arises that each person perceives the sensitivity of each attribute individually. However, tendencies can be recognised. For example, the full address is generally perceived more sensitive than the gender. Therefore, the sensitivity of the attributes is determined through an online survey throughout the project. Since the evaluation of the survey (132 students aged 18–29 years) is ongoing, we use "high", "medium" and "low" as values for sensitivity, to indicate our first results.

5   Implementation

For the first prototype we chose Twitter because the settings options are not as complex as the options on Facebook, which is suitable for testing purposes. We decided to develop a browser extension because it has the advantage that we can use the current session while the user is logged on to Twitter. Since many users remain logged on their personal computer, users will not need to authenticate themselves again which benefits the usability of the tool. Credentials are not saved or forwarded to any back-end server.

Currently, the user has to visit www.twitter.com and log on. The extension calculates the current PIDX and prints the number in the icon in the top right corner. For a detailed view, the user can click on the extension button. There is a view for the user as shown in Fig. 2. With a click on the "Adapt Settings" button, the plugin will change the settings so that the new PIDX is better than the desired one.

The extension is completely running on client side and is only using HTML, CSS and JavaScript. For the PIDX calculation, the extension is sending an AJAX GET request to Twitter's settings page. Therefore, the user does not have to visit any particular page and is not being redirected. After parsing the settings to a JavaScript object, we calculate the visibility and change the settings, based on the algorithm developed in Sect. 3. To finally change the settings, we send an AJAX POST request to Twitter. A specialty for Twitter is that Twitter is requesting a second user verification when changing the settings.

Fig. 2. Prototype 1 - Chrome extension, Twitter

After some tests on Twitter we faced a problem as Twitter might change the settings page. This already happened once since we started testing. The issue here is to somehow notice that a social network changed its settings page, because this will eventually affect the functionality of the tool.

In the current state of the project, we are developing a second, more detailed prototype which is extended to the social network Xing. With this prototype, we will recheck and optimise our theoretical approach.

6   Discussion and Future Work

Since the project is still going on, there are some issues that have to be considered and will be discussed in this section.

In Sect. 2.2, it was mentioned to use $wPIDX$ for practical reasons of the prototype. Until now, $wPIDX$ leads to promising results. However, it has to be evaluated if $cPIDX$ leads to more accurate results. Wang and Nepali claim $cPIDX$ to be the most accurate since it weighs the attribute with the maximum privacy impact most [4]. We plan to verify in several test cases if this statement is true for the desired purposes and if it leads to more accurate results regarding the desired privacy level.

Furthermore, a current task of the project is to evaluate if the concept of virtual attributes described in Sect. 2.2 can be applied for our purposes. A valid alternative could be to group similar attributes from the very beginning. The reduced complexity of the latter approach could lead to a better comparison of attributes across multiple social networks.

The optimisation algorithm introduced in Sect. 3 meets exactly the project's requirements and works reliably. First test cases with the prototype implementation prove that. Currently, the test cases only run on Twitter for practical reasons. However, deeper testing needs to be done, especially borderline test cases. In order to check if the results are equivalent regarding the privacy level, the extended prototype, which includes Twitter and Xing, will be used.

As described in Sect. 4, a survey was conducted to determine the values for sensitivity of each attributes. Meanwhile, the survey has around 150 participants. Therefore, representative values for the sensitivity of the attributes can be specified. We are currently evaluating the results of the survey.

7   Conclusion

One Click Privacy for online social networks aims to provide users a service to easily manage their privacy settings across social networks. The paper concludes with three contributions. Firstly, we developed an algorithm that uses $wPIDX$ which was introduced by Wang and Nepali in [4]. The algorithm is capable of adjusting privacy settings and not exceeding a desired privacy level. With this approach, it is possible to compare privacy settings across multiple social networks. Secondly, we conducted a survey which determines the values for sensitivity. In addition, we have grouped all relevant privacy settings of the chosen social networks in a single file. Last, but not least, the third contribution is the development of a prototype that proves that our approach is working and leads to promising results.

We hope to raise the user's awareness of his privacy, as privacy is not only a question of proper settings, it is also a matter of handling personal data properly.

References

1. Statista: Global social network users growth 2020—statistic (2014). https://www.statista.com/statistics/270919/worldwide-social-network-user-growth/
2. Statista: Anteil der internetnutzer, die in den letzten drei monaten an sozialen netzwerken im internet teilgenommen haben, nach altersgruppen in deutschland im jahr 2016 (2016). https://de.statista.com/statistik/daten/studie/509345/umfrage/anteil-der-nutzer-von-sozialen-netzwerken-nach-altersgruppen-in-deutschland/
3. Statista: Anteil der nutzer von social networks nach altersgruppen in den usa in den jahren 2005 bis 2016 (2016). https://de.statista.com/statistik/daten/studie/500829/umfrage/anteil-der-nutzer-von-sozialen-netzwerken-nach-altersgruppen-in-den-usa/
4. Wang, Y., Nepali, R.K.: Privacy measurement for social network actor model. In: International Conference on Social Computing (SocialCom), pp. 659–664. IEEE, Piscataway (2013)

2nd International Workshop on Timing Performance in Safety Engineering (TIPS 2017)

2nd International Workshop on Timing Performance in Safety Engineering (TIPS 2017)

Chokri Mraidha[1], Laurent Rioux[2], Julio L. Medina[3],
and Marc Geilen[4]

[1] CEA, LIST, Point Courrier 174, 91191 Gif-sur-Yvette, France
chokri.mraidha@cea.fr
[2] Thales R&T, 1 Avenue Augustin Fresnel, 91767 Palaiseau Cedex, France
laurent.rioux@thalesgroup.com
[3] Department of Computer Science and Electronics, University of Cantabria,
Cantabria, Spain
julio.medina@unican.es
[4] Eindhoven University of Technology, Eindhoven, The Netherlands
m.c.w.geilen@tue.nl

1 Introduction

Welcome to the second edition of the workshop on Timing Performance in Safety Engineering (TIPS'17), which has been held in conjunction with the International Conference on Computer Safety, Reliability and Security (SafeComp 2017).

Safety and certification are key issues in various domains such as automotive, medical, avionics and space. Today, designing safety critical real-time systems becomes more and more complex not only because the safety standards are more strict and rigorous, but also because the number of functions to realize is increasing while timing performance must continue to be guaranteed within an acceptable overall cost. For such systems, an increasing portion of design effort is therefore spent on timing performance verification and the corresponding safety and certification argumentations.

Currently, in the industrial design practices, performance engineering and safety engineering are rarely interconnected or integrated, thus requiring additional efforts from the timing performance verification community to fill the gap between the design model and its temporal semantics with techniques to produce proofs and argumentations required by the safety and certification standards. The challenge addressed by this workshop is therefore to link both engineering activities to increase the design efficiency of safety critical real-time systems.

2 Program

We are pleased to announce a program that covers some of the latest research and development activities on timing, safety and security analysis and their integration challenges in various application domains. This year's program consists of four presentations that will promote discussions and foster collaborations between workshop attendees.

Acknowledgments. We thank the SafeComp Workshop Chairs and the SafeComp Organizing Committee for providing the opportunity to organize this workshop. Finally, we are deeply grateful to all the members of our Technical Program Committee, as well as the authors, presenters, and attendees of the TIPS`17 workshop, the community with and for whom all these efforts are done.

TIPS 2017 Program Committee

Liliana Cucu-Grosjean	Inria, France
Zain A.H. Hammadeh	TU Braunschweig, Germany
Huascar Espinoza	Tecnalia, Spain
Loic Frejoz	Realtime@work, France
Bran Selic	Malina Software Corp., Canada
José Merseguer	Univ. de Zaragoza, Spain
Rafik Henia	THALES, France
Bernhard Schatz	Fortiss, Germany
De-Jiu Chen	KTH, Sweden
Dorina C. Petriu	Carleton University, Canada
Yiannis Papadopoulos	University of Hull, UK
Emmanuel Grolleau	ENSMA, France

RobMoSys: Towards Composable Models and Software for Robotics Systems

(Abstract of an Invited Paper)

Selma Kchir, Matteo Morelli, Chokri Mraidha, Ansgar Radermacher,
and Sara Tucci-Piergiovanni

CEA, LIST, PC 174, F-91191 Gif-sur-Yvette Cedex, France
{selma.kchir,matteo.morelli,chokri.mraidha,
ansgar.radermacher,sara.tucci}@cea.fr

RobMoSys is a collaborative project co-funded by the European Union's Horizon 2020 research and innovation programme.

RobMoSys aims to coordinate the whole community's best and consorted effort to build an open and sustainable, agile and multi-domain European robotics software ecosystem. RobMoSys envisions an integration approach built on-top-of, or rather around, the current code-centric robotic platforms, by means of the systematic application of model-driven methods and tools that explicitly focus on systems integration. As proven in many other engineering domains, model-driven approaches are the most suitable to manage integration that is intended to be "all-inclusive" with respect to technologies and groups of stakeholder. The project will drive the non-competitive part of building the eco-system aiming at turning community involvement into active support for an ecosystem of professional quality and scope. It will provide, based on broad involvement via two Open Calls, important concretizations for many of the common robot functionalities (sensing, planning, control in the broad sense). More details on the RobMoSys project are available on the project website: robmosys.eu

Composition and compositionality are main drivers of RobMoSys to address complexity in robotics and face the integration burden caused by type diversity, target diversity and platform diversity.

The talk will present the RobMoSys objectives and its compositional approach. An emphasis will be made on the challenges of the design of robotics systems software components in terms of their Quality-of-Service including timing and safety requirements.

Modeling Rover Communication Using Hierarchical State Machines with Scala

Klaus Havelund and Rajeev Joshi$^{(\boxtimes)}$

Jet Propulsion Laboratory, California Institute of Technology, Pasadena, USA
{klaus.havelund,rajeev.joshi}@jpl.nasa.gov

We demonstrate the application of a new domain-specific language (DSL) for modeling Hierarchical State Machines (HSMs) to the software that manages communications for the Curiosity Mars rover. The spacecraft software is multi-threaded, where some threads implement an HSM that interacts with hardware devices, operating system services, and with other threads via asynchronous and prioritized message passing. Our DSL is implemented as a shallow embedding within the programming language Scala, which makes our models of HSMs textual, short, readable, and perhaps most importantly: easy to write, modify and test at design time. We also present a notation for writing high-level test scenarios that drive the system, and show how we use class inheritance to compactly express derived tests that are variations of a baseline test scenario. We furthermore apply a monitoring Scala DSL for checking temporal logic properties over the running log of events being generated by the HSMs. We show how our framework can be used to define *reactive monitors* that can be used to modify baseline test scenarios by injecting events when certain temporal constraints are met. We describe how we have used reactive monitors to identify certain timing assumptions made in the design. The work described here is part of a broader effort that is exploring the use of a modern high-level programming language for systems modeling, as an alternative to using a formal specification/modeling language.

1 Introduction

Embedded systems such as spacecraft flight software are typically written in low-level implementation languages like C and C^{++}, which provide the level of control and low overhead that is needed for such systems. However, modern spacecraft software is quite complex, and there has been an increasing trend towards developing intermediate, higher-level formalisms that make it easier for developers to design and write flight software. One formalism that is used at NASA's Jet Propulsion Laboratory (JPL) is Hierarchical State Machines (HSMs) [19]. Conventional finite state machines have a finite number of control states and transitions are labeled with atomic letters over a finite alphabet. HSMs allow the declaration of mutable state variables, which can be used in transition guards, and updated in transition actions. HSMs used in flight software are often difficult to write and understand due to the mixture of control states (the states in

© Springer International Publishing AG 2017
S. Tonetta et al. (Eds.): SAFECOMP 2017 Workshops, LNCS 10489, pp. 447–461, 2017.
DOI: 10.1007/978-3-319-66284-8_38

the state machine), code to be executed when taking transitions, and the presence of timers, device interactions, thread priorities, and asynchronous message communication.

The current approach used at JPL is to design the control structure of these HSMs using a graphical tool or a limited domain-specific language (DSL), and to separately write the code that is executed on transitions directly in the implementation language (C/C^{++}). While this approach helps somewhat by saving the developers from having to manually write code for managing the control states of the HSM, the translation from an intermediate DSL directly to low-level implementation code makes it onerous to experiment with design choices during early development. In this paper, we present the application of an internal Scala DSL (called iHSM) for writing HSMs, initially presented in [14], to the modeling of the software that manages communications for the Curiosity Mars rover. We extend the approach presented there (which models a single HSM) to modeling complex software systems in which multiple HSMs are executing concurrently and interacting with each other using asynchronous messaging. We illustrate how iHSM simplifies prototyping and modeling by integrating the notation for describing the HSM control structure within the same language (Scala) that is used to write the actions executed on transitions. We also introduce a notation for describing high-level test scenarios, that can be used to compactly and quickly specify test cases on which the HSMs can be exercised. We furthermore describe the application of the Daut monitoring framework [12] (also a Scala DSL), which can be used to express properties in temporal logic, allowing developers to quickly write and check temporal properties over HSM runs driven by scenario test cases, as well as writing *reactive monitors* that inject events into a running system when some specified temporal conditions are met. We show how iHSM fills a much-needed modeling formalism that allows developers to quickly prototype and test HSM designs.

The contributions of the paper are as follows. (1) We extend the iHSM notation developed in our previous work [14] to model multi-threaded systems, in which multiple HSMs are running in separate threads and interacting with each other via asynchronous messaging. (2) We apply our approach to a real-life case study[1]: the Coordinated Communications Behavior Module (CBM) used in the Curiosity rover for managing communications with Earth. (3) We develop a simple framework for expressing test constraints and a test engine that can automatically run tests satisfying these constraints. (4) We apply the Daut monitoring framework we have developed that allows writing properties in temporal logic and checking these properties during test runs. Our approach is part of a broader effort exploring the use of a modern high-level programming language for systems modeling, as an alternative to using a formal specification language such as VDM or a semi-formal modeling language such as SysML, as discussed in [6,11]. We have chosen Scala for our work as it is a statically typed object-oriented functional programming language which provides many

---

[1] Due to JPL restrictions on sharing of flight artifacts, neither the full case study in C, nor its complete formalization in Scala, can be made publicly available.

convenient features (such as implicit functions, partial functions, call-by-name) that make it easy to develop internal DSLs.

The paper is organized as follows. Section 2 describes related work. Section 3 provides a high-level overview of the architecture of the flight software running on the Curiosity rover, and of the CBM module that is the target of our case study. Section 4 describes how the HSM for the CBM module is modeled in the iHSM notation, how test scenarios are expressed in iHSM, how monitors are expressed in Daut, and how they can be used to check timing assumptions. Finally, Sect. 5 concludes the paper.

2   Related Work

The state pattern [10] is commonly used for modeling state machines in object-oriented programming languages. A state machine is implemented by defining each state as a derived class of the state pattern interface, and by implementing state transitions as methods. The original state pattern does not, however, support hierarchical state machines. A variant of the state pattern to cover HSMs for C and C^{++} is described in [19]. This is a very comprehensive implementation compared to our less than 200 lines of code. However, using C and C^{++} is cumbersome for early modeling and analysis of a design. The Akka framework provides features for concurrent programming and fault protection for the JVM, and in particular it includes a library for writing non-hierarchical finite state machines (FSM) in Scala [1]. The Daut DSL for monitoring event sequences is related to numerous runtime verification frameworks, including [3,5,13,17]. An approach to use state charts for monitoring is described in [9]. Other internal Scala monitoring DSLs have been developed [4,13,16]. Daut itself is a simplification of the earlier TraceContract monitoring framework in Scala [4].

A standard way of formally verifying state machines is to encode them in the input language for, say, a model checker. However, this creates a gap between the modeling language and the implementation language. Model checkers have been developed for programming languages, for example Java PathFinder (JPF) [15] (JPF was originally developed to also support Java as a modeling language). $P^{\#}$ [7] is an extension of $C^{\#}$ with concurrently executing non-hierarchical state machines, communicating asynchronously using message passing. It is inspired by the P external DSL [8] for modeling and programming in the same language, translated to C. $P^{\#}$ supports specification of an environment also as a state machine. Monitors are written as state machines as well, distinguishing between cold and hot (eventually) states, as in Daut. However, these monitors do not support the temporal logic like notation or data parameterized monitors that are expressible in Daut. $P^{\#}$ programs can be analyzed statically for data races, and explored dynamically using randomized testing, exploiting the static analysis results.

Our HSMs differ from UML statecharts (SCs) [2] in a number of ways. First, in UML SCs any state can consist of orthogonal regions executing in parallel. In our approach orthogonal regions are only allowed at the outermost level, where

multiple HSMs run concurrently. Thus, concepts such as fork and join found
in UML SCs are not available in HSMs. Second, while communication between
UML SCs can be synchronous or asynchronous, the communication between
HSMs is asynchronous: a message sent from a machine A to a machine B ends
up in B's input queue and is only consumed by B when its associated thread
runs. Third, UML SCs support a built-in limited notion of timers, whereas HSMs
support explicit programming of timers, which is needed to model JPL flight
software faithfully. HSMs do not currently support history states, but we plan
to add this in the future.

3   Overview of the Curiosity Flight Software Architecture

In this section, we give a brief overview of the flight software (FSW) architecture
for the Curiosity rover. The main computer on Curiosity is a radiation-hardened
PowerPC processor (the BAE RAD750) running the WindRiver VxWorks Operating System, with a priority-preemptive scheduler[2]. The Curiosity FSW consists of around 150 threads that communicate with each other via asynchronous
messaging. In the following subsections, we describe the Curiosity software architecture in more detail.

3.1   Threads and Message Handling

Each thread has an associated incoming queue for storing messages sent to that
thread. A thread T_1 may send a message M to any thread T_2 in the system
(including itself). The message M is appended to the incoming queue for T_2.
A key property of the Curiosity FSW is that sending a message is a nonblocking
operation[3]. However, receiving a message from a queue is a blocking operation,
which causes the thread to be suspended until a message becomes available.
Figure 1 shows an outline of the main loop that is run by each thread.

As shown in the figure, each thread executes an infinite loop that waits
for a message to become available in its incoming queue; when a message m

```
1  while (true) {
2    m = msg_receive()      // blocks until a message is available
3    message_handler(m)     // nonblocking code, may only send messages
4  }
```

Fig. 1. Outline of main thread loop

---

[2] A priority-preemptive scheduler schedules for execution the highest priority task
that is ready to run.
[3] If a message queue is full, an attempt to send a message to that queue results in
either the message being dropped (for noncritical messages), or causes a system
exception (for critical messages).

becomes available, the thread is unblocked and then executes the message_handler function, which processes m. As noted above, as per the architectural rules, the message_handler function is required to be nonblocking, so it may only send messages; it is not allowed to receive any messages.

One quirk of the Curiosity FSW design is that messages delivered to a thread are not consumed in a strict FIFO order. Instead, a thread's incoming queue consists of an ordered sequence $Q_1, Q_2, .. Q_n$ of *subqueues*. The ordering of subqueues denotes message priority, so messages in subqueue Q_k have higher priority than messages in subqueue Q_{k+1}. When a message is delivered to a thread, it is appended to one of the subqueues (depending on the priority associated with the message). Additionally, each subqueue Q_i is associated with a boolean flag B_i, which indicates whether the subqueue is *enabled* for receiving. We say a message M is *pending* for a thread if M is at the head of an enabled subqueue Q_i (that is, such that B_i is true). The msg_receive operation then retrieves the highest priority message that is pending for a thread. If there are no pending messages (that is, all enabled subqueues are empty), then the msg_receive blocks the calling thread. This unusual design of prioritized subqueues was introduced to support the following use case: a thread T_1 receives a message M_1 whose processing requires it to send a request message to another thread T_2 and wait for a reply. As per the architectural pattern, T_1 cannot make a blocking call to T_2, so it must go back to the head of its main thread loop (line 2 in Fig. 1) and wait for the reply from T_2. However, while it is waiting for this reply, we would like to avoid processing new requests sent to T_1 (as this would make the implementation of T_1 more complicated). To achieve this, T_1 uses two subqueues (one for requests and one for replies), and it disables the request subqueue when it sends a request to T_2. Now, any new requests will be ignored until T_1 receives the reply from T_2 (which is delivered to the reply subqueue), at which point T_1 re-enables the request subqueue and processes the next waiting request.

3.2   Hierarchical State Machines (HSMs)

As mentioned earlier, spacecraft software (and embedded software in general) is often designed and implemented using hierarchical state machines (HSMs). HSMs can be characterized as state machines with an imposed hierarchy, allowing states to contain (sub) state machines, to an arbitrary depth. In addition, every state has optional associated *entry* and *exit* actions. When an HSM receives an event E in a state S, it finds the closest ancestor state A of S which has a transition α defined for event E to a target state T. It then computes the least common ancestor state P between A and T. It then executes the exit actions of all states (in order) along the path from S to P, then executes the action associated with the transition α, and finally executes the entry actions (in order) along the path from P to T. In the Curiosity FSW, each HSM is implemented by a thread, which receives events as *messages* sent to the thread's incoming queue. (That is, each received message corresponds to a single event, and the message handler corresponds to the action associated with the transition.)

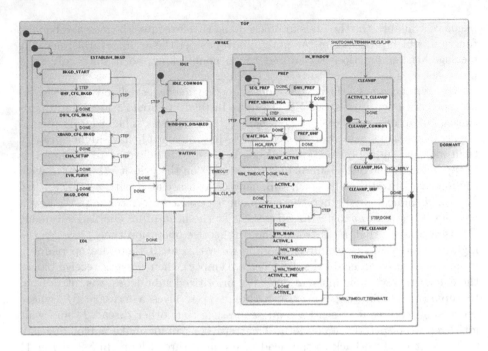

Fig. 2. Full HSM for the communication behavior module

Figure 2 shows a graphical view of the complete HSM for the Communications Behaviors (CBM) module that we are modeling for our case study. This informal diagram was created by the module developer during design and was not intended to depict all the details; it is only included here to show the overall complexity. For instance, none of the transitions are annotated with conditions or action code. The black circles with an incoming edge and multiple outgoing edges represent conditional transitions (where the branch conditions are not shown). The CBM module coordinates the activities needed to prepare the spacecraft for communication sessions (called *windows*) with Earth. Each window has an associated start and end time, and the set of future windows is stored in a table. Windows are added and deleted by ground operators. CBM selects the earliest window in the table and ensures that the telecommunications hardware is configured in time for the window (for instance, by ensuring that the antenna is pointed to and tracking Earth). While we have modeled the entire module HSM as part of our case study, in the interest of readability, we only discuss a small (slightly simplified) fragment of this HSM in this paper. This fragment is shown in Fig. 3. As shown in the figure, there is a state top that contains all other states. Following usual HSM notation, the filled out black circles indicate the initial substate that is entered whenever the parent state is entered. (Thus, for instance, a transition to the in_window state causes the HSM to transition to the xband_prep substate.) Associated with each state are also two optional code fragments, the *entry* and *exit* actions. The *entry* action associated with a state is executed whenever the HSM enters that state, whereas the *exit* action is executed

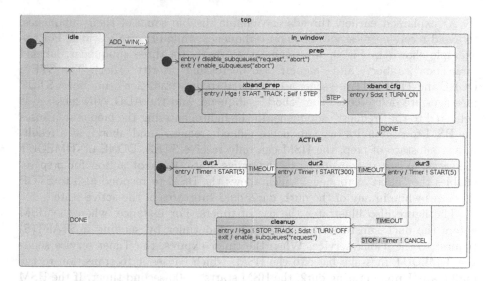

Fig. 3. Fragment of HSM for the CBM module

whenever the HSM leaves that state. Finally, the labeled arrows between states show the transitions that are caused in response to messages received by the HSM. A label has the form MESSAGE/code, which denotes that the transition is triggered when the HSM receives the specified MESSAGE. In response, the HSM transitions to the target state, and executes the (optional) code fragment. For instance, suppose the HSM is in state dur2, and it receives the STOP message. This causes the HSM to perform the following actions (in order): (1) the *exit* action for the state dur2, (2) the *exit* action for the state active, (3) the action Timer ! CANCEL, which cancels an existing timer, and (4) the *entry* action for the state cleanup.

3.3 Interactions Between HSMs, Devices and Timers

The execution of an action may result in the HSM sending messages to other entities in the system, such as other threads (also possibly implemented as HSMs), to devices (for instance, powering on a radio), or to system services (for instance, the timer service, discussed below). Message transmissions are denoted as recv ! M where recv is the receiver to which the message M is sent. In our example, the receivers Hga and Sdst denote devices (the high-gain antenna and an X-Band radio, respectively), whereas the receiver Timer denotes the timer service. The receiver Self denotes the HSM itself; for instance, in state xband_prep, the entry action results in the HSM sending the START_TRACK message to the Hga device, and the STEP message to itself; the latter in turn causes the HSM to transition from the xband_prep to the xband_cfg state, while sending the TURN_ON message to the Sdst device. (Messages to Self allow a thread to break up its processing into smaller units of computation, thereby allowing the processing to be interrupted by other, higher-priority messages.)

As explained earlier, threads can enable/disable some of their subqueues, to avoid receiving messages on those subqueues while in certain states. For the example shown in Fig. 3, we assume that there are three subqueues, labeled "transition", "abort" and "request" (in decreasing priority order). The STEP, DONE and TIMEOUT messages are delivered to the "transition" subqueue, STOP messages are delivered to the "abort" subqueue, and the ADD_WIN message is delivered to the "request" subqueue. In the figure, entering the prep state causes the HSM to disable its two subqueues named "request" and "abort"; as a result, in any substate of prep, the HSM can only receive STEP, DONE or TIMEOUT messages. When it transitions to the active state, the exit action for prep re-enables the "abort" subqueue, which allows the HSM to respond also to STOP messages while in any of the dur1, dur2, dur3 substates of the active state.

The figure also illustrates the use of timers. For instance, when the HSM enters the dur1 substate, it starts a 5-second timer by sending a START(5) request to the Timer service. When the timer expires, the Timer service sends the TIMEOUT message back to the HSM, which causes it to transition to the dur2 state. Upon entering dur2, the HSM starts a 300-second timer. If the HSM receives a STOP message while in a substate of the active state, it cancels the outstanding timer by sending a CANCEL message to the Timer service, and transitions to the cleanup state[4].

3.4   Event Logs

During execution, threads generate a stream of telemetry that is periodically sent to Earth so that ground operators can assess the success of requested activities and the health of various spacecraft subsystems. A key element of the telemetry stream is an *event log* that contains a log of timestamped events that happened on the spacecraft. Event logs are used by engineers to assess if the system is behaving as designed, and are often checked (either manually or using ad-hoc scripts) to verify that the HSM behavior satisfies expected properties. As we discuss in a later subsection, in our approach, we provide a formal, declarative notation (based on temporal logic) in which properties may be expressed, and then the Daut runtime monitoring engine is used to check that the HSM behaviors satisfy these properties. Figure 4 shows fragments of event logs from two runs of the HSM. (In Sect. 4.2, we describe how these runs are generated from test scenarios.) The number before each event denotes the time of the event.[5] The log on the left shows a nominal run, where the HSM enters state dur2 at time 1090 and starts a 300-second timer, which expires at time 1390, after which the window completes nominally. The log on the right shows a run in which a STOP request is sent to

---

[4] In the interests of readability, the simplified HSM shown here does not handle the case where a timer expires right when a CANCEL message is sent; the full HSM handles this condition gracefully.

[5] In our somewhat simplified execution model, we currently assume that entering and exiting states does not take any time; thus several such related events have the same timestamp.

the HSM at time 1380, which causes it to abort the window by canceling the timer and transitioning to the cleanup state. The figure shows how the logs differ after time 1380, showing the different system behaviors.

1085 : HSM_EVR_ENTER_STATE(active)	1085 : HSM_EVR_ENTER_STATE(active)
1085 : IPC_EVR_QUEUE_ENABLE(cbm,abort)	1085 : IPC_EVR_QUEUE_ENABLE(cbm,abort)
1085 : HSM_EVR_ENTER_STATE(dur1)	1085 : HSM_EVR_ENTER_STATE(dur1)
1085 : TIM_EVR_STARTED(1090)	1085 : TIM_EVR_STARTED(1090)
1090 : TIM_EVR_FIRED(1090)	1090 : TIM_EVR_FIRED(1090)
1090 : IPC_EVR_RECV(cbm,transition,TIMEOUT)	1090 : IPC_EVR_RECV(cbm,transition,TIMEOUT)
1090 : HSM_EVR_EXIT_STATE(dur1)	1090 : HSM_EVR_EXIT_STATE(dur1)
1090 : HSM_EVR_ENTER_STATE(dur2)	1090 : HSM_EVR_ENTER_STATE(dur2)
1090 : TIM_EVR_STARTED(1390)	1090 : TIM_EVR_STARTED(1390)
1390 : TIM_EVR_FIRED(1390)	1380 : IPC_EVR_RECV(cbm,abort,STOP)
1390 : IPC_EVR_RECV(cbm,transition,TIMEOUT)	1380 : HSM_EVR_EXIT_STATE(dur2)
1390 : HSM_EVR_EXIT_STATE(dur2)	1380 : HSM_EVR_EXIT_STATE(active)
1390 : HSM_EVR_ENTER_STATE(dur3)	1380 : TIM_EVR_CANCELED(1390)
	1380 : HSM_EVR_ENTER_STATE(cleanup)

Fig. 4. Sample event logs for two runs of the HSM in Fig. 3

4   Modeling and Testing the Communications HSM

4.1   The Communications HSM in iHSM

Figure 5 shows how the Communications Behavior Manager (CBM) HSM shown in Fig. 3 is formalized in our iHSM notation. (In the interests of space, we show only a few states; the others follow a similar pattern.) Lines 1–5 show the definition of message types that are to be handled by the HSM. Lines 7–35 define the state machine as the class CbmHsm extending the MslHsm class, which itself extends the generic HSM class implementing our DSL. Line 8 defines the three subqueue priorities, along with the capacity of each subqueue. Line 9 defines the window table. Line 10 defines the outermost top state of the HSM. The handler for the ADD_WIN message (line 13) results in a transition to the in_window state. Lines 17–20 define the prep state, which has entry and exit actions. The entry action (line 18) results in the "request" and "abort" queues being disabled when the state is entered, whereas the exit action (line 19) results in the "abort" queue being re-enabled. (Note that the "request" queue stays disabled.) The entry action for the xband_prep state causes two messages to be sent: the message START_TRACK is sent to the Hga thread (corresponding to a request for the high-gain antenna to start tracking Earth), and then the HSM sends a STEP message to itself. The thread will then receive this STEP message and execute the transition on line 23, which causes the HSM to transition to the xband_cfg state. The entry action for the xband_cfg state results in the HSM sending (line 26) a TURN_ON message to the Sdst thread. When it receives (line 28) the DONE reply from the Sdst, the HSM transitions to the active state. In the interests of space and readability, we have shown only a simplified fragment of the communications behavior HSM used on Curiosity. We have encoded the full CBM HSM in our iHSM notation. (The full HSM consists of 45 states and substates and over 130 transitions among these states.)

```
1    case object STEP extends CbmMessage("transition")
2    case object DONE extends CbmMessage("transition")
3    case object TIMEOUT extends CbmMessage("transition")
4    case object STOP extends CbmMessage("abort")
5    case class ADD_WIN(start: Int, ...) extends CbmMessage("request")
6
7    class CbmHsm extends MslHsm {
8      queues(("transition", 3), ("abort", 1), ("request", 17))
9      var table = new WindowTable()
10     object top extends state() {}
11     object idle extends state(top, true) {
12       when {
13         case ADD_WIN(..) ⇒ in_window exec { table.add(..) }
14       }
15     }
16     object in_window extends state(top) { }
17     object prep extends state(in_window, true) {
18       entry { disable_subqueues("request", "abort") }
19       exit { enable_subqueues("abort") }
20     }
21     object xband_prep extends state(prep, true) {
22       entry { Hga ! START_TRACK ; Self ! STEP }
23       when { case STEP ⇒ xband_cfg }
24     }
25     object xband_cfg extends state(prep) {
26       entry { Sdst ! TURN_ON }
27       when {
28         case DONE ⇒ active
29       }
30     }
31     object active extends state(in_window) {
32       when { case STOP ⇒ cleanup exec { Timer ! CANCEL } }
33     }
34     ...
35   }
```

Fig. 5. The CBM HSM expressed in iHSM

4.2   Extensible Test Scenarios

In order to test HSMs, we developed a notation for writing test cases. Our notation allows users to specify *test scenarios* that result in certain messages being sent to HSMs in the system at specified times. Figure 6 illustrates two such test scenarios. The notation at(100) exec Cbm ! M indicates that the message M is to be sent to the Cbm HSM at time 100. Note that, because our scenarios are Scala code, we can easily define a local variable S and specify that 3 messages be sent at specified times relative to S. The figure also illustrates how the use of Scala allows us to conveniently define new scenarios as extensions of existing scenarios using class inheritance. As shown, we define the stopTest scenario as an extension of the hgaTest scenario by specifying that an additional STOP message be sent to the HSM at time (S+510). Execution of these two scenarios results in the logs shown in Fig. 4.

class hgaTest **extends** TestScenario {
  val S = 1000
  at(S)   exec Cbm ! SET_BKID("TEST")
  at(S+1) exec Cbm ! SET_MODE(NORMAL)
  at(S+2) exec Cbm ! ADD_WIN(311,...)
}
	class stopTest **extends** hgaTest {
	  at(S+510) exec Cbm ! STOP()
	}

Fig. 6. Two sample test scenarios

4.3   Monitoring Temporal Properties

Next, we describe how to monitor HSMs using a monitoring framework that can check temporal properties. Figure 7 shows two example properties for the CBM HSM. The first property (lines 1–5) checks the state invariant that whenever the HSM is in the prep state, the "abort" subqueue is disabled. The predicate Cbm.inState(re) returns true if the HSM Cbm is in a state whose name matches the regular expression re. The second property (lines 7–13) checks that if a timer has been started, then the HSM either waits for the timer to fire, or it cancels the timer, before starting a new timer. The body of the class is an always-formula (line 9). The function always takes as argument a partial function from events to monitor states. In this case, whenever an TIM_STARTED event is observed, the monitor moves to a watch state, in which it waits for either a TIM_FIRED or a TIM_CANCELED event, but declares an error if another TIM_STARTED event is seen before.

```
1    // In state prep, the "abort" subqueue is disabled
2    class QueueCheck extends MSLMonitor {
3      invariant ("abortDisabled") {
4        Cbm.inState("prep") ==⇒ !Cbm.isEnabled("abort")
5    }}
6
7    // Timer is not started unless previous timer has expired or been canceled
8    class TimerCheck extends MSLMonitor {
9      always {
10       case TIM_STARTED(_) ⇒ watch {
11         case TIM_FIRED(_) | TIM_CANCELED(_) ⇒ ok
12         case TIM_STARTED(_) ⇒ error("Timer restarted")
13   }}}
```

Fig. 7. Two temporal properties monitored

4.4   Derived Test Scenarios with Reactive Monitors

A key feature of our approach using the Daut framework is that monitors are written in Scala, and thus monitor evaluation can execute any Scala code, including sending of messages to the HSM being monitored. We refer to such monitors as *reactive monitors*. Figure 8 shows an example of how a reactive monitor allows us to express complex test scenarios in a compact and readable way. The InjectStop monitor looks for an event indicating that an HSM has entered the "active_1" state; and when this event is seen, it executes the code shown on line 4, which waits for 2 s and then sends a STOP message to the HSM. Note that unlike the stopTest scenario test in Fig. 6 above, which required that a message be sent at a specified time, the use of a reactive monitor allows a message to be sent when a monitored property becomes true, which makes it easier to write test scenarios.

```
1    // 2 seconds after the HSM enters the "active_2" state, send a STOP
2    class InjectStop extends MSLMonitor {
3      always {
4        case HSM_ENTER_STATE("active_1") ⇒ after(2) { Cbm ! STOP() }
5    }}
```

Fig. 8. A reactive monitor

4.5   Checking Timing Properties

In this section, we illustrate how reactive monitors allow us to easily analyze the HSM design in order to check timing assumptions. Figure 9 shows an untimed monitor NoHgaReply that checks if a HGA_START_TRACK is followed by a NO_HGA_REPLY. (This happens when the CBM HSM does not receive a reply from the high-gain antenna in response to a start tracking request). The figure also shows the reactive monitor InjectHgaDelay that waits for the HSM to enter the prep_xband_hga state, and then injects a delay D (which is a parameter to the monitor) before the hga_track_reply message is delivered to the HSM.

Next, in Fig. 10, we show how we can use these monitors to check timing assumptions. The figure shows a Scala method search which takes a time range (lo, hi), and looks for the smallest value m in that range for which the provided function f throws a RuntimeException. This is achieved by iterating over the value of m (line 5) and calling f(m) in each iteration. If all iterations complete without an exception, the method returns None indicating the search was unsuccessful. However, as soon as an exception is encountered, the catch block (lines 7–9) returns with the value of m that caused the exception.

The next method, findMinHgaTimeout uses this search method to find the smallest delay d that can be injected into the system (using the InjectHgaDelay reactive monitor) that results in a violation of the property NoHgaReply.

```
1    // Check if HGA tracking was started but no reply was received
2    class NoHgaReply extends MSLMonitor {
3      always {
4        case HGA_START_TRACK() ⇒ watch {
5          case NO_HGA_REPLY() ⇒ error
6      }}
7    }
8
9    // Delay reply from HGA by D seconds
10   class InjectHgaDelay(D: Int) extends MSLMonitor {
11     always {
12       case HSM_ENTER_STATE("prep_xband_hga") ⇒
13         lpc.delay(D, "cbm", "hga_track_reply")
14   }}
```

Fig. 9. Timing monitors for the CBM case study

```
1    // Find the least value of m for which f(m) throws an exception
2    def search(lo: Int, hi: Int)(f: PartialFunction[Int, Unit]): Option[Int] = {
3      var m = lo
4      try {
5        while (m < hi) { f(m) ; m += 1 }
6        None
7      } catch {
8        case e: RuntimeException ⇒ Some(m)
9    }}
10
11   // Find the least delay that results in violation of NoHgaReply
12   def findMinHgaTimeout {
13     search(400, 500) {
14       case d ⇒ run(new hgaTest, new NoHgaReply, new InjectHgaDelay(d))
15     } match {
16       case Some(m) ⇒ println("Detected failure with value " + m)
17       case None    ⇒ println ("No failures found")
18     }
19   }
```

Fig. 10. Functions for finding smallest delay that causes NoHgaReply to fail

As shown in the figure, the method searches for a delay in the range 400..500 (line 13), and passes in a partial function that, given a delay value d, runs the hgaTest scenario with property monitor NoHgaReply and an instance of reactive monitor InjectHgaDelay(d). It then checks the value returned by the search method (lines 15–17). If the value returned is Some(m), it reports the value that caused the failure; else if the value is None, it reports that no failure was found. Running this search for the CBM HSM revealed that a delay of 409 s or longer results in a violation of the NoHgaReply property.

5   Conclusion

In this paper, we have built upon our previous work using an internal DSL in Scala for writing HSMs. We have described how this DSL is used to model systems with many HSMs, each implemented by a thread, which interact with each other and with devices and system services using asynchronous messaging. We have applied our ideas to a case study modeling a critical HSM that manages communications of the Curiosity rover with Earth. We have shown how to check that these HSMs satisfy properties written in a temporal logic, by integrating a monitoring framework (also written in Scala) that processes event logs generated by the HSMs. Finally, we have described a notation for writing high-level test specifications, which makes it convenient to write complex test cases by specifying a set of stimuli that are to be provided to the system when various constraints are satisfied. Our test specifications are expressed as Scala classes, which allows tests to be extended using inheritance, making it easy to develop multiple test variants from a baseline scenario. Our work is based on using a modern high-level programming language for modeling, testing and monitoring spacecraft software. We are working on making our test specification language more expressive by allowing more complex constraints (and then using an SMT solver to generate test instances). Work on visualizing HSMs from the Scala source code is in progress. We are also investigating more powerful verification techniques, such as model checking and theorem-proving (using the Viper framework [18]) that can be used to formally verify HSM properties.

Acknowledgments. The research performed was carried out at Jet Propulsion Laboratory, California Institute of Technology, under a contract with the National Aeronautics and Space Administration.

References

1. Akka FSMs. http://doc.akka.io/docs/akka/current/scala/fsm.html
2. Unified Modeling Language. http://www.uml.org. Accessed 06 Aug 2017
3. Barringer, H., Falcone, Y., Havelund, K., Reger, G., Rydeheard, D.: Quantified event automata: towards expressive and efficient runtime monitors. In: Giannakopoulou, D., Méry, D. (eds.) FM 2012. LNCS, vol. 7436, pp. 68–84. Springer, Heidelberg (2012). doi:10.1007/978-3-642-32759-9_9
4. Barringer, H., Havelund, K.: TRACECONTRACT: a scala DSL for trace analysis. In: Butler, M., Schulte, W. (eds.) FM 2011. LNCS, vol. 6664, pp. 57–72. Springer, Heidelberg (2011). doi:10.1007/978-3-642-21437-0_7
5. Basin, D., Klaedtke, F., Marinovic, S., Zălinescu, E.: Monitoring of temporal first-order properties with aggregations. In: Legay, A., Bensalem, S. (eds.) RV 2013. LNCS, vol. 8174, pp. 40–58. Springer, Heidelberg (2013). doi:10.1007/978-3-642-40787-1_3
6. Broy, M., Havelund, K., Kumar, R.: Towards a unified view of modeling and programming. In: Margaria, T., Steffen, B. (eds.) ISoLA 2016. LNCS, vol. 9953, pp. 238–257. Springer, Cham (2016). doi:10.1007/978-3-319-47169-3_17

7. Deligiannis, P., Donaldson, A.F., Ketema, J., Lal, A., Thomson, P.: Asynchronous programming, analysis and testing with state machines. In: Proceedings of the 36th ACM SIGPLAN Conference on Programming Language Design and Implementation, PLDI 2015, NY, USA, pp. 154–164 (2015). http://doi.acm.org/10.1145/2737924.2737996

8. Desai, A., Gupta, V., Jackson, E., Qadeer, S., Rajamani, S., Zufferey, D.: P: Safe asynchronous event-driven programming. In: Proceedings of PLDI 2013, pp. 321–332 (2013). http://doi.acm.org/10.1145/2491956.2462184

9. Drusinsky, D.: Modeling and Verification using UML Statecharts. Elsevier, ISBN-13: 978-0-7506-7949-7, 400 p (2006)

10. Gamma, E., Helm, R., Johnson, R., Vlissides, J.: Design Patterns: Elements of Reusable Object-oriented Software. Addison-Wesley, Boston (1995)

11. Hassard, J.: Closing. In: Dias, M., Eick, C.J., Brantley-Dias, L. (eds.) Science Teacher Educators as K-12 Teachers. ASSE, vol. 1, pp. 287–302. Springer, Dordrecht (2014). doi:10.1007/978-94-007-6763-8_20

12. Havelund, K.: Data automata in Scala. In: Proceedings of the 8th International Symposium on Theoretical Aspects of Software Engineering, TASE 2014 (2014)

13. Havelund, K.: Rule-based runtime verification revisited. Int. J. Softw. Tools Technol. Transf. **17**(2), 143–170 (2015)

14. Havelund, K., Joshi, R.: Modeling and monitoring of hierarchical state machines in Scala. In preparation

15. Havelund, K., Visser, W.: Program model checking as a new trend. STTT **4**(1), 8–20 (2002)

16. Kauffman, S., Havelund, K., Joshi, R.: nfer – a notation and system for inferring event stream abstractions. In: Falcone, Y., Sánchez, C. (eds.) RV 2016. LNCS, vol. 10012, pp. 235–250. Springer, Cham (2016). doi:10.1007/978-3-319-46982-9_15

17. Meredith, P., Jin, D., Griffith, D., Chen, F., Roşu, G.: An overview of the MOP runtime verification framework. J. Softw. Tools Technol. Transf. pp. 1–41 (2011). http://dx.doi.org/10.1007/s10009-011-0198-6

18. Müller, P., Schwerhoff, M., Summers, A.J.: Viper: a verification infrastructure for permission-based reasoning. In: Jobstmann, B., Leino, K.R.M. (eds.) VMCAI 2016. LNCS, vol. 9583, pp. 41–62. Springer, Heidelberg (2016). doi:10.1007/978-3-662-49122-5_2

19. Samek, M.: Practical UML Statecharts in C/C++, Event-Driven Programming for Embedded Systems, 2nd edn. Newnes, MA, USA (2009)

Towards Component-Based (max,+) Algebraic Throughput Analysis of Hierarchical Synchronous Data Flow Models

Mladen Skelin[✉] and Marc Geilen

Eindhoven University of Technology, Eindhoven, The Netherlands
{m.skelin,m.c.w.geilen}@tue.nl

Abstract. Synchronous (or static) dataflow (SDF) is deemed the most stable and mature model to represent streaming systems. It is useful, not only to reason about functional behavior and correctness of such systems, but also about non-functional aspects, in particular timing and performance constraints. When talking about performance, throughput is a key metric. Within the SDF domain, hierarchical SDF models are of special interest as they enable compositional modeling, which is a necessity in the design of large systems.

Techniques exist to analyze throughput of synchronous dataflow models. If the model is hierarchical, it first needs to be flattened before these techniques can be applied (for exact analysis at least). Furthermore, all of these techniques are adversely affected by the increase in the graph's repetition vector entries. In this paper, for a loosely defined class of hierarchical synchronous dataflow models, we argue that these dependence issues can be mitigated by taking advantage of the hierarchical structure rather than by flattening the graph. We propose a hierarchical extension to an existing technique that is based on the (max,+) algebraic semantics of SDF.

Keywords: Dataflow · Performance analysis · Hierarchy · (max,+) algebra

1 Introduction

Dataflow models of computation are widely used to represent streaming systems. This is thanks to their simple graphical representation, compactness and the ability to express parallelism inherent to many streaming systems. In dataflow, a system is represented by a directed graph where nodes are called *actors* and edges are called *channels*. Actors represent computational kernels while channels typically capture data, control and resource dependencies between actors. The quanta of information exchanged across channels are called *tokens*. Actors involve themselves into communication with other actors by *firing*. The firing represents the quantum of computation during which actors consume tokens

© Springer International Publishing AG 2017
S. Tonetta et al. (Eds.): SAFECOMP 2017 Workshops, LNCS 10489, pp. 462–476, 2017.
DOI: 10.1007/978-3-319-66284-8_39

from their input channels and produce tokens in their output channels. Preconditions for firing are given by firing rules [20]. The numbers of tokens produced and consumed are called *rates*. In the timed versions of dataflow that we are investigating in this paper, actor firings have a duration that we call the actor *firing delay*.

There exists quite a number of dataflow models. They can be roughly divided into decidable [18] and dynamic dataflow models [4]. Decidable dataflow models can be considered versions of dataflow with restricted semantics so that the model can be scheduled at design-time as well as analyzed for boundedness, deadlock and its timing properties. Examples of decidable dataflow formalisms are synchronous dataflow (SDF), cyclo-static dataflow [6] and scalable SDF [24]. Dynamic dataflow models offer more expressive power in exchange for a decrease in analyzability and implementation efficiency [26]. Well-known examples are boolean dataflow and dynamic dataflow [7].

All in all, in terms of support for design and analysis of timing predictable and repeatable systems (and most predictable systems are at first *real-time systems*), among dataflow models, decidable dataflow models still play a more pronounced role than the echelons of emerging dynamic dataflow models. This in particular refers to SDF as the most stable and mature flavor of decidable dataflow that is characterized by its predictability, strong formal properties and amenability to powerful optimization techniques [5]. In SDF rates are fixed and known at compile time. The firing rules of SDF are conjunctive [20] in the sense that for an actor to fire, every of its inbound channels must contain the number of tokens prescribed by the port rate defined by the actor and the inbound channel in consideration. Furthermore, they are distributive [20] in the sense that when the actor fires all outbound channels receive tokens in the quantity prescribed by the corresponding port rates. As we will further elaborate in the paper, SDF graphs evolve in iterations. An iteration is a set of actor firings that have no net effect on the token distribution of the graph. The number of firings of a particular actor in an iteration is given in the so-called repetition vector of the graph. In this paper we consider the so-called self-timed execution of SDF graphs, which means that actors must fire as soon as they are enabled.

Several examples of use of SDF in design and analysis of predictable and repeatable systems can be found in [2, 22, 28]. If we study these papers, we see the SDF formalism is not only useful for reasoning about the functional behavior and correctness of systems, but also, in its timed version [25], can be used when one needs to derive or prove worst-case performance guarantees, in particular throughput that is a vital performance indicator in streaming systems and that is defined as the long run average number of completed iteration per time-unit. Many authors [12, 13, 16, 17, 25] have dealt with the problem of performance analysis of SDF models. The common characteristic of all of the approaches is that they are in terms of performance adversely affected by the increase of repetition vector entries of the graph. In particular, the performance will scale at least linearly with the sum of the repetition vector entries [14].

However, monolithic SDF models are inconvenient for capturing large designs. Therefore, allowing for compositional modeling is a necessity in the design of large systems as it enforces good engineering practices such as modularity, design reuse and improves readability. Hierarchy has been introduced to SDF [3,10,23,29]. To apply the existing *exact* throughput analysis algorithms to hierarchical dataflow models, however, they first need to be flattened.

In this paper we propose a modular technique for throughput analysis of a subclass of hierarchical SDF graphs with arbitrary number of hierarchy levels that removes the need for flattening the graph. This is achieved by using (max,+)-based state-space representations of hierarchical actors instead of the flattenings in the context of existing throughput analysis techniques based on symbolic simulation. Furthermore, as our technique is able to take advantage of the hierarchical semantics of SDF, we argue that our technique helps mitigate the adverse effect of increase in graph's repetition vector entries on the performance of existing performance analysis techniques. This is due to the fact that no matter how many times a hierarchical actor is scheduled in the composition, we do not need to replicate the firings of all the actors embodied in the hierarchical actor as the existing techniques do, but only use it's *more compact* state-space representation to capture the effects its firing has on the rest of the composition.

The remainder of the paper is organized as follows. Section 2 discusses related work, Sect. 3 covers the concepts needed to understand the remainder of the paper, Sect. 4 presents our throughput analysis technique, while Sect. 5 concludes.

2   Related Work

Roughly, state-of-the-art techniques for throughput analysis of SDF graphs can be divided in two groups. The first group of approaches is based on the conversion of SDF graphs to equivalent homogeneous SDF (HSDF). HSDF is a special kind of SDF where all rates equal 1. The basic algorithm for the conversion is described in [25]. The drawback of these approaches is that the size of the graph may expand exponentially [25]. However, advances have been made by authors of [17] wherein the size of the expansion can be significantly reduced by construction of a so-called linear constraint graph (LCG) from the original SDF graph. With LCG in particular, the compaction is achieved by taking advantage of its redundancy and regularity. Still, some graphs as reported in [17] cannot be represented compactly by the LCG.

The second group of approaches are the simulation-based approaches. The seminal work of [16] performs explicit state-space exploration of the operational semantics of SDF. Despite its worst-case complexity, the method works well in practice, while the techniques based on the conversion of [25] often fail.

Symbolic simulation-based approach described in [12,13] uses (max,+) algebra to capture the self-timed execution of SDF graphs. In particular, the graph's evolution is sublimed into a simple recursive (max,+) linear matrix equation. The

matrix in the equation is derived by symbolic simulation of one iteration of the
SDF graph. This matrix can be considered the incidence matrix of a weighted
digraph, the maximum cycle mean of which is equal to the inverse of the graph's
throughput.

All the exact techniques mentioned have a common characteristic that the
increase of the repetition vector entries in the graph will adversely affect their
performance. In addition, the technique of [16] is also sensitive to the length of
the graph's transient[1]. Furthermore, none of the exact techniques are directly
applicable to hierarchical SDF structures, i.e., the hierarchical model should be
flattened before. There is a technique that targets hierarchical SDF structures [9]
but it is not exact which means that it can only give a conservative throughput
estimate but not the exact value.

3 Preliminaries

This section recaps the (max,+) algebra, the basic SDF concepts and the
(max,+) linear system-theoretic aspects of SDF that are used in this paper.

3.1 (max,+) Algebra

Let $\mathbb{R}_{max} = \mathbb{R} \cup \{-\infty\}$ where $\mathbb{R}$ is the set of real numbers. For elements $a, b \in$
$\mathbb{R}_{max}$, we define operations $\oplus$ and $\otimes$ with max as addition ($a \oplus b \overset{\text{def}}{=} \max(a, b)$)
and + as product ($a \otimes b \overset{\text{def}}{=} a + b$). The set $\mathbb{R}_{max}$ together with operations $\oplus$ and
$\otimes$ extended to matrices and vectors in the same way as in conventional linear
algebra is called (max,+) algebra. The set of n-dimensional (max,+) vectors is
denoted $\mathbb{R}_{max}^{n}$, while $\mathbb{R}_{max}^{n \times n}$ denotes the set of $n \times n$ (max,+) matrices. The (sup-)
sum of matrices $A, B \in \mathbb{R}_{max}^{n \times n}$, denoted by $A \oplus B$ is defined by $[A \oplus B]_{i,j} =$
$[A]_{i,j} \oplus [B]_{i,j}$ where $[A]_{i,j}$ and $[B]_{i,j}$ are entries of matrices A and B with indices
i and j. The matrix product $A \otimes B$ is defined by $[A \otimes B]_{i,j} = \bigoplus_{k=1}^{n} [A]_{i,k} \otimes [B]_{k,j}$.

3.2 Synchronous Dataflow

Figure 1 shows an SDF graph. The graph has six actors, In, D, E, F, G and
Out. Actor firing delays are denoted next to actor names. Rates are denoted
next to channel ends with a convention that the omission of a rate value implies
the value of 1. Notice that the graph in the figure has two feedback loops, one
going from actor E to D across F, and a so-called self-edge from actor G back to
itself. Such feedback loops can cause the graph to deadlock because actors in the
loops depend on each other for tokens. Therefore, feedback loops must include
a certain number of *initial tokens* that specify the initial condition from which

---

[1] Self-timed execution of an SDF graph consists of a periodic phase preceded by a
so-called transient phase.

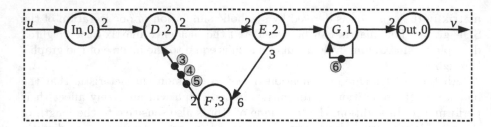

Fig. 1. Example of an SDF graph.

the execution starts. In the figure these are depicted using black dots and are marked as follows: ③, ④, ⑤, ⑥. SDF graphs evolve in iterations. An iteration is a set of actor firings that have no net effect on the token distribution in the graph. The numbers of firings are stored in the repetition vector of the graph Γ. For the graph in Fig. 1, $\Gamma(In, D, E, F, G, Out) = [1, 2, 2, 1, 2, 1]^T$. This vector can be obtained by solving the so-called set of balance equations for an SDF graph [21]. Notice that iterations can overlap in time, i.e. they can be pipelined. An SDF graph can be *closed* or *open* [29] depending on whether all input ports are connected or not, respectively. The graph in Fig. 1 is open as not all its input ports are connected.

3.3   (max,+) Semantics of Synchronous Dataflow

We use (max,+) algebra [1] to model timed SDF graphs. It is a natural choice as it has two operations that determine the self-timed execution of SDF graphs: synchronization and delay. Synchronization manifests itself when an actor waits for all its input tokens to become available ($\oplus$ in (max,+)) before firing. The delay manifests itself in the fact that tokens will be produced only after an amount of time corresponding to the actor firing delay after the firing has begun ($\otimes$ in (max,+)). We mentioned that SDF graphs evolve in iterations that restore the graph back to its initial state. The initial state is determined by the distribution of initial tokens over graph's channels. Thus, in terms of time, the evolution of an SDF graph can be represented as a sequence of vectors $\mathbf{x}(k)$ where each entry of the vector stores the availability time of a token produced in place of a particular initial token after the kth iteration of the graph. Geilen [13] shows that this sequence (for closed SDF graphs) can be determined by a (max,+) linear recursive equation

$$\mathbf{x}(k+1) = M \otimes \mathbf{x}(k), \tag{1}$$

where M is the (max,+) matrix of the graph that defines its state-space representation. For open SDF graphs, whose inputs are fed by the token sequence $\mathbf{u}(k)$, and that produce tokens the timestamps of which are stored in sequence $\mathbf{v}(k)$, (1) can be generalized by the following form

$$\begin{bmatrix} \mathbf{x}(k+1) \\ \mathbf{v}(k) \end{bmatrix} = \begin{bmatrix} M^A & M^B \\ M^C & M^D \end{bmatrix} \otimes \begin{bmatrix} \mathbf{x}(k) \\ \mathbf{u}(k) \end{bmatrix}, \tag{2}$$

where M^A is the state matrix, M^B is the input matrix, M^C is the output matrix and M^D the feedthrough matrix [15]. These matrices (as in conventional linear system theory) encode mutual dependencies between inputs, outputs and internal state. They can be derived via symbolic simulation of one iteration of the graph as described in [13]. We illustrate how to do this on the example SDF graph in Fig. 1. To establish the relationship between the timestamps of tokens contained in (2) we need to express the timestamps of tokens produced in positions of initial tokens after the $(k + 1)$st iteration and tokens produced at the outputs of the graph as (max,+) linear combinations of the timestamps of the same tokens after the kth graph iteration and the input tokens. For the graph of Fig. 1, $t_{\textcircled{3}} = [0 \; -\infty \; -\infty \; -\infty \; -\infty] \otimes [\mathbf{x}(k) \; \mathbf{u}(k)]^T$, $t_{\textcircled{4}} = [-\infty \; 0 \; -\infty \; -\infty \; -\infty] \otimes [\mathbf{x}(k) \; \mathbf{u}(k)]^T$, all the way up to $t_u = [-\infty \; -\infty \; -\infty \; -\infty \; 0] \otimes [\mathbf{x}(k) \; \mathbf{u}(k)]^T$. We call these timestamps symbolic timestamps. We now perform symbolic simulation. The iteration is given by the schedule $In \; D^2 E^2 F G^2 \; Out$ where powers represent actor repetition counts. The iteration starts by actor In firing. This firing consumes the input token u and produces two tokens in channel (In, D) carrying the symbolic timestamp $t_u \otimes 0 = [-\infty \; -\infty \; -\infty \; -\infty \; 0]$. These tokens along with initial tokens in channel (F, D) fuel two firings of actor D as follows. The firings produce two tokens each. The first two have the symbolic timestamp $([-\infty \; -\infty \; -\infty \; -\infty \; 0] \oplus t_{\textcircled{3}}) \otimes 2 = [2 \; -\infty \; -\infty \; -\infty \; 2]$. The remaining are of the following symbolic timestamp $([-\infty \; -\infty \; -\infty \; -\infty \; 0] \oplus t_{\textcircled{4}}) \otimes 2 = [-\infty \; 2 \; -\infty \; -\infty \; 2]$. Then we proceed with actor E the first firing of which is intialized by the tokens produced by the first firing of actor D. The firing results in production of three tokens in channel (E, F) and one token in channel (E, G) with the timestamp $[2 \; -\infty \; -\infty \; -\infty \; 2] \otimes 2 = [4 \; -\infty \; -\infty \; -\infty \; 4]$. The tokens produced by the second firing are available at $[-\infty \; 2 \; -\infty \; -\infty \; 2] \otimes 2 = [-\infty \; 4 \; -\infty \; -\infty \; 4]$. This enables actor F to fire and restore tokens in position $\textcircled{4}$ and $\textcircled{5}$ with the symbolic timestamps $t'_{\textcircled{4}} = t'_{\textcircled{5}} = [7 \; 7 \; -\infty \; -\infty \; 7]$. Note that token $\textcircled{5}$ was not consumed in the current iteration but was shifted in position of token $\textcircled{3}$. Thus, $t'_{\textcircled{3}} = t_{\textcircled{5}} = [-\infty \; -\infty \; 0 \; -\infty \; -\infty]$. Similarly, actor G fires and its second firing results in restoration of token in position $\textcircled{6}$ that ends up with the timestamp $t'_{\textcircled{6}} = [6 \; 5 \; -\infty \; 2 \; 6]$. This is also the timestamp of the token produced on the output, i.e. $t_v = t'_{\textcircled{6}}$. If we gather the symbolic timestamps $t'_{\textcircled{3}}, t'_{\textcircled{4}}, t'_{\textcircled{5}}, t'_{\textcircled{6}}$ and t_v row-by-row into a matrix we obtain

$$
\begin{bmatrix} \mathbf{x}(k+1) \\ \mathbf{v}(k) \end{bmatrix} =
\left[\begin{array}{cccc|c}
-\infty & -\infty & 0 & -\infty & -\infty \\
7 & 7 & -\infty & -\infty & 7 \\
7 & 7 & -\infty & -\infty & 7 \\
6 & 5 & -\infty & 2 & 6 \\ \hline
6 & 5 & -\infty & 2 & 6
\end{array} \right]
\otimes \begin{bmatrix} \mathbf{x}(k) \\ \mathbf{u}(k) \end{bmatrix}
\tag{3}
$$

where $\mathbf{x}(k+1) = [t'_{\textcircled{3}} \; t'_{\textcircled{4}} \; t'_{\textcircled{5}} \; t'_{\textcircled{6}}]^T$, $\mathbf{v}(k) = [t_v]^T$, $\mathbf{x}(k) = [t_{\textcircled{3}} \; t_{\textcircled{4}} \; t_{\textcircled{5}} \; t_{\textcircled{6}}]^T$ and $\mathbf{u}(k) = [t_u]^T$.

3.4   Hierarchy in SDF Graphs

In this paper, following the terminology of [29], when we talk about hierarchical SDF graphs, we mean graphs that contain hierarchical actors. Unlike atomic actors, a hierarchical actor encapsulates an SDF graph. Hierarchical actors can then be connected to other SDF actors, either atomic or hierarchical to form hierarchies of arbitrary depths.

An example of a hierarchical SDF graph is shown in Fig. 2.

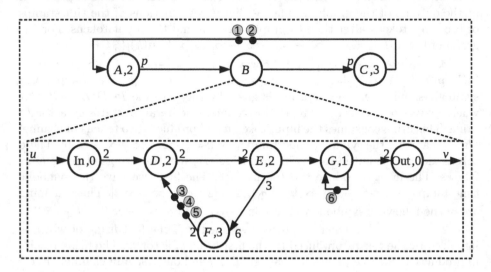

Fig. 2. Example of a hierarchical SDF graph.

In the figure, the top level graph is composed out of three actors A, B and C. Actors A and C are atomic, while actor B is a hierarchical actor that encapsulates the SDF graph of Fig. 1. In this particular example, the output port of actor A is connected to the input port of actor In, while the input port of actor C is connected to the output port of actor Out of the encapsulated graph of hierarchical actor B.

Although hierarchical SDF models are widely used (e.g. in the well-known Ptolemy II framework [11]), care must be taken as there is one complication. In general, hierarchical SDF models are not compositional. In particular, a hierarchical SDF actor cannot be represented by an atomic SDF actor without loss of information that can lead to inconsistency and deadlock [29]. In this paper we assume that only valid aggregations are specified.

4   Throughput Analysis of Hierarchical SDF Models

In this section we discuss throughput analysis for a class of hierarchical SDF models where starting from the bottom level of the hierarchy, the firing of every hierarchical actor implies the execution of one **full** iteration of the encapsulated graph.

In particular, we propose a technique that is an enhancement of the symbolic simulation procedure of [13] that is able to take advantage of the SDF hierarchy semantics. Our technique combines symbolic simulation and the system theoretic view on SDF graphs as (max,+) linear systems that recognize the "usual" state-space representation based on the state, input, output and feedthrough matrices (cf. (2)).

4.1   Our Algorithm

We give a high-level overview of our algorithm in Algorithm 1.

Algorithm 1. Throughput analysis for hierarchical SDF models.

---

input : A hierarchical SDF graph G
output: Throughput Thr of G

1 $H = \texttt{IsolateHierarchyLevels}(G)$
2 **foreach** *hierarchy level h in H* **do**
3   **foreach** *hierarchical actor a in h* **do**
4          $M = \texttt{SymbolicSimulation+}(a,\ S[h-1][:])$
5          $S[h][a] = M$
6   **end**
7 **end**
8 $Cg = \texttt{CommunicationGraph}(M)$
9 $Thr = 1/\texttt{MCM}(Cg)$

The input to the algorithm is a hierarchical SDF graph G, while the output of the algorithm is throughput Thr of the graph. We begin the procedure by isolating the hierarchy levels of the graph starting in a bottom up manner (cf. Line 1). This can be done by employing a fitted flavor of reverse breadth-first search algorithm. Thereafter for each hierarchical actor (cf. Line 3) at the current hierarchy level (cf. Line 2) we perform symbolic simulation in order to obtain the relevant state-space representation of the hierarchical actor (cf. Line 4). The representation (composite matrix that includes the state, input, output and feedthrough submatrices) is stored because later on the symbolic simulation at a higher hierarchy level will need this representation (note that the symbolic simulation in Line 4 is invoked with all the state-space representations belonging to the previous hierarchy level). Finally, when we reach the highest hierarchy level, the symbolic simulation will produce a state-space representation of G for which we construct the corresponding communication graph (cf. Line 8). For details on how construct the communication graph of a (max,+) matrix we refer the interested reader to [19]. The throughput of the graph equals to the inverse of the maximum cycle mean of the communication graph (cf. Line 9).

Note that the algorithm assumes the existence of a hierarchy in the sense that a graph composed only of atomic actors is assumed to be a hierarchical graph composed of one hierarchical actor that encapsulates the atomic actor composition.

4.2   Symbolic Simulation

Algorithm 1 as its core part uses symbolic simulation. The symbolic simulation as originally proposed by [13] cannot take advantage of semantics of hierarchical SDF models. This means that if we are to use the techniques of [13] to compute the throughput of a hierarchical SDF model, we first need to flatten the hierarchy, i.e. to transform the graph to one without it.

As explained in Sect. 3.3, symbolic simulation derives the state-space representation of an SDF graph by simulating the graph for exactly one iteration following the iteration schedule. In the schedule every actor is fired the number of times corresponding to the repetition vector entry for that actor. The procedure requires administration of every token produced and consumed during the iteration. Thus for graphs with large repetition vector entries, the symbolic simulation can become a bottleneck in the overall throughput analysis flow.

In case of hierarchical SDF models (regardless whether the hierarchy is extracted from a flat graph or comes in the specification) we argue that one can avoid the administration of every token. To explain: given a hierarchical actor, the symbolic simulation of [13] would simulate the firing of the actor the number of times given by the encapsulating graph's repetition vector. This implies the firing of every actor (and administration of tokens produced and consumed) of the encapsulation for the same number of times multiplied by the corresponding repetition vector entry in the encapsulation itself and so until the deepest level of the hierarchy. E.g., for the graph of Fig. 2, actor D would have to be fired $p \cdot 2$ times. It is clear that, across hierarchy levels, depending on the repetition vectors at different levels, we may experience (in the worst-case) an exponential rise in complexity.

We argue that we can mitigate the impact that this rise has on the efficiency of symbolic simulation by taking advantage of the hierarchy semantics of SDF. In particular, by using the system theoretic view on SDF sublimed in (2), we propose a way to avoid administration of all actor firings and token consumptions/productions of the encapsulation by using its state-space representation. In particular, to compute the new state of the hierarchical actor and the timestamps of tokens that are produced at its output interface, it is more beneficial, lightweight and elegant to perform a matrix multiplication (cf. (2)) than to simulate the encapsulation symbolically. This way we focus only on the tokens that are part of the state (initial ones) and need not to care about others. Furthermore, particular actor firings are compactly encoded in a single matrix. We argue that in case of hierarchical SDF models with large repetition vectors across the hierarchy this approach will mitigate the adverse effect the increase of graph's repetition vector entries has to the throughput analysis algorithm performance.

The modified algorithm for symbolic simulation is outlined in Algorithm 2.

Algorithm 2. Compute state-space representation of a hierarchical SDF actor.

---

input : A hierarchical or atomic actor a
input : State-space representations of actors in lower hierarchy level
$\quad\quad S[h][:]$
output: State space representation M of a

1 $\Sigma = \texttt{SeqSchedule}(a)$
2 $T = \emptyset$
3 **for** $i = 1$ **to** $\texttt{Length}(\Sigma)$ **do**
4 $\quad\quad a = \Sigma[i]$
5 $\quad\quad$ **if** a *is hierarchical* **then**
6 $\quad\quad\quad |\quad T += \texttt{Fire+}(a,\, S[h][a])$
7 $\quad\quad$ **end**
8 $\quad\quad$ **else**
9 $\quad\quad\quad |\quad T += \texttt{Fire}(a)$
10 $\quad\quad$ **end**
11 **end**
12 $M = \texttt{ConstructStateSpaceRepresentation}(T)$

The algorithm is a modification of Algorithm 1 of [13]. The inputs to the algorithm is the very structure of the hierarchical actor a and the state-space representations ((max,+) matrices) of actors of previous hierarchy levels as the hierarchical actor may as well encapsulate a hierarchical actor from a lower hierarchy level. The output is the state-space representation of the hierarchical actor, i.e. the matrix of (2).

The algorithm first computes the iteration schedule of the actor (cf. Line 1) that gives the ordering of actor firings within the iteration. The schedule is then traversed (cf. Line 3). The firing of each actor is simulated with all the tokens consumed and produced by the firing being administered in container T (cf. Line 2). The crucial difference between Algorithm 2 and Algorithm 1 of [13] is that here, if the actor is hierarchical, we use it state-space representation to compute its new state as well as the symbolic timestamps of tokens it produces in its output channels (cf. Line 6). This way we have avoided the need for flattening the structure and having to administer all the actor firings and tokens consumed and produced by these firings. This has the effect of a compression, as we only focus on initial tokens that are part of the overall state and are carried over to the next hierarchy level. Finally, the tokens can be gathered in the state-space representation for the current actor (cf. Line 12).

4.3 Example

We demonstrate the operating principles of Algorithms 1 and 2 using the running example graph with $p = 2$.

We begin with Algorithm 1. We can isolate two hierarchy levels in the structure. Going bottom up the algorithm encounters the hierarchical actor B for which a state-space representation is derived using Algorithm 2 in the usual manner of [13] as the encapsulation has only atomic actors. The state-space representation is given by (3). Algorithm 1 now visits the top level of the hierarchy on which it employs Algorithm 2. Consequently the iteration schedule is computed which has the form AB^2C. The schedule is now simulated. Actor A fires first by consuming token ①. The two tokens produced by its firing carry the symbolic timestamp

$$\begin{bmatrix} 0 & -\infty & -\infty & -\infty & -\infty & -\infty \end{bmatrix} \otimes 2 = \begin{bmatrix} 2 & -\infty & -\infty & -\infty & -\infty & -\infty \end{bmatrix}. \qquad (4)$$

Note that the symbolic timestamps account for all tokens across all hierarchy levels while the ordering in the vector is given by initial token indices in the figure. After actor A, the schedule dictates that actor B is fired. However, now, to perform this firing, we do not flatten the graph but we use the state-space representation of B of (3). The timestamp of the token produced by the first firing of hierarchical actor B can be directly computed from (2) as follows

$$\begin{bmatrix} 6 & 5 & -\infty & 2 \end{bmatrix} \otimes \begin{bmatrix} -\infty & -\infty & 0 & -\infty & -\infty & -\infty \\ -\infty & -\infty & -\infty & 0 & -\infty & -\infty \\ -\infty & -\infty & -\infty & -\infty & 0 & -\infty \\ -\infty & -\infty & -\infty & -\infty & -\infty & 0 \end{bmatrix} \oplus 6 \otimes \begin{bmatrix} 2 & -\infty & -\infty & -\infty & -\infty & -\infty \end{bmatrix}$$

$$= \begin{bmatrix} -\infty & -\infty & 6 & 5 & -\infty & 2 \end{bmatrix} \oplus \begin{bmatrix} 8 & -\infty & -\infty & -\infty & -\infty & -\infty \end{bmatrix}$$

$$= \begin{bmatrix} 8 & -\infty & 6 & 5 & -\infty & 2 \end{bmatrix}.$$

$$(5)$$

According to (2), the internal state of B advances as follows

$$\begin{bmatrix} -\infty & -\infty & 0 & -\infty \\ 7 & 7 & -\infty & -\infty \\ 7 & 7 & -\infty & -\infty \\ 6 & 5 & -\infty & 2 \end{bmatrix} \otimes \begin{bmatrix} -\infty & -\infty & 0 & -\infty & -\infty & -\infty \\ -\infty & -\infty & -\infty & 0 & -\infty & -\infty \\ -\infty & -\infty & -\infty & -\infty & 0 & -\infty \\ -\infty & -\infty & -\infty & -\infty & -\infty & 0 \end{bmatrix}$$

$$\oplus \begin{bmatrix} -\infty \\ 7 \\ 7 \\ 6 \end{bmatrix} \otimes \begin{bmatrix} 2 & -\infty & -\infty & -\infty & -\infty & -\infty \end{bmatrix}$$

$$(6)$$

$$= \begin{bmatrix} -\infty & -\infty & -\infty & -\infty & 0 & -\infty \\ -\infty & -\infty & 7 & 7 & -\infty & -\infty \\ -\infty & -\infty & 7 & 7 & -\infty & -\infty \\ -\infty & -\infty & 6 & 5 & -\infty & 2 \end{bmatrix} \oplus \begin{bmatrix} -\infty & -\infty & -\infty & -\infty & -\infty & -\infty \\ 9 & -\infty & -\infty & -\infty & -\infty & -\infty \\ 9 & -\infty & -\infty & -\infty & -\infty & -\infty \\ 8 & -\infty & -\infty & -\infty & -\infty & -\infty \end{bmatrix}$$

$$= \begin{bmatrix} -\infty & -\infty & -\infty & -\infty & 0 & -\infty \\ 9 & -\infty & 7 & 7 & -\infty & -\infty \\ 9 & -\infty & 7 & 7 & -\infty & -\infty \\ 8 & -\infty & 6 & 5 & -\infty & 2 \end{bmatrix}.$$

This leads us to the second firing of B. The hierarchical actor is now initialized with the state of (6) while consuming the second token produced by A that carries the symbolic timestamp of (4). The symbolic timestamp of the second token produced by B is therefore calculated as follows

$$\begin{bmatrix} 6 & 5 & -\infty & 2 \end{bmatrix} \otimes \begin{bmatrix} -\infty & -\infty & -\infty & -\infty & 0 & -\infty \\ 9 & -\infty & 7 & 7 & -\infty & -\infty \\ 9 & -\infty & 7 & 7 & -\infty & -\infty \\ 8 & -\infty & 6 & 5 & -\infty & 2 \end{bmatrix}$$

$$\oplus\, 6 \otimes \begin{bmatrix} 2 & -\infty & -\infty & -\infty & -\infty & -\infty \end{bmatrix}$$

$$= \begin{bmatrix} 14 & -\infty & 12 & 12 & 6 & 4 \end{bmatrix} \oplus \begin{bmatrix} 8 & -\infty & -\infty & -\infty & -\infty & -\infty \end{bmatrix}$$

$$= \begin{bmatrix} 14 & -\infty & 12 & 12 & 6 & 4 \end{bmatrix}$$

(7)

Similarly, as in the case of (6) we can calculate the new state of the encapsulated actor B

$$\begin{bmatrix} -\infty & -\infty & 0 & -\infty \\ 7 & 7 & -\infty & -\infty \\ 7 & 7 & -\infty & -\infty \\ 6 & 5 & -\infty & 2 \end{bmatrix} \otimes \begin{bmatrix} -\infty & -\infty & -\infty & -\infty & 0 & -\infty \\ 9 & -\infty & 7 & 7 & -\infty & -\infty \\ 9 & -\infty & 7 & 7 & -\infty & -\infty \\ 8 & -\infty & 6 & 5 & -\infty & 2 \end{bmatrix}$$

$$\oplus \begin{bmatrix} -\infty \\ 7 \\ 7 \\ 6 \end{bmatrix} \otimes \begin{bmatrix} 2 & -\infty & -\infty & -\infty & -\infty & -\infty \end{bmatrix}$$

(8)

$$= \begin{bmatrix} 9 & -\infty & 7 & 7 & -\infty & -\infty \\ 16 & -\infty & 14 & 14 & 7 & -\infty \\ 16 & -\infty & 14 & 14 & 7 & -\infty \\ 14 & -\infty & 12 & 12 & 6 & 4 \end{bmatrix} \oplus \begin{bmatrix} -\infty & -\infty & -\infty & -\infty & -\infty & -\infty \\ 9 & -\infty & -\infty & -\infty & -\infty & -\infty \\ 9 & -\infty & -\infty & -\infty & -\infty & -\infty \\ 8 & -\infty & -\infty & -\infty & -\infty & -\infty \end{bmatrix}$$

$$= \begin{bmatrix} 9 & -\infty & 7 & 7 & -\infty & -\infty \\ 16 & -\infty & 14 & 14 & 7 & -\infty \\ 16 & -\infty & 14 & 14 & 7 & -\infty \\ 14 & -\infty & 12 & 12 & 6 & 4 \end{bmatrix}.$$

Finally, actor C can fire by consuming the tokens produced by B (cf. (5) and (7)) and producing the token carrying the symbolic timestamp

$$\left(\begin{bmatrix} 8 & -\infty & 6 & 5 & -\infty & 2 \end{bmatrix} \oplus \begin{bmatrix} 14 & -\infty & 12 & 12 & 6 & 4 \end{bmatrix} \right) \otimes 3 = \begin{bmatrix} 14 & -\infty & 12 & 12 & 6 & 4 \end{bmatrix}. \quad (9)$$

The firing of C completes the iteration and the tokens produced in positions of initial tokens can be gathered up to compose the state-space representation of the graph. In particular, the tokens produced in places of the initial tokens of the underlying encapsulated graph of B (tokens ③, ④, ⑤, ⑥) are available in (8). Token ② is not consumed in the current iteration as at its end it has moved in position of token ①. Therefore, the token in position ① after the iteration has the symbolic timestamp

$$\begin{bmatrix} -\infty & 0 & -\infty & -\infty & -\infty & -\infty \end{bmatrix}. \quad (10)$$

The token produced in place of initial token ② is the result of the firing of actor C and carries the symbolic timestamp of (9). When we arrange these tokens into a matrix, we obtain the desired state-space representation of the running example SDF model

$$M = \begin{bmatrix} -\infty & 0 & -\infty & -\infty & -\infty & -\infty \\ 14 & -\infty & 12 & 12 & 6 & 4 \\ 9 & -\infty & 7 & 7 & -\infty & -\infty \\ 16 & -\infty & 14 & 14 & 7 & -\infty \\ 16 & -\infty & 14 & 14 & 7 & -\infty \\ 14 & -\infty & 12 & 12 & 6 & 4 \end{bmatrix}. \tag{11}$$

From the communication graph of this matrix, we can obtain the throughput of the graph by applying a maximum cycle mean algorithm [8]. In this case the throughput of the graph is 1/14 iterations per time-unit.

From the performance perspective, by doing symbolic simulation in this manner, for the graph of Fig. 2, we have replaced p standard symbolic simulations of the encapsulation of B with p matrix multiplications of (2). We argue that this is a more performance-friendly way for constructing state-space representations of SDF graphs exposing hierarchy and featuring repetition vectors with large entries. In our example, using the SDF^3 toolsuite [27] running on an Intel i7-6500U machine operating at 2.50 GHz, we have observed that even for the simple structure of Fig. 2 with $p = 10,000$ symbolic simulation of [13] will take about 20 s, while the version introduced in this paper will complete in about 0.5 s.

5   Conclusion and Future Work

In this work we focused on throughput analysis of hierarchical dataflow models. We have set way to development of new methods that can take advantage of the hierarchical semantics of SDF. We base our method on the existing state-of-the-art symbolic simulation method that we combine with the system theoretic view on SDF graphs where hierarchy elements need not to be flattened during the symbolic simulation but where their state-space representation can be used instead. This way we remove the need for the repeated simulation of encapsulated subgraphs of hierarchical actors that includes the administration of actor firings and all of the produced and consumed tokens. By using state-space representation we can only focus on the tokens that are part of the state by means of matrix multiplications. We believe that symbolic simulation endowed with this feature can help mitigate the difficulties that the standard flavor experiences when dealing with graphs with large repetition vectors. As for future work we plan to evaluate our technique using realistic case-studies in an automated environment.

References

1. Baccelli, F., Cohen, G., Olsder, G.J., Quadrat, J.P.: Synchronization and linearity: an algebra for discrete event systems (2001). https://www.rocq.inria.fr/metalau/cohen/SED/book-online.html

2. Bekooij, M., Moreira, O., Poplavko, P., Mesman, B., Pastrnak, M., van Meerbergen, J.: Predictable Embedded Multiprocessor System Design, pp. 77–91. Springer, Heidelberg (2004). doi:10.1007/978-3-540-30113-4_7
3. Bhattacharya, B., Bhattacharyya, S.: Parameterized dataflow modeling for DSP systems. Signal Process. IEEE Trans. **49**(10), 2408–2421 (2001)
4. Bhattacharyya, S.S., Deprettere, E.F., Theelen, B.D.: Dynamic dataflow graphs. In: Bhattacharyya, S.S., Deprettere, E.F., Leupers, R., Takala, J. (eds.) Handbook of Signal Processing Systems, pp. 905–944. Springer, New York (2013). doi:10. 1007/978-1-4614-6859-2_28
5. Bhattacharyya, S.S., Deprettere, E.F., Theelen, B.D.: Dynamic Dataflow Graphs. Springer, New York, NY (2013). doi:10.1007/978-1-4614-6859-2_28
6. Bilsen, G., Engels, M., Lauwereins, R., Peperstraete, J.: Cycle-static dataflow. Signal Process. IEEE Trans. **44**(2), 397–408 (1996)
7. Buck, J.T.: Scheduling dynamic dataflow graphs with bounded memory using the token flow model. Ph.D. thesis, EECS Department, University of California, Berkeley (1993)
8. Dasdan, A., Irani, S.S., Gupta, R.K.: Efficient algorithms for optimum cycle mean and optimum cost to time ratio problems. In: Proceedings of the 36th Annual ACM/IEEE Design Automation Conference, DAC 1999, pp. 37–42. ACM, New York, NY, USA (1999). http://doi.acm.org/10.1145/309847.309862
9. Deroui, H., Desnos, K., Nezan, J.F., Munier-Kordon, A.: Throughput evaluation of DSP applications based on hierarchical dataflow models. In: International Symposium on Circuits and Systems (ISCAS) (2017)
10. Desnos, K., Pelcat, M., Nezan, J.F., Bhattacharyya, S.S., Aridhi, S.: PiMM: parameterized and interfaced dataflow meta-model for MPSoCs runtime reconfiguration. In: 2013 International Conference on Embedded Computer Systems: Architectures, Modeling, and Simulation (SAMOS), pp. 41–48, July 2013
11. Eker, J., Janneck, J.W., Lee, E.A., Liu, J., Liu, X., Ludvig, J., Neuendorffer, S., Sachs, S., Xiong, Y.: Taming heterogeneity - the Ptolemy approach. Proc. IEEE **91**(1), 127–144 (2003)
12. Geilen, M.: Reduction techniques for synchronous dataflow graphs. In: Proceedings of the 46th Annual Design Automation Conference, pp. 911–916. DAC 2009, ACM, New York, NY, USA (2009). http://doi.acm.org/10.1145/1629911.1630146
13. Geilen, M.: Synchronous dataflow scenarios. ACM Trans. Embed. Comput. Syst. **10**(2), 16:1–16:31 (2011). doi:10.1145/1880050.1880052
14. Geilen, M., Stuijk, S.: Worst-case performance analysis of synchronous dataflow scenarios. In: Proceedings of the Eighth IEEE/ACM/IFIP International Conference on Hardware/Software Codesign and System Synthesis, CODES/ISSS 2010, pp. 125–134. ACM, New York, NY, USA (2010), http://doi.acm.org/10.1145/1878961.1878985
15. Geilen, M., Tripakis, S., Wiggers, M.: The earlier the better: a theory of timed actor interfaces. Technical Report UCB/EECS-2010-130, EECS Department, University of California, Berkeley, October 2010. http://www2.eecs.berkeley.edu/Pubs/TechRpts/2010/EECS-2010-130.html
16. Ghamarian, A.H., Geilen, M.C.W., Stuijk, S., Basten, T., Theelen, B.D., Mousavi, M.R., Moonen, A.J.M., Bekooij, M.J.G.: Throughput analysis of synchronous data flow graphs. In: Proceedings of the Sixth International Conference on Application of Concurrency to System Design, ACSD 2006, pp. 25–36. IEEE Computer Society, Washington (2006). http://dx.doi.org/10.1109/ACSD.2006.33

17. de Groote, R., Kuper, J., Broersma, H., Smit, G.J.M.: Max-plus algebraic through-put analysis of synchronous dataflow graphs. In: 2012 38th Euromicro Conference on Software Engineering and Advanced Applications, pp. 29–38 (Sept 2012)

18. Ha, S., Oh, H.: Decidable Dataflow Models for Signal Processing: Synchronous Dataflow and Its Extensions. Springer, New York (2013). doi:10.1007/978-1-4614-6859-2_33

19. Heidergott, B., Olsder, G.J., Van Der Woude, J.: Max Plus at work: modeling and analysis of synchronized systems: a course on Max-Plus algebra and its applications. Princeton University Press, Princeton (2014)

20. Kavi, K.M., Buckles, B.P., Bhat, U.N.: A formal definition of data flow graph models. IEEE Trans. Comput. **C–35**(11), 940–948 (1986)

21. Lee, E., Messerschmitt, D.: Synchronous data flow. Proc. IEEE **75**(9), 1235–1245 (1987)

22. Nelson, A., Goossens, K., Akesson, B.: Dataflow formalisation of real-time streaming applications on a composable and predictable multi-processor SOC. J. Syst. Archit. **61**(9), 435–448 (2015). http://www.sciencedirect.com/science/article/pii/S1383762115000181

23. Piat, J., Bhattacharyya, S.S., Raulet, M.: Interface-based hierarchy for synchronous data-flow graphs. In: 2009 IEEE Workshop on Signal Processing Systems. pp. 145–150, October 2009

24. Ritz, S., Pankert, M., Zivojinovic, V., Meyr, H.: Optimum vectorization of scalable synchronous dataflow graphs. In: Proceedings of the International Conference on Application-Specific Array Processors, 1993, pp. 285–296, October 1993

25. Sriram, S., Bhattacharyya, S.S.: Embedded Multiprocessors: Scheduling and Synchronization, 2nd edn. CRC Press Inc., Boca Raton (2009)

26. Stuijk, S., Geilen, M., Theelen, B., Basten, T.: Scenario-aware dataflow: modeling, analysis and implementation of dynamic applications. In: 2011 International Conference on Embedded Computer Systems (SAMOS), pp. 404–411, July 2011

27. Stuijk, S., Geilen, M., Basten, T.: SDF[3]: SDF For Free. In: Proceedings of the 6th International Conference on Application of Concurrency to System Design, ACSD 2006, pp. 276–278. IEEE Computer Society Press, Los Alamitos, CA, USA. http://www.es.ele.tue.nl/sdf3

28. Stuijk, S.: Predictable mapping of streaming applications on multiprocessors. Ph.D. thesis, Eindhoven University of Technology (2007)

29. Tripakis, S., Bui, D., Geilen, M., Rodiers, B., Lee, E.A.: Compositionality in synchronous data flow: Modular code generation from hierarchical SDF graphs. ACM Trans. Embed. Comput. Syst. **12**(3), 1–26 (2013). doi:10.1145/2442116.2442133

Author Index

Printed in the United States
By Bookmasters